PRINCIPLES OF BUSINESS INFORMATION SYSTEMS

SECOND EDITION

**RALPH STAIR,
GEORGE REYNOLDS
AND THOMAS CHESNEY**

PRINCIPLES OF BUSINESS INFORMATION SYSTEMS

SECOND EDITION

**RALPH STAIR,
GEORGE REYNOLDS
AND THOMAS CHESNEY**

COURSE TECHNOLOGY
CENGAGE Learning

Australia • Brazil • Japan • Korea • Mexico • Singapore • Spain • United Kingdom • United States

COURSE TECHNOLOGY
CENGAGE Learning™

Principles of Business Information Systems

Ralph Stair, George Reynolds and Thomas Chesney

Publisher: Andrew Ashwin

Development Editor: Abigail Jones

Content Project Editor: Sue Povey

Manufacturing Buyer: Elaine Willis

Marketing Manager: Vicky Fielding

Typesetter: Cenveo Publisher Services

Cover design: Adam Renvoize

Text design: Design Deluxe Ltd, Bath, UK

For product information and technology assistance, contact **emea.info@cengage.com**.

For permission to use material from this text or product, and for permission queries, email **emea.permissions@cengage.com**.

This work is adapted from Principles of Information Systems 7th edition by Ralph M. Stair and George Reynolds published by Course Technology, a division of Cengage Learning, Inc. © 2006.

British Library Cataloguing-in-Publication Data
A catalogue record for this book is available from the British Library.

ISBN: 978-1-4737-0388-9

Cengage Learning EMEA
Cheriton House, North Way, Andover, Hampshire, SP10 5BE United Kingdom

Cengage Learning products are represented in Canada by Nelson Education Ltd.

For your lifelong learning solutions, visit **www.cengage.co.uk**

Purchase your next print book, e-book or e-chapter at **www.cengagebrain.com**

Printed in China by RR Donnelley
Print Number 01 Print Year 2015

For Tahseena

For Tahseena

Brief Contents

Contents

1   Overview 1

2 Information Technology Concepts 65

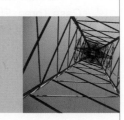

3 Business Information Systems 239

4 Systems Development

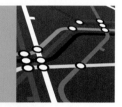

5 Information Systems in Business and Society 455

Preface

As organizations continue to operate in an increasingly competitive and global marketplace, workers in all areas of business including accounting, finance, human resources, marketing, operations management and production must be well prepared to make the significant contributions required for success. Regardless of your future role, you will need to understand what information systems can and cannot do and be able to use them to help you accomplish your work. You will be expected to discover opportunities to use information systems and to participate in the design of solutions to business problems employing information systems. You will be challenged to identify and evaluate information systems options. To be successful, you must be able to view information systems from the perspective of business and organizational needs. For your solutions to be accepted, you must recognize and address their impact on fellow workers, customers, suppliers, and other key business partners. For these reasons, a course in information systems is essential for students in today's high-tech world.

The primary objective of *Principles of Business Information Systems second edition* is to provide the best information systems text and accompanying materials for the first information technology course required of all business students. We want you to learn to use information technology to ensure your personal success in your current or future job and to improve the success of your organization. Principles of Business Information Systems stands proudly at the beginning of the information systems (IS) curriculum and remains unchallenged in its position as the only IS principles text offering the basic IS concepts that every business student must learn to be successful.

This text has been written specifically for the introductory course in the IS curriculum. *Principles of Business Information Systems* treats the appropriate computer and IS concepts together with a strong managerial emphasis on meeting business and organizational needs.

Approach of the Text

Principles of Business Information Systems offers the traditional coverage of computer concepts, but it places the material within the context of meeting business and organizational needs. Placing IS concepts in this context and taking a general management perspective sets the text apart from general computer books thus making it appealing not only to those studying for IS degrees but also to students from other fields of study. The text isn't overly technical, but rather deals with the role that information systems play in an organization and the key principles a manager needs to grasp to be successful. These principles of IS are brought together and presented in a way that is both understandable and relevant. In addition, this book offers an overview of the entire IS discipline, while giving students a solid foundation for further study in advanced IS courses as programming, systems analysis and design, project management, database management, data communications, website and systems development, electronic commerce and mobile commerce applications, and decision support. As such, it serves the needs of both general business students and those who will become IS professionals.

IS Principles First, Where They Belong

Exposing students to fundamental IS principles is an advantage for students who do not later return to the discipline for advanced courses. Since most functional areas in business rely on information systems, an understanding of IS principles helps students in other course work. In addition, introducing students to the principles of IS helps future business function managers employ information systems successfully and avoid mishaps that often result in unfortunate consequences. Furthermore, presenting IS concepts at the introductory level creates interest among general business students who may later choose information systems as a field of concentration.

Goals of this Text

Principles of Business Information Systems has four main goals:

1 To provide a core of IS principles with which every business student should be familiar.
2 To offer a survey of the IS discipline that will enable all business students to understand the relationship of IS courses to their curriculum as a whole.
3 To present the changing role of the IS professional.
4 To show the value of the discipline as an attractive field of specialization.

By achieving these goals, *Principles of Business Information Systems* will enable students to understand and use fundamental information systems principles so that they can function more efficiently and effectively as workers, managers, decision-makers and organizational leaders.

IS Principles

Principles of Business Information Systems, although comprehensive, cannot cover every aspect of the rapidly changing IS discipline. The authors, having recognized this, provide students an essential core of guiding IS principles to use as they face career challenges ahead. Think of principles as basic truths or rules that remain constant regardless of the situation. As such, they provide strong guidance in the face of tough decisions. A set of IS principles is highlighted at the beginning of each chapter. The ultimate goal of *Principles of Business Information Systems* is to develop effective, thinking, action-oriented employees by instilling them with principles to help guide their decision making and actions.

Survey of the IS Discipline

This text not only offers the traditional coverage of computer concepts but also provides a broad framework to impart students with a solid grounding in the business uses of technology. In addition to serving general business students, this book offers an overview of the entire IS discipline and solidly prepares future IS professionals for advanced IS courses and their careers in the rapidly changing IS discipline.

Changing Role of the IS Professional

As business and the IS discipline have changed, so too has the role of the IS professional. Once considered a technical specialist, today the IS professional operates as an internal consultant to all functional areas of the organization, being knowledgeable about their needs and competent in bringing the power of information systems to bear throughout the organization. The IS professional views issues through a global perspective that encompasses the entire organization and the broader industry and business environment in which it operates.

The scope of responsibilities of an IS professional today is not confined to just his or her employer but encompasses the entire interconnected network of employees, suppliers, customers, competitors, regulatory agencies and other entities, no matter where they are located. This broad scope of responsibilities creates a new challenge: how to help an organization survive in a highly interconnected, highly competitive global environment. In accepting that challenge, the IS professional plays a pivotal role in shaping the business itself and ensuring its success. To survive, businesses must now strive for the highest level of customer satisfaction and loyalty through competitive prices and ever-improving product and service quality. The IS professional assumes the critical responsibility of determining the organization's approach to both overall cost and quality performance and therefore plays an important role in the ongoing survival of the organization. This new duality in the role of the IS employee – a professional who exercises a specialist's skills with a generalist's perspective – is reflected throughout the book.

IS as a Field for Further Study

Employment of computer and information systems managers is expected to grow much faster than the average for all occupations. Technological advancements will boost the employment of computer-related workers; in turn, this will boost the demand for managers to direct these workers. In addition, job openings will result from the need to replace managers who retire or move into other occupations.

A career in IS can be exciting, challenging and rewarding! It is important to show the value of the discipline as an appealing field of study and that the IS graduate is no longer a technical recluse. Today, perhaps more than ever before, the IS professional must be able to align IS and organizational goals and ensure that IS investments are justified from a business perspective. The need to draw bright and interested students into the IS discipline is part of our ongoing responsibility. Upon graduation, IS graduates at many schools are among the highest paid of all business graduates. Throughout this text, the many challenges and opportunities available to IS professionals are highlighted and emphasized.

Changes to the Second Edition

Principles of Business Information Systems is an adaptation of the popular US textbook *Principles of Information Systems*, now in its eleventh edition. With a more international outlook, this book is suitable for students in the UK, Europe and South Africa on introductory BIS or MIS courses. The new title reflects the fact that this book has boosted its business emphasis but retained its technology focus.

Continuing to present IS concepts with a managerial emphasis, this edition retains the overall vision, framework and pedagogy that made the previous US editions so popular:

- *Principles of Business Information Systems* keeps the same five-part structure, is packed with new real world examples and business cases, and highlights ethical issues throughout.
- It is still an IS text aimed at those studying business and management.

However, in order to increase its international relevance, we have made a number of changes. The main improvements are:

- Cases are more international in flavour, including examples from South Africa, Australia and Europe, and have a broader sector spread, reflecting a wider variety of business types (including SMEs).
- The book has been brought completely up to date in terms of innovations in IT.
- Legal and ethical issues in IT have been made more international.
- Instead of a separate e-commerce chapter, e-commerce is treated alongside other operational systems, where it should be – it has become another essential that businesses must have.
- A chapter on pervasive computing, reflects the move of the computer away from the desktop to enter almost every aspect of our lives.
- Separate information systems are still discussed in Chapters 7, 8, 9 and 10 (all of Section 3) but we recognise that many large – and some small – companies take a more integrated approach and this is covered at the start of Section 3.

Structure of the Text

Principles of Business Information Systems is organized into five parts – an overview of information systems, an introduction to information technology concepts, an examination of different classes of business information systems, a study of systems development and a focus on information systems in business and the wider society.

The content of each chapter is as follows:

Chapter 1 An Introduction to Information Systems

Chapter 1 creates a framework for the entire book. Major sections in this chapter become entire chapters in the text. This chapter describes the components of an information system and introduces major classes of business information systems. It offers an overview of systems development and outlines some major challenges that IS professionals face.

Chapter 2 Information Systems in Organizations

Chapter 2 gives an overview of business organizations and presents a foundation for the effective and efficient use of IS in a business environment. We have stressed that the traditional mission of IS is to deliver the right information to the right person at the right time. In the section on virtual organizational structure, we discuss that virtual organizational structures allow work to be separated from location and time. Work can be done anywhere, anytime. The concept of business process reengineering (BPR) is introduced and competitive advantage is examined – higher quality products, better customer service and lower costs.

Chapter 3 Hardware: Input, Processing, Output and Storage Devices

This chapter concentrates on the hardware component of a computer-based information system (CBIS) and reflects the latest equipment and computer capabilities – computer memory is explained and a variety of hardware platforms are discussed including mobile technology.

Chapter 4 Software: Systems and Application Software

You cannot come into contact with a computer, without coming into contact with software. This chapter examines a wide range of software and related issues including operating systems and application software, open source and proprietary software, software for mobile devices and copyrights and licenses.

Chapter 5 Organizing and Storing Data

Databases are the heart of almost all IS. A huge amount of data is entered into computer systems every day. Chapter 5 examines database management systems and how they can help businesses. The chapter includes a brief overview of how to organize data in a database, a look at database administration and discusses how data can be used competitively by examining both data mining and business intelligence.

Chapter 6 Computer Networks

The power of information technology greatly increases when devices are linked or networked, which is the subject of this chapter. Today's decision makers need to access data wherever it resides. They must be able to establish fast, reliable connections to exchange messages, upload and download data and software, route business transactions to processors, connect to databases and network services, and send output to printers. This chapter examines the hardware involved and examines the world's biggest computer network, the Internet.

Chapter 7 Operational Systems

Operational systems, such as transaction processing systems allow firms to buy and sell. Without systems to perform these functions, the firm could not operate. Organizations today are moving from a collection of non-integrated transaction processing systems to highly integrated enterprise resource planning systems to perform routine business processes and maintain records about them. These systems support a wide range of business activities associated with supply chain management and customer relationship management. This chapter examines transaction processing systems and enterprise resource planning systems.

Chapter 8 Management Information and Decision Support Systems

This chapter begins with a discussion of decision making and examines the decision-making process. Both management information systems and decision support systems are examined in detail. Their ability to help managers make better decisions is emphasized.

Chapter 9 Knowledge Management and Specialized Information Systems

A discussion of knowledge management leads onto a discussion of some of the special-purpose systems discussed in the chapter, including expert and knowledge-based systems. The other topics discussed include robotics, vision systems, virtual reality and a variety of other special-purpose systems. We discuss embedded artificial intelligence, where artificial intelligence capabilities and applications are placed inside products and services.

Chapter 10 Pervasive Computing

The move of information systems to leave the office desktop and enter every aspect of our lives is well underway. Many businesses are exploiting this to their advantage, as are their customers. This chapter examines some of the technologies that are enabling all of this to happen. New ones are being introduced almost every month. It is important that businesses understand the potential benefits they can bring.

Chapter 11 Systems Analysis

This chapter and the next examine where information systems come from. Systems investigation and systems analysis, the first two steps of the systems development, are discussed. This chapter provides specific examples of how new or modified systems are initiated and analyzed in a number of industries. This chapter emphasizes how a project can be planned, aligned with corporate goals and rapidly developed.

Chapter 12 Systems Design and Implementation

This chapter looks at how the analysis discussed in Chapter 11 can be used to design and build IT solutions. The chapter mainly looks at developing a new system but also examines solving a problem by buying an existing IS that has already been developed.

Chapter 13 Security, Privacy and Ethical Issues in Information Systems

This last chapter looks at security, privacy and ethical issues, something that is in the background throughout the text. A wide range of non-technical issues associated with the use of information systems provide both opportunities and threats to modern organizations. The issues span the full spectrum – from preventing computer waste and mistakes, to avoiding violations of privacy, to complying with laws on collecting data about customers, to monitoring employees.

About the Authors

Ralph Stair received a BS in Chemical Engineering from Purdue University, an MBA from Tulane University, and a PhD from the University of Oregon. He has taught information systems at many universities. He has published numerous articles and books, including *Succeeding With Technology, Programming in BASIC* and many more.

George Reynolds is an assistant professor in the Information Systems department of the College of Business at the University of Cincinnati. He received a BS in Aerospace Engineering from the University of Cincinnati and an MS in Systems Engineering from West Coast University. He taught part-time at Xavier University, the University of Cincinnati, Miami University and the College of Mount Saint Joseph while working full-time in the information systems industry, including positions at the Manned Spacecraft Center in Houston, Texas; the Jet Propulsion Lab in Pasadena, California; and Procter and Gamble in Cincinnati, Ohio.

Thomas Chesney is an associate professor of information systems at Nottingham University Business School where he studies the behaviour of networked individuals. His work has appeared in the Information Systems Journal and Decision Support Systems. Thomas has a PhD in Information Systems from Brunel University an MSc in Informatics from Edinburgh University where his specialism was knowledge management and engineering and a BSc in Information Management from the Queen's University of Belfast. He is a fellow of the Higher Education Academy and a member of the Association for Information Systems.

Acknowledgements

We are indebted to the following reviewers for their perceptive feedback and expert insight on early drafts of this text:

- Scott Bingley, Victoria University, Australia
- Timothy Cleary, London Metropolitan University, UK
- Amare Desta, London South Bank University, UK
- Jane Nash, Rhodes University, South Africa
- Holly Tootell, University of Wollongong, Australia
- Indrit Troshani, University of Adelaide Business School, Australia

DIGITAL SUPPORT RESOURCES

Dedicated Instructor Resources

All of our Higher Education textbooks are accompanied by a range of digital support resources. Each title's resources are carefully tailored to the specific needs of the particular book's readers. Examples of the kind of resources provided include:

- A password protected area for instructors with, for example, a testbank, PowerPoint slides, and an instructor's manual
- An open-access area for students including, for example, useful weblinks and glossary terms

Lecturers: to discover the dedicated lecturer digital support resources accompanying this textbook please register here for access: **http://login.cengage.com**.

Students: to discover the dedicated student digital support resources accompanying this textbook, please search for PRINCIPLES OF BUSINESS INFORMATION SYSTEMS on: **www. cengagebrain.co.uk**

Overview

01

An Introduction to Information Systems

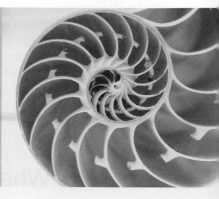

Principles

The value of information is directly linked to how it helps decision makers achieve organizational goals.

Computers and information systems are constantly making it possible for organizations to improve the way they conduct business.

Knowing the potential impact of information systems and having the ability to put this knowledge to work can result in a successful personal career, organizations that reach their goals and a society with a higher quality of life.

System users, business managers and information systems professionals must work together to build a successful information system.

Information systems must be applied thoughtfully and carefully so that society, business and industry can reap their enormous benefits.

Learning Objectives

- Discuss why it is important to study and understand information systems.
- Describe the characteristics used to evaluate the quality of data.

- Name the components of an information system and describe several system characteristics.

- Identify the basic types of business information systems and discuss who uses them, how they are used and what kinds of benefits they deliver.

- Identify the major steps of the systems development process and state the goal of each.

- Describe some of the threats to security and privacy that information systems and the Internet can pose.
- Discuss the expanding role and benefits of information systems in business and industry.

Information systems are used in almost every imaginable profession. Sales representatives use information systems to advertise products, communicate with customers and analyze sales trends. Managers use them to make major decisions, such as whether to build a manufacturing plant or research a cancer drug. From a small music store to huge multinational companies, businesses of all sizes could not survive without information systems to perform accounting and finance operations. Regardless of your chosen career, you will use information systems to help you achieve goals.

This chapter presents an overview of information systems. The sections on hardware, software, databases, telecommunications, e-commerce and m-commerce, transaction processing and enterprise resource planning, information and decision support, special purpose systems, systems development, and ethical and societal issues are expanded to full chapters in the rest of the book. We will start by exploring the basics of information systems.

1.1   What is an Information System?

People and organizations use information every day. Many retail chains, for example, collect data from their shops to help them stock what customers want and to reduce costs. Businesses use information systems to increase revenues and reduce costs. We use automated teller machines outside banks and access information over the Internet. Information systems usually involve computers, and, together, they are constantly changing the way organizations conduct business. Today we live in an information economy. Information itself has value, and commerce often involves the exchange of information rather than tangible goods. Systems based on computers are increasingly being used to create, store and transfer information. Using information systems, investors make multimillion-euro decisions, financial institutions transfer billions of euros around the world electronically, and manufacturers order supplies and distribute goods faster than ever before. Computers and information systems will continue to change businesses and the way we live. To define an information system, we will start by examining what a system is.

What is a System?

system A set of elements or components that interact to accomplish goals.

A central concept of this book is that of a **system**. A system is a set of elements or components that interact to accomplish goals. The elements themselves and the relationships among them determine how the system works. Systems have inputs, processing mechanisms, outputs and feedback (see Figure 1.1). A system processes the input to create the output. For example, consider an automatic car wash. Tangible inputs for the process are a dirty car, water and various cleaning ingredients. Time, energy, skill and knowledge also serve as inputs to the system because they are needed to operate it.

Figure 1.1 Components of a System *A system's four components consist of input, processing, output and feedback.*

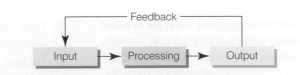

The processing mechanisms consist of first selecting which cleaning option you want (wash only, wash with wax, wash with wax and hand dry, etc.) and communicating that to the operator of the car wash. Liquid sprayers shoot clear water, liquid soap or car wax depending on where your car is in the process and which options you selected. The output is a clean car. As in all systems, independent elements or components (the liquid sprayer, foaming brush and air dryer) interact to create a clean car. A feedback mechanism is your assessment of how clean the car is.

System performance can be measured in various ways. **Efficiency** is a measure of what is produced divided by what is consumed. For example, the efficiency of a motor is the energy produced (in terms of work done) divided by the energy consumed (in terms of electricity or fuel). Some motors have an efficiency of 50 per cent or less because of the energy lost to friction and heat generation.

efficiency A measure of what is produced divided by what is consumed.

Effectiveness is a measure of the extent to which a system achieves its goals. It can be computed by dividing the goals actually achieved by the total of the stated goals. For example, a company might want to achieve a net profit of €100 million for the year with a new information system. Actual profits, however, might only be €85 million for the year. In this case, the effectiveness is 85 per cent (85/100 = 85 per cent).

effectiveness A measure of the extent to which a system achieves its goals; it can be computed by dividing the goals actually achieved by the total of the stated goals.

Evaluating system performance also calls for using performance standards. A **system performance standard** is a specific objective of the system. For example, a system performance standard for a marketing campaign might be to have each sales representative sell €100 000 of a certain type of product each year (see Figure 1.2a). A system performance standard for a manufacturing process might be to provide no more than 1 per cent defective parts (see Figure 1.2b). After standards are

system performance standard A specific objective of the system.

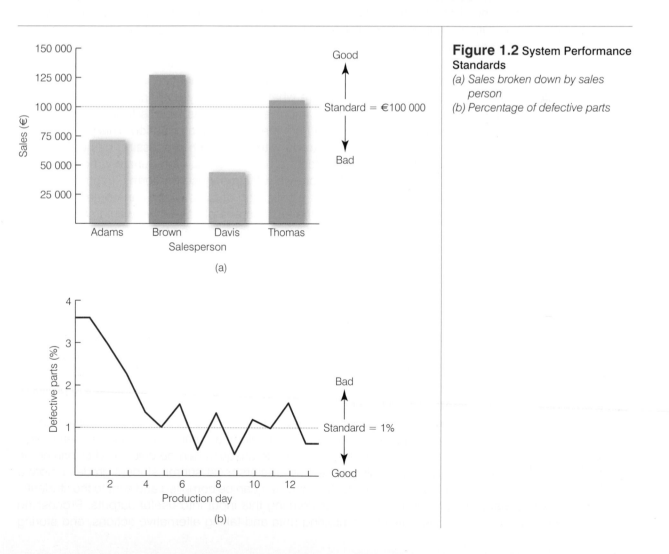

Figure 1.2 System Performance Standards
(a) Sales broken down by sales person
(b) Percentage of defective parts

established, system performance is measured and compared with the standard. Variances from the standard are determinants of system performance.

What is Information?

Information is one of those concepts that we all seem intuitively able to grasp, but find tricky to define. In the 1940s, mathematician Claude Shannon defined it as: information is that which reduces uncertainty. Shannon was working on the technical problems involved in sending messages over communication networks and his concept of information is actually quite different from what we in business information systems mean by 'information'. Nevertheless, we can use his definition as a starting point. Imagine you are unsure of what today's weather will be like. Getting out of bed you open the curtains to see that the sun is shining. You now know a bit more about what's it's going to be like: your uncertainty about the weather has been reduced. Therefore looking out the window gave you information. When you turn on your radio and hear a detailed weather report, your uncertainty has been reduced further. When you look at the temperature gauge in your car, again your uncertainty has gone down. According to Shannon's definition, each of these events has therefore given you information.

However his definition does not really capture what we would think of when we consider the information in, say, a management report. Therefore we simply define information as a collection of facts. These facts can take many forms. The temperature gauge in the car gives information in the form of a number. The radio gives audio information. Looking out of the window gives visual information. Other forms of information include text, images, and video clips.

Another term that is closely related to information is 'data'. It's not intuitive but a philosopher might define data as 'variation'. To explain this: a blank page contains no data, but as soon as there is a mark on the page, that is, as soon as there is variation in the blankness, then data exist. Again this doesn't really capture what we mean by data in the context of business information systems. The traditional information systems view is that the input to an information system is data, and the output from the system is information. This means therefore that the difference between them is to do with how much processing has been done: unprocessed facts are data, processed facts are information. Unfortunately, however, this distinction is of little practical use. Therefore we will simply use the terms 'information' and 'data' interchangeably and define them as a collection of facts which can come in a variety of formats. (Incidentally, strictly speaking the term data is plural, so we would say 'data are used' rather than 'data is used'. However this is often not adhered to and we won't worry too much about it here.)

What is an Information System?

information system (IS) A set of interrelated components that collect, manipulate, store and disseminate information and provide a feedback mechanism to meet an objective.

input The activity of gathering and capturing data.

processing Converting or transforming input into useful outputs.

Now that we have defined the terms 'system' and 'information', we can define an information system: an **information system (IS)** is a set of interrelated components that collect, manipulate, store and disseminate information and provide a feedback mechanism to meet an objective. It is the feedback mechanism that helps organizations achieve their goals, such as increasing profits or improving customer service.

In information systems, **input** is the activity of gathering and capturing data. In producing paycheques, for example, the number of hours every employee works must be collected before the cheques can be calculated or printed. In a university grading system, instructors must submit student grades before a summary of grades for the semester can be compiled and sent to the students.

Processing means converting or transforming this input into useful outputs. Processing can involve making calculations, comparing data and taking alternative actions, and storing data for future use. In a payroll application, the number of hours each employee worked must be converted into net, or take-home, pay. Other inputs often include employee ID number and department. The required processing can first involve multiplying the number of hours worked by the employee's hourly pay rate to get gross pay. If weekly hours worked exceed 35 hours, overtime pay might also be included. Then tax must be deducted along with contributions to health and life insurance or savings plans to get net pay.

After these calculations and comparisons are performed, the results are typically stored. Storage involves keeping data and information available for future use, including output.

Output involves producing useful information, usually in the form of documents and reports. Outputs can include paycheques for employees, reports for managers, and information supplied to stockholders, banks, government agencies and other groups. In addition, output from one system can become input for another. For example, output from a system that processes sales orders can be used as input to a customer billing system. Computers typically produce output on printers and display screens. Output can also be handwritten or manually produced reports, although this is not common.

output Production of useful information, often in the form of documents and reports.

Lastly, **feedback** is information from the system that is used to make changes to input or processing activities. For example, errors or problems might make it necessary to correct input data or change a process. Consider a payroll example. Perhaps the number of hours an employee worked was entered as 400 instead of 40 hours. Fortunately, most information systems check to make sure that data falls within certain ranges. For number of hours worked, the range might be from 0 to 100 hours because it is unlikely that an employee would work more than 100 hours in a week. The information system would determine that 400 hours is out of range and provide feedback. The feedback is used to check and correct the input on the number of hours worked to 40.

feedback Output that is used to make changes to input or processing activities.

Feedback is also important for managers and decision makers. For example, a furniture maker could use a computerized feedback system to link its suppliers and manufacturing plants. The output from an information system might indicate that inventory levels for mahogany and oak are getting low – a potential problem. A manager could use this feedback to decide to order more wood from a supplier. These new inventory orders then become input to the system. In addition to this reactive approach, a computer system can also be proactive – predicting future events to avoid problems. This concept, often called **forecasting**, can be used to estimate future sales and order more inventory before a shortage occurs. Forecasting is also used to predict the strength of hurricanes and possible landing sites, future stock-market values and who will win a political election.

forecasting Predicting future events.

The Characteristics of Valuable Information

To be valuable to managers and decision makers, information should have some and possibly all of the characteristics described in Table 1.1. Many shipping companies, for example, can determine the exact location of inventory items and packages in their systems, and this information makes them responsive to their customers. In contrast, if an organization's information is not accurate or complete, people can make poor decisions costing thousands, or even millions, of euros. Many claim, for example, that the collapse and bankruptcy of some companies, such as drug companies and energy-trading firms, was a result of inaccurate accounting and reporting information, which led investors and employees alike to misjudge the actual state of the company's finances and suffer huge personal losses. As another example, if an inaccurate forecast of future demand indicates that sales will be very high when the opposite is true, an organization can invest millions of euros in a new plant that is not needed. Furthermore, if information is not relevant, not delivered to decision makers in a timely fashion, or too complex to understand, it can be of little value to the organization.

The value of information is directly linked to how it helps decision makers achieve their organization's goals. For example, the value of information might be measured in the time required to

Table 1.1 Characteristics of Valuable Information

Characteristics	Definitions
Accessible	Information should be easily accessible by authorized users so they can obtain it in the right format and at the right time to meet their needs
Accurate	Accurate information is error free. In some cases, inaccurate information is generated because inaccurate data is fed into the transformation process
Complete	Complete information contains all the important facts, but not more facts than are necessary (see the Simple characteristic below)
Economical	Information should also be relatively economical to produce. Decision makers must always balance the value of information with the cost of producing it
Flexible	Flexible information can be used for a variety of purposes. For example, information on how much inventory is on hand for a particular part can be used by a sales representative in closing a sale, by a production manager to determine whether more inventory is needed, and by a financial executive to determine the total value the company has invested in inventory
Relevant	Relevant information is important to the decision maker
Reliable	Reliable information can be depended on. In many cases, the reliability of the information depends on the reliability of the data-collection method. In other instances, reliability depends on the source of the information. A rumor from an unknown source that oil prices might go up may soon not be reliable (even though it might be useful)
Secure	Information should be secure from access by unauthorized users
Simple	Information should be simple, not overly complex. Sophisticated and detailed information might not be needed. In fact, too much information can cause information overload, whereby a decision maker has too much information and is unable to determine what is really important
Timely	Timely information is delivered when it is needed. Knowing last week's weather conditions will not help when trying to decide what coat to wear today
Verifiable	Information should be verifiable. This means that you can check it to make sure it is correct, perhaps by checking many sources for the same information

make a decision or in increased profits to the company. Consider a market forecast that predicts a high demand for a new product. If you use this information to develop the new product and your company makes an additional profit of €10 000, the value of this information to the company is €10 000 minus the cost of the information.

Manual and Computerized Information Systems

An information system can be manual or computerized. For example, some investment analysts manually draw charts and trend lines to assist them in making investment decisions. Tracking data on stock prices (input) over the last few months or years, these analysts develop patterns on graph paper (processing) that help them determine what stock prices are likely to do in the next few days or weeks (output). Some investors have made millions of euros using manual stock analysis information systems. Of course, today many excellent computerized information systems follow stock indexes and markets and suggest when large blocks of stocks should be purchased or sold to take advantage of market discrepancies.

A **computer-based information system (CBIS)** is a single set of hardware, software, databases, telecommunications, people and procedures that are configured to collect, manipulate, store and process data into information. For example, a company's payroll, order entry or inventory-control system is an example of a CBIS. CBISs can also be embedded into products. Some new cars and home appliances include computer hardware, software, databases and even telecommunications to control their operations and make them more useful. This is often called 'embedded', 'pervasive' or 'ubiquitous' computing. CBISs have evolved into sophisticated analysis tools.

The components of a CBIS are illustrated in Figure 1.3. Information technology (IT) refers to hardware, software, databases and telecommunications. A business's **technology infrastructure** includes all the hardware, software, databases, telecommunications, people and procedures that are configured to collect, manipulate, store and process data into information. The technology infrastructure is a set of shared IS resources that form the foundation of each computer-based information system.

Hardware

Hardware consists of computer equipment used to perform input, processing and output activities. Input devices include keyboards, mice and other pointing devices, automatic scanning devices and equipment that can read magnetic ink characters. Investment firms often use voice-response technology to allow customers to access their balances and other information with spoken commands. Processing devices include computer chips that contain the central processing unit and main memory. One processor chip, called the 'Bunny Chip' by some,

computer-based information system (CBIS) A single set of hardware, software, databases, telecommunications, people and procedures that are configured to collect, manipulate, store and process data into information.

technology infrastructure All the hardware, software, databases, telecommunications, people and procedures that are configured to collect, manipulate, store and process data into information.

hardware Any machinery (most of which uses digital circuits) that assists in the input, processing, storage and output activities of an information system.

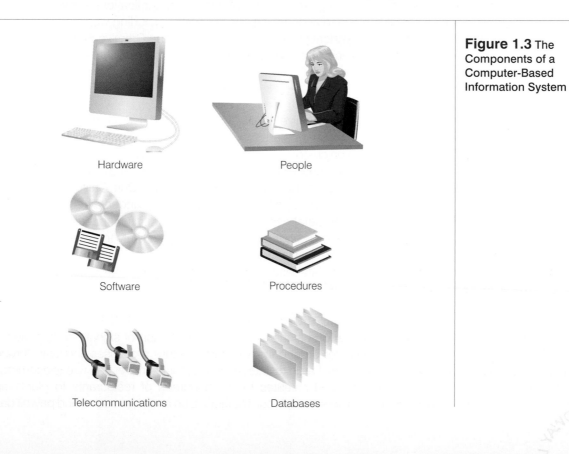

Figure 1.3 The Components of a Computer-Based Information System

Hardware

People

Software

Procedures

Telecommunications

Databases

mimics living organisms and can be used by the drug industry to test drugs instead of using animals, such as rats or bunnies.[1] The experimental chip could save millions of euros and months of time in drug research costs. Processor speed is also important. The TOP500 project (www.top500.org) has collected statistics on the world's fastest computers since 1993. Currently the fastest is Tianhe-2, a supercomputer developed by China's National University of Defense Technology (NUDT) which is capable of performing 33.86 petaflop/s (quadrillions of calculations per second). NUDT say it will be used for business opinion analysis, government security and nuclear fusion research.[2]

The many types of output devices include printers and computer screens. Bond traders, for example, often use an array of six or more computer screens to monitor bond prices and make split-second trades throughout each day. Another type of output device is a printer to print photos from a digital camera. Such printers accept the memory card direct from the camera. There are also many special-purpose hardware devices. Computerized event data recorders (EDRs) are now being placed into vehicles. Like an airplane's black box, EDRs record a vehicle's speed, possible engine problems, a driver's performance and more. The technology is being used to monitor vehicle operation, determine the cause of accidents and investigate whether truck drivers are taking required breaks.

Software

software The computer programs that govern the operation of the computer.

Software consists of the computer programs that govern the operation of the computer. These programs allow a computer to process payroll, send bills to customers, and provide managers with information to increase profits, reduce costs and provide better customer service. With software, people can work anytime at any place. Software, along with manufacturing tools, for example, can be used to fabricate parts almost anywhere in the world.[3] Software called 'Fab Lab' controls tools, such as cutters, milling machines and other devices. A Fab Lab system, which costs about €15 000, has been used to make radio frequency tags to track animals in Norway, engine parts to allow tractors to run on processed castor beans in India and many other fabrication applications.

The two types of software are system software, such as Microsoft Windows, which controls basic computer operations, including start-up and printing; and applications software, such as Microsoft Office, which allows you to accomplish specific tasks, including word processing and drawing charts. Sophisticated application software, such as Adobe Creative Suite, can be used to design, develop, print and place professional-quality advertising, brochures, posters, prints and videos on the Internet.

Databases

database An organized collection of information.

A **database** is an organized collection of facts and information, typically consisting of two or more related data files. An organization's database can contain information on customers, employees, inventory, competitors' sales, online purchases and much more. Most managers and executives consider a database to be one of the most valuable parts of a computer-based information system. One California real estate development company uses databases to search for homes that are undervalued and purchase them at bargain prices.[4] It uses the database to analyze crime statistics, prices, local weather reports, school districts and more to find homes whose values are likely to increase. The database has helped the company realize an average 50 per cent return on investment. Increasingly, organizations are placing important databases on the Internet, which makes them accessible to many, including unauthorized users.

Telecommunications, Networks, and the Internet

telecommunications The electronic transmission of signals for communications; enables organizations to carry out their processes and tasks through effective computer networks.

Telecommunications is the electronic transmission of signals for communications, which enables organizations to carry out their processes and tasks through computer networks. Large restaurant chains, for example, can use telecommunications systems and satellites to link hundreds of restaurants to plants and headquarters to speed credit card authorization and report sales and payroll data.

Networks connect computers and equipment in a building, around the country or around the world to enable electronic communication. Investment firms can use wireless networks to connect thousands of investors with brokers or traders. Many hotels use wireless telecommunications to allow guests to connect to the Internet, retrieve voice messages and exchange email without plugging their computers or mobile devices into a phone socket. Wireless transmission also allows drones, such as Boeing's Scan Eagle, to fly using a remote control system and monitor buildings and other areas.

network Computers and equipment that are connected in a building, around the country or around the world to enable electronic communications.

The **Internet** is the world's largest computer network, actually consisting of thousands of interconnected networks, all freely exchanging information. Research firms, colleges, universities, schools and businesses are just a few examples of organizations using the Internet. People use the Internet to research information, buy and sell products and services, make travel arrangements, conduct banking, and download music and videos, among other activities. After downloading music, you can use audio software to change a song's tempo, create mixes of your favourite tunes and modify sound tracks to suit your personal taste. You can even mix two or more songs simultaneously, which is called 'mashing'. You can also use many of today's mobile phones to connect to the Internet from around the world and at high speeds.[5] This not only speeds communications, but allows you to conduct business electronically. Some airline companies are providing Internet service on their flights so that travellers can send and receive email, check investments and browse the Internet. Internet users can create blogs (weblogs) to store and share their thoughts and ideas with others around the world.[6] You can also record and store TV programmes on computers or special viewing devices and watch them later.[7] Often called 'place shifting', this technology allows you to record TV programmes at home and watch them at a different place when it's convenient.

internet The world's largest computer network, actually consisting of thousands of interconnected networks, all freely exchanging information.

The World Wide Web (WWW), or the web, is a network of links on the Internet to documents containing text, graphics, video and sound. Information about the documents and access to them are controlled and provided by tens of thousands of special computers called 'web servers'. The web is one of many services available over the Internet and provides access to many hundreds of millions of documents. Widely available Internet access has allowed the development of **cloud computing**, where software and data storage are provided as an Internet service and are accessed via a web browser.

cloud computing: A computing environment where software and storage are provided as an Internet service and are accessed via a web browser.

The technology used to create the Internet is also being applied within companies and organizations to create **intranets**, which allow people within an organization to exchange information and work on projects. One company, for example, uses an intranet to connect its 200 global operating companies and 20 000 employees. An **extranet** is a network based on web technologies that allows selected outsiders, such as business partners and customers, to access authorized resources of a company's intranet. Companies can move all or most of their business activities to an extranet site for corporate customers. Many people use extranets every day without realizing it – to track shipped goods, order products from their suppliers or access customer assistance from other companies. If you log on to the FedEx site (www.fedex.com) to check the status of a package, for example, you are using an extranet.

intranet An internal company network built using Internet and World Wide Web standards and products that allows people within an organization to exchange information and work on projects.

extranet A network based on web technologies that allows selected outsiders, such as business partners, suppliers or customers, to access authorized resources of a company's intranet.

People

People are the most important element in most computer-based information systems. The people involved include users of the system and information systems personnel, including all the people who manage, run, program and maintain the system.

procedures The strategies, policies, methods and rules for using a CBIS.

Procedures

Procedures include the strategies, policies, methods, and rules for using the CBIS, including the operation, maintenance and security of the computer. For example, some procedures describe when each program should be run. Others describe who can access facts in the database, or what to do if a disaster, such as a fire, earthquake or hurricane, renders the CBIS unusable. Good procedures can help companies take advantage of new opportunities and avoid potential disasters. Poorly developed and inadequately implemented procedures, however, can cause people to waste their time on useless rules or result in inadequate responses to disasters, such as hurricanes or tornadoes.

1.2 Business Information Systems

The most common types of information systems used in business organizations are those designed for electronic and mobile commerce, transaction processing, management information and decision support. In addition, some organizations employ special-purpose systems, such as virtual reality, that not every organization uses. Together, these systems help employees in organizations accomplish routine and special tasks – from recording sales, processing payrolls and supporting decisions in various departments, to examining alternatives for large-scale projects and opportunities. Often in large organizations one information system is used to accomplish all of these tasks. In others, separate systems are used. When one system is used it is called an Enterprise System, and it does most if not all of the tasks of the other systems shown

Information Systems @ Work

Cybernest Reduces Energy Used to Store Data in South Africa

Telkom is Africa's largest communications company, providing solutions to an entire range of customers. Based in South Africa they offer phone and Internet access along with related services to business, residential and payphone customers. At the end of 2013 they had approximately 3.7 million telephone access lines in service. One of their related services is data hosting. From six data centres – four in Gauteng and two in the Western Cape – employing over 600 IT specialists, Telkom gives customers the ability to store their data securely and reliably without the need to worry about purchasing their own expensive physical infrastructure. Collectively the six centres are known as Cybernest.

The company promotes the security of its operation and its ability to help clients protect themselves from disasters such as fire and flood which could destroy their IT. Client data are backed up so that if a disaster hits one centre, a copy is held at another. Many companies cannot afford to have their own 'off-site' backups.

Cybernest also promotes its green credentials. In a data centre the computing equipment itself consumes a relatively small part – around 30 per cent – of the total power used. Most of the energy consumed, as high as 45 per cent, is taken by the cooling systems. Any reduction in this has immediate financial and environmental benefits. Cybernest expects to achieve an overall energy saving of 34 per cent a year by embedding green principles into the design of its newest data centre and by using free cooling. Free cooling uses the external air temperature to chill water which is then used to remove the heat generated by the data centre. At Cybernest's newest data centre two cooling modes are in place: the usual chiller system and free air cooling. The latter is used when the weather allows it – when the ambient temperature outside falls below 24 degrees Celsius. On these days, cool outside air is filtered in and hot air is vented out. The temperature inside older data centres tends to be uncomfortably cold for humans because air conditioners chill the entire environment, not just the computers. New-generation centres are more selective. They don't cool every-thing, only the components that need cooling. Using the principle that hot air rises and cold air sinks, they have alternating hot and cold aisles, with each cold aisle blowing cool air upwards through the floor and a hot aisle above, sucking warm air out through the ceiling. The components that need to be cool are positioned to face the cold aisle, ensuring the best use of cool air flowing in and hot air flowing out.

Other energy-efficient techniques in use include eco-friendly forms of uninterruptable power supply which are needed in order to safely shut the computers down in case of power failure. According to Althon Beukes, Cybernest's Executive of Infrastructure Operations, 'Some people ask where the wind turbines and solar panels are. The answer is that these solutions aren't yet feasible in a data centre environment. We focus on green technologies that also make business sense.'

Questions

1 What are some of the dangers a company faces when it uses a third party to store and manage its information?

2 Should energy reduction be a priority for all organizations?

3 Can you think of any other services Cybernest could provide?

4 Do you think clients actually care that Cybernest has green credentials, or are they just interested in the cost of the service?

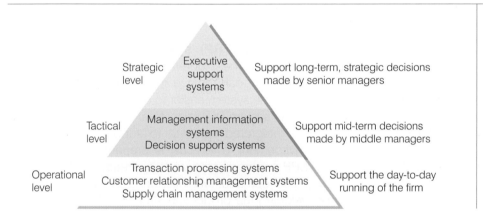

Figure 1.4 Business Information Systems
The triangle shows the main types of information system used in businesses and the level within the business where they tend to be used.

in Figure 1.4. These systems are discussed next and each one is treated separately but you should be aware that they can be combined together to form an enterprise system. You should also be aware that there is no agreed definition on the minimum set of tasks that a system has to do in order for it to be considered an enterprise system but the expectation is that it must do more than any one of the following.

Enterprise Systems: Transaction Processing Systems and Enterprise Resource Planning

Transaction Processing Systems

Since the 1950s, computers have been used to perform common business applications. Many of these early systems were designed to reduce costs by automating routine, labour-intensive business transactions. A **transaction** is any business-related exchange, such as payments to employees, sales to customers or payments to suppliers. Thus, processing business transactions was the first computer application developed for most organizations. A **transaction processing system (TPS)** is an organized collection of people,

transaction Any business-related exchange, such as payments to employees, sales to customers and payments to suppliers.

transaction processing system (TPS) An organized collection of people, procedures, software, databases and devices used to record completed business transactions.

procedures, software, databases and devices used to record completed business transactions. If you understand a transaction processing system, you understand basic business operations and functions.

Enterprise systems help organizations perform and integrate important tasks, such as paying employees and suppliers, controlling inventory, sending out invoices and ordering supplies. In the past, companies accomplished these tasks using traditional transaction processing systems. Today, they are increasingly being performed by enterprise resource planning systems. For example, Whirlpool Corporation, the large appliance maker, used enterprise resource planning to reduce inventory levels by 20 per cent and cut about 5 per cent from its freight and warehousing costs by providing managers with information about inventory levels and costs.[8] The new system may have also helped the company increase its revenues by about €0.7 billion.

One of the first business systems to be computerized was the payroll system. The primary inputs for a payroll TPS are the number of employee hours worked during the week and the pay rate. The primary output consists of paycheques. Early payroll systems produced employee paycheques and related reports required by tax authorities. Other routine applications include sales ordering, customer billing and customer relationship management, and inventory control. Some car companies, for example, use their TPSs to buy billions of euros of needed parts each year through websites. Because these systems handle and process daily business exchanges, or transactions, they are all classified as TPSs.

Enterprise Resource Planning

enterprise resource planning (ERP) system A set of integrated programs capable of managing a company's vital business operations for an entire multi-site, global organization.

An **enterprise resource planning (ERP) system** is a set of integrated programs that manages the vital business operations for an entire multi-site, global organization. An ERP system can replace many applications with one unified set of programs, making the system easier to use and more effective.

Although the scope of an ERP system might vary from company to company, most ERP systems provide integrated software to support manufacturing and finance. In such an environment, a forecast is prepared that estimates customer demand for several weeks. The ERP system checks what is already available in finished product inventory to meet the projected demand. Manufacturing must then produce inventory to eliminate any shortfalls. In developing the production schedule, the ERP system checks the raw materials and packing-materials inventories and determines what needs to be ordered to meet the schedule. Most ERP systems also have a purchasing subsystem that orders the needed items. In addition to these core business processes, some ERP systems can support functions such as human resources, sales, and distribution. The primary benefits of implementing an ERP system include easing adoption of improved work processes and increasing access to timely data for decision making.

e-commerce Any business transaction executed electronically between companies (business-to-business), companies and consumers (business-to-consumer), consumers and other consumers (consumer-to-consumer), business and the public sector, and consumers and the public sector.

mobile commerce (m-commerce) Conducting business transactions electronically using mobile devices such as smartphones.

An important type of transaction processing system handles transaction made electronically over the web. **E-commerce** involves any business transaction executed electronically between companies (business-to-business, 'B2B'), companies and consumers (business-to-consumer, 'B2C'), consumers and other consumers (consumer-to-consumer, 'C2C'), business and the public sector, and consumers and the public sector. You might assume that e-commerce is reserved mainly for consumers visiting websites for online shopping, but web shopping is only a small part of the e-commerce picture; the major volume of e-commerce – and its fastest growing segment – is business-to-business (B2B) transactions that make purchasing easier for corporations. This growth is being stimulated by increased Internet access, growing user confidence, better payment systems, and rapidly improving Internet and web security. E-commerce also offers opportunities for small businesses to market and sell at a low cost worldwide, allowing them to enter the global market. **Mobile commerce (m-commerce)** refers to transactions conducted anywhere, anytime. M-commerce relies on wireless communications that managers and corporations use to place orders and conduct business with hand-held computers, portable phones, laptop computers connected to a network and other mobile devices.

E-commerce offers many advantages for streamlining work activities. Figure 1.5 provides a brief example of how e-commerce can simplify the process of purchasing new office furniture from an office-supply company. In the manual system, a corporate office worker must get approval for a purchase that exceeds a certain amount. That request goes to the purchasing department, which generates a formal purchase order to procure the goods from the approved vendor. Business-to-business e-commerce automates the entire process. Employees go directly to the supplier's website, find the item in a catalogue, and order what they need at a price set by their company. If approval is required, the approver is notified automatically. As the use of e-commerce systems grows, companies are phasing out their traditional systems. The resulting growth of e-commerce is creating many new business opportunities.

E-commerce can enhance a company's stock prices and market value. Today, several e-commerce firms have teamed up with more traditional brick-and-mortar businesses to draw from each other's strengths. For example, e-commerce customers can order products on a website and pick them up at a nearby store.

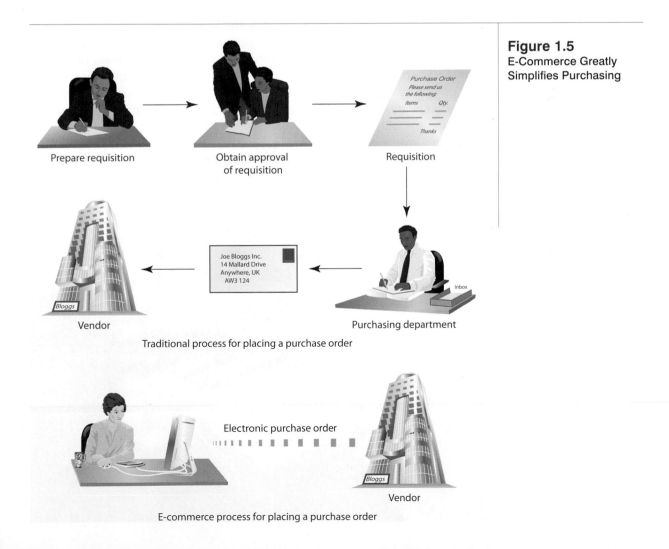

Figure 1.5
E-Commerce Greatly
Simplifies Purchasing

Prepare requisition

Obtain approval
of requisition

Requisition

Joe Bloggs Inc.
14 Mallard Drive
Anywhere, UK
AW3 124

Inbox

Vendor

Purchasing department

Traditional process for placing a purchase order

Electronic purchase order

Vendor

E-commerce process for placing a purchase order

In addition to e-commerce, business information systems use telecommunications and the Internet to perform many related tasks. Electronic procurement (e-procurement), for example, involves using information systems and the Internet to acquire parts and supplies. **Electronic business (e-business)** goes beyond e-commerce and e-procurement by using information systems and the Internet to perform all business-related tasks and functions, such as accounting, finance, marketing, manufacturing and human resource activities. E-business also includes working with customers, suppliers, strategic partners and stakeholders. Compared with traditional business strategy, e-business strategy is flexible and adaptable.

electronic business (e-business) Using information systems and the Internet to perform all business-related tasks and functions.

MIS and DSS

The benefits provided by an effective TPS are tangible and justify their associated costs in computing equipment, computer programs, and specialized personnel and supplies. A TPS can speed business activities and reduce clerical costs. Although early accounting and financial TPSs were already valuable, companies soon realized that they could use the data stored in these systems to help managers make better decisions, whether in human resource management, marketing or administration. Satisfying the needs of managers and decision makers continues to be a major factor in developing information systems.

Management Information Systems

management information system (MIS) An organized collection of people, procedures, software, databases and devices that provides routine information to managers and decision makers.

A **management information system (MIS)** is an organized collection of people, procedures, software, databases and devices that provides routine information to managers and decision makers. An MIS focuses on operational efficiency. Marketing, production, finance and other functional areas are supported by MISs and linked through a common database. MISs typically provide standard reports generated with data and information from the TPS, meaning the output of a TPS is the input to a MIS. Producing a report that describes inventory that should be ordered is an example of an MIS.

MISs were first developed in the 1960s and typically use information systems to produce managerial reports. In many cases, these early reports were produced periodically – daily,

Figure 1.6 Contactless payment *M-commerce means that it is possible to pay for items using a smartphone or other mobile device.*

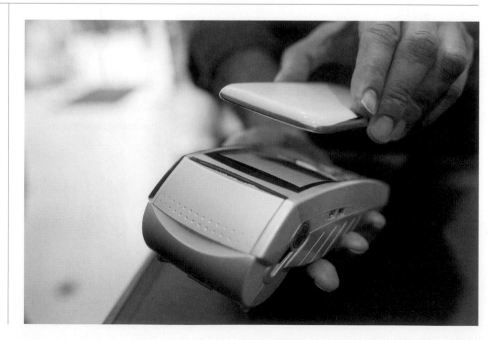

weekly, monthly or yearly. Because of their value to managers, MISs have proliferated through-out the management ranks. For instance, the total payroll summary report produced initially for an accounting manager might also be useful to a production manager to help monitor and control labour and job costs.

Decision Support Systems

By the 1980s, dramatic improvements in technology resulted in information systems that were less expensive but more powerful than earlier systems. People at all levels of organizations began using personal computers to do a variety of tasks; they were no longer solely dependent on the IS depart-ment for all their information needs. People quickly recognized that computer sys-tems could support additional decision-making activities. A **decision support system (DSS)** is an organized collection of people, procedures, software, data-bases and devices that support problem-specific decision making. The focus of a DSS is on making effective decisions. Whereas an MIS helps an organization 'do things right', a DSS helps a manager 'do the right thing'.

decision support system (DSS) An organized collection of people, procedures, software, databases and devices used to support problem-specific decision making.

In addition to assisting in all aspects of problem-specific decision making, a DSS can support customers by rapidly responding to their phone and email enquiries. A DSS goes beyond a traditional MIS by providing immediate assistance in solving problems. Many of these problems are unique and complex, and information is often difficult to obtain. For instance, a car manufacturer might try to determine the layout for its new manufacturing facility. Traditional MISs are seldom used to solve these types of problems; a DSS can help by suggest-ing alternatives and assisting in final decision making.

Decision support systems are used when the problem is complex and the information needed to make the best decision is difficult to obtain and use. So a DSS also involves managerial judegment and perspective. Managers often play an active role in developing and implementing the DSS. A DSS recognizes that different managerial styles and decision types require different systems. For example, two production managers in the same position trying to solve the same problem might require different information and support. The overall emphasis is to support, rather than replace, managerial decision making.

The essential elements of a DSS include a collection of models used to support a decision maker or user (model base), a collection of facts and information to assist in decision mak-ing (database), and systems and procedures (dialogue manager or user interface) that help decision makers and other users interact with the DSS. Software is often used to manage the database – the database management system (DBMS) – and the model base – the model management system (MMS).

In addition to DSSs for managers, group decision support systems and executive support systems use the same approach to support groups and executives.[9] A group decision support system, also called a group support system, includes the DSS elements just described and software, called group-ware, to help groups make effective decisions. An executive support system, also called an executive information system, helps top-level managers, including a firm's president, vice presidents and mem-bers of the board of directors, make better decisions. An executive support system can assist with strategic planning, top-level organizing and staffing, strategic control and crisis management.

Knowledge Management, Artificial Intelligence, Expert Systems and Virtual Reality

In addition to TPSs, MISs and DSSs, organizations often rely on specialized systems. Many use knowledge management systems (KMSs), an organized collection of people, procedures, software, databases and devices to create, store, share and use the organization's knowledge and experience. According to a survey of CEOs, firms that use KMSs are more likely to innovate and perform better.[10]

In addition to knowledge management, companies use other types of specialized systems. The Nissan Motor Company, for example, has developed a specialized system for their vehicles called 'Lane Departure Prevention' that nudges a car back into the correct lane if it veers off course.[11] The system uses cameras and computers to adjust braking to get the vehicle back on course. The system switches off when the driver uses turn signals to change lanes. Other specialized systems are based on the notion of **artificial intelligence (AI)**, in which the computer system takes on the characteristics of human intelligence. The field of artificial intelligence includes several sub-fields (see Figure 1.7). Some people predict that in the future, we will have nanobots, small molecular-sized robots, travelling throughout our bodies and in our bloodstream, keeping us healthy.[12] Other nanobots will be embedded in products and services, making our lives easier and creating new business opportunities.

artificial intelligence (AI) The ability of computer systems to mimic or duplicate the functions or characteristics of the human brain or intelligence.

Artificial Intelligence

Robotics is an area of artificial intelligence in which machines take over complex, dangerous, routine or boring tasks, such as welding car frames or assembling computer systems and components. Vision systems allow robots and other devices to 'see', store and process visual images. Natural language processing involves computers understanding and acting on verbal or written commands in English, Spanish or other human languages. Learning systems allow computers to learn from past mistakes or experiences, such as playing games or making business decisions, and neural networks is a branch of AI that allows computers to recognize and act on patterns or trends. Some successful stock, options and futures traders use neural networks to spot trends and make them more profitable with their investments. State of the art artificial intelligence is impressive. In 2011 the IBM supercomputer Watson competed against and beat two human champions in the game show Jeopardy. By the end of 2018, Google expects to be selling cars with 'driverless' features, using artificial intelligence in the vehicles to avoid passenger injuries.[13]

expert system A system that gives a computer the ability to make suggestions and act like an expert in a particular field.

Expert Systems

Expert systems give the computer the ability to make suggestions and act like an expert in a particular field. It can help the novice user perform at the level of an

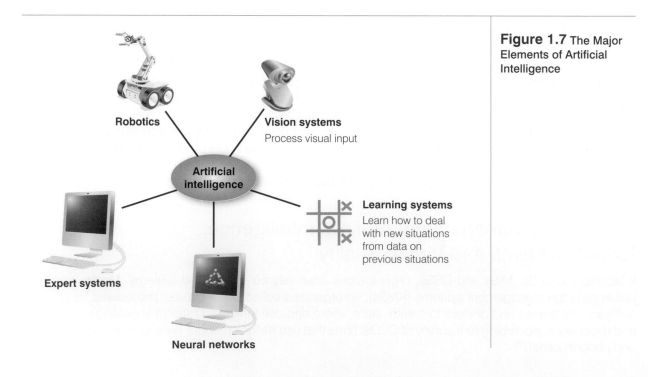

Figure 1.7 The Major Elements of Artificial Intelligence

Robotics

Vision systems
Process visual input

Artificial intelligence

Learning systems
Learn how to deal with new situations from data on previous situations

Expert systems

Neural networks

expert. The unique value of expert systems is that they allow organizations to capture and use the wisdom of experts and specialists. Therefore, years of experience and specific skills are not completely lost when a human expert dies, retires or leaves for another job. Expert systems can be applied to almost any field or discipline. They have been used to monitor nuclear reactors, perform medical diagnoses, locate possible repair problems, design and configure IS components, perform credit evaluations, and develop marketing plans for a new product or new investment strategy. The collection of data, rules, procedures and relationships that must be followed to achieve value or the proper outcome is contained in the expert system's **knowledge base**.

knowledge base A component of an expert system that stores all relevant information, data, rules, cases and relationships used by the expert system.

Virtual Reality

Virtual reality is the simulation of a real or imagined environment that can be experienced visually in three dimensions. Originally, virtual reality referred to immersive virtual reality, which means the user becomes fully immersed in an artificial, computer-generated 3D world. The virtual world is presented in full scale and relates properly to the human size. It can represent any 3D setting, real or abstract, such as a building, an archaeological excavation site, the human anatomy, a sculpture or a crime scene reconstruction. Virtual worlds can be animated, interactive and shared. Through immersion, the user can gain a deeper understanding of the virtual world's behaviour and functionality. Virtual reality can also refer to applications that are not fully immersive, such as mouse-controlled navigation through a 3D environment on a graphics monitor, stereo viewing from the monitor via stereo glasses, stereo projection systems and others.

virtual reality The simulation of a real or imagined environment that can be experienced visually in three dimensions.

A variety of input devices, such as head-mounted displays, data gloves, joysticks and hand-held wands, allow the user to navigate through a virtual environment and to interact with virtual objects. Directional sound, tactile and force feedback devices, voice recognition and other technologies enrich the immersive experience. Because several people can share and interact in the same environment, virtual reality can be a powerful medium for communication, entertainment and learning.

It is difficult to predict where information systems and technology will be in 10 to 20 years. It seems, however, that we are just beginning to discover the full range of their usefulness. Technology has been improving and expanding at an increasing rate; dramatic growth and change are expected for years to come. Without question, a knowledge of the effective use of information systems will be critical for managers both now and in the long term. But how are these information systems created?

1.3 Systems Development

Systems development is the activity of creating or modifying business systems. Systems development projects can range from small to very large in fields as diverse as stock analysis and video game development. People inside a company can develop systems, or companies can use outsourcing, hiring an outside company to perform some or all of a systems development project. Outsourcing allows a company to focus on what it does best and delegate other functions to companies with expertise in systems development. Outsourcing, however, is not the best alternative for all companies. An alternative is agile systems development where systems developed rapidly in close partnership with users. Working together, parts of the system are developed, tested, modified and refined over and over again until a usable system emerges.

systems development The activity of creating or modifying existing business systems.

Developing information systems to meet business needs is highly complex and difficult – so much so that it is common for IS projects to overrun budgets and exceed scheduled completion dates. Her Majesty's Revenue and Customs (HMRC), which collects taxes in the UK, settled out of court with an outsourcing company to recover funds lost due to a tax-related mistake caused

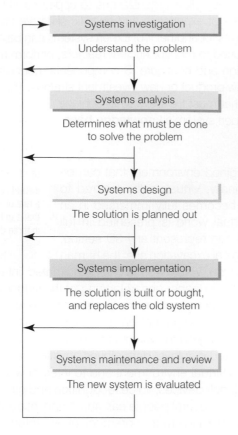

Figure 1.8 An Overview of Systems Development

by a failed systems development project.[14] The failed project overpaid about €2.5 billion to some families with children or taxpayers in a low-income tax bracket. One strategy for improving the results of a systems development project is to divide it into several steps, each with a well-defined goal and set of tasks to accomplish (see Figure 1.8). These steps are summarized next.

Systems Investigation and Analysis

The first two steps of systems development are systems investigation and analysis. The goal of the systems investigation is to gain a clear understanding of the problem to be solved or opportunity to be addressed. A cruise line company, for example, might launch a systems investigation to determine whether a development project is feasible to automate purchasing at ports around the world. After an organization understands the problem, the next question is, 'Is the problem worth solving?' Given that organizations have limited resources – people and money – this question deserves careful consideration. If the decision is to continue with the solution, the next step, systems analysis, defines the problems and opportunities of the existing system. During systems investigation and analysis, as well as design maintenance and review, discussed next, the project must have the complete support of top-level managers and focus on developing systems that achieve business goals.[15]

Systems Design, Implementation, and Maintenance and Review

Systems design determines how the new system will work to meet the business needs defined during systems analysis. Systems implementation involves creating or acquiring the various system components (hardware, software, databases, etc.) defined in the design step, assembling them, and putting the new system into operation. The purpose of systems maintenance and review is to check and modify the system so that it continues to meet changing business needs.

1.4 Information Systems in Society, Business and Industry

Information systems have been developed to meet the needs of all types of organizations and people, and their use is spreading throughout the world to improve the lives and business activities of many citizens. To provide their enormous benefits, however, information systems must be implemented with thought and care. The speed and widespread use of information systems opens users to a variety of threats from unethical people.

Ethical and Societal Issues

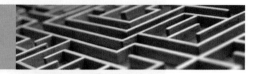

Industrial Scale Cheating

A Massive Open Online Course (MOOC) is an educational course designed to allow as many people as possible to participate via the web. Often these courses are offered for free. In the past few years, millions of students have signed up for courses from some of the world's top universities including Stanford and the Massachusetts Institute of Technology. Students are assessed and if successful receive a certificate of completion. One of the biggest online course providers is Coursera which was set up by Stanford academics and is backed by Silicon Valley investors. With the high cost of physically attending a university, online courses are seen as a way of reaching many more people for much less money, but a major stumbling block has been how such digital courses are assessed: when students are at home how you do know the identity of the person answering the questions? For online courses to gain value they need a credible way of assessing students and an important part of that is preventing fraud.

The Open University has been the leader in distance learning in the UK for several decades. "We're looking at whether we can do online examinations so the student doesn't have to come in to a hall, they just need to be sitting in front of their computer at a particular time when the exam is released to their computer,' says Peter Taylor, chair of the Open University's academic conduct group. 'There are vari-

ous ways you can identify a person. One system we looked at meant that you had to type in a particular phrase – and the rate and the particular way you type is effectively a signature of the individual.' Prof. Taylor says he would expect such technology to be in place within the next five years. He also says that there is no reason to think more people would necessarily cheat online. 'Let's face it, in a large examination hall, each individual student isn't going to be closely watched. The idea of people bringing notes up their sleeves remains a problem.'

Stanford University computer scientist and co-founder of Coursera, Andrew Ng, agrees and thinks that the technology Peter Taylor refers to, called keystroke dynamics, is a solution worth pursuing. Keystroke dynamics is detailed timing information about exactly when a person presses and releases a computer key and can be used to identify them.

An alternative approach is being taken by the Massachusetts Institute of Technology and Harvard, who want to make more use of physical exam halls rather than less. Students taking their online courses will be able to sit their final exams in an international network of test centres. These will be formally supervised exams where the student answers questions on a computer. It is important that the exams are run on computer, because no human is going to mark them – they will be marked automatically.

(continued)

However this may not be enough – students want human feedback, says another Coursera's co-founder Daphne Koller. To achieve this, Coursera has been experimenting with peer assessment, where students grade each other's work, following guidelines set by the teacher. This allows for the marking capacity to grow with the class size – but it also depends on the reliability of fellow students.

Questions

1 Could a series of MOOCs ever capture a 'university experience'? What if they were supported by other online services? What would those online services have to be?

2 What are the advantages and disadvantages of automatic marking from the students' perspective and from the university's?

3 If peers are assessing each other's work, they are likely to discuss what they are doing on their blogs and social media. What would some of the problems with this be and how might a MOOC provider counter them?

4 Why do you think big name universities are offering courses online for free?

Security, Privacy and Ethical Issues in Information Systems and the Internet

Although information systems can provide enormous benefits, they do have some drawbacks.[16] Computer-related mistakes are also a concern. In Japan, a financial services firm had trading losses of ¥245 million due to a typing mistake in entering a trade. In another case, criminals stole carbon credits worth about £30 million from a European carbon credit market.[17]

Increasingly, the ethical use of systems has been highlighted in the news. Ethical issues concern what is generally considered right or wrong. Some IS professionals believe that computers may create new opportunities for unethical behaviour. For example, a faculty member of a medical school falsified computerized research results to get a promotion – and a higher salary. In another case, a company was charged with using a human resource information system to time employee layoffs and firings to avoid paying pensions. More and more, the Internet is also associated with unethical behaviour. Unethical investors have placed false rumours or incorrect information about a company on the Internet and tried to influence its stock price to make money.

Information theft, such as stealing credit card numbers and other personal information, is another issue.

To protect against these threats, you can install security and control measures. For example, many software products can detect and remove viruses and spam, or unwanted e-mail, from computer systems. Information systems can help reduce other types of crime as well. In a New Zealand city, a free computer centre has cut vandalism by keeping young people off the street and giving residents a sense of pride. When a pair of headphones disappeared from the centre, the community rallied to make sure that they were promptly returned.

You can install firewalls (software and hardware that protect a computer system or network from outside attacks) to avoid viruses and prevent unauthorized people from gaining access to your computer system. You can also use identification numbers and passwords. Some security experts propose installing web cameras and hiring 'citizen spotters' to monitor them. Use of information systems also raises work concerns, including job loss through increased efficiency and some potential health problems from making repetitive motions. Ergonomics, the study of designing and positioning workplace equipment, can help you avoid health-related problems of using computer systems.

Computer and Information Systems Literacy

In the twenty-first century, business survival and prosperity has continued to become more difficult. For example, increased mergers among former competitors to create global conglomerates, continued downsizing of corporations to focus on their core businesses and to improve efficiencies, efforts to reduce trade barriers, and the globalization of capital all point to the increased internationalization of business organizations and markets. In addition, business issues and decisions are becoming more complex and must be made faster. Whatever career path you take, understanding information systems will help you cope, adapt and prosper in this challenging environment.

A knowledge of information systems will help you make a significant contribution on the job. It will also help you advance in your chosen career or field. Managers are expected to identify opportunities to implement information systems to improve their business. They are also expected to lead IS projects in their areas of expertise. To meet these personal and organizational goals, you must acquire both computer literacy and information systems literacy. **Computer literacy** is a knowledge of computer systems and equipment and the ways they function. It stresses equipment and devices (hardware), programs and instructions (software), databases and telecommunications.

computer literacy Knowledge of computer systems and equipment and the ways they function; it stresses equipment and devices (hardware), programs and instructions (software), databases and telecommunications.

Information systems literacy goes beyond knowing the fundamentals of computer systems and equipment. **Information systems literacy** is the knowledge of how data and information are used by individuals, groups and organizations. It includes knowledge of computer technology and the broader range of information systems. Most important, however, it encompasses how and why this technology is applied in business. Knowing about various types of hardware and software is an example of computer literacy. Knowing how to use hardware and software to increase profits, cut costs, improve productivity and increase customer satisfaction is an example of information systems literacy. Information systems literacy can involve recognizing how and why people (managers, employees, stockholders and others) use information systems; being familiar with organizations, decision-making approaches, management levels and information needs; and understanding how organizations can use computers and information systems to achieve their goals. Knowing how to deploy transaction processing, management information, decision support and expert systems to help an organization achieve its goals is a key aspect of information systems literacy.

information systems literacy Knowledge of how data and information are used by individuals, groups and organizations.

Information Systems in the Functional Areas of Business

Information systems are used in all functional areas and operating divisions of business. In finance and accounting, information systems forecast revenues and business activity, determine the best sources and uses of funds, manage cash and other financial resources, analyze investments, and perform audits to make sure that the organization is financially sound and that all financial reports and documents are accurate. Sales and marketing use information systems to develop new goods and services (product analysis), select the best location for production and distribution facilities (place or site analysis), determine the best advertising and sales approaches (promotion analysis), and set product prices to get the highest total revenues (price analysis).

In manufacturing, information systems process customer orders, develop production schedules, control inventory levels and monitor product quality. In addition, information systems help to design products (computer-assisted design or CAD), manufacture items (computer-assisted manufacturing or CAM), and integrate machines or pieces of equipment (computer-integrated manufacturing or CIM). Human resource management uses information systems to screen applicants, administer performance tests to employees, monitor employee productivity and more. Legal information systems analyze product liability and warranties and help to develop important legal documents and reports.

Information Systems in Industry

In addition to being used in every department in a company, information systems are used in almost every industry or field in business. The airline industry develops Internet auction sites to offer discount fares and increase revenue. Investment firms use information systems to analyze stocks, bonds, options, the futures market and other financial instruments, and provide improved services to their customers. Banks use information systems to help make sound loans and good investments, as well as to provide online cheque payment for account holders. The transportation industry uses information systems to schedule trucks and trains to deliver goods and services at the lowest cost. Publishing companies use information systems to analyze markets and to develop and publish newspapers, magazines and books. Healthcare organizations use information systems to diagnose illnesses, plan medical treatment, track patient records and bill patients. Retail companies are using the web to take orders and provide customer service support. Retail companies also use information systems to help market products and services, manage inventory levels, control the supply chain and forecast demand. Power management and utility companies use information systems to monitor and control power generation and usage. Professional services firms employ information systems to improve the speed and quality of services they provide to customers. Management consulting firms use intranets and extranets to offer information on products, services, skill levels and past engagements to their consultants. These industries are discussed in more detail as we continue through the book.

1.5 Global Challenges in Information Systems

Changes in society as a result of increased international trade and cultural exchange, often called globalization, have always had a big impact on organizations and their information systems. In his book *The World Is Flat*, Thomas Friedman describes three eras of globalization (see Table 1.2).[18] According to Friedman, we have progressed from the globalization of countries to the globalization of multinational corporations and individuals. Today, people in remote areas can use the Internet to compete with, and contribute to, other people, the largest corporations and entire countries. These workers are empowered by high-speed Internet access, making

Table 1.2 Eras of Globalization

Era	Dates	Characterized by
Globalization 1	Late 1400–1800	Countries with the power to explore and influence the world
Globalization 2	1800–2000	Multinational corporations that have plants, warehouses and offices around the world
Globalization 3	2000–today	Individuals from around the world who can compete and influence other people, corporations and countries by using the Internet and powerful technology tools

the world seem smaller and effectively levelling the global playing field. In the Globalization 3 era, designing a new aeroplane or computer can be separated into smaller subtasks and then completed by a person or small group that can do the best job. These workers can be located in India, China, Russia, Europe and other areas of the world. The subtasks can then be combined or reassembled into the complete design. This approach can be used to prepare tax returns, diagnose a patient's medical condition, fix a broken computer and many other tasks.

Today's information systems have led to greater globalization. High-speed Internet access and networks that can connect individuals and organizations around the world create more international opportunities. Global markets have expanded. People and companies can get products and services from around the world, instead of around the corner or across town. These opportunities, however, introduce numerous obstacles and issues, including challenges involving culture, language and many others.

- *Cultural challenges:* Countries and regional areas have their own cultures and customs that can significantly affect individuals and organizations involved in global trade.
- *Language challenges:* Language differences can make it difficult to translate exact meanings from one language to another.
- *Time and distance challenges:* Time and distance issues can be difficult to overcome for individuals and organizations involved with global trade in remote locations. Large time differences make it difficult to talk to people on the other side of the world. With long distance, it can take days to get a product, a critical part or a piece of equipment from one location to another location.
- *Infrastructure challenges:* High-quality electricity and water might not be available in certain parts of the world. Telephone services, Internet connections and skilled employees might be expensive or not readily available.
- *Currency challenges:* The value of different currencies can vary significantly over time, making international trade more difficult and complex.
- *Product and service challenges:* Traditional products that are physical or tangible, such as a car or bicycle, can be difficult to deliver to the global market. However, electronic products (e-products) and electronic services (e-services) can be delivered to customers electronically, over the phone, networks, through the Internet or other electronic means. Software, music, books, manuals, and help and advice can all be delivered over the Internet.
- *Technology transfer issues:* Most governments don't allow certain military-related equipment and systems to be sold to some countries. Even so, some believe that foreign companies are stealing the intellectual property, trade secrets, copyrighted materials and counterfeiting products and services.[19]

■ *National laws:* Every country have a set of laws that must be obeyed by citizens and organizations operating in the country. These laws can deal with a variety of issues, including trade secrets, patents, copyrights, protection of personal or financial data, privacy and much more. Laws restricting how data enters or exits a country are often called 'trans-border data-flow laws'. Keeping track of these laws and incorporating them into the procedures and computer systems of multinational and trans-national organizations can be very difficult and time consuming, requiring expert legal advice.

■ *Trade agreements:* Countries often enter into trade agreements with each other. The EU has trade agreements among its members.[20] The North American Free Trade Agreement (NAFTA) and the Central American Free Trade Agreement (CAFTA) are other examples.[21] Others include the Australia–United States Free Trade Agreement and agreements between Bolivia and Mexico, Canada and Costa Rica, Canada and Israel, Chile and Korea, Mexico and Japan, the USA and Jordan and many others.[22]

Summary

The value of information is directly linked to how it helps decision makers achieve the organizational goals. Information systems are used in almost every imaginable career area. Regardless of your chosen career, you will find that information systems are indispensable tools to help you achieve your goals. Learning about information systems can help you get your first job, earn promotions and advance your career.

Information is a collection of facts. To be valuable, information must have several characteristics: It should be accurate, complete, economical to produce, flexible, reliable, relevant, simple to understand, timely, verifiable, accessible and secure. The value of information is directly linked to how it helps people achieve their organization's goals.

Computers and information systems are constantly making it possible for organizations to improve the way they conduct business. A system is a set of elements that interact to accomplish a goal or set of objectives. The components of a system include inputs, processing mechanisms and outputs. A system uses feedback to monitor and control its operation to make sure that it continues to meet its goals and objectives.

System performance is measured by its efficiency and effectiveness. Efficiency is a measure of what is produced divided by what is consumed; effectiveness measures the extent to which a system achieves its goals. A system's performance standard is a specific objective.

Knowing the potential impact of information systems and having the ability to put this knowledge to work can result in a successful personal career, organizations that reach their goals and a society with a higher quality of life. Information systems are sets of interrelated elements that collect (input), manipulate and store (process), and disseminate (output) data and information. Input is the activity of capturing and gathering new data, processing involves converting or transforming data into useful outputs, and output involves producing useful information. Feedback is the output that is used to make adjustments or changes to input or processing activities.

The components of a computer-based information system (CBIS) include hardware, software, databases, telecommunications and the Internet, people and procedures. The types of CBISs that organizations use can be classified into: (1) e-commerce and m-commerce, TPS and ERP systems, (2) MIS and DSS, and (3) specialized business information systems. The key to understanding these types of systems begins with learning their fundamentals.

E-commerce involves any business transaction executed electronically between parties such as companies (business to business), companies and consumers (business to consumer), business and the public sector, and consumers and the public sector. The major volume of e-commerce and its fastest-growing segment is business-to-business transactions that make purchasing easier for big corporations. E-commerce also offers opportunities for small businesses to market and sell at a low cost worldwide, thus allowing them to enter the global market right from start-up. M-commerce involves 'anytime, anywhere' computing that relies on wireless networks and systems.

The most fundamental system is the transaction processing system (TPS). A transaction is any business-related exchange. The TPS handles the large volume of business transactions that occur daily within an organization. An enterprise resource planning (ERP) system is a set of integrated programs that can manage the vital business operations for an entire multi-site, global organization. A management information system (MIS) uses the information from a TPS to generate information useful for management decision making.

A decision support system (DSS) is an organized collection of people, procedures, databases and devices that help make problem-specific decisions. A DSS differs from an MIS in the support given to users, the emphasis on decisions, the development and approach, and the system components, speed and output.

Specialized business information systems include knowledge management, artificial intelligence, expert, and virtual reality systems. Knowledge management systems are organized collections of people, procedures, software, databases and devices used to create, store, share and use the organization's knowledge and experience. Artificial intelligence (AI) includes a wide range of systems in which the computer takes on the characteristics of human intelligence. Robotics is an area of artificial intelligence in which machines perform complex, dangerous, routine or boring tasks, such as welding car frames or assembling computer systems and components. Vision systems allow robots and other devices to have 'sight' and to store and process visual images. Natural language processing involves computers interpreting and acting on verbal or written commands in English, Spanish or other human languages. Learning systems let computers learn from past mistakes or experiences, such as playing games or making business decisions, while neural networks is a branch of artificial intelligence that allows computers to recognize and act on patterns or trends. An expert system (ES) is designed to act as an expert consultant to a user who is seeking advice about a specific situation. Originally, the term 'virtual reality' referred to immersive virtual reality, in which the user becomes fully immersed in an artificial,

computer-generated 3D world. Virtual reality can also refer to applications that are not fully immersive, such as mouse-controlled navigation through a 3D environment on a graphics monitor, stereo viewing from the monitor via stereo glasses, stereo projection systems and others.

System users, business managers, and information systems professionals must work together to build a successful information system. Systems development involves creating or modifying existing business systems. The major steps of this process and their goals include systems investigation (gain a clear understanding of what the problem is), systems analysis (define what the system must do to solve the problem), systems design (determine exactly how the system will work to meet the business needs), systems implementation (create or acquire the various system components defined in the design step), and systems maintenance and review (maintain and then modify the system so that it continues to meet changing business needs).

Information systems must be applied thoughtfully and carefully so that society, business and industry can reap their enormous benefits. Information systems play a fundamental and ever-expanding role in society, business and industry. But their use can also raise serious security, privacy and ethical issues. Effective information systems can have a major impact on corporate strategy and organizational success. Businesses around the globe are enjoying better safety and service, greater efficiency and effectiveness, reduced expenses, and improved decision making and control because of information systems. Individuals who can help their businesses realize these benefits will be in demand well into the future.

Computer and information systems literacy are prerequisites for numerous job opportunities, and not only in the IS field. Computer literacy is knowledge of computer systems and equipment, and information systems literacy is knowledge of how data and information are used by individuals, groups and organizations. Today, information systems are used in all the functional areas of business, including accounting, finance, sales, marketing, manufacturing, human resource management and legal information systems. Information systems are also used in every industry, such as airlines, investment firms, banks, transportation companies, publishing companies, healthcare, retail, power management, professional services and more.

Self-Assessment Test

1 A(n) _____ is a set of interrelated components that collect, manipulate and disseminate data and information and provide a feedback mechanism to meet an objective.

2 A(n) _____ is a set of elements or components that interact to accomplish a goal.

3 What is a measure of what is produced divided by what is consumed?
   a. efficiency
   b. effectiveness
   c. performance
   d. productivity

4 Graphs, charts and figures are examples of physical models. True or false?

5 A(n) _____ consists of hardware, software, databases, telecommunications, people and procedures.

6 Computer programs that govern the operation of a computer system are called _____.
   a. feedback
   b. feedforward
   c. software
   d. transaction processing systems

7 What is an organized collection of people, procedures, software, databases and devices used to create, store, share and use the organization's experience and knowledge?
   a. TPS (transaction processing system)
   b. MIS (management information system)
   c. DSS (decision support system)
   d. KMS (knowledge management system)

8 _____ involves anytime, anywhere commerce that uses wireless communications.

9 What determines how a new system will work to meet the business needs defined during systems investigation?
   a. systems implementation
   b. systems review
   c. systems development
   d. systems design

10 _____ literacy is a knowledge of how data and information are used by individuals, groups, and organizations.

Review Questions

1 What is an information system? Explain some of the ways in which information systems are changing our lives.

2 Define the term 'system'. Give several examples.

3 What are the components of any information system?

4 What is feedback? What are possible consequences of inadequate feedback?

5 What is a computer-based information system? What are its components?

6 Identify three functions of a transaction processing system.

7 What is the difference between an intranet and an extranet?

8 What is m-commerce? Describe how it can be used.

9 Identify three elements of artificial intelligence.

10 Identify the steps in the systems development process and state the goal of each.

Discussion Questions

1 Describe how information systems are used in your college or university.

2 Explain using examples the difference between e-commerce and m-commerce.

3 Discuss how you might judge whether a computer is displaying intelligence.

4 Discuss the potential use of virtual reality to enhance the learning experience for new automobile drivers. How might such a system operate? What are the benefits and potential disadvantages of such a system?

5 Discuss how information systems are linked to the business objectives of an organization.

Web Exercises

1 Throughout this book, you will see how the Internet provides a vast amount of information to individuals and organizations. We will stress the World Wide Web, or simply the web, which is an important part of the Internet. Most large universities and organizations have an address on the Internet, called a website or home page. The address of the website for this publisher is www.cengage.co.uk. You can gain access to the Internet through a browser, such as Microsoft Internet Explorer or Safari. Using an Internet browser, go to the Cengage Learning website. Try to obtain information on this book. You might be asked to develop a report or send an email message to your instructor about what you found.

2 Go to an Internet search engine, such as www.google.co.uk, and search for information about knowledge management. Write a brief report that summarizes what you found and the companies that provide knowledge management products.

3 Using the Internet, search for information on the use of information systems in a company or organization that interests you. How does the organization use technology to help accomplish its goals?

Case One

Deep Learning at Google[x]

Google[x] is Google's secret lab, set up in 2010 to take scientific and engineering risks, just to see what might happen. 'Google[x]' is genuinely how they spell the name, and it's seen as a secret lab because it doesn't have a webpage, something unusual at Google. Google[x]'s most famous product is probably Google Glass, the Internet connected spectacles. A lesser known project is Google Brain.

Early on in the lab's history, its researchers asked whether it is possible for a computer to learn to detect faces using only unlabelled images. In other words, can a computer be shown a series of images and figure out on its own which are human and which are not? To re-state the problem: the computer will be shown images and told to classify (or group) them. The question is, will one of the classifications bring together all of the pictures of humans in one group. This is a tricky problem which has been worked on since the 1950s. To answer it, the Google team used an approach called Deep Learning.

Deep learning systems draw their inspiration from what we know of the human brain. Our brains are made up of millions of neurons with billions of interconnections between them. Google Brain is a series of 1000 computers programmed to simulate about 1 million neurons with 1 billion connections between them. Each neuron is a block of computer code that accepts input signals from the neurons that connect into it. Each signal is essentially a number. A neuron takes all the numbers sent to it and performs a calculation on them, and sends the results out to the other neurons that it is connected into. The calculation that a neuron performs involves multiplying its input by numbers called weights. Learning occurs by setting values for what these weights should be. For example, if a particular input is very unimportant its weight might be close to zero. If it is important its weight will be set to be high.

A deep learning strategy calls for the neurons to be organized into several layers. When looking at pictures, the first layer of learning might be to classify dark and light pixels (a pixel is the smallest element in a computerized image). This classification gets passed to the next layer which might distinguish edges in the picture. This then gets passed to the next layer which might recognize features such as eyes.

The Google[x] researchers took 10 million still images from YouTube and fed them into Google Brain. After three days studying them, the system learned to accurately identify certain categories: human faces, human bodies and cats, achieving a 70 per cent relative improvement over the previous state-of-the-art techniques. (The cat category reflects the fact that YouTube is full of videos of cats.)

When Google adopted deep-learning-based speech recognition in its Android smartphone operating system, it achieved a 25 per cent reduction in word errors. 'That's the kind of drop you expect to take ten years to achieve,' says computer scientist Geoffrey Hinton of the University of Toronto in Canada – a reflection of just how difficult it has been to make progress in this area. 'That's like ten break-throughs all together.'

Questions

1 Why do you think Google funds a lab like Google[x]?

2 Many problems can be re-stated as classification tasks. Telling the difference between humans and cats is one. Can you describe how speech recognition is a classification task? Can language translation be stated as classification task? What others can you think of?

3 Use a search engine to find as much information as you can on Google[x]. Imagine you were their chief research scientist – what problems would you set your team to work on next?

4 Do you think artificial intelligence researchers should look to biology (the human brain) for inspiration or might there be a better metaphor for computer intelligence?

Case Two

Nissan's 180-Degree Turn with Parts Distribution

The region of Castilla-La Mancha in central Spain covers over 30 000 square miles, or almost 80 000 square kilometres. With a population of over two million people spread over such a large region, Castilla-La Mancha has the lowest population density of any Spanish region. More than half of its 919 communities have fewer than 500 inhabitants. As Pedro-Jesus Rodriguez Gonzalez, head of Information Technology (IT) and Internet for the regional government of Castilla-La Mancha, puts it, 'This environment presents one of Spain's most challenging demographics for delivering public services. Although much of the population lives in five major cities, a significant portion of its citizens are widely dispersed.'

The government of Castilla-La Mancha has used computers to help it deal with the challenges of delivering public services such as access to social benefits for many years, although limited by the finite resources available to any government agency. Recently, the regional government modernized its technological infrastructure to save money and improve its responsiveness to citizens. It adopted the approach of cloud computing: central applications and data accessed over the Internet, much as people access web pages. By using a cloud-computing approach, Castilla-La Mancha could centralize its data centres, reducing 18 main sites and 30 smaller facilities to two centres. Direct savings as a result of centralizing the data centres are more than half a million dollars.

To develop its new infrastructure, Castilla-La Mancha chose the Vblock system from the Virtual Computing Environment (VCE) Company, LLC. VCE is a joint venture of networking company Cisco and storage supplier EMC, with additional investment by VMware and Intel. Using the combined strengths of their sponsors, VCE can provide solutions that handle all aspects of creating a cloud platform while avoiding the need for users to deal with multiple suppliers.

The first application Castilla-La Mancha developed to take advantage of the new cloud system was Papas 2.0 (Parents 2.0), a program that enables collaboration among parents, teachers, and pupils and facilitates daily work in twenty-first-century classrooms equipped with information systems. Papás 2.0 was introduced to users in November 2010. 'Papás 2.0 Virtual Classroom [gives] teachers and pupils the opportunity to incorporate an online collaborative working environment into the school's daily dynamics,' says Tomás Hervás, general secretary of the Council of Education, Science and Culture. Teachers can follow pupils, set tasks and send messages to parents; families can access data on their children's performance through an Internet connection. Gonzalez adds, 'IT is no longer just a subject, but a main part of the student's daily routine. The students are being educated with the tools they will be using in their future workplace.' When fully rolled out, Papás 2.0 will support 345 000 pupils along with their families and teachers.

The new infrastructure also provides considerable cost savings by consolidating what were previously separate systems into a shared data centre. This data centre will eventually replace about 130 server computers, reducing energy consumption along with space and cooling requirements. Castilla-La Mancha forecasts savings of 20 per cent within the first year, with savings continuing to grow as more of the infrastructure is used to replace older, outmoded computers.

Agustina Piedrabuena, Castilla-La Mancha's chief information officer, summarizes: 'The project has not only helped us to consolidate and simplify our data centre, it also allows us to be completely independent of which department uses the service, where the application is hosted, or what resources it consumes; we are simply automating the provision of applications by means of the cloud.'

Questions

1 What are the main advantages for the government of using cloud computing in this way?

2 What are the advantages and disadvantages of Papas 2.0 for teachers, students and parents?

3 What features do you think a virtual classroom should have?

4 Can you list the hardware, software, telecommunication, people and procedure needed by Papas 2.0?

Case Three

Penda Health

Penda Health provides high-quality, affordable, outpatient healthcare across Kenya through a chain of health clinics. By 2020 they plan to operate over 100 clinics across the country serving millions of patients. Penda Health aims to be affordable to everyone in Kenya, including low- and middle-income population. It launched its first clinic in the town of Kitengela in February 2012. In the first 7 months of business it had over 3 000 patient visits. Their services range from reproductive health, maternal health and family planning for women to full check-ups for men and children. The clinic also specializes in women's services such as breast and cervical cancer screening and family planning.

Penda founder Stephanie Koczela claims she was motivated by seeing deaths from treatable diseases: 'I had just attended too many funerals, people dying from completely preventable causes and treatable diseases. Standing at the sides of the graves and holding the babies of parents who had died from basic infections that are treatable in other parts of the world.' Co-founder Beatrice Ongoce says that 'in Kenya, healthcare quality is associated with being rich, being able to pay more, and bad options are related to being poor'. She wanted to change this.

Technology pays a large part in keeping keep their service affordable. 'I think that most of the healthcare providers that we're competing with don't use technology at all to supplement their systems,' says Ms Koczela. 'They're all paper records, their drugs are often out of stock. We have a system that gives us a warning if any of our drugs are expired, and it forces our providers to dispose of those drugs immediately. Technology allows us to have quality healthcare at scale. With one clinic you could imagine we could monitor our drug supplies and do chart review with paper and all those things? But with a hundred clinics that's just not possible. The only way to do that is to leverage amazing systems.'

Penda Health's system is bespoke and tracks stock and expiry dates through a simple interface accessible from a PC. When supplies run low, a warning is triggered to make sure more is ordered. 'It raises our medical quality. One of the most common problems with healthcare providers in Kenya is that they don't have the equipment that's necessary to provide medical care. This system ensures that we will always have what's necessary for our patients.'

The clinic uses mobile broadband, meaning the system is completely portable – and mobile technology is useful in other ways. Staff text patients to make sure they're taking their drugs at the right times and in the right way, or to tell groups of patients that a specialist is visiting. They also accept payments via the e-money system M-PESA. M-PESA lets customers borrow, withdraw and pay money using text messaging. In a culture where many people are unable to open bank accounts and must therefore carry cash, it has the potential to revolutionize lives. The system gives security, and allows easily and safe transfer of cash from relatives in the first world. According to the World Bank, this happens a lot – over 200 million migrants worldwide sent £120 billion to their families in 2005, a figure which is more than double the volume of official aid.

Penda is now working on develping their own electronic medical records system that ultimately will allow them to share those records if need be with specialists both within Kenya and internationally.

'We want to be the most friendly and highest quality provider for the low and middle-income Kenyan, and in order to do that we need to have tech systems that are backing our chain,' says Ms Koczela.

Questions

1 What sort of information system is Penda using?

2 How does the system help Penda control their costs?

3 What is the system's input and output?

4 What are the advantages and disadvantages of using your mobile phone as your bank account?

Notes

1 Schupak, Amanda, 'The Bunny Chip', *Forbes,* 15 August 2005, p. 53.

2 Dongarra, J. 2013. Visit to the National University for Defense Technology Changsha, China. Available from: www.netlib.org/utk/people/ JackDongarra/PAPERS/tianhe-2-dongarra-report. pdf. Accessed 7 January 2014.

3 Port, Otis, 'Desktop Factories', *Business Week*, 2 May 2005, p. 22.

4 Barron, Kelly, 'Hidden Value', *Fortune,* 27 June 2005, p. 184[B].

5 Yun, Samean, 'New 3G Cell Phones Aim to Be Fast', *Rocky Mountain News*, 1 August 2005, p. 1B.

6 Tynan, Dan, 'Singing the Blog Electric', *PC World,* August 2005, p. 120.

7 Mossberg, Walter, 'Device Lets You Watch Shows on a Home TV, TiVo from Elsewhere', *Wall Street Journal*, 30 June 2005, p. B1.

8 Anthes, Gary, 'Supply Chain Whirl', *Computerworld*, 8 June 2005, p. 27.

9 Majchrzak, Ann, et al., 'Perceived Individual Collaboration Know-How Development', *Information Systems Research,* March 2005, p. 9.

10 Darroch, Jenny, 'Knowledge Management, Innovation, and Firm Performance', *Journal of Knowledge Management*, Vol. 9, No. 3, March 2005, p. 101.

11 Staff, 'Nissan Developing Smart Cars', *CNN Online,* 1 March 2005.

12 Kurzweil, Ray, 'Long Live AI', *Forbes,* 15 August 2005, p. 30.

13 Nichols, S., 11 February 2013. 'Google Wants Some Form of Self-Driving Cars on Roads by 2018', TechRadar. Available from: www.techradar. com/news/car-tech/google-wants-some-form-of-self-driving-cars-on-roads-by-2018-1130660. Accessed 10 January 2014.

14 Staff, 'Tax Credit Fiasco Costs EDS £71m', bbc. co.uk, 22 November 2005.

15 Hess, H.M., 'Aligning Technology and Business', *IBM Systems Journal*, Vol. 44, No. 1, 2005, p. 25.

16 Cavusoglu, Huseyin, et al., 'The Value of Intrusion Detection Systems in Information Technology Security Architecture', *Information Systems Research*, March 2005, p. 28.

17 G. Jelten, T. Cyberthieves Target European Carbon Credit Market. National Public Radio. Available from: www.npr.org. Accessed 22 January 2011.

18 Friedman, Thomas, 'The World Is Flat', *Farrar, Straus and Giroux*, 2005, p. 488.

19 Balfour, Frederik, 'Invasion of the Brain Snatchers', *Business Week*, 9 May 2005, p. 24.

20 Europa – The European Union On-Line, www.europa.eu.int, 15 January 2006.

21 Smith, Geri, et al., 'Central America Is Holding Its Breath', *Business Week*, 20 June 2005, p. 52.

22 SICE – Foreign Trade Information System. Available from: www.sice.oas.org/tradee.asp. Accessed 15 January 2006.

02

Information Systems in Organizations

Principles

The use of information systems to add value to the organization is strongly influenced by organizational structure, and the organization's attitude and ability to change.

Because information systems are so important, businesses need to be sure that improvements to existing systems or completely new systems help lower costs, increase profits, improve service or achieve a competitive advantage.

Cooperation between business managers and IS personnel is the key to unlocking the potential of any new or modified system.

Learning Objectives

- Identify the value-adding processes in the supply chain and describe the role of information systems within them.
- Provide a clear definition of 'organizational structure' and 'organizational change' and discuss how these affect the implementation of information systems.

- Identify some of the strategies employed to lower costs or improve service.
- Define the term 'competitive advantage' and discuss how organizations are using information systems to achieve such an advantage.
- Discuss how organizations justify the need for information systems.

- Define the types of roles, functions and careers available in information systems.

2

Why Learn About Information Systems in Organizations?

The impact that computers have had in organizations cannot be overstated. Office work has been transformed almost beyond all recognition, and many workers could not operate without their computer. All of this happened before the rise in popularity of the Internet as a channel for sharing information. When that happened, the Internet changed everything all over again! No matter what path your career takes, you will almost certainly come into contact with information systems every day. Marketing departments, accounts departments, order processing, shipping and logistics all rely on information systems. Researchers, medical doctors, mechanics – it is difficult to think of a profession where the computer does not play a central role. Even musicians use information systems to get the sound they want. In this chapter, you will see how the use of information systems in every part of organizations can help produce higher-quality products and increase their returns on investment.

2.1 An Introduction to Organizations

organization A formal collection of people and other resources established to accomplish a set of goals.

An **organization** is a formal collection of people and other resources established to accomplish a set of goals. The primary goal of a for-profit organization is to maximize shareholder value, often measured by the price of the company stock. Non-profit organizations include social groups, religious groups, universities, charities and other organizations that do not have profit as their goal.

An organization is a system, which, as you will recall from Chapter 1, means that it has inputs, processing mechanisms, outputs and feedback. Resources such as materials, people and money serve as inputs to the organizational system from the environment, go through a transformation mechanism, and then are produced as outputs to the environment. The outputs from the transformation mechanism are usually goods or services, which are of higher relative value than the inputs alone. Through adding value or worth, organizations attempt to achieve their goals.

How does the organizational system increase the value of resources? In the transformation mechanism, subsystems contain processes that help turn inputs into goods or services of increasing value. These processes increase the relative worth of the combined inputs on their way to becoming final outputs. Consider a car maker. Its inputs are the staff it has hired, the assembly equipment it has bought, raw materials such as metal and plastic and pre-assembled components such car radios. The processing that it does is turning the materials into finished vehicles, which are the output. The finished product is worth more than the cost of the components. This amount is the value that has been added.

value chain A series (chain) of activities that includes inbound logistics, warehouse and storage, production, finished product storage, outbound logistics, marketing and sales and customer service.

The **value chain**, popularized by Michael Porter in his book, *Competitive Strategy*,[1] is a useful tool for analyzing where and how this value gets added. The value chain is a series (chain) of activities that includes inbound logistics, warehouse and storage, production, finished product storage, outbound logistics, marketing and sales, and customer service. The value chain of a manufacturing company is shown in Figure 2.1.

Analyzing value chains when developing information systems often results in efficient transaction processing systems (explained fully in a later chapter), an expanding market and the sharing of information.[2] The value chain is used to examine what happens to raw material to add value to them before the finished product is sold to customers. Information systems can be focused on those activities that add the most value. The value chain can also reveal linkages between different activites (say marketing and production) which can be exploited using IS (to increase communication between the two for instance).

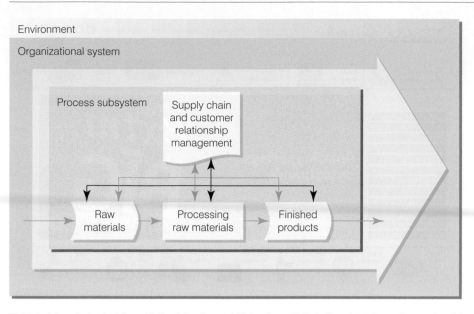

Figure 2.1 The Value Chain of a Manufacturing Company *Managing raw materials, inbound logistics, and warehouse and storage facilities is called 'upstream management', and managing finished product storage, outbound logistics, marketing and sales, and customer service is called 'downstream management'.*

The value chain is just as important (although it can be a little more difficult to apply) to companies that don't manufacture products, but provide services, such as tax preparers and legal firms. By adding a significant amount of value to their products and services, companies ensure success.

Supply chain management (SCM) and customer relationship management (CRM) are two key parts of managing the value chain. SCM helps determine what supplies are required for the value chain, what quantities are needed to meet customer demand, how the supplies should be processed (manufactured) into finished goods and services, and how the shipment of supplies and products to customers should be scheduled, monitored and controlled.[3] For example, in the car manufacturing company mentioned on page 36, SCM can identify key suppliers and parts, negotiate with vendors for the best prices and support, make sure that all supplies and parts are available to manufacture cars, and send finished products to dealerships around the country when they are needed. Increasingly, SCM is accomplished using the Internet and electronic marketplaces (e-marketplaces).[4] When an organization has many suppliers, it can use business-to-business exchanges such as eBay Business (http://business.ebay.co.uk) to negotiate good prices and service.

CRM programs help a company manage all aspects of customer encounters, including marketing and advertising, sales, customer service after the sale, and help retain loyal customers. CRM can assist a company with collecting data on customers, contacting customers, informing them about new products, and actively selling products to existing and new customers. Often, CRM software uses a variety of information sources, including sales from retail stores, surveys, email, and Internet browsing habits, to compile comprehensive customer profiles. CRM systems can also collect customer feedback which can be used to design new products and services. Tesco, the UK's largest retail operation, encourages its customers to use its Clubcard, which allows it to collect information on customer transactions. It uses this information to provide outstanding customer service and deliver loyalty rewards and perks to valued customers[5]. In return, customers are rewarded with discounts on Tesco products, holidays and other deals.

What role does an information system play in these processes? A traditional view of information systems holds that organizations use them to control and monitor processes and ensure

Figure 2.2 Tesco
Website *Tesco uses
its website to help with
customer relationship
management.*

effectiveness and efficiency. Under this view, the output from a company's information systems is used to make changes to company processes. These changes could involve using different raw materials (inputs), designing new assembly-line procedures (product transformation) or developing new products and services (outputs). Here, the information system is external to the process and serves to monitor or control it.

A more contemporary view, however, holds that information systems are often so intimately involved that they are part of the process itself. From this perspective, the information system plays an integral role in the process, whether providing input, aiding product transformation or producing output. Consider a telephone directory business that creates telephone books for international businesses. A customer requests a telephone directory listing all steel suppliers in Western Europe. Using its information system, the directory business can sort files to find the suppliers' names and telephone numbers and organize them into an alphabetical list. The information system itself is an inseparable part of this process. It does not just monitor the process externally but works as part of the process to transform raw data into a product. In this example, the information system turns input (names and telephone numbers) into a sellable output (a telephone directory). The same system might also provide the input (the files storing the data) and output (printed pages for the directory).

This latter view provides a new perspective on how and why businesses can use information systems. Rather than attempting to understand information systems independently of the organization, we must consider the potential role of information systems within the process itself, often leading to the discovery of new and better ways to accomplish the process.

organizational structure
Organizational subunits and the
way they relate to the overall
organization.

Organizational Structures

Organizational structure refers to organizational subunits and the way they relate to each other. An organization's structure depends on its approach to management, and can affect how it views and uses information systems. The types of organizational structures typically include traditional, project, team and virtual.

Traditional Organizational Structure

A **traditional organizational structure**, also called a hierarchical structure, is like a managerial pyramid where the hierarchy of decision making and authority flows from the strategic management at the top, down to operational management and non-management employees. Compared to lower levels, the strategic level, including the managing director of the company and directors, has a higher degree of decision authority, more impact on business goals, and more unique problems to solve (see Figure 2.3).

traditional organizational structure An organizational structure similar to a managerial pyramid, where the hierarchy of decision making and authority flows from strategic management at the top down to operational management and non-management employees. Also called a hierarchical structure.

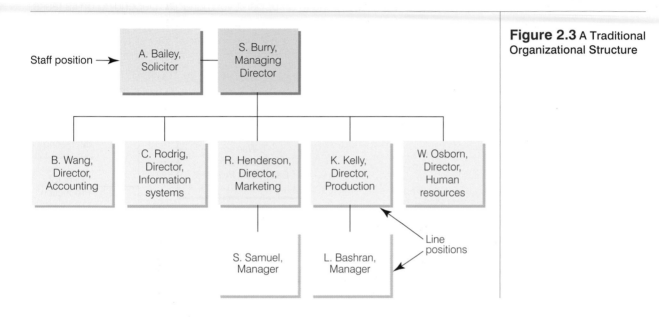

Figure 2.3 A Traditional Organizational Structure

In most cases, department heads report to a managing director or top-level manager. The departments are usually divided according to function and can include marketing, production, information systems, finance and accounting, research and development, and so on. The positions or departments that are directly associated with making, packing, or shipping goods are called line positions. A production manager who reports to a director of production is an example of a line position. Other positions might not be directly involved with the formal chain of command but instead assist a department or area. These are staff positions, such as a solicitor reporting to the managing director.

Today, the trend is to reduce the number of management levels, or layers, in the traditional organizational structure. This type of structure, often called a **flat organizational structure**, empowers employees at lower levels to make decisions and solve problems without needing permission from mid-level managers. **Empowerment** gives employees and their managers more responsibility and authority to make decisions, take action and have more control over their jobs. For example, an empowered shop assistant can respond to customer requests and problems without needing permission from a manager. In a factory, empowerment might mean that an assembly-line worker can stop production to correct a problem before the product is passed to the next station.

flat organizational structure An organizational structure with a reduced number of management layers.

empowerment Giving employees and their managers more responsibility and authority to make decisions, take certain actions, and have more control over their jobs.

Information systems can be a key element in empowering employees because they provide the information employees need to make decisions. The employees might also be empowered to develop or use their own personal information systems, such as a simple forecasting model or spreadsheet.

Project and Team Organizational Structures

A **project organizational structure** is centred on major products or services. For example, in a manufacturing firm that produces baby food and other baby products, each line is produced by a separate unit. Traditional functions such as marketing, finance and production are positioned within these major units (see Figure 2.4). Many project teams are temporary – when the project is complete, the members go on to new teams formed for another project.

The **team organizational structure** is centred on work teams or groups. In some cases, these teams are small; in others, they are very large. Typically, each team has a leader who reports to an upper-level manager. Depending on its tasks,

project organizational structure A structure centred on major products or services.

team organizational structure A structure centred on work teams or groups.

Figure 2.4 A Project Organizational Structure

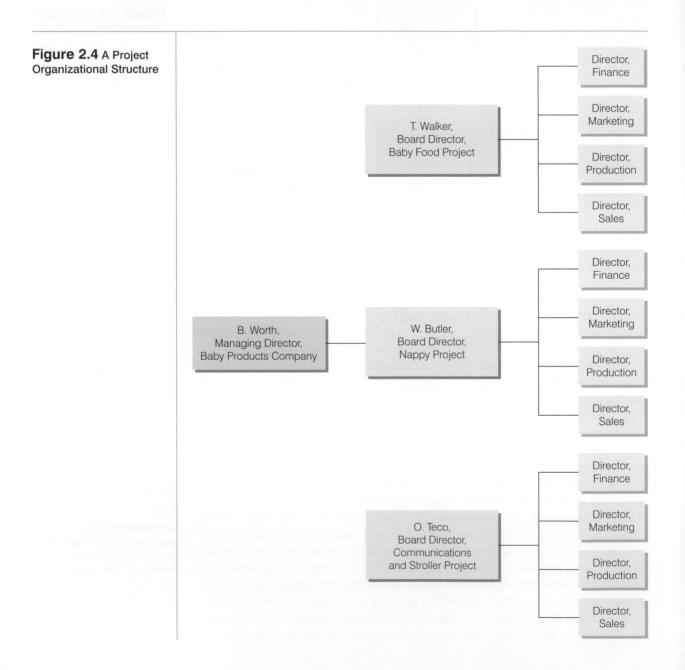

the team can be temporary or permanent. A healthcare company, for example, can form small teams to organize its administrators, physicians and others to work with individual patients.

Virtual Organizational Structure

A **virtual organizational structure** is made up of individuals, teams or complete business units that work with other individuals, teams or complete business units in different geographic locations. This almost always requires the use of the Internet (or other telecommunications) and the teams can exist for a few weeks or years. The people involved might be in different countries and operating in different time zones. In other words, virtual organizational structures allow people who work together to be separated by location and time. The people might never meet physically, which explains the use of the word 'virtual'. In Chapter 10 we will examine some of the technologies that make this form of collaborative work possible. Despite their physical separation, members of a virtual organization can collaborate on any aspect of a project, such as supplying raw materials, producing goods and services, and delivering goods and services to the marketplace.

virtual organizational structure A structure that employs individuals, groups or complete business units in geographically dispersed areas that can last for a few weeks or years, often requiring telecommunications or the Internet.

A company can use a virtual organizational structure with its own dispersed workers who have distinct skills and abilities to reduce costs. PriceWaterhouseCoopers, a global accounting giant, uses virtual teams of five to 50 people in the learning and education department.[6] According to Peter Nicolas, the company's Learning Solutions manager, 'Virtual teaming is the norm for us'. The company takes advantage of software and technology, including Microsoft Live Meeting, Centra Software's Virtual-Classroom Application and Lotus Notes from IBM, to help the teams work from distant locations.

In addition to reducing costs or increasing revenues, a virtual organizational structure can provide an extra level of security. For instance, dispersing employees and using a virtual structure can provide an ability to deal with a disaster at the primary location. If this happened, the company would still have sufficient employees at other locations to keep the business running. Today's workers are performing company work at home, at a customer's location, in coffee shops, on pleasure boats and at convenient work centres in suburbia. People can work at any time. Using the Internet and email, workers can put the finishing touches on a new business proposal in Europe or Asia, while co-workers in North America are sleeping.

Successful virtual organizational structures share key characteristics. One strategy is to have in-house employees concentrate on the firm's core businesses and use virtual employees, groups or businesses to do everything else. Using information systems to manage the activities of a virtual structure is essential, often requiring specialized software to coordinate joint work. Even with sophisticated IS tools though, teams may still need face-to-face meetings, especially at the beginning of new projects.

Organizational Change

Most organizations are constantly undergoing change, both minor and major. The need for **organizational change** can be caused by internal factors, such as those initiated by employees at all levels, or external factors, such as activities wrought by competitors, stockholders, new laws, community regulations, natural occurrences (such as hurricanes) and general economic conditions. In the 1990s, the Internet caused massive changes in the way millions of organizations did business.

organizational change The responses that are necessary so that for-profit and non-profit organizations can plan for, implement and handle change.

Change can be sustaining or disruptive. Sustaining change such as new or cheaper production equipment can help an organization improve its operation. For example, many factories are now able to use robots because prices for robots are falling and their useful lifetime is increasing, leading to a big market in second-hand robots.[7]

2

Disruptive change, on the other hand, often harms an organization's performance or even puts it out of business. In general, disruptive technologies might not originally have good performance, low cost or even strong demand. Over time, however, they often replace existing technologies. They can cause good, stable companies to fail when they don't change or adopt the new technology. VoIP telephone technology is currently disrupting the business models of established companies such as BT (www.bt.com) who, in response, are moving towards providing broadband Internet connections as their main product.

Overcoming resistance to change, especially disruptive change, can be the hardest part of bringing information systems into a business. Occasionally, employees even attempt to sabotage a new information system because they do not want to learn the new procedures and commands. The best way to avoid this resistance is to involve the employees in the decision to implement the change, and consult them on the development or purchase of the information system.

When a company introduces a new information system, a few members of the organization must become agents of change – champions of the new system and its benefits. Understanding the dynamics of change can help them confront and overcome resistance so that the new system can be used to maximum efficiency and effectiveness.

A significant portion of an organization's expenses are used to hire, train and compensate talented staff. So organizations try to control costs by determining the number of employees they need to maintain high-quality goods and services. Strategies to contain costs are outsourcing, on-demand computing and downsizing.

outsourcing Contracting with outside professional services to meet specific business needs.

Outsourcing involves contracting with outside professional services to meet specific business needs. Often, companies outsource a specific business process, such as recruiting and hiring employees, developing advertising materials, promoting product sales or setting up a global telecommunications network. Organizations often outsource a process to focus more closely on their core business – and target limited resources to meet strategic goals. Everton Football Club, for example, has recently outsourced all processing of credit and debit card payments from its stadium shop, online store and call centres because it had become a complex operation that was not part of its core operation. They were able to save time and money by not having to train their staff to do this.[8]

Other reasons for outsourcing are to trim expenses or benefit from the expertise of a service provider. A growing number of organizations, however, are finding that outsourcing does not necessarily lead to reduced costs. One of the primary reasons for cost increases is poorly written contracts that tack on charges from the outsourcing vendor for each additional task. Other potential drawbacks of outsourcing include loss of control and flexibility, overlooked opportunities to strengthen core competency and low employee morale.

on-demand computing Contracting for computer resources to rapidly respond to an organization's varying workflow. Also called 'on-demand business' and 'utility computing'.

On-demand computing is an extension of the outsourcing approach, and many companies offer on-demand computing to business clients and customers. On-demand computing, also called on-demand business and utility computing, involves rapidly responding to the organization's flow of work as the need for computer resources varies. It is often called 'utility computing' because the organization pays for computing resources from a computer or consulting company just as it pays for electricity from a utility company. This approach treats the information system – including hardware, software, databases, telecommunications, personnel and other components – more as a service than as separate products. In other words, instead of purchasing hardware, software and database systems, the organization only pays a fee for the systems it needs at peak times. The approach can save money because the organization does not pay for systems that it doesn't routinely need. It also allows the organization's IS staff to concentrate on more strategic issues.

Downsizing involves reducing the number of employees to cut costs. The term 'rightsizing' is also used. Rather than pick a specific business process to downsize, companies usually look to downsize across the entire company. Downsizing clearly reduces total payroll costs, although employee morale can suffer.

downsizing Reducing the number of employees to cut costs.

Employers need to be open to alternatives for reducing the number of employees and use layoffs as the last resort. It's simpler to encourage people to leave voluntarily through early retirement or other incentives. Voluntary downsizing programmes often include a buyout package offered to certain classes of employees (for example, those over 50 years old). The buyout package offers employees certain benefits and cash incentives if they voluntarily retire from the company. Other options are job sharing and transfers.

Organizational learning is closely related to organizational change. According to the concept of organizational learning, organizations adapt to new conditions or alter their practices over time. Assembly-line workers, secretaries, shop assistants, managers and executives all learn better ways of doing business and incorporate them into their day-to-day activities. Collectively, these adjustments based on experience and ideas are called 'organizational learning'. In some cases, the adjustments can be a radical redesign of business processes, often called 'reengineering'. In other cases, these adjustments can be more incremental, a concept called 'continuous improvement'. Both adjustments reflect an organization's strategy: the long-term plan of action for achieving their goals.

organizational learning The adaptations to new conditions or alterations of organizational practices over time.

Ethical and Societal Issues

For Sale: Access to Corporate Computers

For many firms, offering employees the chance to work from home makes good business sense. It gives their workforce flexibility and could improve morale. It also helps the firm reduce overheads by not having to pay to heat and light an office every day. For convenience, many firms that allow teleworking use remote desktop software.

Remote desktop refers to a system that allows a computer to be run remotely from another computer. The other computer can access the software and files stored on the first computer, and can use it to process work. Often there is a graphical interface so the remote user can see on their screen what they would see if they were at their work computer. Employees must log in to use remote desktop but unfortunately some people are using passwords that are easy to guess, allowing cybercriminals to gain control.

One such illegal service, accessed through a website called Dedicatexpress, was discovered by security researcher Brian Krebs who spent two weeks tracking the site, accessing its forums and getting hold of a list of the corporate networks to which it offered access. At the time the site had about 17 000 servers available but Mr Krebs estimates that about 300 000 have been listed since the site started in 2010. On the site members can buy the login details for a computer which is part of a firm's network, including some firms on the Fortune 500 list, and use them to send spam or as a springboard for a hacking attempt on another company.

Dedicatexpress puts some restrictions on what customers can do with the hacked servers, Mr Krebs said. Paypal fraud, online gambling and dating site scams are among the activities that are banned. While openly selling access to computers may come as a surprise or a shock to some, Mr Krebs said it was likely that the computers had been compromised for a long time. 'My sense is that

(continued)

2

a lot of these systems are probably abused quite a bit before they get to this point,' he said. 'They may have been wrung out in other ways before they are sold to a service like this.' The site is now closed but the owners have probably simply moved the content elsewhere.

So what can a company do to help prevent unauthorized access via remote desktop? The standard advice is that users should create a strong password that is not easy to guess, limit the users who can log on to the host computer, limit the number of password attempts the system allows before the user is locked out, and only allow certain computers access to the remote desktop. This is done by specifying the Internet address of the computers that are allowed to use it.

Questions

1 What is a strong password? How would you go about guessing someone's password?

2 What are some of the advantages and disadvantages of using remote desktop software?

3 What are some of the other concerns firms may have in letting their employees telework?

4 How can firms ensure that employees act responsibly when using software such as remote desktop?

Reengineering and Continuous Improvement

reengineering Also known as 'process redesign' and 'business process reengineering' (BPR). The radical redesign of business processes, organizational structures, information systems and values of the organization to achieve a breakthrough in business results.

To stay competitive, organizations must occasionally make fundamental changes in the way they do business. In other words, they must change the activities tasks, or processes they use to achieve their goals. **Reengineering**, also called 'process redesign' and 'business process reengineering' (BPR), involves the radical redesign of business processes, organizational structures, information systems and values of the organization to achieve a breakthrough in business results. Reengineering can reduce delivery times, increase product and service quality, enhance customer satisfaction, and increase revenues and profitability. When Mittal Steel South Africa's Vanderbijlpark Plant reengineered its steel-making operations, introducing new automated systems, it was able to reduce the amount of raw materials used in its processes and increase its output of steel, which was of a higher quality than before. They were also able to reduce processing time and improve plant availability.[9]

In contrast to simply automating the existing work process, reengineering challenges the fundamental assumptions governing their design. It requires finding and vigorously challenging old rules blocking major business process changes. These rules are like anchors weighing down a firm and keeping it from competing effectively. Table 2.1 provides some examples of such rules.

Table 2.1 Selected Business Rules that Affect Business Processes

Rule	Original Rationale	Potential Problem
Hold small orders until full lorry load shipments can be assembled	Reduce delivery costs	Customer delivery is slow
Do not accept an order until customer credit is approved	Reduce potential for bad debt	Customer service is poor
Let headquarters make all merchandising decisions	Reduce number of items carried in inventory	Customers perceive organization has limited product selection

The Northern Ireland Civil Service is introducing an electronic and document records management system (EDRM) to improve its efficiency. Processes have been reengineered so that instead of records being held in different departments and in different formats (on paper, in databases and even in email), a centralized system will provide access to up-to-date and secure information. It is hoped the system will also reduce the amount of paper the service uses.[10]

In contrast to reengineering, the idea of **continuous improvement** is to constantly seek ways to improve business processes and add value to products and services. This continual change will increase customer satisfaction and loyalty and ensure long-term profitability. Manufacturing companies make continual product changes and improvements. Service organizations regularly find ways to provide faster and more effective assistance to customers. By doing so, these companies increase customer loyalty, minimize the chance of customer dissatisfaction and diminish the opportunity for competitive inroads. Table 2.2 compares these two strategies.

continuous improvement Constantly seeking ways to improve business processes to add value to products and services.

Table 2.2 Comparing Business Process Reengineering and Continuous Improvement

Business Process Reengineering	Continuous Improvement
Strong action taken to solve serious problem	Routine action taken to make minor improvements
Top-down change driven by senior executives	Bottom-up change driven by workers
Broad in scope; cuts across departments	Narrow in scope; focus is on tasks in a given area
Goal is to achieve a major breakthrough	Goal is continuous, gradual improvements
Often led by outsiders	Usually led by workers close to the business
Information system integral to the solution	Information systems provide data to guide the improvement team

User Satisfaction and Technology Acceptance

To be effective, reengineering and continuous improvement efforts must result in satisfied users and be accepted and used throughout the organization. You can determine the actual usage of an information system by the amount of technology diffusion and infusion. **Technology diffusion** is a measure of how widely technology is spread throughout an organization. An organization has a high level of technology diffusion if computers and information systems are located in most departments. Some online merchants, such as BT (www.bt.com), have a high diffusion and use computer systems to perform most of their business functions, including marketing, purchasing and billing.

technology diffusion A measure of how widely technology is spread throughout the organization.

Technology infusion, on the other hand, is the extent to which technology permeates an area or department. In other words, it is a measure of how deeply embedded technology is in an area of the organization. Some architectural firms, for example, use computers in all aspects of designing a building from drafting to final blueprints. The design area, thus, has a high level of infusion. Of course, a firm can have a high level of infusion in one part of its operations and a low level of diffusion overall. The architectural firm might use computers in all aspects of design (high infusion in the design area), but not to perform other business functions, including billing, purchasing and marketing (low diffusion). Diffusion and infusion often depend on the technology available

technology infusion The extent to which technology is deeply integrated into an area or department.

now and in the future, the size and type of the organization, and the environmental factors that include the competition, government regulations, suppliers and so on. This is often called the 'technology, organization and environment' (TOE) framework.[11]

An active research area in IS involves identifying why people accept and use one system, but dislike and therefore don't use another. One early model, the Technology Acceptance Model (TAM), shows that people will use a system if it is easy to use and useful to them. This in itself is unhelpful to IS developers, however TAM has been the basis for an large body of research that is ongoing, and which hopes to produce more practical results.

Although an organization might have a high level of diffusion and infusion with computers throughout the organization, this does not necessarily mean that information systems are being used to their full potential.

Information Systems @ Work

Better Fit for Online Shoppers

Many shoppers who buy clothes online are unsure about what size to order. In fact some shoppers deliberately order several sizes of the same garment and return all of them except the one that fits. 'Almost one in four garments are being returned – 70 per cent of those returns are because the customers got the wrong size,' says Heikki Haldre, chief executive and founder of London-based Fits.me.

Fits.me has developed software that allows shoppers to enter some basic measurements that they have taken themselves and a virtual mannequin is created which fits their dimensions. The mannequin can then be dressed with clothes of different styles and sizes allowing shoppers to see how different garments will fit before making their purchase. More than 30 retailers have already signed up to the service, including Superdry, Hugo Boss and Thomas Pink. 'Being more confident about getting clothes that fit also means shoppers buy more,' says Mr Haldre.

However, with this system the basic problem remains – customers are responsible for taking their own measurements, something no tailor would recommend. So entrepreneur Carlos Solorio has come up with the Tailor Truck. His customized van is equipped with 14 Kinect sensors, which together scan customers' bodies, taking more than 3.5 million body point measurements. These are then sent to a production facility in Asia, allowing a customer to order a tailor-made suit.

'Customers get a custom suit with a price ranging from $500–1500 (€400–1000), which is lower than your typical custom suit,' says Mr Solorio. 'Custom suiting was really limited towards wealthy individuals, and the experience wasn't the best.'

While better than customers trying to measure themselves, the system still doesn't really deliver the convenience promised by online shopping. Therefore computer scientists at the London College of Fashion are developing software that allows shoppers to use their own camera equipment to try to find the perfect fit.

Using their webcam or smartphone, a shopper takes an image of themselves and uploads it to a website. They tell the computer where on the photo their hands and feet are and provide some basic data like their height, weight, age and gender. This information is used to identify the shopper's body shape.

'We realize people might have busy backgrounds [in their photos], so we developed this technology so that it can be used anywhere. Even if you have a busy background, this algorithm will be able to pick that person out,' Mr Al-Sayegh says.

Using garment data provided by the retailer, the software is able to make a size recommendation for the shopper. Mr Al-Sayegh hopes it won't be long before the technology is available in most online clothing stores.

Questions

1 What are the advantages and disadvantages of the London College of Fashion system to retailers and customers?

2 Who do you think might use the London College of Fashion system, and who would not? What sort of retailers would be attracted to this system and why?

3 Outline a policy that an online clothes seller might have about returns. To help, search online for some real policies. How can you make it fair for both the seller and buyer?

4 Would you, or have you, bought clothes online? Discuss your experiences.

The Applications Portfolio

In Chapter 1 we looked at how information systems can be classified by the management level of the user. The **applications portfolio** is perhaps a more useful classification scheme. It sorts information systems according to the contribution they make to the business. According to the applications portfolio, there are four types of system:

1 Support: **Support applications** are nice to have, but are not essential. They include things that are convenient but without them the organization can still conduct business. Typical support applications include electronic diaries and instant messaging software, used to let employees in an office communicate with each other.

2 Key operational: **Key operational applications** are essential. Without them the organization would not be able to do business. Transaction processing systems, mentioned in Chapter 1 and discussed fully in Chapter 8, are an example. If the checkout system at a Tesco shop malfunctions, Tesco would be unable to sell goods until it was repaired. The website of every e-commerce business is key operational.

applications portfolio A scheme for classifying information systems according to the contribution they make to the organization.

support application Support applications make work more convenient but are not essential.

key operational application Key operational applications are essential. Without them the organization could not conduct business.

strategic application A strategic application gives a firm a competitive advantage.

3 Strategic: A **strategic application** is an information system that gives a business an advantage over some or all of its competitors. Some ideas for what this advantage might be are discussed later in this chapter in the section on Competitive Advantage (page 49). The term 'strategic' should not be confused with the same term used to describe senior management in a business. A strategic system could appear anywhere in the company hierarchy.

future strategic application Future strategic applications are ideas for systems which, if fully developed and deployed, might one day become strategic applications.

4 Future strategic: A **future strategic application** (also known as a 'potential strategic' or 'high potential' application) is an idea for, or a prototype of, an information system which, if developed, might one day become a strategic system. A company may have ten future strategic systems and decide to only invest in one. This decision is often a judgement call made by senior management. It may be that the technology to develop a future strategic system is currently too expensive and the company is waiting for prices to fall.

There is an endless cycle at work with systems starting life in one part of the portfolio, and finishing in another. Typically an innovative, leading company will come up with an idea for a potential strategic system. If they invest it in and, if it is successful, it becomes a strategic system. Their competitors see that they have an advantage and so create their own versions of the system. Eventually, the system will become industry standard and now be key operational. In the meantime, the innovative company will have had more ideas for future strategic systems, and so the cycle starts again. Companies that see themselves as industry followers rather than industry leaders will not have strategic or future strategic systems in their portfolio.

Success Factors

Many writers have suggested reasons why some information systems are implemented successfully and why others are not. It is of vital importance that a company's information systems are aligned with the company's goals. Misalignment is a frequently cited reason for information systems failure. The main way of achieving **alignment** is for senior managers to consider the business processes they have in place to achieve company goals, and ask what information systems are needed to support these business processes. Less frequently a business, typically a small business or even a single entrepreneur, will consider what technology is available and ask what business goals can be achieved using it. In this case, information technology is dictating business strategy instead of business strategy dictating what information technology is used. Both are valid paths to alignment.

alignment When the output from an information system is exactly what is needed to help a company achieve its strategic goals, the two are said to be in alignment.

Other common success factors are:

■ Senior management must be committed to the development or purchase of the information system and support it fully.

■ End-users of the system should be involved as early, and as much as possible, in the development or purchase or the system.

requirements engineering Also known as 'requirements analysis' and 'requirements capture'. Identifying what an information system is needed (required) to do. Once the requirements have been identified, a solution can then be designed.

■ Time must be taken to carefully determine what the system must do, something known as **requirements engineering**. Requirements must be clearly stated and understood and accepted by everyone involved.

■ Strong project management in the development or purchase of the information system.

Later on in this text we will examine Joint Application Development, a method for creating IS which places users at the centre of the development.

2.2 Competitive Advantage

A **competitive advantage** is the ability of a firm to outperform its industry, that is, to earn a higher rate of profit than the industry norm[12] and can result from higher-quality products, better customer service and lower costs. Establishing and maintaining a competitive advantage is complex. An organization often uses its information system to help it do this. Ultimately, it is not how much a company spends on information systems but how it makes and manages investments in technology. Companies can spend less and get more value.

> **competitive advantage** The ability of a firm to outperform its industry; that is, to earn a higher rate of profit than the industry norm.

Factors that Lead Firms to Seek Competitive Advantage

A number of factors can lead a company to seek to attain a competitive advantage. Michael Porter, a prominent management theorist, suggested a simple but widely accepted model of the competitive forces in an industry, also called the **five-forces model**. A strong force can put a business at a disadvantage and lead it to invest in technology that can weaken it. The five forces are: (1) the rivalry among existing competitors, (2) the threat of new entrants, (3) the threat of substitute products and services, (4) the bargaining power of buyers, and (5) the bargaining power of suppliers. The more these forces combine in any instance, the more likely firms will seek competitive advantage and the more dramatic the results of such an advantage will be.

> **five-forces model** A widely accepted model that identifies five key factors that can lead to attainment of competitive advantage, including (1) the rivalry among existing competitors, (2) the threat of new entrants, (3) the threat of substitute products and services, (4) the bargaining power of buyers, and (5) the bargaining power of suppliers.

Given the five market forces just mentioned, Porter and others have proposed a number of strategies to attain competitive advantage, including cost leadership, differentiation, niche strategy, altering the industry structure, creating new products and services, and improving existing product lines and services.[13] In some cases, one of these strategies becomes dominant. For example, with a cost leadership strategy, cost can be the key consideration, at the expense of other factors if need be.

Cost Leadership

The intent of a cost leadership strategy is to deliver the lowest possible products and services. In the UK, supermarket Asda has used this strategy for years. Cost leadership is often achieved by reducing the costs of raw materials through aggressive negotiations with suppliers, becoming more efficient with production and manufacturing processes, and reducing warehousing and shipping costs. Some companies use outsourcing to cut costs when making products or completing services.

Differentiation

The intent of differentiation as a strategy is to deliver different products and services. This strategy can involve producing a variety of products, giving customers more choices, or delivering higher-quality products and services. Many car companies make different models that use the same basic parts and components, giving customers more options. Other car companies attempt to increase perceived quality and safety to differentiate their products. Some consumers are willing to pay higher prices for vehicles that differentiate on higher quality or better safety.

Niche Strategy

A niche strategy will deliver to only a small, niche market. Porsche, for example, doesn't produce inexpensive estate cars or saloons. It makes high-performance sports cars and four-wheel drives. Rolex only makes high-quality, expensive watches. It doesn't make inexpensive, plastic watches that can be purchased for €20 or less.

Altering the Industry Structure

Changing the industry to become more favourable to the company or organization is another strategy companies use. The introduction of low-fare airline carriers, such as EasyJet, has forever changed the airline industry, making it difficult for traditional airlines to make high profit margins. To fight back, airlines such as British Airways cut their flight prices and started to emphasize their strengths over low-cost airlines in their advertising. These include landing in central airports rather than airports many miles out of the city they supposedly serve, and extra staff and resources to cope if there is a fault with an aircraft, or adverse weather grounds all planes. Creating **strategic alliances** can also alter the industry structure. A strategic alliance, also called a 'strategic partnership', is an agreement between two or more companies that involves the joint production and distribution of goods and services.

strategic alliance (strategic partnership) An agreement between two or more companies that involves the joint production and distribution of goods and services.

Creating New Products and Services

Some companies introduce new products and services periodically or frequently as part of their strategy. This strategy can help a firm gain a competitive advantage, especially in the computer industry and other high-tech businesses. If an organization does not introduce new products and services every few months, the company can quickly stagnate, lose market share and decline. Companies that stay on top are constantly developing new products and services.

Improving Existing Product Lines and Service

Making real or perceived improvements to existing product lines and services is another strategy. Manufacturers of household products are always advertising 'new and improved' products. In some cases, the improvements are more perceived than real refinements; usually, only minor changes are made to the existing product, such as reducing the amount of sugar in a breakfast cereal. Some mail order companies are improving their service by using Radio Frequency Identification (RFID) tags to identify and track the location of their products as they are shipped from one location to another. Customers and managers can instantly locate products as they are shipped from suppliers to the company, to warehouses and finally to customers.

Other potentially successful strategies include being the first to market, offering customized products and services, and hiring talented staff, the assumption being that the best people will determine the best products and services to deliver to the market and the best approach to deliver these products and services. Companies can also combine one or more of these strategies.

2.3 Evaluating IS

Once an information system has been implemented, management will want to assess how successful it has been in achieving its goals. Often this is a difficult thing to do, and many businesses do not attempt to take anything more than an informal approach to evaluation.[14] Business can use measurements of productivity, return on investment (ROI), net present value and other measures of performance to evaluate the contributions their information systems make to their businesses.

Productivity

Developing information systems that measure and control productivity is a key element for most organizations. **Productivity** is a measure of the output achieved divided by the input required. A higher level of output for a given level of input means greater productivity; a lower level of output for a given level of input means lower productivity. The numbers assigned to productivity

productivity A measure of the output achieved divided by the input required. Productivity = (Output / Input) × 100%.

levels are not always based on labour hours – productivity can be based on factors such as the amount of raw materials used, resulting quality, or time to produce the goods or service. The value of the productivity number is not as significant as how it compares with other time periods, settings and organizations.

After a basic level of productivity is measured, an information system can monitor and compare it over time to see whether productivity is increasing. Then a company can take corrective action if productivity drops below certain levels. In addition to measuring productivity, an information system can be used within a process to significantly increase productivity. Thus, improved productivity can result in faster customer response, lower costs and increased customer satisfaction.

In the late 1980s and early 1990s, overall productivity did not seem to improve as a company increased its investments in information systems. Often called the productivity paradox, this situation troubled many economists who were expecting to see dramatic productivity gains. In the early 2000s, however, productivity again seemed on the rise.

Return on Investment and the Value of Information Systems

One measure of IS value is **return on investment (ROI)**. This measure investigates the additional profits or benefits that are generated as a percentage of the investment in IS technology. A small business that generates an additional profit of €20 000 for the year as a result of an investment of €100 000 for additional computer equipment and software would have a return on investment of 20 per cent (€20 000/€100 000). In many cases, however, it can be difficult to accurately measure ROI.[15]

return on investment (ROI)
One measure of IS value that investigates the additional profits or benefits that are generated as a percentage of the investment in IS technology.

Earnings Growth

Another measure of IS value is the increase in profit, or earnings growth, it brings. For instance, a mail-order company might install an order-processing system that generates a 7 per cent earnings growth compared with the previous year.

Market Share

Market share is the percentage of sales that a product or service has in relation to the total market. If installing a new online catalogue increases sales, it might help a company to increase its market share by 20 per cent.

Customer Awareness and Satisfaction

Although customer satisfaction can be difficult to quantify, about half of today's best global companies measure the performance of their information systems based on feedback from internal and external users. Some companies use surveys and questionnaires to determine whether the IS investment has increased customer awareness and satisfaction.

Total Cost of Ownership

Another way to measure the value of information systems was developed by the Gartner Group and is called the **total cost of ownership (TCO)**. This approach breaks total costs into areas such as the cost to acquire the technology, technical support, administrative costs, and end-user operations. Other costs in TCO include retooling and training costs. TCO can help to develop a more accurate estimate of the total costs for systems that range from desktop computers to large mainframe systems. Market research groups often use TCO to compare products and services.

total cost of ownership (TCO)
The measurement of the total cost of owning computer equipment, including desktop computers, networks and large computers.

Return on investment, earnings growth, market share, customer satisfaction and TCO are only a few measures that companies use to plan for and maximize the value of their IS investments. Regardless of the difficulties, organizations must attempt to evaluate the contributions that information systems make to assess their progress and plan for the future. Information technology and personnel are too important to leave to chance.

Risk

In addition to the return-on-investment measures of a new or modified information system, managers should also consider the risks of designing, developing and implementing these systems. Information systems can sometimes be costly failures. Some companies, for example, have attempted to implement enterprise resource planning (ERP) systems (see Chapter 7) and failed, costing them millions of dollars. In other cases, e-commerce applications have been implemented with little success. The costs of development and implementation can be greater than the returns from the new system.

2.4 Careers in Information Systems

Realizing the benefits of any information system requires competent and motivated IS personnel, and many companies offer excellent job opportunities. Professionals with careers in information systems typically work in an IS department as web developers, computer programmers, systems analysts, database developers and administrators, computer operators, technical support or in other positions. In addition to technical skills, they need skills in written and verbal communication, an understanding of organizations and the way they operate, and the ability to work with people and in groups. Today, many good information, business, and computer science schools require these business and communications skills of their graduates.

In general, IS professionals are charged with maintaining the broadest perspective on organizational goals. Most medium to large organizations manage information resources through an IS department. In smaller businesses, one or more people might manage information resources, with support from outsourced services. As shown in Figure 2.5, the IS department has three primary responsibilities: operations, systems development and support.

Operations

People in the operations component of a typical IS department work with information systems in corporate or business unit computer facilities. They tend to focus more on the efficiency of IS functions rather than their effectiveness.

System operators primarily run and maintain IS equipment, and are typically trained at technical schools or through on-the-job experience. They are responsible for starting, stopping and correctly operating mainframe systems, networks, back-up drives, disc devices, printers and so on. Other operations include scheduling, hardware maintenance, and preparing input and output. Data-entry operators convert data into a form the computer system can use. They can use terminals or other devices to enter business transactions, such as sales orders and payroll data. Increasingly, data entry is being automated – captured at the source of the transaction rather than entered later. In addition, companies might have local area network (LAN) and web operators who run the local network and any websites the company has.

Systems Development

The systems development component of a typical IS department focuses on specific development projects and ongoing maintenance and review. Systems analysts and programmers, for

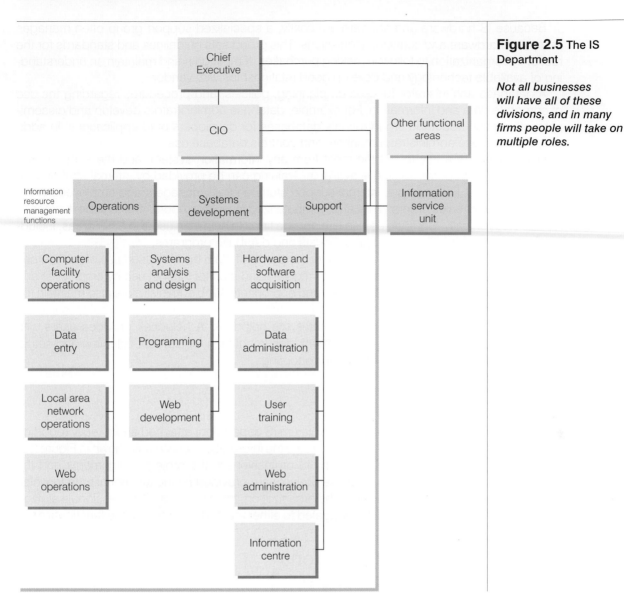

Figure 2.5 The IS Department

Not all businesses will have all of these divisions, and in many firms people will take on multiple roles.

example, address these concerns to achieve and maintain IS effectiveness. The role of a systems analyst is multifaceted. Systems analysts help users determine what outputs they need from the system and construct plans for developing the necessary programs that produce these outputs. Systems analysts then work with one or more programmers to make sure that the appropriate programs are purchased, modified from existing programs or developed. A computer programmer uses the plans the systems analyst created to develop or adapt one or more computer programs that produce the desired outputs.

With the dramatic increase in the use of the Internet, intranets and extranets, many companies have web or Internet developers who create effective and attractive websites for customers, internal personnel, suppliers, stockholders and others who have a business relationship with the company.

Support

The support component of a typical IS department provides user assistance in hardware and software acquisition and use, data administration, user training and assistance, and web administration. In many cases, support is delivered through an information centre.

Because IS hardware and software are costly, a specialized support group often manages computer hardware and software acquisitions. This group sets guidelines and standards for the rest of the organization to follow in making purchases. It must gain and maintain an understanding of available technology and develop good relationships with vendors.

A database administrator focuses on planning, policies, and procedures regarding the use of corporate data and information. For example, database administrators develop and disseminate information about the organization's databases for developers of IS applications. In addition, the database administrator monitors and controls database use.

User training is a key to get the most from any information system, and the support area ensures that appropriate training is available. Training can be provided by internal staff or from external sources. For example, internal support staff can train managers and employees in the best way to enter sales orders, to receive computerized inventory reports and to submit expense reports electronically. Companies also hire outside firms to help train users in other areas, including the use of word processing, spreadsheets and database programs.

Web administration is another key area for support staff. With the increased use of the Internet, web administrators are sometimes asked to regulate and monitor Internet use by employees and managers to make sure that it is authorized and appropriate. Web administrators also maintain the organization's website to keep it accurate and current, which can require substantial resources.

The support component typically operates the helpdesk. A helpdesk provides users with assistance, training, application development, documentation, equipment selection and setup, standards, technical assistance and troubleshooting.

Information Service Units

An information service unit is basically a miniature IS department attached and directly reporting to a functional area in a large organization. Notice the information service unit shown in Figure 2.5. Even though this unit is usually staffed by IS professionals, the project assignments and the resources necessary to accomplish these projects are provided by the functional area to which it reports. Depending on the policies of the organization, the salaries of IS professionals staffing the information service unit might be budgeted to either the IS department or the functional area.

Typical IS Titles and Functions

The organizational chart shown in Figure 2.5 is a simplified model of an IS department in a typical medium or large organization. Many organizations have even larger departments, with increasingly specialized positions such as librarian or quality assurance manager. Smaller firms often combine the roles shown in Figure 2.5 into fewer formal positions.

The Chief Information Officer

The role of the chief information officer (CIO) is to employ an IS department's equipment and personnel to help the organization attain its goals. The CIO is a senior manager concerned with the overall needs of the organization, and sets organization-wide policies, and plans, manages and acquires information systems. Some of the CIO's top concerns include integrating IS operations with business strategies, keeping up with the rapid pace of technology, and defining and assessing the value of systems development projects. The high level of the CIO position reflects that information is one of the organization's most important resources. A CIO works with other high-level officers of an organization, including the finance director and the executive officer, in managing and controlling total corporate resources. CIOs must also work closely with advisory committees, stressing effectiveness and teamwork and viewing information systems as an integral part of the organization's business processes – not an adjunct to the organization. Thus, CIOs need both technical and business skills.

LAN Administrator

Local area network (LAN) administrators set up and manage the network hardware, software, and security processes. They manage the addition of new users, software, and devices to the network. They also isolate and fix operations problems. LAN administrators are in high demand and often solve both technical and non-technical problems. Database administrators manage the use, maintenance and security of a company's databases. Often a database administrator will help users extract the data they need in the format they require.

local area network (LAN) A computer network that connects computer systems and devices within a small area, such as an office, home or several floors in a building.

Internet Careers

These careers are in the areas of web operations, web development and web administration. As with other areas in IS, many top-level administrative jobs are related to the Internet. These career opportunities are found in both traditional companies and those that specialize in the Internet.

Internet jobs within a traditional company include Internet strategists and administrators, Internet systems developers, Internet programmers and Internet or website operators.

Systems Developers

Systems developers design and write software. Typically developers will be graduates with degrees in technical subjects such as computer science, mathematics or engineering. However, many big employers have graduate recruitment schemes where degree subject is less important than an ability to learn. On such schemes, graduates are taught the skills they need. The skills needed by developers include the ability to design solutions to problems and communicate these solutions to other developers and to users, and the technical skill to create these solutions. Software development can be extremely challenging and exciting.

Often, systems developers are employed to create software to support business goals, such as develop the organization's transaction processing system. Alternatively, systems developers may work in a software house, where the software they write is the product the organization sells. One of the fastest growing areas of software development is the games industry, with many universities now offering degrees in games development.

Other IS Careers

Other IS career opportunities include technical writing (creating technical manuals and user guides) and user interface design.

Often, the people filling IS roles have completed some form of certification. **Certification** is a process for testing skills and knowledge resulting in an endorsement by the certifying authority that an individual is capable of performing a particular job. Certification frequently involves specific, vendor-provided or vendor-endorsed coursework. Popular certification programs include Microsoft Certified Systems Engineer, Certified Information Systems Security Professional (CISSP), Oracle Certified Professional and many others.

certification A process for testing skills and knowledge, which results in a statement by the certifying authority that states an individual is capable of performing a particular kind of job.

Summary

The use of information systems to add value to the organization is strongly influenced by organizational structure, and the organization's attitude and ability to change. An organization is a formal collection of people and other resources established to accomplish a set of goals. The primary goal of a for-profit organization is to maximize shareholder value. Non-profit organizations include social groups, religious groups, universities and other organizations that do not have profit as the primary goal.

Organizations are systems with inputs, transformation mechanisms and outputs. Value-added processes increase the relative worth of the combined inputs on their way to becoming final outputs of the organization. The value chain is a series (chain) of activities that includes (1) inbound logistics, (2) warehouse and storage, (3) production, (4) finished product storage, (5) outbound logistics, (6) marketing and sales, and (7) customer service.

Organizational structure refers to how organizational subunits relate to the overall organization. Several basic organizational structures include traditional, project, team and a virtual one. A virtual organizational structure employs individuals, groups or complete business units in geographically dispersed areas. These can involve people in different countries operating in different time zones and different cultures. Organizational change deals with how profit and non-profit organizations plan for, implement and handle change. Change can be caused by internal or external factors. According to the concept of organizational learning, organizations adapt to new conditions or alter practices over time.

Because information systems are so important, businesses need to be sure that improvements to existing systems, or completely new systems, help lower costs, increase profits, improve service or achieve a competitive advantage. Business process reengineering involves the radical redesign of business processes, organizational structures, information systems and values of the organization, to achieve a breakthrough in results. Continuous improvement to business processes can add value to products and services.

The extent to which technology is used throughout an organization can be a function of technology diffusion, infusion and acceptance. Technology diffusion is a measure of how widely technology is in place throughout an organization. Technology infusion is the extent to which technology permeates an area or department. User satisfaction with a computer system and the information it generates depends on the quality of the system and the resulting information.

Outsourcing involves contracting with outside professional services to meet specific business needs. This approach allows the company to focus more closely on its core business and to target its limited resources to meet strategic goals. Downsizing involves reducing the number of employees to reduce payroll costs; however, it can lead to unwanted side effects.

Competitive advantage is usually embodied in either a product or service that has the most added value to consumers and that is unavailable from the competition or in an internal system that delivers benefits to a firm not enjoyed by its competition. The five-forces model explains factors that lead firms to seek competitive advantage: The rivalry among existing competitors, the threat of new market entrants, the threat of substitute products and services, the bargaining power of buyers, and the bargaining power of suppliers. Strategies to address these factors and to attain competitive advantage include cost leadership, differentiation, niche strategy, altering the industry structure, creating new products and services, improving existing product lines and services, and other strategies.

Cooperation between business managers and IS personnel is the key to unlocking the potential of any new or modified system. Information systems personnel typically work in an IS department. The chief information officer (CIO) employs an IS department's equipment and personnel to help the organization attain its goals. Systems analysts help users determine what outputs they need from the system and construct the plans needed to develop the necessary programs that produce these outputs. Systems analysts then work with one or more system developers to make sure that the appropriate programs are purchased, modified from existing programs or developed. The major responsibility of a computer programmer is to use the plans developed by the systems analyst to build or adapt one or more computer programs that produce the desired outputs.

Computer operators are responsible for starting, stopping and correctly operating mainframe systems, networks, tape drives, disc devices, printers and so on. LAN administrators set up and manage the network hardware, software and security processes. Trained personnel are also needed to set up and manage a company's Internet site, including Internet strategists, Internet systems developers, Internet programmers and website operators. Information systems personnel can also support other functional departments or areas.

In addition to technical skills, IS personnel need skills in written and verbal communication, an understanding of organizations and the way they operate, and the ability to work with people (users). In general, IS personnel are charged with maintaining the broadest enterprise-wide perspective.

Self-Assessment Test

1 The value chain is a series of activities that includes inbound logistics, warehouse and storage, production, finished product storage, outbound logistics, marketing and sales, and customer service. True or false?

2 A(n) _____ is a formal collection of people and other resources established to accomplish a set of goals.

3 User satisfaction with a computer system and the information it generates often depends on the quality of the system and the resulting information. True or false?

4 The concept in which organizations adapt to new conditions or alter their practices over time is called _____.
   a. organizational learning
   b. organizational change
   c. continuous improvement
   d. reengineering

5 _____ involves contracting with outside professional services to meet specific business needs.

6 Technology infusion is a measure of how widely technology is spread throughout an organization. True or false?

7 Reengineering is also called _____.

8 What is a measure of the output achieved divided by the input required?
   a. efficiency
   b. effectiveness
   c. productivity
   d. return on investment

9 _____ is a measure of the additional profits or benefits generated as a percentage of the investment in IS technology.

10 Who is involved in helping users determine what outputs they need and constructing the plans needed to produce these outputs?
   a. CIO
   b. applications programmer
   c. systems programmer
   d. systems analyst

11 The systems development component of a typical IS department focuses on specific development projects and ongoing maintenance and review. True or false?

12 The _____ is typically in charge of the IS department or area in a company.

Review Questions

1 What is the value chain?

2 What is the difference between a virtual organizational structure and a traditional organizational structure?

3 What is reengineering? What are the potential benefits of performing a process redesign?

4 What is the difference between technology infusion and technology diffusion?

5 List and define the basic organizational structures.

6 What is downsizing? How is it different from outsourcing?

7 What are some general strategies employed by organizations to achieve competitive advantage?

8 What are several common justifications for implementing an information system?

9 What is on-demand computing? What two advantages does it offer to a company?

10 What is the role of a systems developer? What is the role of a programmer? Are they different and, if so, how?

Discussion Questions

1 You have decided to open an Internet site to buy and sell used music CDs to other students. Describe the value chain for your new business.

2 What are the advantages of using a virtual organizational structure? What are the disadvantages?

3 How might you measure user satisfaction with a registration program at a college or university? What are the important features that would make students and faculty satisfied with the system?

4 There are many ways to evaluate the effectiveness of an information system. Discuss two methods and describe when one method would be preferred over another method.

5 A company has a prototype that it classes in the applications portfolio as potential strategic. If they develop it and it turns out to be strategic, is there any way they can sustain the advantage it brought? Or will it be destined to be copied by competitors which will errode its advantage?

Web Exercises

1 This book emphasizes the importance of information. You can get information from the Internet by going to a specific address, such as www.ibm.com, the home page of the IBM corporation, or a search engine such as www. google.co.uk.

Using Google, search for information about a company or topic discussed in Chapters 1 or 2. You might be asked to develop a report or send an email message to your instructor about what you find.

2 Use the Internet to search for information about user satisfaction. You can use a search engine or a database at your college or university. Write a brief report describing what you find.

Case One

Connecting with Customers through Information

Tesco has come a long way since it began as a market stall selling surplus groceries in London's East End in 1919. It is now the UK's largest food seller, although the company has expanded into general merchandise as well. It operates in 14 countries across Europe, Asia and North America, has over 5000 stores (about half outside the UK), and has annual revenues of £67.6 billion for fiscal 2011(€80 billion).

Despite its history of nearly a century, Tesco is up to date with today's information systems. One way it uses these systems is to understand its customers better. As former CEO Sir Terry Leahy put it in April

2011, 'The hardest thing to know is where you stand relative to your customers, your suppliers and your competitors. Collecting, analyzing, and acting on the insights revealed by customer behaviour, at the [cash register] and online, allowed Tesco to find the truth.' He added, 'Customers [are] the best guide. They have no axe to grind. You have to follow the customers.'

To track and analyze customer information, Tesco invested in a data warehousing system from Teradata along with reporting software from Business Objects. A data warehouse is a large collection of historical data to use for analysis and decision making. At Tesco, 'large' is no exaggeration: its data warehouse contains over 100 TB (terabytes) of data. By comparison, a high-end personal computer in 2011 might have a total storage of 1 TB.

Connecting with customers, though, isn't a one-way process of collecting data about them. Connecting also means reaching out to customers, allowing them to interact in new ways. Tesco is doing that, too. Using augmented reality technology from Kishino AR, Tesco lets customers see products online almost as if they were physically in a store. (You can see this in action in the Kishino AR video listed under Sources.) Tesco will also put computers in eight of its UK stores that allow customers to check out more products than a store can stock and look at heavy, bulky items from all angles. In Korea, Tesco has opened a complete virtual store: customers can view over 500 items, scan their bar codes using a special smartphone app, and order products. The products can be delivered later that same day if they order by 1 pm.

Recognizing that many of the customers it wants to connect with are members of social networking sites, Tesco has also developed a Facebook application in which Clubcard holders (or most of its regular customers, 16 million in the UK alone) can vote on products they want added to its Big Price Drop promotion. Richard Brasher, CEO of Tesco UK, explains, 'We are committed to doing all we can to help our customers, and our new Facebook application will enable them to tell us directly where they most value reduced prices.' Aside from the benefits of lower prices, voting on which prices should be lowered gives customers a feeling of being connected with the store and participating in decisions.

Tesco's applications require modern information systems. More importantly, however, they require the ability to see the value of information and conceive of innovative ways to use it. In this chapter you'll see how that can happen.

Questions

1 Do you think a 'virtual Tesco' would be popular where you live? Why or why not?

2 Is the Tesco Facebook app a good idea in your opinion? Do you think it would be popular with Facebook users?

3 Tesco stores information about the products that its customers purchase. What do you think they could do with this information? (Hint: it's a lot more than you might at first imagine.)

4 What are some of the concerns customers might have about Tesco storing so much data? What could Tesco do to reassure customers?

Case Two

Community Management at Over 6 Million Comments a Month

Organizations and individuals who set up community websites have to be prepared to handle a lot of user generated content. The Huffington Post is a news website covering politics, business, entertainment, environment, technology and local news. Registered users can comment on the articles published, and they do – in 2012 the website handled over 70 million comments leaving some commentators wondering what the point is. In among 70 million comments how could one person's voice be meaningfully heard?

In fact Huffington Post's former community manager Justin Isaf said that many of the comments on the site were made in direct response to the comments of others, meaning that people are talking to each other and debating the issues. 'For us, the solution has been to work really hard to keep the community safe and enjoyable by investing significant time and energy into pre-moderation,' he says.

First of all, the site has a networking feature where users can follow each other to engage with people they find interesting. The system makes sure that old friends can find each other easily, but at the same time it tries to introduce users to new people. The site then employs a team of around 30 full-time moderators working 24 hours a day in six-hour shifts to read comments and ensure they meet community standards. Those who post offensive material can find themselves banned from the site.

However it's just not possible for 30 people to monitor many millions of comments. That's why in 2010 The Huffington Post bought Adaptive Semantics, a small technology company with expertise in automatically analyzing the meaning of text. Adaptive Semantics' main technology is JuLiA, which stands for "Just a Linguistic Algorithm". JuLiA is an artificial intelligence which reads every comment posted to The Huffington Post website and flags up those that contain inappropriate comments, spam and abusive language. JuLiA has the ability to learn and is helped in this regard by the moderators who tag comments as examples of what JuLiA should look out for. The human team also deals with grey-area comments that JuLiA isn't sure about, as well as those needing special care moderation such as the death of a celebrity.

'We have several stories and sections of the site that are sadly controversial and some that are sensitive – our Voices [section], articles about people's appearance, etc.' Mr Isaf says. 'We want to make sure that we have more human involvement because they touch so many real lives, and affect real feelings. So we want to make sure people with feelings and lives are involved. JuLiA is the sensitive type, but she doesn't always "get it" when it's emotional.'

Questions

1 Why do you think people post comments on news websites? Do you think this activity attracts certain types of individual?

2 How do you think the system should introduce people to each other? Should they have similar or different views?

3 List some of the challenges JuLiA faces when trying to moderate user comments.

4 Why do you think The Huffington Post moderates comments at all? Why not just let everyone write what they like?

Case Three

Gaining the Edge

To succeed, a business needs an edge over its competitors: a *competitive advantage*. A big part of creating a competitive advantage is using information systems effectively, meaning a business can't simply buy computers and expect good results. As Oscar Berg puts it in his blog *The Content Economy*, 'What [creates] competitive advantage is how we use technologies, how we let them affect our practices and behaviours... If technologies are carefully selected and applied, they can help to create competitive advantage.'

This chapter discusses the five forces that define any competitive situation: rivalry among existing firms in an industry, the threats of new competitors and of substitute products/services, and a firm's relationships with suppliers and customers. Firms use these forces to achieve a *sustainable* competitive advantage, which is one that others cannot copy immediately to eliminate the edge an innovator can have.

TUI Deutschland is Germany's leading tour operator. Targeted pricing is vital in its market, with the travel company that sets prices to accommodate customers' preferences and habits gaining a competitive advantage. For a large tour operator like TUI, setting optimal prices is not easy. Each season, the employee responsible for a particular tour must set around 100 000 prices for each destination region. The factors that affect the final price of hotel rooms, for example, include facilities, types of rooms, arrival dates and expected demand.

'In the past, decision-making processes were not clear,' explains Matthias Wunderlich, head of Business Intelligence at TUI Deutschland GmbH. 'There were too many gaps in the system, since the information needed to make pricing decisions was hidden in different places. The result was a pricing process that was complex, laborious, time-consuming, and occasionally inconsistent.'

Wunderlich's team developed a new information system to make this process more effective. Used for the first time for the destination of Tenerife in 2010, it organizes historical booking data, making relevant information available to pricing specialists. They define the desired margin for a destination and specify parameters for results. The system calculates combinations and dependencies until the optimum result is achieved. It forecasts which group of customers will drive demand for particular accommodations at each point of the season, from coastal hotels for families during the school holidays to luxury hotels with first-class amenities for premium customers during the low season.

'We have to ensure that a four-star hotel, for example, is always cheaper on a given date than a five-star hotel in the same customer segment,' explains Wunderlich. 'With the new solution, this is guaranteed. There is no need for a time-consuming manual procedure to ensure it is done correctly.'

Because the new pricing process is based on customer data, it reflects the needs and habits of customers. A pricing specialist can set prices that are attractive to customers while still achieving desired margins.

'Traditional pricing methods are no longer appropriate for today's travel and tourism market,' says Wunderlich. 'In the past it was practically impossible to set prices in a way that was flexible and customer-focused. This has all changed. The pricing specialist in effect becomes an expert in a particular customer group and knows exactly what a certain customer is prepared to pay for a certain travel service. This increases profits, but not at the expense of our customers.'

Questions

1 Are there any losers with the TUI system described in this case? If so, who are they? Is this system justified despite creating losers?

2 Of the five competitive forces discussed in this case, which do you think TUI's system affects?

3 What are some of difficulties a firm has in identifying its competitive forces?

4 Consider a book store that gives customers a card to be punched for each book they buy. With ten punches, they get a free paperback of their choice. This low-tech system leverages the force of customer power: By promising customers future benefits, it reduces their motivation to switch suppliers even if another store sells books for less. How could a book store use technology to make this loyalty program more effective in retaining customers?

Notes

1 Porter, M.E., 1980, *Competitive Strategy,* Free Press, New York.
2 Zhu, K., Kraemer, K., 'Post-Adoption Variations in Usage and Value of E-Business by Organizations', *Information Systems Research*, March 2005, p. 61.
3 McDougall, Paul, 'Tools to Tune Supply Chains', *Information Week*, 9 January 2006, p. 62.
4 Grey, W., et al., 'The Role of E-Marketplaces in Relationship-Based Supply Chains', *IBM Systems Journal*, Vol. 44, No. 1, 2005, p. 109.
5 Rowley, Jennifer, 'Customer Relationship Management Through the Tesco Clubcard Loyalty Scheme', *International Journal of Retail & Distribution Management*, 1 March 2005, p. 194.
6 Gordon, Jack, 'Do Your Virtual Teams Deliver Only Virtual Performance?', *Training Magazine*, 1 June 2005.
7 Robotwork Website. Available from: www.robots.com, 31 October, 2007.
8 Dav Friedlos, 'Everton Kicks Off Outsourced Contract', *Computing,* 16 January 2007.
9 See Siemens VAI Website. Available from: www.industry.siemens.com/metals-mining/en/index.htm/. Accessed 31 October 2007.
10 Kelly, Lisa, 'Northern Ireland Civil Service Goes Electronic', *Computing*, 16 January 2007.
11 Tornatzky, L., Fleischer, M., 'The Process of Technological Innovation', *Lexington Books*

(Lexington, MA, 1990), and Zhu, K. and Kraemer, K., 'Post-Adoption Variations in Usage and Value of E-Business by Organizations', *Information Systems Research,* March, 2005, p. 61.

[12] Besanko, D., Dranove, D., Shanley, M. and Schaefer, S., *Economics of Strategy,* 4th ed. (Hoboken, NJ: Wiley, 2007).

[13] Porter, M.E. and Millar, V., 'How Information Systems Give You Competitive Advantage', *Journal of Business Strategy*, Winter 1985. See also Porter,

M.E., *Competitive Advantage* (New York: Free Press, 1985).

[14] Irani, Z. and Love, P.E.D., 'Evaluating the Impact of IT on the Organization' in Galliers, R. and Leidner, D. (eds), *Strategic Information Management,* 3rd ed. (Burlington, MA: Butterworth-Heinemann, 2003).

[15] Huber, Nick, 'Return on Investment: Analysts to Offer Tips on Measuring the Value of IT', *Computer Weekly,* 26 April 2005, p. 20.

World Views Case

High Performance Computing in South Africa: Computing in Support of African Development

Alan Hogarth
Glasgow Caledonian University

South Africa has been in the process of expanding its scientific research and innovation base with a direct link to social and economic development. Part of this process was the recognition that an Information and Communications Technology (ICT) strategy was needed. Two major enabling domains were highlighted and these were Computational Science and High Performance Computing. Major examples in this regard are Biotechnology, particularly with reference to research into the major infectious diseases such as HIV/AIDS and tuberculosis, advanced manufacturing technology, technologies to utilise and protect natural resources and ensure food security (e.g., climate systems analysis and disaster forecasting), and technology for poverty reduction (e.g., behavioural modelling in social research; financial management; HPC in SMEs). Funding for three years (2006–2008) was secured for the high performance computing initiative. In addition, parallel investment in a South African National Research Network (SANReN), intended to provide high bandwidth connectivity for South African researchers, was planned.

In his 2002 State of the Nation address, President Thabo Mbeki of South Africa singled out Information and Communication Technology (ICT) as *'a critical and pervasive element in economic development,'* and recommended the establishment of an *'ICT University.'* This led to the establishment of the Meraka Institute of which The Centre for High Performance Computing (CHPC) is a component.

These developments within South Africa are aligned with initiatives to stimulate research, development and technology across the African continent. A 'Plan for Collective Action' was adopted by African Ministers of Science and Technology in Dakar in November 2005, in a meeting organized jointly by New Partnership for Africa's Development (Nepad) and the African Union (AU). It highlights initiatives and projects that are crucial to enabling Africa to mobilize and strengthen its capacities to engage effectively in scientific and technological development.

The three conceptual pillars of the 'Plan for Collective Action' are capacity building, knowledge production, and technological innovation. The Plan has twelve sub-programmes based on specific content areas, one of which is Information and Communications Technology. The ICT sub-programme was aimed at establishing a continental research network on ICTs. It brought together leading universities and research centres to design and implement projects that generate software to use with African content. Its specific goals are to:

- stimulate technical change and innovation in ICTs
- build skills in local software research and development; and
- build knowledge of Open Source Software and promote its application in education, health and conduct of science.

However, one drawback is the exorbitant price of bandwidth on the African continent.

Funding, largely from the government, was secured for the establishment of the central physical facility together with the appointment of scientific and technical staff by mid-2006. Cooperation with similar facilities in developing countries such as Brazil and India were seen as essential to the success of the South African project, given this country's largely developing economy. Discussions were held with colleagues in India with a view to establishing a relationship similar to that envisaged with those colleagues in Brazil.

A key objective was that of identifying projects that would be supported through the CHPC. These projects were identified and selected on the basis of national importance and also those which were deemed to be appropriate for location in the CHPC. In the future we will see the use of computers become critical to problems as diverse as drug design to combat diseases malaria and HIV/AIDS through the development of models for predicting drought and preventing crop failures. High performance computing is now being positioned at the centre of innovative technologies. The impact of design through scientific computing on economies driven by innovation will be significant.

The creation of a national Centre for High Performance Computing permits South African scientists and engineers to be active at the cutting edge of their respective research disciplines within a vibrant intellectual atmosphere. The benefits of the linkage between research and innovation that is enabled through the CHPC is felt not only in university laboratories but throughout the wider South African economy. The building of a critical mass in state-of-the-art high-performance computing equipment as well as high-level scientific computing expertise in an intellectual common space is central to achieving the goal of making the African Renaissance a reality.

Questions

1 How important is a national ICT strategy for South Africa? Justify your answer.

2 What benefits could be accrued by the South African population by implementing such a strategy?

3 As a Programme Director of the CHPC in charge of research and development what general criteria would you apply when selecting a proposed project?

4 Given the recognised need for the ICT strategy what areas do you think require the most immediate funding in order that the strategy becomes successful?

PART 2

Information Technology Concepts

03

Hardware: Input, Processing, Output and Storage Devices

Principles

Computer hardware must be carefully selected to meet the evolving needs of the organization and of its supporting information systems.

The computer hardware industry is rapidly changing and highly competitive, creating an environment ripe for technological breakthroughs.

The computer hardware industry and users are implementing green computing designs and products.

Learning Objectives

- Describe the role of the central processing unit and main memory.
- State the advantages of multiprocessing and parallel computing systems and provide examples of the types of problems they address.
- Describe the access methods, capacity and portability of various secondary storage devices.
- Identify and discuss the speed, functionality and importance of various input and output devices.
- Identify the characteristics and discuss the usage of various classes of single-user and multiuser computer systems.

- Describe Moore's Law and discuss its implications for future computer hardware developments.
- Give an example of recent innovations in computer CPU chips, memory devices and input/output devices.

- Define the term green computing and identify the primary goals of this program.
- Identify several benefits of green computing initiatives that have been broadly adopted.

68

Why Learn About Hardware?

Organizations invest in computer hardware to improve worker productivity, increase revenue, reduce costs, provide better customer service, speed up time-to-market and enable collaboration among employees. Organizations that don't make wise hardware investments are often stuck with outdated equipment that is unreliable and that cannot take advantage of the latest software advances. Such obsolete hardware can place an organization at a competitive disadvantage. Managers, no matter what their career field and educational background, are expected to help define the business needs that the hardware must support. In addition, managers must be able to ask good questions and evaluate options when considering hardware investments for their areas of the business. This need is especially true in small organizations, which might not have information system specialists. Managers in marketing, sales and human resources often help IS specialists assess opportunities to apply computer hardware and evaluate the options and features specified for the hardware. Managers in finance and accounting especially must keep an eye on the bottom line, guarding against overspending, yet be willing to invest in computer hardware when and where business conditions warrant it.

Today's use of technology is practical – it's intended to yield real business benefits. Using the latest information technology and providing additional processing capabilities can increase employee productivity, expand business opportunities and allow for more flexibility. This chapter concentrates on the hardware component of a computer-based information system (CBIS). Recall that hardware refers to the physical components of a computer that perform the input, processing, output and storage activities of the computer. When making hardware decisions, the overriding consideration of a business should be how hardware can support the objectives of the information system and the goals of the organization.

3.1 Computer Systems: Integrating the Power of Technology

People involved in selecting their organization's computer hardware must clearly understand current and future business requirements so that they can make informed acquisition decisions. Consider the following examples of applying business knowledge to reach sound decisions on acquiring hardware:

- When Facebook needed to add two new data centres, it elected to build its own custom computers rather than buy off-the-shelf computers from traditional manufacturers such as Dell or HP. The computers installed had only the minimum components needed to perform their specific task and did not include expensive manufacturer upgrade and backup services. As a result, the cost of building and outfitting the data centre was reduced by 24 per cent.[1]

- The Air Force Information Technology Commodity Council, composed of top United States Air Force (USAF) officials, selects the computer hardware vendors that provide wares to the service agency. Recently this group chose a vendor to provide new workstations and desktop personal computers based on a number of criteria but primarily on their performance in environmental extremes of heat, humidity, cold, dryness, and air pollutants including dust and sand. The equipment has to perform reliably in the extremes in which the USAF must carry out its missions.[2]

■ Russell's Convenience Stores operates 24 convenience stores across the US western states and Hawaii. Russell's converted to cloud computing technology, where hardware and software resources are provided by a third party over the Internet, to improve how its employees collaborate with one another and with their licencees, vendors and other business partners. It also believes that cloud computing will provide more flexibility and reduce computing costs over a five-year hardware planning horizon. According to Raymond Huff, president of HJB Convenience Corporation/Russell's Convenience, cloud computing 'is helping our licencees to operate as one business – one that is connected, informed, and cohesive.'[3]

As these examples demonstrate, choosing the right computer hardware requires understanding its relationship to the information systems and the needs of an organization.

Hardware Components

Computer system hardware components include devices that perform input, processing, data storage and output, as shown in Figure 3.1.

Recall that any system must be able to process (organize and manipulate) data, and a computer system does so through an interplay between one or more central processing units and primary storage. Each **central processing unit (CPU)** consists of three associated elements: the arithmetic/logic unit, the control unit and the register areas. The **arithmetic/logic unit (ALU)** performs mathematical calculations and makes logical comparisons. The **control unit** sequentially accesses program instructions, decodes them, and coordinates the flow of data in and out of the ALU, the registers, the primary storage, and even secondary storage and various output devices. **Registers** are high-speed storage areas used to temporarily hold small units of program instructions and data immediately before, during and after execution by the CPU.

central processing unit (CPU) The part of the computer that consists of three associated elements: the arithmetic/logic unit, the control unit and the register areas.

arithmetic/logic unit (ALU) The part of the CPU that performs mathematical calculations and makes logical comparisons.

control unit The part of the CPU that sequentially accesses program instructions, decodes them, and coordinates the flow of data in and out of the ALU, the registers, the primary storage, and even secondary storage and various output devices.

register A high-speed storage area in the CPU used to temporarily hold small units of program instructions and data immediately before, during and after execution by the CPU.

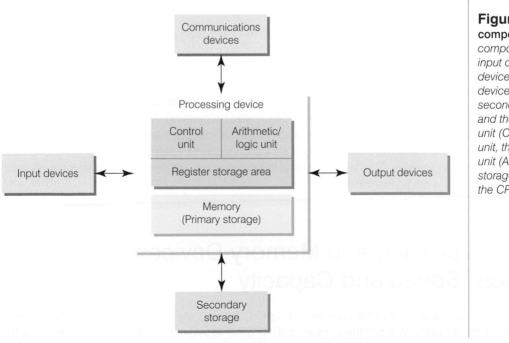

Figure 3.1 Hardware components *These components include the input devices, output devices, communications devices, primary and secondary storage devices, and the central processing unit (CPU). The control unit, the arithmetic/logic unit (ALU), and the register storage areas constitute the CPU.*

primary storage (main memory; memory) The part of the computer that holds program instructions and data.

Primary storage, also called **main memory** or **memory**, is closely associated with the CPU. Memory holds program instructions and data immediately before or after the registers. To understand the function of processing and the interplay between the CPU and memory, let's examine the way a typical computer executes a program instruction.

Hardware Components in Action

Executing any machine-level instruction involves two phases: instruction and execution. During the instruction phase, a computer performs the following steps:

■ Step 1: Fetch instruction. The computer reads the next program instruction to be executed and any necessary data into the processor.

■ Step 2: Decode instruction. The instruction is decoded and passed to the appropriate processor execution unit. Each execution unit plays a different role. The arithmetic/logic unit performs all arithmetic operations; the floating-point unit deals with noninteger operations; the load/store unit manages the instructions that read or write to memory; the branch processing unit predicts the outcome of a branch instruction in an attempt to reduce disruptions in the flow of instructions and data into the processor; the memory-management unit translates an application's addresses into physical memory addresses; and the vector-processing unit handles vector-based instructions that accelerate graphics operations.

instruction time (I-time) The time it takes to perform the fetch instruction and decode instruction steps of the instruction phase.

The time it takes to perform the instruction phase (Steps 1 and 2) is called the **instruction time (I-time)**.

The second phase is execution. During the execution phase, a computer performs the following steps:

■ Step 3: Execute instruction. The hardware element, now freshly fed with an instruction and data, carries out the instruction. This process could involve making an arithmetic computation, logical comparison, bit shift or vector operation.

■ Step 4: Store results. The results are stored in registers or memory.

execution time (e-time) The time it takes to execute an instruction and store the results.

machine cycle The instruction phase followed by the execution phase.

pipelining A form of CPU operation in which multiple execution phases are performed in a single machine cycle.

The time it takes to complete the execution phase (Steps 3 and 4) is called the **execution time (e-time)**.

After both phases have been completed for one instruction, they are performed again for the second instruction and so on. Completing the instruction phase followed by the execution phase is called a **machine cycle**, as shown in Figure 3.2. Some processing units can speed processing by using **pipelining**, whereby the processing unit gets one instruction, decodes another and executes a third at the same time. The Pentium 4 processor, for example, uses two execution unit pipelines. This feature means the processing unit can execute two instructions in a single machine cycle.

3.2 Processing and Memory Devices: Power, Speed and Capacity

The components responsible for processing – the CPU and memory – are housed together in the same box or cabinet, called the *system unit*. All other computer system devices, such as the

Figure 3.2 Execution of an instruction *In the instruction phase, a program's instructions and any necessary data are read into the processor (1). Then the instruction is decoded so that the central processor can understand what to do (2). In the execution phase, the ALU does what it is instructed to do, making either an arithmetic computation or a logical comparison (3). Then the results are stored in the registers or in memory (4). The instruction and execution phases together make up one machine cycle.*

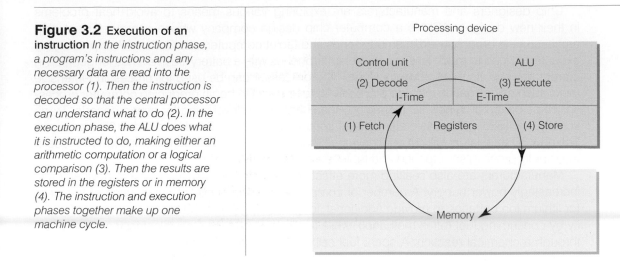

monitor, secondary storage and keyboard, are linked directly or indirectly into the system unit housing. In this section we investigate the characteristics of these important devices.

Processing Characteristics and Functions

Because organizations want efficient processing and timely output, they use a variety of measures to gauge processing speed. These measures include the time it takes to complete a machine cycle and clock speed.

Machine Cycle Time

As you've seen, a computer executes an instruction during a machine cycle. The time in which a machine cycle occurs is measured in *nanoseconds* (one-billionth of one second) and *picoseconds* (one-trillionth of one second). Machine cycle time also can be measured by how many instructions are executed in one second. This measure, called **MIPS**, stands for millions of instructions per second. MIPS is another measure of speed for computer systems of all sizes.

MIPS Millions of instructions per second, a measure of machine cycle time.

Clock Speed

Each CPU produces a series of electronic pulses at a predetermined rate, called the **clock speed**, which affects machine cycle time. The control unit executes instructions in accordance with the electronic cycle, or pulses of the CPU 'clock'. Each instruction takes at least the same amount of time as the interval between pulses. The shorter the interval between pulses, the faster each instruction can be executed.

clock speed A series of electronic pulses produced at a predetermined rate that affects machine cycle time.

Clock speed is often measured in **megahertz** (MHz, millions of cycles per second) or **gigahertz** (GHz, billions of cycles per second). Unfortunately, the faster the clock speed of the CPU, the more heat the processor generates. This heat must be dissipated to avoid corrupting the data and instructions the computer is trying to process. Also, chips that run at higher temperatures need bigger heat sinks, fans, and other components to eliminate the excess heat. This increases the size of the computing device whether it is a desktop computer, tablet computer, or smartphone, which increases the cost of materials and makes the device heavier—counter to what manufacturers and customers desire.

megahertz (MHz) Millions of cycles per second, a measure of clock speed.

gigahertz (GHz) Billions of cycles per second, a measure of clock speed.

Chip designers and manufacturers are exploring various means to avoid heat problems in their new designs. ARM is a computer chip design company whose energy-efficient chip architecture is broadly used in smartphones and tablet computers. Its Cortex-A7 chip design is expected to lead to much less expensive smartphones with a battery life five times longer than in current devices. Its more powerful Cortex-A15 processor can be used for processing-intensive tasks such as navigation or video playback.[4] Intel expects to begin producing computer processor chips based on a new 3D technology that it has been developing for over a decade. Traditionally, transistors, the basic elements of computer chips, are produced in flat 2D structures. The new 3D transistors will cut chip power consumption in half, making the chips ideal for use in the rapidly growing smartphone and tablet computer market.[5]

Manufacturers are also seeking more effective sources of energy as portable devices grow increasingly power hungry. A number of companies are exploring the substitution of fuel cells for lithium ion batteries to provide additional, longer-lasting power. Fuel cells generate electricity by consuming fuel (often methanol), while traditional batteries store electricity and release it through a chemical reaction. A spent fuel cell is replenished in moments by simply refilling its reservoir or by replacing the spent fuel cartridge with a fresh one.

Physical Characteristics of the CPU

Most CPUs are collections of digital circuits imprinted on silicon wafers, or chips, each no bigger than the tip of a pencil eraser. To turn a digital circuit on or off within the CPU, electrical current must flow through a medium (usually silicon) from point A to point B. The speed the current travels between points can be increased by either reducing the distance between the points or reducing the resistance of the medium to the electrical current.

Reducing the distance between points has resulted in ever smaller chips, with the circuits packed closer together. Gordon Moore, who would cofound Intel (the largest maker of microprocessor chips) and become its chairman of the board, hypothesized that progress in chip manufacturing ought to make it possible to double the number of transistors (the microscopic on/off switches) on a single chip every two years. The hypothesis became known as **Moore's Law**, and this 'rule of thumb' has become a goal that chip manufacturers have met more or less for more than four decades.

Moore's Law A hypothesis stating that transistor densities on a single chip will double every two years.

Chip makers have been able to improve productivity and performance by putting more transistors on the same size chip while reducing the amount of power required to perform tasks. Furthermore, because the chips are smaller, chip manufacturers can cut more chips from a single silicon wafer and thus reduce the cost per chip. As silicon-based components and computers perform better, they become cheaper to produce and therefore more plentiful, more powerful and more a part of our everyday lives. This process makes computing devices affordable for an increasing number of people around the world and makes it practical to pack tremendous computing power into the tiniest of devices.

Memory Characteristics and Functions

Main memory is located physically close to the CPU, although not on the CPU chip itself. It provides the CPU with a working storage area for program instructions and data. The chief feature of memory is that it rapidly provides the data and instructions to the CPU.

Storage Capacity

Like the CPU, memory devices contain thousands of circuits imprinted on a silicon chip. Each circuit is either conducting electrical current (on) or not conducting current (off). Data is stored in memory as a combination of on or off circuit states. Usually, 8 bits are used to represent a character, such as the letter A. Eight bits together form a **byte (B)**. In most cases, storage capacity is measured in

byte (B) Eight bits that together represent a single character of data.

bytes, with 1 byte equivalent to one character of data. The contents of the Library of Congress, with over 126 million items and 530 miles of bookshelves, would require about 20 petabytes of digital storage. It is estimated that all the words ever spoken represented in text form would equal about 5 exabytes of information.[6] Table 3.1 lists units for measuring computer storage.

Table 3.1 Computer Storage Units

Name	Abbreviation	Number of Bytes
Byte	B	1
Kilobyte	KB	2^{10} or approximately 1024 bytes
Megabyte	MB	2^{20} or 1024 kilobytes (about 1 million)
Gigabyte	GB	2^{30} or 1024 megabytes (about 1 billion)
Terabyte	TB	2^{40} or 1024 gigabytes (about 1 trillion)
Petabyte	PB	2^{50} or 1024 terabytes (about 1 quadrillion)
Exabyte	EB	2^{60} or 1024 petabytes (about 1 quintillion)

Types of Memory

Computer memory can take several forms. Instructions or data can be temporarily stored in and read from **random access memory (RAM)**. As currently designed, RAM chips are volatile storage devices, meaning they lose their contents if the current is turned off or disrupted (as happens in a power surge, brownout or electrical noise generated by lightning or nearby machines). RAM chips are mounted directly on the computer's main circuit board or in other chips mounted on peripheral cards that plug into the main circuit board. These RAM chips consist of millions of switches that are sensitive to changes in electric current.

random access memory (RAM)
A form of memory in which instructions or data can be temporarily stored.

RAM comes in many varieties: static random access memory (SRAM) is byte-addressable storage used for high-speed registers and caches; dynamic random access memory (DRAM) is byte-addressable storage used for the main memory in a computer; and double data rate synchronous dynamic random access memory (DDR SDRAM) is an improved form of DRAM that effectively doubles the rate at which data can be moved in and out of main memory. Other forms of RAM memory include DDR2 SDRAM and DDR3 SDRAM.

Read-only memory (ROM), another type of memory, is nonvolatile, meaning that its contents are not lost if the power is turned off or interrupted. ROM provides permanent storage for data and instructions that do not change, such as programs and data from the computer manufacturer, including the instructions that tell the computer how to start up when power is turned on. ROM memory also comes in many varieties: programmable read-only memory (PROM), which is used to hold data and instructions that can never be changed; erasable programmable read-only memory (EPROM), which is programmable ROM that can be erased and reused; and electrically erasable programmable read-only memory (EEPROM), which is user-modifiable read-only memory that can be erased and reprogrammed repeatedly through the application of higher than normal electrical voltage.

read-only memory (ROM)
A nonvolatile form of memory.

Chip manufacturers are competing to develop a nonvolatile memory chip that requires minimal power, offers extremely fast write speed, and can store data accurately even after a large number of write-erase cycles. Such a chip could eliminate the need for RAM and simplify and speed up memory processing. Phase change memory (PCM) is one potential approach to provide such a memory device. PCM employs a specialized glass-like material that can change its physical state, shifting between a low-resistance crystalline state to a high-resistance gaseous state by applying voltage to rearrange the atoms of the material. This technology is expected to perform 100 times faster than flash memory and may be used by server computers by 2016.[7]

Although microprocessor speed has roughly doubled every 24 months over the past decades, memory performance has not kept pace. In effect, memory has become the principal bottleneck to system performance. **Cache memory** is a type of high-speed memory that a processor can access more rapidly than main memory to help to ease this bottleneck (see Figure 3.3). Frequently used data is stored in easily accessible cache memory instead of slower memory such as RAM. Because cache memory holds less data, the CPU can access the desired data and instructions more quickly than when selecting from the larger set in main memory. Thus, the CPU can execute instructions faster, improving the overall performance of the computer system. Cache memory is available in three forms. The level 1 (L1) cache is on the CPU chip. The level 2 (L2) cache memory can be accessed by the CPU over a high-speed dedicated interface. The latest processors go a step further and place the L2 cache directly on the CPU chip itself and provide high-speed support for a tertiary level 3 (L3) external cache.

cache memory A type of high-speed memory that a processor can access more rapidly than main memory.

3

Figure 3.3 Cache memory *Processors can access this type of high-speed memory faster than main memory. Located on or near the CPU chip, cache memory works with main memory. A cache controller determines how often the data is used, transfers frequently used data to cache memory, and then deletes the data when it goes out of use.*

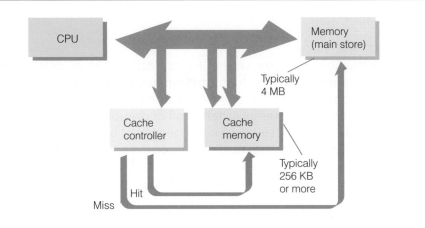

Memory capacity contributes to the effectiveness of a computer. For example, complex processing problems, such as computer-assisted product design, require more memory than simpler tasks such as word processing. Also, because computer systems have different types of memory, they might need other programs to control how memory is accessed and used. In other cases, the computer system can be configured to maximize memory usage. Before purchasing additional memory, an organization should address all these considerations.

Multiprocessing

multiprocessing The simultaneous execution of two or more instructions at the same time.

coprocessor The part of the computer that speeds processing by executing specific types of instructions while the CPU works on another processing activity.

Generally, **multiprocessing** involves the simultaneous execution of two or more instructions at the same time. One form of multiprocessing uses coprocessors. A **coprocessor** speeds processing by executing specific types of instructions while the CPU works on another processing activity. Coprocessors can be internal or external to the CPU and may have different clock speeds than the CPU. Each type of coprocessor performs a specific function.

For example, a maths coprocessor chip speeds mathematical calculations, while a graphics coprocessor chip decreases the time it takes to manipulate graphics.

A **multicore microprocessor** combines two or more independent processors into a single computer so that they share the workload and boost processing capacity. In addition, a dual-core processor enables people to perform multiple tasks simultaneously, such as playing a game and burning a CD.

multicore microprocessor
A microprocessor that combines two or more independent processors into a single computer so that they share the workload and improve processing capacity.

AMD and Intel are battling for leadership in the multicore processor marketplace, with both companies offering quad-core, six-core and eight-core CPU chips that can be used to build powerful desktop computers. AMD announced that its eight-core desktop processors based on its so-called Bulldozer architecture broke the world's record for clock speed by running at 8.5 GHz.[8]

You need to use multithreaded software designed to take full advantage of the computing power of multicore processors. Scientists at the Jet Propulsion Laboratory are planning to take advantage of the full capabilities of multicore processors to perform image analysis and other tasks on future space missions.[9]

When selecting a CPU, organizations must balance the benefits of processing speed with energy requirements and cost. CPUs with faster clock speeds and shorter machine cycle times require more energy to dissipate the heat generated by the CPU and are bulkier and more expensive than slower ones.

Parallel Computing

Parallel computing is the simultaneous execution of the same task on multiple processors to obtain results faster. Systems with thousands of such processors are known as **massively parallel processing systems**, a form of multiprocessing that speeds processing by linking hundreds or thousands of processors to operate at the same time, or in parallel, with each processor having its own bus, memory, discs, copy of the operating system and applications. The processors might communicate with one another to coordinate when executing a computer program, or they might run independently of one another but under the direction of another processor that distributes the work to the other processors and collects their results. The dual-core processors mentioned earlier are a simple form of parallel computing.

parallel computing The simultaneous execution of the same task on multiple processors to obtain results faster.

massively parallel processing systems A form of multiprocessing that speeds processing by linking hundreds or thousands of processors to operate at the same time, or in parallel, with each processor having its own bus, memory, discs, copy of the operating system and applications.

The most frequent uses for parallel computing include modelling, simulation and analyzing large amounts of data. Parallel computing is used in medicine to develop new imaging systems to complete ultrasound scans in less time with greater accuracy, enabling doctors to provide better diagnosis to patients, for example. Instead of building physical models of new products, engineers can create a virtual model of them and use parallel computing to test how the products work and then change design elements and materials as needed. Astrophysicists at the University of Nottingham in the United Kingdom are using parallel computing to build a simulation of the early universe. The computer they are using, called Curie, is based in France and has more than 92 000 computer units and offers 2 petaflops of power – the equivalent of 2 million billion operations per second.[10]

Grid computing is the use of a collection of computers, often owned by multiple individuals or organizations, to work in a coordinated manner to solve a common problem. Grid computing is a low-cost approach to parallel computing. The grid can include dozens, hundreds or even thousands of computers that run collectively to solve extremely large processing problems. Key to the success of grid computing is a central server that acts as the grid leader and traffic monitor. This controlling server divides the computing task

grid computing The use of a collection of computers, often owned by multiple individuals or organizations, to work in a coordinated manner to solve a common problem.

into subtasks and assigns the work to computers on the grid that have (at least temporarily) surplus processing power. The central server also monitors the processing and, if a member of the grid fails to complete a subtask, it restarts or reassigns the task. When all the subtasks are completed, the controlling server combines the results and advances to the next task until the whole job is completed.

CERN is the European Organization for Nuclear Research and its main area of research is the study of the fundamental constituents of matter and the forces acting between them.[11] CERN uses grid computing with the processing power of over 300 000 high-end personal computers. This computing power is needed to process some 25 petabytes of data generated each year by the Large Hadron Collider (LHC) particle accelerator looking for evidence of new particles that can provide clues to the origins of our universe.[12]

3.3 Secondary Storage

Storing data safely and effectively is critical to an organization's success. Driven by many factors – such as needing to retain more data longer to meet government regulatory concerns, storing new forms of digital data such as audio and video, and keeping systems running under the onslaught of increasing volumes of email – the estimated amount of data that companies store digitally is growing so rapidly that by 2020 storage requirements will be 44 times what they were in 2009 (an average compounded growth rate of 42 per cent per year).[13] International Data Corporation (IDC) estimates that more than 1.8 zettabytes (10^{21} bytes) of information was created and stored in 2011 alone.[14]

The Indian government is undertaking a massive effort (estimated cost is more than €3 billion) to register its 1.2 billion residents in a universal citizen ID system. When complete, the result will be the world's largest database of biometric data including retina scans, fingerprints and multiple facial images of each individual. The database will have many applications including use at India's borders to recognize travellers and to identify people who should not be in controlled areas such as the hangar area of an airport. The system can also be used in crowd control to recognize the gender and age of a crowd of people and identify where security personnel might be most needed.[15] Advanced data storage technologies will be required to store the large quantity of data and enable users to gain quick access to the information.

secondary storage Devices that store large amounts of data, instructions and information more permanently than allowed with main memory.

For most organizations, the best overall data storage solution is likely a combination of different **secondary storage** options that can store large amounts of data, instructions and information more permanently than allowed with main memory. Compared with memory, secondary storage offers the advantages of nonvolatility, greater capacity and greater economy. On a cost-per-megabyte basis, secondary storage is considerably less expensive than primary memory (see Table 3.2). The selection of secondary storage media and devices requires understanding their primary characteristics: access method, capacity and portability.

As with other computer system components, the access methods, storage capacities and portability required of secondary storage media are determined by the information system's objectives. An objective of a credit card company's information system might be to rapidly retrieve stored customer data to approve customer purchases. In this case, a fast access method is critical. In other cases, such as equipping the Coca-Cola field sales force with pocket-sized personal computers, portability and storage capacity might be major considerations in selecting and using secondary storage media and devices.

In addition to cost, capacity and portability, organizations must address security issues to allow only authorized people to access sensitive data and critical programs. Because the data and programs kept on secondary storage devices are so critical to most organizations, all of these issues merit careful consideration.

Table 3.2 Cost Comparison for Various Forms of Storage

All forms of secondary storage cost considerably less per gigabyte of capacity than SDRAM, although they have slower access times. A data cartridge costs about €0.015 per gigabyte, while SDRAM can cost around €12 per gigabyte – 800 times more expensive.

Description	Cost	Storage Capacity GB)	Cost Per GB
1.6 TB 4 mm backup data tape cartridge	€30.17	1,600	€0.015
1 TB desktop external hard drive	€68.71	1000	€0.07
25 GB rewritable Blu-ray disc	€2.17	25	€0.083
500 GB portable hard drive	€58.89	500	€0.11
72 GB DAT 72 data cartridge	€12.80	72	€0.18
50 4.7 GB DVD+R discs	€56.59	235	€0.23
4 GB flash drive	€7.51	4	€1.87
9.1 GB write-once, read-many optical disc	€55.84	9.1	€6.13
1 GB DDR2 SDRAM computer memory upgrade	€12.04	1	€12.04

Access Methods

Data and information access can be either sequential or direct. **Sequential access** means that data must be accessed in the order in which it is stored. For example, inventory data might be stored sequentially by part number, such as 100, 101, 102 and so on. If you want to retrieve information on part number 125, you must read and discard all the data relating to parts 001 through 124.

Direct access means that data can be retrieved directly without the need to pass by other data in sequence. With direct access, it is possible to go directly to and access the needed data – for example, part number 125 – without having to read through parts 001 through 124. For this reason, direct access is usually faster than sequential access. The devices used only to access secondary storage data sequentially are called **sequential access storage devices (SASDs)**; those used for direct access are called **direct access storage devices (DASDs)**.

sequential access A retrieval method in which data must be accessed in the order in which it is stored.

direct access A retrieval method in which data can be retrieved without the need to read and discard other data.

sequential access storage device (SASD) A device used to sequentially access secondary storage data.

direct access storage device (DASD) A device used for direct access of secondary storage data.

Secondary Storage Devices

Secondary data storage is not directly accessible by the CPU. Instead, computers usually use input/output channels to access secondary storage and transfer the desired data using intermediate areas in primary storage. The most common forms of secondary storage devices are magnetic, optical and solid state.

Magnetic Secondary Storage Devices

Magnetic storage uses tape or disc devices covered with a thin magnetic coating that enables data to be stored as magnetic particles. **Magnetic tape** is

magnetic tape A type of sequential secondary storage medium, now used primarily for storing backups of critical organizational data in the event of a disaster.

a type of sequential secondary storage medium, which is now used primarily for storing back-ups of critical organizational data in the event of a disaster. Examples of tape storage devices include cassettes and cartridges measuring a few millimeters in diameter, requiring very little storage space. Magnetic tape has been used as storage media since the time of the earliest computers, such as the 1951 Univac computer.[16]

Australia Wide IT offer clients a robotic tape backup system, where a robotic arm automatically loads tapes into the tape drive to be read to use for storage.[17]

magnetic disc A direct access storage device with bits represented by magnetized areas.

3

A **magnetic disc** is a direct access storage device that represents bits using small magnetized areas and uses a read/write head to go directly to the desired piece of data. Because direct access allows fast data retrieval, this type of storage is ideal for companies that need to respond quickly to customer requests, such as airlines and credit card firms. For example, if a manager needs information on the credit history of a customer or the seat availability on a particular flight, the information can be obtained in seconds if the data is stored on a direct access storage device. Magnetic disc storage varies widely in capacity and portability. Hard discs, though more costly and less portable, are more popular because of their greater storage capacity and quicker access time.

IBM is building a data repository nearly 10 times larger than anything in existence. This huge storehouse consists of 200 000 conventional hard discs working together to provide a storage capacity of 120 petabytes – large enough to hold 60 copies of the 150 billion pages needed to backup the web. An unnamed client will use the storage device with a supercomputer to perform detailed simulations of real-world events such as weather forecasts, seismic processing for the petroleum industry, or molecular studies of genomes or proteins.[18]

Putting an organization's data online involves a serious business risk – the loss of critical data can put a corporation out of business. The concern is that the most critical mechanical components inside a magnetic disc storage device – the disc drives, the fans and other input/output devices – can fail. Thus organizations now require that their data storage devices be fault tolerant; that is, they can continue with little or no loss of performance if one or more key components fail.

redundant array of independent/inexpensive discs (RAID) A method of storing data that generates extra bits of data from existing data, allowing the system to create a 'reconstruction map' so that, if a hard drive fails, the system can rebuild lost data.

A **redundant array of independent/inexpensive discs (RAID)** is a method of storing data that generates extra bits of data from existing data, allowing the system to create a 'reconstruction map' so that, if a hard drive fails, it can rebuild lost data. With this approach, data is split and stored on different physical disc drives using a technique called *striping* to evenly distribute the data. RAID technology has been applied to storage systems to improve system performance and reliability.

disc mirroring A process of storing data that provides an exact copy that protects users fully in the event of data loss.

RAID can be implemented in several ways. In the simplest form, RAID subsystems duplicate data on drives. This process, called **disc mirroring**, provides an exact copy that protects users fully in the event of data loss. However, to keep complete duplicates of current backups, organizations need to double the amount of their storage capacity. Other RAID methods are less expensive because they only duplicate part of the data, allowing storage managers to minimize the amount of extra disc space they must purchase to protect data. Optional second drives for personal computer users who need to mirror critical data are available for less than €75.5.

Advanced Audio Rentals produced the soundtrack for the movie *Avatar*. They used 3 GB and 6 GB RAID storage devices to store the film's soundtracks and to ensure smooth, efficient data transfers to guarantee high, consistent performance.[19]

virtual tape A storage device for less frequently needed data so that it appears to be stored entirely on tape cartridges, although some parts of it might actually be located on faster hard discs.

Virtual tape is a storage technology for less frequently needed data so that it appears to be stored entirely on tape cartridges, although some parts might actually be located on faster hard discs. The software associated with a virtual tape system is sometimes called a *virtual tape server*. Virtual tape can be used with a sophisticated storage-management system that moves data to slower but less costly forms of storage media as people use the data less often. Virtual tape technology can decrease data access time, lower the total cost of ownership and reduce the amount of floor space consumed by tape operations.

Baldor Electric Company designs, manufactures and markets industrial electric motors, transmission products, drives and generators. The firm implemented a virtual tape system to replace its tape-based storage system consisting of thousands of magnetic tapes. Baldor uses the new virtual tape system to back up its five production databases twice a day and stores the data for 14 days. The time to create backups has been cut by 40 per cent, and the new system takes up about 100 square feet less of data-centre floor space.[20]

Optical Secondary Storage Devices

An **optical storage device** uses special lasers to read and write data. The lasers record data by physically burning pits in the disc. Data is directly accessed from the disc by an optical disc device, which operates much like a compact disc player. This optical disc device uses a low-power laser that measures the difference in reflected light caused by a pit (or lack thereof) on the disc.

optical storage device A form of data storage that uses lasers to read and write data.

A common optical storage device is the **compact disc read-only memory (CD-ROM)** with a storage capacity of 740 MB of data. After data is recorded on a CD-ROM, it cannot be modified – the disc is 'read-only'. A CD burner, the informal name for a CD recorder, is a device that can record data to a compact disc. *CD-recordable (CD-R)* and *CD-rewritable (CD-RW)* are the two most common types of drives that can write CDs, either once (in the case of CD-R) or repeatedly (in the case of CD-RW). CD-RW technology allows PC users to backup data on CDs.

compact disc read-only memory (CD-ROM) A common form of optical disc on which data cannot be modified once it has been recorded.

A **digital video disc (DVD)** looks like a CD but can store about 135 minutes of digital video or several gigabytes of data. Software, video games and movies are often stored and distributed on DVDs. At a data transfer rate of 1.352 MB per second, the access speed of a DVD drive is faster than that of the typical CD-ROM drive.

digital video disc (DVD) A storage medium used to store software, video games and movies.

DVDs have replaced recordable and rewritable CD discs (CD-R and CD-RW) as the preferred format for sharing movies and photos. Whereas a CD can hold about 740 MB of data, a single-sided DVD can hold 4.7 GB, with double-sided DVDs having a capacity of 9.4 GB. Several types of recorders and discs are currently in use. Recordings can be made on record-once discs (DVD-R and DVD+R) or on rewritable discs (DVD-RW, DVD+RW and DVD-RAM). Not all types of rewritable DVDs are compatible with other types.

The US Naval Air Warfare Center Weapons Division at China Lake, California, is testing various brands of archival-quality DVDs for longevity and reliability. It has a need to store large volumes of data for generations.[21]

The Blu-ray high-definition video disc format, based on blue laser technology, stores at least three times as much data as a DVD. The primary use for this new format is in home entertainment equipment to store high-definition video, although this format can also store computer data. A dual-layer Blu-ray disc can store 50 GB of data.

The Holographic Versatile Disc (HVD) is an advanced optical disc technology still in the development stage that will store more data than even the Blu-ray optical disc system. HVD is the same size and shape as a regular DVD but can hold 1 terabyte (or more) of information. One HVD approach records data through the depth of the storage media in three dimensions by splitting a laser beam in two – the signal beam carries the data, and the reference beam positions where the data is written and read. HVD will make it possible to view 3D visuals on home TVs.[22]

Solid State Secondary Storage Devices

Solid state storage devices (SSDs) store data in memory chips rather than magnetic or optical media. These memory chips require less power and provide faster data access than magnetic data storage devices. While hard drives can provide 250 to 350 IOPS (input/output operations per second or read/write operations per second), advanced SSDs can perform at the rate of one-half million IOPS.[23]

In addition, SSDs have few moving parts, so they are less fragile than hard disc drives. All these factors make the SSD a preferred choice for portable computers. Two current disadvantages of SSD are their high cost per GB of data storage (roughly a 5:1 disadvantage compared to hard discs) and lower capacity compared to current hard drives. However, SSD is a rapidly developing technology, and future improvements will lower its cost and increase its capacity.

A Universal Serial Bus (USB) flash drive is one example of a commonly used SSD. USB flash drives are external to the computer and are removable and rewritable. Most weigh less than an ounce and can provide storage of 1 to 64 GB. For example, SanDisk manufactures its Ultra Backup USB Flash Drive with a storage capacity of 64 GB for around €151, which includes password protection and hardware encryption.[24]

Qualcomm is a US global communications company that designs, manufactures and markets wireless communications products and services. Its information systems organization used SSD to reduce the time required to boot up its employees' notebook computers, speed up overall system performance and reduce downtime caused by hard disc failures.[25]

The Vaillant Group and its over 12 000 employees provide heating, ventilation and air conditioning (HVAC) products and systems worldwide. Vaillant converted from the use of traditional hard drive storage systems to SSD to improve the performance of its key business systems. Critical business interactive transactions as well as batch processing jobs were dramatically improved, taking one-tenth or less of the time required using the old technology.[26]

Enterprise Storage Options

Businesses need to store large amounts of data created throughout an organization. Such large secondary storage is called *enterprise storage* and comes in three forms: attached storage, network-attached storage (NAS) and storage area networks (SANs).

Attached Storage

Attached storage methods include the tape, hard discs and optical devices discussed previously, which are connected directly to a single computer. Attached storage methods, though simple and cost effective for single users and small groups, do not allow systems to share storage, and they make it difficult to backup data.

Because of the limitations of attached storage, firms are turning to network-attached storage (NAS) and storage area networks (SANs). These alternatives enable an organization to share data storage resources among a much larger number of computers and users, resulting in improved storage efficiency and greater cost effectiveness. In addition, they simplify data backup and reduce the risk of downtime. Nearly one-third of system downtime is a direct result of data storage failures, so eliminating storage problems as a cause of downtime is a major advantage.

Network-Attached Storage

network-attached storage (NAS)
Hard disc storage that is set up with its own network address rather than being attached to a computer.

Network-attached storage (NAS) is hard disc storage that is set up with its own network address rather than being attached to a computer. Figure 3.4 shows a NAS storage device. NAS includes software to manage storage access and file management, relieving the users' computers of those tasks. The result is that both application software and files can be served faster because they are not competing for the same processor resources. Computer users can share and access the same information, even if they are using different types of computers. Common applications for NAS include consolidated storage, Internet and e-commerce applications, and digital media.

Figure 3.4 NAS storage device *The Seagate BlackArmor NAS 440 has a capacity of 4 to 12 terabytes at a cost of less than €0.20 per GB.*

One of the most popular Swiss skiing destinations is the Davos Klosters resort with more than 300 kilometres of ski slopes, five mountain railways, and 22 hotels with 1700 beds. Resort guests expect hassle-free hotel check-ins, an always available online ticket shop, reliable information display boards, and efficient and on-time mountain railways. It takes powerful information systems to meet these expectations. The resort decided to implement NAS storage devices to make sure its information systems are reliable and provide fast access to data, dependable backups of operational data and easy expansion of storage capacity.[27]

Storage Area Network

A **storage area network (SAN)** is a special-purpose, high-speed network that provides direct connections among data storage devices and computers across the enterprise (see Figure 3.5). A SAN also integrates different types of storage subsystems, such as multiple RAID storage devices and magnetic tape backup systems, into a single storage system. Use of a SAN offloads the network traffic associated with storage onto a separate network. The data can then be copied to a remote location, making it easier for companies to create backups and implement disaster recovery policies.

storage area network (SAN) A special-purpose, high-speed network that provides high-speed connections among data storage devices and computers over a network.

Using a SAN, an organization can centralize the people, policies, procedures and practices for managing storage, and a data storage manager can apply the data consistently across an enterprise. This centralization eliminates inconsistent treatment of data by different system administrators and users, providing efficient and cost-effective data storage practices.

NorthgateArinso is a global human resources services provider that equips its clients with HR solutions using advanced technology, outsourcing and consulting. The firm's systems support multicountry payroll, training, recruiting and talent management.[28] NorthgateArinso implemented two integrated data centres, one in London and one in Brussels, with an information systems architecture based on standard servers from a single supplier and data storage provided by SAN hardware and software. The SAN makes the total data stored available to all users. The company's prior collection of separate servers, applications and databases is now integrated

Figure 3.5 Storage
area network *A SAN
provides high-speed
connections among
data-storage devices and
computers over a network.*

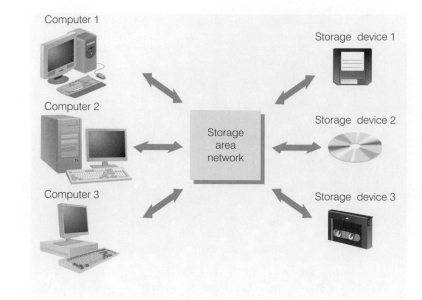

3

into an infrastructure that is easier to manage and can more flexibly meet the challenges of a highly fluctuating workload.[29]

A fundamental difference between NAS and SAN is that NAS uses file input/output, which defines data as complete containers of information, while SAN deals with block input/output, which is based on subsets of data smaller than a file. SAN manufacturers include EMC, Hitachi Data Systems Corporation, Xiotech and IBM.

As organizations set up large-scale SANs, they use more computers and network connections than in a NAS environment and, consequently, the network becomes difficult to manage. In response, software tools designed to automate storage using previously defined policies are finding a place in the enterprise. Known as **policy-based storage management**, the software products from industry leaders such as Veritas Software Corporation, Legato Systems, EMC and IBM automatically allocate storage space to users, balance the loads on servers and discs, and reroute network traffic when systems go down – all based on policies set up by system administrators.

policy-based storage management Automation of storage using previously defined policies.

The trend in secondary storage is toward higher capacity, increased portability, and automated storage management. Organizations should select a type of storage based on their needs and resources. In general, storing large amounts of data and information and providing users with quick access makes an organization more efficient.

Storage as a Service

storage as a service A data storage model where a data storage service provider rents space to individuals and organizations.

Storage as a service is a data storage model in which a data storage service provider rents space to people and organizations. Users access their rented data storage via the Internet. Such a service enables the users to store and backup their data without requiring a major investment to create and maintain their own data storage infrastructure. Businesses can also choose pay-per-use services, where they rent space on massive storage devices housed either at a service provider (such as Hewlett-Packard or IBM) or on the customers' premises, paying only for the amount of storage they use. This approach is sensible for organizations with wildly fluctuating storage needs, such as those involved in the testing of new drugs or in developing software.

Amazon, Google, Microsoft, Stortech based in South Africa, HP and IBM are a few of the storage-as-a-service providers used by organizations. Amazon.com's Simple Storage Service (S3) provides storage as a service with a monthly cost of roughly €0.10 per GB stored and €0.075 per GB of data transferred into the Amazon.com storage.

Box.net, Carbonite, SugarSynch, Symantec and Mozy are a few of the storage-as-a-service providers used by individuals. This set of providers all charge less than €6 per month for up to 5 GB of storage.

A Mozy customer who had his laptop stolen was able to provide police with photos of the thief because Mozy continued to backup data after the laptop was stolen, including the thief's photos and documents. The customer accessed the photos from his online storage site, and police captured the thief and returned the laptop.[30]

3.4 Input and Output Devices: The Gateway to Computer Systems

Your first experience with computers is usually through input and output devices. These devices are the gateways to the computer system – you use them to provide data and instructions to the computer and receive results from it. Input and output devices are part of a computer's user interface, which includes other hardware devices and software that allow you to interact with a computer system.

As with other computer system components, an organization should keep its business goals in mind when selecting input and output devices. For example, many restaurant chains use handheld input devices or computerized terminals that let food servers enter orders efficiently and accurately. These systems have also cut costs by helping to track inventory and market to customers.

Characteristics and Functionality

In general, businesses want input devices that let them rapidly enter data into a computer system, and they want output devices that let them produce timely results. When selecting input and output devices, businesses also need to consider the form of the output they want, the nature of the data required to generate this output, and the speed and accuracy they need for both. Some organizations have very specific needs for output and input, requiring devices that perform specific functions. The more specialized the application, the more specialized the associated system input and output devices.

The speed and functions of input and output devices should be balanced with their cost, control and complexity. More specialized devices might make it easier to enter data or output information, but they are generally more costly, less flexible and more susceptible to malfunction.

The Nature of Data

Getting data into the computer – input – often requires transferring human-readable data, such as a sales order, into the computer system. 'Human-readable' means data that people can read and understand. A sheet of paper containing inventory adjustments is an example of human-readable data. In contrast, machine-readable data can be read by computer devices (such as the universal barcode on many grocery and retail items) and is typically stored as bits or bytes. Inventory changes stored on a disc is an example of machine-readable data.

Some data can be read by people and machines, such as magnetic ink on bank cheques. Usually, people begin the input process by organizing human-readable data and transforming it into machine-readable data. Every keystroke on a keyboard, for example, turns a letter symbol of a human language into a digital code that the machine can manipulate.

Data Entry and Input

data entry Converting human-readable data into a machine-readable form.

data input Transferring machine-readable data into the system.

Getting data into the computer system is a two-stage process. First, the human-readable data is converted into a machine-readable form through **data entry**. The second stage involves transferring the machine-readable data into the system. This is **data input**.

Today, many companies are using online data entry and input: they communicate and transfer data to computer devices directly connected to the computer system. Online data entry and input place data into the computer system in a matter of seconds. Organizations in many industries require the instantaneous updating offered by this approach. For example, when ticket agents enter a request for concert tickets, they can use online data entry and input to record the request as soon as it is made. Ticket agents at other terminals can then access this data to make a seating check before they process another request.

Source Data Automation

source data automation Capturing and editing data where it is initially created and in a form that can be directly entered into a computer, thus ensuring accuracy and timeliness.

Regardless of how data gets into the computer, it should be captured and edited at its source. **Source data automation** involves capturing and editing data where it is originally created and in a form that can be directly entered into a computer, thus ensuring accuracy and timeliness. For example, using source data automation, salespeople enter sales orders into the computer at the time and place they take the orders. Any errors can be detected and corrected immediately. If an item is temporarily out of stock, the salesperson can discuss options with the customer. Prior to source data automation, orders were written on paper and entered into the computer later (usually by a clerk, not by the person who took the order). Often the handwritten information wasn't legible or, worse yet, got lost. If problems occurred during data entry, the clerk had to contact the salesperson or the customer to 'recapture' the data needed for order entry, leading to further delays and customer dissatisfaction.

Input Devices

Data entry and input devices come in many forms. They range from special-purpose devices that capture specific types of data to more general-purpose input devices. Some of the special-purpose data entry and input devices are discussed later in this chapter. First, we focus on devices used to enter and input general types of data, including text, audio, images and video for personal computers.

Personal Computer Input Devices

A keyboard and a computer mouse are the most common devices used for entry and input of data such as characters, text and basic commands. Some companies are developing keyboards that are more comfortable, more easily adjusted and faster to use than standard keyboards. These ergonomic keyboards, such as the split keyboard offered by Microsoft and others, are designed to avoid wrist and hand injuries caused by hours of typing. Other keyboards include touchpads that let you enter sketches on the touchpad while still using keys to enter text. Other innovations are wireless mice and keyboards, which keep a physical desktop free from clutter.

You use a computer mouse to point to and click symbols, icons, menus and commands on the screen. The computer takes a number of actions in response, such as placing data into the computer system.

Speech-Recognition Technology

Using **speech-recognition technology**, a computer equipped with a source of speech input, such as a microphone, can interpret human speech as an alternative means of providing data or instructions to the computer. The most basic systems require you to train the system to recognize your speech patterns or are limited to a small vocabulary of words. More advanced systems can recognize continuous speech without requiring you to break your speech into discrete words. Interactive voice response (IVR) systems allow a computer to recognize both voice and keypad inputs.

speech-recognition technology Input devices that recognize human speech.

Companies that must constantly interact with customers are eager to reduce their customer support costs while improving the quality of their service. Time Warner Cable implemented a speech-recognition application as part of its customer call centre. Subscribers who call customer service can speak commands to begin simple processes such as 'pay my bill' or 'add Show-Time'. The voice recognition system saves time and money even though most people would prefer to speak to a live person. 'We have roughly 13 million customers, and a few seconds or minutes here or there for each customer can really add up to longer hold times and higher staffing costs – which makes cable rates climb,' says Time Warner spokesman Matthew Tremblay.[31]

Digital Cameras

Digital cameras record and store images or video in digital form, so when you take pictures, the images are electronically stored in the camera. You can download the images to a computer either directly or by using a flash memory card. After you store the images on the computer's hard disc, you can then

digital camera An input device used with a PC to record and store images and video in digital form.

edit and print them, send them to another location or paste them into another application. This digital format saves time and money by eliminating the need to process film in order to share photos. For example, you can download a photo of your project team captured by a digital camera and then post it on a website or paste it into a project status report. Digital cameras have eclipsed film cameras used by professional photographers for photo quality and features such as zoom, flash, exposure controls, special effects and even video-capture capabilities. With the right software, you can add sound and handwriting to the photo. Many computers and smartphones come equipped with a digital camera to enable their users to place video calls and take pictures and videos.

Canon, Casio, Nikon, Olympus, Panasonic, Pentax, Sony and other camera manufacturers offer full-featured, high-resolution digital camera models at prices ranging from €190 to €2600. Some manufacturers offer pocket-sized camcorders for less than €110.

The police department in Wallis, Mississippi, consists of only five officers but is one of the first departments in the USA to use tiny digital cameras that clip onto the front pocket of the officers' uniforms. The cameras are the size of a pack of gum and come with a memory card capable of holding hours of evidence. The cameras record each police stop in its entirety and provide evidence that supports prosecution of suspects.[32]

Scanning Devices

Scanning devices capture image and character data. A page scanner is like a copy machine. You either insert a page into the scanner or place it face down on the glass plate of the scanner and then scan it. With a handheld scanner, you manually move or roll the scanning device over the image you want to scan. Both page and handheld scanners can convert monochrome or colour pictures, forms, text and other images into machine-readable digits. Considering that US enterprises generate an estimated 1 billion pieces of paper daily, many companies are looking to scanning devices to help them manage their documents and reduce the high cost of using and processing paper.

Silicon Valley Bank (SVB) Financial Group is headquartered in Santa Clara, California, and is surrounded by hundreds of high-tech companies and start-up ventures in the life science,

3

clean technology, venture capital, private equity and premium wine markets.[33] SVB used to store loan and deposit documents for some 4000 clients in paper files at its headquarters. The firm received more than 75 requests per day from branches for copies of documents, with each request taking about 15 minutes to process. SVB implemented document-scanning hardware and software that can create a digital, online copy of all documents. Now users can immediately access the documents online, leading to improvements in customer service and reductions in administrative costs.[34]

Optical Data Readers

You can also use a special scanning device called an *optical data reader* to scan documents. The two categories of optical data readers are for optical mark recognition (OMR) and optical character recognition (OCR). You use OMR readers for grading tests and other purposes such as forms. With this technology, you use pencils to fill in bubbles or check boxes on OMR paper, which is also called a 'mark sense form'. OMR systems are used in standardized tests, including the SAT and GMAT tests, and to record votes in elections. In contrast, most OCR readers use reflected light to recognize and scan various machine-generated characters. With special software, OCR readers can also convert handwritten or typed documents into digital data. After being entered, this data can be shared, modified and distributed over computer networks to hundreds or thousands of people.

Magnetic Ink Character Recognition (MICR) Devices

In the 1950s, the banking industry became swamped with paper cheques, loan applications, bank statements and so on. The result was the development of magnetic ink character recognition (MICR), a system for reading banking data quickly. With MICR, data is placed on the bottom of a cheque or other form using a special magnetic ink. Using a special character set, data printed with this ink is readable by people and computers (see Figure 3.6).

Figure 3.6 MICR
device *Magnetic ink
character recognition
technology codes data on
the bottom of a cheque or
other form using special
magnetic ink, which
is readable by people
and computers. For an
example, look at the bottom
of a bank cheque.*

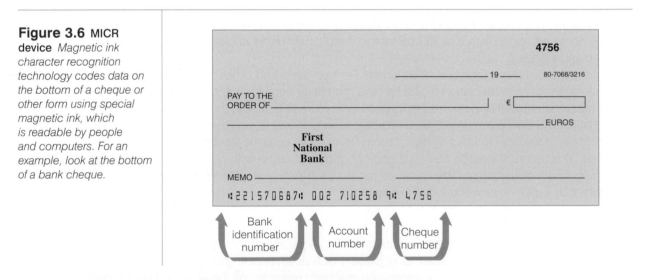

Magnetic Stripe Cards

magnetic stripe card A type
of card that stores a limited
amount of data by modifying the
magnetism of tiny iron-based
particles contained in a band on
the card.

A **magnetic stripe card** stores a limited amount of data by modifying the magnetism of tiny iron-based particles contained in a band on the card. The magnetic stripe is read by physically swiping the card at a terminal. For this reason, such cards are called a contact card. Magnetic stripe cards are commonly used in credit cards, transportation tickets and drivers' licences.

Chip-and-PIN Cards

Most European countries as well as many countries in Asia and South America are converting to the chip-and-PIN (personal identification number) card, which uses 'smart card' technology.[35] These cards are also known as EMV-enabled cards because they are named after their developers Europay, MasterCard and Visa.[36] This technology employs a computer chip that communicates with a card reader using radio frequencies, which means the cards do not need to be swiped at a terminal. **Chip-and-PIN cards** require different terminals from those used for magnetic stripe cards. For security, the card holder is also required to enter a PIN at the point of sale, making such cards more effective at preventing fraud. Although credit card fraud is a problem, credit card issuers cannot force merchants to invest in the new terminals required for chip-and-PIN cards. As a result, deployment of this technology is lagging.

chip-and-PIN card A type of card that employs a computer chip that communicates with a card reader using radio frequencies; it does not need to be swiped at a terminal.

Cardholders of Chase's premium Palladium card and a test market sample of some 15 000 Wells Fargo customers who are frequent overseas travellers will be issued cards with both the magnetic stripe and chip-and-PIN technology.[37]

Contactless Cards

A **contactless card** has an embedded chip that only needs to be held close to a terminal to transfer its data; no PIN needs to be entered. MasterCard is testing the use of contactless-based payments aboard flights of WestJet, a Canadian airline. One problem with the current method of payment using regular credit cards is that these transactions are conducted in an offline mode with no credit check authorization possible. With contactless cards, it will eventually be possible to support online credit card authorization, thus reducing the potential of fraud. This fraud protection will open the door to expanding in-flight sales beyond drinks and refreshments to the sale of wine and apparel that is delivered to the passengers' homes when they land.[38]

contactless card A card with an embedded chip that only needs to be held close to a terminal to transfer its data; no PIN needs to be entered.

Point-of-Sale Devices

Point-of-sale (POS) devices are terminals used to capture data for data entry. They are frequently used in retail operations to enter sales information into the computer system. The POS device then computes the total charges, including tax. In medical settings, POS devices are often used for remote monitoring in hospitals, clinics, laboratories, doctors' offices and patients' homes. With network-enabled POS equipment, medical professionals can instantly get an update on the patient's condition from anywhere at any time via a network or the Internet. POS devices use various types of input and output devices, such as keyboards, barcode readers, scanning devices, printers and screens. Much of the money that businesses spend on computer technology involves POS devices.

point-of-sale (POS) device A terminal used to enter data into the computer system.

La Paz is an upscale Mexican restaurant in Atlanta, Georgia. However, its POS was outdated, and workers needed hours each night to close out and balance the books. The restaurant replaced its POS with a new system that provides useful payroll and management reporting features such as tracking tips and sales. Workers also like the feature that lets them close books rapidly and accurately.[39]

Special input devices can be attached to smartphones and computers to accept payments from credit and debit cards for goods and services. Intuit Go Payment and Square can provide a small credit card scanner that plugs into your smartphone.[40]

Automated Teller Machine (ATM) Devices

Another type of special-purpose input/output device, the automated teller machine (ATM) is a terminal that bank customers use to perform transactions with their bank accounts. Companies use various ATM devices, sometimes called *kiosks*, to support their business processes. Some can dispense tickets, such as for airlines, concerts and soccer games. Some colleges use them to produce transcripts.

Pen Input Devices

By touching the screen with a pen input device, you can activate a command or cause the computer to perform a task, enter handwritten notes, and draw objects and figures. Pen input requires special software and hardware. Handwriting recognition software, for example, converts handwriting on the screen into text. The Tablet PC from Microsoft and its hardware partners can transform handwriting into typed text and store the 'digital ink' just the way a person writes it. People can use a pen to write and send email, add comments to Word documents, mark up PowerPoint presentations, and even hand-draw charts in a document. The data can then be moved, highlighted, searched and converted into text. If perfected, this interface is likely to become widely used. Pen input is especially attractive if you are uncomfortable using a keyboard. The success of pen input depends on how accurately and at what cost handwriting can be read and translated into digital form.

Audi AG installed interactive white boards at its five technical training locations in Germany. PowerPoint presentations can be projected on the screen, and trainers can draw over the image and highlight features by circling or underlining. Consequently, static presentations have become more interactive.[41]

Touch-Sensitive Screens

Advances in screen technology allow display screens to function as input as well as output devices. By touching certain parts of a touch-sensitive screen, you can start a program or trigger other types of action. Touch-sensitive screens can remove the need for a keyboard, which conserves space and increases portability. Touchscreens are frequently used at petrol stations to allow customers to select grades of petrol and request a receipt; on photocopy machines for selecting options; at fast-food restaurants for entering customer choices; at information centres for finding facts about local eating and drinking establishments; and at amusement parks to provide directions to patrons. They also are used in kiosks at airports and department stores. Touch-sensitive screens are also being considered for gathering votes in elections.

As touchscreens get smaller, the user's fingers begin to block the information on the display. Nanotouch technology is being explored as a means of overcoming this problem. Using this technology, users control the touchscreen from its backside so that fingers do not block the display. As the user's finger moves on the back of the display, a tiny graphical finger is projected onto the touchscreen. Such displays are useful for mobile audio players the size of a coin.

Barcode Scanners

A barcode scanner employs a laser scanner to read a barcoded label and pass the data to a computer. The barcode reader may be stationary or hand-held to support a wide variety of uses. This form of input is used widely in store checkouts and warehouse inventory control. Barcodes are also used in hospitals, where a nurse scans a patient's wristband and then a barcode on the medication about to be administered to prevent medication errors.

Mobio, an international mobile payments and marketing company, has developed an iPhone application that it is testing with fans of the Jacksonville Jaguars football team. The fans use the application to scan a barcode at their seat and a menu of food and beverage items is displayed on their phone. Fans then select and pay for the items they want using the iPhone application, and the order is then delivered to their seat.[42]

Radio Frequency Identification

radio frequency identification (RFID) A technology that employs a microchip with an antenna to broadcast its unique identifier and location to receivers.

Radio frequency identification (RFID) is a technology that employs a microchip with an antenna to broadcast its unique identifier and location to receivers. The purpose of an RFID system is to transmit data by a mobile device, called a tag (see Figure 3.7), which is read by an RFID reader and

Figure 3.7 RFID tag
An RFID tag is small compared to current barcode labels used to identify items.

processed according to the needs of a computer program. One popular application of RFID is to place microchips on retail items and install in-store readers that track the inventory on the shelves to determine when shelves should be restocked. The RFID tag chip includes a special form of EPROM memory that holds data about the item to which the tag is attached. A radio frequency signal can update this memory as the status of the item changes. The data transmitted by tahe tag might provide identification, location information or details about the product tagged, such as date manufactured, retail price, colour or date of purchase.

The Canadian government is supporting a move to require the sheep industry to use RFID chips to enable a 'farm to fork' traceability system.[43]

Output Devices

Computer systems provide output to decision makers at all levels of an organization so they can solve a business problem or capitalize on a competitive opportunity. In addition, output from one computer system can provide input into another computer system. The desired form of this output might be visual, audio or even digital. Whatever the output's content or form, output devices are designed to provide the right information to the right person in the right format at the right time.

Display Monitors

The display monitor is a device used to display the output from the computer. Because early monitors used a cathode-ray tube to display images, they were sometimes called *CRTs*. The cathode-ray tubes generate one or more electron beams. As the beams strike a phosphorescent compound (phosphor) coated on the inside of the screen, a dot on the screen called a pixel lights up. A **pixel** is a dot of colour on a photo image or a point of light on a display screen. It appears in one of two

pixel A dot of colour on a photo image or a point of light on a display screen.

3

modes: on or off. The electron beam sweeps across the screen so that as the phosphor starts to fade, it is struck and lights up again.

plasma display A type of display using thousands of smart cells (pixels) consisting of electrodes and neon and xenon gases that are electrically turned into plasma (electrically charged atoms and negatively charged particles) to emit light.

A **plasma display** uses thousands of smart cells (pixels) consisting of electrodes and neon and xenon gases that are electrically turned into plasma (electrically charged atoms and negatively charged particles) to emit light. The plasma display lights up the pixels to form an image based on the information in the video signal. Each pixel is made up of three types of light – red, green and blue – with the plasma display varying the intensities of the lights to produce a full range of colours. Plasma displays can produce high resolution and accurate representation of colours to create a high-quality image.

LCD display Flat display that uses liquid crystals – organic, oil-like material placed between two polarizers – to form characters and graphic images on a backlit screen.

LCD displays are flat displays that use liquid crystals – organic, oil-like material placed between two polarizers – to form characters and graphic images on a backlit screen. These displays are easier on your eyes than CRTs because they are flicker-free, brighter and do not emit the type of radiation that concerns some CRT users. In addition, LCD monitors take up less space and use less than half of the electricity required to operate a comparably sized CRT monitor. *Thin-film transistor (TFT) LCDs* are a type of liquid crystal display that assigns a transistor to control each pixel, resulting in higher resolution and quicker response to changes on the screen. TFT LCD monitors have displaced the older CRT technology and are available in sizes from 12 to 30 inches. Many companies now provide multimonitor solutions that enable users to see a wealth of related information at a single glance.

organic light-emitting diode (OLED) display Flat display that uses a layer of organic material sandwiched between two conductors, which in turn are sandwiched between a glass top plate and a glass bottom plate so that when electric current is applied to the two conductors, a bright, electroluminescent light is produced directly from the organic material.

Organic light-emitting diode (OLED) uses a layer of organic material sandwiched between two conductors, which in turn are sandwiched between a glass top plate and a glass bottom plate. When electric current is applied to the two conductors, a bright, electroluminescent light is produced directly from the organic material. OLEDs can provide sharper and brighter colours than LCDs and CRTs, and, because they do not require a backlight, the displays can be half as thick as LCDs, and are flexible. Another big advantage is that OLEDs do not break when dropped. OLED technology can also create 3D video displays by taking a traditional LCD monitor and then adding layers of transparent OLED films to create the perception of depth without the need for 3D glasses or laser optics. The iZ3D monitor is capable of displaying in both 2D and 3D modes. The manufacturer offered a 22-inch version of the monitor at a price of €226.53 to coincide with the debut of *Avatar*, a film directed by James Cameron.

Because most users leave their computers on for hours at a time, power usage is an important factor when deciding which type of monitor to purchase. Although the power usage varies from model to model, LCD monitors generally consume between 35 and 50 per cent less power than plasma screens.[44] OLED monitors use even less power than LCD monitors.

Aspect ratio and screen size describe the size of the display screen. Aspect ratio is the ratio of the width of the display to its height. An aspect ratio of 4 to 3 is common. For widescreen LCD monitors used for viewing DVD movies in widescreen format, playing games or displaying multiple screens side-by-side, an aspect ratio of 16 to 10 or 15 to 9 is preferred. The screen size is measured diagonally from the outside of the screen casing for CRT monitors and from the inside of the screen casing for LCD displays.

With today's wide selection of monitors, price and overall quality can vary tremendously. The quality of a screen image is measured by the number of horizontal and vertical pixels used to create it. Resolution is the total number of pixels contained in the display; the more pixels, the clearer and sharper the image. The size of the display monitor also affects the quality of the viewing. The same pixel resolution on a small screen is sharper than on a larger screen, where the same number of pixels is spread out over a larger area. Over the years, display monitor sizes have increased and display standards and resolutions have changed, as shown in Table 3.3.

Table 3.3 Common Display Monitor Standards and Associated Resolutions

Standard	Resolution (number of horizontal pixels × vertical pixels)
WSXGA (Wide SGXA plus)	1680 × 1050
UXGA (Ultra XGA)	1600 × 1200
WUXGA (Wide Ultra XGA)	1920 × 1200
QXGA (Quad XGA)	2048 × 1536

Another way to measure image quality is the distance between one pixel on the screen and the next nearest pixel, which is known as *dot pitch*. The common range of dot pitch is from 0.25 mm to 0.31 mm. The smaller the dot pitch, the better the picture. A dot pitch of 0.28 mm or smaller is considered good. Greater pixel densities and smaller dot pitches yield sharper images of higher resolution.

The characteristics of screen colour depend on the quality of the monitor, the amount of RAM in the computer system, and the monitor's graphics adapter card. Digital Video Interface (DVI) is a video interface standard designed to maximize the visual quality of digital display devices such as flat-panel LCD computer displays.

Companies are competing on the innovation frontier to create thinner display devices for computers, mobile phones and other mobile devices. In its effort to gain an edge, LG Phillips has developed an extremely thin display that is only 0.15 mm thick, or roughly as thick as a human hair. The display is also so flexible that it can be bent or rolled without damage. Nokia has demonstrated a flexible portable computer that you can actually twist and bend to change a music track or adjust the volume.[45] Such screens open possibilities for manufacturers to make mobile phones and laptops with significantly larger displays but without increasing the size of the device itself, as the screen could be rolled up or folded and tucked away into a pocket.

The Microsoft Surface platform is designed to help people learn, collaborate and make decisions. The Surface can be used as a table, mounted on the wall, or embedded in furniture or fixtures. Its large 40-inch screen is an effective way to share photos, maps, modelling and simulations. The Surface allows a single user or multiple users to manipulate digital content by motion of their hands.

The Bank of Canada is Canada's largest bank and uses the Surface as a component of its Discovery Zone, a unique and digitally interactive approach to engage customers to learn more about the bank, its services and its employees. Arbie, an animated character, guides people through various applications with the results displayed on the Surface screen. These applications help people learn which bank services can help them meet their financial needs, demonstrates the value of a Tax Free Savings Account compared with a standard savings account, and provides photos and brief profiles of the local branch staff. The software includes an Instant Win application and puzzles for children to work while their parents do their banking.[46]

Printers and Plotters

One of the most useful and common forms of output is called *hard copy*, which is simply paper output from a printer. The two main types of printers are laser printers and inkjet printers, and they are available with different speeds, features and capabilities. Some can be set up to accommodate paper forms, such as blank cheque forms and invoice forms. Newer printers allow businesses to create customized printed output using full colour for each customer from standard paper and data input. Ticket-receipt printers such as those used in restaurants, ATMs and point-of-sale systems are in widescale use.

The speed of the printer is typically measured by the number of pages printed per minute (ppm). Like a display screen, the quality, or resolution, of a printer's output depends on the number of dots printed per inch (dpi). A 600-dpi printer prints more clearly than a 300-dpi printer. A recurring cost of using a printer is the inkjet or laser cartridge that must be replaced periodically – every few thousand pages for laser printers and every 500 to 900 pages for inkjet printers.

Costing less than €400, laser printers are generally faster than inkjet printers and can handle more volume: 25 to 60 ppm for black and white and 6 to 25 ppm for colour. Inkjet printers that can print 12 to 40 ppm for black and white and 5 to 20 ppm for colour are available for less than €150. For colour printing, inkjet printers print vivid hues with an initial cost much less than colour laser printers and can produce high-quality banners, graphics, greeting cards, letters, text and photo prints.

A number of manufacturers offer multiple-function printers that can copy, print (in colour or black and white), fax and scan. Such multifunctional devices are often used when people need to do a relatively low volume of copying, printing, faxing and scanning. The typical price of multifunction printers ranges from €75 to €400, depending on features and capabilities. Because these devices take the place of more than one piece of equipment, they are less expensive to acquire and maintain than a standalone fax plus a standalone printer, copier and so on. Also, eliminating equipment that was once located on a countertop or desktop clears a workspace for other work-related activities. As a result, such devices are popular in homes and small office settings.

3D printers can be used to turn 3D computer models into 3D objects. One form of 3D printer uses an inkjet printing system to print an adhesive in the shape of a cross-section of the model. Next, a fine powder is sprayed onto the adhesive to form one layer of the object. This process is repeated thousands of times until the object is completed. 3D printing is commonly used by aerospace firms, auto manufacturers and other design-intensive companies. It is especially valuable during the conceptual stage of engineering design, when the exact dimensions and material strength of the prototype are not critical.

Some new printers from Hewlett-Packard and others allow printing without requiring the printer to be connected to a computer. A USB storage device such as a thumb drive can be inserted into a slot in the printer, and the user can specify what is to be printed without entering commands to the computer.[47]

Other mobile print solutions enable users to wirelessly send documents, email messages and attachments, presentations and even boarding passes from any smartphone, tablet computer or laptop to any mobile printer in the world. For example, mobile users who use the PrinterOn service only need to access a directory of PrinterOn printers and locations and then send to the email address of the printer an email with attachment to be printed. American Airlines Admiral Club, Delta Sky Club, Embassy Suites and DoubleTree by Hilton have installed PrinterOn printers at many of their locations.[48]

Plotters are a type of hard-copy output device used for general design work. Businesses typically use plotters to generate paper or acetate blueprints, schematics and drawings of buildings or new products. Standard plot widths are 24 inches and 36 inches, and the length can be whatever meets the need – from a few inches to many feet.

Digital Audio Players

digital audio player A device that can store, organize and play digital music files.

MP3 A standard format for compressing a sound sequence into a small file.

A **digital audio player** is a device that can store, organize and play digital music files. **MP3** (MPEG-1 Audio Layer-3) is a popular format for compressing a sound sequence into a very small file, while preserving the original level of sound quality when it is played. By compressing the sound file, it requires less time to download the file and less storage space on a hard drive.

You can use many different music devices smaller than a deck of cards to download music from the Internet and other sources. These devices have no moving parts and can store hours of music. Apple expanded into the digital music market with an MP3 player (the iPod) and the iTunes Music Store, which allows you to find music online, preview it and download it in a way that is safe, legal and affordable. Other MP3 manufacturers include Dell, Sony, Samsung, Iomega, Creative and Motorola, whose Rokr product is the first iTunes-compatible phone.

The Apple iPod Touch, with a 3.5-inch widescreen, is a music player that also plays movies and TV shows, displays photos, and connects to the Internet. You can, therefore, use it to view YouTube videos, buy music online, check emails, and more. The display automatically adjusts the view when it is rotated from portrait to landscape. An ambient light sensor adjusts brightness to match the current lighting conditions.

E-book Readers

The digital media equivalent of a conventional printed book is called an e-book (short for electronic book). The Project Gutenberg Online Book Catalog lists over 36 000 free e-books and a total of over 100 000 e-books available. E-books can be downloaded from Project Gutenberg (www.gutenberg.org) or many other sites onto personal computers or dedicated hardware devices known as e-book readers. The devices themselves cost from around €150 to €250, and downloads of the bestselling books and new releases cost less than €9.99. The e-book reader has the capacity to store thousands of books. The most current Amazon Kindle, Sony PRS, Kobo e-reader, Barnes & Noble's Nook, and iRiver's Story are popular e-readers that use e-paper displays that either look like printed pages or LCD screens that are bright and shiny but can be difficult to read in bright sunlight.[49] E-books weigh less than three-quarters of a pound, are around one-half inch thick, and come with a display screen ranging from 5 to 8 inches. Thus, these readers are more compact than most paperbacks and can be easily held in one hand. Recent e-book readers display content in 16 million colours and high resolution. On many e-readers, the size of the text can be magnified for readers with poor vision.

3.5 Computer System Types

In general, computers can be classified as either special purpose or general purpose. *Special-purpose computers* are used for limited applications, for example by military, government and scientific research groups such as the CIA and NASA. Other applications include specialized processors found in appliances, cars and other products. For example, automobile repair shops connect special-purpose computers to your car's engine to identify specific performance problems. As another example, IBM is developing a new generation of computer chips to develop so-called cognitive computers that are designed to mimic the way the human brain works. Rather than being programmed as today's computers are, cognitive computers will be able to learn through experiences and outcomes and mimic human learning patterns.[50]

General-purpose computers are used for a variety of applications and to execute the business applications discussed in this text. General-purpose computer systems can be divided into two major groups: systems used by one user at a time and systems used by multiple concurrent users. Table 3.4 shows the general ranges of capabilities for various types of computer systems. General-purpose computer systems can range from small handheld computers to massive supercomputers that fill an entire room. We will first cover single-user computer systems.

Table 3.4 Types of Computer Systems

Single-user computer systems can be divided into two groups: portable computers and nonportable computers.

Factor	Single-User Computers				
	Portable Computers				
	Handheld	Laptop	Notebook	Netbook	Tablet
Cost	€100–€300	€350–€2000	€500–€2000	€150–€600	€150–€400
Weight (pounds)	<.30	4.0–7.0	<4	<2.5	0.75–2.0
Screen size (inches)	2.4–3.6	11.5–15.5	11.6–14.0	7.0–11.0	5.0–14.0
Typical use	Organize personal data	Improve worker productivity	Improve productivity of mobile worker	Access the Internet and email	Capture data via pen input, improve worker productivity

Nonportable Computers			
	Thin Client	Desktop	Nettop	Workstation
Cost	€150–€400	€400–€2000	€100–€300	€600–€4000
Weight (pounds)	1–3	<30	<5	<35
Screen size (inches)	10.0–15.0	13.0–27.0	Comes with or without attached screen	13.0–27.0
Typical use	Enter data and access applications via the Internet	Improve worker productivity	Replace desktop with small, low-cost, low-energy computer	Perform engineering, CAD and software development

Multiple-user computer systems include servers, mainframes and supercomputers.

Factor	Multiple-User Computers		
	Server	Mainframe	Supercomputer
Cost	€400–€40 000	>€75 000	>€200 000
Weight (pounds)	>25	>100	>100
Screen size (inches)	n/a	n/a	n/a
Typical use	Perform network and Internet applications	Perform computing tasks for large organizations and provide massive data storage	Run scientific applications; perform intensive number crunching

Portable Computers

Many computer manufacturers offer a variety of **portable computers**, those that are small enough to carry easily. Portable computers include handheld computers, laptop computers, notebook computers, netbook computers and tablet computers.

Handheld computers are single-user computers that provide ease of portability because of their small size – some are as small as a credit card. These systems often include a variety of software and communications capabilities. Most can communicate with desktop computers over wireless networks. Some even add a built-in GPS receiver with software that can integrate location data into the application. For example, if you click an entry in an electronic address book, the device displays a map and directions from your current location. Such a computer can also be mounted in your car and serve as a navigation system. One of the shortcomings of handheld computers is that they require a lot of power relative to their size.

A **smartphone** is a handheld computer that combines the functionality of a mobile phone, camera, web browser, email tool, MP3 player and other devices into a single device. BlackBerry was one of the earliest smartphone devices, developed by the Canadian company Research in Motion in 1999.

In early 2011, both LG and Motorola announced new smartphones based on dual-core 1 GHz processors that can run in parallel to deliver faster performance, provided the software has been designed to take advantage of the dual-core processing capability. Such chips can enable 3D enabled handsets that would not require users to wear special glasses to view the content.[51]

While Apple with its iPhone dominated the smartphone market for several years, it is now facing stiff competition from Amazon, Samsung, HTC, Motorola, Nokia, Samsung and others. Apple has sued many of its competitors for allegedly violating its patents and trademarks used in mobile devices. In return, many of these competitors have countersued Apple, with Samsung and Apple alone being engaged in 30 legal battles in nine countries.[52] Industry observers point out that such patent wars stifle innovation and competition, but unfortunately they have become a common tactic in dealing with the competition.[53]

The technology market is shifting to low power mobile devices such as smartphones and tablet computers. In 2013, PC sales slipped by 8 per cent while sales of tablets increased 53 per cent.[54]

Increasingly consumers and workers alike will perform data processing, email, web surfing, and database lookup tasks on smartphone-like devices. The number of business applications for smartphones is increasing rapidly to meet this need, especially in the medical field where it is estimated that about 30 per cent of doctors have an iPad and more than 80 per cent carry a smartphone.[55] epSOS is an attempt to offer seamless healthcare to European citizens. Part of the project is a system for electronic prescriptions. Doctors can log in to the epSOS portal and transmit a patient's prescription directly to a pharmacy.[56]

AccessReflex is software that enables users to view Microsoft Access databases from a smartphone.[57] EBSCOhost Mobile offers mobile access to a broad range of full text and bibliographic databases for research.[58] Mobile police officers can use their smartphones to connect to national crime databases, and emergency first responders can use theirs to connect to hazardous materials databases to find advice of how to deal with dangerous spills or fires involving such materials.

portable computer A computer small enough to carry easily.

handheld computer A single-user computer that provides ease of portability because of its small size.

smartphone A handheld computer that combines the functionality of a mobile phone, camera, web browser, email tool, MP3 player and other devices into a single device.

3

Laptop Computers

laptop computer A personal computer designed for use by mobile users, being small and light enough to sit comfortably on a user's lap.

A **laptop computer** is a personal computer designed for use by mobile users, being small and light enough to sit comfortably on a user's lap. Laptop computers use a variety of flat panel technologies to produce a lightweight and thin display screen with good resolution. In terms of computing power, laptop computers can match most desktop computers, as they come with powerful CPUs as well as large-capacity primary memory and disc storage. This type of computer is highly popular among students and mobile workers who carry their laptops on trips and to meetings and classes. Many personal computer users now prefer a laptop computer over a desktop because of its portability, lower energy usage and smaller space requirements.

Notebook Computers

notebook computer Smaller than a laptop computer, an extremely lightweight computer that weighs less than 4 pounds and can easily fit in a briefcase.

Many highly mobile users prefer notebook computers that weigh less than 2 kilograms compared to larger laptops that weigh up to around 3 kilograms. However, there are limitations to these small, lighter laptops. They typically come without optical drives for burning DVDs or playing Blu-ray movies. Because they are thinner, they have less room for larger, longer-life batteries. Their thin profile also does not allow for heat sinks and fans to dissipate the heat generated by fast processors, so they typically have less processing power. Finally, few come with a high-power graphics card so these machines are less popular with gamers.

Netbook Computers

netbook computer A small, light, inexpensive member of the laptop computer family.

Netbook computers are small, light and inexpensive members of the laptop computer family that are great for tasks that do not require a lot of computing power, such as sending and receiving email, viewing DVDs, playing games or accessing the Internet. However, netbook computers are not good for users who want to run demanding applications, have many applications open at one time or need lots of data storage capacity.

Many netbooks use the Intel Atom CPU (the N450), which is specially designed to run on minimal power so that the computer can use small, lightweight batteries and avoid potential overheating problems without the need for fans and large heat sinks. Battery life is a key distinguishing feature when comparing various netbooks, with expected operating time varying from 4 hours to nearly 12 hours depending on the manufacturer and model.

All 320 high school students in Bloomingdale, Michigan, were provided their own netbook computers and free wireless Internet access. The goal of this program is to provide students with additional learning resources and improve the level of instruction. This is important for a community where nearly half of the households are without Internet access. Teachers update the system each day to notify students and parents about missing assignments; they can also attach a worksheet if applicable. Students appreciate the ability to track their homework and to watch online videos covering many topics and providing step-by-step directions on how to complete homework assignments.[59]

Tablet Computers

tablet computer A portable, lightweight computer with no keyboard that allows you to roam the office, home or factory floor, carrying the device like a clipboard.

Tablet computers are portable, lightweight computers with no keyboard that allow you to roam the office, home or factory floor, carrying the device like a clipboard. You can enter text with a writing stylus directly on the screen thanks to built-in handwriting recognition software. Other input methods include an optional keyboard or speech recognition. Tablet PCs that support input only via a writing stylus are called *slate computers*. The *convertible tablet PC* comes with a swivel screen and can be used as a traditional notebook or as a pen-based tablet PC. Most new tablets come with a front-facing camera for videoconferencing and a second camera for snapshot photos and video.[60]

Tablets do not yet have the processing power of desktop computers. They also are limited in displaying some videos because the Flash software does not run at all on an iPad nor does it run reliably on Android tablets.[61] Further, tablet screens of most manufacturers need better antiglare protection before they can be used outside in full sunlight.

Tablet computers are especially popular with students and gamers. They are also frequently used in the healthcare, retail, insurance and manufacturing industries because of their versatility. M&D Oral Care and Maxillofacial Surgery is an oral surgery practice in Connecticut that installed iPads and a Motorola Xoom tablet at five patient chairs in its office so that patients can view their CT scans and X-rays as well as educational videos.[62]

De Santos is a high-end Italian-American restaurant in New York's West Village. Its waiters use tablet computers to take orders and swipe credit cards. In addition to displaying the full menu, the tablet displays the restaurant's table and seating chart. Accordingly, the tablets make the whole process of seating customers, taking orders, sending orders to the kitchen, and paying the bill simpler and more time efficient. By using tablets, waiters can serve more tables and provide improved customer service. 'Nowadays in New York City, the menus don't list the entire specifications of each dish,' says Sebastian Gonella, one of the owners and cofounders of the restaurant. 'With this software, you can show them exactly the dish itself and all the specifications for each dish, so people are really buying what they're seeing and there's no more confusion. It's pretty important.'[63]

The Apple iPad is a tablet computer capable of running the same software that runs on the older Apple iPhone and iPod Touch devices, giving it a library of over 300 000 applications.[64] It also runs software developed specifically for it. The device has a 9.7-inch screen and an on-screen keypad, weighs 1.5 pounds, and supports Internet access over wireless networks.

A number of computer companies are offering tablet computers to compete with Apple's iPad and iPad II, including the Playbook from BlackBerry, the TouchPad from Hewlett-Packard, the Kindle Fire from Amazon, the Streak by Dell, the Tablet S and Tablet P from Sony, the Thrive by Toshiba, the Galaxy Tab from Samsung, the Xoom from Motorola, and the low-cost (less than €50) Aakash and Ubislate from the India-based company Quad.

Nonportable Single-User Computers

Nonportable single-user computers include thin client computers, desktop computers, nettop computers and workstations.

Thin Clients

A **thin client** is a low-cost, centrally managed computer with no extra drives (such as CD or DVD drives) or expansion slots. These computers have limited capabilities and perform only essential applications, so they remain 'thin' in terms of the client applications they include. As stripped-down computers, they do not have the storage capacity or computing power of typical desktop computers, nor do they need it for the role they play. With no hard disc, they never pick up viruses or suffer a hard disc crash. Unlike personal computers, thin clients download data and software from a network when needed, making support, distribution and updating of software applications much easier and less expensive.[65] Thin clients work well in a cloud-computing environment to enable users to access the computing and data resources available within the cloud.[66]

thin client A low-cost, centrally managed computer with essential but limited capabilities and no extra drives (such as CD or DVD drives) or expansion slots.

Jewelry Television is viewed by over 65 million people in the USA and millions more visit its website (www.jtv.com). As a result of this exposure, the company has become one of the world's largest jewellery retailers. Its 300 call centre representatives handle more than 6 million calls per year using thin client computers to access information to respond to customer queries and to place orders.[67]

Desktop Computers

desktop computer A nonportable computer that fits on a desktop and that provides sufficient computing power, memory and storage for most business computing tasks.

Desktop computers are single-user computer systems that are highly versatile. Named for their size, desktop computers can provide sufficient computing power, memory, and storage for most business computing tasks.

The Apple iMac is a family of Macintosh desktop computers first introduced in 1998 in which all the components (including the CPU, disc drives and so on) fit behind the display screen. The Intel iMac is available with Intel's new core i5 or i7 processors making such machines the first quad-core iMacs.

Nettop Computers

nettop computer An inexpensive desktop computer designed to be smaller, lighter and consume much less power than a traditional desktop computer.

A **nettop computer** is an inexpensive (less than €250) desktop computer designed to be smaller and lighter and to consume one-tenth the power of a traditional desktop computer.[68] A nettop is designed to perform basic processing tasks such as exchanging email, Internet surfing and accessing web-based applications. This computer can also be used for home theatre activities such as watching video, viewing pictures, listening to music and playing games. Unlike netbook computers, nettop computers are not designed to be portable, and they come with or without an attached screen. (Nettops with attached screens are called all-in-ones.) A nettop without an attached screen can be connected to an existing monitor or even a TV screen. They also may include an optical drive (CD/DVD). The CPU is typically an Intel Atom or AMD Geode, with a single-core or dual-core processor. Choosing a single-core processor CPU reduces the cost and power consumption but limits the processing power of the computer. A dual-core processor nettop has sufficient processing power to enable you to watch video and do limited processing tasks. Businesses are considering using nettops because they are inexpensive to buy and run, and therefore these computers can improve an organization's profitability.

Workstations

workstation A more powerful personal computer used for mathematical computing, computer-assisted design, and other high-end processing, but still small enough to fit on a desktop.

Workstations are more powerful than personal computers but still small enough to fit on a desktop. They are used to support engineering and technical users who perform heavy mathematical computing, computer-assisted design (CAD), video editing and other applications requiring a high-end processor. Such users need very powerful CPUs, large amounts of main memory and extremely high-resolution graphic displays. Workstations are typically more expensive than the average desktop computer. Some computer manufacturers are now providing laptop versions of their powerful desktop workstations.

Sekotec Security and Communication is a small company that provides video surveillance systems to supermarkets, gas stations, retail stores and hotels throughout Germany. Their customer solutions typically involve clusters of 4, 8, 16 or 32 video cameras linked to a powerful workstation that controls the operation of the cameras and can store multiple terabytes of video data for rapid viewing.[69]

Multiple-User Computer Systems

Multiple-user computers are designed to support workgroups from a small department of two or three workers, to large organizations with tens of thousands of employees and millions of customers. Multiple-user systems include servers, mainframe computers and supercomputers.

Servers

server A computer employed by many users to perform a specific task, such as running network or Internet applications.

A **server** is a computer employed by many users to perform a specific task, such as running network or Internet applications. Servers typically have large memory and storage capacities, along with fast and efficient communications abilities. A web server handles Internet traffic and communications. An enterprise server stores and provides access to programs that meet the needs of an entire organization. A file server stores and coordinates program and data files. Server systems consist of multiuser computers, including supercomputers, mainframes and other servers. Often an organization will house a large number of servers in the same room where access to the machines can be controlled, and authorized support personnel can more easily manage and maintain the servers from this single location. Such a facility is called a *server farm*.

Google runs a server farm in Finland, using wind to power it and sea water to cool it. Google buys electricity from a wind farm in Northern Sweden, and brings in water from the Bay of Finland. The farm is based in an old paper mill which already had massive quarter-mile-long sea water tunnels, which had been used to cool the paper mill's manufacturing systems.[70]

Servers offer great **scalability**, the ability to increase the processing capability of a computer system so that it can handle more users, more data or more transactions in a given period. Scalability is increased by adding more, or more powerful, processors. *Scaling up* adds more powerful processors, and *scaling out* adds many more equal (or even less powerful) processors to increase the total data-processing capacity.

> **scalability** The ability to increase the processing capability of a computer system so that it can handle more users, more data or more transactions in a given period.

Information Systems @ Work

Build Your Own

You've probably heard of people building their own computers, such as hobbyists, or a small business that assembles computers for other local small businesses. It can be a fun hobby or a reasonable way to earn a living. A large international company, of course, would never do such a thing.

Unless you are talking about Facebook.

For most of its history, Facebook bought the same servers everyone else bought. The company probably received big discounts from suppliers because it uses a lot of servers, but the computer designs were the same that anyone else could buy. The servers got the job done, but Facebook thought the job could be done better. So, the company managers did what anyone else could do: they hired hardware designers and told them, 'Come up with something better.'

This does not mean Facebook management thought that engineers at Dell, HP, IBM and all the other server suppliers are incompetent. Far from it. However, the company recognized that those engineers design for a broad market and must satisfy a wide range of customer needs. The customer can specify some server components, such as the number and size of its drives, but the basic design of the

server is fixed. Facebook managers realized that if engineers only need to satisfy the needs of a single company, they can meet those needs more closely. The new hardware designers at Facebook started the Open Compute Project based on the model of open source software projects. Their goal was to create energy-efficient, low-cost servers.

As hardware engineering manager Amir Michael puts it, 'Trying to optimize costs, we took out a lot of components you find in a standard server. That made it easier to service. It made the thermals more efficient because you had less obstructions blocking cool air. And it made it ten pounds lighter. That's ten pounds less material you're buying, ten pounds less you have to lift every time you put it into the rack or pull it out, and ten pounds less you have to recycle when you're done with it.'

The Open Compute Project built a 'vanity-free server' – one free of extras that Facebook wouldn't need. 'We didn't pay attention to how the servers looked,' Michael says. 'There's no paint. There's no buttons on the front. There's no fancy logos or emblems.' But this no-frills approach was also part of the effort to significantly reduce the cost of cooling the machine. With computers using an estimated

2 per cent of the world's power, with much of that going to cooling, reducing cooling costs is significant.

Because of its size, Facebook could do more than just redesign its servers. It also redesigned the building that houses the servers, developing a new data centre from scratch in Prineville, Oregon. The data centre is close to sources of hydroelectric power, benefits from cool winds that can reduce the need for air conditioning, and is designed for minimum power consumption and environmental impact.

Unlike most other high-tech organizations, which keep their development activities quiet, Facebook doesn't mind if you know about its hardware designs. The firm realizes that it's not its hardware that makes it successful; it's what Facebook does with that hardware. You can download Facebook's design documentation at no charge from the Open Compute Project website. If you agree to the terms of its open licence, you can even join the community and contribute your own ideas.

Questions

1 Facebook uses more servers than all but a handful of organizations. Most use far fewer. How can Facebook's experience help smaller organizations? (Use your school/university as an example if you like.)

2 What are some of the design goals Facebook should have when creating their servers? How do these differ from smaller firms?

3 Does Facebook designing its own servers give it a competitive advantage as described in Chapter 2? If so, via which of the five competitive forces does it gain an advantage and how? If not, why would Facebook design its own servers?

4 Suppose you were about to start a social network site to compete with Facebook. Can you find any information from the Open Compute Project website (opencompute.org) to make you more successful than you would be otherwise? Why or why not?

The Intel 10-core Westmere-EX processor is targeted at high-end servers such as those frequently used in data centres to support large databases and other processing intense applications. The processor supports a technology called hyperthreading, which enables each core to conduct two sets of instructions, called threads. Hyperthreading gives each processor the ability to run up to 20 threads simultaneously.[71] Advanced Micro Devices (AMD) has announced the release of a 16-core server chip code-named Interlagos Opteron 6200.[72]

Less powerful servers are often used on a smaller scale to support the needs of many users. For example, the Gashora Girls Academy located in the republic of Rwanda deployed server computers to ensure that its 270 students and 12 teachers could have access to the latest technology.[73] Each server computer supports multiple students, each working independently using their own basic workstation that allows them to run word processing and spreadsheet software, use computer science applications, stream videos and listen to audio programs. This solution minimized the school's investment in hardware and reduced ongoing power and maintenance costs, making it feasible for students to access computing technology to gain the work skills necessary to be successful in the twenty-first century.[74]

Server manufacturers are also competing heavily to reduce the power required to operate their servers and making 'performance per watt' a key part of their product differentiation strategy. Low power usage is a critical factor for organizations that run servers farms of hundreds or even thousands of servers. Typical servers draw up to 220 watts, while new servers based on Intel's Atom microprocessor draw 8 or fewer watts. The annual power savings from such low-energy usage servers can amount to tens of thousands of dollars for operators of a large server farm.

A virtual server is a method of logically dividing the resources of a single physical server to create multiple logical servers, each acting as its own dedicated machine. The server administrator uses software to divide one physical server into multiple isolated virtual environments. For example, a single physical web server might be divided into two virtual private servers. One of the virtual servers hosts the organization's live website, while the other hosts a copy of the website. The second private virtual server is used to test and verify updates to software before changes are made to the live website. The use of virtual servers is growing rapidly. In a typical data centre deployment of several hundred servers, companies using virtualization can build 12 virtual machines for every actual server with a resulting savings in capital and operating expenses (including energy costs) of millions of euros per year.

EZZI.net is a web hosting service provider for many companies including some of the largest *Fortune* 500 companies. It has data centres located in New York City and Los Angeles that employ virtual servers because they are easy to use, can be supported around the clock, and operate with a 99.7 per cent uptime to meet the needs of its many customers.[75]

A **blade server** houses many computer motherboards that include one or more processors, computer memory, computer storage and computer network connections. These all share a common power supply and air-cooling source within a single chassis. By placing many blades into a single chassis, and then mounting multiple chassis in a single rack, the blade server is more powerful but less expensive than traditional systems based on mainframes or server farms of individual computers. In addition, the blade server approach requires much less physical space than traditional server farms.

blade server A server that houses many individual computer motherboards that include one or more processors, computer memory, computer storage, and computer network connections.

Norddeutsche Landesbank (NORD/LB) is a major financial institution with headquarters in Hanover, Germany. The bank was suffering from slow response time for its key systems while trying to meet new business needs. New blade server computers were installed to improve system response time by 40 per cent and provide the bank's departments with the data they need on a timely basis so they could operate efficiently.[76]

Mainframe Computers

A **mainframe computer** is a large, powerful computer shared by dozens or even hundreds of concurrent users connected to the machine over a network. The mainframe computer must reside in a data centre with special HVAC equipment to control temperature, humidity and dust levels. In addition, most mainframes are kept in a secure data centre with limited access. The construction and maintenance of a controlled-access room with HVAC can add hundreds of thousands of dollars to the cost of owning and operating a mainframe computer.

mainframe computer A large, powerful computer often shared by hundreds of concurrent users connected to the machine over a network.

The role of the mainframe is undergoing some remarkable changes as lower-cost, single-user computers become increasingly powerful. Many computer jobs that used to run on mainframe computers have migrated onto these smaller, less expensive computers. This information-processing migration is called *computer downsizing*.

The new role of the mainframe is as a large information-processing and data storage utility for a corporation – running jobs too large for other computers, storing files and databases too large to be stored elsewhere, and storing backups of files and databases created elsewhere. For example, the mainframe can handle the millions of daily transactions associated with airline, automobile and hotel/motel reservation systems. It can process the tens of thousands of daily queries necessary to provide data to decision support systems. Its massive storage and input/output capabilities enable it to play the role of a video computer, providing full-motion video to multiple, concurrent users.

3

Payment Solution Providers (PSP) is a Canadian corporation specializing in e-payment networks and the integration of financial transaction processing systems. PSP recently selected an IBM system z mainframe computer on which to run its credit card processing business. Other alternatives examined lacked the security PSP requires and would make it difficult to meet the banking industry's compliance standards for increasing controls around cardholder data to reduce credit card fraud. In addition, consolidation of operations onto a single mainframe provides a compact, efficient infrastructure that minimizes space requirements and reduces costs for IT management, power and cooling, and software licences by 35 per cent.[77]

Supercomputers

supercomputers The most powerful computer systems with the fastest processing speeds.

Supercomputers are the most powerful computers with the fastest processing speed and highest performance. They are special-purpose machines designed for applications that require extensive and rapid computational capabilities. Originally, supercomputers were used primarily by government agencies to perform the high-speed number crunching needed in weather forecasting, earthquake simulations, climate modelling, nuclear research, study of the origin of matter and the universe, and weapons development and testing. They are now used more broadly for commercial purposes in the life sciences and the manufacture of drugs and new materials. For example, Procter & Gamble uses supercomputers in the research and development of many of its leading commercial brands such as Tide and Pampers to help develop detergent with more soap suds and improve the quality of its nappies.[78]

A Japanese supercomputer built by Fujitsu named simply 'K' and capable of making 8.2 quadrillion calculations per second (8.2 petaflops, where flop is floating point operation per second) was identified as the world's fastest computer in June 2011. This machine has the computing power of one million laptop computers working in tandem. Although considered energy efficient, the computer requires enough electricity to operate 10 000 homes at a cost of €7.55 million per year. This computer is three times faster than the previous speed champion, the Tianhe-1A supercomputer at the National Supercomputing Center in Tianjin, China.[79]

The K and the Tianhe-1A supercomputers are based on a new architecture that employs both

graphics processing unit (GPU) A specialized circuit that is very efficient at manipulating computer graphics and is much faster than the typical CPU chip at performing floating point operations and executing algorithms for which processing of large blocks of data is done in parallel.

graphics processing unit (GPU) chips to perform high-speed processing. The GPU chip is a specialized circuit that is very efficient at manipulating computer graphics and is much faster than the typical CPU chip at performing floating point operations and executing algorithms for which processing of large blocks of data is done in parallel. This maths is precisely the type performed by supercomputers.[80]

The fastest operational US supercomputer as of this writing is the XT-5 Jaguar built by Cray and residing at the Department of Energy's Oak Ridge Laboratory in Tennessee. This computer was recently used to conduct simulations of the airflow around 18-wheeler tractor trailers to prove that outfitting these trailers with a set of integrated aerodynamic truck parts would substantially reduce gas consumption and the production of carbon dioxide. Use of the XT-5 shortened the computing time required from days to a few hours and avoided the need to build time-consuming and expensive physical prototypes. All told, running the simulations on the XT-5 cut the time required to go from concept to design of the necessary truck parts from 3.5 years to just 1.5 years.[81] Table 3.5 lists the three most powerful supercomputers in use as of June 2014.

Watson, an IBM supercomputer, is best known for defeating former *Jeopardy!* quiz champions. The contest was a means to demonstrate the various systems, data management and analytics technology that can be applied in business and across different industries.[82]

Table 3.5 The Three Most Powerful Operational Supercomputers (June 2014)

Rank	System	Manufacturer	Research Centre	Location	Speed (teraflops)
1	Tianhe-2	NUDT	National Super Computer Centre in Guangzhou	China	33 000
2	Titan	Cray	Oak Ridge National Laboratory	USA	18 000
3	Sequoia	IBM	Lawarence Livermore National Laboratory	USA	17 000

Watson is being 'trained' by the insurance company WellPoint to diagnose treatment options for patients.[83]

There are plans to develop a new supercomputer (called Titan) with a computing power of 20 petaflops at the Oak Ridge Laboratory. This machine will employ the new architecture using a combination of GPU chips from Nvidia and CPU chips from Intel and Advanced Micro Devices.[84] Table 3.6 lists the processing speeds of supercomputers.

Table 3.6 Supercomputer Processing Speeds

Speed	Meaning
GigaFLOPS	1×10^9 FLOPS
TeraFLOPS	1×10^{12} FLOPS
PetaFLOPS	1×10^{15} FLOPS
ExaFLOPS	1×10^{18} FLOPS

3.6 Green Computing

Green computing is concerned with the efficient and environmentally responsible design, manufacture, operation and disposal of IS-related products, including all types of computers, printers and printer materials such as cartridges and toner. Business organizations recognize that going green is in their best interests in terms of public relations, safety of employees and the community at large. They also recognize that green computing presents an opportunity to substantially reduce total costs over the lifecycle of their IS equipment. Green computing has three goals: reduce the use of hazardous material, allow companies to lower their power-related costs (including potential cap and trade fees), and enable the safe disposal or recycling of computers and computer-related equipment. According to Greenpeace, 50 million tons of computers, monitors, laptops, printers, disc drives, mobile phones, DVDs and CDs are discarded worldwide each year.[85]

green computing A program concerned with the efficient and environmentally responsible design, manufacture, operation and disposal of IS-related products.

Computers contain many toxic substances including beryllium, brominated flame retardants, cadmium, lead, mercury, polyvinyl chloride and selenium. As a result, electronic manufacturing

3

employees and suppliers at all steps along the supply chain and in the manufacturing process are at risk of unhealthy exposure. Computer users can also be exposed to these substances when using poorly designed or damaged devices.

Because it is impossible to ensure safe recycling or disposal, the best practice is to eliminate the use of toxic substances, particularly since recycling of used computers, monitors and printers has raised concerns about toxicity and carcinogenicity of some of the substances. Safe disposal and reclamation operations must be extremely careful to avoid exposure in recycling operations and leaching of materials such as heavy metals from landfills and incinerator ashes. In many cases, recycling companies export large quantities of used electronics to companies in undeveloped countries. Unfortunately, many of these countries do not have strong environmental laws, and they sometimes fail to recognize the potential dangers of dealing with hazardous materials. In their defense, these countries point out that the USA and other first-world countries were allowed to develop robust economies and rise up out of poverty without the restrictions of strict environmental policies.

One of the earliest initiatives toward green computing in the USA was the voluntary labelling programme known as Energy Star. It was conceived of by the Environmental Protection Agency in 1992 to promote energy efficiency in hardware of all kinds. This program resulted in the widespread adoption of sleep mode for electronic products. For example, Energy Star monitors have the capability to power down into two levels of 'sleep'. In the first level, the monitor energy consumption is less than or equal to 15 Watts, and in the second power consumption reduces to 8 Watts, which is less than 10 per cent of its operating power consumption.[86]

The European Union Directive 2002/95/EC required that as of July 2006 new electrical and electronic equipment cannot contain any of six banned substances in quantities exceeding certain maximum concentration values. The six banned substances are lead, mercury, cadmium, hexavalent chromium, polybrominated biphenyls and polybrominated diphenylethers. The directive was modified in September 2011 to exclude lead and cadmium because of the impracticality of finding suitable substitutes for these materials.[87] This directive applies to US organizations selling equipment to members of the European Union (EU) and has encouraged US manufacturers to meet the standards as well.

The Green Electronics Council manages the Electronic Product Environment Assessment Tool (EPEAT) to assist in the evaluation and purchase of green computing systems. The EPEAT assesses products against 51 lifecycle environmental criteria developed by representatives of the environmental community, manufacturers, private and public purchasers, resellers, recyclers, and other interested parties. These criteria are documented in IEEE Standard 1680 and have to do with the reduction of hazardous materials, the use of recycled materials, the design for recovery through recycling systems, product longevity, energy conservation, end of life management, the manufacturer's corporate environmental policy and packaging.[88] The products evaluated against the EPEAT criteria are placed into one of three tiers based on their rating, as shown in Table 3.7.

Table 3.7 EPEAT Product Tiers

Tier	Number of Required Criteria that Must be Met	Number of Optional Criteria that Must be Met
Bronze	All 23	None
Silver	All 23	At least 50%
Gold	All 23	At least 75%

Ethical and Societal Issues

Australian police print a gun that is dangerous at both ends

Twenty-seven hours, a high-tech printer and instructions downloaded from the Internet were all it took for Australian police to fabricate a gun powerful enough to kill. In May 2013, police in New South Wales created and tested two guns using a AUD$1700 3D printer and blueprints produced by US firm Defense Distributed. Tests conducted with the guns produced both a 'catastrophic failure' that could be deadly for the individual wielding the firearm, as well as a shot capable of killing a target. 'Make no mistake they will kill at both ends,' New South Wales Police Commissioner Andrew Scipione said.

3D printing is an additive technology in which objects are built up in a great many very thin layers. There are a number of ways this can be achieved but one approach is to stick powder granules together by applying heat to them. A well-established 3D printing technology that works in this manner is selective laser sintering (SLS). This builds objects by laying down a fine layer of powder and then using a laser to selectively fuse some of the granules together. At present, SLS 3D printers can output objects using a wide range of powdered materials. These include wax, polystyrene, nylon, glass, ceramics, stainless steel, titanium, aluminium and various alloys including cobalt chrome. During printing, non-bonded powder granules support the object as it is constructed. Once printing is complete, almost all the excess power is able to be recycled.

When printing their guns, New South Wales police printed the parts separately and then assembled them. All of the parts were plastic expect for the tiny firing pin which needed to be metal and in fact was not printed by the police – they used an existing part. However, in February 2014 the first metal gun was printed using SLS. Made up of over 30 parts it was fired by a company called Solid Concepts who claimed it could be used to accurately fire 50 rounds. 'We weren't trying to figure out a cheaper, easier, better way to make a gun. That wasn't the point at all. What we were trying to do is dispel the commonly held notion that [selective laser sintering] parts are not strong enough or accurate enough for real-world applications,' said Phillip Conner, project manager at the company.

These are worrying trends for some. The possibility of undetectable firearms made from plastic has huge implications for airport security, and the possibility of downloading blueprints from the Internet that can create a gun using such cheap technology is also a big concern.

Questions

1 How do you think 3D printing will change manufacturing?

2 Can you come up with a business plan for a small business using 3D printing? Do you think you could sell to the same markets without using 3D printing?

3 Do you think it is possible to police or control 3D printed guns? How?

4 How do you think airport security should react to the possibility of undetectable firearms?

Computer manufacturers such as Apple, Dell and Hewlett-Packard have long competed on the basis of price and performance. As the difference among the manufacturers in these two arenas narrows, support for green computing is emerging as a new business strategy for these companies to distinguish themselves from the competition. Apple claims to have the 'greenest lineup of notebooks' and is making progress at removing toxic chemicals. Dell's new mantra is to become 'the greenest technology company on Earth'. Hewlett-Packard highlights its long tradition of environmentalism and is improving its packaging to reduce the use of materials. It is also urging computer users around the world to shut down their computers at the end of the day to save energy and reduce carbon emissions.

Summary

Principle:

Computer hardware must be carefully selected to meet the evolving needs of the organization and its supporting information systems. Computer hardware should be selected to meet specific user and business requirements. These requirements can evolve and change over time.

The central processing unit (CPU) and memory cooperate to execute data processing. The CPU has three main components: the arithmetic/logic unit (ALU), the control unit, and the register areas. Instructions are executed in a two-phase process called a machine cycle, which includes the instruction phase and the execution phase.

Computer system processing speed is affected by clock speed, which is measured in gigahertz (GHz). As the clock speed of the CPU increases, heat is generated that can corrupt the data and instructions the computer is trying to process. Bigger heat sinks, fans and other components are required to eliminate the excess heat. This excess heat can also raise safety issues. Chip designers and manufacturers are exploring various means to avoid heat problems in their new designs.

Primary storage, or memory, provides working storage for program instructions and data to be processed and provides them to the CPU. Storage capacity is measured in bytes.

A common form of memory is random access memory (RAM). RAM is volatile; loss of power to the computer erases its contents. RAM comes in many different varieties including dynamic RAM (DRAM), synchronous DRAM (SDRAM), double data rate SDRAM and DDR2 SDRAM.

Read-only memory (ROM) is nonvolatile and contains permanent program instructions for execution by the CPU. Other nonvolatile memory types include programmable read-only memory (PROM), erasable programmable read-only memory (EPROM), electrically erasable PROM (EEPROM) and flash memory.

Cache memory is a type of high-speed memory that CPUs can access more rapidly than RAM.

A multicore microprocessor is one that combines two or more independent processors into a single computer so that they can share the workload. Intel and AMD have introduced eight-core processors that are effective in working on problems involving large databases and multimedia.

Parallel computing is the simultaneous execution of the same task on multiple processors to obtain results faster. Massively parallel processing involves linking many processors to work together to solve complex problems.

Grid computing is the use of a collection of computers, often owned by multiple individuals or organizations, to work in a coordinated manner to solve a common problem.

Computer systems can store larger amounts of data and instructions in secondary storage, which is less volatile and has greater capacity than memory. The primary characteristics of secondary storage media and devices include access method, capacity, portability and cost. Storage media can implement either sequential access or direct access. Common forms of secondary storage include magnetic storage devices such as tape, magnetic disc and virtual tape; optical storage devices such as optical disc, digital video disc (DVD) and holographic versatile disc (HVD); and solid state storage devices such as flash drives.

Redundant array of independent/inexpensive discs (RAID) is a method of storing data that generates extra bits of data from existing data, allowing the system to more easily recover data in the event of a hardware failure.

Network-attached storage (NAS) and storage area networks (SAN) are alternative forms of data storage that enable an organization to share data resources among a much larger number of computers and users for improved storage efficiency and greater cost effectiveness.

Storage as a service is a data storage model in which a data storage service provider rents space to people and organizations.

Input and output devices allow users to provide data and instructions to the computer for processing, and allow subsequent storage and output. These devices are part of a user interface through which human beings interact with computer systems.

Data is placed in a computer system in a two-stage process: data entry converts human-readable data into machine-readable form; data input then transfers it to the computer. Common input devices include a keyboard, a mouse, speech recognition, digital cameras, terminals, scanning devices, optical data readers, magnetic ink character recognition devices, magnetic stripe cards, chip-and-PIN cards, contactless cards, point-of-sale devices, automated teller machines, pen input devices, touch-sensitive screens, barcode scanners and radio frequency identification tags.

Display monitor quality is determined by aspect ratio, size, colour and resolution. Liquid crystal display and organic light-emitting diode technology is enabling improvements in the resolution and size of computer monitors. Other output devices include printers, plotters, Surface touch tables, digital audio players and e-book readers.

Computer systems are generally divided into two categories: single user and multiple users. Single-user systems include portable computers such as hand-held, laptop, notebook, netbook and tablet computers. Nonportable single-user systems include thin client, desktop, nettop and workstation computers.

Multiuser systems include servers, blade servers, mainframes and supercomputers.

Principle:

The computer hardware industry is rapidly changing and is highly competitive, creating an environment ripe for technological breakthroughs. CPU processing speed is limited by physical constraints such as the distance between circuitry points and circuitry materials. Moore's Law is a hypothesis stating that the number of transistors on a single chip doubles every two years. This hypothesis has been accurate since it was introduced in 1970.

Manufacturers are competing to develop a non-volatile memory chip that requires minimal power, offers extremely fast write speed, and can store data accurately even after it has been stored and written over many times. Such a chip could eliminate the need for RAM forms of memory.

Principle:

The computer hardware industry and users are implementing green computing designs and products. Green computing is concerned with the efficient and environmentally responsible design, manufacture, operation and disposal of IT-related products.

Business organizations recognize that going green can reduce costs and is in their best interests in terms of public relations, safety of employees and the community at large.

Three specific goals of green computing are reduce the use of hazardous material, lower power-related costs, and enable the safe disposal and/or recycling of IT products.

Three key green computing initiatives are the Energy Star programme to promote energy efficiency, the European Union Directive 2002/95/EC to reduce the use of hazardous materials, and the use of the EPEAT tool to evaluate and purchase green computing systems.

Self-Assessment Test

Computer hardware must be carefully selected to meet the evolving needs of the organization and its supporting information systems.

1 All organizations require the most powerful and most current software to remain competitive. True or false?

2 The faster the clock speed of the CPU, the more heat the processor generates. True or false?

3 The overriding consideration for a business in making hardware decisions should be how the hardware supports the _____ _____ of the information system and goals of the organization.

4 Which represents the largest amount of data – an exabyte, terabyte or gigabyte?

5 Which of the following CPU components provides a high-speed storage area to temporarily hold small units of program instruction and data immediately before, during and after execution by the CPU?
a. control unit
b. register
c. ALU
d. main memory

6 Executing an instruction by the CPU involves two phases: the _____ phase and the execution phase.

7 _____ involves capturing and editing data when it is originally created and in a form that can be directly entered into a computer, thus ensuring accuracy and timeliness.

The computer hardware industry is rapidly changing and highly competitive, creating an environment ripe for technological breakthroughs.

8 Many computer jobs that used to run on mainframe computers have migrated onto smaller, less expensive computers. This information-processing migration is called _____.

9 The transistor densities on a single chip double every two years. True or false?

The computer hardware industry and users are implementing green computing designs and products.

10 Green computing is about saving the environment; there are no real business benefits associated with this programme. True or false?

11 The disposal and reclamation operations for IT equipment must be careful to avoid unsafe exposure to _____.

Review Questions

1 What is a virtual tape system and what is it used for?

2 How does the role of primary storage differ from secondary storage?

3 Identify and briefly discuss the fundamental characteristic that distinguishes RAM from ROM memory.

4 What is RFID technology? Identify three practical uses for this technology.

5 What is a fuel cell? What advantages do fuel cells offer over batteries for use in portable electronic devices? Do they have any disadvantages?

6 What is the difference between a CPU chip and a GPU chip?

7 What is RAID storage technology?

8 Outline and briefly explain the two-phase process for executing machine-level instructions.

9 What is a massively parallel processing computer system? How is grid computing different from such a system? How is it similar?

10 Identify the three components of the CPU and explain the role of each.

11 Distinguish between a netbook computer and laptop computer. Distinguish between a nettop and desktop computer.

12 Identify and briefly describe the various classes of single-user, portable computers.

13 What is a solid state storage device?

14 Define the term green computing and state the primary goals of this programme.

15 What is the EPEAT tool? How is it used?

Discussion Questions

1 Discuss the role of the business manager in helping to determine the computer hardware to be used by the organization.

2 Explain why the clock speed is not directly related to the true processing speed of a computer.

3 Briefly describe the concept of multiprocessing. How does parallel processing differ from multiprocessing?

4 What issues can arise when the CPU runs at a very fast clock speed? What measures are manufacturers taking to deal with this problem?

5   Briefly discuss the advantages and disadvantages of installing thin clients for use in a university computer lab versus desktop computers.

6   What is an eight-core processor? What advantages does it offer users over a single-core processor? Are there any potential disadvantages?

7   Outline the Electronic Product Environment Assessment for rating computer products.

8   Briefly describe Moore's Law. What are the implications of this law? Are there any practical limitations to Moore's Law?

9   Identify and briefly discuss the advantages and disadvantages of solid state secondary storage devices compared to magnetic secondary storage devices.

10   Briefly discuss the advantages and disadvantages of attached storage, network-attached storage and storage area networks in meeting enterprise data storage challenges.

11   If cost were not an issue, describe the characteristics of your ideal computer. What would you use it for? Would you choose a handheld, portable, desktop or workstation computer? Why?

12   Briefly explain the differences between the magnetic stripe card and the chip-and-PIN card.

13   Discuss potential issues that can arise if an organization is not careful in selecting a reputable service organization to recycle or dispose of its IS equipment.

Web Exercises

1   There is great competition among countries and manufacturers to develop the fastest supercomputer. Do research on the web to identify the current three fastest supercomputers and how they are being used. Write a brief report summarizing your findings.

2   Do research on the web to learn more about the Electronic Product Environment Assessment Tool and the criteria it uses to evaluate products. Use the EPEAT to find out the rating for your current computer. Which company seems to have the greenest notebook computers? Write a brief report summarizing your findings.

Case One

Sending Computers into the Cloud

Since the modern electronic computer was invented in the 1940s, the trend has been towards reducing the size of the computer while increasing its capability. The logical end of this trend is to remove the physical computer altogether. While that isn't likely to happen in business, companies have found ways to make their central computers disappear.

Central computers still exist, of course, but if you look around business offices, follow the cables from a desktop or wireless router through walls and down halls, you may not find a central computer. What you'll find instead in more and more organizations are sig-

nals going 'into the cloud', That saying refers to *cloud computing*, which provides computing services and database access over the Internet that are accessible from anywhere in the world rather than from a specific computer in a specific location.

Deutsche Bank (DB), the German financial services firm, made a decision to send its computers into the cloud. As Alistair McLaurin of its Global Technology Engineering group put it, the bank 'wanted to create something radically different,' to 'challenge assumptions around what centrally provided IT services could be and how much they must cost'. DB created a system in which computing is done by *virtual machines (VMs)*: software-managed 'slices' of real computers that behave in every respect like a full computer but that share the hardware of one real computer with many other VMs. A virtual machine is an extension of the familiar concept of running more than one program at a time. In a VM, you run more than one operating system at a time, with each completely isolated from the others. The result is substantial savings in hardware cost and everything that goes with it, such as space and electricity. By putting the computers that host their virtual machines in the cloud, DB freed themselves from the constraints of being at a particular physical location. DB can thus optimize the use of these virtual computers across the entire company.

Another advantage of the virtual approach is that someone who needs a new computer doesn't have to purchase one. Instead, they can use a virtual computer inside a real computer that the company already has; such a VM is easier to set up than a new system. In fact, 'a user who is a permanent employee, who wants a new Virtual Machine for their own use only, can do it by visiting one website, selecting an operating system [Windows, Solaris or Linux] and clicking three buttons. The new VM will be ready and available for them within an hour.'

The Open Data Center Alliance recently chose DB as the grand prize winner of its Conquering the Cloud Challenge. The specific basis for the award was the way DB's cloud-based system manages user identities. When a user requests a virtual machine, the system already knows who has

to approve the request (if anyone), where its cost should be billed and who should be allowed to administer the machine. The cloud-based system means users don't have to worry about how virtual machines are created, making it more practical to use them. Because a virtual machine is less expensive than a new desktop computer, DB management wanted to encourage employees to use the virtual machines. Removing barriers to their adoption was important, which is why they designed the cloud-based system to manage user identities.

Currently, programmers and other system developers use DB's cloud system for application development and testing. If a developer is working with a computer that runs Solaris and wants to test an application under Windows 7 or Windows Vista, he or she can do so using a virtual machine quickly and efficiently. The cloud system will be used next for DB production applications, except for those that need 100 per cent uptime (such as the one that operates a network of ATMs). After that? Who knows?

Questions

1   Describe the hardware requirements of a company wanting to use cloud computing.

2   What are some of the advantages of using cloud computing in a business context?

3   What are the security issues around using cloud computing and how would you combat them?

4   How does the location independence of cloud computing help Deutsche Bank?

Case Two

Extreme Storage

The amount of data stored in the world's computers is growing faster than drive capacities are growing to hold it.

The United States Library of Congress processes about 40 TB of data each week. That's about 20 times the capacity of the largest commonly available disc drives. The library uses nearly 20 000 disc drives to store over 3 petabytes (PB)

of data in total. Thomas Youkel, group chief of enterprise systems engineering at the library, estimates that the library's data load will quadruple in the next few years. The library realized that it had to manage this data intelligently to cope with its size. One method the library used was to separate the actual content, which is usually needed only at the end of a search, from the information about the content (*metadata*) used in searching. Only the metadata is kept in high-speed storage, with the content kept offline or on low-speed, less expensive storage media.

On a smaller (but still large) scale, Mazda Motor Corporation has 'only' about 90 TB of data. To trade off access time and cost, the firm divides its data into four levels. The most frequently needed data is kept in solid state storage. The next level of data is stored on high-performance 15 000-RPM drives; next, on less expensive 7200-RPM drives; and, finally, on magnetic tape. The top and bottom tiers each store about 20 per cent of the total, with the remaining 60 per cent on the middle magnetic-disc tiers.

Whether an organization has extraordinary storage requirements like the Library of Congress or more manageable requirements like Mazda, the amount of data organizations need to store is exploding for several reasons. One is the accumulation of years of data, which companies are reluctant to discard since it may be of value in the future. Another is the proliferation of storage-intensive data types such as photos and video, which occupy more space than letters and numbers. Advanced data analysis methods, which help extract value from this data, are another business reason to collect data. As a report from the Data Warehousing Institute puts it, 'The fastest growing use case for big data analytics is advanced data visualization. A growing number of companies are running sophisticated analytics tools on big data sets in order to build highly complex visual representations of their data.' This representation helps managers make better decisions but uses a lot of storage space.

Storage vendors compete to meet the demand for greater storage capacity by using the enterprise storage system types discussed earlier in this chapter. A recent article by Desmond Fuller in *Computerworld* discusses how businesses use NAS to handle data storage needs such as those of the Library of Congress and Mazda:

> A larger business might use a low-cost NAS box to offload stagnant, rarely used data from more expensive, high-performance storage. Or it might place one alongside a virtual server farm to store virtual machine images or ship

one to a satellite office to serve as low-cost file storage. For a small to medium-size business, one of these NAS boxes would serve the needs for daily file storage, with the bonus that nontechnical staff could set it up and start using it without professional IT help.

Fuller goes on to review five NAS offerings, noting, 'I found the richest sets of business features – straightforward setup, easy remote access, plentiful backup options – at the higher end of the scale.' It's important for a business to analyze its needs carefully before looking at what's available. Some features will only come at a price, and the business shouldn't pay that price if it doesn't need the features.

The range of storage area network (SAN) offerings is equally wide. Blackpool and the Fylde College, north of Liverpool in England, chose a NetApp SAN to support its faculty, staff, and 20 000+ students. Network manager Simon Bailey says, 'Previously, we had over 100 servers with attached storage to manage. These were constantly running out of disc space and we were forever trying to cram in extra disc capacity. To be honest, the situation had got past manageable.' Today, after expanding its initial SAN, the college has centralized 99 per cent of its storage. 'The centralized NetApp storage system has allowed us to implement a scalable data management strategy in line with organizational growth,' says Bailey. 'It's flexible, scalable and affordable – we wouldn't be without it.'

Questions

1 Suppose you use about 500 GB (0.5 TB) of storage in your personal system, filling about two-thirds of its 750 GB disc. Most of that storage is used by your video library. Photos, music and software (including the operating system) use about 20 GB. Traditional data files, such as word processing files, spreadsheets and emails, require less than 1 GB. Which of the technologies and strategies discussed in this case might be of practical value to you? Why?

2 Both SAN and NAS systems can use RAID internally (see discussion earlier in this chapter). Why might this be a good idea?

3

3 Consider the Library of Congress's 15 000 to 18 000 disc drives. The mean time between failures (MTBF) of a typical disc drive has been estimated at about 50 years. If that figure is correct, the library will have 300 to 360 drive failures every year, an average of about one a day. What does that mean for managing its hardware? How is that different from the way a small business with five or six disc drives should manage its hardware?

4 Both Mazda and the Library of Congress divide their data into multiple tiers to manage it effectively and cost effectively. SAN systems can support this strategy by incorporating several types of storage into one SAN. How could your college or university take advantage of this concept? Outline three tiers of data it could have, with two specific examples of data that would be in each tier. (For example, records of students who graduated or left at least ten years ago could be in the lowest tier.)

Case Three

Tracking Laptops as they Enter and Leave a Building

Based in Pretoria, South Africa, Techsolutions is a leading provider of solutions for tracking laptop computers, returnable goods such as pallets, crates, bins and containers, as well as other assets. The company uses a variety of technologies to do this, including RFID tags. RFID tags can be attached to just about anything – clothing, missiles, pets or, in the case of Techsolutions' clients, laptops and other valuable goods. RFID tags can work in several ways but essentially a reader sends out a radio signal which the tag responds to in a way that the reader can detect. This allows the reader to identify the product that the tag is attached to. Some tags have batteries or other power sources and can be used over long distances, but others – known as passive tags – have no power source at all. Instead they harvest power from the radio signals sent out by the reader, and convert this into the energy they need to respond. This can only happen over short distances, maybe just a metre or so.

Techsolutions first deployed SmartAsset for Laptops in 2008, for the Department of Trade and Industry. Their solution includes hardware, software, tags and integration services to integrate with access control or other systems. SmartAsset is offered with either passive or active tags, depending on the requirements of the client. Smart-Asset has also been integrated into CCTV and physical security systems.

SmartAsset Laptop is offered with either manual or automated asset identification. In the case of manual, the RFID asset tag is linked with the details of an employee and their ID photograph. When the RFID tag on a laptop passes a security point, the screen situated at the security personnel desk will display the photograph of the employee linked to the asset. This allows security personnel a highly efficient method for authenticating employees and laptops as they enter or leave a facility.

In the case of automated identification, an employee is also issued with an RFID tag which is linked to the RFID tags of the assets issued to them. When an RFID tagged asset passes the security checkpoint, SmartAsset will look in the database for the linked employee. If the linked employee is also found to be at the checkpoint, the system will log the movement. But if the linked employee is not found to be present, the system will generate an alarm and display the details of the asset and the linked employee to the security personnel for investigation.

SmartAsset for Laptops reduces security personnel workload in a busy facility and increases security significantly as every laptop gets automatically authenticated in and out of the building with an audit trail of date, time and location. This can also enable emergency exits and alternative non-manned points of egress to have an authentication station with a simple web camera, so that every time there is a read event (a laptop leaving the building) an image file is taken from the webcam and added to the database. That way, if something is discovered missing even weeks later, a picture of that asset leaving the facility is stored securely in the database.

RFID is similar to barcode technology except that it works over longer distances and does not require 'line of sight' – a barcode reader needs to 'see' the barcode, whereas an RFID tag can be detected inside a briefcase or jacket pocket.

Questions

1 Describe if and how RFID technology could be used to protect data (rather than hardware).

2 How else could a company protect its laptops?

3 Does using this system indicate that a company has a lack of trust in its employees? How could a company overcome this?

4 What else could this technology be used for?

Notes

1 King, Ian and Bass, Dina, 'Dell Loses Orders as Facebook Do-It-Yourself Servers Gain: Tech', *Bloomberg News*. Available from: www.bloomberg.com/news/2011–09-12/dell-loses-orders-as-facebook-do-it-yourself-servers-gain-tech.html, 12 September 2011.

2 Staff, 'US Air Force Chooses HP as Key Technology Provider', *Market Watch*, 29 August 2011.

3 Staff, 'Convenience Store Chain Chooses IBM to Collaborate in the Cloud', IBM Press Release, 16 August 2011.

4 Arthur, Charles, 'ARM Chip Offers Cheaper Smartphones with Longer Battery Life by 2013', *The Guardian*, 20 October 2011.

5 D'Altorio, Tony, 'Intel's 3D Chip Challenge'. Available from: www.investmentu.com/2011/May/intel-chip-challenges-arm.html, 12 May 2011.

6 Seubert, Curtis, 'How Many Bytes Is an Exabyte?' Available from: www.ehow.com/about_6370860_many-bytes-exabyte_.html. Accessed 21 October 2011.

7 Lee, Kevin, 'IBM's Next-Gen Memory Is 100 Times Faster Than Flash', *PC World*, 30 June 2011.

8 Shah, Agam, 'AMD's First Eight-Core Desktop Processors Detailed', *PC World*, 6 October 2011.

9 Bronstein, Benjamin, et al., 'Using a Multicore Processor for Rover Autonomous Science', IEEEAC paper, no. 1104, version 1. Available from: http://ase.jpl.nasa.gov/public/papers/bornstein_ieeeaero2011_using.pdf, 10 January 2011.

10 University of Nottingham, 2014. Available from: www.nottingham.ac.uk/news/pressreleases/2014/february/powerful-supercomputer-to-offer-a-glimpse-of-the-early-universe.aspx. Accessed 18 July 2014.

11 European Organization for Nuclear Research Website, 'The Name CERN'. Available from: http://public.web.cern.ch/public/en/About/Name-en.html. Accessed 21 October 2011.

12 The Best Physics Videos Website, 'What's New @ CERN?' Available from: http://bestphysicsvideos.blogspot.com/2011/12/whats-new-cern-n3-grid-computing.html, 5 December 2011.

13 Cariaga, Vance, 'Teradata Helps Corporations Save Vast Amounts of Data', *Investor's Business Daily*, 21 October 2011.

14 Kerschberg, Ben, 'Names to Know in Big Data: Hitachi Data Systems', *Forbes*, 25 October 2011.

15 Jellinek, Dan, 'India Builds World's Largest Biometric ID Database'. Available from; www.ukauthority.com/Headlines/tabid/36/NewsArticle/tabid/64/Default.aspx?id=3371. Accessed 17 October 2011.

16 Mims, Christopher, 'And the Longest Running Digital Storage Media is …'. Available from: www.technologyreview.com/blog/mimssbits/26990, 13 July 2011.

17 Australia Wide IT, 2014. Available from: http://australiawideit.com.au/services/backup-systems. Accessed 18 July 2014.

18 Simonite, Tom, 'IBM Builds Biggest Data Drive Ever', *Technology Review*, 25 August 2011.

19 ATTO Technology Website, 'Avatar "Sounds Off" Using ATTO's Technology'. Available from: www.attotech.com/pdfs/Advanced-AudioRentals.pdf. Accessed 27 October 2011.

20 IBM Success Stories, 'Baldor Electric Opts for IBM ProtecTIER and IBM XIV'. Available from: www-01.ibm.com/software/success/cssdb.nsf/CS/DLAS-8JYRFM?OpenDocument&Site=corp&cty=en_us. Accessed 26 July 2011.

3

21 Millenniata Website, 'Millenniata Partners with Hitachi-LG Data Storages'. Available from: http://millenniata.com/2011/08/24/millenniata-partners-with-hitachi-lg-data-storage, 15 August 2011.

22 Holographics Projectors Website, Holographic Video Disk page. Available from: www.holographicprojectors.com.au/hvd, 27 October 2011.

23 Staff, 'Vaillant Accelerates SAP Environment through the Use of SSD Technology'. Available from: www.ramsan.com/resources/successStories/91, 10 October 2011.

24 SanDisk Website, 'SanDisk Ultra Backup USB Flash Drive'. Available from: www.sandisk.com/products/usb-flash-drives/sandisk-ultra-backup-usb-flash-drive. Accessed 28 October 2011.

25 Kingston Technology Website, 'SSD Performance and Productivity Revitalize Notebook Assets'. Available from: http://media.kingston.com/images/branded/MKF_357_Qualcomm_Case_study.pdf. Accessed 19 December 2011.

26 Staff, 'Vaillant Accelerates SAP Environment through the Use of SSD Technology'. Available from: www.ramsan.com/resources/successStories/91, 19 October 2011.

27 HP Website, 'High-availability IT for Swiss Holiday Destination, Davos Klosters, HP Customer Case Study'. Available from: h20195.www2.hp.com/v2/GetPDF.aspx/4AA3–4360EEW.pdf. Accessed 29 October 2011.

28 NorthgateArinso Website, 'Delivering HR Excellence'. Available from: http://ngahr.com. Accessed 30 October 2011.

29 IBM Success Stories, 'NorthgateArinso Builds Compact, Energy-efficient and Scalable Solution'. Available from: www-01.ibm.com/software/success/cssdb.nsf/CS/STRD-8GXE3S?OpenDocument&Site=corp&cty=en_us, 18 May 2011.

30 Mozy Website, 'I Found My Stolen Laptop'. Available from: http://mozy.com/home/reviews. Accessed 30 October 2011.

31 Spangler, Todd, 'Time Warner Cable Adds Speech Recognition to Customer Service'. Available from: www.multichannel.com/article/464064-Time_Warner_Cable_Adds_Speech_Recognition_To_Customer_Service_Line.php. Accessed 16 February 2011.

32 Prann, Elizabeth, 'Police Officers Find Tiny Pocket Cams Are Silent Partners'. Available from: www.foxnews.com/scitech/2011/07/04/police-officers-find-tiny-pocket-cams-are-silent-partners, 4 July 2011.

33 Silicon Valley Bank Website, 'About SVB Financial Group'. Available from: www.svb.com/Company/About-SVB-Financial-Group. Accessed 29 October 2011.

34 PSIGEN Software Website, 'Silicon Valley Bank'. Available from: www.psigen.com/industry_solutions/banking_finanical_services_scanning_capture_imaging_software_industry_solution.aspx. Accessed 29 October 2011.

35 Perkins, Ed, 'Travel-Friendly Chip-and-Pin Credit Cards Coming to US', *USA Today*, 4 April 2011.

36 Herron, Janna, 'US Credit Cards Add Chip and PIN Security'. Available from: www.foxbusiness.com/personal-finance/2011/10/20/us-credit-cards-add-chip-and-pin-security. Accessed 21 October 2011.

37 Perkins, Ed, 'Travel-Friendly Chip-and-Pin Credit Cards Coming to US', *USA Today*, 21 April 2011.

38 Fitzgerald, Kate, 'MasterCard Testing Contactless Payments for In-Flight Purchases'. Available from: www.paymentssource.com/news/mastercard-testing-contactless-payments-in-flight-guestlogix-3008292–1.html?zkPrintable=1&nopagination=1, 25 October 2011.

39 First Data Website, 'A First Data Customer Success Story: First Data's POS Restaurant Solution Helps La Paz Restaurant Improve Operations and Offer Gift Cards'. Available from: www.firstdata.com/en_us/insights/lapaz-case-study.html?cat=Success+Stories&tag=POS+Payments+%26+Customer+Contact. Accessed 20 December 2011.

40 Mastin, Michelle, 'Square vs. Intuit Go Payment: Mobile Credit Card Systems Compared', *PC World*. Available from: www.pcworld.com/businesscenter/article/239250/square_vs_intuit_gopayment_mobile_credit_card_systems_compared.html#tk.mod_rel, 6 September 2011.

41 SMART Customer Stories, 'Audi AG Advancement through Technology at Audi AG'. Available from: www.smarttech.com/us/Customer%20Stories/Browse%20Stories?q=1&business=1&allstories=1. Accessed 27 December 2011.

42 Barcode.com Website, 'Mobio Uses Barcode to Enhance Game Day,' http://barcode.com/mobio-uses-barcodes-to-enhance-game-day.html. Accessed 31 October 2011.

43 Canadian Sheep Federation, 'Sheep Industry Continues toward Mandatory RFID Tags'. Available from: www.seregonmap.com/repository/wool/scm/uploads/CSF-Mandatory-RFID-Tags-English.pdf, 20 June 2011.

44 Kondolojy, Amanda, 'LCD vs Plasma Monitors'. Available from: www.ehow.com/about_4778386_ lcd-vs-plasma-monitors.html. Accessed 1 November 2011.

45 Grubb, Ben, 'Nokia Demos Flexible Mobile and Smudge-Free Screen Technology', www.theage.com. au/digital-life/mobiles/nokia-demos-flexible-mobile-and-smudgefree-screen-technology-20111028– 1mmhe.html. Accessed 28 October 2011.

46 Microsoft Case Studies, 'Royal Bank of Canada Delights Customers with Innovative Microsoft Surface Experience'. Available from: www. microsoft.com/casestudies/Microsoft-Surface/ Royal-Bank-of-Canada/Royal-Bank-of-Canada-delights-customers-with-innovative-Microsoft-Surface-experience/4000011029, 25 August 2011.

47 HP Website, 'HP ePrint Enterprise Mobile Printing'. Available from: http://h71028.www7.hp.com/ enterprise/us/en/ipg/HPeprint-solution.html. Accessed 6 November 2011.

48 PrinterOn Website, 'Mobile Printing Solutions'. Available from: www.printeron.com. Accessed 6 November 2011.

49 Kozlowski, Michael, 'Inspiring Technologies in e-Readers during 2011', http://goodereader.com/ blog/electronic-readers/inspiring-technologies-in-e-readers-during-2011. Accessed 7 November 2011.

50 IBM Website, 'IBM Unveils Cognitive Computing Chips'. Available from: www-03.ibm.com/press/us/ en/pressrelease/35251.wss, 18 August 2011.

51 Lomas, Natasha, 'Dual Core Smartphones: The Next Mobile Arms Race'. Available from: www. silicon.com/technology/mobile/2011/01/12/dual-core-smartphones-the-next-mobile-arms-race, 11 January 2011.

52 Ji-hyun, Cho, 'Samsung, Google Gain in Apple Patent Fight'. Available from: Asia News Network, www.asianewsnet.net/home/news. php?id=23574. Accessed 11 July 2011.

53 Chen, Brian X., 'Samsung Wins a Round in Patent Fight with Apple', New York Times, 9 December 2011.

54 Gartner, 2013. Available from: http://www.gartner. com/newsroom/id/2610015. Accessed 3 October 2014.

55 Fuquay, Jim, 'Doctors Using Smartphones, Tablets to Access Medical Data', Star-Telegram, 6 July, 2011.

56 epSOS, 2014. Available from: www.epsos.eu/ epsos-services/eprescription.html. Accessed 18 July 2014.

57 AccessReflex Website, 'Stay Connected with Your MS Access'. Available from: http://access. mobilereflex.com/features.html. Accessed 7 November 2011.

58 EBSCO Publishing Website. Available from: www. ebscohost.com/schools/mobile-access. Accessed 8 November 2011.

59 Mack, Julie, 'Bloomingdale High School Students Each Given Netbook Computer, Internet Access'. Available from: Kalamazoo Gazette, 12 October 2011.

60 Strohmeyer, Robert and Perenson Melissa, J., 'Why Your Next PC Will Be a Tablet', PC World, January 2011.

61 Wenzel, Elsa, 'Slates Enable a Surgery Practice to Improve Patient Care', PC World, 1 October 2011.

62 Wenzel, Elsa, 'Tablets Help a Business Stand Out, Improve Client Care', PC World, 24 July 2011.

63 Smith, Dave, 'The Birth of the iRestaurant', Inc., 16 August 2011.

64 Strohmeyer, Robert and Perenson Melissa, J., 'Why Your Next PC Will Be a Tablet', PC World, January 2011.

65 Wyse Website, 'Wyse Thin Clients', http://wyse. com/products/hardware/thinclients/index.asp. Accessed 19 October 2011.

66 Deboosere, Lien, et al., 'Cloud-based Desktop Services for Thin Clients'. Available from: http://doi. ieeecomputersociety.org/10.1109/MIC.2011.139, 9 October 2011.

67 Wyse Website, 'Wyse TV Jewelry Case Study'. Available from: www.wyse.com/resources/ casestudies/CS-JTV-register.asp. Accessed 19 October 2011.

68 Wiesen, G., 'What Is a Nettop?' www.wisegeek. com/what-is-a-nettop.htm. Accessed 19 October 2011.

69 Dell Website, 'Zooming in on Time-Savings'. Available from: http://i.dell.com/ sites/content/corporate/case-studies/en/ Documents/2010-sekotec-10008226.pdf. Accessed 1 April 2010.

70 www.google.co.uk/about/datacenters/inside/ locations/hamina. Accessed 18 July 2014.

71 Parrish, Kevin, 'Intel to Ship 10-Core CPUs in the First Half of 2011', IDG New Service, 11 February 2011.

72 Morgan, Timothy Prickett, 'AMD Shoots Lower with Opteron 3000 Chips', The Register. Available from: www.theregister.co.uk/2011/11/14/amd_ opteron_3000_server_chip, 14 November 2011.

73 Microsoft Case Studies, 'Gashora Girls Academy', www.microsoft.com/casestudies/Case_Study_Detail.aspx?CaseStudyID=4000010078. Accessed 26 May 2011.

74 North, Jeffrey, 'The Total Economic Impact of Microsoft Windows MultiPoint Server 2011', Forrester Consulting Project, April 2011.

75 PRWeb, 'Companies on Tight Budgets Thrive with Low Prices on EZZI.net Dedicated Servers, Dedicated Cloud Servers, and Virtual Private Servers'. Available from: http://news.yahoo.com/companies-tight-budgets-thrive-low-prices-ezzi-net-110250858.html. Accessed 20 October 2011, and EZZI.net Website, 'Virtual Private Servers'. Available from: www.ezzi.net/vps.php. Accessed 21 October 2011.

76 IBM Success Stories, 'Top German Bank NORD/LB Improves Business and Technical Efficiencies Using IBM and SAP'. Available from: www-01.ibm.com/software/success/cssdb.nsf/CS/STRD-8M4GN6?OpenDocument&Site=default&cty=en_us. Accessed 27 September 2011.

77 Taft, Darryl K., 'IBM Mainframe Replaces HP, Oracle Systems for Payment Solutions', *eWeek*, 19 April 2011.

78 ChemInfo Website, 'Supercomputer Center Partners with P&G on Simulation'. Available from: www.chem.info/News/2011/02/Software-Supercomputer-Center-Partners-with-PG-on-Simulation. Accessed 28 February 2011.

79 Staff, 'Japanese Supercomputer Is the Most Powerful', *Thaindian News*, 20 June 2011.

80 Hesseldahl, Arik, 'Nvidia Chips to Power World's Most Powerful Computer'. Available from: http://allthingsd.com/?p=130810&ak_action=printable, 11 October 2011.

81 Staff, 'Big Rigs Go Aerodynamic, Thanks to Supercomputers', *TechNewsDaily*, 9 February 2011.

82 IBM Website, 'IBM's Watson, What is Watson?'. Available from: www-03.ibm.com/innovation/us/watson/what-is-watson/index.html. Accessed 23 December 2011.

83 Technology staff, 'IBM's Watson Supercomputer to Give Instant Medical Diagnosis', *Los Angeles Times*, 12 September 2011.

84 Hesseldahl, Arik, 'Nvidia Chips to Power World's Most Powerful Computer'. Available from: http://allthingsd.com/?p=130810&ak_action=printable. Accessed 11 October 2011.

85 Parsons, June and Oja, Dan, *New Perspectives on Computer Concepts 2011* (Boston, MA: Cengage Learning, 2011), p. 106.

86 US Department of Energy Website, 'Energy Savers – When to Turn off Your Computer'. Available from: www.energysavers.gov/your_home/appliances/index.cfm/mytopic=10070. Accessed 8 November 2011.

87 Staff, 'Commission Decision of September 8, 2011', *Official Journal of the European Union*, 10 September 2011.

88 EPEAT Website, 'Welcome to EPEAT', www.epeat.net. Accessed 8 November 2011.

04

Software: Systems and Application Software

Principles

Systems and application software are critical in helping individuals and organizations achieve their goals.

Organizations use off-the-shelf application software for common business needs and proprietary application software to meet unique business needs and provide a competitive advantage.

Organizations should choose programming languages with functional characteristics that are appropriate for the task at hand and well suited to the skills and experience of the programming staff.

The software industry continues to undergo constant change; users need to be aware of recent trends and issues to be effective in their business and personal life.

Learning Objectives

- Identify and briefly describe the functions of the two basic kinds of software.
- Outline the role of the operating system and identify the features of several popular operating systems.

- Discuss how application software can support personal, workgroup and enterprise business objectives.
- Identify three basic approaches to developing application software and discuss the pros and cons of each.

- Outline the overall evolution and importance of programming languages and clearly differentiate among the generations of programming languages.

- Identify several key software issues and trends that have an impact on organizations and individuals.

Why Learn about Systems and Application Software?

Software is indispensable for any computer system and the people using it. In this chapter you will learn about systems and application software. Without systems software, computers would not be able to accept data input from a keyboard, process data or display results. Application software is one of the keys to helping you achieve your career goals. Sales representatives use software on their smartphones and tablet computers to enter sales orders and help their customers get what they want. Stock and bond traders use software to make split-second decisions involving millions of dollars. Scientists use software to analyze the threat of climate change. Regardless of your job, you most likely will use software to help you advance in your career and earn higher wages. You can also use software to help you prepare your personal income taxes, keep a budget, and keep in contact with friends and family online. Software can truly advance your career and enrich your life. We begin with an overview of software.

Software has a profound impact on individuals and organizations. It can make the difference between profits and losses and between financial health and bankruptcy. As Figure 4.1 shows, companies recognize this impact, spending more on software than on computer hardware.

Figure 4.1 Importance of Software in Business
Since the 1950s, businesses have greatly increased their expenditures on software compared with hardware.

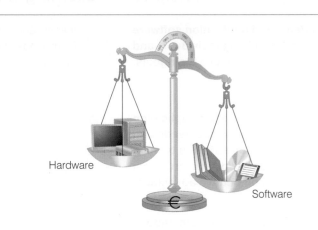

Hardware

Software

4.1 An Overview of Software

computer programs Sequences of instructions for the computer.

documentation Text that describes a program's functions to help the user operate the computer system.

As you learned in Chapter 1, software consists of computer programs that control the workings of computer hardware. **Computer programs** are sequences of instructions for the computer. **Documentation** describes the program functions to help the user operate the computer system. Some documentation is given on-screen or online, while other forms appear in external resources, such as printed manuals. Software is a growing and dynamic industry. In 2011, for example, China's software industry grew almost 30 per cent.[1] Some believe that software development and sales have more growth potential than hardware.[2] According to an early Internet pioneer and board of directors member of Hewlett-Packard, 'This week, Hewlett-Packard (where I am on the board) announced that it is exploring jettisoning its struggling PC business in favour of investing more heavily in software, where it sees better potential for growth.'

Systems Software

Systems software is the set of programs that coordinates the activities and functions of the hardware and other programs throughout the computer system. Each type of systems software is designed for a specific CPU and class of hardware. The combination of a hardware configuration and systems software is known as a computer system platform.

Application Software

Application software consists of programs that help users solve particular computing problems.[3] An architectural firm in Boise, Idaho, for example, used ProjectDox software to streamline the paperwork required to get approval and permits for building projects.[4] According to one architect from the firm, 'The nice thing is that most files, whether it be a PDF or Word document, can be dropped into different folders online and sent. It's not a big deal like it was before.' Software from Amcom allows companies such as Eddie Bauer to provide the exact location of someone who calls from an Eddie Bauer retail location to emergency call centres.[5] According to a company technical analyst, 'We take communications and security very seriously. The Amcom system is a perfect communications safety net in case someone dials 911 and can't explain where they are.'

In most cases, application software resides on the computer's hard disc before it is brought into the computer's memory and run. Application software can also be stored on CDs, DVDs and even USB flash drives. An increasing amount of application software is available on the web. Sometimes referred to as a *rich Internet application (RIA)*, a web-delivered application combines hardware resources of the web server and the PC to deliver valuable software services through a web browser interface. Before a person, group or enterprise decides on the best approach for acquiring application software, they should analyze their goals and needs carefully.

Supporting Individual, Group and Organizational Goals

Every organization relies on the contributions of people, groups and the entire enterprise to achieve its business objectives. One useful way of classifying the many potential uses of information systems is to identify the scope of the problems and opportunities that an organization addresses. This scope is called the *sphere of influence*. For most companies, the spheres of influence are personal, workgroup and enterprise. Table 4.1 shows how various kinds of software support these three spheres.

Information systems that operate within the **personal sphere of influence** serve the needs of individual users. These information systems help users improve their personal effectiveness, increasing the amount and quality of work

personal sphere of influence The sphere of influence that serves the needs of an individual user.

Table 4.1 Software Supporting Individuals, Workgroups and Enterprises

Software	Personal	Workgroup	Enterprise
Systems software	Smartphone, tablet computer, personal computer and workstation operating systems	Network operating systems	Server and mainframe operating systems
Application software	Word processing, spreadsheet, database and graphics	Electronic mail, group scheduling, shared work and collaboration	General ledger, order entry, payroll and human resources

personal productivity software The software that enables users to improve their personal effectiveness, increasing the amount of work and quality of work they can do.

workgroup Two or more people who work together to achieve a common goal.

workgroup sphere of influence The sphere of influence that helps workgroup members attain their common goals.

enterprise sphere of influence The sphere of influence that serves the needs of the firm in its interaction with its environment.

they can do. Such software is often called **personal productivity software**. For example, MindManager software from Mindjet provides tools to help people diagram complex ideas and projects using an intuitive graphic interface.[6]

When two or more people work together to achieve a common goal, they form a **workgroup**. A workgroup might be a large formal, permanent organizational entity, such as a section or department or a temporary group formed to complete a specific project. An information system in the **workgroup sphere of influence** helps workgroup members attain their common goals. Often, software designed for the personal sphere of influence can extend into the workgroup sphere. For example, people can use online calendar software such as Google Calendar to store personal appointments but also to schedule meetings with others.

Information systems that operate within the **enterprise sphere of influence** support the firm in its interaction with its environment, which includes customers, suppliers, shareholders, competitors, special-interest groups, the financial community and government agencies. This means the enterprise sphere of influence includes business partners, such as suppliers that provide raw materials; retail companies that store and sell a company's products; and shipping companies that transport raw materials to the plant and finished goods to retail outlets. For example, many enterprises use IBM Cognos software as a centralized web-based system where employees, partners and stakeholders can report and analyze corporate financial data.[7]

4.2 Systems Software

Controlling the operations of computer hardware is one of the most critical functions of systems software. Systems software also supports the application programs' problem-solving capabilities. Types of systems software include operating systems, utility programs and middleware.

Operating Systems

operating system (OS) A set of computer programs that controls the computer hardware and acts as an interface with applications.

An **operating system (OS)** is a set of programs that controls the computer hardware and acts as an interface with applications (see Figure 4.2). Operating systems can control one or more computers, or they can allow multiple users to interact with one computer. The various combinations of OSs, computers and users include the following:

■ **Single computer with a single user.** This system is commonly used in a personal computer, tablet computer or a smartphone that supports one user at a time. Examples of OSs for this setup include Microsoft Windows, Mac OS X and Google Android.

Figure 4.2 Role of Operating Systems *The role of the operating system is to act as an interface between application software and hardware.*

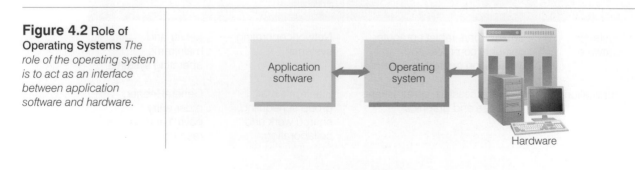

Application software ← Operating system → Hardware

■ **Single computer with multiple simultaneous users.** This system is typical of larger server or mainframe computers that can support hundreds or thousands of people, all using the computer at the same time. Examples of OSs that support this kind of system include UNIX, z/OS and HP UX.

■ **Multiple computers with multiple users.** This type of system is typical of a network of computers, such as a home network with several computers attached or a large computer network with hundreds of computers attached supporting many users, sometimes located around the world. Most PC operating systems double as network operating systems. Network server OSs include Red Hat Linux, Windows Server and Mac OS X Server.

■ **Special-purpose computers.** This type of system is typical of a number of computers with specialized functions, such as those that control sophisticated military aircraft, space shuttles, digital cameras or home appliances. Examples of OSs for these purposes include Windows Embedded, Symbian and some distributions of Linux.

The OS, which plays a central role in the functioning of the complete computer system, is usually stored on disc on general-purpose computers and in solid state memory on special-purpose computers such as mobile phones and smartphones. After you start, or 'boot up', a computer system, portions of the OS are transferred to memory as the system needs them. This process can take anywhere from a split second on a smartphone, to a few minutes on a desktop PC, to hours on a large mainframe or distributed computer systems. OS developers are continuously working to shorten the time required to boot devices from being shut down and wake devices from sleep mode.

You can also boot a computer from a CD, DVD or even a USB flash drive. A storage device that contains some or all of the OS is often called a *rescue disc* because you can use it to start the computer if you have problems with the primary hard disc.

The set of programs that make up the OS performs a variety of activities, including the following:

■ performing common computer hardware functions

■ providing a user interface and input/output management

■ providing a degree of hardware independence

■ managing system memory

■ managing processing tasks

■ sometimes providing networking capability

■ controlling access to system resources

■ managing files.

The **kernel**, as its name suggests, is the heart of the OS and controls its most critical processes. The kernel ties all of the OS components together and regulates other programs. For a really gentle introduction on how to write an operating system, head to the University of Cambridge Computer Laboratory at www.cl.cam.ac.uk/projects/raspberrypi/tutorials/os. The tutorial will show you how to write a simple kernel for the Rasberry Pi computer.

kernel The heart of the operating system, which controls its most critical processes.

Common Hardware Functions

All applications must perform certain hardware-related tasks, such as the following:

■ Get input from the keyboard or another input device.

■ Retrieve data from discs.

■ Store data on discs.

■ Display information on a monitor or printer.

Each of these tasks requires a detailed set of instructions. The OS converts a basic request into the instructions that the hardware requires. In effect, the OS acts as an intermediary between the application and the hardware. The OS uses special software provided by device manufacturers, called device drivers, to communicate with and control a device. Device drivers are installed when a device is initially connected to the computer system.

User Interface and Input/Output Management

user interface The element of the operating system that allows people to access and interact with the computer system.

command-based user interface A user interface that requires you to give text commands to the computer to perform basic activities.

One of the most important functions of any OS is providing a **user interface**, which allows people to access and interact with the computer system. The first user interfaces for mainframe and personal computer systems were command based. A **command-based user interface** requires you to give text commands to the computer to perform basic activities. For example, the command ERASE 00TAXRTN would cause the computer to erase a file named 00TAXRTN. RENAME and COPY are other examples of commands used to rename files and copy files from one location to another. Today's systems engineers and administrators often use a command-based user interface to control the low-level functioning of computer systems. Most modern OSs (including popular graphical user interfaces such as Windows) provide a way to interact with the system through a command line.

graphical user interface (GUI) An interface that displays pictures (icons) and menus that people use to send commands to the computer system.

A **graphical user interface (GUI)** displays pictures (called *icons*) and menus that people use to send commands to the computer system. GUIs are more intuitive to use because they anticipate the user's needs and provide easy to recognize options. Microsoft Windows is a popular GUI. As the name suggests, Windows is based on the use of a window, or a portion of the display screen dedicated to a specific application. The screen can display several windows at once.

While GUIs have traditionally been accessed using a keyboard and mouse, more recent technologies allow people to use touch screens and spoken commands. Today's mobile devices and some PCs, for example, use a touch user interface also called a *natural user interface (NUI)* or multitouch interface by some. Apple's Mountain Lion operating system, for example, uses a touch user interface to allow people to control the personal computer by touching the screen.[8] Speech recognition is also available with some operating systems.[9] By speaking into a microphone, the operating system commands and controls the computer system. Sight interfaces use a camera on the computer to determine where a person is looking on the screen and performs the appropriate command or operation. Some companies are also experimenting with sensors attached to the human brain (brain interfaces) that can detect brain waves and control a computer as a result. Sight and brain interfaces can be very helpful to disabled individuals.

Hardware Independence

application program interface (API) Tools software developers use to build application software without needing to understand the inner workings of the OS and hardware.

Software applications are designed to run on a particular operating system by using the operating system's **application program interface (API)**, which provides software developers with tools they use to build application software without needing to understand the inner workings of the OS and hardware (see Figure 4.3). Being able to develop software without concern for the specific underlying hardware is referred to as *hardware independence*. When new hardware technologies are introduced, the operating system is required to adjust to address those changes, not the application software that runs on the operating system.

Memory Management

The OS also controls how memory is accessed, maximizing the use of available memory and storage to provide optimum efficiency. The memory-management feature of many OSs allows

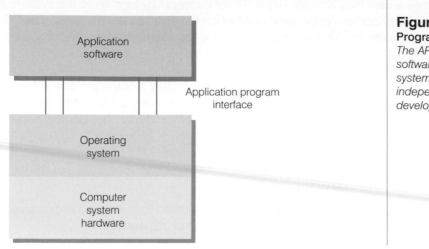

Figure 4.3 Application Program Interface (API)
The API links application software to the operating system, providing hardware independence for software developers.

4

the computer to execute program instructions effectively and to speed processing. One way to increase the performance of an old computer is to upgrade to a newer OS and increase the amount of memory.

Most OSs support *virtual memory*, which allocates space on the hard disc to supplement the immediate, functional memory capacity of RAM. Virtual memory works by swapping programs or parts of programs between memory and one or more disc devices – a concept called paging. This procedure reduces CPU idle time and increases the number of jobs that can run in a given time span.

Processing Tasks

The task-management features of today's OSs manage all processing activities. Task management allocates computer resources to make the best use of each system's assets. Task-management software lets one user run several programs or tasks at the same time (multitasking) and allows several users to use the same computer at the same time (time sharing).

An OS with multitasking capabilities allows a user to run more than one application at the same time. While you're working in the *foreground* in one program, one or more other applications can be churning away, unseen, in the *background*. Background activities include tasks such as sorting a database, printing a document, or performing other lengthy operations that otherwise would monopolize your computer and leave you staring at the screen unable to perform other work. Multitasking can save users a considerable amount of time and effort. *Time sharing* allows more than one person to use a computer system at the same time. For example, 15 customer service representatives might enter sales data into a computer system for a mail-order company at the same time. The ability of the computer to handle an increasing number of concurrent users smoothly is called *scalability*. This feature is critical for systems expected to handle a large and possibly fluctuating number of users, such as a mainframe computer or a web server.

Networking Capability

Most operating systems include networking capabilities so that computers can join together in a network to send and receive data and share computing resources. Operating systems for larger server computers are designed specifically for computer networking environments.

Access to System Resources and Security

Because computers often handle sensitive data that can be accessed over networks, the OS needs to provide a high level of security against unauthorized access to the users' data and programs. Typically, the OS establishes a logon procedure that requires users to enter an identification code, such as a user name and a matching password. Operating systems may also control what system resources a user may access. When a user successfully logs on to the system, the OS restricts access to only portions of the system for which the user has been cleared. The OS records who is using the system and for how long, and reports any attempted breaches of security.

File Management

The OS manages files to ensure that files in secondary storage are available when needed and that they are protected from access by unauthorized users. Many computers support multiple users who store files on centrally located discs or tape drives. The OS keeps track of where each file is stored and who can access them.

Current Operating Systems

Today's operating systems incorporate sophisticated features and impressive graphic effects. Table 4.2 classifies a few current OSs by sphere of influence.

Table 4.2 Operating Systems Serving Three Spheres of Influence

Personal	Workgroup	Enterprise
Microsoft Windows	Microsoft Windows Server	Microsoft Windows Server
Mac OS X, Mac OS X iPhone	Mac OS X Server	
Linux	Linux	Linux
Google Android, Chrome OS		
HP webOS		
	UNIX	UNIX
	IBM i and z/OS	IBM i and z/OS
	HP-UX	HP-UX

Microsoft PC Operating Systems

Since a once small company called Microsoft developed PC-DOS and MS-DOS to support the IBM personal computer introduced in the 1980s, personal computer OSs have steadily evolved. PC-DOS and MS-DOS had command-driven interfaces that were difficult to learn and use. MS-DOS gave way to Windows, which opened the PC market to everyday users. Windows evolved through several versions, including Windows 1.01, 2.03, 3.0 and 3.1, Windows 95, 98 and Me, Windows NT, Windows 2000, Windows XP, Windows Vista, Windows 7 and Windows 8.

Windows XP (XP reportedly stands for the positive experience that you will have with your personal computer) was released in the autumn of 2001. In 2007, Microsoft released *Windows Vista* to the public, introducing it as the most secure version of Windows ever. The next version, *Windows 7*, was released in 2009 with improvements and new features. Many analysts classified Windows 7 as 'Vista done right'. Windows 7 has strong support for touch displays and netbooks, ushering in a new era of mobile computing devices. Windows 7 is available in configurations designed for 32-bit or 64-bit processors. Users running newer computers are advised to install the 64-bit version, if their computers can support it, to experience faster processor performance.[10]

Microsoft Windows 8, released in 2012, offers a number of enhancements, including features for tablet computers.[11] Windows 8 includes a touch interface and many new features for the consumer market.[12] The home screen displays colourful application 'tiles' instead of icons.[13] Windows 8 is available for a number of platforms, including smartphones, tablet computers, PCs and servers.[14] According to one industry analyst, 'They're betting the farm on this one. Microsoft's problem is how do they keep the existing customer base with Windows while addressing touch?' Many smartphone and mobile device makers plan to use Microsoft's Windows operating system in their devices.[15]

Apple Computer Operating Systems

In July 2001, Mac OS X was released as an entirely new OS for the Mac based on the UNIX operating system. It included a new user interface, which provided a new visual appearance for users – including luminous and semitransparent elements, such as buttons, scroll bars, windows and fluid animation to enhance the user's experience.

Since its first release, Apple has upgraded OS X several times. OS X v 10.10 Yosemite is Apple's latest operating system.[16] It offers multitouch, full-screen applications, mission control features and other innovations. It also incorporates many features of Apple's mobile devices into Apple's desktop and laptop computers.[17] Yosemite can also automatically save a document every time a change is made to an application, such as a word-processing or spreadsheet application. In one survey, ease of use, the number of available applications, and overall user appeal for Apple's mobile operating system (iOS) received high ratings.[18]

Because Mac OS X runs on Intel processors, Mac users can set up their computer to run both Windows and Mac OS X and select which platform they want to work with when they boot their computer. Such an arrangement is called *dual booting*. While Macs can dual boot into Windows, the opposite is not true. Apple does not allow OS X to be run on any machine other than an Apple. However, Windows PCs can dual boot with Linux and other OSs.

Linux

Linux is an OS developed by Linus Torvalds in 1991 as a student in Finland. The OS is distributed under the *GNU General Public Licence*, and its source code is freely available to everyone. It is, therefore, called an *open-source* operating system. This designation doesn't mean, however, that Linux and its assorted distributions are necessarily free – companies and developers can charge money for a distribution as long as the source code remains available. Linux is actually only the kernel of an OS, the part that controls hardware, manages files, separates processes and so forth.

Several combinations of Linux are available, with various sets of capabilities and applications to form a complete OS. Each of these combinations is called a *distribution* of Linux. Many distributions are available as free downloads.

Linux is available on the Internet and from other sources. Popular versions include Red Hat Linux, OpenSUSE and Caldera OpenLinux. Several large computer vendors, including IBM, Hewlett-Packard and Intel, support the Linux operating system. Although Linux is free software, Red Hat had revenues of about $0.75 billion in 2011 distributing and servicing the software.[19]

Information Systems @ Work

Linux in Business

If you use a computer as a university business student, odds are that it runs either Microsoft Windows or Apple Mac OS. Few students outside computer science, and even fewer business school computer labs, use any other platform.

That's not the case in business. In May 2012 about 65 per cent of 662 million web servers surveyed used the Linux operating system, described in this chapter, to run a web server application called Apache. Apache's market share fluctuates but has

(continued)

been above 40 per cent since 1997. Linux is popular among businesses in other application areas as well.

Why do businesses use Linux? Their reasons for choosing it vary. For PrintedArt, an online shop that sells limited editions of fine art photography, the reasons involved the availability of open-source applications developed for Linux. President and CEO of PrintedArt, Klaus Sonnenleiter, explains the company's choice of the open-source package Drupal for managing web content. 'Before settling on Drupal, we went through a major evaluation shoot-out between the different CMS [Content Management System] options. After looking at a fairly large number of options, Joomla, Drupal, Alfresco and Typo3 became the finalists. Drupal came out on top because of its layered API [Application Program Interface] that lets PrintedArt … create their own integrations and modules.'

Ubercart, the free open-source e-commerce shopping cart module, is also a core part of the PrintedArt system. 'In addition, we use Capsule running as a Google App as our CRM', Sonnenleiter adds. 'We also use MailChimp, and we are evaluating Producteev as our project and to do-list manager.'

Gompute of Göteborg, Sweden, is larger than the six-person PrintedArt. Gompute operates a cluster of 336 IBM servers to provide high-performance computing on demand for technical and scientific users. Those people use Gompute's computers in fields such as fluid dynamics, stress analysis and computational chemistry. Linux gives them the ability to run the variety of applications that the company's customers require. These include proprietary applications such as ANSYS for computer-aided engineering and PERMAS for structural analysis for which users must purchase a licence, and open-source programs such as OpenFOAM for advanced computation, which are free for anyone

to use. If none of these applications meet a user's needs, users can write their own programs and then run them on Gompute's advanced hardware.

The Linux groundswell in business is so strong that not even Microsoft is immune. In June 2012 Microsoft announced that its Azure cloud-computing service will let customers run Linux as well as Windows. Linux provides important features in this environment, such as the ability to retain data even after a virtual machine is rebooted. By offering Linux, Microsoft can pursue customers that need data retention and other Linux capabilities.

Questions

1 If you use Windows or Mac OS, did you consider Linux as a possible operating system when you bought your present computer? If not, why not? If you did consider Linux, why did you reject it? If you use Linux, why did you choose Linux over Windows and Mac OS? What advantages and disadvantages have you found since you made that choice? Would you make the same choice again?

2 As the case mentions, about two-thirds of all web servers run Linux but only about 1 per cent of personal computers do. What factors do you think account for this difference?

3 Basic applications are available for all operating systems. Beyond those applications, some users depend on packages while others tend to write their own applications. How does application availability affect their choice of an operating system?

4 Microsoft support for Linux in its Azure cloud-computing service could increase Azure revenue but could also decrease Windows revenue. Discuss the pros and cons of offering Azure support from a business standpoint.

Google

Over the years, Google has extended its reach from providing the most popular search engine to application software (Google Docs), mobile operating system (Android), web browser (Chrome) and, more recently, PC operating system – *Chrome OS*.[20] Today, over 100 million people are using Google's Android operating system in smartphones and mobile devices.[21] This number is up from less than 10 million users in 2009. Some believe that the number of Android users could explode to more than 200 million in a few years or less.

Google's Gingerbread operating system was designed for smartphones and other mobile devices, such as Samsung's Galaxy Note.[22] Chrome OS is a Linux-based operating system for netbooks and nettops, which are notebooks and desktop PCs primarily used to access web-based information and services such as email, web browsing, social networks and Google online applications. The OS is designed to run on inexpensive low-power computers. Chrome OS for personal computers doesn't need application software.[23] All applications can be accessed through the Internet. An open-source version of Chrome OS, named Chromium OS, was made available at the end of 2009. Because it is open-source software, developers can customize the source code to run on different platforms, incorporating unique features.

Workgroup Operating Systems

To keep pace with user demands, the technology of the future must support a world in which network usage, data-storage requirements and data-processing speeds increase at a dramatic rate. Powerful and sophisticated OSs are needed to run the servers that meet these business needs for workgroups.

Windows Server

Microsoft designed *Windows Server* to perform a host of tasks that are vital for websites and corporate web applications. For example, Microsoft Windows Server can be used to coordinate large data centres. It delivers benefits such as a powerful web server management system, virtualization tools that allow various operating systems to run on a single server, advanced security features and robust administrative support. Windows Home Server allows individuals to connect multiple PCs, storage devices, printers and other devices into a home network.[24] It provides a convenient way to store and manage photos, video, music and other digital content. It also provides backup and data recovery functions.

UNIX

UNIX is a powerful OS originally developed by AT&T for minicomputers – the predecessors of servers that are larger than PCs and smaller than mainframes. Ken Thompson, one of the creators of the UNIX operating system, was awarded the Japan Prize, a prize for outstanding contribution to science and technology.[25] UNIX can be used on many computer system types and platforms including workstations, servers and mainframe computers. UNIX also makes it much easier to move programs and data among computers or to connect mainframes and workstations to share resources. There are many variants of UNIX, including HP/UX from Hewlett-Packard, AIX from IBM and Solaris from Oracle. Oracle's Solaris operating system manages eBay's systems, including database servers, web servers, tape libraries and identity management systems. The online auction company found that when it switched to Solaris, system performance increased.[26]

Red Hat Linux

Red Hat Software offers a Linux network OS that taps into the talents of tens of thousands of volunteer programmers who generate a steady stream of improvements for the Linux OS. The *Red Hat Linux* network OS is very efficient at serving web pages and can manage a cluster of up to eight servers. Distributions such as SuSE and Red Hat have proven Linux to be a very stable and efficient OS. Red Hat's newest version of Red Hat Enterprise Virtualization (RHEV) software no longer requires Windows Server software to operate.[27] According to a director of Red Hat's virtualization business, 'We're in a really good position to capitalize on the growing demand for alternatives to VMware.' RHEV provides virtualization capabilities for servers and desktop computers.[28] Other vendors are also investigating virtualization for open-source software such as Linux.[29]

Mac OS X Server

The *Mac OS X Server* is the first modern server OS from Apple Computer and is based on the UNIX OS. The most recent version is OS X v 10.10 Yosemite Server. It includes support for 64-bit processing, along with several server functions and features that allow the easy management of network and Internet services such as email, website hosting, calendar management and sharing, wikis and podcasting.

Enterprise Operating Systems

Mainframe computers, often referred to as 'Big Iron', provide the computing and storage capacity to meet massive data-processing requirements and offer many users high performance and excellent system availability, strong security and scalability. In addition, a wide range of application software has been developed to run in the mainframe environment, making it possible to purchase software to address almost any business problem. Examples of mainframe OSs include z/OS from IBM, HP-UX from Hewlett-Packard and Linux. The *z/OS* is IBM's first 64-bit enterprise OS. It supports IBM's mainframes that can come with up to sixteen 64-bit processors.[30] (The z stands for zero downtime.) The *HP-UX* is a robust UNIX-based OS from Hewlett-Packard designed to handle a variety of business tasks, including online transaction processing and web applications. HP-UX supports Hewlett-Packard's computers and those designed to run Intel's Itanium processors.

Operating Systems for Small Computers, Embedded Computers and Special-Purpose Devices

New OSs are changing the way we interact with smartphones, mobile phones, digital cameras, TVs and other digital electronics devices. Companies around the world are developing operating systems for these devices. Alibaba Cloud Computing, a part of the Chinese Alibaba Group, has developed an operating system for smartphones and mobile devices.[31] This operating system will compete with operating systems from Google, Apple and Microsoft in China.[32] Hewlett-Packard is hoping that car and appliance makers will increasingly use its webOS operating system.[33] The webOS uses a touch interface and allows people to connect to the Internet.[34] According to a company spokesperson, 'We're looking at expanding the base and bringing to the webOS an ecosystem that inspires developers.'

These OSs are also called *embedded operating systems* or just *embedded systems* because they are typically embedded within a device. Embedded systems are typically designed to perform specialized tasks. For example, an automotive embedded system might be responsible for controlling fuel injection. A digital camera's embedded system supports taking and viewing photos and may include a limited set of editing tools. A GPS device uses an embedded system to help people find their way around town or more remote areas. Some of the more popular OSs for devices are described in the following section.

Mobile Phone Embedded Systems and Operating Systems

Mobile phones have traditionally used embedded systems to provide communication and limited personal information management services to users. *Symbian*, a popular mobile phone embedded OS, has traditionally provided voice and text communication, an address book and a few other basic applications. Nokia has introduced three new mobile phones using its updated Symbian operating system.[35] According to the head of sales for Nokia, 'We will use Symbian to introduce competitive products that offer more choice at affordable prices to people all over this world.' When RIM introduced the BlackBerry smartphone in 2002, the mobile phone's capabilities were vastly expanded.[36] Since then, mobile phone embedded systems have transformed into full-fledged personal computer OSs such as the iPhone OS, Google Android and Microsoft Windows Mobile. Even traditional embedded systems such as Palm OS (now webOS) and Symbian have evolved into PC operating systems with APIs and software development kits that allow developers to design hundreds of applications providing a myriad of mobile services.

Windows Embedded

Windows Embedded is a family of Microsoft OSs included with or embedded into small computer devices.[37] Windows Embedded includes several versions that provide computing power for TV set top boxes, automated industrial machines, media players, medical devices, digital cameras, PDAs, GPS receivers, ATMs, gaming devices and business devices such as cash registers. Windows Embedded Automotive provides a computing platform for automotive software such as Ford Sync. The Ford Sync system uses an in-dashboard display and wireless networking technologies to link automotive systems with mobile phones and portable media players.[38]

Proprietary Linux-Based Systems

Because embedded systems are usually designed for a specific purpose in a specific device, they are usually proprietary or custom-created and owned by the manufacturer. Sony's Wii, for example, uses a custom-designed OS based on the Linux kernel. Linux is a popular choice for embedded systems because it is free and highly configurable. It has been used in many embedded systems, including e-book readers, ATM machines, mobile phones, networking devices and media players.

Utility Programs

Utility programs help to perform a variety of tasks. For example, some utility programs merge and sort sets of data, keep track of computer jobs being run, compress files of data before they are stored or transmitted over a network (thus saving space and time) and perform other important tasks. Parallels Desktop is a popular utility that allows Apple Mac computers to run Windows programs.[39] The utility, which costs under €75, creates a virtual Windows machine inside a Mac computer.

utility program Program that helps to perform maintenance or correct problems with a computer system.

Another type of utility program allows people and organizations to take advantage of unused computer power over a network. Often called *grid computing*, this approach can be very efficient and less expensive than purchasing additional hardware or computer equipment. CERN, home of the Large Hadron Collider (LHC), the world's largest scientific instrument, is also home to one of the world's largest scientific grid computing and storage systems. The LHC Computing Grid (LCG) project provides scientists around the world with access to shared computer power and storage systems over the Internet.[40] In 2012, this project helped identify a particle that may be the Higgs boson, also called the 'God Particle' by some people.

Although many PC utility programs come installed on computers, you can also purchase utility programs separately. The following sections examine some common types of utilities.

Hardware Utilities

Some hardware utilities are available from companies such as Symantec, which produces Norton Utilities. Hardware utilities can check the status of all parts of the PC, including hard discs, memory, modems, speakers and printers. Disc utilities check the hard disc's boot sector, file allocation tables and directories, and analyze them to ensure that the hard disc is not damaged. Disc utilities can also optimize the placement of files on a crowded disc.

Security Utilities

Computer viruses and spyware from the Internet and other sources can be a nuisance – and sometimes can completely disable a computer. Antivirus and antispyware software can be installed to constantly monitor and protect the computer. If a virus or spyware is found, most of the time it can be removed. It is also a good idea to protect computer systems with firewall software. Firewall software filters incoming and outgoing packets, making sure that neither hackers nor their tools are attacking the system. Symantec, McAfee and Microsoft are the most popular providers of security software.

File-Compression Utilities

File-compression programs can reduce the amount of disc space required to store a file or reduce the time it takes to transfer a file over the Internet. Both Windows and Mac operating systems let you compress or decompress files and folders. A zip file has a .zip extension, and its contents can be easily unzipped to the original size. *MP3 (Motion Pictures Experts Group-Layer 3)* is a popular file-compression format used to store, transfer and play music and audio files, such as podcasts – audio programs that can be downloaded from the Internet.

Spam-Filtering Utilities

Receiving unwanted email (spam) can be a frustrating waste of time. Email software and services include spam-filtering utilities to assist users with these annoyances. Email filters identify spam by learning what the user considers spam and routing it to a junk mail folder. However, this method is insufficient for protecting enterprise-level email systems where spam containing viruses is a serious threat. Businesses often use additional spam-filtering software from companies including Cisco, Barracuda Networks and Google at the enterprise level to intercept dangerous spam as it enters the corporate email system.

Network and Internet Utilities

A broad range of network- and systems-management utility software is available to monitor hardware and network performance and trigger an alert when a server is crashing or a network problem occurs.[41] IBM's Tivoli Netcool and Hewlett-Packard's Automated Network Management Suite can be used to solve computer-network problems and help save money.[42] In one survey, about 60 per cent of responding organizations used monitoring software to determine if their Internet sites and Internet applications were running as expected.

Server and Mainframe Utilities

Some utilities enhance the performance of servers and mainframe computers. James River Insurance uses a utility program from Confio to help it monitor the performance of its computer systems and databases.[43] According to a manager for James River, 'We take a proactive approach to database management to ensure we maintain high availability and performance in our virtual and physical environments.' IBM and other companies have created systems-management software that allows a support person to monitor the growing number of desktop computers attached to a server or mainframe computer. Similar to the virtual machine software discussed earlier, *server virtualization software* allows a server to run more than one operating system at the same time. For example, you could run four different virtual servers simultaneously on one physical server.

Other Utilities

Utility programs are available for almost every conceivable task or function. Managing the vast array of operating systems for smartphones and mobile devices, for example, has been difficult for many companies. In one survey, two-thirds of responding organizations allowed managers and workers to connect to corporate databases using smartphones and mobile devices with very little or no guidance or supervision.[44] Utility programs can help. Research in Motion (RIM) has developed a utility program that helps companies manage mobile phones and mobile devices from its company and others.[45] Often called *mobile device management (MDM)*, this type of software should help companies as smartphones and other mobile devices become more popular for managers and workers in a business setting. MDM software helps a company manage security, enforce corporate strategies, and control downloads and content streaming from corporate databases into smartphones and mobile devices. In addition, a number of companies, such as CNET, offer utilities that can be downloaded for most popular operating systems.[46]

Middleware

Middleware is software that allows various systems to communicate and exchange data. It is often developed to address situations where a company acquires different types of information systems through mergers, acquisitions, or expansion and wants the systems to share data and interact. Middleware can also serve as an interface between the Internet and private corporate systems. For example, it can be used to transfer a request for information from a corporate customer on the corporate website to a traditional database on a mainframe computer and return the results to the customer on the Internet.

The use of middleware to connect disparate systems has evolved into an approach for developing software and systems called SOA. A **service-oriented architecture (SOA)** uses modular application services to allow users to interact with systems and systems to interact with each other. Systems developed with SOA are flexible and ideal for businesses that need a system to expand and evolve over time. SOA modules can be reused for a variety of purposes, thus reducing development time. Because SOA modules are designed using programming standards so that they can interact with other modules, rigid custom-designed middleware software is not needed to connect systems.

middleware Software that allows various systems to communicate and exchange data.

service-oriented architecture (SOA) A modular method of developing software and systems that allows users to interact with systems and systems to interact with each other.

4

4.3 Application Software

As discussed earlier in this chapter, the primary function of application software is to apply the power of the computer to give people, workgroups and the entire enterprise the ability to solve problems and perform specific tasks. One debt collection agency, for example, was able to save more than €180 000 annually by using application software from Latitude to monitor people not paying their bills on time.[47] Applications help you perform common tasks, such as create and format documents, perform calculations or manage information. Some applications are more specialized. Accenture, for example, offers application software specifically for the property and causality insurance industry.[48] NB Publishers in South Africa use application software to format books so they can be read on e-readers.[49] Yusen Logistics in Australia uses application software to calculate its costs and to route packages from sender to receiver.[50] New passenger-screening software at the Tulsa International Airport has streamlined the check-in process and reduced privacy concerns.[51] The software, called automated target recognition, uses a new full-body scanning technology. The US Army is testing new application software on smartphones and tablet computers in combat zones.[52] The military software will help commanders and combat troops analyze surveillance video and data from battlefields to help them locate and eliminate enemy troops, giving new meaning to the term 'killer app'.

Overview of Application Software

Proprietary software and off-the-shelf software are important types of application software. **Proprietary software** is one-of-a-kind software designed for a specific application and owned by the company, organization or person that uses it. Proprietary software can give a company a competitive advantage by providing services or solving problems in a unique manner, better than methods used by a competitor. **Off-the-shelf software** is mass-produced by software vendors to address needs that are common across businesses, organizations or individuals. For example, Amazon uses the same off-the-shelf payroll software as many businesses, but the company uses custom-designed

proprietary software One-of-a-kind software designed for a specific application and owned by the company, organization, or person that uses it.

off-the-shelf software Software mass-produced by software vendors to address needs that are common across businesses, organizations or individuals.

proprietary software on its website that allows visitors to more easily find items to purchase. The relative advantages and disadvantages of proprietary software and off-the-shelf software are summarized in Table 4.3.

Table 4.3 Comparison of Proprietary and Off-the-Shelf Software

Proprietary Software		Off-the-Shelf Software	
Advantages	**Disadvantages**	**Advantages**	**Disadvantages**
You can get exactly what you need in terms of features, reports and so on	It can take a long time and significant resources to develop required features	The initial cost is lower because the software firm can spread the development costs over many customers	An organization might have to pay for features that are not required and never used
Being involved in the development offers control over the results	In-house system development staff may be hard pressed to provide the required level of ongoing support and maintenance because of pressure to move on to other new projects	The software is likely to meet the basic business needs – you can analyze existing features and the performance of the package before purchasing	The software might lack important features, thus requiring future modification or customization. This lack can be very expensive because users must adopt future releases of the software as well
You can modify features that you might need to counteract an initiative by competitors or to meet new supplier or customer demands	The features and performance of software that has yet to be developed present more potential risk	The package is likely to be of high quality because many customer firms have tested the software and helped identify its bugs	The software might not match current work processes and data standards

Many companies use off-the-shelf software to support business processes. Key questions for selecting off-the-shelf software include the following. First, will the software run on the OS and hardware you have selected? Second, does the software meet the essential business requirements that have been defined? Third, is the software manufacturer financially solvent and reliable? Finally, does the total cost of purchasing, installing and maintaining the software compare favourably to the expected business benefits?

Some off-the-shelf programs can be modified, in effect blending the off-the-shelf and customized approaches. For example, El Camino Hospital in Mountain View, California, customized Microsoft's e-health management system, Amalga, to track patients with the H1N1 flu and those that may have been exposed to it.[53]

application service provider (ASP) A company that provides the software, support and computer hardware on which to run the software from the user's facilities over a network.

Another approach to obtaining a customized software package is to use an application service provider. An **application service provider (ASP)** is a company that can provide the software, support and computer hardware on which to run the software from the user's facilities over a network. Some vendors refer to the service as *on-demand software*.

software as a service (SaaS) A service that allows businesses to subscribe to web-delivered application software.

Today, many companies are running software on the web. This approach is called **Software as a Service (SaaS)**, which allows businesses to subscribe to web-delivered application software. In most cases, the company pays a monthly service charge or a per-use fee.[54] Guardian Life Insurance, for example, implemented an actuarial application by using Amazon's Ec2 SaaS approach.[55]

According to the CIO of the company, 'We don't do anything because it's Cloud. But if the financials look right, if the risk profile looks right, if the richness and robustness look right, we go with that solution.' Like ASP, SaaS providers maintain software on their own servers and provide access to it over the Internet. SaaS usually uses a web browser-based user interface. Many business activities are supported by SaaS. Vendors include Oracle, SAP, Net Suite, Salesforce and Google. Tidewell, a hospice that serves about 8000 Florida families, acquired software from Salesforce.com to save money and streamline its operations.[56] SaaS can reduce expenses by sharing its running applications among many businesses. Some people, however, are concerned about the security of data and programs on the Internet using the SaaS approach.[57]

SaaS and new web development technologies have led to a new paradigm in computing called cloud computing.[58] *Cloud computing* refers to the use of computing resources, including software and data storage, on the Internet (the cloud) rather than on local computers. Google, for example, is launching new personal computers built by Samsung and Acer called Chromebooks that include only an Internet browser. All of the software applications are accessed through an Internet connection.[59] Businesses can get a Chromebook and Chrome OS for under €22 per user.[60] In addition, Google's email and productivity suite can be purchased for about €37 per month per individual. Rather than installing, storing and running software on your own computer, with cloud computing, you use the web browser to access software stored and delivered from a web server. Typically the data generated by the software is also stored on the web server. For example, Tableau software allows users to import databases or spreadsheet data to create powerful visualizations that provide useful information.[61] Cloud computing also provides the benefit of being able to easily collaborate with others by sharing documents on the Internet.

ASP, SaaS and cloud computing, however, involve some risks. For example, sensitive information could be compromised in a number of ways, including unauthorized access by employees or computer hackers; the host might not be able to keep its computers and network up and running as consistently as necessary; or a disaster could disable the host's data centre, temporarily putting an organization out of business. In addition, these approaches are not accepted and used by everyone.[62] According to one survey, about 15 per cent of enterprises are either using the SaaS approach or plan to use the approach in the next year. It can also be difficult to integrate the SaaS approach with existing software. According to the CIO of Hostess Brands, "Figuring out integration requirements and how providers handle those and getting everything in sync have been among our tougher challenges.'

Personal Application Software

Hundreds of computer applications can help people at school, home and work. New computer software under development and existing GPS technology, for example, will allow people to see 3D views of where they are, along with directions and 3D maps to where they would like to go. Absolute software, which uses GPS technology, helps people and organizations retrieve stolen computers. The company has recovered almost 10 000 devices worth over €7 million.[63] According to a special investigator for the Detroit Public Schools (DPS), 'At DPS, we've already seen the effect of these recoveries. We would have never recovered any of the 300 plus laptops stolen from our district without the aid of Absolute Software.'

The features of some popular types of personal application software are summarized in Table 4.4. In addition to these general-purpose programs, thousands of other personal computer applications perform specialized tasks that help you do your taxes, get in shape, lose weight, get medical advice, write wills and other legal documents, repair your computer, fix your car, write music, and edit your pictures and videos. This type of software, often called *user software* or *personal productivity software*, includes the general-purpose tools and programs that support individual needs.

Word-Processing

Word-processing applications are installed on most PCs today. These applications come with a vast array of features, including those for checking spelling, creating tables, inserting formulas,

Table 4.4 Examples of Personal Application Software

Type of Software	Explanation	Example
Word-processing	Create, edit and print text documents	Microsoft Word Google Docs Apple Pages Open Office Writer
Spreadsheet	Provide a wide range of built-in functions for statistical, financial, logical, database, graphics, and date and time calculations	Microsoft Excel IBM Lotus 1-2-3 Google Spreadsheet Apple Numbers Open Office Calc
Database	Store, manipulate and retrieve data	Microsoft Access IBM Lotus Approach Borland dBASE Google Base Open Office Base
Graphics	Develop graphs, illustrations and drawings	Adobe Illustrator Adobe FreeHand Microsoft PowerPoint Open Office Impress
Project management	Plan, schedule, allocate and control people and resources (money, time and technology) needed to complete a project according to schedule	Microsoft Project Symantec On Target Scitor Project Scheduler Symantec Time Line
Financial management	Provide income and expense tracking and reporting to monitor and plan budgets (some programs have investment portfolio management features)	Intuit Quicken
Desktop publishing (DTP)	Use with personal computers and high-resolution printers to create high-quality printed output, including text and graphics; various styles of pages can be laid out; art and text files from other programs can also be integrated into published pages	Quark Xpress Microsoft Publisher Adobe PageMaker Corel Ventura Publisher Apple Pages

creating graphics and much more. Much of the work required to create this book used the popular word-processing software, Microsoft Word.

A team of people can use a word-processing program to collaborate on a project. The authors and editors who developed this book, for example, used the Track Changes and Reviewing features of Microsoft Word to track and make changes to chapter files. With these features, you can add comments or make revisions to a document that a coworker can review and either accept or reject.

Spreadsheet Analysis

Spreadsheets are powerful tools for manipulating and analyzing numbers and alphanumeric data. Individuals and organizations use spreadsheets. Features of spreadsheets include formulas, statistical analysis, built-in business functions, graphics, limited database capabilities and much more. The business functions include calculation of depreciation, present value, internal rate of return and the monthly payment on a loan, to name a few. Optimization is another powerful feature of many spreadsheet programs. *Optimization* allows the spreadsheet to maximize or minimize a quantity subject to certain constraints. For example, a small furniture manufacturer that produces chairs and tables might want to maximize its profits. The constraints could be a limited supply of lumber, a limited number of workers who can assemble the chairs and tables, or a limited amount of various hardware fasteners that might be required. Using an optimization feature, such as Solver in Microsoft Excel, the spreadsheet can determine what number of chairs and tables to produce with labour and material constraints to maximize profits.

Database Applications

Database applications are ideal for storing, organizing and retrieving data. These applications are particularly useful when you need to manipulate a large amount of data and produce reports and documents. Database manipulations include merging, editing and sorting data. The uses of a database application are varied. You can keep track of a CD collection, the items in your apartment, tax records and expenses. A student club can use a database to store names, addresses, phone numbers and dues paid. In business, a database application can help process sales orders, control inventory, order new supplies, send letters to customers and pay employees. Database management systems can be used to track orders, products and customers; analyze weather data to make forecasts for the next several days; and summarize medical research results. A database can also be a front end to another application. For example, you can use a database application to enter and store income tax information and then export the stored results to other applications, such as a spreadsheet or tax-preparation application.

Presentation Graphics Program

It is often said that a picture is worth a thousand words. With today's graphics programs, it is easy to develop attractive graphs, illustrations and drawings that assist in communicating important information. Presentation graphics programs can be used to develop advertising brochures, announcements and full-colour presentations and to organize and edit photographic images. If you need to make a presentation at school or work, you can use a special type of graphics program called a presentation application to develop slides and then display them while you are speaking. Because of their popularity, many colleges and departments require students to become proficient at using presentation graphics programs.

Many graphics programs, including Microsoft PowerPoint, consist of a series of slides. Each slide can be displayed on a computer screen, printed as a handout or (more commonly) projected onto a large viewing screen for audiences. Powerful built-in features allow you to develop attractive slides and complete presentations. You can select a template for a type of presentation, such as recommending a strategy for managers, communicating news to a sales force, giving a training presentation or facilitating a brainstorming session. The presentation graphics program lets you create a presentation step-by-step, including applying colour and attractive formatting. You can also design a custom presentation using the many types of charts, drawings and formatting available. Most presentation graphics programs come with many pieces of *clip art*, such as drawings and photos of people meeting, medical equipment, telecommunications equipment, entertainment and much more.

Personal Information Managers

Personal information management (PIM) software helps people, groups and organizations store useful information, such as a list of tasks to complete or a set of names and addresses. PIM software usually provides an appointment calendar, an address book or contacts list, and a place to take notes. In addition, information in a PIM can be linked. For example, you can link an appointment with a sales manager in the calendar to information on the sales manager in the address book. When you click the appointment in the calendar, a window opens displaying information on the sales manager from the address book. Microsoft Outlook is an example of very popular PIM software. Increasingly, PIM software is moving online where it can be accessed from any Internet-connected device.

Some PIMs allow you to schedule and coordinate group meetings. If a computer or handheld device is connected to a network, you can upload the PIM data and coordinate it with the calendar and schedule of others using the same PIM software on the network. You can also use some PIMs to coordinate emails inviting others to meetings. As users receive their invitations, they click a link or button to be automatically added to the guest list.

Software Suites and Integrated Software Packages

software suite A collection of single programs packaged together in a bundle.

A **software suite** is a collection of single programs packaged together in a bundle. Software suites can include a word-processor, spreadsheet program, database management system, graphics program, communications tools, organizers and more. Some suites support the development of web pages, note taking and speech recognition so that applications in the suite can accept voice commands and record dictation. Software suites offer many advantages. The software programs have been designed to work similarly so that, after you learn the basics for one application, the other applications are easy to learn and use. Buying software in a bundled suite is cost effective; the programs usually sell for a fraction of what they would cost individually.

Microsoft Office, Corel WordPerfect Office, Lotus SmartSuite and Sun Microsystems Open-Office are examples of popular general-purpose software suites for personal computer users. Microsoft Office has the largest market share. Most of these software suites include a spreadsheet program, word processor, database program and graphics presentation software. All can exchange documents, data and diagrams (see Table 4.5). In other words, you can create a spreadsheet and then cut and paste that spreadsheet into a document created using the word-processing application.

Table 4.5 Major Components of Leading Software Suites

Personal Productivity Function	Microsoft Office	Lotus Symphony	Corel WordPerfect Office	Open Office	AppleiWork	Google
Word-Processing	Word	Documents	WordPerfect	Writer	Pages	Docs
Spreadsheet	Excel	Spreadsheets	Quattro Pro	Calc	Numbers	Spreadsheet
Presentation Graphics	PowerPoint	Presentations	Presentations	Impress and Draw	Keynote	Presentation
Database	Access			Base		

In addition to suites, some companies produce *integrated application packages* that contain several programs. For example, Microsoft Works is one program that contains a basic word processor, spreadsheet, database, address book, calendar and other applications. Although not as powerful as stand-alone software included in software suites, integrated software packages offer a range of capabilities for less money. QuickOffice can be used on tablet computers and smartphones to read and edit Microsoft Office documents.[64] Onlive can also be used to open and edit Microsoft Office documents on an Apple iPad.[65] Some integrated packages cost about €75.

Some companies offer web-based productivity software suites that require no installation – only a web browser. Zoho, Google and Thinkfree offer free online word processor, spreadsheet, presentation and other software that require no installation on the PC. Adobe has developed

Acrobat.com, a suite of programs that can be used to create and combine Adobe PDF (Portable Document Format) files, convert PDF files to Microsoft Word or Excel files, create web forms and more.[66] After observing this trend, Microsoft responded with an online version of some of its popular Office applications. Office 365 offers basic software suite features over the Internet using cloud computing.[67] The cloud-based applications can cost €7 per user per month depending on the features used.[68] Microsoft offers plans for professionals and small businesses, enterprises and education. Some believe that Office 365 has advantages over many other online suites.[69] According to the director of online services at Microsoft, 'With Office 365, businesses of all sizes can get the same robust capabilities that have given larger businesses an edge for years.'[70] The city of Winston-Salem, North Carolina, for example, used Office 365 to save money and place software applications on the Internet. According to the CIO of the city, 'I have to improve technology with a constrained budget. Because we were able to package Microsoft cloud and local products in one enterprise agreement, we ended up with more bang for no additional cost.' The online versions of Word, Excel, PowerPoint and OneNote are tightly integrated with Microsoft's desktop Office suite for easy sharing of documents among computers and collaborators.

Other Personal Application Software

In addition to the software already discussed, people can use many other interesting and powerful application software tools. In some cases, the features and capabilities of these applications can more than justify the cost of an entire computer system. TurboTax, for example, is a popular tax-preparation program. You can find software for creating web pages and sites, composing music, and editing photos and videos. Many people use educational and reference software and entertainment, games and leisure software. Game-playing software is popular and can be very profitable for companies that develop games and various game accessories, including virtual avatars such as colourful animals, fish and people.[71] Game-playing software has even been used as therapy for young children and adults recovering from cancer and other diseases.[72] According to a hospital executive, 'It's a very motivating tool for the patients. It's visual, the feedback is instant, and it's fun.' Some believe that online game players may have solved an important AIDS research question.[73] Engineers, architects and designers often use computer-aided design (CAD) software to design and develop buildings, electrical systems, plumbing systems and more. Autosketch, CorelCAD and AutoCad are examples of CAD software. Other programs perform a wide array of statistical tests. Colleges and universities often have a number of courses in statistics that use this type of application software. Two popular applications in the social sciences are SPSS and SAS.

Mobile Application Software

The number of applications (apps) for smartphones and other mobile devices has exploded in recent years. Besides the valuable mobile applications that come with these devices, tens of thousands of applications have been developed by third parties. For example, iPhone users can download and install thousands of applications using Apple's App Store.[74] Many iPhone apps are free, while others range in price from 99 cents to hundreds of dollars. Thousands of mobile apps are available in the Android Market for users of Android handsets. Microsoft and other software companies are also investing in mobile applications for devices that run on its software.[75] SceneTap, an application for iPhones and Android devices, can determine the number of people at participating bars, pubs or similar establishments, and the ratio of males to females.[76] This approach uses video cameras and facial recognition software to identify males and females. SocialCamera, an application for Android phones, allows people to take a picture of someone and then search their Facebook friends for a match.[77] New facial-recognition software developed at Carnegie Mellon University was able to correctly identify about one-third of the people tested from a simple photograph from a mobile phone or camera.[78] Facial-recognition software, however, could be a potential invasion to privacy.[79] The market for mobile application software for smartphones and mobile devices could reach €60 billion by 2017.[80] Table 4.6 lists a few mobile application categories.

Table 4.6 Categories of Mobile Applications for Smartphones

Category	Description
Books and reference	Access e-books, subscribe to journals or look up information in Webster's or Wikipedia
Business and finance	Track expenses, trade stocks and access corporate information systems
Entertainment	Access all forms of entertainment, including movies, television programs, music videos and local night life
Games	Play a variety of games, from 2D games such as Pacman and Tetris, to 3D games such as Need for Speed, Rock Band and The Sims
Health and fitness	Track workout and fitness progress, calculate calories, and even monitor your speed and progress from your wirelessly connected Nike shoes
Lifestyle	Find good restaurants, select wine for a meal and more
Music	Find, listen to and create music
News and weather	Access major news and weather providers including Reuters, AP, the *New York Times* and the Weather Channel
Photography	Organize, edit, view and share photos taken on your camera phone
Productivity and utilities	Create grocery lists, practice PowerPoint presentations, work on spreadsheets, synchronize with PC files and more
Social networking	Connect with others via major social networks including Facebook, Twitter and MySpace
Sports	Keep up with your favourite team or track your own golf scores
Travel and navigation	Use the GPS in your smartphone to get turn-by-turn directions, find interesting places to visit, access travel itineraries and more

Workgroup Application Software

workgroup application software Software that supports teamwork, whether team members are in the same location or dispersed around the world.

Workgroup application software is designed to support teamwork, whether team members are in the same location or dispersed around the world. This support can be accomplished with software known as *groupware* that helps groups of people work together effectively. Microsoft Exchange Server, for example, has groupware and email features.[81] Also called *collaborative software*, this approach allows a team of managers to work on the same production problem, letting them share their ideas and work via connected computer systems.

Examples of workgroup software include group-scheduling software, electronic mail and other software that enables people to share ideas. Lotus Notes and Domino are examples of workgroup software from IBM. Web-based software is ideal for group use. Because documents are stored on an Internet server, anyone with an Internet connection can access them easily. Google provides options in its online applications that allow users to share documents, spreadsheets, presentations, calendars and notes with other specified users or everyone on the web. This sharing makes it convenient for several people to contribute to a document without concern for software compatibility or storage. Google also provides a tool for creating web-based forms and surveys. When invited parties fill out the form, the data is stored in a Google spreadsheet.

Enterprise Application Software

Software that benefits an entire organization – enterprise application software – can also be developed specifically for the business or purchased off the shelf. The Copper Mountain Ski Resort used Visual One software from Agilysys to manage condominiums and other real estate holdings.[82] According to the information technology director, 'We need a dynamic software system that allows us to manage our rather complex condominium lodging model.' More CPA firms are acquiring sophisticated tax software for their corporate clients.[83] According to a manager at the Citrin Cooper CPA firm, 'The number of available software programs has expanded in recent years. At the same time, more specialized software is available that focuses on individual industries.' Verafin has developed specialized software that helps banks find people and organizations that attempt to launder money.[84] The software works by looking for suspicious transactions or patterns in large databases of financial transactions.[85]

Enterprise software also helps managers and workers stay connected. Traditional email might not be the best approach.[86] According to the vice president of a large publishing company, 'If you have a really important message you need to get to people; email is where it goes to die. People need a sense of ambient awareness.' This type of awareness can come from enterprise software and group support systems, first introduced in Chapter 1. The following are some applications that can be addressed with enterprise software:

Accounts payable	Invoicing
Accounts receivable	Manufacturing control
Airline industry operations	Order entry
Automatic teller systems	Payroll
Cash-flow analysis	Receiving
Check processing	Restaurant management
Credit and charge card administration	Retail operations
Distribution control	Sales ordering
Fixed asset accounting	Savings and time deposits
General ledger	Shipping
Human resource management	Stock and bond management
Inventory control	Tax planning and preparation

According to a survey, cost is the greatest concern for selecting enterprise software.[87] Other factors include the difficulty to install and manage enterprise software and the ability to integrate enterprise software with other software applications. Increasingly, enterprise application software is being found on smartphones and mobile devices. In one survey, over 80 per cent of respondents believe that having enterprise application software that can be used on smartphones and mobile devices was an important factor in selecting enterprise software.[88]

Application Software for Information, Decision Support and Competitive Advantage

Specialized application software for information, decision support and competitive advantage is available in every industry. For example, many schools and colleges use Blackboard or other learning management software to organize class materials and grades. Genetic researchers, as another example, are using software to visualize and analyze the human genome. Music executives use decision support software to help pick the next hit song. Companies seeking a competitive advantage, first discussed in Chapter 2, are increasingly building or developing their own enterprise software.[89] According to the CIO of the New York Stock Exchange Euronext, 'Building is not easy. If it were, everyone would do it and we'd get no edge.' But how are all these systems actually developed and built? The answer is through the use of programming languages, which is discussed next.

4.4 Programming Languages

Both system and application software are written in coding schemes called *programming languages*. The primary function of a programming language is to provide instructions to the computer system so that it can perform a processing activity. Information systems professionals

Ethical and Societal Issues

Software Controls Nuclear Power Plants

The safety of nuclear power plants has always been an important consideration in their design. In the wake of the Fukushima plant failure after a record tsunami in March 2011, safety has an even higher priority. Using software to control power plants offers the potential of increased safety compared to earlier methods.

Duke Energy's Oconee nuclear power plant on the eastern shore of Lake Keowee near Seneca, South Carolina, was commissioned in 1973. As it entered the twenty-first century, its older analogue control systems were showing their age. The plant suffered minor control failures during the 1990s, though no people were injured and no radiation leaked out as a result. Digital controls were added to some parts of the system in the late 1990s and

early 2000s to deal with the most acute problems, but it was clear that Oconee's entire control structure needed to be replaced.

The purpose of a reactor protection system (RPS) is to protect the integrity of the plant's nuclear fuel by monitoring inputs from the reactor core. To accomplish this monitoring, application software must check sensors located throughout the reactor. If any safe operating values are exceeded, the software takes action, such as injecting cooling water or shutting the reactor down by inserting control rods.

After reviewing RPS applications, Duke Energy chose the Teleperm XS (TXS) system from Areva of France because TXS is designed to modernize existing analogue instrumentation and control systems, and because its design includes features to ensure reliability. TXS is licenced in 11 countries and was already in use in other nuclear reactors outside the USA, thus assuring Duke that Oconee would not be a test site. TXS encompasses three functional systems:

■ **Protection**: Monitoring safety parameters, enabling automatic protection and safeguard actions when an initiating event occurs.

■ **Surveillance**: Monitoring the core, rod control and reactor coolant system and performing actions to protect reactor thresholds from being breached.

■ **Priority and actuator control system**: Managing the control and monitoring of operational and safety system actuators.

Reactor Unit 1 of the Oconee facility became the first US nuclear power plant to convert to fully digital control in May 2011. Unit 3 was converted in May 2012, with Unit 2 scheduled for May 2013. The first two conversions took place, and the third will take place, during the respective reactors' scheduled refuelling shutdowns.

The nuclear power industry has recognized the importance of this instrumentation and control system upgrade. In May 2012, the Nuclear Energy Institute awarded Duke Energy its 'Best of the Best' Top Industry Practice award. Speaking at the award ceremony, Preston Gillespie, vice president at the Oconee site, said, 'When I look back over the decision of leaders that I worked for ten years ago, who had the vision of what it would take to install a safety-related digital system, I stand very much in respect of what those leaders did. They knew it would be hard; they knew the cost would be great; they knew they had to find the right partner; they knew they had to get it through the licencing process. All of this, they knew, would result in reliable and safe operation of the plant. Because of that vision, the trail is now blazed for the rest of the industry to take advantage of the fruits of their labour.'

If the conversion goes well, other nuclear power plants will likely follow Oconee's lead as soon as they can afford it, said David Lochbaum, director of the Nuclear Safety Project for the Union of Concerned Scientists: 'There are a lot of eyes on that. If it goes well, you'll probably see many people in the queue making it happen. If it doesn't go well, they are going to wait for Duke Energy to iron out the kinks.'

Questions

1 Does a computer controlling a nuclear power plant need an operating system? Justify your answer in terms of what an operating system does and whether these functions are necessary in an RPS application.

2 Duke Energy selected off-the-shelf software for Oconee rather than writing custom software (or having a software development firm write it for them). Discuss the pros and cons of these two approaches in this situation. Do you think Duke Energy made the correct choice? Why or why not?

3 At first glance, you might think a system that uses computers and software to control a nuclear plant has more ways to fail than a system that doesn't use them and is, therefore, at greater risk of failure. Why is a computer-controlled nuclear power system not at a greater risk of failure?

4 Computers are increasingly used to control systems that affect human lives. Besides nuclear power plants, examples include passenger aircraft, elevators and medical equipment. Should the programmers who write software for those systems be licenced, be certified or be required to pass standardized official examinations?

work with **programming languages**, which are sets of keywords, symbols and rules for constructing statements that people can use to communicate instructions to a computer. Programming involves translating what a user wants to accomplish into a code that the computer can understand and execute. *Program code* is the set of instructions that signal the CPU to perform circuit-switching operations. In the simplest coding schemes, a line of code typically contains a single instruction such as, 'Retrieve the data in memory address X'. As discussed in Chapter 3, the instruction is then decoded during the instruction phase of the machine cycle. Like writing a report or a paper in English, writing a

programming languages Sets of keywords, commands, symbols and rules for constructing statements by which humans can communicate instructions to a computer.

computer program in a programming language requires the programmer to follow a set of rules. Each programming language uses symbols, keywords and commands that have special meanings and usage. Each language also has its own set of rules, called the

syntax A set of rules associated with a programming language.

syntax of the language. The language syntax dictates how the symbols, keywords and commands should be combined into statements capable of conveying meaningful instructions to the CPU. Rules such as 'statements must terminate with a semicolon', and 'variable names must begin with a letter', are examples of a language's syntax. A variable is a quantity that can take on different values. Program variable names such as SALES, PAYRATE and TOTAL follow the syntax because they start with a letter, whereas variables such as %INTEREST, $TOTAL and #POUNDS do not.

The Evolution of Programming Languages

The desire for faster, more efficient, more powerful information processing has pushed the development of new programming languages. The evolution of programming languages is typically discussed in terms of generations of languages (see Table 4.7).

Table 4.7 Evolution of Programming Languages

Generation	Language	Approximate Development Date	Sample Statement or Action
First	Machine language	1940s	00010101
Second	Assembly language	1950s	MVC
Third	High-level language	1960s	READ SALES
Fourth	Query and database languages	1970s	PRINT EMPLOYEE NUMBER IF GROSS PAY > 1000
Beyond Fourth	Natural and intelligent languages	1980s	IF gross pay is greater than 40, THEN pay the employee overtime pay

Visual, Object-Oriented and Artificial Intelligence Languages

Today, programmers often use visual and object-oriented languages. In the future, they may be using artificial intelligence languages to a greater extent. In general, these languages are easier for nonprogrammers to use, compared with older generation languages.

Visual programming uses a graphical or 'visual' interface combined with text-based commands. Prior to visual programming, programmers were required to describe the windows, buttons, text boxes and menus that they were creating for an application by using only text-based programming language commands. With visual programming, the software engineer drags and drops graphical objects such as buttons and menus onto the application form. Then, using a programming language, the programmer defines the capabilities of those objects in a separate code window. Visual Basic was one of the first visual programming interfaces. Today, software engineers use Visual Basic.NET, Visual C++, Visual C# (# is pronounced "sharp" as in music) and other visual programming tools.

Many people refer to visual programming interfaces such as Visual C# as 'visual programming languages'. This custom is fine for casual references, but a lesser-known category of programming language is more truly visual. With a true visual programming language, programmers create software by manipulating programming elements only graphically, without the use of any text-based programming language commands. Examples include Alice, Mindscript and Microsoft Visual Programming Language (VPL). Visual programming languages are ideal for teaching novices the basics about programming without requiring them to memorize programming language syntax.

Some programming languages separate data elements from the procedures or actions that will be performed on them, but another type of programming language ties them together into units called *objects*. An object consists of data and the actions that can be performed on the data. For example, an object could be data about an employee and all the operations (such as payroll calculations) that might be performed on the data. Programming languages that are based on objects are called *object-oriented programming languages*. C ++ and Java are popular general-purpose object-oriented programming languages.[90] Languages used for web development, such as Javascript and PHP, are also object oriented. In fact, most popular languages in use today take the object-oriented approach – and for good reason.

Using object-oriented programming languages is like constructing a building using prefabricated modules or parts. The object containing the data, instructions and procedures is a programming building block. The same objects (modules or parts) can be used repeatedly. One of the primary advantages of an object is that it contains reusable code. In other words, the instruction code within that object can be reused in different programs for a variety of applications, just as the same basic prefabricated door can be used in two different houses. An object can relate to data on a product, an input routine or an order-processing routine. An object can even direct a computer to execute other programs or to retrieve and manipulate data. So, a sorting routine developed for a payroll application could be used in both a billing program and an inventory control program. By reusing program code, programmers can write programs for specific application problems more quickly (see Figure 4.4). By combining existing program objects with new ones, programmers can easily and efficiently develop new object-oriented programs to accomplish organizational goals.

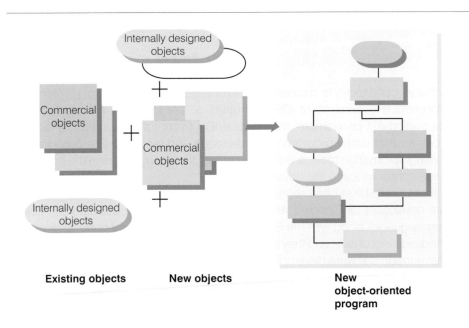

Existing objects   **New objects**   **New object-oriented program**

Figure 4.4 Reusable Code in Object-Oriented Programming *By combining existing program objects with new ones, programmers can easily and efficiently develop new object-oriented programs to accomplish organizational goals. Note that these objects can be either commercially available or designed internally.*

Programming languages used to create artificial intelligence or expert systems applications are often called *fifth-generation languages* (5GLs). Fifth-generation languages are sometimes called *natural languages* because they use even more English-like syntax than 4GLs. They allow programmers to communicate with the computer by using normal sentences. For example, computers programmed in fifth-generation languages can understand queries such as 'How many athletic shoes did our company sell last month?'

With third-generation and higher-level programming languages, each statement in the language translates into several instructions in machine language. A special software program called a **compiler** converts the programmer's source code into the machine-language instructions, which consist of binary digits, as shown in Figure 4.5. A compiler creates a two-stage process for program execution. First, the compiler translates the program into a machine language; second, the CPU executes that program. Another approach is to use an *interpreter*, which is a language translator that carries out the operations called for by the source code. An interpreter does not produce a complete machine-language program. After the statement executes, the machine-language statement is discarded, the process continues for the next statement and so on.

compiler A special software program that converts the programmer's source code into the machine-language instructions, which consist of binary digits.

4

Figure 4.5 How a Compiler Works *A compiler translates a complete program into a complete set of binary instructions (Stage 1). After this is done, the CPU can execute the converted program in its entirety (Stage 2).*

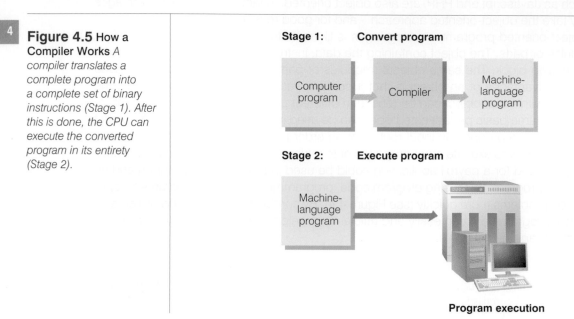

The majority of software used today is created using an integrated development environment. An *integrated development environment,* or *IDE*, combines all the tools required for software engineering into one package. For example, the popular IDE Microsoft Visual Studio includes an editor that supports several visual programming interfaces and languages, a compiler and interpreter, programming automation tools, a debugger (a tool for finding errors in the code) and other tools that provide convenience to the developer.[91]

Software Development Kits (SDKs) often serve the purpose of an IDE for a particular platform. For example, software developers for Google's Android smartphone platform use Java (an object-oriented programming language) along with the Eclipse SDK. They use special code libraries provided by Google for Android functionality, and they test out their applications in an Android Emulator.[92]

IDEs and SDKs have made software development easier than ever. Many novice coders and some who might have never considered developing software are publishing applications for popular platforms such as Facebook and the iPhone.

4.5   Software Issues and Trends

Because software is such an important part of today's computer systems, issues such as software bugs, licencing, upgrades, global software support and taxation have received increased attention. The governor of Colorado and the Colorado General Assembly, for example, repealed a tax on certain types of software.[93] The tax repeal should help Colorado's software industry. Software can also be harmful to companies and countries. For example, a foreign TV programme might have shown software to its viewers designed to attack websites in the US.[94]

Software Bugs

A software bug is a defect in a computer program that keeps it from performing as it is designed to perform.[95] Some software bugs are obvious and cause the program to terminate unexpectedly. Other bugs are subtler and allow errors to creep into your work. Computer and software vendors say that as long as people design and program hardware and software, bugs are inevitable.[96] The following list summarizes tips for reducing the impact of software bugs:

- Register all software so that you receive bug alerts, fixes and patches.
- Check the manual or read-me files for solutions to known problems.
- Access the support area of the manufacturer's website for patches.
- Install the latest software updates.
- Before reporting a bug, make sure that you can recreate the circumstances under which it occurs.
- After you can recreate the bug, call the manufacturer's tech support line.
- Consider waiting before buying the latest release of software, to give the vendor a chance to discover and remove bugs. Many schools and businesses don't purchase software until the first major revision with patches is released.

Copyrights and Licences

Most companies aggressively guard and protect the source code of their software from competitors, lawsuits and other predators.[97] As a result, most software products are protected by law using copyright or licencing provisions. Those provisions can vary, however. In some cases, you are given unlimited use of software on one or two computers. This stipulation is typical with many applications developed for personal computers. In other cases, you pay for your usage: If you use the software more, you pay more. This approach is becoming popular with software placed on networks or larger computers. Most of these protections prevent you from copying software and giving it to others. Some software now requires that you *register* or *activate* it before it can be fully used. This requirement is another way software companies prevent illegal distribution of their products.

When people purchase software, they don't actually own the software, but rather they are licenced to use the software on a computer. This is called a single-user licence. A **single-user licence** permits you to install the software on one or more computers, used by one person. A single-user licence does not allow you to copy and share the software with others. Table 4.8 describes different types of software licences. Licences that accommodate multiple users are usually provided at a discounted price.

single-user licence A software licence that permits you to install the software on one or more computers, used by one person.

Freeware and Open-Source Software

Some software developers are not as interested in profiting from their intellectual property as others and have developed alternative copyrights and licencing agreements. *Freeware* is software that is made available to the public for free.[98] Software developers might give away their product for several reasons. Some want to build customer interest and name recognition. Others simply don't need the money and want to make a valuable donation to society. Still others, such

Table 4.8 Software Licences

Licence	Description
Single-user licence	Permits you to install the software on one computer, or sometimes two computers, used by one person.
Multiuser licence	Specifies the number of users allowed to use the software and can be installed on each user's computer. For example, a 20-user licence can be installed on 20 computers for 20 users.
Concurrent-user licence	Designed for network-distributed software, this licence allows any number of users to use the software but only a specific number of users to use it at the same time.
Site licence	Permits the software to be used anywhere on a particular site, such as a college campus, by everyone on the site.

as those associated with the Free Software Foundation (www.fsf.org), believe that all software should be free. Some freeware is placed in the public domain where anyone can use the software free of charge. (Creative works that reach the end of their term of copyright revert to the public domain.) Table 4.9 shows some examples of freeware.

Table 4.9 Examples of Freeware

Software	Description
Thunderbird	Email and newsgroup software
Pidgin	Instant messaging software
Adobe Reader	Software for viewing Adobe PDF documents
AVG Anti-Virus	Antivirus security software
WinPatrol	Antispyware software
IrfanView	Photo-editing software

Freeware differs slightly from free software. Freeware simply implies that the software is distributed for free. The term free software was coined by Richard Stallman and the Free Software Foundation and implies that the software is not only freeware, but it is also open source. **Open-source software** is distributed, typically for free, with the source code also available so that it can be studied, changed and improved by its users.[99] Open-source software evolves from the combined contribution of its users. The Code For America (CFA) organization, for example, used open-source software in Boston and other American cities to help cities and municipalities solve some of their traffic problems, such as locating fire hydrants that might be completely covered with snow in the winter.[100] CFA made its efforts free to other cities and municipalities. Table 4.10 provides examples of popular open-source software applications.

Open-source software is not completely devoid of restrictions. Much of the popular free software in use today is protected by the GNU General Public Licence (GPL). The GPL grants you the right to do the following:

open-source software Software that is distributed, typically for free, with the source code also available so that it can be studied, changed and improved by its users.

- Run the program for any purpose.
- Study how the program works and adapt it to your needs.
- Redistribute copies so you can help others.
- Improve the program and release improvements to the public.

Table 4.10 Examples of Open-Source Software

Software	Category
Linux	Operating system
Open Office	Application software
MySQL	Database software
Mozilla Firefox	Internet browser
Gimp	Photo editing
OpenProj	Project management
Grisbi	Personal accounting

Software under the GPL is typically protected by a 'copyleft' (a play on the word copyright), which requires that any copies of the work retain the same licence. A copyleft work cannot be owned by any one person, and no one is allowed to profit from its distribution. The Free Software Directory (http://directory.fsf.org) lists over 5000 software titles in 22 categories licenced under the GPL.

Why would an organization run its business using software that's free? Can something that's given away over the Internet be stable, reliable or sufficiently supported to place at the core of a company's day-to-day operations? The answer is surprising – many believe that open-source software is often *more* reliable and secure than commercial software. How can this be? First, because a program's source code is readily available, users can fix any problems they discover. A fix is often available within hours of the problem's discovery. Second, because the source code for a program is accessible to thousands of people, the chances of a bug being discovered and fixed before it does any damage are much greater than with traditional software packages.

However, using open-source software does have some disadvantages. Although open-source systems can be obtained for next to nothing, the up-front costs are only a small piece of the total cost of ownership that accrues over the years that the system is in place. Some claim that open-source systems contain many hidden costs, particularly for user support or solving problems with the software. Licenced software comes with guarantees and support services while open-source software does not. Still, many businesses appreciate the additional freedom that open-source software provides. The question of software support is the biggest stumbling block to the acceptance of open-source software at the corporate level. Getting support for traditional software packages is easy – you call a company's freephone support number or access its website. But how do you get help if an open-source package doesn't work as expected? Because the open-source community lives on the Internet, you look there for help. Through use of Internet discussion areas, you can communicate with others who use the same software, and you might even reach someone who helped develop it. Users of popular open-source packages can get correct answers to their technical questions within a few hours of asking for help on the appropriate Internet forum. Another approach is to contact one of the many companies emerging to support and service such software – for example, Red Hat for Linux and Sendmail, Inc., for Sendmail. These companies offer high-quality, for-pay technical assistance.

Software Upgrades

Software companies revise their programs periodically. Software upgrades vary widely in the benefits that they provide, and what some people call a benefit others might call a drawback.

Deciding whether to upgrade to a new version of software can be a challenge for corporations and people with a large investment in software. Should the newest version be purchased when it is released? Some users do not always get the most current software upgrades or versions unless it includes significant improvements or capabilities. Developing an upgrading strategy is important for many businesses. American Express, for example, has standardized its software upgrade process around the world to make installing updated software faster and more efficient.[101] The standardized process also helps the company make sure that updated software is more stable with fewer errors and problems.

Global Software Support

Large global companies have little trouble persuading vendors to sell them software licences for even the most far-flung outposts of their company. But can those same vendors provide adequate support for their software customers in all locations? Supporting local operations is one of the biggest challenges IS teams face when putting together standardized companywide systems. Slower technology growth markets, such as Eastern Europe and Latin America, might not have any official vendor presence. Instead, large vendors such as Sybase, IBM and Hewlett-Packard typically contract with local providers to support their software.

One approach that has been gaining acceptance in North America is to outsource global support to one or more third-party distributors. The user company can still negotiate its licence with the software vendor directly, but it then hands the global support contract to a third-party supplier. The supplier acts as a middleman between software vendor and user, often providing distribution, support and invoicing.

In today's computer systems, software is an increasingly critical component. Whatever approach people and organizations take to acquire software, everyone must be aware of the current trends in the industry. Informed users are wise consumers.

Summary

Principle:

Systems and application software are critical in helping individuals and organizations achieve their goals. Software consists of programs that control the workings of the computer hardware. The two main categories of software are systems software and application software. Systems software is a collection of programs that interacts between hardware and application software and includes operating systems, utility programs and middleware. Application software can be proprietary or off the shelf and enables people to solve problems and perform specific tasks.

An operating system (OS) is a set of computer programs that controls the computer hardware to support users' computing needs. An OS converts an instruction from an application into a set of instructions needed by the hardware. This intermediary role allows hardware independence. An OS also manages memory, which involves controlling storage access and use by converting logical requests into physical locations and by placing data in the best storage space, including virtual memory.

An OS manages tasks to allocate computer resources through multitasking and time sharing. With multitasking, users can run more than one application at a time. Time sharing allows more than one person to use a computer system at the same time.

The ability of a computer to handle an increasing number of concurrent users smoothly is called *scalability*, a feature critical for systems expected to handle a large number of users.

An OS also provides a user interface, which allows users to access and command the computer. A command-based user interface requires text commands to send instructions. A graphical user interface (GUI), such as Windows, uses icons and menus. Other user interfaces include touch and speech.

Software applications use the OS by requesting services through a defined application program interface (API). Programmers can use APIs to create application software without having to understand the inner workings of the OS. APIs also provide a degree of hardware independence so that the underlying hardware can change without necessarily requiring a rewrite of the software applications.

Over the years, many popular OSs have been developed, including Microsoft Windows, the Mac OS X and Linux. There are several options for OSs in the enterprise as well, depending on the type server. UNIX is a powerful OS that can be used on many computer system types and platforms, from workstations to mainframe systems. Linux is the kernel of an OS whose source code is freely available to everyone. Some OSs, such as Mac OS X iPhone, Windows Embedded, Symbian, Android, webOS and variations of Linux, have been developed to support mobile communications and consumer appliances. When an OS is stored in solid state memory, embedded in a device, it is referred to as an embedded operating system or an embedded system for short.

Utility programs can perform many useful tasks and often come installed on computers along with the OS. This software is used to merge and sort sets of data, keep track of computer jobs being run, compress files of data, protect against harmful computer viruses, monitor hardware and network performance, and perform dozens of other important tasks. Virtualization software simulates a computer's hardware architecture in software so that computer systems can run operating systems and software designed for other architectures or run several operating systems simultaneously on one system. Middleware is software that allows different systems to communicate and transfer data back and forth.

Principle:

Organizations use off-the-shelf application software for common business needs and proprietary application software to meet unique business needs and provide a competitive advantage. Application software applies the power of the computer to solve problems and perform specific tasks. One useful way of classifying the many potential uses of information systems is to identify the scope of problems and opportunities addressed by a particular organization or its sphere of influence. For most companies, the spheres of influence are personal, workgroup and enterprise.

User software, or personal productivity software, includes general-purpose programs that enable users to improve their personal effectiveness, increasing the quality and amount of work that can be done. Software that helps groups work together is often called workgroup application software. It includes group scheduling software, electronic mail and other software that enables people to share ideas. Enterprise software that benefits the entire organization, called enterprise resource planning software, is a set of integrated programs that help manage a company's vital business operations for an entire multisite, global organization.

Three approaches to acquiring application software are to build proprietary application software, buy existing programs off the shelf, or use a combination of customized and off-the-shelf application software. Building proprietary software (in-house or on contract) has the following advantages. The organization gets software that more closely matches its needs. Further, by being involved with the development, the organization has further control over the results. Finally, the organization has more flexibility in making changes. The disadvantages include the following. It is likely to take longer and cost more to develop. Additionally, the in-house staff will be hard pressed to provide ongoing support and maintenance. Lastly, there is a greater risk that the software features will not work as expected or that other performance problems will occur.

Some organizations have taken a third approach – customizing software packages. This approach usually involves a mixture of the preceding advantages and disadvantages and must be carefully managed.

An application service provider (ASP) is a company that provides the software, support and computer hardware on which to run the software from the user's facilities over a network. ASPs customize off-the-shelf software on contract and speed deployment of new applications while helping IS managers avoid implementation headaches. ASPs reduce the need for many skilled IS staff members and also lower a project's start-up expenses. Software as a Service (SaaS) allows businesses to subscribe to web-delivered business application software by paying a monthly service charge or a per-use fee.

SaaS and recent web development technologies have led to a new paradigm in computing called cloud computing. Cloud computing refers to the use of computing resources, including software and data storage, on the Internet (the cloud), not on local computers. Rather than installing, storing and running software on your own computer, with cloud computing you access software stored on and delivered from a web server.

Although hundreds of computer applications can help people at school, home and work, the most popular applications are word-processing, spreadsheet analysis, database, graphics and personal information management. A software suite, such as SmartSuite, WordPerfect, StarOffice or Microsoft Office, offers a collection of these powerful programs sold as a bundle.

Many thousands of applications are designed for businesses and workgroups. Business software generally falls under the heading of information systems that support common business activities, such as accounts receivable, accounts payable, inventory control and other management activities.

Principle:

Organizations should choose programming languages with functional characteristics that are appropriate for the task at hand and well suited to the skills and experience of the programming staff. All software programs are written in coding schemes called *programming languages*, which provide instructions to a computer to perform some processing activity. The several classes of programming languages include machine, assembly, high-level, query and database, object-oriented, and visual programming.

Programming languages have changed since their initial development in the early 1950s. In the first generation, computers were programmed in machine language, and, in the second, assembly languages were used. The third generation consists of many high-level programming languages that use English-like statements and commands. They must be converted to machine language by special software called a compiler. Fourth-generation languages include database and query languages such as SQL.

Fifth-generation programming languages combine rules-based code generation, component management, visual programming techniques, reuse management and other advances. Object-oriented programming languages use groups of related data, instructions and procedures called *objects*, which serve as reusable modules in various programs. These languages can reduce program development and testing time. Java can be used to develop applications on the Internet. Visual programming environments, integrated development environments (IDEs) and software development kits (SDKs) have simplified and streamlined the coding process and have made it easier for more people to develop software.

Principle:

The software industry continues to undergo constant change; users need to be aware of recent trends and issues to be effective in their business and personal life. Software bugs, software licencing and copyrighting, open-source software, shareware and freeware, multiorganizational software development, software upgrades, and global software support are all important software issues and trends.

A software bug is a defect in a computer program that keeps it from performing in the manner intended. Software bugs are common, even in key pieces of business software.

Freeware is software that is made available to the public for free. Open-source software is freeware that also has its source code available so that others may modify it. Open-source software development and maintenance is a collaborative process, with developers around the world using the Internet to download the software, communicate about it, and submit new versions of it.

Software upgrades are an important source of increased revenue for software manufacturers and can provide useful new functionality and improved quality for software users.

Global software support is an important consideration for large global companies putting together standardized companywide systems. A common solution is outsourcing global support to one or more third-party software distributors.

Self-Assessment Test

Systems and application software are critical in helping individuals and organizations achieve their goals.

1 Which of the following is an example of a command-driven operating system?
   a. XP
   b. Yosemite
   c. MS DOS
   d. Windows 7

2 Many of today's mobile devices and some PCs use a touch user interface, also called a *natural user interface (NUI)* or multitouch interface by some. True or false?

3 _____ is an open-source OS that is used in all computer platforms: PC, server, embedded, smartphones and others.

4 Spam filtering is a function of the operating system. True or false?

5 Some companies use _____ to run multiple operating systems on a single computer.
   a. multitasking
   b. middleware
   c. service-oriented architecture
   d. virtualization

Organizations use off-the-shelf application software for common business needs and proprietary application software to meet unique business needs and provide a competitive advantage.

6 Application software that determines the best shipping option for products from a manufacturing company to a consumer is software for the personal sphere of influence. True or false?

7 Software that enables users to improve their personal effectiveness, increasing the amount of work they can do and its quality, is called _____.
   a. personal productivity software
   b. operating system software
   c. utility software
   d. graphics software

8 Optimization can be found in which type of application software?
   a. spreadsheets
   b. word-processing programs
   c. personal information management programs
   d. presentation graphics programs

9 _____ software is one-of-a-kind software designed for a specific application and owned by the company, organization or person that uses it.

10 _____ allows businesses to subscribe to web-delivered business application software by paying a monthly service charge or a per-use fee.
   a. Software as a Service (SaaS)
   b. An application service provider (ASP)
   c. Proprietary software
   d. Off-the-shelf software

Organizations should choose programming languages with functional characteristics that are appropriate for the task at hand and well suited to the skills and experience of the programming staff.

11 Most software purchased to run on a personal computer uses a _____ licence.
   a. site
   b. concurrent-user
   c. multiuser
   d. single-user

12 One of the primary advantages of _____ programming is the use of reusable code modules that save developers from having to start coding from scratch.

13 Each programming language has its own set of rules, called the _____ of the language.

14 An object-oriented language converts a programmer's source code into the machine-language instructions consisting of binary digits. True or false?

The software industry continues to undergo constant change; users need to be aware of recent trends and issues to be effective in their business and personal life.

15 _____ allows users to tweak the software to their own needs.
a. Freeware
b. Off-the-shelf software
c. Open-source software
d. Software in the public domain

16 What type of licence is an enterprise likely to purchase for software that it intends all of its employees to use while on site?

Review Questions

1 What is the difference between systems software and application software? Give four examples of personal productivity software.

2 What steps can a user take to correct software bugs?

3 Identify and briefly discuss two types of user interfaces provided by an operating system. What are the benefits and drawbacks of each?

4 What is a software suite? Give several examples.

5 Name four operating systems that support the personal sphere of influence.

6 What is Software as a Service (SaaS)?

7 What is multitasking?

8 Define the term *utility software* and give two examples.

9 Identify the two primary sources for acquiring application software.

10 What is cloud computing? What are the pros and cons of cloud computing?

11 What is open-source software? What are the benefits and drawbacks for a business that uses open-source software?

12 What does the acronym API stand for? What is the role of an API?

13 Briefly discuss the advantages and disadvantages of frequent software upgrades.

14 List four application software packages that would be useful for an enterprise.

15 What is the difference between freeware and open-source software?

Discussion Questions

1 Assume that you must take a computer-programming course next term. What language do you think would be best for you to study? Why? Do you think that a professional programmer needs to know more than one programming language? Why or why not?

2 You are going to buy a personal computer. What operating system features are important to you? What operating system would you select and why?

3 You have been asked to develop a user interface for someone with limited sight – someone without the ability to recognize shapes on a computer screen. Describe the user interface you would recommend.

4 You are using a new release of an application software package. You think that you have discovered a bug. Outline the approach that you would take to confirm that it is indeed a bug. What actions would you take if it truly were a bug?

5 For a company of your choice, describe the three most important application software packages you would recommend for the company's profitability and success.

6 Define the term *Software as a Service (SaaS)*. What are some of the advantages and disadvantages of employing a SaaS? What precautions might you take to minimize the risk of using one?

7 Describe three personal productivity software packages you are likely to use the most. What personal productivity software packages would you select for your use?

8 Describe the most important features of an operating system for a smartphone.

9 If you were the IS manager for a large manufacturing company, what issues might you have with the use of open-source software? What advantages might there be for use of such software?

10 Identify four types of software licences frequently used. Which approach does the best job of ensuring a steady, predictable stream of revenue from customers? Which approach is most fair for the small company that makes infrequent use of the software?

11 How have software development kits (SDKs) influenced software development?

12 How can virtualization save a company a lot of money?

Web Exercises

1 Use the web to research four productivity software suites from various vendors (see http://en.wikipedia.org/wiki/Office_Suite). Create a table in a word-processing document to show what applications are provided by the competing suites. Write a few paragraphs on which suite you think best matches your needs and why.

2 Use the Internet to search for three popular freeware utilities that you would find useful. Write a report that describes the features of these three utility programs.

3 Use the Internet to search for information on embedded operating systems. Describe how embedded operating systems can be used in vehicles, home appliances, TVs and other devices.

4 Do research on the web about application software that is used in an industry and is of interest to you. Write a brief report describing how the application software can be used to increase profits or reduce costs.

Case One

Tendring District Council: Open for Business Online

Tendring District Council, with a population of about 150 000, is located in the county of Essex in southeast England. Every year the council receives thousands of applications for building permits and other items that could be affected by regulations or could affect other people.

Applications to Tendring District Council span a wide range of requests. Applications received during the week ending 25th May 2012, for example, ranged from a request by Mr A. Maloney of Frinton & Walton to prune a cherry tree in his front garden to a request by Mr T. Munson of Wix to install two wind turbines, 50-feet tall from ground to hub, with 18-foot blades. Installing two wind turbines needs more consideration than pruning a cherry tree, but Tendring District Council must process both

requests and render decisions according to the established rules.

When making decisions, the council solicits the opinions of neighbours, neighbourhood organizations, the Essex County highway department, National Heritage (for buildings or locations of historic importance), and gas, electricity and water companies. In a typical year, Tendring issues about 9000 requests for comments – *consultations*, in the official terminology – and receives about 8000 replies.

Traditionally, the council sent all consultations by mail, which posed three problems:

1 Significant costs are associated with producing multiple copies of the documents and for postage.

2 Sending and receiving paper files delayed planning activities.

3 The consultation process generated a great deal of paper, all of which had to be stored (requiring space) or discarded (having an environmental impact, even with recycling).

To reduce or eliminate those problems, Tendring decided to invest in an electronic document management system (EDMS) using software from Idox. This system generates electronic consultations where the consultee – that is, one with whom Tendring District Council consults – has an email address. The consultation email contains all relevant details of the planning proposal plus a hyperlink the consultee can use to view and comment on the proposal on Tendring's website.

Tendring recognized the importance of adapting the system to its users, not forcing users to adapt to the system. The council knew that instead of using the EDMS, some consultees might prefer to reply by email, while others would prefer to submit hard copy documents. Tendring, therefore, left open the traditional email and hard copy routes for responding but found that few consultees used them. Two reasons might be that the EDMS also allows comments to be public or private and that it maintains appropriate security to ensure the privacy of comments that have been submitted as private.

Today, 99 per cent of planning consultations are handled electronically. (This figure includes both website and email replies.) The district council's finance department calculated total savings at £150 000 (about US$230 000) per year, including £8000 (about US$12 500) on postage alone.

Consultees like the new system, too. Vicky Presland, district manager of the Essex County East Area Highways Office, says 'Consultee Access has saved considerable time in producing our responses to the local Planning Authority, and has allowed us to reduce our own filing systems due to the easy access to ours and other consultees' responses.' This system truly has no losers.

Questions

1 Tendring District Council selected an off-the-shelf package for its document management system rather than developing custom software or having custom software developed for them. Do you agree with this decision? Justify your answer.

2 What is the sphere of influence of the Tendring District Council EDMS and online consultee response application: personal, workgroup or enterprise? Indicate whether the system has aspects of more than one sphere of influence, being as specific as possible.

3 Tendring District Council is responsible for a relatively small area. Larger regional and municipal government agencies have used electronic document systems for much longer than Tendring has. Why do you think other agencies use electronic document systems? Consider both business and technical factors.

4 Suppose Tendring evaluated EDMS systems and found that the best one for its needs was not compatible with its existing operating system. What would you suggest Tendring do? Justify your answer.

Case Two

Microfinance Needs Software

India may be the most entrepreneurial country in the world. However, since most of its new enterprises are small, business owners often don't qualify for conventional banking services. The *microfinance* system has grown up to meet their needs. According to Consultative Group to Assist the Poor (CGAP), which provides microfinance information and services to 'governments, financial service providers, donors and investors', microfinance 'offers poor people access to basic financial services such as loans, savings, money transfer services and insurance'. Unfortunately, as CGAP points out, 'the administrative cost of making tiny loans is much higher in percentage terms than the cost of making

7 IBM Website, www-01.ibm.com/software/data/cognos, accessed 19 September 2011.

8 Mossberg, W., Apple's Lion Brings PCs into the Tablet Era', *The Wall Street Journal*, 21 July 2011, p. D1.

9 Microsoft Website, windows.microsoft.com/en-US/windows7/What-can-I-do-with-Speech-Recognition, accessed 18 September.

10 Microsoft Website, technet.microsoft.com/en-us/windows/dd320286, accessed 12 September 2011.

11 Wingfield, N. and Tibken, S., 'Microsoft to Limit Tablets', *The Wall Street Journal*, 2 June 2011, p. B4.

12 Keizer, G., 'Microsoft Gambles with Windows 8', *Computerworld*, 20 June 2011, p. 6.

13 Grundberg, S. and Ovide, S., 'A Test Ride for Windows 8', *The Wall Street Journal*, 1 March 2012, p. B4.

14 Henderson, Tom, 'Windows 8 Breaks New Ground', *Network World*, 23 January 2012, p. 28.

15 Ramstad, E., 'Samsung Plans to Expand Tablet Line to Use Windows', *The Wall Street Journal*, 9 September 2011, p. B4.

16 Apple Website, www.apple.com/macosx, accessed 18 September 2011.

17 Vascellaro, Jessica, 'Apple's Mac Makeover', *The Wall Street Journal*, 17 February 2012, B1.

18 Nelson, F., 'IT Pro Ranking', *InformationWeek*, 5 September 2011, p. 16.

19 Vance, Ashlee, 'Red Hat Sees Lots of Green', *Bloomberg Businessweek*, 2 April 2012, p. 41.

20 'And Now, Google's Other Operating System', *Bloomberg Businessweek*, 13 June 2011, p. 42.

21 Kowitt, B., 'One Hundred Million Android Fans Can't Be Wrong', *Fortune*, 4 July 2011, p. 93.

22 Mossberg, Walter, 'Mobile Device That's Better for Jotter than a Talker', *The Wall Street Journal*, 16 February 2012, p. D1.

23 Clayburn, T., 'Google Gambles on Chromebooks', *InformationWeek*, 30 May 2011, p. 18.

24 Microsoft Website, www.microsoft.com/windows/products/winfamily/windowshomeserver/default.mspx, accessed 20 September 2011.

25 Binstock, Andrew, 'Q&A: Ken Thompson, Creator of Unix', *InformationWeek*, 27 June 2011, p. 45.

26 Sun Website, www.sun.com/customers/index.xml?c=ebay.xml&submit=Find, accessed 12 September 2011.

27 Red Hat RHEV Freed from Windows Fetters', *Network World*, 22 August 2011, p. 8.

28 Red Hat Website, www.redhat.com/virtualization/rhev, accessed 12 September 2011.

29 Dornan, A., 'Linux Virtualization Finds Some Rich Uncles', *InformationWeek*, 13 June 2011, p. 21.

30 IBM Website, www-03.ibm.com/systems/z/os/zos, accessed 20 September 2011.

31 Fletcher, O., 'Alibaba Develops Cloud Mobile Operating System', *The Wall Street Journal*, 5 July 2011, p. B5.

32 Apple Website, www.apple.com/ios/ios5, accessed 17 September 2011.

33 Sherr, I., 'H-P Looks to Kitchens, Cars', *The Wall Street Journal*, 16 August 2011, p. B5.

34 HP Website, www.hpwebos.com/us/products/software/webos2, accessed 15 September 2011.

35 Lawton, C. and Kim, Y., 'Nokia Updates Smart Phones', *The Wall Street Journal*, 25 August 2011, p. B5.

36 King, C., 'RIM, Dolby Settle Dispute', *The Wall Street Journal*, 13 September 2011, p. B9.

37 Microsoft Website, www.microsoft.com/windowsembedded/en-us/windows-embedded.aspx, accessed 20 September 2011.

38 Ford Motors Website, www.ford.com/technology/sync, accessed 20 September 2011.

39 Mossberg, W., 'A Parallels World Where Windows Zips on Macs', *The Wall Street Journal*, 1 September 2011, p. D1.

40 CERN Website, http://wlcg.web.cern.ch, accessed 12 September 2011.

41 Babcock, C., 'What You Can't See', *InformationWeek*, 5 September 2011, p. 18.

42 Nance, Barry, 'HP, IBM, CA Deliver Powerful Toolkits', *Network World*, 12 March 2012, p. 26.

43 'James River Insurance Selects Confio Software', *Business Wire*, 2 August 2011.

44 Healy, M., 'The OS Mess', *InformationWeek*, 11 July 2011, p. 21.

45 Murphy, C., 'Is Management Software RIM's Secret Weapon?', *InformationWeek*, 5 September 2011, p. 6.

46 CNET Website, www.cnet.com, accessed 20 September 2011.

47 'First Financial Asset Management Deploys Debt Collection Solution from Latitude Software', *Business Wire*, 30 June 2011.

48 'Accenture to Expand Property and Casualty Insurance Software', *Business Wire*, July 2011.

49 www.nb.co.za/History. Accessed 18 July 2014.

50 www.au.yusen-logistics.com. Accessed 18 July 2014.

51 McClatchy, S., 'New Software Installed to Help Speed Airport Screening', *Tribune Business News*, 11 August 2011.

52 Hodge, N., 'Killer App', *The Wall Street Journal*, 3 June 2011, p. A2.

53 El Camino Hospital Website, www.elcaminohospital. org/Locations/El_Camino_Hospital_Mountain_View, accessed 12 September 2011.

54 'Globus Online to Provide Software-as-a-Service for NSF', *PR Newswire*, 2 September 2011.

55 'Big SaaS Done Right', *Computerworld*, 13 February 2012, p. 13.

56 Schultz, B., 'Florida Hospice Saves with SaaS', *Network World*, 6 June 2011, p. 24.

57 Thurman, Mathias, 'Plugging a SaaS Access Hole', *Computerworld*, 12 March 2012, p. 33.

58 Mossberg, W., 'Google Unveils a Laptop with Its Brain in the Cloud', *The Wall Street Journal*, 23 June 2011 p. D1.

59 'And Now, Google's Other Operating System', *Bloomberg Businessweek*, 13 June 2011, p. 42.

60 Clayburn, T., 'Google Gambles on Chromebooks', *InformationWeek*, 30 May 2011, p. 18.

61 Tableau Software Website, www.tableausoftware. com, accessed 20 September 2011.

62 Biddick, M., 'IT Management Goes SaaS', *InformationWeek*, 5 September 2011, p. 33.

63 'Absolute Software Helps Recover 20 000th Stolen Computer', *PR Wire*, June 2011.

64 Burrows, Peter, 'It Looks Like You're Trying to Use Word on an iPad', *Bloomberg Businessweek*, 23 January 2012, p. 35.

65 Mossberg, W., 'Working in Word, Excel, PowerPoint On an iPad', *The Wall Street Journal*, 12 January 2012, p. D1.

66 Adobe Acrobat Website, www.acrobat.com/ welcome/en/home.html, accessed 7 March 2012.

67 Henschen, Doug, 'Microsoft Places Bigger Bet on Cloud Apps', *InformationWeek*, 11 July 2011, p. 10.

68 Microsoft Website, www.microsoft.com/en-us/ office365, accessed 15 September 2011.

69 'Office 365 vs. Google: Advantage Microsoft', *InformationWeek*, 11 July 2011, p. 10.

70 Rizzo, Tom, 'Office 365: Best of Both Worlds', *Network World*, 22 August 2011, p. 20.

71 Wingfield, N., 'Virtual Products, Real Profits', *The Wall Street Journal*, 9 September 2011, p. A1.

72 Ramachandran, S., 'Playing on a Tablet at Therapy', *The Wall Street Journal*, 26 July 2011, p. D1.

73 Horn, Leslie, 'Gamers Unlock Protein Mystery That Baffled AIDS Researchers for Years', www. pcmag.com/ article2/0,2817,2393200,00.asp, accessed 20 September 2011.

74 Satariano, A. and MacMillan, D., 'Anarchy in the App Store', *Bloomberg Businessweek*, 19 March 2012, p. 47.

75 Ovide, Shira and Sherr, Ian, 'Microsoft Banks on Mobile Apps', *The Wall Street Journal*, 6 April 2012, p. B1.

76 Steel, E., 'A Face Launches 1000 Apps', *The Wall Street Journal*, 5 August 2011, p. B5.

77 Android Website, https://market.android.com/ details?id=com.viewdle.socialcamera&hl=en, accessed 15 September 2011.

78 Angwin, J., 'Face-ID Tools Pose New Risk', *The Wall Street Journal*, 1 August 2011, p. B1.

79 Fowler, G. and Lawton, C., 'Facebook Again in Spotlight on Privacy', *The Wall Street Journal*, 9 June 2011, p. B1.

80 'Mobile Software Market to Reach $80 Billion by 2017', *Business Wire*, 16 June 2011.

81 Microsoft Exchange Server Website, microsoft. com/exchange, accessed 20 September 2011.

82 'Copper Mountain Resort Selects Agilysys Visual One', *PR Newswire*, August 2011.

83 Martin, D., 'Software Creates Less-Taxing Environment', *NJ Biz*, 1 August 2011, p. 18.

84 Tozzi, J., 'Bank Data Miner', *Bloomberg Businessweek*, 3 July 2011, p. 41.

85 Verafin Website, verafin.com, accessed 15 September 2011.

86 Burnham, K., 'Spreading the Word', *CIO*, 1 September 2011, p. 11.

87 Biddick, M., 'IT Management Goes SaaS', *InformationWeek*, 5 September 2011, p. 33.

88 '81 Per Cent Find Mobile ERP Software Interface Important', *Business Wire*, 12 July 2011.

89 Nash, K., 'Do It Yourself', *CIO*, 1 September 2011, p. 28.

90 C ++ Website, www.cplusplus.com, accessed 25 Setember 2011.

91 Microsoft Website, www.microsoft.com/ visualstudio/en-us, accessed 25 September 2011.

92 Android Website, developer.android.com/guide / developing/tools/emulator.html, accessed 25 September 2011.

93 'Hickenlooper Merits Praise for Repealing Software Tax', *Boulder County Business Report*, 25 June 2011 p. 30.

94 Page, Jeremy, 'Chinese State TV Alludes to US Website Attacks', *The Wall Street Journal*, 25 August 2011, p. A8.

95 'Malware in Android Apps Rises', *The Tampa Tribune*, 26 March 2012, p. 3.

96 Babcock, Charles, 'Leap Day Bug Caused Azure Outage', *InformationWeek*, 26 March 2012, p. 14.

97 Searcey, D., 'Toyota Maneuvers to Protect Crown Jewels', *The Wall Street Journal*, 22 March 2011, p. B1.

98 Freeware Website, freewarehome.com, accessed 25 September 2011.

99 Binstock, A., 'NET Alternative in Transition', *InformationWeek*, 13 June 2011, p. 42.

100 Matlin, C., 'Innovator', *Bloomberg Businessweek*, 11 April 2011, p. 34.

101 Nash, K., 'Discipline for Unruly Updates', *CIO*, 1 July 2011, p. 14.

05

Organizing and Storing Data

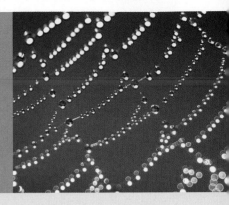

Principles

Data management and modelling are key aspects of organizing data and information.

A well-designed and well-managed database is central to almost all information systems and is an extremely valuable tool in supporting decision making.

The number and type of database applications will continue to evolve and yield real business benefits.

Learning Objectives

- Define general data management concepts and terms, highlighting the advantages of the database approach to data management.
- Describe the relational database model and outline its basic features.

- Identify the common functions performed by all database management systems and identify popular user database management systems.

- Identify and briefly discuss current database applications.

Why Learn About Organizing Data?

Having had an overview of IS in organizations, and examined different types of hardware and software, we now turn to look at using that hardware and software to store and process data. Databases are the heart of almost all IS. A huge amount of data is entered into computer systems every day. In this chapter, you will learn about database management systems and how they can help you. If you become a marketing manager, you can access a vast store of data on existing and potential customers from surveys, their web habits and their past purchases. This information can help you sell products and services. If you work in business law, you will have access to past cases and legal opinions from sophisticated legal databases. This information can help you win cases and protect your organization legally. If you become a human resource (HR) manager, you will be able to use databases to analyze the impact of raises, employee insurance benefits and retirement contributions on long-term costs to your company. Using database management systems will likely be a critical part of your job. In this chapter, you will see how you can use data mining to extract valuable information to help you succeed. This chapter starts by introducing basic concepts of database management systems.

5

5.1 Data Management and Data Modelling

At the centre of almost every information system is a database, used to store data so that it can be processed to provide useful information. A database is used by almost every firm to record a history of that firm's transactions. This historical data can be hugely useful in uncovering patterns and relationships the firm had never even considered before, a practice known as 'data mining', something that is explained later in this chapter. The most common type of database is a relational database, so-named because the basic structure for storing data is a table, and the word relation is another name for a table. A **relational database** is defined as a series of related tables, stored together with a minimum of duplication to achieve consistent and controlled pool of data.

relational database A series of related tables, stored together with a minimum of duplication to achieve consistent and controlled pool of data.

So a relational database is made up of a number of tables. In loose terms, each table stores the data about someone or something of interest to the firm. This someone or something is known as an **entity**. (We will see later that sometimes the data about one entity is stored in two or more tables, and sometimes the data about two or more entities are stored in one table.) For example, a small business selling office furniture might have a customer table to store all the data about their customers, a supplier table to store information about suppliers, and an order table that records all the orders that are placed by its customers. In this example there are three entities – customer, order and supplier.

entity A person, place or thing about whom or about which an organization wants to store data.

The rows in a table collect together all the data about one specific entity. For example, in the customer table, each row stores all the data about one particular customer – Jane Smith, for instance, or Desmond Paton. These rows are known as **records**. The columns in a table are the specific items of data that get stored; for example, first name, surname or telephone number. These columns are known as **fields** or attributes.

record A row in a table; all the data pertaining to one instance of an entity.

field A characteristic or attribute of an entity that is stored in the database.

So a database is made up of tables, which are made up of records, which are made up of fields. This is illustrated in Figure 5.1 using the customer table example. Notice that in the figure each customer has been given a unique customer number. This is because, as can be seen, there are two customers called Jane Wilson. Both work for the same company and therefore have the same address and phone number. The database needs some way of

Customer_Number	First_Name	Surname	Address1	Address2
10	Jane	Wilson	London Road	Oxford
11	John	Smith	Quai d'Orsay	Paris
12	Jane	Wilson	London Road	Oxford
13	Desmond	Paton	Marshall Street	Johannesburg
14	Susan	Haynes	Baker Street	London

Figure 5.1 The Customer Table for an Office Furniture Seller

differentiating between them, and that is the job of the customer number, which is the **primary key**. Every table should have a primary key field used to identify individual records, and also to create relationships between tables, something we will examine next.

The advantages and disadvantages of using a relational database to store data are listed in Table 5.1.

primary key A field in a table that is unique – each record in that table has a different value in the primary key field. The primary key is used to uniquely identify each record and to create relationships between tables.

Table 5.1 Advantages and Disadvantages of the Database Approach

Advantages	Explanation
Improved strategic use of corporate data	Accurate, complete, up-to-date data can be made available to decision makers where, when and in the form they need it. The database approach can also give greater visibility to the organization's data resource
Reduced data redundancy	Data is organized by the database management system (DBMS) and stored in only one location. This results in more efficient use of system storage space
Improved data integrity	With the traditional approach, some changes to data were not reflected in all copies of the data kept in separate files. This is prevented with the database approach because no separate files contain copies of the same piece of data
Easier modification and updating	The DBMS coordinates updates and data modifications. Programmers and users do not have to know where the data is physically stored. Data is stored and modified once. Modification and updating is also easier because the data is stored in only one location in most cases
Data and program independence	The DBMS organizes the data independently of the application program, so the application program is not affected by the location or type of data. Introduction of new data types not relevant to a particular application does not require rewriting that application to maintain compatibility with the data file
Better access to data and information	Most DBMSs have software that makes it easy to access and retrieve data from a database. In most cases, users give simple commands to get important information. Relationships between records can be more easily investigated and exploited, and applications can be more easily combined
Standardization of data access	A standardized, uniform approach to database access means that all application programs use the same overall procedures to retrieve data and information

(continued)

Table 5.1 *Continued*

Advantages	Explanation
A framework for program development	Standardized database access procedures can mean more standardization of program development. Because programs go through the DBMS to gain access to data in the database, standardized database access can provide a consistent framework for program development. In addition, each application program need address only the DBMS, not the actual data files, reducing application development time
Better overall protection of the data	Accessing and using centrally located data is easier to monitor and control. Security codes and passwords can ensure that only authorized people have access to particular data and information in the database, thus ensuring privacy
Shared data and information resources	The cost of hardware, software and personnel can be spread over many applications and users. This is a primary feature of a DBMS

Disadvantages	Explanation
More complexity	DBMS can be difficult to set up and operate. Many decisions must be made correctly for the DBMS to work effectively. In addition, users have to learn new procedures to take full advantage of a DBMS
More difficult to recover from a failure	With the traditional approach to file management, a failure of a file affects only a single program. With a DBMS, a failure can shut down the entire database
More expensive	DBMS can be more expensive to purchase and operate. The expense includes the cost of the database and specialized personnel, such as a database administrator, who is needed to design and operate the database. Additional hardware might also be required

Relationships Between Tables

Consider the customer table (Figure 5.1) and the order table (Figure 5.2) in the office furniture seller's database. It should be obvious that there is a relationship between these two – the firm needs to know which orders have been placed by which customer, otherwise they wouldn't know where to ship the goods, or who to charge for them. How this relationship is created in a database is shown in Figure 5.2, which shows the order table. The fourth record in the table is an order for a computer desk. The first field in the table, Order_Number, is the order table's primary key. Then there are details of what the order is, description, price and colour. The last field on the right-hand side is the Customer_Number. This creates the relationship between an

Figure 5.2 The Order Table for an Office Furniture Seller

Order_Number	Description	Price	Colour	Customer_Number
100	Swivel chair	€89	Black	10
101	Coat rack	€15	Silver	10
102	White board	€23	White	11
103	Computer desk	€150	Brown	13
104	Filing cabinet	€50	Gray	10

order and a customer – customer 13 has ordered the computer desk. To find out who customer 13 is, look back at Figure 5.1, find 13 in the Customer_Number field, and we see it is Desmond Paton. We also find the delivery address – the desk is being shipped to South Africa. The customer number in the order table is known as a **foreign key**. An important concept when setting up relationships is 'referential integrity'. What this means is that you cannot have an instance of a foreign key before it exists as an instance of a primary key. Using the office furniture database as an example, if the database has enforced referential integrity (which it should) it means you can't have an order for Customer_Number 15 unless there actually is a customer with Customer_Number 15 in the customer table.

> **foreign key** When a primary key is posted into another table to create a relationship between the two, it is known as a foreign key.

This is an extremely convenient and useful way of organizing data (refer back to Table 5.1). It means, in this case, that the delivery address doesn't have to be stored twice – once with the order and again with the customer details. Storing the same information twice is very bad practice and leads to all sorts of problems. If a customer moves and one address is updated but the other is not, then the firm has useless data – it is not known which address is the correct one. A large part of organizing data involves deciding which fields are going to be primary keys and identifying where the foreign keys should be. A process for making that decision is described next.

Designing Relational Databases

This section describes an approach to designing a relational database. A database design is also known as a data model or a database schema. It is a list of all the tables in the database, along with all the fields, with any primary and foreign keys identified. The approach has four stages:

1 Identify all entities.
2 Identify all relationships between entities.
3 Identify all attributes.
4 Resolve all relationships.

If you are trying this approach out for yourself, you are unlikely to get the perfect data model first time. The approach is iterative; that is, once you do all four stages once, examine the resulting schema. If it doesn't work perfectly, go back to stage one and adjust your list of entities, then go through the rest of the stages again. Do this over and over again until, eventually, a good data model emerges.

Identify Entities

The first step is to identify all the entities you want to store data about. This is usually done by interviewing the firm's managers and staff. If there are too many of them to interview, sometimes database designers will use a questionnaire to get opinions from as many people as possible. If you are designing a database for a student project, you will probably think that this first step is the easy bit, but in fact getting the right list of entities is vital if your data model is to be useful, and it is often not a trivial task, specifically because you have to interview different people and each might give you a different list! (This problem is examined more closely in a later chapter on system development.)

Identify Relationships

You next need to identify any relationships that exist between entities. The sort of relationships that you have to identify are relationships that the firm wants to store information about. For example, there might be a relationship between customers and suppliers – some of them might play golf together. However, this is unlikely to be the sort of thing the firm will want to store. The relationship between customers and orders is definitely something that the firm will want to store, so that they can see which customers have placed which orders. Like identifying entities, identifying relationships between them is not trivial and may take several attempts to get right.

Once you identify a relationship, there are three things you need to document about it: its degree, cardinality and optionality.

degree The number of entities involved in a relationship.

The **degree** of a relationship is simply how many entities are involved, and this figure is often two. When the degree is two, it is known as a 'binary relationship'.

cardinality In a relationship, cardinality is the number of one entity that can be related to another entity.

The **cardinality** of a relationship is whether each entity in the relationship is related to one or more than one of the other entities. For example, going back to the customer–order relationship, each order is placed by just one customer, but each customer can place many orders. Hence the cardinality in this case is one to many (1 : M). Cardinality for a binary relationship can be one to one (1 : 1), one to many (1 : M) or many to many (M : M).

optionality If a binary relationship is optional for an entity, that entity doesn't have to be related to the other.

Last, the **optionality** documents whether the relationship must exist for each entity or whether it is optional. For instance, an order must be placed by a customer – there is no option. An order can't exist unless a customer has placed it! However, a customer can be in the database even though they have no current orders, so the relationship is optional for the customer.

All of the above is documented in an entity–relationship diagram, shown in Figure 5.3.

Figure 5.3 Entity–Relationship Diagram (E–RD) with Notation Explained

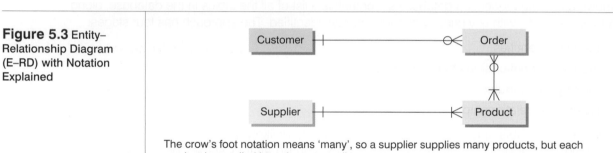

The crow's foot notation means 'many', so a supplier supplies many products, but each product is supplied by only one supplier.

The 0 and | represent optionality – a 0 means the relationship is optional so a customer doesn't have to have an order. A | means not-optional (or 'obligatory') so an order has to have one (and only one) customer.

It is important to note that the database designer doesn't get to make up the degree, cardinality and optionality herself. These are dictated to her by what are known as the **enterprise rules**, which the designer must uncover by, usually, interviewing staff. An example of the enterprise rules describing the customer–order relationship is as follows:

enterprise rules The rules governing relationships between entities.

■ Each order must be placed by one and only one customer.

■ Each customer can place many orders, but some won't have placed any orders.

Enterprise rules are specific to the firm. For example, consider the relationship between employee and car, which a firm wants to store so it can manage its parking spaces. One employee can own as many cars as he can afford, so does that mean this relationship is one to many? Not necessarily. If the firm has decided that it is only going to store information on one car for each of its employees then the relationship is one to one, regardless of how many cars each actually owns. The relationship will probably be optional on one side because not every employee will own a car, but every car in the database will be owned by an employee.

Identify Attributes

The third stage is to identify all the attributes that are going to be stored for each entity. An attribute should be the smallest sensible piece of data that is to be stored. For example, customer name is probably a bad attribute – customer first name and surname would be better (some databases also include title and initial as separate attributes). Why is this? It is so that first name and surname can be accessed separately. For example, if you wanted to start a letter to a customer, 'Dear John', you would be unable to do this if you had stored the name as 'John Smith'. In this case, the letter would have to read 'Dear John Smith'. As before, attributes can be identified by interviewing staff.

Resolve Relationships

The customer–order relationship was implemented by taking the primary key of customer and posting it as a foreign key in the order table. This is essentially what resolving a relationship means – deciding how to implement it. Sometimes a relationship between two entities will result in three tables being implemented, sometimes one, most often two. There is a series of rules to decide what tables to implement and which primary keys to use as a foreign key.

First, let us examine the customer–order relationship more closely to see why we implemented it the way we did. If we had taken the order table primary key (order number) and posted it as a foreign key in the customer table, we would have had two problems, both illustrated in Figure 5.4. First, we have a repeating group – that means we would be trying to squeeze more than one piece of information into one cell in the database, in this case the fact that customer 10 has three orders. We also have a null (blank space) because customers 12 and 14 haven't placed any orders. Posting the customer number into the order table (look back at Figure 5.2) solves both those problems. Basically, the null isn't too big a problem, but a relational database cannot cope with a repeating group. Trying to implement the relationship by posting order number into the customer table simply won't work.

Customer_Number	First_Name	Surname	Address1	Address2	Order_Number
10	Jane	Wilson	London Road	Oxford	100,101,104
11	John	Smith	Quai d'Orsay	Paris	102
12	Jane	Wilson	London Road	Oxford	
13	Desmond	Paton	Marshall Street	Johannesburg	103
14	Susan	Haynes	Baker Street	London	

Figure 5.4 Posting Order Number into Customer for an Office Furniture Seller

A full discussion of resolving relationships is beyond the scope of this book. However, there only are six types of binary relationship. Figure 5.5 gives one example of each and explains how to implement it. Note that the figure illustrates the most 'elegant' way to resolve each relationship, not necessarily the most efficient in terms of access time. A company with a lot of data would implement its database for speed rather than elegance. (What this means in practice is that its database might have some nulls in the foreign keys or store some information twice.)

What you should end up with after you resolve each relationship is a list of tables along with all primary and foreign keys identified, such as that shown in Figure 5.6. This could then be implemented using a database management system.

5

Figure 5.5 The Six Types of Binary Relationship

1. One-to-one relationship, obligatory on both sides.

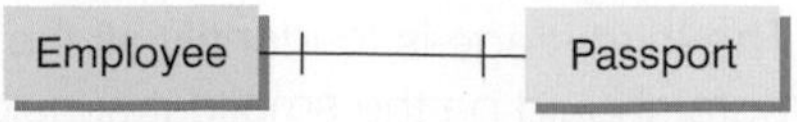

   Employee – Passport

   Each employee must have one and only one passport; each passport must have one and only one employee.

   To resolve this relationship, combine both entities into one table.

2. One-to-one relationship, optional on one side.

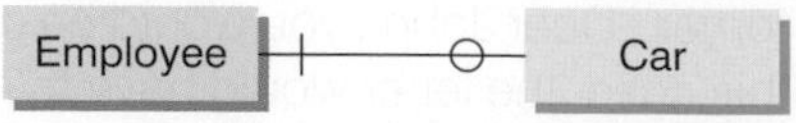

   Employee – Company car

   Each employee might have one and only one company car; each company car is owned by one and only one employee.

   To resolve this relationship, take the primary key from employee and post it as a foreign key in company car.

3. One-to-one relationship, optional on both sides.

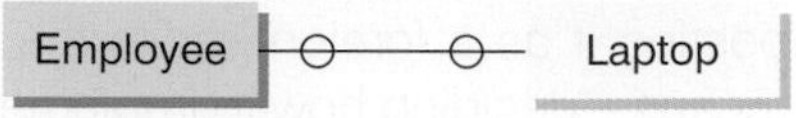

   Employee – Laptop

   Each employee might have one laptop; each laptop might belong to one employee (but some are for general use and therefore won't belong to anyone).

   To resolve this relationship, implement three tables – an employee table, a laptop table and a new table that we will call 'owns'. The owns table only has two fields – employee number and laptop number. The primary key of owns is a 'composite key', i.e. it is the employee number and laptop number combined, and each combination of the two is unique.

4. One-to-many relationship, many side obligatory to one side.

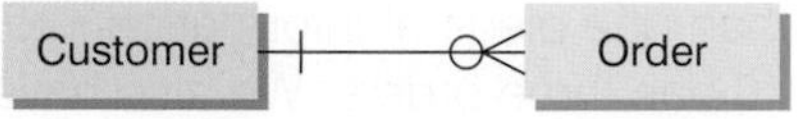

   Customer – Order

   A customer can place many orders; but might have placed no orders, each order must be placed by one and only one employee.

   Resolve this relationship by taking the primary key from customer and posting it as a foreign key in order.

5. One-to-many relationship, many side optional to one side.

   Student – Elective module

   A student might take one elective module; each module is taken by many students (i.e. the students don't have to take an elective module).

   Most companies would implement this in the same way as for Relationship 4 above. However, the way to avoid nulls in the foreign key is to implement three tables – one for student, one for elective module, and one that we'll call 'studies' (as a student studies a module). The studies table has just two fields – student number and module number. The primary key of the studies table is student number (or you could implement a composite key).

6. Many-to-many relationship.

   Student – Tutor

   Each tutor teaches many students; each student is taught by many tutors.

   To resolve this relationship, implement three tables – one for student, one for tutor, and a third we'll call teaches. The teaches table has two fields – student number and tutor number, and its primary key is a composite key, i.e. a combination of student number and tutor number.

Figure 5.6 A Database Design (Also Known as a Data Model or a Database Schema)
Primary keys are identified with a # symbol, foreign keys are underlined.

Customer{Customer_Number#, FirstName, Surname, Telephone}

Order{Order_Number#, Description, Price, Colour, Customer_Number}

Supplier{Supplier_Number#, Company_Name, Contact_FirstName, Contact_Surname, Telephone}

5.2 Database Management Systems

How do we actually create, implement, use and update a database? The answer is found in the database management system. A DBMS is a group of programs used as an interface between a database and application programs or between a database and the user. The capabilities and types of database systems, however, vary, but generally they provide the following.

Creating and Modifying the Database

Schemas or designs are entered into the DBMS (usually by database person- nel) via a data definition language. A **data definition language (DDL)** is a collection of instructions and commands used to define and describe data and relationships in a specific database. A DDL allows the database's creator to describe the data and relationships. Structured Query Language (SQL) is a DDL. Figure 5.7 shows four SQL statements to create a database called Let- tings, a table called Landlords and insert a record about John Smith.

data definition language (DDL) A collection of instructions and commands used to define and describe data and relationships in a specific database.

```
CREATE DATABASE Lettings;

USE Lettings;

CREATE TABLE landlords(
Firstname CHAR(10),
Surname CHAR(10),
Telephone CHAR(10));

INSERT INTO landlords(
'John', 'Smith', '123456');
```

Figure 5.7 SQL as a DDL *SQL code is being used to create a database called 'Lettings' with a table called 'landlords' which has three fields: 'Firstname', 'Surname' and 'Telephone'. The code then enters one landlord called John Smith into the table.*

Another important step in creating a database is to establish a **data dictionary**, a detailed description of all data used in the database. The data dictionary describes all the fields in the database, their range of accepted val- ues, the type of data (such as alphanumeric or numeric), the amount of storage space needed for each, and a note of who can access each and who updates each. Figure 5.8 shows a typical data dictionary entry.

data dictionary A detailed description of all the data used in the database.

Attribute	Data Type	Primary Key?	Required?
Customer_Number	Text	Y	Y
First_Name	Text	N	Y
Surname	Text	N	Y
Date_of_Birth	Date	N	N

Figure 5.8 A Typical Data Dictionary Entry for the Customer Table for an Office Furniture Seller

A data dictionary helps achieve the advantages of the database approach in these ways:

■ *Reduced data redundancy:* By providing standard definitions of all data, it is less likely that the same data item will be stored in different places under different names.

For example, a data dictionary reduces the likelihood that the same part number would be stored as two different items, such as PT_NO and PARTNO.

■ *Increased data reliability:* A data dictionary and the database approach reduce the chance that data will be destroyed or lost. In addition, it is more difficult for unauthorized people to gain access to sensitive data and information.

■ *Assists program development:* With a data dictionary, programmers know what data is stored and what data type each field is. This information is valuable when writing programs that make use of the data.

■ *Easier modification of data and information:* The data dictionary and the database approach make modifications to data easier because users do not need to know where the data is stored. The person making the change indicates the new value of the variable or item, such as part number, that is to be changed. The database system locates the data and makes the necessary change.

Storing and Retrieving Data

One function of a DBMS is to be an interface between an application program and the database. When an application program needs data, it requests that data through the DBMS. Suppose that to calculate the total price of a new car, a car dealer pricing program needs price data on the engine option – six cylinders instead of the standard four cylinders. The application program thus requests this data from the DBMS. In doing so, the application program follows a logical access path. Next, the DBMS, working with various system programs, accesses a storage device, such as disc drives, where the data is stored. When the DBMS goes to this storage device to retrieve the data, it follows a path to the physical location (physical access path) where the price of this option is stored. In the pricing example, the DBMS might go to a disc drive to retrieve the price data for six-cylinder engines. This relationship is shown in Figure 5.9.

Figure 5.9 Logical and Physical Access Paths

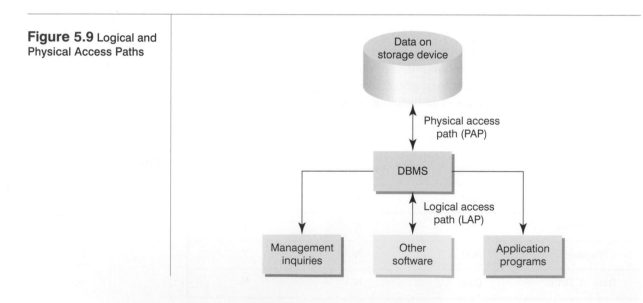

This same process is used if a user wants to get information from the database. First, the user requests the data from the DBMS. For example, a user might give a command, such as LIST ALL OPTIONS FOR WHICH PRICE IS GREATER THAN 200 EUROS. This is the logical access path (LAP). Then, the DBMS might go to the options price section of a disc to get the information for the user. This is the physical access path (PAP).

Two or more people or programs attempting to access the same record in the same database at the same time can cause a problem. For example, an inventory control program might attempt to reduce the inventory level for a product by ten units because ten units were just shipped to a customer. At the same time, a purchasing program might attempt to increase the inventory level for the same product by 200 units because more inventory was just received. Without proper database control, one of the inventory updates might not be correctly made, resulting in an inaccurate inventory level for the product. **Concurrency control** can be used to avoid this potential problem. One approach is to lock out all other application programs from access to a record if the record is being updated or used by another program.

concurrency control A method of dealing with a situation in which two or more people need to access the same record in a database at the same time.

Manipulating Data and Generating Reports

After a DBMS has been installed, employees, managers and consumers can use it to review reports and obtain important information. Some databases use Query-by-Example (QBE), which is a visual approach to developing database queries or requests.

Alternatively, SQL can be used to query the database. For example, SELECT * FROM EMPLOYEE WHERE JOB_CLASSIFICATION = "C2".

This will output all employees who have a job classification of 'C2'. The '*' tells the DBMS to include all columns from the EMPLOYEE table in the results. In general, the commands that are used to manipulate the database are part of the **data manipulation language (DML)**, of which SQL is an example. (So SQL is both a DDL and DML.) SQL commands can be used in a computer program, to query a database, which is convenient for programmers.

data manipulation language (DML) The commands that are used to manipulate the data in a database.

SQL, which is pronounced like the word 'sequel', was developed in the 1970s at the IBM Research Laboratory in San Jose, California. In 1986, the American National Standards Institute (ANSI) adopted SQL as the standard query language for relational databases. Since ANSI's acceptance of SQL, interest in making SQL an integral part of relational databases on both mainframe and personal computers has increased. SQL has many built-in functions, such as average (AVG), find the largest value (MAX), find the smallest value (MIN) and others. Table 5.2 contains examples of SQL commands.

SQL lets programmers learn one powerful query language and use it on systems ranging from PCs to the largest mainframe computers. Programmers and database users also find SQL

Table 5.2 Examples of SQL Commands

SQL Command	Description
SELECT ClientName, Debt FROM Client WHERE Debt > 1000	This query displays all clients (ClientName) and the amount they owe the company (Debt) from a database table called Client for clients who owe the company more than €1000 (WHERE Debt > 1000)
SELECT ClientName, ClientNum, OrderNum FROM Client, Order WHERE Client.ClientNum=Order.ClientNum	This command is an example of a join command that combines data from two tables: the client table and the order table (FROM Client, Order). The command creates a new table with the client name, client number, and order number (SELECT ClientName, ClientNum, OrderNum). Both tables include the client number, which allows them to be joined. This is indicated in the WHERE clause, which states that the client number in the client table is the same as (equal to) the client number in the order table (WHERE Client.ClientNum=Order.ClientNum)
GRANT INSERT ON Client to Guthrie	This command is an example of a security command. It allows Bob Guthrie to insert new values or rows into the Client table

valuable because SQL statements can be embedded into many programming languages (discussed in Chapter 4), such as C11, Visual Basic and COBOL. Because SQL uses standardized and simplified procedures for retrieving, storing and manipulating data in a database system, the popular database query language can be easy to understand and use.

After a database has been set up and loaded with data, it can produce any desired reports, documents and other outputs. These outputs usually appear in screen displays or hard-copy printouts. The output-control features of a database program allow you to select the records and fields to appear in reports. You can also make calculations specifically for the report by manipulating database fields. Formatting controls and organization options (such as report headings) help you to customize reports and create flexible, convenient and powerful information-handling tools.

A DBMS can produce a wide variety of documents, reports and other outputs that can help organizations achieve their goals. The most common reports select and organize data to present summary information about some aspect of company operations. For example, accounting reports often summarize financial data such as current and past-due accounts. Many companies base their routine operating decisions on regular status reports that show the progress of specific orders towards completion and delivery. Polygon, for example, has developed the ColorNet database to help traders of rare gemstones perform routine processing activities, including the buying and selling of precious gemstones.[1]

Databases can also provide support to help executives and other people make better decisions. A database by Intellifit, for example, can be used to help shoppers make better decisions and get clothes that fit when shopping online.[2] The database contains true sizes of apparel from various clothing companies that do business on the web. The process starts when a customer's body is scanned into a database at one of the company's locations, typically in a shopping mall. About 200 000 measurements are taken to construct a 3D image of the person's body shape. The database then compares the actual body dimensions with sizes given by web-based clothing stores to get an excellent fit. According to one company executive, 'We're 90 per cent (accurate) about the sizes and the styles and the brands that will fit you best.'

A database is central to every business selling over the Internet. Amazon, for example, has a huge amount of data that other books sellers must envy, on customers' past purchases, which it uses to make personal recommendations and generate more sales. Each time a returning customer comes back to the website, a report is produced (which becomes part of the webpage itself, something described later in this chapter and again in Case One, page 186) of their recommendations.

Database Administration

database administrator (DBA) The role of the database administrator is to plan, design, create, operate, secure, monitor and maintain databases.

Database systems require a skilled **database administrator (DBA)**. A DBA is expected to have a clear understanding of the fundamental business of the organization, be proficient in the use of selected database management systems, and stay abreast of emerging technologies and new design approaches. The role of the DBA is to plan, design, create, operate, secure, monitor and maintain databases. Typically, a DBA has a degree in computer science or management information systems and some on-the-job training with a particular database product or more extensive experience with a range of database products.

The DBA works with users to decide the content of the database – to determine exactly what entities are of interest and what attributes are to be recorded about those entities. Thus, personnel outside of IS must have some idea of what the DBA does and why this function is important. The DBA can play a crucial role in the development of effective information systems to benefit the organization, employees and managers.

The DBA also works with programmers as they build applications to ensure that their programs comply with database management system standards and conventions. After the database is built and operating, the DBA monitors operations logs for security violations. Database performance is also monitored to ensure that the system's response time meets users' needs and that it operates efficiently. If there is a problem, the DBA attempts to correct it before it becomes serious.

Some organizations have also created a position called the **data administrator**, a non-technical but important role that ensures that data is managed as an important organizational resource. The data administrator is responsible for defining and implementing consistent principles for a variety of data issues, including setting data standards and data definitions that apply across all the databases in an organization. For example, the data administrator would ensure that a term such as 'customer' is defined and treated consistently in all corporate databases. This person also works with business managers to identify who should have read or update access to certain databases and to selected attributes within those databases. This information is then communicated to the database administrator for implementation. The data administrator can be a high-level position reporting to top-level managers.

data administrator A non-technical position responsible for defining and implementing consistent principles for a variety of data issues.

Selecting a Database Management System

The database administrator often selects the database management system for an organization. The process begins by analyzing database needs and characteristics. The information needs of the organization affect the type of data that is collected and the type of database management system that is used. Important characteristics of databases include the following:

- *Database size:* The number of records or files in the database.
- *Database cost:* The purchase or lease costs of the database.
- *Concurrent users:* The number of people who need to use the database at the same time (the number of concurrent users).
- *Performance:* How fast the database is able to update records.
- *Integration:* The ability to be integrated with other applications and databases.
- *Vendor:* The reputation and financial stability of the database vendor.

For many organizations, database size doubles about every year or two.[3] Wal-Mart, for example, adds billions of rows of data to its databases every day. Its database of sales and marketing information is approximately 500 terabytes large. According to Dan Phillips, Wal-Mart's vice president of information systems, 'Our database grows because we capture data on every item, for every customer, for every store, every day.' Wal-Mart deletes data after two years and doesn't track individual customer purchases. Scientific databases are likely the largest in the world. The UK's forensic DNA database is vast and NASA's Stanford Linear Accelerator Center stores about 1000 terabytes of data.[4]

Using Databases with Other Software

Database management systems (DBMSs) are often used with other software packages or the Internet. A DBMS can act as a front-end application or a back-end application. A front-end application is one that directly interacts with people or users. Marketing researchers often use a database as a front end to a statistical analysis program. The researchers enter the results of market questionnaires or surveys into a database. The data is then transferred to a statistical analysis program to determine the potential for a new product or the effectiveness of an advertising campaign. A back-end application interacts with other programs or applications; it only indirectly interacts with people or users. When people request information from a website, the website can interact with a database (the back end) that supplies the desired information.

For example, you can connect to a university website to find out whether the university's library has a book you want to read. The website then interacts with a database that contains a catalogue of library books and articles to determine whether the book you want is available.

5.3 Database Applications

Database applications manipulate the content of a database to produce useful information. Common manipulations are searching, filtering, synthesizing and assimilating the data contained in a database using a number of database applications. These applications allow users to link the company databases to the Internet, set up data warehouses, use databases for strategic business intelligence, place data at different locations, use online processing and open connectivity standards for increased productivity, and search for and use unstructured data, such as graphics, audio and video.[5]

Linking Databases to the Internet

Linking databases to the Internet is an incredibly useful application for organizations and individuals. Every e-commerce website uses database technology to dynamically create its webpages, saving vast amounts of efforts. Every time you visit Amazon, for instance, or the South African fashion retailer Edgars, or one of thousands of other Internet businesses, the pages you see are created at that time from a database of product and customer information. This simplifies the maintenance of the website – to add new stock, all that needs to be done is enter a new record in the product table.

Yahoo! and several educational partners are scanning books and articles into large web-based databases.[6] Called the Open-Content Alliance, they plan to offer free access to material that is no longer under copyright agreements. General Electric and Intermountain Health Care are developing a comprehensive web database on medical treatments and clinical protocols for doctors.[7] The database is expected to cost about €74 million to develop and should help physicians more accurately diagnose patient illnesses. Some banner ads on websites are linked directly with sophisticated databases that contain information on products and services.[8] This allows people to get product and service information without leaving their current website. LetsGoDigital, a company that sells cameras and other digital products over the Internet, based in the Netherlands, uses this approach.

Developing a seamless integration of traditional databases with the Internet is often called a 'semantic web'. A semantic web allows people to access and manipulate a number of traditional databases at the same time through the Internet. Many software vendors – including IBM, Oracle, Microsoft, Macromedia, Inline Internet Systems and Netscape Communications – are incorporating the capability of the Internet into their products. Such databases allow companies to create an Internet-accessible catalogue, which is nothing more than a database of items, descriptions and prices.

In addition to the Internet, organizations are gaining access to databases through networks to get good prices and reliable service. Connecting databases to corporate websites and networks can lead to potential problems, however. One database expert believes that up to 40 per cent of websites that connect to corporate databases are susceptible to hackers taking complete control of the database. By typing certain characters in a form on some websites, a hacker can issue SQL commands to control the corporate database.

Big Data Applications

Much of the data that organizations store comes from their Transaction Processing Systems, which are described fully in Chapter 7. However firms are frequently storing less well-structured data too, such as photos, videos, data from customers' blogs, data from social networks and from their own website including the order people view their webpages. All of this is often called Big Data – large amounts of unstructured data that are difficult or impossible to capture and analyze using traditional database management systems.

Big data can provide valuable insights to help organizations achieve their goals. It can reveal which potential customers are most likely to purchase which products. It can identify where and when a customer tends to shop. It can even determine how much a customer would be willing to pay for a product.

Special big data hardware and software tools have been developed to collect, store and analyze these data. Apache Hadoop is an open-source database that can be used to manage large unstructured datasets in conjunction with relational databases.[9] Yahoo! for example, uses Hadoop to collect and analyze exabytes (millions of terabytes) of data.[10] Oracle has developed Big Data Applicance, which is a combination of hardware and software specifically designed to capture, store and analyze large amounts of unstructured data. IBM has developed InfoSphere BigInsights, which is based on Hadoop, to help organizations analyze continuously created data.

Data Warehouses

5

The data necessary to make sound business decisions is stored in a variety of locations and formats. This data is initially captured, stored and managed by transaction processing systems that are designed to support the day-to-day operations of the organization. For decades, organizations have collected operational, sales and financial data with their transaction processing systems (explained fully in Chapter 7). A **data warehouse** is a database or a collection of databases that holds business information from many sources in the enterprise, covering all aspects of the company's processes, products and customers. The data warehouse provides business users with a multidimensional view of the data they need to analyze business conditions. A data warehouse stores historical data that has been extracted from transaction processing systems, as well as data from external sources (see Figure 5.10).

data warehouse A database or collection of databases that collects business information from many sources in the enterprise, covering all aspects of the company's processes, products and customers.

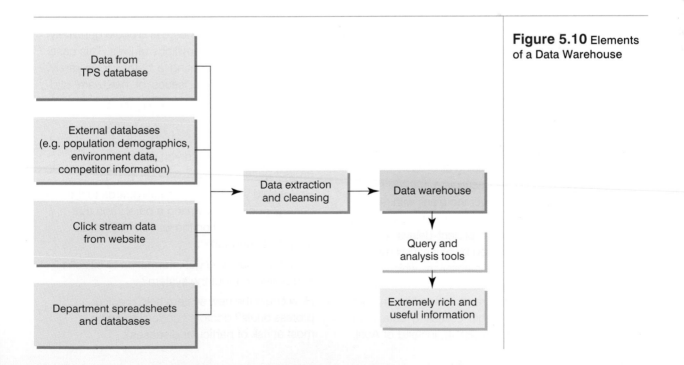

Figure 5.10 Elements of a Data Warehouse

This operational and external data is 'cleaned' to remove inconsistencies and integrated to create a new information database that is more suitable for business analysis.

Data warehouses typically start out as very large databases, containing millions and even hundreds of millions of data records. As this data is collected from various sources, one data warehouse is built that business analysts can use. To keep it accurate, the data warehouse receives regular updates. Old data that is no longer needed is purged. It is common for a data warehouse to contain from three to ten years of current and historical data. Data-cleaning tools can merge data from many sources to make the warehouse, automate data collection and verification, delete unwanted data and maintain the data. Data warehouses can also get data from unique sources. Oracle's Warehouse Management software, for example, can accept information from radio frequency identification (RFID) technology, which is being used to tag

Ethical and Societal Issues

5

Sharing the Big Data of the NHS

The British National Health Service (NHS) is currently implementing a new database which will enable doctors and hospitals to share patient data with each other. Sharing information about patient care will help the NHS to understand the health needs of all patients and the quality of the treatment provided. The system aims to find more effective ways of preventing, treating and managing illnesses, understand who is most at risk of particular diseases and conditions to provide preventative services, and identify who could be at risk of a condition or would benefit from a particular treatment. The system, called Care.Data, will store the NHS Number (a primary key), the date of birth and gender of all patients along with details of treatments received and the outcomes they had.

How, when and with whom the data get shared is strictly controlled by law and confidentiality rules, and British citizens are able to opt out of being included in the system, with every household in the country being sent information explaining all of this. However there has been widespread criticism that the public have been left in the dark over the plans with reports that not everyone has received the leaflet explaining the project. This has led to project delays. Use of the system has been delayed by at least six months while the communications campaign, which gives people the chance to opt out, is improved. An NHS spokesman said: 'To ensure that the concerns are met, NHS England will begin collecting data from GP surgeries in the autumn (2014), instead of April,

to allow more time to build understanding of the benefits of using the information, what safeguards are in place, and how people can opt out if they choose to.' The Association of Medical Research Charities chief executive Sharmila Nebhrajani said that any sharing of data must be done with care, competence and consent. 'Care that respects the sensitivity of the data, competence to ensure that information is held securely, and most importantly with the informed consent of the public,' she said.

The data that Care.Data is planning to store will become an important resource and could genuinely save and improve many millions of lives. This case highlights that implementing a database is rarely just about the technical issues of hardware and software.

Questions

1 What safeguards would you put in place to protect patient privacy?

2 How would you explain the safeguards to the general public? (Try writing a paragraph that would be included on the leaflet – it's not as easy as it sounds!)

3 How else could you get information to citizens and patients about the system?

4 How could the new system help medical professionals? doctors? understand who is most at risk of particular diseases?

products as they are shipped or moved from one location to another.[11] A data warehouse can be extremely difficult to establish, with the typical cost exceeding €2 million.

Data Mining

Data mining is the process of analyzing data to try to discover patterns and relationships within the data. Typically, a data warehouse is mined. Like gold mining, data mining sifts through mountains of data to find a few nuggets of valuable information. There are a number of data mining tools and techniques.

data mining The process of analyzing data to try to discover patterns and relationships within the data.

Association rules algorithms are used to find associations between items in the data. A question that an association rule algorithm might be used to answer is, if someone buys eggs, how likely is it that they will also buy cheese? This information could be used in a supermarket to layout the goods in the best configuration. Rattle (Figure 5.11) is an extremely powerful data mining application which can be used within the programming language R. Both are entirely free and can be downloaded from www.r-project.org/.

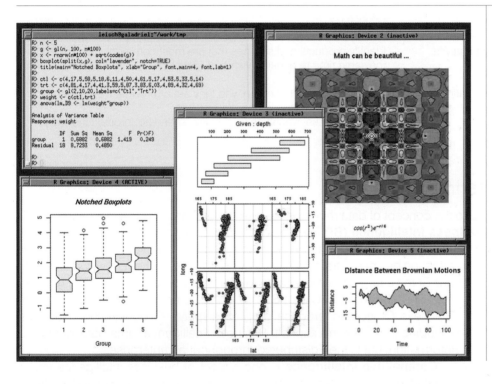

Figure 5.11 Data mining with Rattle *Rattle is a software package that runs in the R programming language. Both are available for free. To get started visit www.r-project.org*

Data mining is used extensively in marketing to improve customer retention; identify cross-selling opportunities; manage marketing campaigns; market, channel and pricing analysis; and customer segmentation analysis (especially one-to-one marketing). Data-mining tools help users find answers to questions they haven't thought to ask.

E-commerce presents another major opportunity for effective use of data mining. Attracting customers to websites is tough; keeping them can be tougher. For example, when retail websites launch deep-discount sales, they cannot easily determine how many first-time customers are likely to come back and buy again. Nor do they have a way of understanding which customers acquired during the sale are price sensitive and more likely to jump on future sales. As a result, companies are gathering data on user traffic through their websites and storing that data in databases. This data is then analyzed using data-mining techniques to personalize and customize the website, and develop sales promotions targeted at specific customers.

Traditional DBMS vendors are well aware of the great potential of data mining. Thus, companies such as Oracle, Sybase, Tandem and Red Brick Systems are all incorporating data-mining functionality into their products. Table 5.3 summarizes a few of the most frequent applications for data mining. See Case Two on page 187 for an explanation of one data-mining algorithm.

Table 5.3 Common Data-Mining Applications

Application	Description
Branding and positioning of products and services	Enable the strategist to visualize the different positions of competitors in a given market using performance (or other) data on dozens of key features of the product and then to condense all that data into a perceptual map of only two or three dimensions
Customer churn	Predict current customers who are likely to switch to a competitor
Direct marketing	Identify prospects most likely to respond to a direct marketing campaign (such as a direct mailing)
Fraud detection	Highlight transactions most likely to be deceptive or illegal
Market basket analysis	Identify products and services that are most commonly purchased at the same time (e.g. nail polish and lipstick)
Market segmentation	Group customers based on who they are or on what they prefer
Trend analysis	Analyze how key variables (e.g. sales, spending, promotions) vary over time

Business Intelligence

Closely linked to the concept of data mining is the use of databases for business-intelligence purposes. **Business intelligence (BI)** involves gathering enough of the right information in a timely manner and usable form and analyzing it so that it can be used to have a positive effect on business strategy, tactics or operations.[12] 'Right now, we are using our BI tools to generate on-demand statistics and process-control reports,' said Steve Snodgrass, CIO of Granite Rock Company.[13] The company uses Business Objects to produce graphic displays of construction supplies, including concrete and asphalt. Business intelligence turns data into useful information that is then distributed throughout an enterprise.

business intelligence The process of gathering enough of the right information in a timely manner and usable form and analyzing it to have a positive impact on business strategy, tactics or operations.

competitive intelligence One aspect of business intelligence limited to information about competitors and the ways that knowledge affects strategy, tactics, and operations.

Competitive intelligence is one aspect of business intelligence and is limited to information about competitors and the ways that knowledge affects strategy, tactics and operations. Competitive intelligence is a critical part of a company's ability to see and respond quickly and appropriately to the changing marketplace. Competitive intelligence is not espionage: the use of illegal means to gather information. In fact, almost all the information a competitive-intelligence professional needs can be collected by examining published information sources, conducting interviews and using other legal, ethical methods. Using a variety of analytical tools, a skilled competitive-intelligence professional can by deduction fill the gaps in information already gathered.

counterintelligence The steps an organization takes to protect information sought by 'hostile' intelligence gatherers.

The term '**counterintelligence**' describes the steps an organization takes to protect information sought by 'hostile' intelligence gatherers. One of the most effective counterintelligence measures is to define 'trade secret' information relevant to the company and control its dissemination.

Information Systems @ Work

Managing the Database: It Can't Stop

A database is like any other organizational asset: someone must watch over it for the organization to obtain the greatest value from its investment. As you read in this chapter, that person is the database administrator (DBA).

In a company like Vodafone, database administration is a big job. Vodafone Group is one of the world's largest mobile communications companies with operations in Europe, the Middle East, Africa, Asia Pacific and the USA (where it owns 45 per cent of Verizon Wireless). Vodafone provides communications services to 391 million registered mobile customers.

Vodafone has 3650 Oracle databases in Europe alone. These databases support critical applications that include online web services, online Vodafone shops, automatic teller machines (ATMs) for prepaid mobile top-ups (refills), and billing systems.

Vodafone needed to manage these databases effectively without increased staffing. It wanted to become proactive in database management to improve overall system stability and availability. Specific challenges included the following:

- Improve reporting to ensure that database configuration issues are flagged and resolved before they become major and affect customer experience.

- Improve system availability and stability to ensure that the business-critical applications (including billing, online web services and retail) are always available.

- Provide faster access to the knowledge of customer support specialists, thus speeding problem resolution.

Fortunately, DBAs need not go into this battle unarmed. The same technology that gave rise to these needs also helps companies deal with them. Oracle's solution, which Vodafone (already a user of Oracle database management software) adopted, is called Oracle Enterprise Manager, now in version 12c. Other database suppliers have corresponding products.

For example, Enterprise Manager 12c has a module called the Automatic Database Diagnostic Monitor (ADDM). Its purpose is to diagnose why a system is slow, a time-consuming task for DBAs. ADDM focuses on activities that are the most time consuming for databases. It drills down through a problem classification tree to find the causes of problems. ADDM's goal is to discover the cause behind performance problems rather than just reporting symptoms. Each ADDM finding has an associated impact and benefit measure to rank issues and respond first to the most critical ones. To better understand the effect of the findings over time, each finding has a descriptive name that DBAs can use to apply filters, search for data and retrieve previous occurrences of the finding in the last 24 hours.

Vodafone began by carrying out a pilot project using Enterprise Manager 12c on 108 of its databases, just under 3 per cent of the total, in the third quarter of 2011. Using data from this pilot project, Vodafone calculated that it would need 85 DBAs in Europe for all its databases, an average of 43 databases each – less than an hour a week per database. The reduction in time spent on technical tasks freed up time for business-generating activities, such as designing improved solutions to business needs.

Using Oracle's support services and Enterprise Manager 12c, 'we have improved response times by more than 50 per cent and are much more proactive, fixing issues before they become a problem for our customers,' reports Peter O'Brien, manager of technology and infrastructure services for Oracle products at Vodafone Group. Informed use of technology support tools clearly pays off for this business.

Questions

1 Database support products are not interchangeable: each vendor's support software is designed to work with its databases. How would you approach the problem of selecting a database supplier if one of them had the best support software but was deficient in

(continued)

other areas? Or if that database was the most expensive?

2 Vodafone's customers make mobile telephone calls at any time. This usage means that at least some of its databases must be available around the clock. Downtime of more than a few seconds will cause Vodafone to lose customers. By contrast, your university could survive a database outage of several minutes to a few hours with little harm beyond annoyance. Should your university invest in a product like Enterprise Manager?

3 Do you think you would enjoy being a database administrator? Do you think you would be good at this job? Explain why.

4 From the description of the difference between the jobs of database administrator and of data administrator, would a data administrator use a product like Enterprise Manager? Why or why not?

Distributed Databases

Distributed processing involves placing processing units at different locations and linking them via telecommunications equipment. A **distributed database** – a database in which the data is spread across several smaller databases connected through telecommunications devices – works on much the same principle. A user in the London branch of a clothing manufacturer, for example, might make a request for data that is physically located at corporate headquarters in Milan, Italy. The user does not have to know where the data is physically stored (see Figure 5.12).

distributed database A database in which the data is spread across several smaller databases connected via telecommunications devices.

Figure 5.12 The Use of a Distributed Database
This figure shows how data from a clothing manufacturer is stored across multiple sites.

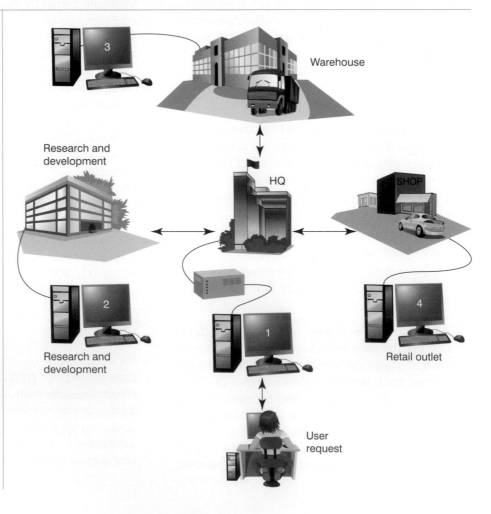

For the clothing manufacturer, computers might be located at the headquarters, in the research and development centre, in the warehouse, and in a company-owned retail store. Telecommunications systems link the computers so that users at all locations can access the same distributed database no matter where the data is actually stored.

Distributed databases give organizations more flexibility in how databases are organized and used. Local offices can create, manage and use their own databases, and people at other offices can access and share the data in the local databases. Giving local sites more direct access to frequently used data can improve organizational effectiveness and efficiency significantly. The New York City Police Department, for example, has about 35 000 officers searching for information located in over 70 offices around the city.[14] According to one database programmer, 'They had a lot of information available in a lot of different database systems and wanted fingertip access to the information in a very user-friendly front-end.' Dimension Data helped the police department by developing an US$11(€8) million system to tie their databases together. 'Now, we can send them critical details before they even arrive at the scene,' said police commissioner Raymond Kelly. The new distributed database is also easier for police officers to use.

Despite its advantages, distributed processing creates additional challenges in integrating different databases (information integration), maintaining data security, accuracy, timeliness and conformance to standards.[15] Distributed databases allow more users direct access at different sites; thus, controlling who accesses and changes data is sometimes difficult.[16] Also, because distributed databases rely on telecommunications lines to transport data, access to data can be slower.

To reduce telecommunications costs, some organizations build a **replicated database**. A replicated database holds a duplicate set of frequently used data. The company sends a copy of important data to each distributed processing location when needed or at predetermined times. Each site sends

replicated database A database that holds a duplicate set of frequently used data.

the changed data back to update the main database on an update cycle. This process, often called data synchronization, is used to make sure that replicated databases are accurate, up to date and consistent with each other. A railway, for example, can use a replicated database to increase punctuality, safety and reliability. The primary database can hold data on fares, routings and other essential information. The data can be continually replicated and downloaded from the master database to hundreds of remote servers across the country. The remote locations can send back the latest figures on ticket sales and reservations to the main database.

Online Analytical Processing (OLAP)

For nearly two decades, databases and their display systems have provided flashy sales presentations and trade show demonstrations. All you have to do is ask where a certain product is selling well, for example, and a colourful table showing sales performance by region, product type and time frame appears on the screen. Called **online analytical processing (OLAP)**, these programs are now being used to store and deliver data warehouse information efficiently. The leading OLAP software vendors include Cognos, Comshare, Hyperion Solutions, Oracle, MineShare, WhiteLight and Microsoft. (Note that, in this context, the word 'online' does not

online analytical processing (OLAP) Software that allows users to explore data from a number of perspectives.

refer to the Internet – it simply means that a query is made and answered immediately, as opposed to a user submitting a query and the processing taking place at some other time, for instance at night when the servers are used less.)

The value of data ultimately lies in the decisions it enables. Powerful information-analysis tools in areas such as OLAP and data mining, when incorporated into a data warehousing architecture, bring market conditions into sharper focus and help organizations deliver greater competitive value. OLAP provides top-down, query-driven data analysis; data mining provides bottom-up, discovery-driven analysis. OLAP requires repetitive testing of user-originated theories; data mining requires no assumptions and instead identifies facts and conclusions based on patterns discovered. OLAP, or multidimensional analysis, requires a great deal of human ingenuity and interaction with the database to find information in the database. A user of a data-mining tool does not need to figure out what questions to ask; instead, the approach is, 'here's the data, tell me what interesting patterns emerge'. For example, a data-mining tool in a credit card company's customer database can construct a profile of fraudulent activity from historical information. Then, this profile can be applied to all incoming transaction data to identify and stop fraudulent behaviour, which might otherwise go undetected. Table 5.4 compares the OLAP and data-mining approaches to data analysis.

Table 5.4 Comparison of OLAP and Data Mining

Characteristic	OLAP	Data Mining
Purpose	Supports data analysis and decision making	Supports data analysis and decision making
Type of analysis supported	Top-down, query-driven data analysis	Bottom-up, discovery-driven data analysis
Skills required of user	Must be very knowledgeable of the data and its business context	Must trust in data-mining tools to uncover valid and worthwhile hypotheses

Visual, Audio and Other Database Systems

Organizations are increasingly finding a need to store large amounts of visual and audio signals in an organized fashion. Credit card companies, for example, enter pictures of charge slips into an image database using a scanner. The images can be stored in the database and later sorted by customer name, printed and sent to customers along with their monthly statements. Image databases are also used by physicians to store x-rays and transmit them to clinics away from the main hospital. Financial services, insurance companies and government branches are using image databases to store vital records and replace paper documents. Drug companies often need to analyze many visual images from laboratories. The PetroView database and analysis tool allows petroleum engineers to analyze geographic information to help them determine where to drill for oil and gas. Recently, a visual-fingerprint database was used to solve a 40-year-old murder case in California. Visual databases can be stored in some object-relational databases or special-purpose database systems. Many relational databases can also store graphic content.

Combining and analyzing data from different databases is an increasingly important challenge. Global businesses, for example, sometimes need to analyze sales and accounting data stored around the world in different database systems. Companies such as IBM are developing virtual database systems to allow different databases to work together as a unified database system. DiscoveryLink, one of IBM's projects, can integrate biomedical data from different sources. The Centre for Disease Control (CDC) also has the problem of integrating more than 100 databases on various diseases.

In addition to visual, audio and virtual databases, there are a number of other special-purpose database systems. Spatial data technology involves using a database to store and access data according to the locations it describes and to permit spatial queries and analysis. MapExtreme is spatial technology software from MapInfo that extends a user's database so that it can store, manage and manipulate location-based data. Police departments, for example, can use this type of software to bring together crime data and map it visually so that patterns are easier to analyze.

Police officers can select and work with spatial data at a specified location, within a rectangle, a given radius or a polygon such as their area of jurisdiction. For example, a police officer can request a list of all alcohol shops within a two-mile radius of the police station. Builders and insurance companies use spatial data to make decisions related to natural hazards. Spatial data can even be used to improve financial risk management, with information stored by investment type, currency type, interest rates and time.

Summary

Data management and modelling are key aspects of organizing data and information. Data is one of the most valuable resources that a firm possesses. The most common way to organize data is in a relational database. A relational database is made up of tables, each table is made up of records and each record is made up of fields. Loosely, each table stores information about an entity. An entity is someone or something that the firm wants to store information about. The fields are the characteristics or attributes about the entity that are stored. A record collects together all the fields of a particular instance of an entity. A primary key uniquely identifies each record.

Designing a database involves identifying entities and the relationships between them, as well as the attributes of each entity. There are rules to follow to convert related entities into a data model, a list of all tables to be implemented in the database, with primary and foreign key identified. Basic data manipulations include selecting, projecting and joining.

A well-designed and well-managed database is central to almost all information systems and is an extremely valuable tool in supporting decision making. A DBMS is a group of programs used as an interface between a database and its users and other application programs. When an application program requests data from the database, it follows a logical access path. The actual retrieval of the data follows a physical access path. Records can be considered in the same way: a logical record is what the record contains; a physical record is where the record is stored on storage devices. Schemas are used to describe the entire database, its record types and their relationships to the DBMS. Schemas are entered into the computer via a data definition language, which

describes the data and relationships in a specific database. Another tool used in database management is the data dictionary, which contains detailed descriptions of all data in the database.

After a DBMS has been installed, the database can be accessed, modified and queried via a data manipulation language. A specialized data manipulation language is Structured Query Language (SQL). SQL is used in several popular database packages today and can be installed on PCs and mainframes.

Popular single-user DBMS include Corel Paradox and Microsoft Access. IBM, Oracle and Microsoft are the leading DBMS vendors.

Selecting a DBMS begins by analyzing the information needs of the organization. Important characteristics of databases include the size of the database, the number of concurrent users, its performance, the ability of the DBMS to be integrated with other systems, the features of the DBMS, the vendor considerations, and the cost of the database management system.

The number and types of database applications will continue to evolve and yield real business benefits. Organizations are building data warehouses, which are relational database management systems specifically designed to support management decision making. Data mining, which is the automated discovery of patterns and relationships in a data warehouse, is emerging as a practical approach to generating hypotheses about the patterns and anomalies in the data that can be used to predict future behaviour.

Predictive analysis is a form of data mining that combines historical data with assumptions about future conditions to forecast outcomes of events such as future product sales or the probability that a customer will default on a loan.

Business intelligence is the process of getting enough of the right information in a timely manner and usable form and analyzing it so that it can have a positive effect on business strategy, tactics or operations. Competitive intelligence is one aspect of business intelligence limited to information about competitors and the ways that information affects strategy, tactics and operations. Competitive intelligence is not espionage – the use of illegal means to gather information. Counterintelligence describes the steps an organization takes to protect information sought by 'hostile' intelligence gatherers.

With the increased use of telecommunications and networks, distributed databases, which allow multiple users and different sites access to data that may be stored in different physical locations, are gaining in popularity. To reduce telecommunications costs, some organizations build replicated databases, which hold a duplicate set of frequently used data.

Online analytical processing (OLAP) programs are being used to store data and allow users to explore the data from a number of different perspectives.

An object-oriented database uses the same overall approach of object-oriented programming, first discussed in Chapter 4. With this approach, both the data and the processing instructions are stored in the database. An object-relational database management system (ORDBMS) provides a complete set of relational database capabilities, plus the ability for third parties to add new data types and operations to the database. These new data types can be audio, video and graphical data that require new indexing, optimization and retrieval features.

In addition to raw data, organizations are increasingly finding a need to store large amounts of visual and audio signals in an organized fashion. There are also a number of special-purpose database systems.

Self-Assessment Test

1 A relational database is made up of _____.
   a. worksheets
   b. documents
   c. tables
   d. files

2 A(n) _____ is a person, place or thing about whom or about which a firm wants to store information.

3 _____ dictate the type of relationships that exist between entities.

4 A(n) _____ uniquely identifies a record.

5 When identifying relationships between entities, you must identify the degree, _____ and optionality.

6 The commands used to access and report information from the database are part of the _____.
   a. data definition language
   b. data manipulation language
   c. data normalization language
   d. schema

7 Access is a popular DBMS for _____.
   a. personal computers
   b. graphics workstations
   c. mainframe computers
   d. supercomputers

8 A(n) _____ holds business information from many sources in the enterprise, covering all aspects of the company's processes, products and customers.

9 An information-analysis tool that involves the automated discovery of patterns and relationships in a data warehouse is called

_____.

   a. a relational database
   b. data mining
   c. predictive analysis
   d. business intelligence

10 _____ allows users to explore corporate data from a number of perspectives.

Review Questions

1 What is an attribute? How is it related to an entity?

2 Define the term 'database'. How is it different from a database management system?

3 What are the advantages of the database approach?

4 What is a database schema, and what is its purpose?

5 What is the difference between a data definition language (DDL) and a data manipulation language (DML)?

6 How do you resolve a many-to-many relationship?

7 What is a distributed database system?

8 What is data mining? What is OLAP? How are they different?

9 What is Big Data? How can it be used?

10 What is business intelligence? How is it used?

Discussion Questions

1 You have been selected to represent the student body on a project to develop a new database for a student club you belong to. What actions might you take to fulfil this responsibility to ensure that the project meets the needs of students and is successful?

2 Your company wants to increase revenues from its existing customers. How can data mining be used to accomplish this objective?

3 Make a list of the databases in which data about you exists. How is the data in each database captured? Who updates each database and how often? Is it possible for you to request a printout of the contents of your data record from each database? What data privacy concerns do you have?

4 You are the vice president of information technology for a large, multinational consumer packaged goods company (such as Procter and Gamble, Unilever or Gillette). You must make a presentation to persuade the board of directors to invest €5 million to establish a competitive-intelligence group – including people, data-gathering services and software tools. What key points do you need to make in favour of this investment? What arguments can you anticipate that others might make?

5 Identity theft, where people steal your personal information, continues to be a threat. Assume that you are the database administrator for a corporation with a large database. What steps would you implement to help you prevent people from stealing personal information from the corporate database?

Web Exercises

1 Use a search engine to find information on specific products for one of the following topics: business intelligence, object-oriented databases or audio databases. Write a brief report describing what you found, including a description of the database products and the companies that developed them.

2 Use a search engine to find three companies in an industry that interests you, that use a database management system. Describe how databases are used in each company. Could the companies survive without the use of a database management system? Why?

Case One

Stocard Reduces Wallet Weight

A recently commissioned consumer study into Australian loyalty programs called 'Share the Love 2014' provides companies with in-depth insights into consumers' relationships with loyalty programs. The research found that almost three-quarters of members are happy to have their buying behaviour monitored in return for personalized offers. The top loyalty programmes include Coles Flybuys, Woolworth's Everyday Rewards and Qantas Frequent Flyer. However, not everyone wants to carry a wallet full of plastic loyalty cards. The Stocard App allows people to store their card details on their mobile phone. Then, when a user shops at a store, instead of hunting for that store's loyalty card, they simply open the Stocard app and have the cashier scan the replica barcode displayed on their smartphone screen – there is no need for the customer to carry the physical card. To add a new card, customers can take a picture of it with their mobile phone camera.

Stocard was founded in 2011 by David Handlos, Björn Goβ and Florian Barth while they were studying at university. Retailers who partner with Stocard can push special offers via the app, which is presumably how the start-up intends to make money. It allows companies to stitch together personal information about a customer, such as where they live and how many children they have, with what products they buy, which is usually called shopping basket data. Below is a picture of a database design that could store this information. 'Shopping' stores information about the date, time and location the customer does a shop. Shopping basket stores a list of all the products a customer bought every time they do a shop.

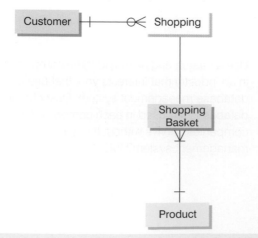

One way that data from this database could be analyzed is with an association rules algorithm. An association rules algorithm is designed to uncover interesting purchase patterns in shopping basket data or, to put it another way, answers the question: what products are often bought together? Consider the following data:

Transaction ID, apples, bananas, potatoes, bread

TRANSACTION (T)	Apples	Bananas	Potatoes	Bread
1	1	1	0	1
2	0	0	1	1
3	1	1	1	0
4	1	1	0	0
5	1	1	0	1
6	0	0	1	1

Let's say that we're interested in what gets bought alongside bread. Transaction 1 gives the first possible rule: IF apples AND bananas ARE PURCHASED THEN bread WILL BE PURCHASED. Transaction 2 gives another: IF potatoes ARE PURCHASED THEN bread WILL BE PURCHASED. Many millions of rules will be produced from a real company database, so how do we decide which rules are any good? We look for two criteria – support and confidence.

Support is how often the first part of the rule comes up. Apples and bananas are bought together 4 times out of 6 so that rule's support is 4/6 or 66 per cent. Confidence is how often the rule is correct in those transactions that feature the first part of the rule. So for the four times that apples and bananas are bought together (it doesn't matter what else was also bought with them), bread is bought twice, so that rule's confidence is 2/4 or 50 per cent. In general, rules with the highest support and confidence are the best.

Armed with the best rules, a company can start to make product recommendations to customers: 'you bought this product, you might also be interested in this other product'. You may have seen messages like this one, especially if you have ever made a purchase on Amazon.

Questions

1 Calculate the support and confidence of the rule: IF potatoes ARE PURCHASED THEN bread WILL BE PURCHASED.

2 What are some of the reasons people sign up for a loyalty programme?

3 What are some of the fears that stop people signing up for a loyalty programme? How could a company overcome these?

4 How else could Stocard make money?

Case Two

Computational Social Scientists Take on Wall Street

The Holy Grail of data mining has for a long time been to be able to predict share prices. However, share price movements have consistently been shown to be no different from randomly generated numbers going up and down without pattern, which makes future prices impossible to predict from past share prices. However, everyone knows that share prices are not random. They vary according to what's going on in the world – news events, the publication of company reports, the behaviour of company executives and employee unions. It's just the timings of these events affect prices in ways that make prices look random.

So is prediction a lost cause?

Not necessarily. Instead of making the prediction based on what share prices were in the past, why not make it on a measure of what's going on in the world – what people are talking about, for instance. If everyone is talking about a company maybe this interest will make the share price jump up (or down). But how to do you know what people are talking about?

Tobias Preis and colleagues think they may have a solution: Google Trend Data. Every time a user searches for something on Google, Google records the search term they used. Maybe if a particular term comes up frequently then that can be used to predict a share price jump. Preis and his colleagues have done an analysis using historical share and trend data and they may be on to something.

They followed a simple strategy: if the word 'debt' was searched for more this week than last week they predicted that the Dow Jones Industrial Average index was about fall, and if debt was searched for less last week than this week, they predicted it was going to rise. An investor who followed this for real (the researchers did not really invest any money) would have made 300 per cent more than someone following a buy and hold strategy (not taking trading fees into account).

Questions

1 Describe a data model (database design) that could be used to store share price data.

2 What else could Google Trend Data be able to predict?

3 Do a Google search for Google Trend Data. What data are you able to access? Why do you think Google give away these data?

4 Who do you think should own Google search terms – the user that wrote them or Google? What implications does your answer have for Internet users and Internet companies?

Case Three

From a Traditional Database to Business Intelligence

Medihelp is South Africa's third largest health insurance company. It covers about 350 000 people with plans ranging from R744 to R4278 (about €70 to €400) per month per person. Medihelp needed a better way to access and analyze data on customers, claims and third-party providers in order to monitor the effectiveness of its insurance products and to fine-tune and create new products as needed.

Medihelp's problem was that its data were stored in a traditional database. As discussed in this chapter, traditional databases are not designed to support decision making. They're not efficient at the types of information retrieval that decision making uses. With Medihelp's existing database, reports took unacceptably long times to run. Reports based on the content of the full database couldn't be run at all. This inefficiency detracted from Medihelp's ability to make informed business decisions.

For example, Medihelp's claim file had about 55 million rows. Each row contained about 35 data values describing medical conditions, treatments and payments. Each row was associated with one of 15 million rows of historical member data, which held another 15 or so data values describing the member and his or her coverage. For claim processing, accessing the data for a single claim was fast and efficient. Combining data from thousands of rows, as decision support calls for, was not.

'Logging into our [traditional] database ... was not providing us the information we needed to make the best business decisions,' explains Jan Steyl, senior manager of business intelligence at Medihelp. 'We needed a dedicated, high-performance data warehouse.'

After looking at several options, Medihelp made a preliminary selection of Sybase IQ as the basis for its data warehouse. Working with B. I. Practice, a Sybase subsidiary in South Africa, Medihelp carried out a proof of concept to confirm that Sybase IQ could deliver the needed performance at an acceptable cost. This procedure involved loading a subset of the tables from the operational database into Sybase IQ, executing queries that used only that subset of the data and evaluating the results.

Because these queries now used a database designed for business intelligence, performance improved dramatically. Response time was reduced by an average of 71.5 per cent. Response time for ad hoc queries, those which were not programmed into the database system ahead of time, was reduced by an average of 74.1 per cent. One query's response time dropped by 92.8 per cent.

Theo Els, Medihelp's senior manager of client relations, likes the new system. 'Health insurers supply data to employer groups. These demographic and claims profiles are essential for employer groups seeking to understand their employees' health risks ... and the consequent impact that risk can have on business productivity. Brokers and healthcare consultants also use this information in their annual client reviews to ensure that employees receive the most suitable coverage. It is imperative that the ... data warehouse provide accurate information in a format that is easily understood.'

The biggest beneficiary of Medihelp's data warehouse is its product development team. The team uses data from the data warehouse to understand trends in claims by benefit code, condition, area, age group and other factors. Medihelp also uses its data warehouse to determine what financial effects changes to a benefit in a specific product will have. This provides the sales force with the right offering at the right price for specific target markets in South Africa.

Questions

1 What is the difference between a database and a data warehouse?

2 How can a data warehouse be used to create business intelligence?

3 How does the structure of a database affect what an organization can do with the information in it?

4 Discuss some of the ethical issues about using business intelligence in this industry. (For instance, what if an insurer could predict whether someone is likely to suffer a particular condition?)

Notes

1 Novellino, Teresa, 'Polygon Launches Colored Gemstone Database', *Business Media*, 24 February 2005.

2 Schuman, Evan, 'Company Offers a High Tech Way to Get Clothes to Fit', *CIO Insight*, 18 March 2005.

3 Staff, 'Data, Data, Everywhere', *Information Week*, 9 January 2006, p. 49.

4 Staff, 'Biggest Brother: DNA Evidence', *The Economist*, 5 January 2006.

5 Gray, Jim and Compton, Mark, 'Long Anticipated, the Arrival of Radically Restructured Database Architectures Is Now Finally at Hand', *ACM Queue*, vol. 3, no. 3, April 2005.

6 Delaney, Kevin, 'Yahoo, Partners Plan Web Database', *Wall Street Journal*, 3 October 2005, p. B6.

7 Kranhold, Kathryn, 'High-Tech Tool Planned for Physicians', *Wall Street Journal*, 17 February 2005, p. D3.

8 Staff, 'In-Ad Search', *New Media Age*, 13 January 2006, p. 28.

9 Vijayan, J., 'Hadoop works alongside RDBMS', *Computerworld*, 22 August 2011, p. 5.

10 Bednarz, A. 'Rise of Hadoop Challenge for IT', *Network World*, 13 February 2012, p. 1.

11 Hall, Mark, 'Databases Can't Handle RFID', *Computerworld,* 7 February 2005, p. 8.

12 Johnson, Avery, 'Hotels Take 'Know Your Customers' to a New Level', *Wall Street Journal*, 7 February 2006, p. D1.

13 McAdams, Jennifer, 'Business Intelligence: Power to the People', *Computerworld*, 2 January 2006, p. 24.

14 Murphy, David, 'Fighting Crime in Real Time', *PC Magazine*, 28 September 2005, p. 70.

15 Kay, Russell, 'Enterprise Information Integration', *Computerworld*, 19 September 2005, p. 64.

16 Babcock, Charles, 'Protection Gets Granular', *InformationWeek*, 23 September 2005, p. 58.

5

06

Computer Networks

Principles	Learning Objectives
Effective communications are essential to organizational success.	■ Define the terms 'communications' and 'telecommunications' and describe the components of a telecommunications system.
Communications technology lets more people send and receive all forms of information over great distances.	■ Identify several communications hardware devices and discuss their function.
	■ Describe many of the benefits associated with a telecommunications network.
	■ Define the term 'communications protocols' and identify several common ones.
The Internet is like many other technologies – it provides a wide range of services, some of which are effective and practical for use today, others are still evolving, and still others will fade away from lack of use.	■ Briefly describe how the Internet works, including alternatives for connecting to it and the role of Internet service providers.
	■ Describe the World Wide Web and the way it works.
	■ Explain the use of web browsers, search engines and other web tools.
	■ Outline a process for creating web content.
Because the Internet and the World Wide Web are becoming more universally used and accepted for business use, management, service and speed, privacy and security issues must continually be addressed and resolved.	■ Define the terms 'intranet' and 'extranet' and discuss how organizations are using them.

Why Learn About Computer Networks?

We have examined hardware and software, and paid special attention to how data is organized for storage. The power of information technology greatly increases when devices are linked or networked, which is the subject of this chapter. Today's decision makers need to access data wherever it resides. They must be able to establish fast, reliable connections to exchange messages, upload and download data and software, route business transactions to processors, connect to databases and network services, and send output to printers. Regardless of your chosen career field, you will need the communications capabilities provided by computer networks. The world's largest network is the Internet. To say that the Internet has had a big impact on organizations of all types and sizes would be a huge understatement. Since the early 1990s, when the Internet was first used for commercial purposes, it has affected all aspects of business. Businesses use the Internet to sell and advertise their products and services, reaching out to new and existing customers. People working in every field and at every level use the Internet in their jobs. Whatever your career, you will probably use the Internet daily.

6.1 Telecommunications

Telecommunications refers to the electronic transmission of signals for communications, by such means as telephone, radio and television. Telecommunications impacts businesses greatly because it lessens the barriers of time and distance. Telecommunications is not only changing the way businesses operate, but also the nature of commerce itself. As networks are connected with one another and transmit information more freely, a competitive marketplace demands excellent quality and service from all organizations.

telecommunications The electronic transmission of signals for communications; enables organizations to carry out their processes and tasks through effective computer networks.

Figure 6.1 shows a general model of telecommunications. The model starts with a sending unit (1), such as a person, a computer system, a terminal or another device, that originates the message. The sending unit transmits a signal (2) to a telecommunications device (3). The telecommunications device – a hardware component that facilitates electronic communication – performs many tasks, which can include converting the signal into a different form or from one type to another. The telecommunications device then sends the signal through a medium (4). A telecommunications medium is any material substance that carries an electronic signal to support communications between a sending and receiving device. Another telecommunications device (5) connected to the receiving computer (6) receives the signal. The process can be reversed, and

Figure 6.1 Elements of a Telecommunications System
Telecommunications devices relay signals between computer systems and transmission media.

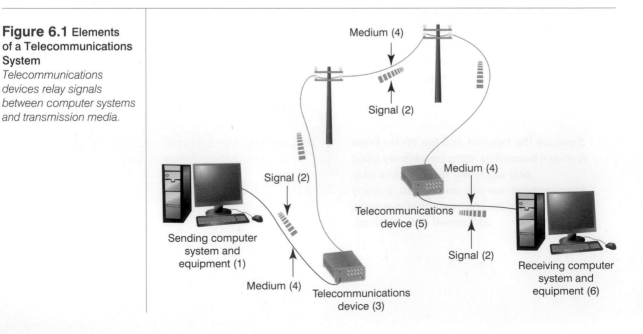

the receiving unit (6) can send another message to the original sending unit (1). An important characteristic of telecommunications is the speed at which information is transmitted, which is measured in bits per second (bps). Common speeds are in the range of thousands of bits per second (Kbps) to millions of bits per second (Mbps) and even billions of bits per second (Gbps).

Advances in telecommunications technology allow us to communicate rapidly with clients and co-workers almost anywhere in the world. Communication between two people can occur synchronously or asynchronously. With synchronous communication, the receiver gets the message almost instantaneously, when it is sent. Phone communication is an example of synchronous communication. With asynchronous communication, there is a measurable delay between the sending and receiving of the message, sometimes hours or even days. Sending a letter through the post office or by email are examples of asynchronous communications. Both types of communications are important in business. However, to use telecommunications effectively, you must carefully analyze telecommunications media and devices.

Channel Bandwidth

Telecommunications **channel bandwidth** refers to the rate at which data is exchanged, usually measured in bits per second (bps) – the broader the bandwidth, the more information can be exchanged at one time. **Broadband communications** can exchange data very quickly, as opposed to **narrowband communications**, which supports a much lower rate of data exchange. Telecommunications professionals consider the capacity of the channel when they recommend transmission media for a business. In general, today's organizations need more bandwidth for increased transmission speed to carry out their daily functions. To increase bandwidth, first consider the different types of telecommunications media you can use.

channel bandwidth The rate at which data is exchanged over a communications channel, usually measured in bits per second (bps).

broadband communications A telecommunications system in which a very high rate of data exchange is possible.

narrowband communications A telecommunications system that supports a much lower rate of data exchange than broadband.

Guided Transmission Media Types

Transmission media can be divided into two broad categories: guided transmission media, in which communications signals are guided along a solid medium; and wireless, in which the communications signal is broadcast over airwaves as a form of electromagnetic radiation.

There are many different guided transmission media types. Table 6.1 summarizes the guided media types by physical media type. Several guided transmission media types are discussed in the sections following the table.

Table 6.1 Guided Transmission Media Types

Guided Media Types			
Media Type	Description	Advantages	Disadvantages
Twisted-pair wire	Twisted pairs of copper wire, shielded or unshielded	Used for telephone service; widely available	Transmission speed and distance limitations
Coaxial cable	Inner conductor wire surrounded by insulation	Cleaner and faster data transmission than twisted-pair wire	More expensive than twisted-pair wire
Fibre-optic cable	Many extremely thin strands of glass bound together in a sheathing; uses light beams to transmit signals	Diameter of cable is much smaller than coaxial; less distortion of signal; capable of high transmission rates	Expensive to purchase and install
Broadband over power lines	Data is transmitted over standard high-voltage power lines	Can provide Internet service to rural areas where cable and phone service may be non-existent	Can be expensive and may interfere with ham radios, and police and fire communications

Twisted-Pair Wire

Twisted-pair wire contains two or more twisted pairs of wire, usually copper (see Figure 6.2a). Proper twisting of the wire keeps the signal from 'bleeding' into the next pair and creating electrical interference. Because the twisted-pair wires are insulated, they can be placed close together and packaged in one group. Hundreds of wire pairs can be grouped into one large wire cable.

Twisted-pair wires are classified by category, depending on the frequency of data transmission. The lower categories are used primarily in homes. Higher categories are sometimes used in smaller networks. Ten gigabit ethernet (labelled IEEE 802.3an) is an emerging standard for transmitting data at the speed of 10 billion bits per second for limited distances over shielded twisted-pair wires. It will be used for the high-speed links that connect groups of computers or to move data stored in large databases on large computers to stand-alone storage devices.[1]

Coaxial Cable

Figure 6.2b shows a typical coaxial cable. Coaxial cable falls in the middle of the guided transmission media in terms of cost and performance. The cable itself is more expensive than twisted-pair wire but less so than fibre-optic cable (discussed next). However, the cost of installation and other necessary communications equipment makes it difficult to compare the total costs of each media. Coaxial cable offers cleaner and crisper data transmission (less noise) than twisted-pair wire. It also offers a higher data transmission rate. Companies such as Virgin Media are aggressively courting customers for telephone service, enticing them away from the phone companies such as BT by bundling Internet and phone services along with TV.

Figure 6.2 Types of Guided Transmission **Media** *(a) Twisted-pair wire (b) Coaxial cable (c) Fibre-optic cable*

(a)

(b)

(continued)

(c)

Figure 6.2 *Continued*

6

Fibre-Optic Cable

Fibre-optic cable, consisting of many extremely thin strands of glass or plastic bound together in a sheathing (a jacket), transmits signals with light beams (see Figure 6.2c). These high-intensity light beams are generated by lasers and are conducted along the transparent fibres. These fibres have a thin coating, called cladding, which effectively works like a mirror, preventing the light from leaking out of the fibre. The much smaller diameter of fibre-optic cable makes it ideal when there is not room for bulky copper wires – for example, in crowded conduits, which can be pipes or spaces carrying both electrical and communications wires. In such tight spaces, the smaller fibre-optic telecommunications cable is very effective. Because fibre-optic cables are immune to electrical interference, they can transmit signals over longer distances with fewer expensive repeaters to amplify or rebroadcast the data. Fibre-optic cable and associated tele-communications devices are more expensive to purchase and install than their twisted-pair wire counterparts, although the cost is decreasing.

Laying thousands of miles of fibre-optic cable across its vast expanses is credited for helping propel India into the high-tech world. With the capability that this infrastructure provided, Indian workers were able to collaborate closely with their Western counterparts even though they were thousands of miles away.[2] As a result, India has emerged as a key business partner to many firms that have outsourced part of their business operations or that use Indian firms for information systems projects.

Broadband Over Power Lines

Many utilities, cities and organizations are experimenting with providing network connections over standard high-voltage power lines. Manassas, Virginia, became the first city in the US to offer this service to all its citizens. To access the Internet, broadband over power lines (BPL) users connect their computer to a special hardware device that plugs into any electrical wall socket. A potential issue with BPL is that transmitting data over unshielded power lines can interfere with both ham radio broadcasts, and police and fire radios. However, BPL can provide Internet service in rural areas where broadband access is unavailable because electricity is prevalent in homes, even more than telephone lines.[3]

Wireless Transmission Media Types

Many technologies are used to transmit communications wirelessly. The major technologies include microwave, satellite, radio and infrared. Their key distinguishing feature is the frequency at which signals are transmitted. These are discussed next.

Microwave Transmission

Microwave is a high-frequency (300 MHz–300 GHz) signal sent through the air (see Figure 6.3). Terrestrial (Earth-bound) microwaves are transmitted by line-of-sight devices, so that the line of sight between the transmitter and receiver must be unobstructed. Typically, microwave stations are placed in a series – one station receives a signal, amplifies it and retransmits it to the next microwave transmission tower. Such stations can be located roughly 30 miles apart before the curvature of the Earth makes it impossible for the towers to 'see one another'. Microwave signals can carry thousands of channels at the same time.

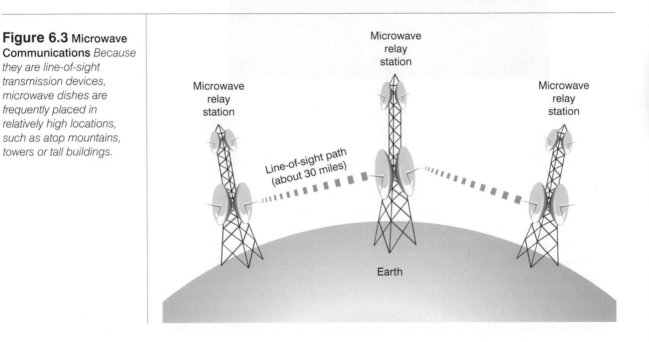

Figure 6.3 Microwave **Communications** *Because they are line-of-sight transmission devices, microwave dishes are frequently placed in relatively high locations, such as atop mountains, towers or tall buildings.*

A communications satellite also operates in the microwave frequency range (see Figure 6.4). The satellite receives the signal from the Earth station, amplifies the relatively weak signal, and then rebroadcasts it at a different frequency. The advantage of satellite communications is that it can receive and broadcast over large geographic regions. Such problems as the curvature of the Earth, mountains and other structures that block the line-of-sight microwave transmission make satellites an attractive alternative. Geostationary, low earth orbit and small mobile satellite stations are the most common forms of satellite communications.

A geostationary satellite orbits the Earth directly over the equator, approximately 35 400 km (22 000 miles) above the Earth so that it appears stationary. Three such satellites, spaced at equal intervals (120 angular degrees apart), can cover the entire world. A geostationary satellite can be accessed using a dish antenna aimed at the spot in the sky where the satellite hovers.

A low earth orbit (LEO) satellite system employs many satellites, each in a circular orbit at an altitude of a few hundred kilometres. The satellites are spaced so that, from any point on the Earth at any time, at least one satellite is on a line of sight.

A very small aperture terminal (VSAT) is a two-way satellite ground station with a dish antenna smaller than three metres in diameter. Many retail chains employ this technology to support

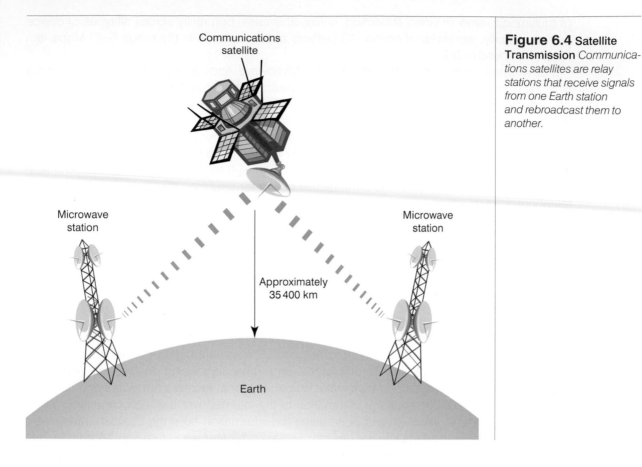

Communications
satellite

Microwave
station

Microwave
station

Approximately
35 400 km

Earth

6

point-of-sale transactions, including credit cards. News organizations employ VSAT dishes that run on battery power to transmit news stories from remote locations. VSAT technology is being used to rebuild the telecommunications infrastructure in Afghanistan and Iraq.

Ford Motor and its service provider Sprint were pioneers in the conversion of employees from using land lines to mobile phone service. In 2005, Ford converted over 8000 employees. The initial deployment covered Ford's product development department, which is a user group that is very collaborative and highly mobile.[4]

3G Wireless Communication

Wireless communication for mobile devices has evolved through four generations of technology and services. The 1G (first generation) of wireless communications standards originated in the 1980s and were based on analogue communications. The 2G (second generation) were fully digital networks that superseded 1G networks in the early 1990s. In 2G, phone conversations were encrypted, mobile phone usage was expanded and short message services (SMS), or texting, was introduced.

3G or third generation wireless communication supports voice and broadband data communications in a mobile environment at speeds of 2–4 Mbps. Additional capabilities include mobile video, e-commerce, location-based services, gaming and music. The wide variety of 3G communications protocols can support many business applications. The challenge is to enable these protocols to intercommunicate and support fast, reliable, global wireless communications.

4G Wireless Communication

The International Telecommunications Union (ITU) has defined 4G as a network that has meaningful improvement over 3G. 4G broadband mobile wireless is delivering enhanced versions of multimedia, smooth video streaming, universal access, portability across all types of device and, eventually, worldwide roaming. 4G delivers access speeds in the range 5–20 Mbps, ten times the speed of 3G.

For example, Worldwide Interoperability for Microwave Access (WiMAX) is a version of 4G which is based on a set of IEEE 802.16 wireless metropolitan area network standards that support various types of communications access. IEEE stands for the Institute of Electrical and Electronic Engineers, a non-profit organization and one of the leading standards-setting organizations. In many respects, WiMAX operates like wi-fi (discussed next) only over greater distances and faster transmission speeds. Fewer WiMAX base stations are therefore required to cover the same geographical area than when using wi-fi technology. Most telecommunications experts agree that WiMAX is an attractive option for countries that lack an existing wired telephone infrastructure.

Wi-Fi

wi-fi A medium-range wireless telecommunications technology brand owned by the Wi-Fi Alliance.

Wi-fi is a wireless telecommunications technology brand owned by the Wi-Fi Alliance, which consists of about 300 technology companies including AT&T, Dell, Microsoft, Nokia and Qualcomm. The alliance exists to improve the interoperability of wireless local area network products based on the IEEE 802.11 series of telecommunications standards.

Wi-fi is a medium-range wireless option typically operating up to about 30 metres around a single building. With a wi-fi network, the user's computer, smartphone or tablet has a wireless adapter that translates data into a radio signal and transmits it using an antenna. A wireless access point, which consists of a transmitter with an antenna, receives the signal and decodes it. The access point then sends the information to the Internet over a wired connection. When receiving data, the wireless access point takes the information from the Internet, translates it into a radio signal, and sends it to the devices wireless adapter (see Figure 6.5). Mobile devices typically come with built-in wireless transmitters and software that enable them to detect the existence of a wi-fi network and alert the user. The area covered by one or more interconnected wireless access points is called a 'hot spot'. Wi-fi has proven so popular that hot spots have been established in many airports, coffee shops, libraries, university campuses and hotels.

Figure 6.5 A Typical Mobile Transmission **Scenario** *Using a mobile phone, the caller dials the number (1). The signal is sent from the phone's antenna to the low-powered mobile antenna located in that area (2). The signal is sent to the regional mobile phone switching office, also called the mobile telephone subscriber office (MTSO) (3). The signal is switched to the local telephone company switching station located nearest the call destination (4). Now integrated into the regular phone system, the call is switched to the number originally dialled (5), all without the need for operator assistance.*

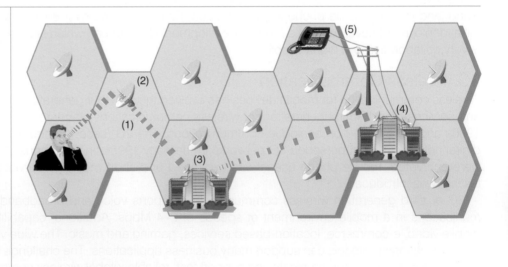

Near Field Communication

Near field communication (NFC) is a very short-range wireless connectivity technology designed for consumer electronics, smartphones and credit cards. Once two NFC-enabled devices are in close proximity (touching or a few centimetres apart), they exchange the necessary communications parameters and passwords to enable bluetooth, wi-fi or other wireless communications between the devices. Because only two devices participate, NFC establishes a peer-to-peer network. Barclays Bank has been one of the first banks in the UK to offer a contactless payment system built into its credit cards. Customers can pay for goods easily and safely by waving their card across a reader in the store. The system uses NFC technology.

near field communication (NFC) A very short-range wireless connectivity technology designed for consumer electronics, smartphones and credit cards.

Bluetooth

Bluetooth is a wireless communications specification that describes how smartphones, computers, printers and other electronic devices can be interconnected over distances of a few metres at a rate or about 2 Mbps. One important application of bluetooth is in hands-free use of mobile phones when driving, using a bluetooth headset to connect to a phone.

bluetooth a wireless communications specification that describes how smartphones, computers, printers and other electronic devices can be interconnected over distances of a few metres at a rate or about 2Mbps.

Ultra Wideband

Ultra wideband (UWB) communications involves the transmission of extremely short electromagnetic pulses lasting just 50 to 1000 picoseconds. (One picosecond is one trillionth, or one-millionth of one-millionth, of a second.) The pulses are capable of supporting data transmission rates of 480 to 1320 Mbps over relatively short ranges of 10 to 50 metres. UWB offers several advantages over other communications means: a high throughput rate, the ability to transmit virtually undetected and impervious to interception or jamming, and a lack of interference with current communications services.

ultra wideband (UWB) A form of short-range communications that employs extremely short electromagnetic pulses lasting 50 to 1000 picoseconds that are transmitted across a broad range of radio frequencies or several gigahertz.

Potential UWB applications include wirelessly connecting printers and other devices to desktop computers or enabling home multimedia networks. Manufacturers of medical instruments are using UWB for video endoscopes, laryngoscopes and ultrasound transducers.[5]

Infrared Transmission

Another mode of transmission, called infrared transmission, sends signals through the air via light waves at a frequency of 300 GHz and above. Infrared transmission requires line-of-sight transmission and short distances – under a few hundred metres. Infrared transmission can be used to connect a display screen, a printer and a mouse to a computer, meaning there are no wires to clutter up the desk. Some special-purpose phones can also use infrared transmission. You can use infrared to establish a wireless network, with the advantage that devices can be moved, removed and installed without expensive wiring and network connections.

The Apple remote is a remote control made for use with Apple products with infrared capabilities. It has just six buttons: Menu, Play/Pause, Volume Up, Volume Down, Previous/Rewind, and Next/Fast-forward. The Mac Mini features an infrared port designed to work with the Apple remote and supports Front Row, a multimedia application that allows users to access shared iTunes and iPhoto libraries and video throughout their home.[6]

Telecommunications Hardware

Telecommunications hardware devices include modems, multiplexers and front-end processors.

Modems

At different stages in the communication process, telecommunications often uses transmission media of different types and capacities. If you use an analogue telephone line to transfer data, it

analogue signal A variable signal continuous in both time and amplitude so that any small fluctuations in the signal are meaningful.

digital signal A signal that represents bits.

modem A telecommunications hardware device that converts (modulates and demodulates) communications signals so they can be transmitted over the communication media.

can only accommodate an **analogue signal** (a variable signal continuous in both time and amplitude so that any small fluctuations in the signal are meaningful). Because a computer generates a **digital signal** representing bits, you need a special device to convert the digital signal to an analogue signal and vice versa (see Figure 6.6). Translating data from digital to analogue is called 'modulation', and translating data from analogue to digital is called 'demodulation'. Thus, these devices are modulation/demodulation devices or **modems**.

Modems can dial telephone numbers, originate message sending, and answer incoming calls and messages. Cellular modems in laptop computers allow people on the go to communicate with other computer systems and devices.

Figure 6.6 How a Modem Works *Digital signals are modulated into analogue signals, which can be carried over existing phone lines. The analogue signals are then demodulated back into digital signals by the receiving modem.*

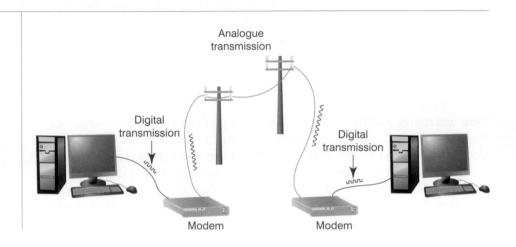

multiplexer A device that encodes data from two or more data sources onto a single communications channel, thus reducing the number of communications channels needed and therefore lowering telecommunications costs.

Multiplexers

A **multiplexer** is a device that encodes data from two or more data sources onto a single communications channel, thus reducing the number of communications channels needed and therefore lowering telecommunications costs (see Figure 6.7).

Figure 6.7 Use of a Multiplexer to Consolidate Data Communications Onto a Single Communications Link

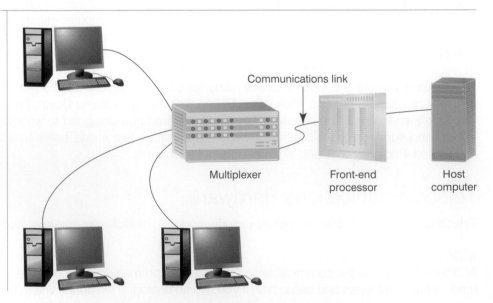

Front-End Processors

Front-end processors are special-purpose computers that manage communications to and from a computer system serving hundreds or even thousands of users. They poll user devices to see if they have messages to send and facilitate efficient, error-free communications. By performing this work, the front-end processor relieves the primary computer system of much of the overhead processing associated with telecommunications.

front-end processor A special-purpose computer that manages communications to and from a computer system serving hundreds or even thousands of users.

Private Branch Exchange

A private branch exchange (PBX) is a telephone switching exchange that serves a single organization. It enables users to share a certain number of outside lines (trunk lines) to make telephone calls to people outside the organization. This sharing reduces the number of trunk lines required, which in turn reduces the organization's telephone costs. A PBX also enables the routing of calls between individuals within the organizations. The PBX can also provide many other functions including voice-mail, voice paging, three-way calling, call transfer and call waiting. A VoIP-PBX can accept Voice over IP (VoIP) calls as well as traditional phone calls. With VoIP calls, the callers' voices are converted into packets of data for routing over the Internet.

private branch exchange (PBX) A telephone switching exchange that serves a single organization.

Switches, Bridges, Routers and Gateways

In addition to communications protocols, certain hardware devices switch messages from one network to another at high speeds. A **switch** uses the physical device address in each incoming message on the network to determine to which output port it should forward the message to reach another device on the same network. A **bridge** connects one LAN to another LAN that uses the same telecommunications protocol. A **router** forwards data packets across two or more distinct networks toward their destinations through a process known as 'routing'. A **gateway** is a network device that serves as an entrance to another network.

switch A telecommunications device that uses the physical device address in each incoming message on the network to determine to which output port it should forward the message to reach another device on the same network.

bridge A telecommunications device that connects one LAN to another LAN that uses the same telecommunications protocol.

router A telecommunications device that forwards data packets across two or more distinct networks towards their destinations, through a process known as routing.

gateway A telecommunications device that serves as an entrance to another network.

computer network The communications media, devices and software needed to connect two or more computer systems and/or devices.

6.2 Networks and Distributed Processing

A **computer network** consists of communications media, devices and software needed to connect two or more computer systems or devices. The computers and devices on the networks are called 'network nodes'. After they are connected, the nodes can share data, information and processing jobs. Increasingly, businesses are linking computers in networks to streamline work processes and allow employees to collaborate on projects. If a company uses networks effectively, it can grow into an agile, powerful and creative organization. Organizations can use networks to share hardware, programs and databases. Networks can transmit and receive information to improve organizational effectiveness and efficiency. They enable geographically separated workgroups to share information, which fosters teamwork, innovative ideas and new business strategies.

Network Types

Depending on the physical distance between nodes on a network and the communications and services it provides, networks can be classified as personal area, local area, metropolitan area or wide area.

Personal Area Networks

personal area network (PAN)
A network that supports the interconnection of information technology within a range of three metres or so.

A **personal area network (PAN)** is a wireless network that connects information technology devices within a range of three metres or so. One device serves as the controller during wireless PAN initialization, and this controller device mediates communication within the PAN. The controller broadcasts a beacon that synchronizes all devices and allocates time slots for the devices. With a PAN, you can connect a laptop, digital camera and portable printer without physical cables. You could download digital image data from the camera to the laptop and then print it on a high-quality printer – all wirelessly. The bluetooth communication protocol is the industry standard for PAN communications.

Metro AG is a major German retailer that owns and operates about 2400 wholesale stores, supermarkets, hypermarkets, department stores and specialty retailers (such as home improvement and consumer electronics). The firm is testing a new voice-operated, smart tag system equipped with bluetooth communications to help warehouse personnel quickly and accurately fill merchandise orders. Item pickers wear a headset to receive instructions on which items to pick. They also wear a high-tech glove that gathers product information from the RFID chip on each item that they pick from the shelves. The glove and RFID chip communicate using bluetooth technology. If workers accidentally pick the wrong product, they receive a message requesting them to repeat the process. The main benefit of the voice-operated RFID picking system is that work sequences aren't interrupted by employees having to manually compare product identification data on the item to the description on a written list.[7]

Local Area Networks

A network that connects computer systems and devices within a small area, such as an office, home or several floors in a building is a local area network (LAN). Typically, LANs are wired into office buildings and factories (see Figure 6.8). Although LANs often use unshielded twisted-pair wire, other media – including fibre-optic cable – is also popular. Increasingly, LANs are using some form of wireless communications.

An example of a sophisticated LAN is the one that DigitalGlobe uses. DigitalGlobe is the company responsible for the detailed satellite images accessed by millions of Google Earth users. The firm uses a high-speed LAN (10 GB/sec) to connect workers to its huge file storage system (200 TB) so that new images can be quickly captured and added to its rapidly growing repository of Earth photos.[8]

A basic type of LAN is a simple peer-to-peer network that a small business might use to share files and hardware devices such as printers. In a peer-to-peer network, you set up each computer as an independent computer, but let other computers access specific files on its hard drive or share its printer. These types of networks have no server. Instead, each computer is connected to the next machine. Examples of peer-to-peer networks include Windows for Workgroups, Windows NT and AppleShare. Performance of the computers on a peer-to-peer network is usually slower because one computer is actually sharing the resources of another computer. However, these networks provide a good foundation from which small businesses can grow. The software cost is minimal, and businesses can use the network cards if they decide to enlarge the system. In addition, peer-to-peer networks are becoming cheaper, faster and easier to use for home-based businesses.

With more people working at home, connecting home computing devices and equipment into a unified network is on the rise. Small businesses are also connecting their systems and equipment. A home or small business can connect network, computers, printers, scanners and other devices. A person working on one computer, for example, can use data and programs stored on another computer's hard disc. In addition, several computers on the network can share a single printer. To make home and small business networking a reality, many companies are offering standards, devices and procedures.

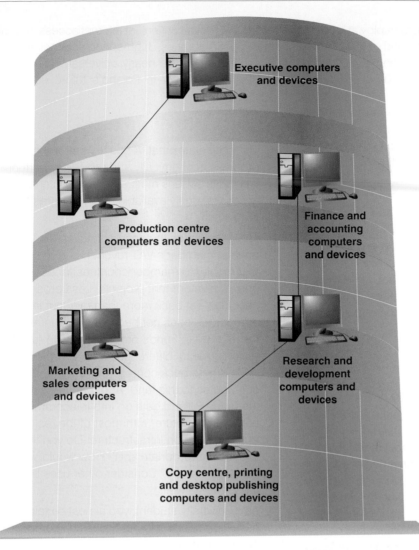

Figure 6.8 A Typical **LAN** *All network users within an office building can connect to each other's devices for rapid communication. For instance, a user in research and development could send a document from her computer to be printed at a printer located in the desktop publishing centre.*

Executive computers and devices

Production centre computers and devices

Finance and accounting computers and devices

Marketing and sales computers and devices

Research and development computers and devices

Copy centre, printing and desktop publishing computers and devices

6

Ethical and Societal Issues

Bringing High-Speed Internet to Poland

Full business or personal participation in today's society is impossible without good Internet access. A country that wants to progress economically and provide opportunities for its citizens must ensure that Internet access is widely available.

The government of Poland understands this principle. The Polish government has taken several steps to make high-speed Internet connections widely available.

In 2009, Poland passed legislation to support and encourage the development of telecommunications networks, reducing regulatory barriers to new infrastructure and increasing competition. Many new projects were initiated after this legislation was adopted. For example, on 14 January 2011, the Łódzkie *voivodship* (province) in central Poland opened the bidding for operating a network that will give all of its nearly 3 million residents Internet access in their homes.

Consistent with this philosophy, in October 2009, the Polish government reached an agreement with the largest telecommunications carrier,

(continued)

Telekomunikacja Polska (TP), to deploy at least 1. 2 million broadband lines by the end of 2012. By the end of 2010, TP had built more than 454 000 such lines, including more than 420 000 over 6 Mbps. The company also increased the percentage that will go into unprofitable rural areas from the initially planned 23 per cent to 30 per cent. In April 2011, TP started regulatory discussions about deploying 3 million Fiber to the Home (FTTH) lines, beginning in 2012.

Other legislation supports this aim. For example, new apartment buildings must have high-speed data connections from the building access point to each unit. Knowing that the most expensive part of broadband installation is already done for them, telecommunications companies are more likely to bring high-speed Internet connections to the building itself and to compete in offering that service to the building's residents.

The European Union (EU) is also contributing to Poland's Internet infrastructure. The EU gets a portion of each member country's value-added tax (VAT revenue) collections and allocates those funds to development projects throughout the EU. The Broadband Network of Eastern Poland will provide broadband Internet access to most residents of the five low-income *voivodships* in that part of the country. This endeavour is the largest EU-funded information technology project anywhere, with a total budget of PLN1. 4 billion (about US$400 million) through 2015. The EU will supply about 85 per cent of that budget, with Poland providing the remaining 15 per cent.

As of the end of 2011, 62 per cent of Poland's residents had high-speed Internet access. This percentage is above the worldwide average of 32.7 per cent but below the EU average of 71.5 per cent. Poland's current efforts should increase the percentage to the European average – which is, of course, a moving target as all EU countries are also moving forward. The International Telecommunications Union estimates that 90 per cent of all Poles will have broadband Internet access at a fixed location by the end of 2015. Since many of the remaining 10 per cent will have mobile access and since many of those who have no personal

access will have convenient Internet access through their public libraries, high-speed Internet access in some form will be nearly universal. This access will be a key factor in Poland's future economic success.

Questions

1 The case states that 'A country that wants to progress economically and provide opportunities for its citizens must ensure that Internet access is widely available.' Do you agree? Why or why not?

2 The case states that the EU takes a fraction of each member's VAT revenue and returns that money to member countries for economic development projects. Less prosperous countries get back more than they put in; more prosperous ones get back less. The intent of this European Funds programme is to reduce developmental differences among regions. Poland gets back considerably more than it contributes to this fund. About 30 per cent of the funds Poland gets go into telecommunications infrastructure, with most of the rest going to transportation infrastructure. Do you think this is an appropriate split? How would you divide these funds? Consider other uses besides these two as well.

3 As a university student, you almost certainly have high-speed Internet access on campus and most likely where you live as well. If you did not have such access, what difficulties would you encounter? How hard would it be to do the job you hope to have after graduation without good Internet access?

4 As of 31 March 2012, 7.5 million Poles out of a population of 38.5 million were Facebook members – slightly less than 20 per cent. The corresponding fraction for the US was just over 50 per cent. How much of the difference do you think is due to lack of high-speed Internet access and how much to other factors? What do you think will be the effect of better high-speed Internet availability on Facebook membership in Poland?

Metropolitan Area Networks

A **metropolitan area network (MAN)** is a telecommunications network that connects users and their computers in a geographical area that spans a campus or city. Most MANs have a range of roughly up to 100 kilometres. For example, a MAN might redefine the many networks within a city into a single larger network or connect several LANs into a single campus LAN. EasyStreet (an Internet service provider) and OnFibre (a metro network solutions provider) designed a MAN for the city of Portland, Oregon, to provide local businesses fast (more than 1 Gps), low-cost Internet connections.[9]

metropolitan area network (MAN) A telecommunications network that connects users and their devices in a geographical area that spans a campus or city.

Wide Area Networks

A **wide area network (WAN)** is a telecommunications network that connects large geographic regions. A WAN might be privately owned or rented and includes public (shared users) networks. When you make a long-distance phone call or access the Internet, you are using a WAN. WANs usually consist of computer equipment owned by the user, together with data communications equipment and telecommunications links provided by various carriers and service providers (see Figure 6.9).

wide area network (WAN) A telecommunications network that ties together large geographic regions.

Figure 6.9 A Wide Area Network *WANs are the basic long-distance networks used around the world. The actual connections between sites, or nodes (shown by dashed lines), might be any combination of satellites, microwave or cabling. When you make a long-distance telephone call or access the Internet, you are using a WAN.*

6

International Networks

international network A network that links users and systems in more than one country.

Networks that link systems among countries are called **international networks**. However, international telecommunications involves special problems. In addition to requiring sophisticated equipment and software, international networks must meet specific national and international laws regulating the electronic flow of data across international boundaries, often called transborder data flow. Some countries have strict laws limiting the use of telecommunications and databases, making normal business transactions such as payroll costly, slow or even impossible. Other countries have few laws concerning telecommunications and database use. These countries, sometimes called data havens, allow other governments and companies to process data within their boundaries. International networks in developing countries can have inadequate equipment and infrastructure that can cause problems and limit the usefulness of the network.

Marks & Spencer PLC has a substantial international presence with 550 stores worldwide operating in 30 countries. It depends on an international network to link all its stores to capture daily sales and track results. It also deals with roughly 2000 direct suppliers of finished products located in places such as Bangalore, Bangladesh, Delhi, Hong Kong, Istanbul and Sri Lanka. Reliable international communications are also required for it to work quickly and effectively with its supply base so that it can acquire goods more efficiently while still meeting the firm's strict trading standards. The firm is working with Cable & Wireless PLC to implement an Internet protocol virtual private network to provide Voice over Internet Protocol (VoIP) at its 400 UK stores and a converged voice/data IP international network for all its operations.[10] The stores involved in the first phase of the development have experienced a great improvement in the response times of customer-facing systems, such as payment processing and customer ordering, as well as stock ticketing, email and personnel management systems.[11]

Mesh Networking

mesh networking A way to route communications between network nodes (computers or other device) by allowing for continuous connections and reconfiguration around blocked paths by 'hopping' from node to node until a connection can be established.

Mesh networking is a way to route communications among network nodes (computers or other devices) by allowing for continuous connections and reconfiguration around blocked paths by 'hopping' from node to node until a connection can be established. In the full mesh topology, each node (workstation or other device) is connected directly to each of the other nodes. In the partial mesh topology, some nodes might be connected to all the others, and other nodes are connected only to nodes with which they frequently exchange communications (see Figure 6.10). Mesh networks are very robust: If one node fails, all the other nodes can still communicate with each other, directly or through one or more intermediate nodes. Mesh networks are being set up to blanket large areas to provide Internet access, secure connections to corporate networks and VoIP calls. Many cities throughout Europe are setting up mesh networks to give residents, sometimes free, Internet access.

Distributed Processing

centralized processing Processing alternative in which all processing occurs at a single location or facility.

decentralized processing Processing alternative in which processing devices are placed at various remote locations.

When an organization needs to use two or more computer systems, it can use one of three basic processing alternatives: centralized, decentralized, or distributed. With **centralized processing**, all processing occurs in a single location or facility. This approach offers the highest degree of control because a single centrally managed computer performs all data processing.

With **decentralized processing**, processing devices are placed at various remote locations. Each computer system is isolated and does not communicate with another system. Decentralized systems are suitable for companies that have independent operating divisions.

With distributed processing, computers are placed at remote locations but connected to each other via telecommunications devices. One benefit of dis-

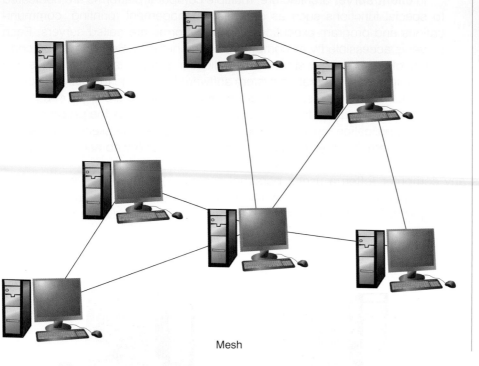

Figure 6.10 Partial
Mesh Network

Mesh

tributed processing is that managers can allocate data to the locations that can process it most efficiently.

The September 11, 2001, terrorist attacks on the World Trade Center in New York and the current relatively high level of natural disasters such as hurricane Katrina in the Gulf of Mexico in the southern US in 2005 sparked many companies to distribute their workers, operations and systems much more widely, a reversal of the recent trend towards centralization. The goal is to minimize the consequences of a catastrophic event at one location while ensuring uninterrupted systems availability.

Client/Server Systems

Users can share data through file server computing, which allows authorized users to download entire files from certain computers designated as file servers. After downloading data to a local computer, a user can analyze, manipulate, format and display data from the file (see Figure 6.11).

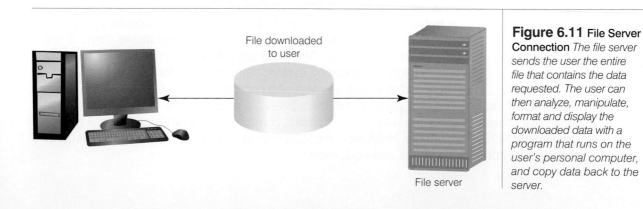

File downloaded
to user

File server

Figure 6.11 File Server
Connection *The file server sends the user the entire file that contains the data requested. The user can then analyze, manipulate, format and display the downloaded data with a program that runs on the user's personal computer, and copy data back to the server.*

client/server An architecture in which multiple computer platforms are dedicated to special functions such as database management, printing, communications and program execution.

In **client/server** architecture, multiple computer platforms are dedicated to special functions such as database management, printing, communications and program execution. These platforms are called servers. Each server is accessible by all computers on the network. Servers can be computers of all sizes; they store both application programs and data files and are equipped with operating system software to manage the activities of the network. The server distributes programs and data to the other computers (clients) on the network as they request them. An application server holds the programs and data files for a particular application, such as an inventory database. The client or the server can do the processing. An email server sends and receives emails. A web server sends out web pages.

A client is any computer (often a user's personal computer) that sends messages requesting services from the servers on the network. A client can converse with many servers concurrently (see Figure 6.12). Table 6.3 lists the advantages and disadvantages of client/ server architecture.

Figure 6.12 Client/ Server Connection
Multiple computer platforms, called servers, are dedicated to special functions. Each server is accessible by all computers on the network. The client requests services from the servers, provides a user interface and presents results to the user.

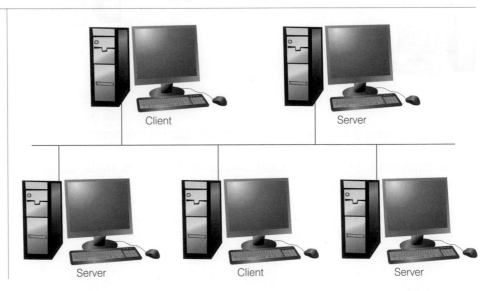

Client Server

Server Client Server

Communications Software

In Chapter 4 you learned that all computers have operating systems that control many functions. When an application program requires data from a disc drive, it goes through the operating system. Now consider a computer attached to a network that connects large disc drives, printers, and other equipment and devices. How does an application program request data from a disc drive on the network? The answer is through the network operating system.

network operating system (NOS) Systems software that controls the computer systems and devices on a network and allows them to communicate with each other.

A **network operating system (NOS)** is systems software that controls the computer systems and devices on a network and allows them to communicate with each other. The NOS performs the same types of functions for the network as operating system software does for a computer, such as memory and task management and coordination of hardware. When network equipment (such as printers, plotters and disc drives) is required, the NOS makes sure that these resources are used correctly. In most cases, companies that produce and sell networks provide the NOS. For example, NetWare is the NOS from Novell, a popular network environment for personal computer systems and equipment.

Software tools and utilities are available for managing networks. With **network-management software**, a manager on a networked personal computer can monitor the use of individual computers and shared hardware (such as printers), scan for viruses and ensure compliance with software licences. Network-management software also simplifies the process of updating files and programs on computers on the network – a manager can make changes through a communications server instead of on individual computers. In addition, network-management software protects software from being copied, modified or downloaded illegally, and performs error control to locate telecommunications errors and potential network problems. Some of the many benefits of network-management software include fewer hours spent on routine tasks (such as installing new software), faster response to problems and greater overall network control.

network-management software
Software that enables a manager on a networked desktop to monitor the use of individual computers and shared hardware (such as printers), scan for viruses and ensure compliance with software licences.

Network management is one of the most important tasks of IS managers. In fact, poor management of the network can cause a whole company to suffer. Because companies use networks to communicate with customers and business partners, network outages or slow performance can even mean a loss of business. Network management includes a wide range of technologies and processes that monitor the infrastructure and help IS staff identify and address problems before they affect customers, business partners or employees.

Fault detection and performance management are the two types of network-management products. Both employ the Simple Network Management Protocol (SNMP) to obtain key information from individual network components. SNMP allows anything on the network, including switches, routers, firewalls, and even operating systems and server products and utilities, to communicate with management software about its current operations and state of health. SNMP can also control these devices and products, telling them to redirect traffic, change traffic priorities or even to shut down.

Fault management software alerts IS staff in real time when a device is failing. Equipment vendors place traps (code in a software program for handling unexpected or unallowable conditions) on their hardware to identify problems. In addition, the IS staff can place agents – automated pieces of software – on networks to monitor functions. When a device exceeds a given performance threshold, the agent sends an alarm to the company's IS fault management program. For example, if a CPU registers that it is more than 80 per cent busy, the agent might trigger an alarm.

Performance management software sends messages to the various devices (i.e. polls them) to sample their performance and to determine whether they are operating within acceptable levels. The devices reply to the management system with performance data that the system stores in a database. This real-time data is correlated to historical trends and displayed graphically so that the IS staff can identify any unusual variations.

Today, most IS organizations use a combination of fault management and performance management to ensure that their network remains up and running and that every network component and application is performing acceptably. With the two technologies, the IS staff can identify and resolve fault and performance issues before they affect customers and service. The latest network-management technology even incorporates automatic fixes – the network-management system identifies a problem, notifies the IS manager, and automatically corrects the problem before anyone outside the IS department notices it.

Sierra Pacific is a wood products provider in the US that, prior to installing network-management software, learned about network problems in the worst way – from users calling the network operations centre to complain. The company has operations in about 50 distributed server locations, including deep in the woods where users are connected through routers to a high-speed network. Sierra Pacific installed Systems Intrusion Analysis and Reporting Environment open-source software on all servers to collect network and performance data around the clock and forward it to a central network server. Now, Sierra Pacific has the data it needs to identify bottlenecks and failed components before users are affected.[12]

Securing Data Transmission

The interception of confidential information by unauthorized individuals can compromise private information about employees or customers, reveal marketing or new product development plans, or cause organizational embarrassment. Organizations with widespread operations need a way to maintain the security of communications with employees and business partners, wherever their facilities are located.

Guided media networks have an inherently secure feature: only devices physically attached to the network can access the data. Wireless networks, on the other hand, are surprisingly often configured by default to allow access to any device that attempts to 'listen to' broadcast communications. Action must be taken to override the defaults.

encryption The process of converting an original message into a form that can be understood only by the intended receiver.

encryption key A variable value that is applied (using an algorithm) to a set of unencrypted text to produce encrypted text or to decrypt encrypted text.

Encryption of data is one approach taken to protect the security of communications over both wired and wireless networks. **Encryption** is the process of converting an original message into a form that can be understood only by the intended receiver. An **encryption key** is a variable value that is applied (using an algorithm) to a set of unencrypted text to produce encrypted text or to decrypt encrypted text (see Figure 6.13). The key is chosen from one of a large number of possible encryption keys. The longer the key, the greater the number of possible encryption keys. An encryption protocol based on a 56-bit key, for example, has 256 different possible keys, while one based on a 128-bit key has 2128 different possible keys. Of course, it is essential that the key be kept secret from possible interceptors. A hacker who obtains the key by whatever means can recover the original message from the encrypted data

6

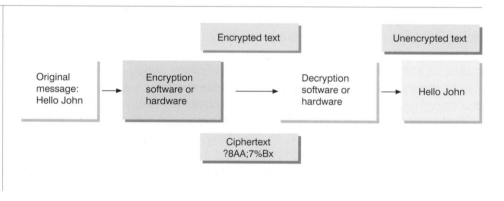

Figure 6.13 Client/ Server Connection
Multiple computer platforms, called servers, are dedicated to special functions. Each server is accessible by all computers on the network. The client requests services from the servers, provides a user interface and presents results to the user.

Encryption methods rely on the limitations of computing power for their security. If breaking a code requires too much computing power, even the most determined hacker cannot be successful.

With headquarters in Dallas, Texas, 7-Eleven operates, franchises or licenses over 8800 stores in North America and another 33 900 in 16 countries. The company uses encryption to secure its email. Todd Cohen, leader of 7-Eleven's Information Security, Risk and Compliance practice, states that 'The protection of sensitive partner information is essential to our leadership as a trusted retailer. Email is a critical communication tool in everyday business with our partners, and [encryption services] enable us to use email securely and confidently.'[13]

Securing Wireless Networks

WEP and WPA are the two main approaches to securing wireless networks such as wi-fi and WiMAX. Wired equivalent privacy (WEP) used to use encryption based on 64-bit key, which has been upgraded to a 128-bit key. WEP represents an early attempt at securing wireless communications and is not difficult for hackers to crack. Most wireless networks now use the Wi-Fi Protected Access (WPA) security protocol that offers significantly improved protection over WEP.

The following steps, while not foolproof, help safeguard a wireless network:

■ Connect to the router and change the default logon (admin) and password (password) for the router. These defaults are widely known by hackers.

■ *Create a service set identifier (SSID).* This is a 32-character unique identifier attached to the header portion of packets sent over a wireless network that differentiates one network from another. All access points and devices attempting to connect to the network must use the same SSID.

■ *Configure the security to WPA.* Surprisingly, many routers are shipped with encryption turned off.

■ *Disable SSID broadcasting.* By default, wireless routers broadcast a message communicating the SSID so wireless devices within range (such as a laptop) can identify and connect to the wireless network. If a device doesn't know the wireless network's SSID, it cannot connect. Disabling the broadcasting of the SSID will discourage all but the most determined and knowledgeable hackers.

■ Configure each wireless computer on the network to access the network by setting the security to WPA and entering the same password entered to the router.

War driving involves hackers driving around with a laptop and antenna trying to detect insecure wireless access points. Once connected to such a network, the hacker can gather enough traffic to analyze and crack the encryption.

Virtual Private Network (VPN)

The use of a virtual private network is another means used to secure the transmission of communications. A **virtual private network (VPN)** is a private network that uses a public network (usually the Internet) to connect multiple remote locations. A VPN provides network connectivity over a potentially long physical distance and thus can be considered a form of wide area network. VPNs support secure, encrypted connections between a company's employees and remote users through a third-party service provider. Telecommuters, salespeople and frequent travellers find the use of a VPN to be a safe, reliable, low-cost way to connect to their corporate intranets. Often, users are provided with a security token that displays a constantly changing password to log onto the VPN (Figure 6.14). This solution avoids the problem of users forgetting their password while providing added security through use of a password constantly changing every 30 to 60 seconds.

virtual private network (VPN) A private network that uses a public network (usually the Internet) to connect multiple remote locations.

Werner Enterprises is a transportation and logistics company with a fleet of 7250 trucks, nearly 25 000 tractors, and more than 13 000 employees and independent contractors.[14] Most

Figure 6.14 RSA SecurID security token
The six digits displayed on the token are used as an access code to gain access to a VPN network. The digits change every 60 seconds.

of its business is in North America, but it is expanding globally with customers in Africa, China, Europe and Latin America. Werner employs a VPN solution to link its Shanghai operations center to its headquarters and data center in Omaha, Nebraska, so that employees can access load management systems to support global operations.[15]

6.3 The Internet

The Internet is the world's largest computer network. Actually, the Internet is a collection of interconnected networks, all freely exchanging information. Nobody knows exactly how big the Internet is because it is a collection of separately run, smaller computer networks. There is no single place where all the connections are registered. Figure 6.15 shows the staggering growth

Figure 6.15 Internet Growth: Number of Internet Domain Names

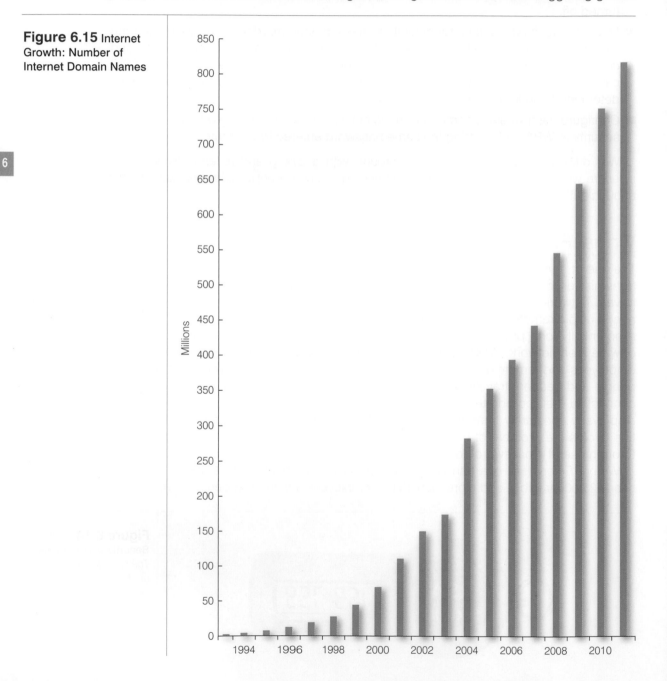

of the Internet, as measured by the number of Internet host sites or domain names. Domain names are discussed later in the chapter.

The Internet is truly international in scope, with users on every continent – including Antarctica. China has spent many billions in its telecommunications infrastructure in the last few years. China, however, restricts the use of the Internet.[16] In 2005, for example, China implemented new Internet rules. According to the Xinhua News Agency of China, '[Only] healthy and civilized news and information that is beneficial to the improvement of the quality of the nation, beneficial to its economic development and conductive to social progress will be allowed. The sites are prohibited from spreading news and information that goes against state security and public interest.' The penalties for sharing unauthorized information are severe, with more than one Internet user being imprisoned for things they have published online.

The ancestor of the Internet was the **ARPANET**, a project started by the US Department of Defense (DoD) in 1969. The ARPANET was both an experiment in reliable networking and a means to link DoD and military research contractors, including many universities doing military-funded research. (ARPA stands for the Advanced Research Projects Agency, the branch of the DoD in charge of awarding grant money. The agency is now known as DARPA – the added D is for Defense.) The ARPANET was highly successful, and every university in the country wanted to use it. This wildfire growth made it difficult to manage the ARPANET, particularly its large and rapidly growing number of university sites. So, the ARPANET was broken into two networks: MILNET, which included all military sites, and a new, smaller ARPANET, which included all the non-military sites. The two networks remained connected, however, through use of the **Internet Protocol (IP)**, which enables traffic to be routed from one network to another as needed. Katie Hafner's book, *Where Wizards Stay Up Late: The Origins of the Internet*, gives a detailed description of the history of the Internet.[17]

ARPANET A project started by the US Department of Defense (DoD) in 1969 as both an experiment in reliable networking and a means to link DoD and military research contractors, including many universities doing military-funded research.

Internet Protocol (IP) A communication standard that enables traffic to be routed from one network to another as needed.

6

Today, people, universities and companies are attempting to make the Internet faster and easier to use. Robert Kahn, who managed the early development of the ARPANET, wants to take the Internet to the next level. He is president of the non-profit organization National Research Initiatives, which provides guidance and funding for the development of a national information infrastructure. The organization is looking into using 'digital objects', which allow all types of computer systems to use and share programs and data. To speed Internet access, a group of corporations and universities called the University Corporation for Advanced Internet Development (UCAID) is working on a faster, new Internet. Called Internet2 (I2), Next Generation Internet (NGI) or Abilene (depending on the universities or corporations involved) the new Internet offers the potential of faster Internet speeds, up to 2 Gbps or more.[18] Some I2 connections can transmit data at 100 Mbps, which is about 200 times faster than dial-up connections. This speed would allow you to transfer the contents of a DVD in less than a minute.

How the Internet Works

The Internet transmits data from one computer (called a host) to another (see Figure 6.16). If the receiving computer is on a network to which the first computer is directly connected, it can send the message directly. If the receiving and sending computers are not directly connected to the same network, the sending computer relays the message to another computer which forwards it on. The message might be sent through a router to reach the forwarding computer. The forwarding host, which needs to be attached to at least one other network, delivers the message directly if it can or passes it to another forwarding host. A message can pass through a dozen or more forwarders on its way from one part of the Internet to another.

The various networks that are linked to form the Internet work much the same way – they pass data around in chunks called packets, each of which carries the addresses of its sender and

Figure 6.16 Routing Messages Over the Internet

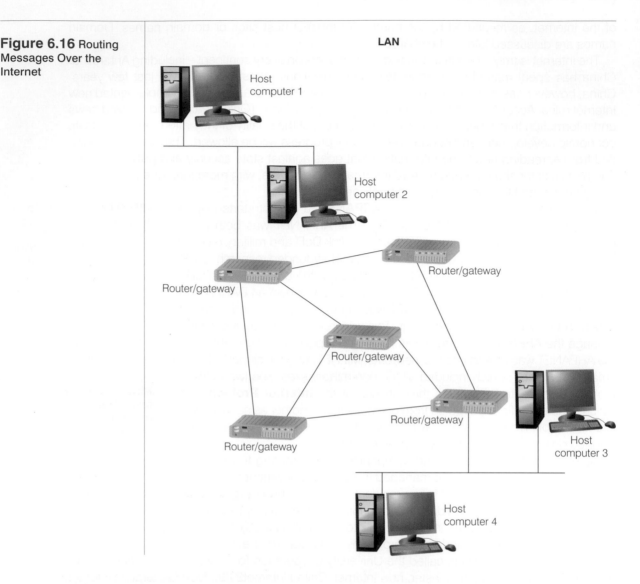

its receiver. The set of conventions used to pass packets from one host to another is known as the Internet Protocol (IP). Many other protocols are used in connection with IP. The best known is the **Transmission Control Protocol (TCP)**, which operates at the transport layer. Many people use TCP/IP as an abbreviation for the combination of TCP and IP used by most Internet applications. After a network following these standards links to a **backbone** – one of the Internet's high-speed, long-distance communications links – it becomes part of the worldwide Internet community.

Each computer on the Internet has an assigned address called its **uniform resource locator (URL)**, to identify it to other hosts. The URL gives those who provide information over the Internet a standard way to designate where Internet elements such as servers, documents and newsgroups can be found. Consider the URL for Cengage Learning, http://www.cengage.co.uk.

The 'http' specifies the access method and tells your software to access a file using the Hypertext Transport Protocol. This is the primary method for interacting with the Internet. In many cases, you don't need to include http:// in a URL because it is the default protocol. Thus, http://www.cengage.co.uk can be abbreviated to www.cengage.co.uk.

Transmission Control Protocol (TCP) The widely used transport-layer protocol that most Internet applications use with IP.

backbone One of the Internet's high-speed, long-distance communications links.

uniform resource locator (URL) An assigned address on the Internet for each computer.

The 'www' part of the address signifies that the files associated with this website reside on the World Wide Web server of 'cengage.co.uk'. The 'cengage.co.uk' itself is the domain name that identifies the Internet host site. Domain names must adhere to strict rules. They always have at least two parts, with each part separated by a dot (full stop). For some Internet addresses, the far right part of the domain name is the country code (such as uk for the United Kingdom, au for Australia, ca for Canada, dk for Denmark, fr for France and jp for Japan). Many Internet addresses have a code denoting affiliation categories. (Table 6.4 contains a few popular categories.) The far left part of the domain name identifies the host network or host provider, which might be the name of a university or business.

Table 6.4 Some Top-Level Domain Affiliations

Affiliation ID	Affiliation
com	Commercial organizations
edu	Educational sites (mostly based in the US)
gov	Government sites (mostly based in the US)
net	Networking organizations
org	Organizations
scot	Related to Scotland and Scottish culture

Originally, Herndon, Virginia-based Network Solutions, Inc. (NSI), was the sole company in the world with the direct power to register addresses using .com, .net or .org domain names. However, its government contract ended in October 1998, as part of the US government's move to turn management of the web's address system over to the private sector. Today, other companies, called registrars, can register domain names, and additional companies are seeking accreditation to register domain names from the Internet Corporation for Assigned Names and Numbers (ICANN). Some registrars are concentrating on large corporations, where the profit margins might be higher, compared with small businesses or individuals.

An **Internet service provider (ISP)** is any company that provides people and organizations with access to the Internet. Thousands of organizations serve as Internet service providers, ranging from universities to major communications giants such as BT and AT&T. To use this type of connection, you must have an account with the service provider and software that allows a direct link via TCP/IP. In most cases, ISPs charge a monthly fee of around €20 for unlimited Internet connection through a standard modem. Some ISPs are experimenting with low-fee or no-fee Internet access, though strings are attached to the no-fee offers in most cases, typically that the user must subscribe to telephone services as well.

Internet service provider (ISP)
Any company that provides people or organizations with access to the Internet.

6.4 Internet Applications

Many people believe the terms 'Internet' and 'World Wide Web' are synonymous. However the web, which is examined next, is just one application of the Internet. Others also discussed in this section are email, telnet and FTP. More applications are given in Chapter 10.

The World Wide Web

The **World Wide Web** was developed by Tim Berners-Lee at CERN, the European Organization for Nuclear Research in Geneva. He originally conceived of it as an internal document-management system. From this modest beginning, the World Wide Web (web, WWW or W3) has grown to a collection of tens of thousands of independently owned computers that work together as one in an Internet service. These computers, called web servers, are scattered all over the world and contain every imaginable type of data. Thanks to the high-speed Internet circuits connecting them and some clever cross-indexing software, users can jump from one web computer to another effortlessly, creating the illusion of using one big computer. Because of its ability to handle multimedia objects, including linking multimedia objects distributed on web servers around the world, the web has become the most popular means of information access on the Internet today.

World Wide Web (WWW or W3) A collection of tens of thousands of independently owned computers that work together as one in an Internet service.

The web is a menu-based system that uses the client/server model. It organizes Internet resources throughout the world into a series of menu pages, or screens, that appear on your computer. Each web server maintains pointers, or links, to data on the Internet and can retrieve that data. However, you need the right hardware and telecommunications connections, or the web can be painfully slow.

Data can exist on the web as ASCII characters, word-processing files, audio files, graphic and video images, or any other sort of data that can be stored in a computer file. A website is like a magazine, with a cover page called a **home page** which includes links to the rest of its material. The words on a website are typically written in hypertext. **Hypertext** allows the linking of certain words to other web pages, so users can click on them to access related material. This feature gives the web its name, as all information is linked together like a spider's web.

home page A cover page for a website that has graphics, titles and text.

hyptertext Text used to connect web pages, allowing users to access information in whatever order they wish.

Hypertext Markup Language (HTML) is the standard page description language for web pages. One way to think about HTML is as a set of highlighter pens that you use to mark up plain text to make it a web page – one colour for the headings, another for bold and so on. The **HTML tags** let the browser know how to format the text: as a heading, as a list or as main text, for example. HTML also tells whether pictures, videos and other elements should be inserted, and where they should go. Users mark up a page by placing HTML tags before and after a word or words. For example, to turn a sentence into a heading, you place the <h1> tag at the start of the sentence. At the end of the sentence, you place the closing tag </h1>. When you view this page in your browser, the sentence will be displayed as a heading. So, an HTML file is made up of two things: text and tags. The text is your message, and the tags are codes that mark the way words will be displayed. All HTML tags are enclosed in a set of angle brackets (< and >), such as <h2>. The closing tag has a forward slash in it, such as </b> for closing bold. Consider the following text and tags:

Hypertext Markup Language (HTML) The standard page description language for web pages.

HTML tags Codes that let the web browser know how to format text – as a heading, as a list, or as body text – and whether images, sound, or other elements should be inserted.

    <h1 align="center">Principles of Business Information Systems</h1>

This HTML code centres Principles of Information Systems as a major, or level 1, heading. The 'h1' in the HTML code indicates a first-level heading. On some web browsers (discussed next), the heading might be 14-point type size with a Times Roman font. On other browsers, it might be a larger 18-point size in a different font. There is a standard, but not all browsers stick to it. Figure 6.17 shows a simple document and its corresponding HTML tags. Notice the <html> tag at the top indicating the beginning of the HTML code. The <title> indicates the beginning of the title: 'Cengage Learning – Shaping the Future of Global Learning' The </title> tag indicates the end of the title.

Figure 6.17 Sample Hypertext Markup Language *Shown at the left on the screen is a document, and at the right are the corresponding HTML tags.*

Some newer web standards are gaining in popularity, including Extensible Markup Language (XML), Extensible Hypertext Markup Language (XHTML), Cascading Style Sheets (CSS), Dynamic HTML (DHTML) and Wireless Markup Language (WML). WML can display web pages on small screens, such as smartphones and PDAs. XHTML is a combination of XML and HTML that has been approved by the World Wide Web Consortium (W3C).

Extensible Markup Language (XML) is a markup language for web documents containing structured information, including words and pictures. XML does not have a predefined tag set. With HTML, for example, the <h1> tag always means a first-level heading. The content and formatting are contained in the same HTML document. With XML, web documents contain the content of a web page. The formatting of the content is contained in a separate style sheet. A few typical instructions in XML follow:

> **Extensible Markup Language (XML)** The markup language for web documents containing structured information, including words, pictures and other elements.

<chapter>Hardware
<topic>Input Devices
<topic>Processing and Storage Devices
<topic>Output Devices

How the preceding content is formatted and displayed on a web page is contained in the corresponding style sheet, such as the following cascading style sheet (CSS). Note that the chapter title 'Hardware' is displayed on the web page in a large font (18 points). 'Hardware' will appear in bold blue text. 'Input Devices' and the other titles will appear in a smaller font (12 points) in italic red text.

chapter: (font-size: 18pt; color: blue; font-weight: bold; display: block; font-family: Arial;margin-top: 10pt; margin-left: 5pt)

topic: (font-size: 12pt; color: red; font-style: italic; display: block; font-family: Arial;margin-left: 12pt)

XML includes the capabilities to define and share document information over the web. A company can use XML to exchange ordering and invoicing information with its customers. CSS improves web page presentation, and DHTML provides dynamic presentation of web content. These standards move more of the processing for animation and dynamic content to the web browser, discussed next, and provide quicker access and displays.

Web Browsers

A **web browser** translates HTML so you can read it. It provides a graphical interface to the web. The menu consists of graphics, titles and text with hypertext links. **Hypermedia** links you to Internet resources, including text documents, graphics, sound files and newsgroup servers. As you choose an item or resource, or move from one document to another, you might be accessing various computers on the Internet without knowing it, while the web handles all the connections. The beauty of web browsers and the web is that they make surfing the Internet fun. Clicking with a mouse on a highlighted word or graphic whisks you effortlessly to computers halfway around the world. Most browsers offer basic features such as support for backgrounds and tables, displaying a web page's HTML source code, and a way to create hot lists of your favourite sites. Web browsers enable net surfers to view more complex graphics and 3D models, as well as audio and video material, and to run small programs embedded in web pages called **applets**. A web browser plug-in is an external program that is executed by a web browser when it is needed. For example, if you are working with a web page and encounter an Adobe pdf file, the web browser will typically run the external Adobe pdf reader program or plug-in to allow you to open the file. Microsoft Internet Explorer and Google Chrome are examples of web browsers for PCs. Safari is a popular web browser from Apple for their Macintosh computer, and Mozilla Firefox is a web browser available in numerous languages that can be used on PCs, computers with the Linux operating system and Apple Mac computers.

web browser Software that creates a unique, hypermedia-based menu on a computer screen, providing a graphical interface to the web.

hypermedia An extension of hypertext where the data, including text, images, video and other media, on web pages is connected allowing users to access information in whatever order they wish.

applet A small program embedded in web pages.

6

Information Systems @ Work

Is Email History?

It's hard to imagine business without email, which is as common as the water cooler – and probably more useful. Is it, however, time to move on?

That's what IT services firm Atos, based in Bezons just outside Paris, France, thinks. It aims to become a 'zero email company' within three years to help tackle what it calls 'information pollution', which Atos sees as bogging down company progress because employees overuse email rather than turning to more effective forms of interaction.

As one example of information pollution, consider a six-person project group. One member sends the others an email with a suggestion. The other five respond, with copies to all group mem-

bers (as is standard business email practice). Three of the members reply to the other comments. Soon each project member receives two or three dozen email messages. Most of those messages repeat the same content with a new sentence or two at the top.

Atos chairman and CEO Thierry Breton, speaking at a conference in February 2011, said he plans to end all internal emails among Atos employees. 'We are producing data on a massive scale that is fast polluting our working environments and also encroaching into our personal lives,' he said. 'We are taking action now to reverse this trend, just as organizations took measures to reduce environmental pollution after the industrial revolution.'

Though its name may not be a household word in the United States, Atos is not a small firm. It has 74 000 employees in 42 countries and annual revenues in excess of US$7.55 billion. If it can eliminate email, size should not prevent other companies from doing the same.

As in most companies, Atos employees regularly use email to communicate with one another and to share documents and other files. What will they use instead? Collaboration and social media tools.

A collaboration tool lets employees use an online discussion group instead of sending emails to each other. (An online discussion group would have helped the six-person project team in the earlier example.) Social media tools include using familiar sites such as Facebook to keep others informed about their business activities. Groups can also use wikis to create shared repositories of information on topics of interest. Atos has found that making such tools available reduces email volume by 10 to 20 per cent immediately.

The effort to reduce email volume concerns internal email messages only. Breton and other Atos managers do not expect customers to stop sending email messages to company employees, nor do they expect employees who receive email enquiries from customers and suppliers to respond in any other way. They just hope to eliminate email as an internal communication medium.

Not everyone thinks that eliminating internal e-mail is practical. Industry analyst Brian Prentice of Gartner Group faults the bureaucracy that leads to overuse of email, not the medium itself. In his view, 'The only solution is to tackle the ballooning administration and bureaucracy overhead in organizations that is fuelling the number of emails being generated. Specifically, our criticism of email as a collaboration tool needs to shift towards the unchecked growth of bureaucracy it enables.' In other words, email is a symptom, not the problem.

Not surprisingly, Hubert Tardieu, an advisor to Atos CEO Breton, disagrees. He believes that email does not lend itself to creating communities of shared interests within an organization but that other forms of electronic communication do. 'Zero mail is not an objective in itself,' he writes, 'but the recognition that companies are suffering from email overload.' While conceding that the root problem is modern bureaucracy, he feels that

email encourages the growth of that bureaucracy while other media don't. Tardieu concludes, 'The bet of the Social Organization is that cooperation within communities associated with appropriate processes will create a new style of organization and a new style of management more suitable to the digital generation. In the Social Organization, we shall communicate through the enterprise social network across the various communities we belong to, reducing the usage of mail to formal communication.'

In early 2012, a year into Atos's three-year effort, the jury is still out. Stay tuned!

Questions

1 Do you agree with Brian Prentice of the Gartner Group that email is a symptom, not the problem itself? Will information overload decline if people start using other tools instead of email?

2 Think about your use of social media such as Facebook. If you could count on all your friends to see updates to your Facebook page and if they knew that was the only way they would hear from you, what fraction of your emails do you think you could avoid sending? Would it be more or less work to update your Facebook page than to send email messages?

3 Recall a group project you completed in university recently, and then answer one of the following questions:

a. If you communicated with group members primarily by email, would the project have gone more smoothly if you had had a different way to communicate? Why or why not? What would be the best way to communicate with each other?

b. If you communicated using a tool other than email, was the tool better than email? Why or why not? Could a third method, neither email nor what you used, be better?

4 Atos is a large firm and can afford to set up several social media and collaboration sites, each of which eliminates some need for email. Suppose you work for a small firm with fewer technology resources and people to support them. Can you use this approach? If not all of it, then can you use any of it? Should you?

Search Engines and Web Research

Looking for information on the web is like browsing in a library – without the alphabetic listing of books in the card catalogue, it is difficult to find information. Web search tools – called **search engines** – take the place of the card catalogue. Most search engines, such as Google, are free. They make money by, among other things, charging advertisers to put ad banners in their search engine results. Companies often pay a search engine for a sponsored link, which is usually displayed at the top of the list of links for an Internet search. Google has over 60 per cent of search volume.[19]

search engine A web search tool.

Search engines that use keyword indexes produce an index of all the text on the sites they examine. Typically, the engine reads at least the first few hundred words on a page, including the title and any keywords or descriptions that the author has built into the page structure. The engine throws out common words such as 'and', 'the', 'by' and 'for'. The engine assumes remaining words are valid page content; it then alphabetizes these words (with their associated sites) and places them in an index where they can be searched and retrieved. Some companies include a meta tag in the HTML header for search engine robots from sites such as Google to find and use. Meta tags are not shown on the web page when it is displayed; they only help search engines discover and display a website. To place the search results in the most relevant order, Google counts the number of links that are made to each from other websites, and puts the one with the most at the top.

Today's search engines do more than look for words, phrases or sentences on the web. For example, you can use Google to search for images and video.[20] You can even search for geographic locations to get a view from the skies using satellites.[21] Google, for example, offers Google Maps and Google Earth to provide aerial views. After downloading and installing Google Earth, you can type an address and Google will show you the neighbourhood or even a house in some cases. Microsoft Virtual Earth and Local Search also give aerial views and close-ups of some locations, including retail stores in some cases.[22] You can also use news organizations' websites, such as the BBC's (http://news.bbc.co.uk/), to access current information on a variety of topics. Some websites maintain versions in different languages, especially for research purposes. In addition, many ordinary web users are publishing lists of their favourite web pages along with explanations of what they are, to classify web content and to make it easier for them (and others) to retrieve information. Such lists are known as 'folksonomies' although this word has been voted one of the most annoying Internet terms.

Web Programming Languages

Java An object-oriented programming language from Sun Microsystems based on C++ that allows small programs (applets) to be embedded within an HTML document.

There are a number of important web programming languages. **Java**, for example, is an object-oriented programming language from Sun Microsystems based on the C++ programming language, which allows small programs – the applets mentioned earlier – to be embedded within an HTML document. When the user clicks the appropriate part of an HTML page to retrieve an applet from a web server, the applet is downloaded onto the client workstation, where it begins executing. Unlike other programs, Java software can run on any type of computer. Programmers use Java to make web pages come alive, adding splashy graphics, animation and real-time updates.

The relationship among Java applets, a Java-enabled browser, and the web is shown in Figure 6.18. To develop a Java applet, the author writes the code for the client computer and installs that on the web server. The user accesses the web page on a personal computer, which serves as a client. The web page contains an additional HTML tag called APP, which refers to the Java applet. A rectangle on the page is occupied by the Java applet. If the user clicks the rectangle to execute the Java applet, the client computer checks to see whether a copy of the applet is already stored locally on its hard drive. If it is not, the computer accesses the web server and requests that the applet be downloaded. The applet can be

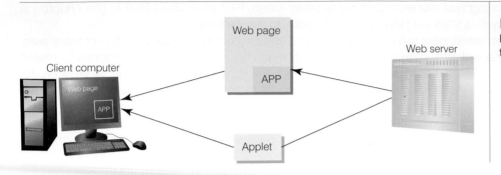

Figure 6.18
Downloading an Applet from a Web Server

located anywhere on the web. If the user has a Java-enabled browser (such as Sun HotJava or Netscape Navigator), the applet is downloaded to the user's computer and is executed in the browser.

The user accesses the web page from a web server. If the user clicks the APP rectangle to execute the Java applications, the client's computer checks for a copy on its local hard drive. If it does not find the applet, the client requests the web server to download the applet.

The web server that delivers the Java applet to the web client cannot determine what kind of hardware or software environment the client is running, and the developer who creates the Java applet does not have to worry about whether it will work correctly on Windows, UNIX or Mac OS. Java is thus often described as a 'cross-platform' programming language.

In addition to Java, companies use a variety of other programming languages and tools to develop websites. JavaScript, VBScript and ActiveX (used with Internet Explorer) are Internet languages used to develop web pages and perform important functions, such as accepting user input. Hypertext Preprocessor, or PHP, is an open-source programming language. PHP code or instructions can be embedded directly into HTML code. Unlike some other Internet languages, PHP can run on a web server, with the results being transferred to a client computer. PHP can be used on a variety of operating systems. It can also be used with a variety of database management systems, such as DB2, Oracle, Informix, MySQL and many others. These characteristics – running on different operating systems and database management systems, and being an open source language – make PHP popular with many web developers.

Developing Web Content

The art of web design involves working within the technical limitations of the web and using a set of tools to make appealing designs. A study at Glamorgan University Business School in Wales, for example, concluded that women prefer web pages with more colour in the background and informal pictures and images.[23] Men prefer darker colours and like 3D, moving images. You can create a web page using one of the following approaches: (a) write your copy with a word processor, and then use an HTML converter to convert the page into HTML format; (b) use an HTML editor to write text (it will add HTML tags at the same time); (c) edit an existing HTML template (with all the tags ready to use) to meet your needs; and (d) use an ordinary text editor such as Notepad and type the start and end tags for each item.

After you develop web content, your next step is to place, or publish, the content on a web server, so others can access it. Popular publishing options include using ISPs, free sites and web hosting. BT's starter package comes with 5 GB of web space and users can pay to increase this.[24] Free sites offer limited space for a website. In return, free sites often require the user to view advertising or agree to other terms and conditions. Web hosting services provide space on their websites for people and businesses that don't have the financial resources, time or skills to host their own website. A web host charges a monthly fee, depending on services offered. Some web hosting sites include domain name registration, web authoring software, and activity reporting and monitoring of the website. Often, FTP (described later in this chapter) is used to copy files from the developer's computer to the web server.

Some web developers are creating programs and procedures to combine two or more websites into one website, called a 'mash-up'.[25] A mash-up is named for the process of mixing two or more (often hip-hop) songs into one song. A website containing crime information, for example, can be mashed up with a mapping website to produce a website with crime information placed on top of a map of a metropolitan area. People are becoming very creative in how they mash up several websites into new ones. Mashing up websites is becoming popular, but not everyone is happy with the practice. Some companies are trying to block the mash-up of the content on their website without permission.

After a website has been constructed, a content management system (CMS) can keep the website running smoothly. CMS consists of both software and support. Companies that provide CMS can charge from €11 000 to more than €400 000 annually, depending on the complexity of the website being maintained and the services being performed. Adobe Experience Manager is an example of a CMS.

Many products make it easy to develop web content and interconnect web services, discussed in the next section. Microsoft, for example, has introduced a development and web services platform called .NET. The .NET platform allows developers to use different programming languages to create and run programs, including those for the web. The .NET platform also includes a rich library of programming code to help build XML web applications.

Web Services

web services Standards and tools that streamline and simplify communication among websites for business and personal purposes.

Web services consist of standards and tools that streamline and simplify communication among websites, promising to revolutionize the way we develop and use the web for business and personal purposes. Internet companies, including Amazon, eBay and Google, are now using web services. Amazon, for example, has developed Amazon Web Services (AWS) to make the contents of its huge online catalogue available by other websites or software applications.

The key to web services is XML. Just as HTML was developed as a standard for formatting web content into web pages, XML is used within a web page to describe and transfer data between web service applications. XML is easy to read and has wide industry support. Besides XML, three other components are used in web service applications:

1 SOAP (Simple Object Access Protocol) is a specification that defines the XML format for messages. SOAP allows businesses, their suppliers and their customers to communicate with each other. It provides a set of rules that makes it easier to move information and data over the Internet.

2 WSDL (Web Services Description Language) provides a way for a web service application to describe its interfaces in enough detail to allow a user to build a client application to talk to it. In other words, it allows one software component to connect to and work with another software component on the Internet.

3 UDDI (Universal Discovery Description and Integration) is used to register web service applications with an Internet directory so that potential users can easily find them and carry out transactions over the web.

Developing Web Content and Applications

Popular tools for creating web pages and managing websites include Adobe Dreamweaver, Microsoft Expression Web and the open source alternative Nvu. Such software allows users to create web pages using an interface similar to a word-processor. The software converts what the user types into HTML code and creates hyperlinks to connect the pages. Web application frameworks have arisen to simplify web development by providing the foundational code – or framework – for a professional interactive website which users can customize as they need. Websites are usually developed on a user's computer and then uploaded to a web server. Although a business may manage its own web server, the job is often outsourced to a web-hosting company.

Email

Email or electronic mail is a method of sending communications over computer networks. It is no longer limited to simple text messages. Depending on your hardware and software, and the hardware and software of your recipient, you can embed sound and images in your message and attach files that contain text documents, spreadsheets, graphics or executable programs. Email travels through the systems and networks that make up the Internet. Gateways can receive email messages from the Internet and deliver them to users on other networks. Thus, you can send email messages to anyone in the world if you know that person's email address and you have access to the Internet or another system that can send email. For large organizations whose operations span a country or the world, email allows people to work around the time zone changes. Some users of email claim that they eliminate two hours of verbal communications for every hour of email use.

Some companies use bulk email to send legitimate and important information to sales representatives, customers and suppliers around the world. With its popularity and ease of use, however, some people feel they are drowning in too much email. Many emails are copies sent to a large list of corporate users. Users are taking a number of steps to cope with and reduce their mountain of email. For instance, some users only look at their in-boxes once each day. Many companies have software scan incoming messages for possible junk or bulk email, called spam, and delete it or place it in a separate file. Some have banned the use of copying others in on emails unless it is critical.

Telnet and FTP

Telnet is a terminal emulation protocol that enables you to log on to other computers on the Internet to gain access to their publicly available files. Telnet is particularly useful for perusing library holdings and large databases. It is also called 'remote logon'.

File Transfer Protocol (FTP) is a protocol that describes a file transfer process between a host and a remote computer. Using FTP, users can copy files from one computer to another. Companies, for example, use it to transfer vast amounts of business transactional data to the computers of its customers and suppliers. You can also use FTP to gain access to a wealth of free software on the Internet. FTP can be used to upload or download content to a website.

Telnet A terminal emulation protocol that enables users to log on to other computers on the Internet to gain access to public files.

File Transfer Protocol (FTP) A protocol that describes a file transfer process between a host and a remote computer and allows users to copy files from one computer to another.

Cloud computing

Cloud computing refers to a computing environment where software and storage are provided as an Internet service and accessed with a web browser. Apple Computer has developed a service called iCloud to allow users to store their music, photos and other information. Google Docs, Zoho, 37signals, Flypaper, Adobe Buzzword and others provide web-delivered productivity and information management software including word-processors, spreadsheets and presentation software.

Cloud computing offers many advantages to companies. By outsourcing business information systems to the cloud, a business saves on system design, installation and maintenance. No universally accepted standard exists yet for cloud computing and managing applications can

cloud computing A computing environment where software and storage are provided as an Internet service and are accessed via a web browser.

be difficult when many providers are involved. A company wanting to make full use of the cloud will need a clear cloud computing strategy.

6.5 Intranets and Extranets

An intranet is an internal company network built using Internet and World Wide Web standards and products. Employees of an organization use it to gain access to company information. After getting their feet wet with public websites that promote company products and services, corporations are seizing the web as a swift way to streamline – even transform – their organizations. A big advantage of using an intranet is that many people are already familiar with Internet technology, so they need little training to make effective use of their corporate intranet.

An intranet is an inexpensive yet powerful alternative to other forms of internal communication, including conventional computer setups. One of an intranet's most obvious virtues is its ability to reduce the need for paper. Because web browsers run on any type of computer, the same electronic information can be viewed by any employee. That means that all sorts of documents (such as internal phone books, procedure manuals, training manuals and requisition forms) can be inexpensively converted to electronic form on the web and be constantly updated. An intranet provides employees with an easy and intuitive approach to accessing information that was previously difficult to obtain. For example, it is an ideal solution to providing information to a mobile sales force that needs access to rapidly changing information.

A rapidly growing number of companies offer limited access to their intranet to selected customers and suppliers. Such networks are referred to as extranets, and connect people who are external to the company. An extranet is a network that links selected resources of the intranet of a company with its customers, suppliers or other business partners. Again, an extranet is built around web technologies. Eikos Risk Applications in South Africa, for example, uses an extranet to provide tailored content to its clients. The firm is an insurance broker and their extranet gives clients access to policy information, information about claims and facility management reports. Clients log in to the extranet on a secure web page.

Security and performance concerns are different for an extranet than for a website or network-based intranet. User authentication and privacy are critical on an extranet so that information is protected. Obviously, performance must be good to provide quick response to customers and suppliers. Table 6.5 summarizes the differences between users of the Internet, intranets and extranets.

Table 6.5 Summary of Internet, Intranet and Extranet Users

Type	Users	Need User ID and Password?
Internet	Anyone	No
Intranet	Employees and managers	Yes
Extranet	Employees, managers and business partners	Yes

Summary

Effective communications are essential to organizational success. Telecommunications refers to the electronic transmission of signals for communications, including telephone, radio and television. Telecommunications is creating profound changes in business because it removes the barriers of time and distance.

The elements of a telecommunications system include a sending unit, such as a person, a computer system, a terminal, or another device, that originates the message. The sending unit transmits a signal to a telecommunications device, which performs a number of functions such as converting the signal into a different form or from one type to another. A telecommunications device is a hardware component that facilitates electronic communication. The telecommunications device then sends the signal through a medium, which is anything that carries an electronic signal and serves as an interface between a sending device and a receiving device. The signal is received by another telecommunications device that is connected to the receiving computer. The process can then be reversed, and another message can pass from the receiving unit to the original sending unit. With synchronous communications, the receiver gets the message instantaneously, when it is sent. Voice and phone communications are examples. With asynchronous communications there is a delay between sending and receiving the message. A communications channel is the transmission medium that carries a message from the source to its receivers.

Communications technology lets more people send and receive all forms of information over greater distances. The telecommunications media that physically connect data communications devices can be divided into two broad categories: guided transmission media, in which communications signals are guided along a solid medium, and wireless media, in which the communications signal is sent over airwaves. Guided transmission media include twisted-pair wire cable, coaxial cable, fibre-optic cable and broadband over power lines. Wireless media types include microwave, cellular and infrared.

A modem is a telecommunications hardware device that converts (modulates and demodulates) communications signals so they can be transmitted over the communication media.

A multiplexer is a device that encodes data from two or more data sources onto a single communications channel, thus reducing the number of communications channels needed and, therefore, lowering telecommunications costs.

A front-end processor is a special-purpose computer that manages communications to and from a computer system serving hundreds or even thousands of users.

Telecommunications carriers offer a wide array of phone and dialling services, including digital subscriber line (DSL) and wireless telecommunications.

The effective use of networks can turn a company into an agile, powerful and creative organization, giving it a long-term competitive advantage. Networks let users share hardware, programs and databases across the organization. They can transmit and receive information to improve organizational effectiveness and efficiency. They enable geographically separated workgroups to share documents and opinions, which fosters teamwork, innovative ideas and new business strategies.

The physical distance between nodes on the network and the communications and services provided by the network determines whether it is called a personal area network (PAN), local area network (LAN), metropolitan area network (MAN) or wide area network (WAN). A PAN connects information technology devices within a range of about 10 metres. The major components in a LAN are a network interface card, a file server and a bridge or gateway. A MAN connects users and their computers in a geographical area larger than a LAN but smaller than a WAN. WANs link large geographic regions, including communications between countries, linking systems from around the world. The electronic flow of data across international and global boundaries is often called transborder data flow.

A mesh network is a way to route communications between network nodes (computers or other device) by allowing for continuous connections and reconfiguration around blocked paths by 'hopping' from node to node until a connection can be established.

A client/server system is a network that connects a user's computer (a client) to one or more host computers (servers). A client is often a PC that requests services from the server, shares processing tasks with the server and displays the results. Many companies have reduced their use of mainframe computers in favour of client/server systems using midrange or personal computers to achieve cost savings, provide more control over the desktop, increase flexibility and become more responsive to business changes. The start-up costs of these systems can be high, and the systems are more complex than a centralized mainframe computer.

When people on one network want to communicate with people or devices in a different organization on another network, they need a common communications protocol and various network devices to do so. A communications protocol is a set of rules that govern the exchange of information over a communications channel. There are a myriad of communications protocols, including international, national and industry standards.

In addition to communications protocols, telecommunications uses various devices. A switch uses the physical device address in each incoming message on the network to determine which output port to forward the message to in order to reach another device on the same network. A bridge is a device that connects one LAN to another LAN that uses the same telecommunications protocol. A router forwards data packets across two or more distinct networks towards their destinations, through a process known as routing. A gateway is a network device that serves as an entrance to another network.

When an organization needs to use two or more computer systems, it can follow one of three basic data-processing strategies: centralized, decentralized or distributed. With centralized processing, all processing occurs in a single location or facility. This approach offers the highest degree of control. With decentralized processing, processing devices are placed at various remote locations. The individual computer systems are isolated and do not communicate with each other. With distributed processing, computers are placed at remote locations but are connected to each other via telecommunications devices. This approach helps minimize the consequences of a catastrophic event at one location, while ensuring uninterrupted systems availability.

Communications software performs important functions, such as error checking and message formatting. A network operating system controls the computer systems and devices on a network, allowing them to communicate with one another. Network-management software enables a manager to monitor the use of individual computers and shared hardware, scan for viruses and ensure compliance with software licences.

The Internet is like many other technologies – it provides a wide range of services, some of which are effective and practical for use today, others are still evolving, and still others will fade away from lack of use. The Internet started with ARPANET, a project sponsored by the US Department of Defense (DoD). Today, the Internet is the world's largest computer network. Actually, it is a collection of interconnected networks, all freely exchanging information. The Internet transmits data from one computer (called a host) to another. The set of conventions used to pass packets from one host to another is known as the Internet Protocol (IP). Many other protocols are used with IP. The best known is the Transmission Control Protocol (TCP). TCP is so widely used that many people refer to the Internet protocol as TCP/IP, the combination of TCP and IP used by most Internet applications. Each computer on the Internet has an assigned address to identify it from other hosts, called its uniform resource locator (URL). There are several ways to connect to the Internet: via a LAN whose server is an Internet host or via an online service that provides Internet access.

An Internet service provider is any company that provides access to the Internet. To use this type of connection, you must have an account with the service provider and software that allows a direct link via TCP/IP. Among the value-added services ISPs provide are electronic commerce, intranets and extranets, website hosting, web transaction processing, network security and administration, and integration services.

Because the Internet and the World Wide Web are becoming more universally used and accepted for business use, management, service and speed, privacy and security issues must continually be addressed and resolved. A rapidly growing number of companies are doing business on the web and enabling shoppers to search for and buy products online. For many people, it is easier to shop on the web than search through catalogues or trek to the high street.

The steps to creating a web page include organizing storage space on a web server; writing your copy with a word-processor, using an HTML editor, editing an existing HTML document, or using an ordinary text editor to create your page; opening the page using a browser, viewing the result on a web browser, and correcting any tags; adding links to your home page to take viewers to another home page; adding pictures and sound; uploading the HTML file to your website; reviewing the web page to make sure that all links are working correctly; and advertising your web page. After a website has been constructed, a content management system (CMS) can be used to keep the website running smoothly. Web services are also used to develop web content. Web services consist of a collection of standards and tools that streamline and simplify communication among websites, which could revolutionize the way people develop and use the web for business and personal purposes.

An intranet is an internal corporate network built using Internet and World Wide Web standards and products. It is used by the employees of an organization to gain access to corporate information. Computers using web server software store and manage documents built on the web's HTML format. With a web browser on your PC, you can call up any web document – no matter what kind of computer it is on. Because web browsers run on any type of computer, the same electronic information can be viewed by any employee. That means all sorts of documents can be converted to electronic form on the web and constantly be updated.

An extranet is a network that links selected resources of the intranet of a company with its customers, suppliers or other business partners. It is also built around web technologies. Security and performance concerns are different for an extranet than for a website or network-based intranet. User authentication and privacy are critical on an extranet. Obviously, performance must be good to provide quick response to customers and suppliers.

Management issues and service and speed affect all networks. No centralized governing body controls the Internet. Also, because the amount of Internet traffic is so large, service bottlenecks often occur. Privacy, fraud and security issues must continually be addressed and resolved.

Self-Assessment Test

1 Voice and phone communications are examples of asynchronous communications. True or false?

2 Two broad categories of transmission media are _____.
   a. guided and wireless
   b. shielded and unshielded
   c. twisted and untwisted
   d. infrared and microwave

3 Some utilities, cities and organizations are experimenting with the use of _____ to provide network connections over standard high-voltage power lines.

4 Which of the following is a telecommunications service that delivers high-speed Internet access to homes and small businesses over existing phone lines?
   a. BPL
   b. DSL
   c. wi-fi
   d. ethernet

5 A device that encodes data from two or more devices onto a single communications channel is called a(n) _____.

6 A(n) _____ is a network that can connect technology devices within a range of 10 metres (33 feet) or so.

7 A(n) _____ is a company that provides people and organizations with access to the Internet.

8 What is the standard page description language for web pages?
   a. Home Page Language
   b. Hypermedia Language
   c. Java
   d. Hypertext Markup Language (HTML)

9 A(n) _____ is a network based on web technology that links customers, suppliers and others to the company.

10 An intranet is an internal corporate network built using Internet and World Wide Web standards and products. True or false?

Review Questions

1 What is the difference between synchronous and asynchronous communications? Give examples.

2 What advantages and disadvantages are associated with the use of client/server computing?

3 Describe a local area network and its various components.

4 What is a metropolitan area network?

5 List some uses for a personal area network.

6 What is a domain name?

7 What are Telnet and FTP used for?

8 What is the web?

9 What is an intranet? Provide three examples of the use of an intranet.

10 What is an extranet? How is it different from an intranet?

Discussion Questions

1 How might you use a local area network in your home? What devices might eventually connect to such a network?

2 Why is an organization that employs centralized processing likely to have a different management decision-making philosophy than an organization that employs distributed processing?

3 Identify three companies with which you are familiar that are using the web to conduct business. Describe their use of the web.

4 One of the key issues associated with the development of a website is getting people to visit it. If you were developing a website, how would you inform others about it and make it interesting enough that they would return and also tell others about it?

5 How could you use the Internet if you were a travelling salesperson?

Web Exercises

1 The Internet can be a powerful source of information about various industries and organizations. Locate several industry or organization websites. Which website is the best designed? Which one provides the most amount of information?

2 Research some of the potential disadvantages of using the Internet, such as privacy, fraud or unauthorized websites. Write a brief report on what you have found.

Case One

University of Sydney Redesigns Its Website

Since its founding in 1850, the University of Sydney has grown to dozens of faculties, schools and centres. Naturally, each one needed a website. The university eventually had over 600 distinct sites with millions of individual pages. These sites included intranets, online learning systems, and information for staff, students and external stakeholders. Each unit chose its own tools to build its site, which was then hosted on one of more than 200 servers.

As often happens when a website 'just grows', the result was a hodgepodge. The university had no site standards so that its sites did not have a consistent look and feel. Sites often contained duplicated, out-of-date or inaccurate information.

Web publishing was also cumbersome. Many faculty members wanted to publish content themselves, but had to go through their unit's IT department. This requirement created an annoying bottleneck.

To address these challenges, the university needed publishing standards. University managers also wanted to remove IT bottlenecks by enabling faculty staff to publish web content themselves. 'As well as a technology solution, we needed to change the way people thought about how information could be structured to meet users' needs', said web services manager Charlie Forsyth.

The University of Sydney decided to implement a content management system. They hired advisory firm Gartner to draw up a short list of vendors before asking for bids. Gartner provides industry analysis, evaluating products for a range of users, and offers consulting services to customize the general analysis to the needs of a specific organization. With its Asia/Pacific headquarters in North Sydney and a research service solely for educational institutions, Gartner was a reasonable choice.

The content management bid was won by Hewlett-Packard subsidiary Autonomy. 'Autonomy TeamSite had the scalability and power to tackle our mountain of content, the size of our web presence, and the number of users we needed to service,' said Forsyth. 'Because TeamSite is a file-based, rather than database-driven, system, it requires a lower infrastructure cost than other enterprise-grade products.' Marian Theobald, director of community engagement, adds that this 'solution has given our staff a level of control and professionalism in presentation that was not available previously'.

Initial implementation took four months. After that, the solution was rolled out to the group responsible for the central university site. This procedure allowed the university to develop processes and guidelines that it would later apply across its entire web presence. In the next phase, the university created 130 websites with 25 000 pages of content. Today, content owners throughout the university can contribute directly to their sites while maintaining consistent presentation.

The university has leveraged this investment in other ways. Every year, its faculties publish 16 student handbooks with information on courses and units of study as well as academic regulations. Most run to hundreds of pages. These handbooks now use templates that each unit can populate, speeding their creation while ensuring presentation consistency. Students can get handbooks in the format they prefer: they can read a handbook online, view it as an e-book, receive it on a CD-ROM, or print it as a hard copy. The small number of students who choose printing has enabled the university to reduce handbook printing costs by 21 per cent.

The new designs have cut the time it takes to find information. Before redeveloping the websites, a student survey showed 69 per cent found it 'easy to very easy' to find information on the university's main site. After redevelopment, this figure rose to 79 per cent. Another success indicator is that the number of telephone enquiries from prospective students halved within two years, from 5886 to 3014, during a period of growth. The university attributes this decrease to improved information available on the web.

Questions

1 Examine different parts of your college or university website. Does the site have a consistent look and feel? If you look at the Athletics section, the Admissions section, and the description of your academic programme, can you tell at a glance that they belong to the same institution? If you can't, how would your college or university benefit from a more consistent appearance? If they are consistent, what would your college or university lose if they were not?

2 Suppose it costs twice as much to print a single copy of a handbook on demand as it costs to print each copy when they are printed in volume. What fraction of the students must use alternative access methods in order for the university to save 21 per cent of its printing cost for handbooks overall? What if the cost ratio of single-copy printing to the cost of each copy when printed in volume is 5:1? If 85 per cent of the students access handbooks online, how much more expensive can single-copy printing be for the university to break even on printing handbooks?

3 Instead of implementing content management software, the University of Sydney could have issued website guidelines to its units and motivated them to use the same website development software by negotiating a site-wide licence and offering training. How effective would that approach have been? Which of the benefits in this case study would the university probably have achieved in full, which would it probably have achieved in part, and which would it not have achieved at all? Should the university have considered this less expensive approach at all? Why or why not?

4 The case study gives one of the benefits for the new approach as the ability of individual faculty members to publish their own web content. What are some disadvantages of this ability? On balance, do you think it is a good idea? Why or why not? Does a university differ from a profit-making corporation or a religious organization in this regard? If you think it does, what are the differences, and how do they affect this issue? If you think it doesn't differ, why don't other differences affect this issue?

Case Two

Social Networking inside a Business

PepsiCo Russia, an organizational element of PepsiCo Europe, is the largest food and beverage business in Russia and the countries of the former Soviet Union. Much of PepsiCo Russia's growth has been through acquisitions, since PepsiCo management recognizes the business potential of Russia and neighbouring countries. For example, its €2.87 billion acquisition of 18 000-employee Will-Bimm-Dann, completed in 2011, is the largest foreign investment to date in the Russian food industry. PepsiCo had previously acquired a majority stake in JSC Lebedyanski, Russia's leading juice producer and a major baby food company, for €1.06 billion. Because of these and other acquisitions, PepsiCo Russia now consists of dozens

of employee groups that have no shared history. Making them work as a unit creates a management challenge.

To deal with this challenge, PepsiCo Russia decided to create an employee intranet portal with a social focus. To learn what users expect of social sites, the project team looked at Facebook, VK (previously VKontakte, a Russian social site comparable to Facebook), LinkedIn and Google+. 'We studied the [user] experience of the world's best social networking sites, and combined it with the concepts of enterprise portals,' says project leader Eugene Karpov.

PepsiCo Russia used Microsoft SharePoint collaboration software to integrate social networking concepts with its portal. The current SharePoint release has social networking features: users can find information from others with matching interests; they can bookmark, tag and rate content, making it accessible to those on a team; and they get consolidated views of what other users are tracking or have written. Wikis also made their debut in Share-Point 2010. SharePoint 15, anticipated for 2013, is expected to extend the package's social networking capabilities.

The intranet uses a Quick Poll feature to gauge employee sentiment on topics of interest and to provide feedback on the portal itself. For example, the Quick Poll of 15 March 2012, asked, 'What news does the portal lack?' It offered five choices: PepsiCo Russia business achievements, PepsiCo global news, news from plants and regions, corporate citizenship, and life at PepsiCo (sports, contests and so on). Like most other content, this poll can be displayed in either Russian or English as a user prefers.

Since PepsiCo Russia's programmers had little experience with Share-Point, the company partnered with an experienced SharePoint developer to build its intranet site. This firm, WSS Consulting, carried out the project for a total cost of €75 510, not including SharePoint licence fees. One reason WSS could do it for this rela-tively small sum is that it had already developed a general-purpose portal for SharePoint: WSS Portal. WSS Portal provided a ready-made basis for PepsiCo Russia's portal, thus reducing its cost, shortening its development time and ensuring good performance: the server typically returns pages in less than 0.2 seconds.

Features of the new portal include social profiles, community membership, quick polls, document management and location-specific information such as weather. In March 2012, 5000 office employees had portal access, but access will be extended to thousands of factory-floor workers in the future. Employee reception of the portal has been positive, and there are many plans for future enhancements.

Questions

1   What could employees use the social networking features of SharePoint for? What would be the business benefit?

2   What could the poll feature be used for?

3   Do you think SharePoint would be a good way for PepsiCo Russia to communicate with its suppliers and customers?

4   What is a wiki and what could employees use one for?

Case Three

NetHope Worldwide Disaster Relief

When disaster strikes, it has both an economic and human impact. People who are not affected by the disaster often feel a moral obligation to come to the aid of the disaster's victims. People feel this obligation even more strongly if they have specific skills that can help alleviate the effects of the disaster.

One skill needed in many natural disasters is the ability to set up networks so the people affected, their governments, and organizations that want to help can communicate with each other. That need for long-distance communication places a particular responsibility on the technology community. Many high-tech companies fulfil this responsibility under the auspices of NetHope, a group of large humanitarian relief organizations.

Consider, for example, the 2010 floods in Pakistan. They affected over 20 million people and had an economic impact estimated at €7.17 billion. If relief is not provided quickly in such situations, the effects of a disaster can worsen and spread.

NetHope and its partners have been on site in all recent natural disasters. In the first two months after the Haiti earthquake of 2010, NetHope and its partner Microsoft helped launch a website for interagency collaboration, set up cloud computing solutions for Haiti's government and for organizations working in the country, and had Bing and MSN each set up web pages where people could donate to Haiti. Communication between Haitians and aid workers was hampered because few workers spoke Haitian Creole. To solve this problem, Microsoft added Haitian Creole to Microsoft Translator, a free automatic translation tool, and provided the tool to aid workers.

In the 2011 tsunami in Japan, NetHope partners provided a cloud-based community communication portal for Second Harvest Japan. The organization uses the portal to coordinate food donors, transportation providers, and distributors in the Japanese relief effort. Cloud services avoid problems such as damaged infrastructure and equipment, power shortages and telecommunications service interruptions.

One of NetHope's five major missions is connectivity. According to the NetHope website, the connectivity objective is to 'improve communications between organizations and field offices in remote parts of the world, where infrastructure is limited or absent'. Until recently, NetHope tried to meet this objective by placing very small aperture terminals (VSATs) in remote areas with little to no terrestrial infrastructure. VSAT systems include an Earth station (usually less than 3 metres, or 10 feet, wide) placed outdoors in line of sight to the sky to link to a satellite in geosynchronous orbit. The satellite can relay messages to anywhere else on Earth, permitting communication with isolated areas.

However, as Gisli Olafsson, Emergency Response Director of NetHope (and a former Microsoft employee) learned, 'using VSAT as the preferred way to connect is not always the most effective and economical method'. Olafsson continues: 'With most countries moving toward a 3G wireless broadband mobile network, ... we have seen that mobile networks are becoming more resilient to large-scale disasters, with core services generally being available within two weeks of a major incident. It is more economical and easier to stockpile and transfer 3G modems than VSAT kits.'

Technology, of course, is never the entire answer. People are an important part of any system. After the 2010 Haiti earthquake, NetHope launched NetHope Academy to provide IT skills training and on-the-job work experience to unemployed Haitians so they could build in-country technical expertise. The first group of NetHope Academy interns spent three weeks in intensive boot camp-style classroom training. They were then placed with teams rebuilding devastated areas of Haiti, using their new skills to help team members keep in touch with people outside their immediate area.

In addition to Microsoft, NetHope partners include such well-known technology firms as Accenture, Cisco, Hewlett-Packard and Intel. The technology community can be proud of its commitment to humanitarian aid and economic recovery.

Questions

1 What good would telecommunications be in an affected area just after a natural disaster?

2 Why is 3G making telecommunications networks more resilient to disaster?

3 Outline an information technology strategy that a company might use to protect itself from failure in the event of a disaster?

4 In what ways could cloud computing help to prepare/deal with natural disaster?

Notes

1 Webster, John S., 'Ethernet Over Copper', *Computerworld*, 27 March 2006.

2 Di Stefano, Theodore F., 'India's Hi-Tech Dominance: How Did IT Happen?' *E-Commerce Times,* 14 April 2006.

3 Orzech, Dan, 'Surfing Through the Power Grid', *Wired News,* 20 October 2005.

4 Pappalardo, Denise, 'Ford Not Quite in Cruise Control'. Available from: *Network World*, www.networkworld.com, 27 February 2006.

5 Gelke, H. 'Harnessing Ultra-Wideband for Medial Applications', Medical Electronic Design. Available from: www.medicalelectronicsdesign.com/article/harnessing-ultra-wideband-medical-applications. Accessed 30 April 2014.

6 Honan, Mathew, 'Apple Unveils Intel-Powered Mac Minis', *Computerworld,* 28 February 2006.

7 Blau, John, 'Metro Shows Voice-Operated RFID Device at CeBIT', *Computerworld,* 8 March 2006.

8 Mearian, Lucas, 'Google Earth's Photographer Builds Out Infrastructure', *Computerworld*, 1 March 2006.

9 Staff, 'EasyStreet and OnFibre Bring State-of-the-Art Network to Portland', Press Releases, OnFibre. Available from: www.onfibre.com, 20 January 2005.

10 Betts, Mitch, 'Global Dispatches: Hitachi Replacing PCs with Thin Clients to Boost Security', *Computerworld*, 30 May 2005.

11 About Us – Strategic Relationships – Marks & Spencer – Cable & Wireless. Available from: www.cw.com/US/about_us/strategic_relationships/cisco/cisco_customers_ms.html.

12 Dubie, Denise, 'Sierra Pacific Taps Open Source Management Tools', *Network World*, 12 December 2005.

13 4-Traders Web site, "ZIX: 08/23/2011 7-Eleven Expands Secure Email Services with ZIX Corporation," 4-Traders, www.4-traders.com/ZIX-CORPORATION-11477/news/ZIX-08-23-2011-7-Eleven-Expands-Secure-Email-Serviceswith-Zix-Corporation-13767214, 24 August 2011.

14 Werner EnterprisesWeb site, "AboutWerner," www.werner.com/content/about, accessed 15 December 2011.

15 AT&T Case Study, "Werner Enterprises Sees Green Light for Growth in China," www.business.att.com/enterprise/resource_item/Insights/Case_Study/werner_enterprises, accessed 15 December 2011.

16 Staff, 'China Tightens Web-Content Rules', *Wall Street Journal*, 26 September 2005, p. B3.

17 Hafner, Katie, 'Where Wizards Stay Up Late: The Origins of the Internet', Touchstone, Rockefeller Center, New York, 1996.

18 Internet2 Website. Available from: www. internet2.edu, 29 November 2005.

19 Miller, Michael, 'Web Portals Make a Comeback', *PC Magazine*, 4 October 2005, p. 7.

20 Pike, Sarah, 'The Expert's Guide to Google, Yahoo!, MSN, and AOL', *PC Magazine,* 4 October 2005, p. 112.

21 Guth, Robert, et al., 'Sky-High Search Wars', *The Wall Street Journal*, 24 May 2005, p. B1.

22 Staff, 'Microsoft Looks for a Place Among Competitors with MSN Local Search', *Rocky Mountain News,* 21 June 2005, p. 6B.

23 Staff, 'Study: Web Site's Appearance Matters', *CNN Online*, 11 August 2005.

24 BT Website, 2014. Available from: http://business.bt.com/domains-and-hosting/web-hosting. Accessed 15 July 2014.

25 Hof, Robert, 'Mix, Match, and Mutate', *Business Week*, 25 July 2005, p. 72.

World Views Case

How to Build a Calculator with Stuff You Probably Have Lying Around the House

Computers can be made to work in a number of ways.

Every computer has a set of electronic components that manage the flow of data around it, known as its chipset. There are a number of ways that these could be configured to make a working computer. Each configuration comes with its own set of basic commands or instruction set to make it work. The computer's operating system has to be written so that everything it does will get translated into the basic commands that a particular chipset uses.

In the early days of Microsoft, engineers took great care to make sure their software could be used by different operating systems, and therefore potentially on computers with different chipsets. Microsoft engineer Charles Simonyi who managed the original development of Microsoft Office put a lot of effort into making sure Word and Excel would run on different types of computer, however as it turned out this effort was not really needed because Microsoft's own operating system rapidly became very popular. You might have heard of Charles Simonyi – he funded the Professor for Public Understanding of Science post at the University of Oxford that Richard Dawkins held for over a decade, and he also was an early space tourist.

Anyway, whatever a computer's instruction set is, when it gets down to it, all that a digital computer is doing is converting zeros to ones and back again, and passing the results around itself and out to other computers and devices. Converting ones to zeros is how a computer adds numbers, and adding is a computer's fundamental operation. It doesn't matter what a computer looks like it is doing, what it is actually doing is adding binary numbers together. The numbers are stored as electric charge – essentially a tiny magnet where positive and negative charges represent 1 and 0. Each of these is referred to as a bit.

How a computer works is not actually that complicated, although it's too complicated to explain in the space we have here. Instead we will look at how a computer could add binary numbers. To start, how could we add just two bits together?

Well, we'll need two inputs and two outputs.

Inputs 0 + 0 will output 00. (The inputs will actually be 00 – the plus sign is just to make this a little more readable.) 0 + 1 (or 1 + 0) will output 01. The result of 1 + 1 will be 10 which is the binary number two.

When adding numbers that are longer than one bit each, then from the two bit results above the right hand bit will be the result and the left hand bit will be carried into the next column, just like you probably learned to add at school. It looks like this:

```
   1 0 1 1
+  1 0 1 1 0
  ---------
  1 0 0 0 1
```

In this addition, 1 + 1 comes up three times, so three times a 1 has been carried into the next column. What this means is that when you add a binary number, the adder needs to be able to handle three bits: The two bits that are being added plus a bit that might have been carried from the previous column. An adder that just handles two bits is called a half adder; an adder that handles three bits is a full adder.

The behaviour of a full adder can be shown like this:

Input 1	Input 2	Carried bit	Output 1	Output 2
0	0	0	0	0
0	0	1	0	1
0	1	0	0	1
0	1	1	1	0
1	0	0	0	1
1	0	1	1	0
1	1	0	1	0
1	1	1	1	1

The Carried bit is a bit that has been carried over from the previous sum. Output 2 is the result, and Output 1 is the bit that gets carried over to the next sum. A half adder is a bit simpler. Its behaviour looks like this:

Input 1	Input 2	Output 1	Output 2
0	0	0	0
0	1	0	1
1	0	0	1
1	1	1	0

This can be read as:
0 plus 0 equals 0
0 plus 1 equals 1
1 plus 0 equals 1
1 plus 1 equals 2 which, as said before, in binary is 10

So how do we build a half adder?

Stand-up comedian and mathematician Matt Parker has designed and constructed a beautiful half adder using dominos. Two elements (they are called `logic gates') are needed. The first is called AND. It takes two inputs and outputs; a 1 if both of the inputs are 1, and 0 otherwise. In dominos an AND gates looks like this:

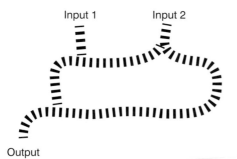

If you stack up a set of dominos as above and knock none of them over nothing happens (which means the output is 0). If you knock one of them over the line of dominos connected to the output gets broken and again nothing is output. Only if both inputs are knocked over does the output fall which represents an output of 1. Try it!

The second element is called XOR. It takes two inputs and outputs 1 if either input is 1, and 0 if the inputs are 00 or 11. In dominos Matt Parker's XOR gate looks like this:

Input 1   Input 2

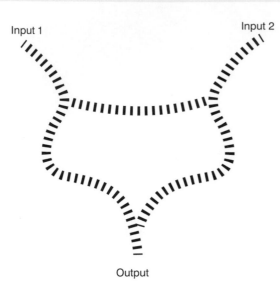

Output

If you knock down none, there is no output. If you knock down either input you get an output of 1. If you knock down both inputs the falling dominos bump into each other, cancelling themselves out and there is no output. Again try it and see.

To create a half adder you need to arrange your dominos like this:

Input 1   Input 2

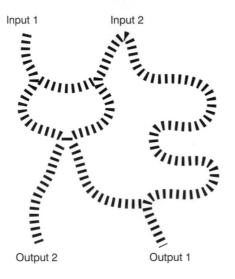

Output 2   Output 1

So how does it work? Well, if nothing is input, nothing is output so $0 + 0 = 00$.

If either input is knocked down then the left hand side of dominos fall in such a way that a break is caused just before Output 1 so Output 1 doesn't fall, but Output 2 does. The reason the line going to Output 1 loops around is to cause a delay to give the break time to work. So $1 + 0 = 01$ and $0 + 1 = 01$. (Notice that in the figure Output 2 and 1 are the wrong way around – this is OK, but it means you really should be looking at this figure upside down.)

Finally if both inputs are knocked over then the XOR gate cancels both the break and Output 2, so only Output 1 falls over. So $1 + 1 = 10$. If you have enough dominos you can try this one too.

Matt and his team went ahead and built a full adder from dominos, 10 000 of them! Basically you need to chain together two half adders to make a full adder, and chain together a series of full adders to add together binary digits which are made up of more than one bit. Chaining full adders is how a computer adds up.

On YouTube you can watch the 10,000 domino computer working (search for 'domino computer'), or if you have a spare afternoon you could try designing it yourself.

Questions

1 Try designing a set of dominos that will count two bits where Output 1 is carried into a second full adder. The second one will have to have three inputs – two bits plus the carried bit.

2 How could an adder be made to subtract? (Hint: the structure of the adder doesn't change – all the dominos stay exactly as they are. Only the input changes. Think about how you can subtract numbers only by using adding for a few minutes, and then search for 'two's complement' online.)

3 How could an adder be made to multiply?

4 Other people have built computers using all manner of raw materials. Run a search to find some of them. A particularly interesting one has been made out of John Conway's Game of Life.

PART 3

Business Information Systems

PART 3

Business Information Systems

07

Operational Systems

Principles

An organization must have information systems that support the routine, day-to-day activities that occur in the normal course of business and help a company add value to its products and services.

Traditional transaction processing systems support the various business functions of organizations that have not yet implemented enterprise resource planning systems.

Electronic and mobile commerce allow transactions to be made by the customer, with less need for sales staff, and open up new opportunities for conducting business.

A company that implements an enterprise resource planning system is creating a highly integrated set of systems, which can lead to many business benefits.

Learning Objectives

- Identify the basic activities and business objectives common to all transaction processing systems.
- Identify key control and management issues associated with transaction processing systems.

- Describe the inputs, processing and outputs for the transaction processing systems associated with the order processing, purchasing and accounting business functions.

- Define e- and m-commerce and describe various forms of e-commerce.

- Identify the challenges multinational corporations must face in planning, building and operating their transaction processing systems.
- Discuss the advantages and disadvantages associated with the implementation of an enterprise resource planning system.

Why Learn About Operational Systems?

You might recall from Chapter 2 that operational systems support the day-to-day running of a firm. Operational systems, such as transaction processing systems (TPS), allow firms to buy and sell. Without systems to perform these functions, the firm could not operate. Organizations today are moving from a collection of non-integrated transaction processing systems to highly integrated enterprise resource planning systems to perform routine business processes and maintain records about them. These systems support a wide range of business activities associated with supply chain management and customer relationship management (as mentioned in Chapter 1). Although they were initially thought to be cost-effective only for very large companies, even small and mid-sized companies are now implementing these systems to reduce costs and improve service.

Employees who work directly with customers – whether in sales, customer service or marketing – require high-quality transaction processing systems and their associated information to provide good customer service. Companies selling online need electronic- and mobile-commerce software to allow customers to perform transactions. No matter what your role, it is very likely that you will provide input to or use the output from your organization's systems. Your effective use of these systems will be essential to raise the productivity of your firm, improve customer service and enable better decision making. Thus, it is important that you understand how these systems work and what their capabilities and limitations are.

7.1 Introduction

Part 3 of this book describes the main types of business information system. This chapter looks at those systems that manage the day-to-day running of the firm. Without them an organization couldn't operate. They include systems that sell products and services to customers (transaction processing systems), systems that buy materials from suppliers (supply chain management systems), systems that help manage the after-sales service (customer relationship management systems) and systems that maintain tax records (accounting systems). Then Chapter 8 looks at systems used by the organization to manage its longer-term operations and make decisions about product offerings and marketing campaigns. Chapter 9 looks at more specialized systems including robotics and artificial intelligence. Chapter 10 then looks at the ways information technology has become part of our work and home environment.

Often, especially with the systems described in this chapter and the next, the output from one of the systems is the input to another of the systems. An alternative approach to having separate systems do all of the jobs that are discussed, is to have one enterprise-wide system that does all of them. This is the enterprise resource planning (ERP) approach, which is described at the start of this chapter. ERP doesn't really fit into either the day-to-day running category or the long-term planning category since it does both and the decision to include it in this chapter rather than the next is fairly arbitrary. Also there is no agreed minimum set of tasks that a system has to perform in order for it to be classed as an ERP. However the expectation is that an ERP does some of the tasks described in this chapter, plus some of the tasks described in the next chapter. One way of looking at the material in Chapters 7 and 8 is that if an organization has an ERP, then the systems described are sub-systems of their ERP. If an organization does not have an ERP, then the systems described are stand-alone information systems in their own right.

7.2 Enterprise Resource Planning

Enterprise resource planning (ERP) systems evolved from systems (called materials requirements planning or MRP systems) that allowed companies to plan out how much raw materials they would need at a certain time in the future, plan their production, control their inventory and manage their purchasing process. Many organizations recognized that their existing systems lacked the integration needed to coordinate these activities and also to share valuable information across all the business functions of the firm. As a result, costs were higher and customer service suffered. This led firms to start to create new systems, which came to be known as enterprise resource planning systems. Large organizations, especially members of the Fortune 1000, were the first to take on the challenge of implementing ERP. An ERP is a system that manages an entire company's vital business information. Many firms consider themselves to have an ERP if the system manages most, rather than all, of their information.

Advantages of ERP

Increased global competition, executives' desire for control over the total cost and product flow through their enterprises, and ever-more-numerous customer interactions drive the demand for enterprise-wide access to real-time information. ERP offers integrated software from a single vendor to help meet those needs. The primary benefits of implementing ERP include improved access to data for operational decision making, elimination of inefficient or outdated systems, improvement of work processes, and technology standardization. ERP vendors have also developed specialized systems for specific applications and market segments.

Improved Access to Data for Operational Decision Making

ERP systems operate via an integrated database, using one set of data to support all business functions. The systems can support decisions on optimal sourcing or cost accounting, for instance, for the entire enterprise or for business units, rather than gathering data from multiple business functions and then trying to coordinate that information manually or reconciling it with another application. The result is an organization that looks seamless, not only to the outside world but also to the decision makers who are deploying resources within that organization. The data is integrated to facilitate operational decision making and allows companies to provide greater customer service and support, strengthen customer and supplier relationships, and generate new business opportunities.

   The British company Flambeau produces a wide range of plastic products and employs thousands of workers in eight manufacturing locations worldwide. It has grown through acquisition, and out of necessity was running multiple, disparate legacy information systems that drew data from multiple databases. The firm had to resort to the use of spreadsheets to manually track critical business information used for cost and inventory control. This inevitably led to errors and poor decision making. Finally the company implemented an ERP system to deliver timely, consistent data for both production and financial management purposes. Flambeau has used the system to lower its inventory costs, better manage its production operations, and provide access to a single set of data used to run the business.[1]

Elimination of Costly, Inflexible Legacy Systems

Adoption of an ERP system enables an organization to eliminate dozens or even hundreds of separate systems and replace them with a single, integrated set of applications for the entire enterprise. In many cases, these systems are decades old, the original developers are long gone, and the systems are poorly documented. As a result, the systems are extremely difficult to fix when they break, and adapting them to meet business needs takes too long. They become an anchor around the organization that keeps it from moving ahead and remaining competitive. An ERP system helps match the capabilities of an organization's information systems to its business needs – even as these needs evolve.

Improvement of Work Processes

Competition requires companies to structure their business processes to be as effective and customer oriented as possible. ERP vendors do considerable research to define the best business processes. They gather the requirements of leading companies within an industry and combine them with findings from research institutions and consultants. The individual application modules included in the ERP system are then designed to support these best practices, which should be one of the most efficient and effective ways to complete a business process. Thus, implementation of an ERP system ensures good work processes based on best practices. For example, for managing customer payments, the ERP system's finance module can be configured to reflect the most efficient practices of leading companies in an industry. This increased efficiency ensures that everyday business operations follow the optimal chain of activities, with all users supplied the information and tools they need to complete each step.

With 22 000 employees serving 4.7 million customers and generating revenue of €14 billion, Achmea is the largest insurance company in the Netherlands. The company had grown rapidly through acquisition and had evolved to using a mix of manual data collection and reporting processes. The company converted to an ERP system to standardize on a set of industry best practices, streamlined work processes, and sophisticated data analysis tools across all divisions and operating companies. As a result, the company could reduce staffing levels in some areas of the business by as much as 30 per cent, thus improving productivity and cutting costs. In addition, the time required to complete month-end financial reporting was reduced by 30 per cent, with an increase in the accuracy and reliability of the data.[2]

Upgrade of Technology Infrastructure

When implementing an ERP system, an organization has an opportunity to upgrade the information technology (hardware, operating systems, databases, etc.) that it uses. While centralizing and formalizing these decisions, the organization can eliminate the multiple hardware platforms, operating systems and databases it is currently using – most likely from a variety of vendors – and standardize on fewer technologies and vendors. This reduces ongoing maintenance and support costs as well as the training load for those who must support the infrastructure.

Barloworld Handling UK is the United Kingdom distributor of Hyster forklifts. It also provides parts and service through 26 service locations that field customer service calls, schedule and dispatch field techs, and manage the ordering and delivery of parts. This highly decentralized service operation resulted in inefficient work processes, high costs and inconsistent service levels. Barloworld reengineered its service operations to squeeze out waste and inefficiency. Service technicians were issued handheld computers programmed to follow the new work processes. The handheld devices could also access work orders, equipment information and inventory data held in the firm's ERP database. By integrating mobile devices with improved work processes and access to ERP data, the firm achieved 'paperless, real-time data entry; immediate parts lookup and availability checks with overnight delivery; time sheets completed as work progresses; and automatic dispatch of work orders,' according to Robert S. Tennant, the firm's CIO. The number of service locations was reduced from 26 to 6, service tech efficiency was increased by 10 per cent, and annual revenue increased by more than €500 000.[3]

- *Process da
  capture, pi
  ness activi
  tions espe

- *Maintain a
  accuratel)
  to execute
  shipment:

- *Avoid pro
  processir
  bank, rec
  transactic
  organiza

- *Produce
  quickly c
  are sent
  ing the f
  firms en

- *Increase
  required
  ness tra

- *Help ir
  providi

- *Help b
  to com
  ers sat
  of con
  their o
  shopp

- *Achie
  and n
  oped
  long-
  some
  comp

Tran

TPS ca
update
outside
proce:
data m

Data

Captu
action
as by
card
speci

Disadvantages of ERP Systems

Unfortunately, implementing ERP systems can be difficult and can disrupt current business practices. Some of the major disadvantages of ERP systems are the expense and time required for implementation, the difficulty in implementing the many business process changes that accompany the ERP system, the problems with integrating the ERP system with other systems, difficulty in loading data into the new system, the risks associated with making a major commitment to a single vendor, and the risk of implementation failure.

Expense and Time in Implementation

Getting the full benefits of ERP takes time and money. Although ERP offers many strategic advantages by streamlining a company's TPS, large firms typically need three to five years and spend tens of millions of euros to implement a successful ERP system.

Difficulty Implementing Change

In some cases, a company has to radically change how it operates to conform to the ERP's work processes – its best practices. These changes can be so drastic to long-time employees that they retire or quit rather than go through the change. This exodus can leave a firm short of experienced workers. Sometimes, the best practices simply are not appropriate for the firm and cause great work disruptions.

Difficulty Integrating with Other Systems

Most companies have other systems that must be integrated with the ERP system, such as financial analysis programs, e-commerce operations and other applications. Many companies have experienced difficulties making these other systems operate with their ERP system. Other companies need additional software to create these links.

Difficulty in Loading Data into New ERP System

A major amount of work is required to load existing data from various sources into the new ERP database. The new ERP system may have the capability to store hundreds or even thousands of data items (e.g. customer name, bill to address, product description, etc.). The data items that will be required depend on the scope of ERP implementation. If certain processes or transactions are not included within the scope of implementation, there will be less data to load.

Data mapping is the examination of each data item required for the new ERP system and determining where that data item will come from. While most of the data for the new system will come from the files of existing legacy systems, some data items may need to be pulled from manual systems or may even need to be created for the new system. Data clean-up is required because the legacy systems are likely to contain data that is inaccurate, incomplete or inconsistent. For example, the same customer may be listed multiple times in existing customer files with varying bill to addresses or products may appear in the existing inventory files that have not been produced for years. Data loading can be performed either by using data conversion software that reads the old data and converts it into a format for loading into the database or by end-users entering data via the input screens of the new system.

Risks in Using One Vendor

The high cost to switch to another vendor's ERP system makes it extremely unlikely that a firm will do so. After a company has adopted an ERP system, the vendor has less incentive to listen and respond to customer concerns. The high cost to switch also comes with the risk that the ERP vendor allows its product to become outdated or goes out of business.

Selecting an ERP system involves not only choosing the best software product, but also the right long-term business partner. It was unsettling for many companies that had implemented example, are hard-copy documents produced by a payroll TPS, whereas an outstanding balance report for invoices might be a soft-copy report displayed by an accounts receivable TPS.

In addition to major documents such as cheques and invoices, most TPS provide other useful management information and decision support, such as printed or on-screen reports that help managers and employees perform various activities. A report showing current inventory is one example; another might be a document listing items ordered from a supplier to help an administrator check the order for completeness when it arrives. A TPS can also produce reports required by law, such as tax statements.

Information Systems @ Work

Tesco's Dark Stores

In the world of Tesco online grocery shopping, the person on the checkout is no longer the only face of the company. Delivery drivers play a new part in representing the company and they are hired not on the basis of their driving skills but on whether or not Tesco think you would want them in your house. 'They go into customers' kitchens, they're brand ambassadors for us and they need to be service superstars,' says Simon Belsham, managing director of Tesco grocery online.

In densely populated areas where many people shop for groceries online, Tesco use a 'dark store': a faceless warehouse, closed to the public, but which inside looks reasonably just like a regular Tesco shop, except there's no advertising posters or checkout tills. Tesco have six dark stores around London. In them, online grocery orders are packed and sent out to customers in the city and southeast England.

The shelves in the dark store get stocked in the afternoon, and then at 8 p.m. the picking starts, to get bags ready for the delivery vans to leave at 6.15 a.m. the next morning, returning throughout the day to be re-filled.

'There's always something going on,' says Chris May, the centre's manager. Instead of retail assistants, there are 'pickers' who fill bags with online orders. Different parts of the store work in different ways. In one section, pickers stay in one spot while a mechanized system – the 'goods-to-person pickstation' – sends infrequently purchased items from storage along a conveyor belt to the picker. For products that Tesco sell more of, like bread and milk, pickers have to go and get them.

'It's a little bit like I imagine going into a Willy Wonka factory,' says Jennifer Creevy, deputy editor of *Retail Week*. 'It looks really whizzy and there's crates moving around. It's really impressive.' Organizing things this way saves space and time, and creates a safer workplace, according to Dematic, the company that built the pickstation system.

Over 35 per cent of all items sold by Tesco online are being added to online shopping baskets on customers' mobile phones and Tesco have capitalized on this by releasing an app to help customers shop for items quickly and conveniently, with their favourite items being particularly easy to find.

Mr Belsham insists, however, that machines cannot replace the personal touch that customers value. He does concede though that focusing on the customer when they aren't there is tricky. To combat the feeling that this giant warehouse is cut off from the outside world, workers are occasionally told to go out with the delivery drivers. That way they get to meet the customers.

Sometimes, the centre's doors are flung open to invite friends and family in. This helps those close to employees to understand the work they do. By the way, Tesco doesn't like the term 'dark store' as they think it sounds sinister. They prefer 'dotcom only'.

Questions

1 In what ways do dark stores benefit Tesco? What alternative models are there?

2 How else could Tesco introduce a 'human touch' for online customers? Would customers want this?

3 How could a local small grocer compete with this system?

4 How could Tesco use the data generated by the system to their advantage? (There are probably too many possibilities to list them all!)

(partially visible left margin from underlying page)

248

252

7

7

7.4 Traditional Transaction Processing Applications

This section presents an overview of several common transaction processing systems that support the order processing, purchasing and accounting business functions (see Table 7.3).

Table 7.3 Systems that Support Order Processing, Purchasing and Accounting Functions

Order Processing	Purchasing	Accounting
Order processing	Inventory control (raw materials, packing materials, spare parts and supplies)	Budget
Sales configuration		Accounts receivable
Shipment planning		Payroll
Shipment execution	Purchase order processing	Asset management
Inventory control (finished product)	Receiving	General ledger
Accounts receivable	Accounts payable	

Order Processing Systems

7

The traditional TPS for order processing include order entry, sales configuration, shipment planning, shipment execution, inventory control and accounts receivable. Running these systems efficiently and reliably is critical to an enterprise. Figure 7.4 is a system-level flowchart that shows the various systems and the information that flows among them. Table 7.4 summarizes the input, processing and output (IPO) of the essential systems that include the traditional order processing systems.

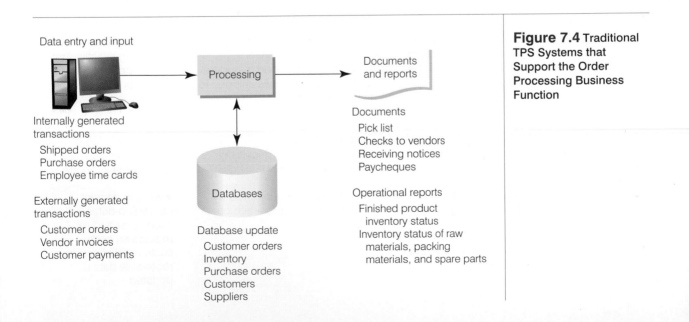

Data entry and input

Internally generated transactions
  Shipped orders
  Purchase orders
  Employee time cards

Externally generated transactions
  Customer orders
  Vendor invoices
  Customer payments

Databases

Database update
  Customer orders
  Inventory
  Purchase orders
  Customers
  Suppliers

Documents and reports

Documents
  Pick list
  Checks to vendors
  Receiving notices
  Paycheques

Operational reports
  Finished product
    inventory status
  Inventory status of raw
    materials, packing
    materials, and spare parts

Figure 7.4 Traditional TPS Systems that Support the Order Processing Business Function

Beaulieu Group LLC is the third-largest carpet manufacturer in the world. Its major customers include US home improvement chains The Home Depot and Lowe's Companies. Its most popular brands are Beaulieu, Coronet, Hollytex, and Laura Ashley Home. In an effort to streamline its traditional order processing process, the firm equipped 250 of its commercial accounts sales staff with an order entry application that runs on a Pocket PC. With the new system, salespeople enter customer orders, access the company's pricing databases and make changes to orders over a wireless network. If a wireless connection cannot be made at the customer's site, the salesperson can enter orders on the Pocket PC and then transmit the data later when communications can be established. The new process has improved the way salespeople interact with customers and reduced the time they spend filling out paperwork. Previously, orders had to be written out at a customer's site and then sent to the company's central office, where clerical workers keyed them into an order processing system. As a result, the salespeople spent too much time on administrative work entering and correcting orders and not enough time selling.

Table 7.4 IPO of the Traditional TPS Systems that Support Order Processing

System	Input	Processing	Output
Order entry	Customer order information via a variety of means: data entry by sales rep, customer input, mail, phone, e-commerce, or computer to computer via EDI or XML formats	Order is checked for completeness and accuracy. On-hand inventory is checked to ensure each item can be shipped in the quantity ordered or a substitute item is suggested	An open order record
Sales configuration	Customer order information including model and options desired	Review customer order information and ensure the configuration will meet the customer's needs; suggest additional options and features when appropriate	Revised customer order
Shipment planning	Open orders, i.e. orders received but not yet shipped	Determine which open orders will be filled, when and from which location each order will be shipped to minimize delivery costs and meet customer desired delivery dates	Pick list for each order to be filled from each shipping location showing the items and quantities needed to fill the order
Shipment execution	Pick list and data entered by warehouse operations personnel as they fill the order	Data entered by warehouse operations personnel captured and used to update record of what was shipped to the customer	A shipped order record specifying exactly what was shipped to the customer – this can be different than what was ordered
Inventory control (finished product)	Record of each item picked to fill a customer order	Inventory records are updated to reflect current quantity of each item	Updated inventory database and various management reports
Accounts receivable	Shipped order records received from shipment execution that show precisely what was shipped on each order; payments from customers	Determine amount owed by each customer for each order placed	Invoice statement containing details of each order and its associated costs; customers' accounts receivable data is updated

Purchasing Systems

The traditional TPS that support the purchasing business function include inventory control, purchase order processing, receiving and accounts payable (see Figure 7.5). Table 7.5 shows the input, processing and output associated with this collection of systems. Figure 7.6 shows how RFID technology is helping inventory control.

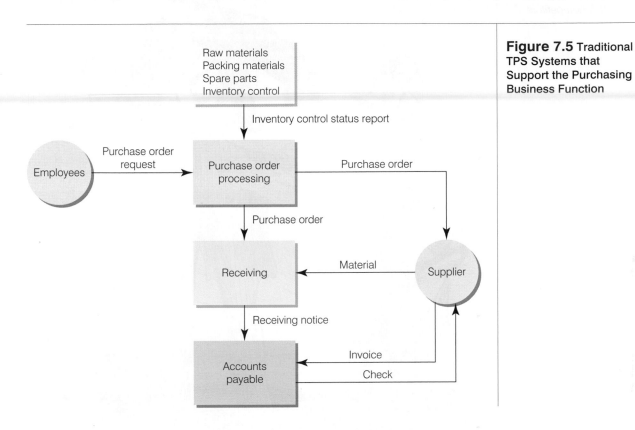

Figure 7.5 Traditional TPS Systems that Support the Purchasing Business Function

Table 7.5 IPO for the Traditional TPS Systems that Support Purchasing

System	Input	Processing	Output
Inventory control	Records reflecting any increase or decrease in the inventory of specific items of raw materials, packing materials or spare parts	Withdrawals are subtracted from inventory counts of specific items; additions are added to the inventory count	The inventory record of each item is updated to reflect its current count
Purchase order processing	Inventory records, employee-prepared purchase order requests, information on preferred suppliers	Items that need to be ordered are identified, quantities to be ordered are determined, qualified supplier with whom to place the order is identified	Purchase orders are placed with preferred suppliers for items
Receiving	Information on the quantity and quality of items received	Receipt is matched to purchase order, input data is edited for accuracy and completeness	Receiving report is created, inventory records are updated to reflect new receipts
Accounts payable	Purchase orders placed, information on receipts, supplier invoices	Supplier invoice matched to original purchase order and receiving report	Payment generated to supplier

Figure 7.6 An early transaction processing system? *The boys are trying to transact with the gent, who looks like he's already done a deal with one of their competitors.*

7

Accounting Systems

accounting systems Systems that include budget, accounts receivable, payroll, asset management, and general ledger.

The primary **accounting systems** include the budget, accounts receivable, payroll, asset management, and general ledger (see Figure 7.7). Table 7.6 shows the input, processing, and output associated with these systems.

7.5 Electronic and Mobile Commerce

Electronic Commerce

electronic commerce Conducting business transactions (e.g. distribution, buying, selling and servicing) electronically over computer networks such as the Internet, extranets and corporate networks.

Electronic commerce is conducting a business transaction (e.g. distribution, buying, selling and servicing) electronically over computer networks, primarily the Internet but also extranets and corporate networks. An e-commerce system is a type of transaction processing system. Business activities that are strong candidates for conversion to e-commerce are paper

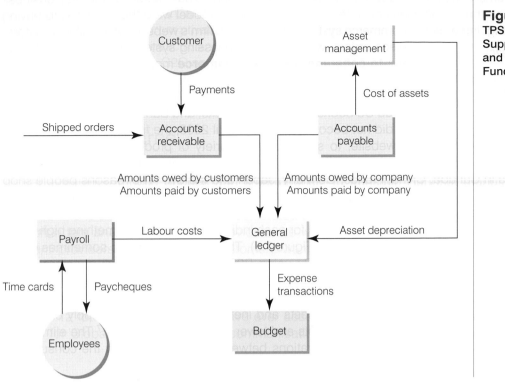

Figure 7.7 Traditional TPS Systems that Support the Accounting and Finance Business Function

Table 7.6 IPO for the Traditional TPS Systems that Support Accounting

System	Input	Processing	Output
Budget	Amounts budgeted for various categories of expense	Accumulates amount spent in each budget category	Budget status report showing amount under/over budget
Accounts receivable	Shipment records specifying exactly what was shipped to a customer	Determines amount to be paid by customer including delivery costs and taxes	Customer bills and monthly statements, management reports summarizing customer payments
Payroll	Number of hours worked by each employee, employee pay rate, employee tax and withholding information	Calculates employee gross pay and net pay and amount to be withheld for various taxing agencies and employee benefit programmes	Payroll cheque and stub, payroll register (a summary report of all payroll transactions), W2 forms
Asset management	Data regarding the purchase of capital assets	Calculates depreciation and net value of all corporate assets	Listing of all assets showing purchase price and current value after depreciation
General ledger	All transactions affecting the financial standing of the firm	Posts financial transactions to appropriate accounts specified in the firm's chart of accounts	Financial reports such as the profit and loss statement, balance sheet

Fortunately, FPWR could choose from many available CRM packages – even if the C is taken as Constituent rather than Customer, as is more appropriate when donors are part of the picture. Unfortunately, the very abundance of CRM packages makes it difficult to choose one. FPWR's limited budget was a critical factor in selecting a CRM package. When the foundation learned of CiviCRM, designed specifically for charitable organizations and available at no charge, that system became the obvious answer.

CiviCRM is designed specifically for donor tracking. It can record contributions of cash, items or services of value (in-kind), and volunteer time. It can handle one-time gifts, recurring gifts, pledges of future gifts and more. It can track offline gifts to provide a complete picture of a donor's contributions through all channels. The system also differentiates grants (which obligate FPWR to do something in return) from contributions (which don't). It tracks household and workplace affiliations to indicate who is connected to whom. It also lets the organization manage volunteers by skills and availability and create membership levels with various criteria and benefits.

Three people from FPWR plus a hired developer set up CiviCRM, and FPWR now takes in over €528 570 annually through online donations.

FPWR used CiviCRM to launch its OneSmallStep for Research initiative (OSS) in 2011. This initiative brought together over 500 fundraisers in 53 cities around the world to raise money for PWS research. OSS organizers in each city used CiviCRM to establish their campaigns and recruit fundraisers who,

in turn, solicit donations. CiviCRM handles multiple currencies, languages and payment processors as well as manages the legal donation tracking requirements of different countries. Through the first four months of 2012, OSS raised €126 856.8 towards its goal of €0.75 million. Without CiviCRM, this achievement would not have been possible.

Questions

1 Other than a smaller budget, how are charities different from companies that sell products by e-commerce? How are they similar?

2 Your university almost certainly solicits donations from its graduates. How do its donor management requirements differ from those of FPWR? How are they similar?

3 Anything involving children's health, such as PWS, has an emotional appeal to donors. Most products sold online have less emotional appeal but greater practical value. How does the emotional appeal of a product or service affect the information a CRM system should store in its database for each constituent (donor or customer)?

4 Using the relational database concepts you learned in Chapter 5, figure out what entities, attributes and relationships the CiviCRM database design should include. Then, using the ERD concepts you learned there, draw a data model for it. Include all the entities and relationships that are needed for the CiviCRM features described in the case.

for mobile telephony.) The Internet Corporation for Assigned Names and Numbers (ICANN) created a .mobi domain in late 2005 to help attract mobile users to the web.[9] mTID Top Level Domain Ltd of Dublin, Ireland, is responsible for administration of this domain and helping to ensure that the .mobi destinations work fast, efficiently and effectively with user handsets.[10] In most western European countries, communicating via wireless devices is common, and consumers are much more willing to use m-commerce. Japanese consumers are generally enthusiastic about new technology and are much more likely to use mobile technologies for making purchases.

For m-commerce to work effectively, the interface between the wireless device and its user needs to improve to the point that it is nearly as easy to purchase an item on a wireless device as it is to purchase it on a home computer. In addition, network speed must improve so that users do not become frustrated. Security is also a major concern, particularly in two areas: the security of the transmission itself and the trust that the transaction is being made with the intended party. Encryption can provide secure transmission. Digital certificates can ensure that transactions are made between the intended parties.

The handheld devices used for m-commerce have several limitations that complicate their use. Their screens are small, perhaps no more than a few square centimetres, and might be able to display only a few lines of text. Their input capabilities are limited to a few buttons, so entering data can be tedious and error prone. They have less processing power and less bandwidth than desktop computers, which are usually hardwired to a high-speed LAN. They also operate on limited-life batteries. For these reasons, it is currently impossible to directly access many websites with a handheld device. Web developers must rewrite web applications so that users with hand-held devices can access them.

7.6 Production and Supply Chain Management

Production and Supply Chain Management systems follow a systematic process for developing a production plan that draws on the information available in the system database.

The process starts with sales forecasting to develop an estimate of future customer demand. This initial forecast is at a fairly high level with estimates made by product group rather than by each individual product item. The sales forecast extends for months into the future. The sales forecast will be produced using specialized software and techniques. Many organizations are moving to a collaborative process with major customers to plan future inventory levels and production rather than relying on an internally generated sales forecast. The sales and operations plan takes demand and current inventory levels into account and determines the specific product items that need to be produced and when to meet the forecast future demand. Production capacity and any seasonal variability in demand must also be considered. The result is a high-level production plan that balances market demand to production capacity. Panasonic and other companies have outsourced the development of a sales and operation plan to i2 Technologies in India. Best Buy, a major Panasonic customer, collects information on sales of Panasonic items at its shops' checkout stations and sends the data to i2. i2 processes the data and sends manufacturing recommendations to Panasonic, which become the basis for factory schedules.[11]

Demand management refines the production plan by determining the amount of weekly or daily production needed to meet the demand for individual products. The output of the demand management process is the master production schedule, which is a production plan for all finished goods.

Detailed scheduling uses the production plan defined by the demand management process to develop a detailed production schedule specifying production scheduling details, such as which item to produce first and when production should be switched from one item to another. A key decision is how long to make the production runs for each product. Longer production runs reduce the number of machine setups required, thus reducing production costs. Shorter production runs generate less finished product inventory and reduce inventory holding costs.

Materials requirement planning determines the amount and timing for placing raw material orders with suppliers. The types and amounts of raw materials required to support the planned production schedule are determined based on the existing raw material inventory and the bill of materials or BOM, a sort of 'recipe' of ingredients needed to make each product item. The quantity of raw materials to order also depends on the lead time and lot sizing. Lead time is the time it takes from the time a purchase order is placed until the raw materials arrive at the production facility. Lot size has to do with discrete quantities that the supplier will ship and the amount that is economical for the producer to receive and/or store. For example, a supplier might ship a certain raw material in batches of 80 000 units. The producer might need 95 000 units. A decision must be made to order one or two batches.

Purchasing uses the information from materials requirement planning to place purchase orders for raw materials and transmit them to qualified suppliers. Typically, the release of these

- A dock worker enters a receipt of purchased materials from a supplier and the ERP system automatically creates a general ledger entry to increase the value of inventory on hand.
- A production worker withdraws raw materials from inventory to support production and the ERP system generates a record to reduce the value of inventory on hand.

Thus, the ERP system captures transactions entered by workers in all functional areas of the business. The ERP system then creates the associated general ledger record to track the financial impact of the transaction. This set of records is an extremely valuable resource that companies can use to support financial accounting and managerial accounting.

Financial accounting consists of capturing and recording all the transactions that affect a company's financial state and then using these documented transactions to prepare financial statements to external decision makers, such as stockholders, suppliers, banks and government agencies. These financial statements include the profit and loss statement, balance sheet and cash flow statement. They must be prepared in strict accordance to rules and guidelines of the governing agencies.

All transactions that affect the financial state of the firm are captured and recorded in the data-base of the ERP system. This data is used in the financial accounting module of the ERP system to prepare the statements required by various constituencies. The data can also be used in the managerial accounting module of the ERP system along with various assumptions and forecasts to perform various analyses such as generating a forecasted profit and loss statement to assess the firm's future profitability.

Hosted Software Model for Enterprise Software

Business application software vendors are experimenting with the hosted software model to see if the approach meets customer needs and is likely to generate significant revenue. This pay-as-you-go approach is appealing to small businesses because they can then experiment with powerful software capabilities without making a major financial investment. Also, using the hosted software model means the small business firm does not need to employ a full-time IT person to maintain key business applications. The small business firm can expect additional savings from reduced hardware costs and costs associated with maintaining an appropriate computer environment (such as air conditioning, power and an uninterruptible power supply).

Not only is the hosted software model attractive to small and medium-sized firms, even some large companies are experimenting with it. DuPont, the large, multinational chemical company, is one of the early adopters of the hosted software model. The firm is retooling its sales force by leveraging best practices and focusing its e-business and marketing capabilities into 16 high-powered global centres. As part of the change, DuPont plans to use the hosted SAP Sales on Demand software across the enterprise to provide a common systems platform and a common set of business processes for DuPont's entire sales force. It hopes to integrate the hosted system with its SAP ERP software and retire some of its legacy CRM applications. The business goal is to make sure that the firm presents itself as one DuPont to customers who buy from different DuPont businesses. Its largest customers are served as 'corporate accounts' with a point of contact who can manage all their interactions with DuPont to ensure the maximum benefit to the customer.[13]

7.9 International Issues Associated with Operational Systems

Operational systems must support businesses that interoperate with customers, suppliers, business partners, shareholders and government agencies in multiple countries. Different languages and cultures, disparities in IS infrastructure, varying laws and customs rules, and multiple currencies are among the challenges that must be met by an operational system of a multinational company. The following sections highlight these issues.

Different Languages and Cultures

Teams composed of people from several countries speaking different languages and familiar with different cultures might not agree on a single work process. In some cultures, people do not routinely work in teams in a networked environment. Despite these complications, many multinational companies can establish close connections with their business partners and roll out standard IS applications for all to use. However, sometimes they require extensive and costly customization. For example, even though English has become a standard business language among executives and senior managers, many people within organizations do not speak English. As a result, software might need to be designed with local language interfaces to ensure the successful implementation of a new system. Other customizations will also be needed; date fields for example: the European format is day/month/year, Japan uses year/month/day, and the US date format is month/day/year. Sometimes, users might also have to implement manual processes to override established formatting to enable systems to function correctly.

Disparities in Information System Infrastructure

The lack of a robust or a common information infrastructure can also create problems. For example, much of Latin America lags behind the rest of the world in Internet usage, and online marketplaces are almost non-existent there. This gap makes it difficult for multinational companies to get online with their Latin American business partners. Even something as mundane as the fact that the power plug on a piece of equipment built in one country might not fit into the power socket of another country can affect the infrastructure.

Varying Laws and Customs Rules

Numerous laws can affect the collection and dissemination of data. For example, labour laws in some countries prohibit the recording of worker performance data. Also, some countries have passed laws limiting the transborder flow of data linked to individuals. Specifically, European Community Directive 95/96/EC of 1998 requires that any company doing business within the borders of the 25 European Union member nations protect the privacy of customers and employees. It bars the export of data to countries that do not have data-protection standards comparable to the European Union's.

Trade custom rules between nations are international laws that set practices for two or more nations' commercial transactions. They cover imports and exports and the systems and procedures dealing with quotas, visas, entry documents, commercial invoices, foreign trade zones, payment of duty and taxes and many other related issues. For example, the North American Free Trade Agreement (NAFTA) of 1994 created trade custom rules to address the flow of goods throughout the North American continent. Most of these custom rules and their changes over time create headaches for people who must keep systems consistent with the rules.

Multiple Currencies

The enterprise system of multinational companies must conduct transactions in multiple currencies. To do so, a set of exchange rates is defined, and the information systems apply these rates to translate from one currency to another. The systems must be current with foreign currency exchange rates, handle reporting and other transactions such as cash receipts, issue vendor payments and customer statements, record retail store payments, and generate financial reports in the currency of choice.

Summary

An organization must have information systems that support the routine, day-to-day activities that occur in the normal course of business and help a company add value to its products and services. Transaction processing systems (TPS) are at the heart of most information systems in businesses today. A TPS is an organized collection of people, procedures, software, databases and devices used to capture fundamental data about events that affect the organization (transactions). All TPS perform the following basic activities: data collection, which involves the capture of source data to complete a set of transactions; data editing, which checks for data validity and completeness; data correction, which involves providing feedback of a potential problem and enabling users to change the data; data manipulation, which is the performance of calculations, sorting, categorizing, summarizing and storing data for further processing; data storage, which involves placing transaction data into one or more databases; and document production, which involves outputting records and reports.

The methods of transaction processing systems include batch and online. Batch processing involves the collection of transactions into batches, which are entered into the system at regular intervals as a group. Online transaction processing (OLTP) allows transactions to be entered as they occur.

Organizations expect TPS to accomplish a number of specific objectives, including processing data generated by and about transactions, maintaining a high degree of accuracy and information integrity, compiling accurate and timely reports and documents, increasing labour efficiency, helping provide increased and enhanced service, and building and maintaining customer loyalty. In some situations, an effective TPS can help an organization gain a competitive advantage.

Traditional TPS support the various business functions of organizations that have not yet implemented enterprise resource planning systems. Many organizations conduct ongoing TPS audits to prevent accounting irregularities or loss of data privacy. The audit can be performed by the firm's internal audit group or by an outside auditor for greater objectivity.

The traditional TPS systems that support the order processing business functions include order entry, sales configuration, shipment planning, shipment execution, inventory control and accounts receivable.

The traditional TPS that support the purchasing function include inventory control, purchase order processing, accounts payable and receiving.

The traditional TPS that support the accounting business function include the budget, accounts receivable, payroll, asset management and general ledger.

Electronic and mobile commerce allow transactions to be made by the customer, with less need for sales staff, and open up new opportunities for conducting business. E-commerce is the conducting of business activities electronically over networks. Business-to-business (B2B) e-commerce allows manufacturers to buy at a low cost worldwide, and it offers enterprises the chance to sell to a global market. Business-to-consumer (B2C) e-commerce enables organizations to sell directly to consumers, eliminating intermediaries. In many cases, this squeezes costs and inefficiencies out of the supply chain and can lead to higher profits and lower prices for consumers. Consumer-to-consumer (C2C) e-commerce involves consumers selling directly to other consumers. Online auctions are the chief method by which C2C e-commerce is currently conducted.

Mobile commerce is the use of wireless devices such as PDAs, mobile phones, and smartphones to facilitate the sale of goods or services – anytime, anywhere. The market for m-commerce in North America is expected to mature much later than in western Europe and Japan. Although some industry experts predict great growth in this arena, several hurdles must be overcome, including improving the ease of use of wireless devices, addressing the security of wireless transactions, and improving network speed. M-commerce provides a unique opportunity to establish one-on-one marketing relationships and support communications anytime and anywhere.

A company that implements an enterprise resource planning system is creating a highly integrated set of systems, which can lead to many business benefits. Enterprise resource planning (ERP) software supports the efficient operation of business processes by integrating activities throughout a business, including sales, marketing, manufacturing, logistics, accounting and staffing. Implementation of an ERP system can provide many advantages, including providing access to data for operational decision making; elimination of costly, inflexible legacy systems; providing improved work processes; and creating the opportunity to upgrade technology infrastructure. Some of the disadvantages associated with an ERP system are that they are time consuming, difficult and expensive to implement.

Although the scope of ERP implementation can vary from firm to firm, most firms use ERP systems to support production and supply chain management, customer relationship management and sales ordering, and financial and managerial accounting.

The production and supply chain management process starts with sales forecasting to develop an estimate of future customer demand. This initial forecast is at a fairly high level with estimates made by product group rather than by each individual product item. The sales and operations plan takes demand and current inventory levels into account and determines the specific product items that need to be produced and when to meet the forecast future demand. Demand management refines the production plan by determining the amount of weekly or daily production needed to meet the demand for individual products. Detailed scheduling uses the production plan defined by the demand management process to develop a detailed production schedule specifying production scheduling details such as which item to produce first and when production should be switched from one item to another. Materials requirement planning determines the amount and timing for placing raw material orders with suppliers. Purchasing uses the information from materials requirement planning to place purchase orders for raw materials and transmit them to qualified suppliers. Production uses the detailed schedule to plan the details of running and staffing the production operation.

Numerous complications arise that multinational corporations must address in planning, building and operating their TPS. These challenges include dealing with different languages and cultures, disparities in IS infrastructure, varying laws and customs rules, and multiple currencies.

Self-Assessment Test

1 Identify the missing TPS basic activity: data collection, data editing, data _____, data manipulation, data storage and document production.

2 The primary objective of any TPS is to capture, process and store transactions, and to produce a variety of documents related to routine business activities. True or false?

3 Which of the following are not one of the basic components of a TPS?
   a. databases
   b. networks
   c. procedures
   d. analytical models

4 Data should be captured at its source and recorded accurately in a timely fashion, with minimal manual effort, and in an electronic or digital form that can be directly entered into the computer are the principles behind _____.

5 Inventory control, purchase order processing, receiving, and accounts payable systems make up a set of systems that support the _____ business function.

6 eBay is an example of which of the following forms of e-commerce?
   a. G2G
   b. B2B
   c. B2C
   d. C2C

7 Amazon is an example of which of the following forms of e-commerce?
   a. G2G
   b. B2B
   c. B2C
   d. C2C

8 E-commerce websites should be rewritten for mobile devices, to allow for mobile commerce. True or false?

9 Which of the following is a primary benefit of implementing an ERP system?
   a. elimination of inefficient systems
   b. easing adoption of improved work processes
   c. improving access to data for operational decision making
   d. all of the above

10 Only large, multinational companies can justify the implementation of ERP systems. True or false?

Review Questions

1 List several characteristics that distinguish a TPS from an MIS.

2 What basic transaction processing activities are performed by all transaction processing systems?

3 Define e-commerce.

4 List and explain four different types of e-commerce.

5 Identify and briefly describe three limitations that complicate the use of handheld devices used for m-commerce.

6 What is source data automation? Give an example.

7 Identify four complications that multinational corporations must address in planning, building and operating their ERP systems.

8 How does materials requirement planning support the purchasing process? What are some of the issues and complications that arise in materials requirement planning?

9 What systems are included in the traditional TPS systems that support the accounting business function?

10 List and briefly describe the set of activities that must be performed by the sales ordering module of an ERP system to capture a customer sales order.

Discussion Questions

1 Explain the difference between B2C and B2Me e-commerce. Give examples of each.

2 What do you think are the biggest barriers to wide-scale adoption of m-commerce by consumers? Who do you think is working on solutions to these problems and what might the solutions entail?

3 If a customer prints an order form downloaded from a website, completes it using a black pen, and faxes it off to a company, does this constitute e-commerce? Why or why not?

4 What are the advantages of implementing ERP as an integrated solution to link multiple business processes versus a series of non-integrated TPS systems? Can you identify any disadvantages?

5 What sort of benefits should the suppliers and customers of a firm that has successfully implemented an ERP system see? What sort of issues might arise for suppliers and customers during an ERP implementation?

Web Exercises

1 Visit eBay or another online auction website and choose an item on which to bid. Before entering the bid process, research the site for information about any rules associated with bidding and how to bid effectively. Follow the suggested processes and record your results. Write a brief memo to your instructor summarizing your experience.

2 Do research on the web and identify the most popular ERP system solution for small and medium-sized businesses. Why is this solution the most popular? Develop a one-page report or send an email message to your instructor about what you found.

Case One

GMC Puts ERP in the Cloud

GMC Global, part of the 4000-employee, Australia-based management consultants SMEC Group, is a world leader in helping mining companies create efficient and effective operations. The company applies the same drive for efficiency and effectiveness to its own operations. 'Our business depends on effective resource management and accurate tracking of time, so having access to timely data that we can easily convert into an invoice is critical for us,' said Thomas Hynes, executive general manager of global operations.

Before 2012, GMC Global used a variety of functional applications. It had one system for inventory, invoicing and financial management and one for time and expenses, as well as a home-grown spreadsheet-based systems in North and South America. None of these systems were integrated with each other. That led to inconsistent processes from location to location, which in turn made it difficult to assign staff effectively or to ensure consistent client results. Forrester Research gives these additional dangers of poorly integrated applications in a project-oriented services business such as GMC Global's:

- With no clear picture of each project and the overall business, there is no solid information basis for decision making.

- Errors creep into project management data, making it more likely that the team will miss project milestones.

- Project managers who must work with multiple systems have less time to manage their projects actively and to engage with customers and prospects.

- Lack of consistent project metrics leads to lack of insight into staff and team performance, making it hard for a firm to optimize its resources.

Integrating applications requires those applications to share data. The best way to share data is usually by using a shared database. However, in early 2012, GMC Global had active projects in 14 countries, covering every continent except Europe and Antarctica. Over 80 per cent of the firm's employees are consultants who spend the great majority of their time in remote locations. They could be in different places every year. Accessing a fixed database would be quick from wherever the database is located but could become a bottleneck elsewhere in the world because the consultants would have to access it remotely and share its physical connection to the Internet.

GMC Global's solution was cloud computing. It chose Professional Services Automation (PSA) integrated software from NetSuite, Inc.. After an eight-week period for installation and training, GMC Global went live in March 2012. Its 180 employees now use PSA for project tracking and resource management, time and expense accounting, billing and reporting.

GMC Global isn't finished. The firm plans to upgrade to NetSuite's Services Resource Planning (SRP) software suite to provide even greater financial control of its global business. SRP is the service-oriented equivalent of ERP in production-based organizations. 'Moving to NetSuite SRP will complete the picture for us and enable some of the things that are restricting us at the moment, like global accessibility and managing processes consistently across all regions,' said Hynes. 'Once we get there, we expect to have a far better view of our overall business.'

Questions

1 You read about cloud computing in Chapter 3, which discusses it as it applies to all types of applications. What are the specific advantages and disadvantages of cloud computing for ERP?

2 How would moving to a single shared database, used by all applications, address the concerns that Forrester lists as dangers of poor integration?

3 How can a university, which is also a service organization, benefit from integrated software? (Contrast integrated software with applications that are not integrated. List the specific applications you have in mind.)

4 GMC Global is a service organization. Do you think the applicability of cloud computing to its ERP requirements would be different for a manufacturing firm of comparable size? What about the applicability of cloud ERP to a chain of retail stores?

Case Two

MobiKash: Bringing Financial Services to Rural Africa

Full participation in the twenty-first-century economy requires access to financial services. However, this access is a luxury for many citizens of African nations. Due to the long distances between bank branches and the lack of rapid, cost-effective transportation to the urban areas in which banks are typically found, fewer than 10 per cent of Africans participate in formal banking. Those who do often face time-consuming inefficiencies.

A new company, MobiKash Afrika, hopes to change this by empowering people in Africa with a secure and independent mobile commerce system that is easy to use. In planning its system, MobiKash established several standards:

■ The service must be independent of specific mobile telephone operators.

■ The service must be independent of specific banks or financial institutions.

■ The service must work with all bill issuers.

■ The service must not require smartphones or high-end feature phones.

MobiKash offers its members five services, all accessible from a mobile phone: loading money into their MobiKash account from any bank account, paying bills, sending money to any other mobile phone user or bank account, managing a bank or MobiKash account, and obtaining or depositing cash. Only the last pair of services requires members to visit a physical location where cash can be handled, but that site doesn't have to be a bank. MobiKash agents in market towns, convenient to rural areas, can handle transactions that require cash. (As of the end of 2011,

3000 MobiKash agents were operating in Kenya. The firm expected to cover all 47 Kenyan counties by mid-2012.) Account holders don't even need to visit a bank to set up their MobiKash accounts: in fact, anyone with a mobile phone to whom a MobiKash user sends money becomes a MobiKash user automatically.

MobiKash charges for some services. Withdrawing cash costs 25 to 75 Kenya shillings (Kshs), about €0.23 to €0.68, for withdrawals up to Kshs 10 000 (about €15), with higher fees for larger withdrawals. Paying bills from a mobile phone incurs a fixed fee of Kshs 25, no matter how large the bill is. The largest fee that MobiKash charges is Kshs 350, about €3, for cash withdrawals in excess of Kshs 75 000, about €679.60. This fee schedule is consistent with the financial resources of MobiKash users and the value those users place on each financial service.

The MobiKash system is based on Sybase 365m Commerce software. Several factors contributed to this choice, including the local presence of Sybase in Africa with experience in similar applications, its understanding of how to integrate with African financial institutions, and the system's ability to work with any mobile telephone. It operates from an existing Sybase data centre in Frankfurt, Germany.

In early 2012, MobiKash services were available only in Kenya. However, MobiKash is expanding in east, west and southern Africa, starting with Zimbabwe, and is planning to cover at least nine countries by the end of 2012. It is working with Masary, an Egyptian e-wallet firm, to cover northern Africa as well. Work is also under way to support intercontinental fund transfers to and from North America, Europe and the Middle East. As for the future, at the end of 2011, CEO Duncan Otieno said, 'We see MobiKash in the next five years playing with the international or global mobile commerce space in at least 40 countries. The plans for building this network are already in progress.'

Questions

1 Firms can base m-commerce systems on commercially available software, as MobiKash did here. Alternatively, they can write their own software. List three pros and cons of each approach. Do you think MobiKash made the right choice?

2 What is the value of each of the four MobiKash standards listed near the beginning of this case study?

3 MobiKash is not the only mobile money system in Kenya. Safaricom M-Pesa is the oldest and largest of the other mobile money systems. However, the others are tied to specific banks or network operators. Using the competitive concepts you studied in Chapter 2, how can MobiKash compete against established firms in this market?

4 Contrast your m-commerce needs with those of a typical rural African. Would you find the MobiKash offering attractive in full, in part (which parts?) or not at all?

Case Three

Kerry Group Is on Your Table

In business, sourcing is the set of activities involved in finding, evaluating and then engaging suppliers of goods or services. Before a business can start to manage its supply chain, as described in this chapter, it must complete a sourcing process.

Ireland's Kerry Group, a supplier of food ingredients and flavours to the worldwide food industry and of consumer food products to the British Isles, requires a wide range of raw materials from many suppliers. With annual revenue of €5.3 billion (about US $7 billion) in 2011, it needs a lot of those materials. With plants in 25 countries and 40 per cent of revenue from outside Europe, it is impossible for the people in one plant to know about all possible suppliers worldwide, but making local sourcing decisions would reduce economies of scale. With the thin profit margins of the food industry, good sourcing decisions are vital to Kerry Group profitability. Software to manage the sourcing process is one way to help make those decisions.

Kerry Group was already a SAP customer when it chose SAP Sourcing OnDemand, having used SAP ERP systems since 2009. The advantage of obtaining a new system from its existing ERP supplier is assured compatibility with applications the company already uses. 'What we needed was an intuitive sourcing system that would be completely integrated with our SAP back-office for an end-to-end procurement process,' said Peter Fotios, Kerry Group's director of e-procurement services.

SAP Sourcing OnDemand uses the cloud computing concept. As its OnDemand name suggests, customers do not have to dedicate computing resources to the software. They use SAP resources on demand as their needs require, paying on a per-user, per-month subscription basis. Meanwhile, SAP is responsible for administrative tasks such as data backup and, if necessary, restoration.

Kerry Group implemented SAP Sourcing On Demand by beginning with a pilot plant. 'We rolled it out smoothly in Ireland first, then England and then throughout our global operations in 23 countries,' explains Fotios. If any problems appeared in Ireland, the pilot site, Kerry Group could have focused all its problem-solving resources on that location. Fortunately, no major issues arose.

Another thing that Kerry Group did right at implementation time was training. Recognizing that it had competent in-house trainers and competent technical professionals, but few if any who were both, the firm engaged SAP's Irish training partner Olas to assist with that end of the project. Olas brought SAP expertise to the training team, completing the required set of capabilities.

Moving forward, Kerry Group has project plans extending into 2016 for the full roll-out of all its planned SAP ERP capabilities. The smoothness of its Sourcing OnDemand implementation, which took a total of four weeks elapsed time because the software was already running in the cloud when they began, is a good indication that the rest of the project (which is in many ways more complex) will probably go well. If Kerry Group is to carry out its mission statement, which includes being 'the world leader in food ingredients and flavours serving the food and beverage industry,' the roll-out will have to be smooth.

Questions

1 According to Peter Fotios, one of Kerry Group's top requirements was ease of integration with its existing SAP system. Why might a company select a sourcing system that was not as easy to integrate with its existing SCM software?

2 Kerry Group is taking a slow and methodical approach to implementing the parts of SAP ERP software it will use, extending that implementation over six years. What does the company gain and what does it lose by taking its time in this way?

3 Why should Kerry Group standardize on one ERP package? Wouldn't it be simpler and less expensive to let each plant and sales operation choose its own software, as long as it can report its financial results to headquarters in a standard form?

4 As the largest ERP vendor, SAP can support Kerry Group in 45 countries where the latter has manufacturing facilities or sales operations, providing a local contact for training, problem-solving and requesting new features. These factors are important. However, others are important also. Suppose another ERP supplier didn't have this depth of local support but offered software that met Kerry Group's needs better, cost less or both. Rank those factors for importance and discuss how you would make this vendor selection decision.

Notes

1 IQMS Website. Available from: www.iqms.com/company/flambeau. Accessed 5 August 2014.
2 Briefings Direct, 2013. ERP for IT Helps Dutch Insurance Giant Achmea to Reinvent IT Processes to Improve Business Performance Across the Board. Available from: http://briefingsdirect.blogspot.co.uk/2013/03/erp-for-it-helps-dutch-insurance-giant.html. Accessed 10 October 2014.
3 SAP Industry Executive Overview. Barloworld Handling UK: Driving Optimal Performance with Mobile Technology. Available from: www.sap.com. Accessed 10 October 2014.
4 Marlin, Steven, 'Bank Deploys Anti-Money Laundering System', *Information Week*, 11 October 2005.
5 Sullivan, Laurie, 'Bad Online Shopping Experiences Are Bad for Business', *Information Week*, 24 January 2005.
6 Perez, Juan Carlos, 'Amazon Turns 10, Helped by Strong Tech, Service', *Computerworld*, 15 July 2005.
7 Javed, Naseem, 'Move Over B2B, B2C – It's M2E Time,' *E-Commerce Times*, 17 August 2005.
8 'Investor Relations', eBay Website, http://investor.ebay.com/fundamentals.cfm. Accessed 4 May 2006.
9 Mello, John P. Jr, 'New .mobi Domain Approved but Challenges Remain', *TechNewsWorld*, 11 May 2006.
10 Ibid.
11 Anthes, Gary, 'Sidebar: It's All Global Now', *Computerworld*, 20 February 2006.
12 McDougall, Paul, 'Closing the Last Supply Gap', *Information Week*, 8 November 2005.
13 Songini, Marc, 'SAP Launches First Piece of Hosted CRM Service', *Computerworld*, 16 February 2006.

08

Management Information and Decision Support Systems

Principles

Good decision-making and problem-solving skills are the key to developing effective information and decision support systems.

A management information system (MIS) must provide the right information to the right person in the right format at the right time.

Decision support systems (DSSs) support decision-making effectiveness when faced with unstructured or semi-structured business problems.

Specialized support systems, such as group support systems (GSSs) and executive support systems (ESSs), use the overall approach of a DSS in situations such as group and executive decision making.

Learning Objectives

- Define the stages of decision making.
- Discuss the importance of implementation and monitoring in problem solving.

- Explain the uses of MIS and describe their inputs and outputs.
- Discuss information systems in the functional areas of business organizations.

- List and discuss important characteristics of DSSs that give them the potential to be effective management support tools.
- Identify and describe the basic components of a DSS.

- State the goals of a GSS and identify the characteristics that distinguish it from a DSS.
- Identify the fundamental uses of an ESS and list the characteristics of such a system.

Why Learn About Management Information Systems and Decision Support Systems?

The previous chapter looked at systems at the operational level of a firm (see also Figure 1.5 and Figure 8.11). This chapter considers systems higher up, at the tactical and strategic levels. The true potential of information systems in organizations is in helping employees make more informed decisions, something that is supported by both management information and decision support systems. Transportation coordinators can use management information reports to find the least expensive way to ship products to market and to solve bottlenecks. A bank or credit union can use a group support system to help it determine who should receive a loan. Shop managers can use decision support systems to help them decide what and how much inventory to order to meet customer needs and increase profits. An entrepreneur who owns and operates a temporary storage company can use vacancy reports to help determine what price to charge for new storage units. Everyone wants to be a better problem solver and decision maker. This chapter shows you how information systems can help. It begins with an overview of decision making and problem solving.

8.1 Decision Making and Problem Solving

Organizations need to make good decisions. In most cases, strategic planning and the overall goals of the organization set the course for decision making, helping employees and business units achieve their objectives and goals. Often, information systems also assist with strategic planning, helping top management make better decisions.

In business, one of the highest compliments you can receive is to be recognized by your colleagues and peers as a 'real problem solver'. Problem solving is a critical activity for any business organization. After identifying a problem, you begin the problem-solving process with decision making. A well-known model developed by Herbert Simon divides the **decision-making phase** of the problem-solving process into three stages: intelligence, design and choice. This model was later incorporated by George Huber into an expanded model of the entire problem-solving process (see Figure 8.1).

decision-making phase The first part of problem solving, including three stages: intelligence, design and choice.

Figure 8.1 How Decision Making Relates to Problem Solving

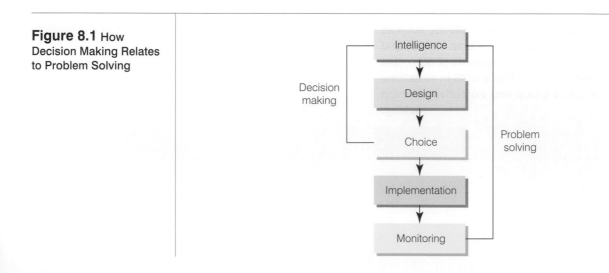

The three stages of decision making – intelligence, design and choice – are augmented by implementation and monitoring to result in problem solving.

The first stage in the problem-solving process is the **intelligence stage**. During this stage, you identify and define potential problems or opportunities. For example, you might learn about the need for an intervention or change in an unsatisfactory situation. During the intelligence stage, you also investigate resource and environmental constraints. For example, if you were a French farmer, during the intelligence stage you might explore the possibilities of shipping apples from your farm to shops in Ireland. The perishability of the fruit and the maximum price that consumers in Ireland are willing to pay for the fruit are problem constraints. Aspects of the problem environment that you must consider include import/export laws regarding the shipment of food products.

> **intelligence stage** The first stage of decision making, in which potential problems or opportunities are identified and defined.

In the **design stage**, you develop alternative solutions to the problem. In addition, you evaluate the feasibility of these alternatives. In the fruit shipping example, you would consider the alternative methods of shipment, including the transportation times and costs associated with each.

> **design stage** The second stage of decision making, in which alternative solutions to the problem are developed.

The last stage of the decision-making phase, the **choice stage**, requires selecting a course of action. Here you might select the method of shipping fruit by air from you as the solution. The choice stage would then conclude with selection of an air carrier. As you will see later, various factors influence choice; the act of choosing is not as simple as it might first appear.

> **choice stage** The third stage of decision making, which requires selecting a course of action.

Problem solving includes and goes beyond decision making. It also includes the **implementation stage**, when the solution is put into effect. For example, if your decision is to ship fruit to Ireland as air freight using a specific air freight company, implementation involves informing your farming staff of the new activity, getting the fruit to the airport and actually shipping the product.

> **problem solving** A process that goes beyond decision making to include the implementation and monitoring stages.

> **implementation stage** A stage of problem solving in which a solution is put into effect.

The final stage of the problem-solving process is the **monitoring stage**. In this stage, decision makers evaluate the implementation to determine whether the anticipated results were achieved and to modify the process in light of new information. Monitoring can involve feedback and adjustment. For example, you might need to change your air carrier if it regularly has shipping delays.

> **monitoring stage** The final stage of the problem-solving process, in which decision makers evaluate the implementation.

Programmed versus Non-Programmed Decisions

In the choice stage, various factors influence the decision maker's selection of a solution. One such factor is whether the decision can be programmed. **Programmed decisions** are made using a rule, procedure, or quantitative method. For example, to say that inventory should be ordered when inventory levels drop to 100 units is a programmed decision because it adheres to a rule. Programmed decisions are easy to computerize using traditional information systems. The relationships between system elements are fixed by rules, procedures, or numerical relationships. In other words, they are structured and deal with routine, well-defined decisions.

> **programmed decision** A decision made using a rule, procedure or quantitative method.

Non-programmed decisions, however, deal with unusual or exceptional situations. In many cases, these decisions are difficult to quantify. Determining the appropriate training programme for a new employee, deciding whether to start a new type of product line, and weighing the benefits and drawbacks of installing a new pollution control system are examples. Each of these decisions contains unique characteristics, and standard rules or procedures might not apply to them. Today, decision support systems help solve many non-programmed decisions, in which the problem is not routine, and rules and relationships are not well defined (unstructured or ill-structured problems).

> **non-programmed decision** A decision that deals with unusual or exceptional situations that can be difficult to quantify.

Optimization, Satisficing and Heuristic Approaches

In general, computerized decision support systems can either optimize or satisfice. An optimization model finds the best solution, usually the one that will best help the organization meet its goals. For example, an optimization model can find the appropriate number of products that an organization should produce to meet a profit goal, given certain conditions and assumptions. Optimization models use problem constraints. A limit on the number of available work hours in a manufacturing facility is an example of a problem constraint. Some spreadsheet programs, such as Microsoft Excel, have optimizing features. A business such as an appliance manufacturer can use an optimization program to reduce the time and cost of manufacturing appliances and increase profits. Optimization software also allows decision makers to explore various alternatives.

Consider a few examples of how you can use optimization to achieve huge savings. Bombardier Flexjet, a company that sells fractional ownership of jets, used an optimization program to save almost €22 million annually to better schedule its aircraft and crews.[1] Hutchinson Port Holdings, the world's largest container terminal, saved even more – over €37 million annually.[2] The company processes a staggering 10 000 trucks and 15 ships every day, and used optimization to maximize the use of its trucks. Deere & Company, a manufacturer of commercial vehicles and equipment, increased shareholder value by over €75 million annually by using optimization to minimize inventory levels and by enhancing customer satisfaction.[3]

Laps Care from TietoEnatorAM is an information system that used optimization to assign medical personnel to home health-care patients in Sweden while minimizing costs. The system has improved care while increasing efficiency by 10 to 15 per cent and lowering costs by €20 million.[4]

A **satisficing model** is one that finds a good – but not necessarily the best – problem solution. Satisficing is usually used because modelling the problem properly to get an optimal decision would be too difficult, complex or costly. Satisficing normally does not look at all possible solutions but only at those likely to give good results. Consider a decision to select a location for a new manufacturing plant. To find the optimal (best) location, you must consider all cities in Europe. A satisficing approach is to consider only five or ten cities that might satisfy the company's requirements. Limiting the options might not result in the best decision, but it will likely result in a good decision, without spending the time and effort to investigate all cities. Satisficing is a good alternative modelling method because it is sometimes too expensive to analyze every alternative to find the best solution.

satisficing model A model that will find a good – but not necessarily the best – problem solution.

Heuristics, often referred to as 'rules of thumb' – commonly accepted guidelines or procedures that usually find a good solution – are often used in decision making. An example of a heuristic is to order four months' supply of inventory for a particular item when the inventory level drops to 20 units or less; although this heuristic might not minimize total inventory costs, it can serve as a good rule of thumb to avoid running out of stock without maintaining excess inventory. Trend Micro, a provider of antivirus software, has developed an antispam product that is based on heuristics. The software examines emails to find those most likely to be spam. It doesn't examine all emails.

heuristics Commonly accepted guidelines or procedures that usually find a good solution.

Sense and Respond

Sense and Respond (SaR) involves determining problems or opportunities (sense) and developing systems to solve the problems or take advantage of the opportunities (respond).[5] SaR often requires nimble organizations that replace traditional lines of authority with those that are flexible and dynamic. IBM, for example, used SaR with its microelectronics division to help with inventory control. It used mathematical models and optimization routines to control inventory levels. The models sensed when a shortage of inventory for customers was likely and responded by backlogging and storing extra inventory to avoid the shortages. In this application, SaR identified potential problems and solved them before they became a reality. SaR can also identify opportunities, such as new products or marketing approaches, and then respond by building the new products or starting new marketing campaigns. One way to implement the SaR approach is through management information and decision support systems, discussed in the next section.

Big Data

The amount of data that some companies are currently collecting is becoming so huge that it is difficult to process using traditional database technology. This phenomenon is referred to as Big Data, and it is currently a hot research topic in information systems. Big Data is of interest because of the additional insight it can offer into customer behaviour, logistics, factory design and a host of other applications. Big Data involves new ways of capturing data, processing it and visualizing the patterns and trends in it. Often processing Big Data requires many computers operating in parallel.

8.2 An Overview of Management Information Systems

A management information system (MIS) is an integrated collection of people, procedures, databases, hardware and software that provides managers and decision makers with information to help achieve organizational goals. The primary purpose of an MIS is to help an organization achieve its goals by providing managers with insight into the regular operations of the organization so that they can control, organize and plan more effectively. One important role of the MIS is to provide the right information to the right person in the right format at the right time. In short, an MIS provides managers with information, typically in reports, that supports effective decision making and provides feedback on daily operations. For example, a manager might request a report of weekly sales, broken down by area. On the basis of this information, she might decide to redistribute her mobile sales staff to have greater coverage in one place, less in another.

Figure 8.2 shows the role of an MIS within the flow of an organization's information. Note that business transactions can enter the organization through traditional methods or via the Internet or an extranet connecting customers and suppliers to the firm's ERP or transaction processing systems. The use of MIS spans all levels of management. That is, they provide support to and are used by employees throughout the organization.

Inputs to a Management Information System

As shown in Figure 8.2, data that enters an MIS originates from both internal and external sources, including the company's supply chain, first discussed in Chapter 2. The most significant internal data sources for an MIS are the organization's various TPS and ERP systems. As discussed in Chapter 5, companies also use data warehouses to store valuable business information. Other internal data comes from specific functional areas throughout the firm.

External sources of data can include customers, suppliers, competitors and stockholders whose data is not already captured by the TPS, as well as other sources, such as the Internet. In addition, many companies have implemented extranets to link with selected suppliers and other business partners to exchange data and information.

Figure 8.2 Sources of Managerial Information
The MIS is just one of many sources of managerial information. Decision support systems, executive support systems and expert systems also assist in decision making.

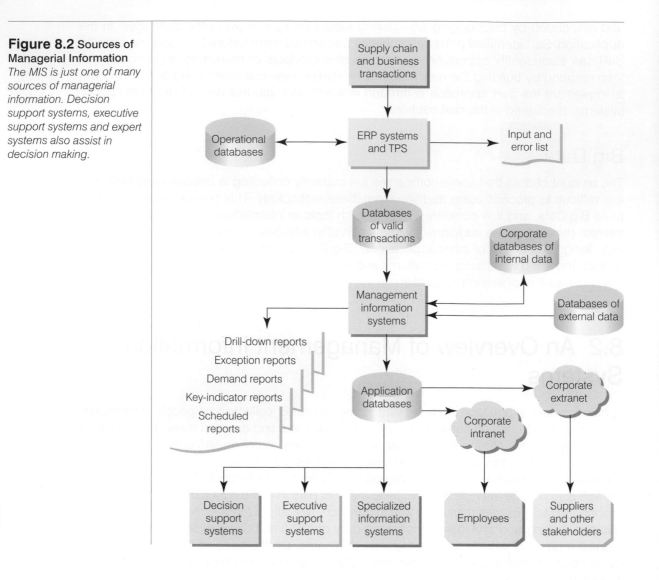

8

The MIS uses the data obtained from these sources and processes it into information more usable by managers, primarily in the form of predetermined reports. For example, rather than simply obtaining a chronological list of sales activity over the past week, a national sales manager might obtain his or her organization's weekly sales data in a format that allows him or her to see sales activity by region, by local sales representative, by product and even in comparison with last year's sales.

Outputs of a Management Information System

The output of most management information systems is a collection of reports that are distributed to managers. These can include tabulations, summaries, charts and graphs. Management reports can come from various company databases, data warehouses and other sources. These reports include scheduled reports key-indicator reports, demand reports, exception reports and drill-down reports (see Figure 8.3).

scheduled report A report produced periodically, or on a schedule, such as daily, weekly or monthly.

Scheduled Reports

Scheduled reports are produced periodically, or on a schedule, such as daily, weekly or monthly. For example, a production manager could use a weekly summary report that lists total payroll costs to monitor and control labour and job costs. A manufacturing report generated once per day to monitor the production of a new item is another example of a scheduled report. Other scheduled reports can help managers control customer credit, performance of sales representatives, inventory levels and more.

A **key-indicator report** summarizes the previous day's critical activities and is typically available at the beginning of each workday. These reports can summarize inventory levels, production activity, sales volume and the like. Key-indicator reports are used by managers and executives to take quick, corrective action on significant aspects of the business.

key-indicator report A summary of the previous day's critical activities; typically available at the beginning of each workday.

Demand Reports

Demand reports are developed to give certain information upon request. In other words, these reports are produced on demand. Like other reports discussed in this section, they often come from an organization's database system. For example, an executive might want to know the production status of a particular item – a demand report can be generated to provide the requested information by querying the company's database. Suppliers and customers can also use demand reports. FedEx, for example, provides demand reports on its website to allow its customers to track packages from their source to their final destination. Other examples of demand reports include reports requested by executives to show the hours worked by a particular employee, total sales to date for a product and so on.

demand report A report developed to give certain information at someone's request.

Exception Reports

Exception reports are reports that are automatically produced when a situation is unusual or requires management action. For example, a manager might set a parameter that generates a report of all items which have been purchased and then returned by more than five customers. Such items may need to be looked at to identify any production problem, for instance. As with key-indicator reports, exception reports are most often used to monitor aspects important to an organization's success. In general, when an exception report is produced, a manager or executive takes action. Parameters, or trigger points, for an exception report should be set carefully. Trigger points that are set too low might result in too many exception reports; trigger points that are too high could mean that problems requiring action are overlooked. For example, if a manager wants a report that contains all projects over budget by €1000 or more, the system might retrieve almost every company project. The €1000 trigger point is probably too low. A trigger point of €10000 might be more appropriate.

exception report A report automatically produced when a situation is unusual or requires management action.

Drill-Down Reports

Drill-down reports provide increasingly detailed data about a situation. Through the use of drill-down reports, analysts can see data at a high level first (such as sales for the entire company), then at a more detailed level (such as the sales for one department of the company) and then a very detailed level (such as sales for one sales representative). Managers can drill down into more levels of detail to individual transactions if they want.

drill-down report A report providing increasingly detailed data about a situation.

Developing Effective Reports

Management information system reports can help managers develop better plans, make better decisions and obtain greater control over the operations of the firm, but, in practice, the types of reports can overlap. For example, a manager can demand an exception report or set trigger points for items contained in a key-indicator report. In addition, some software packages can be used to produce, gather and distribute reports from different computer systems. Certain guidelines should be followed in designing and developing reports to yield the best results. Table 8.1 explains some of these guidelines.

Figure 8.3 Reports
Generated by an MIS

The types of reports are
(a) scheduled, (b) key
indicator, (c) demand,
(d) exception and (e–h) drill
down.

(a) Scheduled Report

Daily Sales Detail Report

Prepared: 08/10/14

Order #	Customer ID	Salesperson ID	Planned Ship Date	Quantity	Item #	Amount
P12453	C89321	CAR	08/12/14	144	P1234	€3214
P12453	C89321	CAR	08/12/14	288	P3214	€5660
P12454	C03214	GWA	08/13/14	12	P4902	€1224
P12455	C52313	SAK	08/12/14	24	P4012	€2448
P12456	C34123	JMW	08/13/14	144	P3214	€720
....	....	....	....	....	....	....

(b) Key-Indicator Report

Daily Sales Key-Indicator Report

	This Month	Last Month	Last Year
Total Orders Month to Date	€1808	€1694	€1914
Forecasted Sales for the Month	€2406	€2224	€2608

(c) Demand Report

Daily Sales by Salesperson Summary Report

Prepared: 08/10/14

Salesperson ID	Amount
CAR	€42 345
GWA	€38 950
SAK	€22 100
JWN	€12 350
....	....
....	....

(d) Exception Report

Daily Sales Exception Report – Orders Over 10 000

Prepared: 08/10/14

Order #	Customer ID	Salesperson ID	Planned Ship Date	Quantity	Item #	Amount
P12345	C89321	GWA	08/12/14	576	P1234	€12 856
P22153	C00453	CAR	08/12/14	288	P2314	€28 800
P23023	C32832	JMN	08/11/14	144	P2323	€14 400
....	....	....	....	....	....	....
....	....	....	....	....	....	....

Characteristics of a Management Information System

In general, MIS perform the following functions:

■ *Provide reports with fixed and standard formats.* For example, scheduled reports for inventory control can contain the same types of information placed in the same locations on the reports. Different managers can use the same report for different purposes.

Figure 8.3 *Continued*

(e) First-Level Drill-Down Report

Earnings by Quarter (Millions)			
	Actual	Forecast	Variance
2nd Qtr 2014	€12.6	€11.8	6.8%
1st Qtr 2014	€10.8	€10.7	0.9%
4th Qtr 2014	€14.3	€14.5	−1.4%
3rd Qtr 2014	€12.8	€13.3	−3.8%

(f) Second-Level Drill-Down Report

Sales and Expenses (Millions)			
Qtr: 2nd Qtr 2014	Actual	Forecast	Variance
Gross Sales	€110.9	€108.3	2.4%
Expenses	€ 98.3	€ 96.5	1.9%
Profit	€ 12.6	€ 11.8	6.8%

(g) Third-Level Drill-Down Report

Sales by Division (Millions)			
Qtr: 2nd Qtr 2014	Actual	Forecast	Variance
Beauty Care	€ 34.5	€ 33.9	1.8%
Health Care	€ 30.0	€ 28.0	7.1%
Soap	€ 22.8	€ 23.0	−0.9%
Snacks	€ 12.1	€ 12.5	−3.2%
Electronics	€ 11.5	€ 10.9	5.5%
Total	€110.9	€108.3	2.4%

(h) Fourth-Level Drill-Down Report

Sales by Product Category (Millions)			
Qtr: 2nd Qtr 2014 Division: Health Care	Actual	Forecast	Variance
Toothpaste	€12.4	€10.5	18.1%
Mouthwash	€ 8.6	€ 8.8	−2.3%
Over-the-Counter Drugs	€ 5.8	€ 5.3	9.4%
Skin Care Products	€ 3.2	€ 3.4	−5.9%
Total	€30.0	€28.0	7.1%

■ *Produce hard-copy and soft-copy reports.* Some MIS reports are printed on paper, which are hard-copy reports. Most output soft copy, using visual displays on computer screens. Soft-copy output is typically formatted in a report format. In other words, a manager might display an MIS report directly on the computer screen, but the report would still appear in the standard hard-copy format.

Table 8.1 Guidelines for Developing MIS Reports

Guidelines	Reason
Tailor each report to user needs	The unique needs of the manager or executive should be considered, requiring user involvement and input
Spend time and effort producing only reports that are useful	After being instituted, many reports continue to be generated even if no one uses them anymore
Pay attention to report content and layout	Prominently display the information that is most desired. Do not clutter the report with unnecessary data. Use commonly accepted words and phrases. Managers can work more efficiently if they can easily find desired information
Use management-by-exception reporting	Some reports should be produced only when a problem needs to be solved or an action should be taken
Set parameters carefully	Low parameters might result in too many reports; high parameters mean valuable information could be overlooked
Produce all reports in a timely fashion	Outdated reports are of little or no value
Periodically review reports	Review reports at least once per year to make sure they are still needed. Review report content and layout. Determine whether additional reports are needed

■ *Use internal data stored in the computer system.* MIS reports use primarily internal sources of data that are contained in computerized databases. Some MISs also use external sources of data about competitors, the marketplace and so on. The web is a frequently used source for external data.

■ *Allow users to develop their own custom reports.* Although analysts and programmers might be involved in developing and implementing complex MIS reports that require data from many sources, users are increasingly developing their own simple programs to query databases and produce basic reports. This capability, however, can result in several users developing the same or similar reports, which can increase the total time expended and require more storage, compared with having an analyst develop one report for all users.

■ *Require users to submit formal requests for reports to systems personnel.* When IS personnel develop and implement MIS reports, they typically require others to submit a formal request to the IS department. If a manager, for example, wants a production report to be used by several people in his or her department, a formal request for the report is often required. User-developed reports require much less formality.

8.3 Functional MIS

Most organizations are structured along functional lines or areas. This functional structure is usually apparent from an organization chart. Some traditional functional areas are finance, manufacturing, marketing and human resources, among others. The MIS can also be divided along those functional lines to produce reports tailored to individual functions (see Figure 8.4).

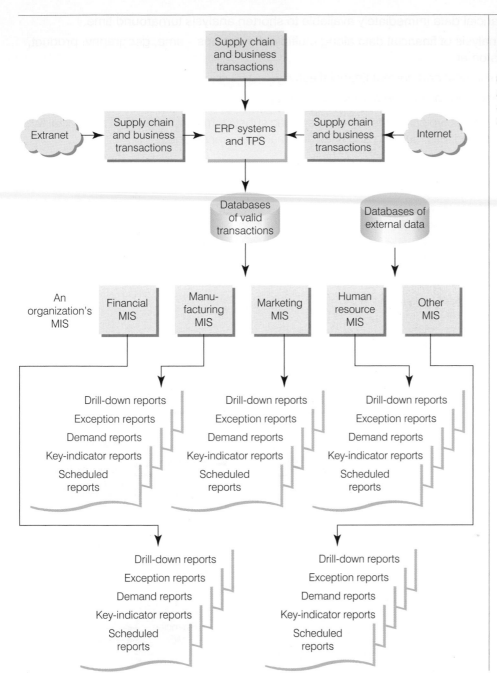

Figure 8.4 An Organization's MIS
The MIS is an integrated collection of functional information systems, each supporting particular functional areas.

Financial Management Information Systems

A **financial MIS** provides financial information not only for executives but also for a broader set of people who need to make better decisions on a daily basis. Financial MISs are used to streamline reports of transactions. Most financial MIS perform the following functions:

- Integrate financial and operational information from multiple sources, including the Internet, into a single system.

- Provide easy access to data for both financial and non-financial users, often through the use of a corporate intranet to access corporate web pages of financial data and information.

financial MIS A management information system that provides financial information not only for executives but also for a broader set of people who need to make better decisions on a daily basis.

■ Make financial data immediately available to shorten analysis turnaround time.

■ Enable analysis of financial data along multiple dimensions – time, geography, product, plant, customer.

■ Analyze historical and current financial activity.

■ Monitor and control the use of funds over time.

Figure 8.5 shows typical inputs, function-specific subsystems and outputs of a financial MIS, including profit and loss, auditing and uses and management of funds.

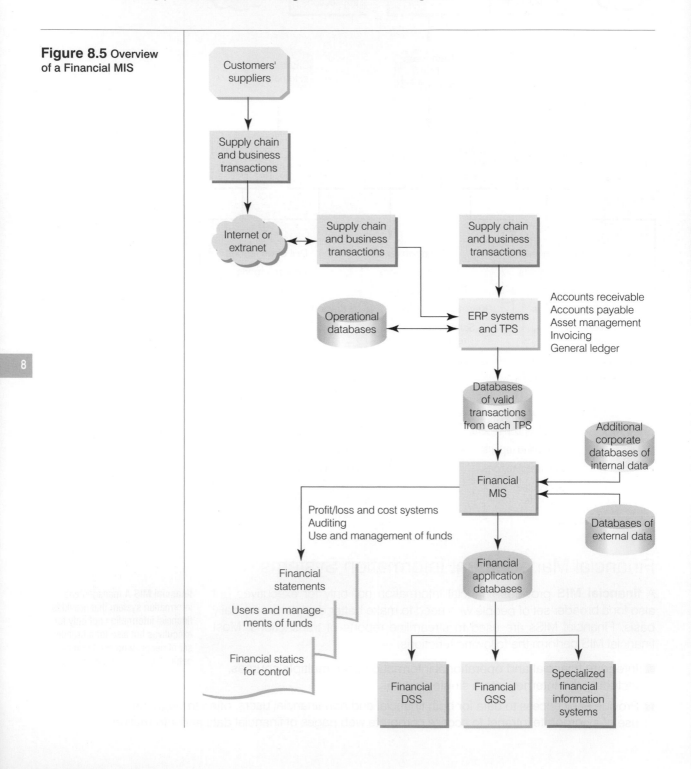

Figure 8.5 Overview of a Financial MIS

Financial MIS are used to compute revenues, costs, profits and for **auditing**. Auditing involves analyzing the financial condition of an organization and determining whether financial statements and reports produced by the financial MIS are accurate. Financial MISs are also used to manage funds. Internal uses of funds include purchasing additional inventory, updating plants and equipment, hiring new employees, acquiring other companies, buying new computer systems, increasing marketing and advertising, purchasing raw materials or land, investing in new products, and increasing research and development. External uses of funds are typically investment related. Companies often invest excess funds in such external revenue generators as bank accounts, stocks, bonds, bills, notes, futures, options and foreign currency using financial MISs.

> **auditing** Analyzing the financial condition of an organization and determining whether financial statements and reports produced by the financial MIS are accurate.

Manufacturing Management Information Systems

More than any other functional area, advances in information systems have revolutionized manufacturing. As a result, many manufacturing operations have been dramatically improved over the last decade. Also, with the emphasis on greater quality and productivity, having an effective manufacturing process is becoming even more critical. The use of computerized systems is emphasized at all levels of manufacturing – from the shop floor to the executive suite. People and small businesses, for example, can benefit from manufacturing MISs that once were only available to large corporations. Personal fabrication systems, for example, can make circuit boards, precision parts, radio tags and more.[6] Personal fabrication systems include precise machine tools, such as milling machines and cutting tools, and sophisticated software. The total system can cost €15 000. For example, in a remote area of Norway, Maakon Karlson uses a personal fabrication system that makes radio tags to track sheep and other animals. The use of the Internet has also streamlined all aspects of manufacturing. Figure 8.6 gives an overview of some of the manufacturing MIS inputs, subsystems and outputs.

The manufacturing MIS subsystems and outputs monitor and control the flow of materials, products and services through the organization. As raw materials are converted to finished goods, the manufacturing MIS monitors the process at almost every stage. New technology could make this process easier. Using specialized computer chips and tiny radio transmitters, companies can monitor materials and products through the entire manufacturing process. Car manufacturers, who convert raw steel, plastic and other materials into a finished automobile, also monitor their manufacturing processes. Auto manufacturers add thousands of dollars of value to the raw materials they use in assembling a car. If the manufacturing MIS also lets them provide additional services, such as customized paint colours, on any of their models, it has added further value for customers. In doing so, the MIS helps provide the company the edge that can differentiate it from competitors. The success of an organization can depend on the manufacturing function. Some common information subsystems and outputs used in manufacturing are discussed next.

- ■ *Design and engineering.* Manufacturing companies often use computer-aided design (CAD) with new or existing products (Figure 8.7). For example, Boeing uses a CAD system to develop a complete digital blueprint of an aircraft before it ever begins its manufacturing process. As mock-ups are built and tested, the digital blueprint is constantly revised to reflect the most current design. Using such technology helps Boeing reduce its manufacturing costs and the time to design a new aircraft.

- ■ *Master production scheduling and inventory control.* Scheduling production and controlling inventory are critical for any manufacturing company. The overall objective of master production scheduling is to provide detailed plans for both short-term and long-range scheduling of manufacturing facilities. Many techniques are used to minimize

Figure 8.6 Overview of a Manufacturing MIS

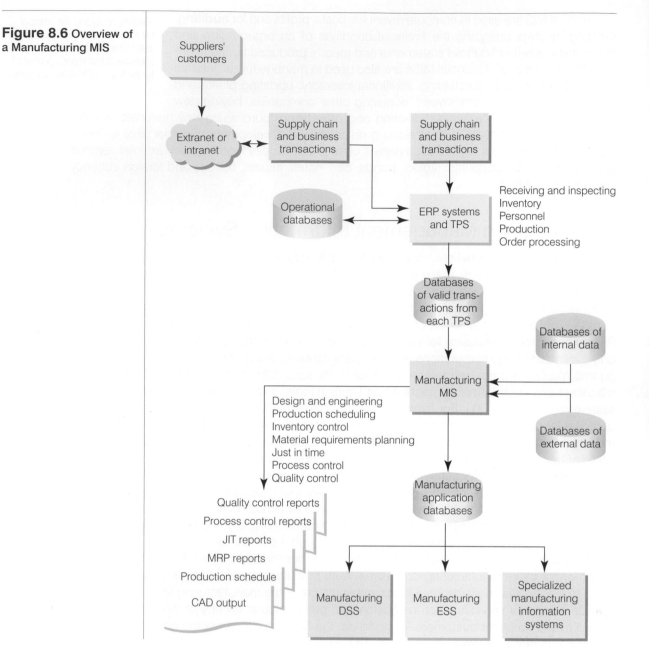

economic order quantity (EOQ) The quantity that should be reordered to minimize total inventory costs.

reorder point (ROP) A critical inventory quantity level.

material requirements planning (MRP) A set of inventory-control techniques that help coordinate thousands of inventory items when the demand of one item is dependent on the demand for another.

inventory costs. Most determine how much and when to order inventory. One method of determining how much inventory to order is called the **economic order quantity (EOQ)**. This quantity is calculated to minimize the total inventory costs. The when-to-order question is based on inventory usage over time. Typically, the question is answered in terms of a **reorder point (ROP)**, which is a critical inventory quantity level. When the inventory level for a particular item falls to the reorder point, or critical level, the system generates a report so that an order is immediately placed for the EOQ of the product. Another inventory technique used when the demand for one item depends on the demand for another is called **material requirements planning (MRP)**. The basic goal of MRP is to determine when finished products, such as automobiles or aeroplanes,

Figure 8.7 A Vanguard-class nuclear powered submarine.
This submarine carries UK Trident nuclear missiles and is soon to be retired from service. Computer aided design will be used in all aspects of the design of its replacement.

are needed and then to work backward to determine deadlines and re-sources needed, such as engines and tires, to complete the final product on schedule. **Just-in-time (JIT)** inventory and manufacturing is an approach that maintains inventory at the lowest levels without sacrificing the availability of finished products. With this approach, inventory and materials are delivered just before they are used in a product. A JIT inventory system would arrange for a car windscreen to be delivered to the assembly line just before it is secured to the automobile, rather than storing it in the manufacturing facility while the car's other components are being assembled. JIT, however, can result in some organizations running out of inventory when demand exceeds expectations.[7]

just-in-time (JIT) inventory A philosophy of inventory management in which inventory and materials are delivered just before they are used in manufacturing a product.

■ *Process control.* Managers can use a number of technologies to control and streamline the manufacturing process. For example, computers can directly control manufacturing equipment, using systems called **computer-aided manufacturing (CAM)**. CAM systems can control drilling machines, assembly lines and more. **Computer-integrated manufacturing (CIM)** uses computers to link the components of the production process into an effective system. CIM's goal is to tie together all aspects of production, including order processing, product design, manufacturing, inspection and quality control, and shipping. A **flexible manufacturing system (FMS)** is an approach that allows manufacturing facilities to rapidly and efficiently change from making one product to another. In the middle of a production run, for example, the production process can be changed to make a different product or to switch manufacturing materials. By using an FMS, the time and cost to change manufacturing jobs can be substantially reduced, and companies can react quickly to market needs and competition.

computer-aided manufacturing (CAM) A system that directly controls manufacturing equipment.

computer-integrated manufacturing (CIM) Using computers to link the components of the production process into an effective system.

flexible manufacturing system (FMS) An approach that allows manufacturing facilities to rapidly and efficiently change from making one product to making another.

■ *Quality control and testing.* With increased pressure from consumers and a general concern for productivity and high quality, today's manufacturing organizations are placing

quality control A process that
ensures that the finished product
meets the customers' needs.

more emphasis on **quality control**, a process that ensures that the finished product meets the customers' needs. Information systems are used to monitor quality and take corrective steps to eliminate possible quality problems.

Marketing Management Information Systems

A **marketing MIS** supports managerial activities in product development, distribution, pricing decisions, promotional effectiveness and sales forecasting. Marketing functions are increasingly being performed on the Internet. Many companies are developing Internet marketplaces to advertise and sell products. The amount spent on online advertising is worth billions of euros annually. Software can measure how many customers see the advertising. Some companies use software products to analyze customer loyalty. Some marketing departments are actively using blogs to publish company-related information and interact with customers.[8]

marketing MIS An information
system that supports managerial
activities in product development,
distribution, pricing decisions and
promotional effectiveness.

Customer relationship management (CRM) programs, available from some ERP vendors, help a company manage all aspects of customer encounters. CRM software can help a company collect customer data, contact customers, educate customers on new products and sell products to customers through a website. An airline, for example, can use a CRM system to notify customers about flight changes. New Zealand's Jade Stadium, for example, uses CRM software from GlobalTech Solutions to give a single entry point to its marketing efforts and customer databases, instead of using about 20 spreadsheets.[9] The CRM software will help Jade Stadium develop effective marketing campaigns, record and track client contacts, and maintain an accurate database of clients. Yet, not all CRM systems and marketing sites on the Internet are successful. Customization and ongoing maintenance of a CRM system can be expensive. Figure 8.8 shows the inputs, subsystems and outputs of a typical marketing MIS.

Subsystems for the marketing MIS include marketing research, product development, promotion and advertising, and product pricing. These subsystems and their outputs help marketing managers and executives increase sales, reduce marketing expenses, and develop plans for future products and services to meet the changing needs of customers.

- *Marketing research.* The purpose of marketing research is to conduct a formal study of the market and customer preferences. Computer systems are used to help conduct and analyze the results of surveys, questionnaires, pilot studies and interviews. Messages on social media sites such as Facebook and Twitter are regularly used for market research, as companies search for their brand names to see what people are saying about them.

- *Product development.* Product development involves the conversion of raw materials into finished goods and services and focuses primarily on the physical attributes of the product. Many factors, including plant capacity, labour skills, engineering factors, and materials are important in product development decisions. In many cases, a computer program analyzes these various factors and selects the appropriate mix of labour, materials, plant and equipment, and engineering designs. Make-or-buy decisions can also be made with the assistance of computer programs.

- *Promotion and advertising.* One of the most important functions of any marketing effort is promotion and advertising. Product success is a direct function of the types of advertising and sales promotion done. Increasingly, organizations are using the Internet to advertise and sell products and services. With the use of GPS, marketing firms can promote products such as local shops and restaurants to mobile devices like phones and tablets that are close by. You could receive a discount coupon for a shop as you walk past it!

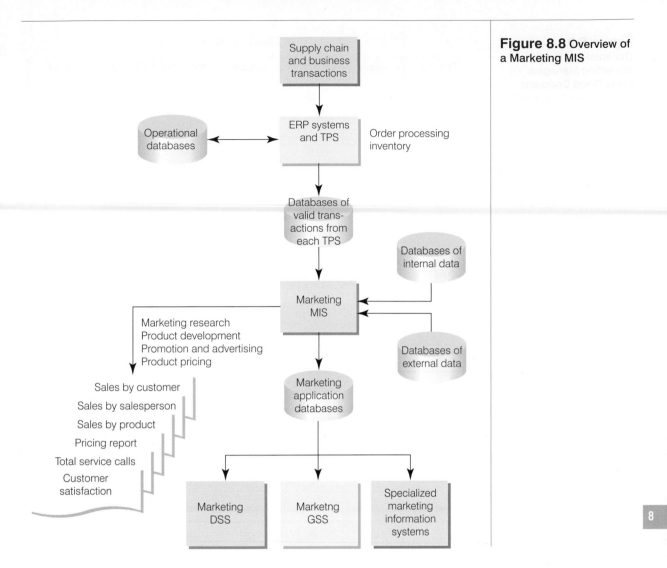

Figure 8.8 Overview of a Marketing MIS

- *Product pricing.* Product pricing is another important and complex marketing function. Retail price, wholesale price and price discounts must be set. Most companies try to develop pricing policies that will maximize total sales revenues. Computers are often used to analyze the relationship between prices and total revenues. Some companies are using Internet behavioural pricing, where the price customers pay online depends on what they might be willing to pay based on information on past transactions and Internet searches that reveal individual shopping behaviours.

- *Sales analysis.* Computerized sales analysis is important to identify products, sales personnel and customers that contribute to profits and those that do not. Several reports can be generated to help marketing managers make good sales decisions (see Figure 8.9). The sales-by-product report lists all major products and their sales for a period of time, such as a month. This report shows which products are doing well and which need improvement or should be discarded altogether. The sales-by-salesperson report lists total sales for each salesperson for each week or month. This report can also be subdivided by product to show which products are being sold by each salesperson. The sales-by-customer report is a tool that can be used to identify high- and low-volume customers.

Figure 8.9 Reports
Generated to Help
Marketing Managers
Make Good Decisions
*(a) This sales-by-product
report lists all major
products and their sales
for the period from August
to December. (b) This
sales-by-salesperson report
lists total sales for each
salesperson for the same
time period. (c) This sales-
by-customer report lists
sales for each customer
for the period. Like all MIS
reports, totals are provided
automatically by the system
to show managers at a
glance the information
they need to make good
decisions.*

(a) Sales by product

Product	August	September	October	November	December	Total
Product 1	34	32	32	21	33	152
Product 2	156	162	177	163	122	780
Product 3	202	145	122	98	66	633
Product 4	345	365	352	341	288	1691

(b) Sales by salesperson

Salesperson	August	September	October	November	December	Total
Jones	24	42	42	11	43	162
Kline	166	155	156	122	133	732
Lane	166	155	104	99	106	630
Miller	245	225	305	291	301	1367

(c) Sales by customer

Customer	August	September	October	November	December	Total
Ang	234	334	432	411	301	1712
Braswell	56	62	77	61	21	277
Celec	1202	1445	1322	998	667	5634
Jung	45	65	55	34	88	287

Human Resource Management Information Systems

A **human resource MIS (HRMIS)**, also called a personnel MIS, is concerned with activities related to previous, current and potential employees of the organization. Because the personnel function relates to all other functional areas in the business, the human resource (HR) MIS plays a valuable role in ensuring organizational success. Some of the activities performed by this important MIS include workforce analysis and planning, hiring, training, job and task assignment, and many other personnel-related issues. An effective HRMIS allows a company to keep personnel costs at a minimum, while serving the required business processes needed to achieve corporate goals. Although human resource information systems focus on cost reduction, many of today's HR systems concentrate on hiring and managing existing employees to get the total potential of the human talent in the organization. According to the High Performance Workforce Study conducted by Accenture, the most important HR initiatives include improving worker productivity, improving adaptability to new opportunities and facilitating organizational change. Figure 8.10 shows some of the inputs, subsystems and outputs of the HRMIS.

human resource MIS (HRMIS)
An information system that is concerned with activities related to employees and potential employees of an organization, also called a personnel MIS.

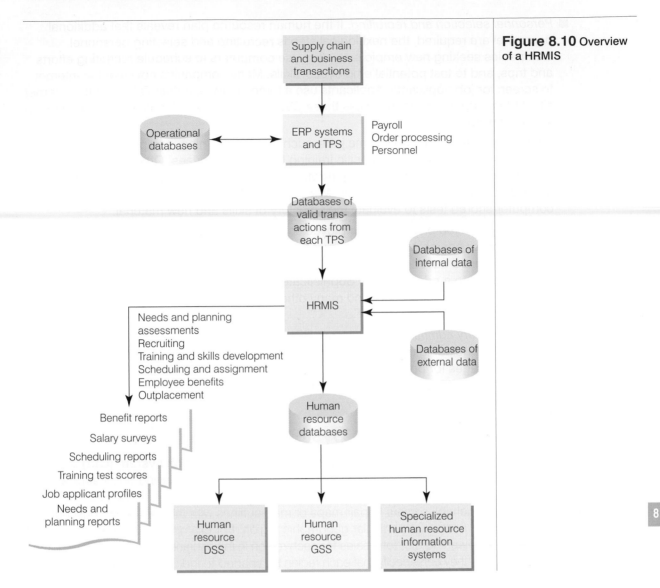

Figure 8.10 Overview of a HRMIS

Human resource subsystems and outputs range from the determination of human resource needs and hiring through retirement and outplacement. Most medium and large organizations have computer systems to assist with human resource planning, hiring, training and skills inventorying, and wage and salary administration. Outputs of the human resource MIS include reports, such as human resource planning reports, job application review profiles, skills inventory reports and salary surveys.

■ *Human resource planning.* One of the first aspects of any HRMIS is determining personnel and human needs. The overall purpose of this MIS subsystem is to put the right number and kinds of employees in the right jobs when they are needed. Effective human resource planning can require computer programs, such as SPSS and SAS, to forecast the future number of employees needed and anticipating the future supply of people for these jobs. IBM is using an HR pilot program, called Professional Marketplace, to plan for workforce needs, including the supplies and tools the workforce needs to work efficiently.[10] Professional Marketplace helps IBM to catalogue employees into a glossary of skills and abilities. Like many other companies, HR and workforce costs are IBM's biggest expense.

■ *Personnel selection and recruiting.* If the human resource plan reveals that additional personnel are required, the next logical step is recruiting and selecting personnel. Companies seeking new employees often use computers to schedule recruiting efforts and trips, and to test potential employees' skills. Many companies now use the Internet to screen for job applicants. Applicants use a template to load their CVs onto the Internet site. HR managers can then access these CVs and identify applicants they are interested in interviewing.

■ *Training and skills inventory.* Some jobs, such as programming, equipment repair and tax preparation, require very specific training for new employees. Other jobs may require general training about the organizational culture, orientation, dress standards and expectations of the organization. When training is complete, employees often take computer-scored tests to evaluate their mastery of skills and new material.

■ *Scheduling and job placement.* Employee schedules are developed for each employee, showing his or her job assignments over the next week or month. Job placements are often determined based on skills inventory reports, which show which employee might be best suited to a particular job. Sophisticated scheduling programs are often used in the airline industry, the military and many other areas to get the right people assigned to the right jobs at the right time.

■ *Wage and salary administration.* Another HRMIS subsystem involves determining salaries and benefits, including medical insurance and pension payments. Wage data, such as industry averages for positions, can be taken from the corporate database and manipulated by the HRMIS to provide wage information reports to higher levels of management.

Geographic Information Systems

Although not yet common in organizations, a **geographic information system (GIS)** is a computer system capable of assembling, storing, manipulating and displaying geographically referenced information; that is, data identified according to its location. A GIS enables users to pair maps or map outlines with tabular data to describe aspects of a particular geographic region. For example, sales managers might want to plot total sales for each region in the countries they serve. Using a GIS, they can specify that each region be shaded to indicate the relative amount of sales – no shading or light shading represents no or little sales, and deeper shading represents more sales. Staples Inc., the large office supply store chain, used a geographic information system to select about 100 new store locations, after considering about 5000 possible sites.[11] Finding the best location is critical. It can cost up to €750 000 for a failed store because of a poor location. Staples uses a GIS tool from Tactician Corporation along with software from SAS. Although many software products have seen declining revenues, the use of GIS software is increasing.

geographic information system (GIS) A computer system capable of assembling, storing, manipulating and displaying geographic information; that is, data identified according to its location.

8.4 Decision Support Systems

Management information systems provide useful summary reports to help solve structured and semi-structured business problems. Decision support systems (DSSs) offer the potential to assist in solving both semi-structured and unstructured problems. A DSS is an organized collection of people, procedures, software, databases, and devices used to help make decisions that solve problems. The focus of a DSS is on decision-making effectiveness when faced with unstructured or semi-structured business problems. As with a TPS and an MIS, a DSS should be designed, developed and used to help an organization achieve its goals and objectives. Decision support systems offer the potential to generate higher profits, lower costs, and better products and services.

Decision support systems, although skewed somewhat towards the top levels of management, are used at all levels. To some extent, today's managers at all levels are faced with less structured, non-routine problems, but the quantity and magnitude of these decisions increase as a manager rises higher in an organization. Many organizations contain a tangled web of complex rules, procedures and decisions. DSSs are used to bring more structure to these problems to aid the decision-making process. In addition, because of the inherent flexibility of decision support systems, managers at all levels are able to use DSSs to assist in some relatively routine, programmable decisions in lieu of more formalized management information systems.

Characteristics of a Decision Support System

Decision support systems have many characteristics that allow them to be effective management support tools, some of which are listed here. Of course, not all DSSs work the same.

- *Provide rapid access to information.* DSSs provide fast and continuous access to information.

- *Handle large amounts of data from different sources.* For instance, advanced database management systems and data warehouses have allowed decision makers to search for information with a DSS, even when some data resides in different databases on different computer systems or networks. Other sources of data can be accessed via the Internet or over a corporate intranet. Using the Internet, an oil giant can use a decision support system to save hundreds of millions of euros annually by coordinating a large amount of drilling and exploration data from around the globe.

- *Provide report and presentation flexibility.* Managers can get the information they want, presented in a format that suits their needs. Furthermore, output can be displayed on computer screens or printed, depending on the needs and desires of the problem solvers.

- *Offer both textual and graphical orientation.* DSSs can produce text, tables, line drawings, pie charts, trend lines and more. By using their preferred orientation, managers can use a DSS to get a better understanding of a situation and to convey this understanding to others.

- *Support drill-down analysis.* A manager can get more levels of detail when needed by drilling down through data. For example, a manager can get more detailed information for a project – viewing the overall project cost, then drilling down and seeing the cost for each phase, activity and task.

- *Perform complex, sophisticated analysis and comparisons using advanced software packages.* Marketing research surveys, for example, can be analyzed in a variety of ways using programs that are part of a DSS. Many of the analytical programs associated with a DSS are actually stand-alone programs, and the DSS brings them together.

- *Support optimization, satisficing and heuristic approaches.* By supporting all types of decision-making approaches, a DSS gives the decision maker a great deal of flexibility in computer support for decision making. For example, **what-if analysis**, the process of making hypothetical changes to problem data and observing the impact on the results, can be used to control inventory. Given the demand for products, such as automobiles, the computer can determine the necessary parts and components, including engines, transmissions, windows and so on. With what-if analysis, a manager can make changes to problem data, say the number of cars needed for next month, and immediately see the impact on the parts requirements.

> **what-if analysis** The process of making hypothetical changes to problem data and observing the impact on the results.

- *Perform goal-seeking analysis.* **Goal-seeking analysis** is the process of determining the problem data required for a given result. For example, a

> **goal-seeking analysis** The process of determining the problem data required for a given result.

financial manager might be considering an investment with a certain monthly net income, and the manager might have a goal to earn a return of 9 per cent on the investment. Goal seeking allows the manager to determine what monthly net income (problem data) is needed to yield a return of 9 per cent (problem result). Some spreadsheets can be used to perform goal-seeking analysis.

■ *Perform simulation.* **Simulation** is the ability of the DSS to duplicate the features of a real system. In most cases, probability or uncertainty is involved. For example, the number of repairs and the time to repair key components of a manufacturing line can

simulation The ability of the DSS to duplicate the features of a real system.

be calculated to determine the impact on the number of products that can be produced each day. Engineers can use this data to determine which components need to be reengineered to increase the mean time between failures and which components need to have an ample supply of spare parts to reduce the mean time to repair. Drug companies are using simulated trials to reduce the need for human participants and reduce the time and costs of bringing a new drug to market. Drug companies are hoping that this use of simulation will help them identify successful drugs earlier in development. Corporate executives and military commanders often use computer simulations to allow them to try different strategies in different situations. Corporate executives, for example, can try different marketing decisions under various market conditions. Military commanders often use computer war games to fine-tune their military strategies in different warfare conditions. The Turkish army, for example, uses simulation to help coordinate its fuel-supply system.[12]

Capabilities of a Decision Support System

Developers of decision support systems strive to make them more flexible than management information systems and to give them the potential to assist decision makers in a variety of situations. DSSs can assist with all or most problem-solving phases, decision frequencies and different degrees of problem structure. DSS approaches can also help at all levels of the decision-making process. A single DSS might provide only a few of these capabilities, depending on its uses and scope.

■ *Support for problem-solving phases.* The objective of most decision support systems is to assist decision makers with the phases of problem solving. As previously discussed, these phases include intelligence, design, choice, implementation and monitoring. A specific DSS might support only one or a few phases. By supporting all types of decision-making approaches, a DSS gives the decision maker a great deal of flexibility in getting computer support for decision-making activities.

■ *Support for different decision frequencies.* Decisions can range on a continuum from one-of-a-kind to repetitive decisions. One-of-a-kind decisions are typically

ad hoc DSS A DSS concerned with situations or decisions that come up only a few times during the life of the organization.

institutional DSS A DSS that handles situations or decisions that occur more than once, usually several times per year or more. An institutional DSS is used repeatedly and refined over the years.

handled by an ad hoc DSS. An **ad hoc DSS** is concerned with situations or decisions that come up only a few times during the life of the organization; in small businesses, they might happen only once. For example, a company might need to change the layout of its open plan offices. Repetitive decisions are addressed by an institutional DSS. An **institutional DSS** handles situations or decisions that occur more than once, usually several times per year or more. An institutional DSS is used repeatedly and refined over the years. For example, a DSS used to assist help desk staff solve employees' computer problems and queries.

■ *Support for different problem structures.* As discussed previously, decisions can range from highly structured and programmed to unstructured and non-programmed. **Highly structured problems** are straightforward, requiring known facts and relationships. **Semi-structured or unstructured problems**, on the other hand, are more complex. The relationships among the pieces of data are not always clear, the data might be in a variety of formats, and it is often difficult to manipulate or obtain. In addition, the decision maker might not know the information requirements of the decision in advance.

highly structured problems
Problems that are straightforward and require known facts and relationships.

semi-structured or unstructured problems More complex problems in which the relationships among the pieces of data are not always clear, the data might be in a variety of formats, and the data is often difficult to manipulate or obtain.

■ *Support for various decision-making levels.* Decision support systems can provide help for managers at different levels within the organization. Operational managers can get assistance with daily and routine decision making. Tactical decision makers can use analysis tools to ensure proper planning and control. At the strategic level, DSSs can help managers by providing analysis for long-term decisions requiring both internal and external information (see Figure 8.11).

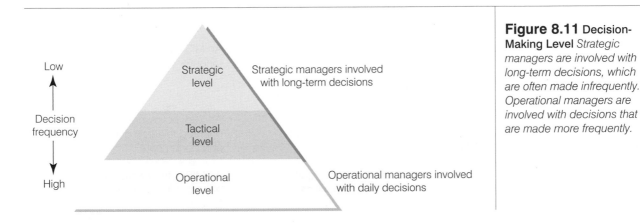

Figure 8.11 Decision-Making Level *Strategic managers are involved with long-term decisions, which are often made infrequently. Operational managers are involved with decisions that are made more frequently.*

A Comparison of a DSS and an MIS

A DSS differs from an MIS in numerous ways, including the type of problems solved, the support given to users, the decision emphasis and approach, and the type, speed, output and development of the system used. Table 8.2 lists brief descriptions of these differences. You should note that entity resource planning systems include both MISs and DSSs (and, as discussed in the previous chapter, TPS).

Components of a Decision Support System

At the core of a DSS are a database and a model base. In addition, a typical DSS contains a user interface, also called **dialogue manager**, that allows decision makers to easily access and manipulate the DSS and to use common business terms and phrases. Finally, access to the Internet, networks and other computer-based systems permits the DSS to tie into other powerful systems, including the TPS or function-specific subsystems. Internet software agents, for example, can be used in creating powerful decision

dialogue manager A user interface that allows decision makers to easily access and manipulate the DSS and to use common business terms and phrases.

Table 8.2 Comparison of a DSS and an MIS

Factor	DSS	MIS
Problem Type	A DSS can handle unstructured problems that cannot be easily programmed	An MIS is normally used only with structured problems
Users	A DSS supports individuals, small groups and the entire organization. In the short run, users typically have more control over a DSS	An MIS supports primarily the organization. In the short run, users have less control over an MIS
Support	A DSS supports all aspects and phases of decision making; it does not replace the decision maker – people still make the decisions	This is not true of all MIS systems – some make automatic decisions and replace the decision maker
Emphasis Approach	A DSS emphasizes actual decisions and decision-making styles. A DSS is a direct support system that provides interactive reports on computer screens	An MIS usually emphasizes information only. An MIS is typically an indirect support system that uses regularly produced reports
Speed	Because a DSS is flexible and can be implemented by users, it usually takes less time to develop and is better able to respond to user requests	An MIS's response time is usually longer
Output	DSS reports are usually screen oriented, with the ability to generate reports on a printer	An MIS, however, typically is oriented towards printed reports and documents
Development	DSS users are usually more directly involved in its development. User involvement usually means better systems that provide superior support. For all systems, user involvement is the most important factor for the development of a successful system	An MIS is frequently several years old and often was developed for people who are no longer performing the work supported by the MIS

Information Systems @ Work

Harnessing citizen scientists to map pollution

When you hear the word pollution you probably think of air quality and unclean water. You might not immediately think of street lights. Light pollution refers to excessive artificial light, often aimed into the sky. Light pollution represents wasted energy and can have a negative impact on animals and plants. For instance, birds, insects, even fish and amphibians navigate by using the night sky. Humans are affected too: light represents a major factor which influences our health and wellbeing. Too much light at inappropriate times can interfere with us and our performance and health can suffer. Light pollution also limits our ability to star gaze, and has been called the most dramatic change we have made to our biosphere. Hong Kong is one of the worst affected places. Its night sky is as much as 1000 times brighter than international norms. One study has found that even rural areas of Hong

Kong, including the nearby island of Lantau and the city's Wetland Park to the north – a world famous staging post for migratory birds – are being affected by man-made lighting.

The Globe at Night programme is an international citizen-science project to raise public awareness of the impact of light pollution. The luminance of the night sky at locations on the Earth's surface is very poorly known and the campaign, which has been running since 2006, is making a major contribution to science by mapping it. Citizen-science uses information technology to form online communities of interested amateur scientists who together collect vast amounts of data to study some phenomenon. The Globe at Night project invites citizen-scientists to measure the brightness of their night sky. Individuals can upload measurements made anywhere on Earth using a special mobile phone app. Observers go outside at least one hour after sunset and compare their view of a constellation to that shown in a series of star charts, which are generated specially for each observer based on their location. The app allows the observer to record their exact latitude and longitude using their mobile's GPS, and displays the star charts. Nearly 100 000 measurements have been made from people in 115 countries. The project coordinators are keen to get children involved and encourage observers to learn about their star constellations.

Using the terminology of business information systems, the app itself (which is called Loss Of The Night) can be thought of as a transaction processing system with each observation being one transaction. The transactions are then sent to a central system which summarises and analyzes these transactions to track worldwide lighting changes. The central system is equivalent to a management information system.

Questions

1 Why do you think people take part in citizen-science projects? What benefits do you think citizen-scientists get out of the Globe at Night project?

2 What sort of decisions could be made using this data? Could the data be used for other purposes?

3 Using mobile information technology, what else could citizen-scientists be asked to track? What about other hobbies – trainspotting for instance? Visit the website www.wheresgeorge.com for another idea.

4 Using Google or similar, search for other citizen-science projects. Selecting one, investigate the information technology it uses.

support systems. Figure 8.12 shows a conceptual model of a DSS although specific DSSs might not have all these components.

The Database

The database management system allows managers and decision makers to perform qualitative analysis on the company's vast stores of data in databases, data warehouses (discussed

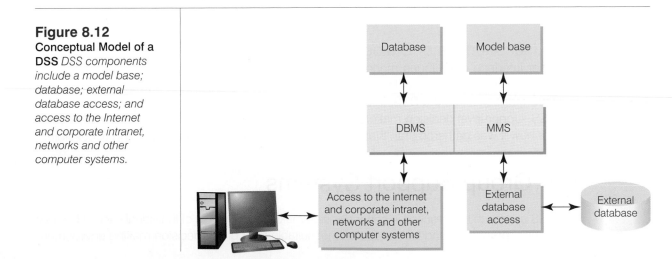

Figure 8.12
Conceptual Model of a DSS *DSS components include a model base; database; external database access; and access to the Internet and corporate intranet, networks and other computer systems.*

in Chapter 5). DSSs tap into vast stores of information contained in the corporate database, retrieving information on inventory, sales, personnel, production, finance, accounting and other areas.[13] Data mining and business intelligence, introduced in Chapter 5, are often used in DSSs. Airline companies, for example, use a DSS to help it identify customers for round-trip flights between major cities. The DSS can be used to search a data warehouse to contact thousands of customers who might be interested in an inexpensive flight. A casino can use a DSS to search large databases to get detailed information on patrons. It can tell how much each patron spends per day on gambling, and more. Opportunity International uses a DSS to help it make loans and provide services to tsunami victims and others in need around the world.[14] According to the information services manager of Opportunity International, 'We need to pull all the data . . . to one central database that we can analyze, and we need a way to get that information back out to people in the field.' A DSS can also be used in emergency medical situations to make split-second, life-or-death treatment decisions.[15]

A database management system can also connect to external databases to give managers and decision makers even more information and decision support. External databases can include the Internet, libraries, government databases and more. The combination of internal and external database access can give key decision makers a better understanding of the company and its environment.

The Model Base

In addition to the data, a DSS needs a model of how elements of the data are related, in order to help make decisions. The **model base** allows managers and decision makers to perform quantitative analysis on both internal and external data.[16] The model base gives decision makers access to a variety of models so that they can explore different scenarios and see their effects. Ultimately, it assists them in the decision-making process. Procter & Gamble, maker of Pringles potato crisps, Pampers nappies and hundreds of other consumer products, use DSSs to streamline how raw materials and products flow from its suppliers to its customers, saving millions of euros.[17] Scientists and mathematicians also use DSSs.[18] DSSs can be excellent at predicting customer behaviours.[19] Most banks, for example, use models to help forecast which customers will be late with payments or might default on their loans.

model base Part of a DSS that provides decision makers access to a variety of models and assists them in decision making.

The models and algorithms used in a DSS are often reviewed and revised over time.[20] As a result of Hurricane Katrina in the US, for example, American insurance companies plan to revise their models about storm damage and insurance requirements.[21]

model management software Software that coordinates the use of models in a DSS.

Model management software (MMS) is often used to coordinate the use of models in a DSS, including financial, statistical analysis, graphical and project-management models. Depending on the needs of the decision maker, one or more of these models can be used (see Table 8.3).

The User Interface or Dialogue Manager

The user interface or dialogue manager allows users to interact with the DSS to obtain information. It assists with all aspects of communications between the user and the hardware and software that constitute the DSS. In a practical sense, to most DSS users, the user interface is the DSS. Upper-level decision makers are often less interested in where the information came from or how it was gathered than that the information is both understandable and accessible.

8.5 Group Support Systems

The DSS approach has resulted in better decision making for all levels of individual users. However, many DSS approaches and techniques are not suitable for a group decision-making environment.

Table 8.3 Model Management Software

DSS often use financial, statistical, graphical and project-management models

Model Type	Description	Software
Financial	Provides cash flow, internal rate of return and other investment analysis	Spreadsheet, such as Microsoft Excel
Statistical	Provides summary statistics, trend projections, hypothesis testing and more	Statistical program, such as SPSS or SAS
Graphical	Assists decision makers in designing, developing and using graphic displays of data and information	Graphics programs, such as Microsoft PowerPoint
Project Management	Handles and coordinates large projects; also used to identify critical activities and tasks that could delay or jeopardize an entire project if they are not completed in a timely and cost-effective fashion	Project management software, such as Microsoft Project

Although not all workers and managers are involved in committee meetings and group decision-making sessions, some tactical and strategic-level managers can spend more than half their decision-making time in a group setting. Such managers need assistance with group decision making. A **group support system (GSS)**, also called a group decision support system, consists of most of the elements in a DSS, plus software to provide effective support in group decision-making settings (see Figure 8.13).[22]

Group support systems are used in most industries. Architects are increasingly using GSSs to help them collaborate with other architects and builders to develop the best plans and to compete for contracts. Manufacturing companies use GSSs to link raw material suppliers to their own company systems.

group support system (GSS)
Software application that consists of most elements in a DSS, plus software to provide effective support in group decision making; also called 'group decision support system'.

8

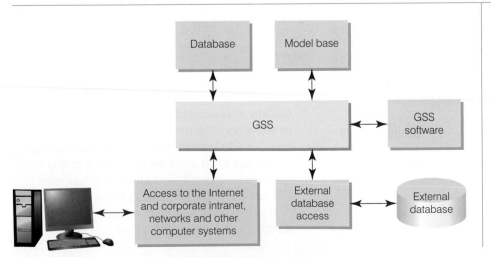

Figure 8.13
Configuration of a GSS
A GSS contains most of the elements found in a DSS, plus software to facilitate group member communications.

Ethical and Societal Issues

You Want to Put That *Where*?

Land use is often a contentious topic. Every-one wants the benefits that airports, electricity-generating plants, prisons and all-night railroad freight car classification yards bring to society. Still, few people want to live next door to one of these operations.

Fortunately, geographic information systems (GISs) can help sort out the issues involved with sit-ing these and other operations, including those that are not necessarily as objectionable. The govern-ment of Queensland, Australia, used a GIS to figure out the best locations for poultry farms in the south-ern part of that state.

As background, chicken passed beef and veal in 2007 to become the most popular form of meat for Australians. Queensland has about 20 per cent of Australia's population and produces about 20 per cent of its chicken. Chicken farming is split be-tween two major centres: near the town of Mareeba in the north and near the capital city of Brisbane in the south. Owing to the larger number of com-peting land uses near Brisbane, the government of Queensland needed to develop objective ways to allocate this scarce resource.

Poultry farms are not nearly as objectionable as some other operations that modern society finds necessary, but many factors still determine the best places to put them. William Mortimer, senior spa-tial analyst at Queensland Government, writes that 'Geographic information systems and spatial analy-sis tools enable the departmental decision makers to visualize and understand complex issues on a site specific and regional scale basis.' Among these issues are what he calls *primary constraints*. The lo-cation of a poultry farm *may* not be:

- Too close (under 1 km, about 0.6 miles) to an-other poultry farm.
- In a key mineral resource extraction area.
- In an urban or residential area (a 2 km buffer, about 1.2 miles, is desirable).
- In an area of high ecological significance.
- In a low-lying, flood-prone area.

- In a koala conservation area.
- In a designated water catchment area.
- Within the Royal Australian Air Force base at Amberley.

As secondary constraints, a poultry farm *should* not be:

- On land that is too steep (over 10 per cent slope).
- Next to a watercourse.
- On good quality agricultural land.
- On land suitable for strategic crops.
- In a national park or other protected area.
- On an oil or gas pipeline.
- On acid sulphate soil.

Conversely, it is desirable for a poultry farm to be:

- Near poultry processing plants.
- Near paved roads.
- Near a reliable supply of clean water.
- Near a supply of electricity.
- Near poultry feed mills.

Using these constraints and ESRI's ArcGIS software, the Queensland government was able to produce maps of the southern part of Queensland, showing areas that were suitable for new poultry farms, calculating automatically the amount of land available in each of them, and showing areas of different sizes in different colours. This mapping provides a good basis for future planning – both for the poultry industry and for those affected by it.

Questions

1 Assume the area under consideration for possible poultry farms is about 1000 square miles, or 2500 square km, and that the resulting maps have to be accurate to 100 feet, or 30 m. Estimate how long it would take to draw maps that reflect all 20 of the factors listed in this box by hand. You will have to make additional as-sumptions; be sure to state them.

2 How could this approach be used to help choose locations for new solar electricity-generating fields? What would have to be changed? What could stay essentially the same?

3 Suppose your university outgrew its present facilities and needed to build a new campus. List primary constraints, secondary constraints and desirable factors for its choice of location.

4 You have probably used a different type of geographic information system for navigation. Ignore its GPS aspect, which serves only to determine your location, and consider its maps. How do those maps differ from those that a land-use information system would have? How are they similar?

Characteristics of a GSS that Enhance Decision Making

It is often said that two heads are better than one. When it comes to decision making, GSS unique characteristics have the potential to result in better decisions. Developers of these systems try to build on the advantages of individual support systems while adding new approaches, unique to group decision making. For example, some GSSs can allow the exchange of information and expertise among people without direct face-to-face interaction. The following sections describe some characteristics that can improve and enhance decision making.

■ *Design for groups.* The GSSs approach acknowledges that special procedures, devices and approaches are needed in group decision-making settings. These procedures must foster creative thinking, effective communications and good group decision-making techniques.

■ *Ease of use.* Like an individual DSS, a GSS must be easy to learn and use. Systems that are complex and hard to operate will seldom be used. Many groups have less tolerance than do individual decision makers for poorly developed systems.

■ *Flexibility.* Two or more decision makers working on the same problem might have different decision-making styles and preferences. Each manager makes decisions in a unique way, in part because of different experiences and cognitive styles. An effective GSS not only has to support the different approaches that managers use to make decisions, but also must find a means to integrate their different perspectives into a common view of the task at hand.

■ *Decision-making support.* A GSS can support different decision-making approaches such as **brainstorming**, the **group consensus approach** or the **nominal group technique**.

■ *Anonymous input.* Many GSSs allow anonymous input, where group members do not know which of them is giving the input. For example, some organizations use a GSS to help rank the performance of managers. Anonymous input allows the group decision makers to concentrate on the merits of the input without considering who gave it. In other words, input given by a top-level manager is given the same consideration as input from employees or other members of the group. Some studies have shown that groups using anonymous input can make better decisions and have superior results compared with groups that do not use anonymous input. Anonymous input, however, can result in flaming, where an unknown team member posts insults or even obscenities on the GSS.

brainstorming A decision-making approach that often consists of members offering ideas 'off the top of their heads'.

group consensus approach A decision-making approach that forces members in the group to reach a unanimous decision.

nominal group technique A decision-making approach that encourages feedback from individual group members, and the final decision is made by voting, similar to the way public officials are elected.

■ *Reduction of negative group behaviour.* One key characteristic of any GSS is the ability to suppress or eliminate group behaviour that is counterproductive or harmful to effective decision making. In some group settings, dominant individuals can take over the discussion, which can prevent other members of the group from presenting creative alternatives. In other cases, one or two group members can sidetrack or subvert the group into areas that are non-productive and do not help solve the problem at hand. Other times, members of a group might assume they have made the right decision without examining alternatives – a phenomenon called 'groupthink'. If group sessions are poorly planned and executed, the result can be a tremendous waste of time. GSS designers are developing software and hardware systems to reduce these types of problems. Procedures for effectively planning and managing group meetings can be incorporated into the GSS approach. A trained meeting facilitator is often employed to help lead the group decision-making process and to avoid groupthink.

■ *Parallel communication.* With traditional group meetings, people must take turns addressing various issues. One person normally talks at a time. With a GSS, every group member can address issues or make comments at the same time by entering them into a PC or workstation. These comments and issues are displayed on every group member's PC or workstation immediately. Parallel communication can speed meeting times and result in better decisions.

■ *Automated recordkeeping.* Most GSSs can keep detailed records of a meeting automatically. Each comment that is entered into a group member's PC or workstation can be recorded. In some cases, literally hundreds of comments can be stored for future review and analysis. In addition, most GSSs packages have automatic voting and ranking features. After group members vote, the GSS records each vote and makes the appropriate rankings.

8.6 Executive Support Systems

8

executive support system (ESS)
Specialized DSS that includes all hardware, software, data, procedures and people used to assist senior-level executives within the organization.

Because top-level executives often require specialised support when making strategic decisions, many companies have developed systems to assist executive decision making. This type of system, called an **executive support system (ESS)**, is a specialized DSS that includes all hardware, software, data, procedures and people used to assist senior-level executives within the organization. In some cases, an ESS, also called an executive information system (EIS), supports decision making of members of the board of directors, who are responsible to stockholders.

An ESS is a special type of DSS and, like a DSS, an ESS is designed to support higher-level decision making in the organization. The two systems are, however, different in important ways. DSSs provide a variety of modelling and analysis tools to enable users to thoroughly analyze problems – that is, they allow users to answer questions. ESSs present structured information about aspects of the organization that executives consider important. In other words, they allow executives to ask the right questions.

The following are general characteristics of ESSs:

■ *Are tailored to individual executives.* ESSs are typically tailored to individual executives; DSSs are not tailored to particular users. They present information in the preferred format of that executive.

■ *Are easy to use.* A top-level executive's most critical resource can be his or her time. Thus, an ESSs must be easy to learn and use and not overly complex.

■ *Have drill-down abilities.* An ESS allows executives to drill down into the company to determine how certain data was produced. Drilling down allows an executive to get more detailed information if needed.

■ *Support the need for external data.* The data needed to make effective top-level decisions is often external – information from competitors, the federal government, trade associations and journals, consultants and so on. An effective ESS can extract data useful to the decision maker from a wide variety of sources, including the Internet and other electronic publishing sources.

■ *Can help with situations that have a high degree of uncertainty.* Most executive decisions involve a high degree of uncertainty. Handling these unknown situations using modelling and other ESS procedures helps top-level managers measure the amount of risk in a decision.

■ *Have a future orientation.* Executive decisions are future oriented, meaning that decisions will have a broad impact for years or decades. The information sources to support future-oriented decision making are usually informal – from organizing golf partners to tying together members of social clubs or civic organizations.

■ *Are linked with value-added business processes.* Like other information systems, executive support systems are linked with executive decision making about value-added business processes.

Capabilities of Executive Support Systems

The responsibility given to top-level executives and decision makers brings unique problems and pressures to their jobs. The following is a discussion of some of the characteristics of executive decision making that are supported through the ESS approach. ESSs take full advantage of data mining, the Internet, blogs, podcasts, executive dashboards and many other technological innovations. As you will note, most of these decisions are related to an organization's overall profitability and direction. An effective ESS should have the capability to support executive decisions with components such as strategic planning and organizing, crisis management and more.

■ *Support for defining an overall vision.* One of the key roles of senior executives is to provide a broad vision for the entire organization. This vision includes the organization's major product lines and services, the types of businesses it supports today and in the future, and its overriding goals.

■ *Support for strategic planning.* ESSs also support **strategic planning**. Strategic planning involves determining long-term objectives by analyzing the strengths and weaknesses of the organization, predicting future trends, and projecting the development of new product lines. It also involves planning the acquisition of new equipment, analyzing merger possibilities, and making difficult decisions concerning downsizing and the sale of assets if required by unfavourable economic conditions.

strategic planning Determining long-term objectives by analyzing the strengths and weaknesses of the organization, predicting future trends and projecting the development of new product lines.

■ *Support for strategic organizing and staffing.* Top-level executives are concerned with organizational structure. For example, decisions concerning the creation of new departments or downsizing the labour force are made by top-level managers. Overall direction for staffing decisions and effective communication with labour unions are also major decision areas for top-level executives. ESSs can be employed to help analyze the impact of staffing decisions, potential pay raises, changes in employee benefits and new work rules.

■ *Support for strategic control.* Another type of executive decision relates to strategic control, which involves monitoring and managing the overall operation of the organization. Goal seeking can be done for each major area to determine what performance these areas need to achieve to reach corporate expectations. Effective ESS approaches can help top-level managers make the most of their existing resources and control all aspects of the organization.

■ *Support for crisis management.* Even with careful strategic planning, a crisis can occur. Major disasters, including hurricanes, tornadoes, floods, earthquakes, fires and terrorist activities, can totally shut down major parts of the organization. Handling these emergencies is another responsibility for top-level executives. In many cases, strategic emergency plans can be put into place with the help of an ESS. These contingency plans help organizations recover quickly if an emergency or crisis occurs.

Decision making is a vital part of managing businesses strategically. IS systems such as information and decision support, group support and executive support systems help employees by tapping existing databases and providing them with current, accurate information. The increasing integration of all business information systems – from TPS to MIS to DSS to ESS – can help organizations monitor their competitive environment and make better-informed decisions. Organizations can also use specialized business information systems, discussed in the next two chapters, to achieve their goals.

Summary

8

Good decision-making and problem-solving skills are the key to developing effective information and decision support systems. Every organization needs effective decision making and problem solving to reach its objectives and goals. Problem solving begins with decision making. A well-known model developed by Herbert Simon divides the decision-making phase of the problem-solving process into three stages: intelligence, design and choice. During the intelligence stage, potential problems or opportunities are identified and defined. Information is gathered that relates to the cause and scope of the problem. Constraints on the possible solution and the problem environment are investigated. In the design stage, alternative solutions to the problem are developed and explored. In addition, the feasibility and implications of these alternatives are evaluated. Finally, the choice stage involves selecting the best course of action. In this stage, the decision makers evaluate the implementation of the solution to determine whether the anticipated results were achieved and to modify the process in light of

new information learned during the implementation stage.

Decision making is a component of problem solving. In addition to the intelligence, design and choice steps of decision making, problem solving also includes implementation and monitoring. Implementation places the solution into effect. After a decision has been implemented, it is monitored and modified if needed.

Decisions can be programmed or non-programmed. Programmed decisions are made using a rule, procedure or quantitative method. Ordering more inventory when the level drops to 100 units or fewer is an example of a programmed decision. A non-programmed decision deals with unusual or exceptional situations. Determining the best training programme for a new employee is an example of a non-programmed decision.

Decisions can use optimization, satisficing or heuristic approaches. Optimization finds the best solution. Optimization problems often have an objective such as maximizing profits given production and material constraints. When a problem is too complex for optimization, satisficing is often used. Satisficing finds a good, but not necessarily the best, decision. Finally, a heuristic is a 'rule of thumb' or commonly used guideline or procedure used to find a good decision.

A management information system (MIS) must provide the right information to the right person in the right format at the right time. A management information system is an integrated collection of people, procedures, databases and devices that provides managers and decision makers with information to help achieve organizational goals. An MIS can help an organization achieve its goals by providing managers with insight into the regular operations of the organization so that they can control, organize and plan more effectively and efficiently. The primary difference between the reports generated by the TPS and those generated by the MIS is that MIS reports support managerial decision making at the higher levels of management.

Data that enters the MIS originates from both internal and external sources. The most significant internal sources of data for the MIS are the organization's various TPS and ERP systems. Data warehouses and data marts also provide important input data for the MIS. External sources of data for the MIS include extranets, customers, suppliers, competitors and stockholders.

The output of most MIS is a collection of reports that are distributed to managers. Management information systems have a number of common characteristics, including producing scheduled, demand, exception and drill-down reports; producing reports with fixed and standard formats; producing hard-copy and soft-copy reports; using internal data stored in organizational computerized databases; and having reports developed and implemented by IS personnel or end users.

Most MISs are organized along the functional lines of an organization. Typical functional management information systems include financial, manufacturing, marketing, human resources and other specialized systems. Each system is composed of inputs, processing subsystems and outputs.

Decision support systems (DSSs) support decision-making effectiveness when faced with unstructured or semi-structured business problems. DSS characteristics include the ability to handle large amounts of data; obtain and process data from different sources; provide report and presentation flexibility; support drill-down analysis;

perform complex statistical analysis; offer textual and graphical orientations; support optimization, satisficing and heuristic approaches; and perform what-if, simulation, and goal-seeking analysis.

DSSs provide support assistance through all phases of the problem-solving process. Different decision frequencies also require DSS support. An ad hoc DSS addresses unique, infrequent decision situations; an institutional DSS handles routine decisions. Highly structured problems, semi-structured problems and unstructured problems can be supported by a DSS. A DSS can also support different managerial levels, including strategic, tactical and operational managers. A common database is often the link that ties together a company's TPS, MIS and DSS.

The components of a DSS are the database, model base, user interface or dialogue manager, and a link to external databases, the Internet, the corporate intranet, extranets, networks and other systems. The database can use data warehouses and data marts. Access to other computer-based systems permits the DSS to tie into other powerful systems, including the TPS or function-specific subsystems.

Specialized support systems, such as group support systems (GSSs) and executive support systems (ESSs), use the overall approach of a DSS in situations such as group and executive decision making. A group support system (GSS) consists of most of the elements in a DSS, plus software to provide effective support in group decision-making settings. GSSs are typically easy to learn and use, and can offer specific or general decision-making support. GSS software, also called 'groupware', is specially designed to help generate lists of decision alternatives and perform data analysis. These packages let people work on joint documents and files over a network.

The frequency of GSS use and the location of the decision makers will influence the GSS alternative chosen. The decision room alternative supports users in a single location who meet infrequently. Local area networks can be used when group members are located in the same geographic area and users meet regularly. Teleconferencing is used when decision frequency is low and the location of group members is distant. A wide area network is used when the decision frequency is high and the location of group members is distant.

Executive support systems (ESSs) are specialized decision support systems designed to meet the needs of senior management. They serve to indicate issues of importance to the organization, indicate new directions the company might take and help executives monitor the company's progress. ESSs are typically easy to use, offer a wide range of computer resources, and handle a variety of internal and external data. In addition, the ESS performs sophisticated data analysis, offers a high degree of specialization, and provides flexibility and comprehensive communications abilities. An ESS also supports individual decision-making styles. Some of the major decision-making areas that can be supported through an ESS are providing an overall vision, strategic planning and organizing, strategic control and crisis management.

Self-Assessment Test

1   The last stage of the decision making process is the _____.
   a. initiation stage
   b. intelligence stage
   c. design stage
   d. choice stage

2   Problem solving is one of the stages of decision making. True or false?

3   A decision that inventory should be ordered when inventory levels drop to 500 units is an example of a(n) _____.
   a. synchronous decision
   b. asynchronous decision
   c. non-programmed decision
   d. programmed decision

4   A(n) _____ model will find the best solution, usually the one that will best help the organization meet its goals.

5   A satisficing model is one that will find a good problem solution, but not necessarily the best problem solution. True or false?

6   The focus of a decision support system is on decision-making effectiveness when faced with unstructured or semi-structured business problems. True or false?

7   What component of a decision support system allows decision makers to easily access and manipulate the DSS and to use common business terms and phrases?
   a. the knowledge base
   b. the model base
   c. the user interface or dialogue manager
   d. the expert system

8   What allows a person to give his or her input without his or her identity being known to other group members?
   a. groupthink
   b. anonymous input
   c. nominal group technique
   d. delphi

9   The local area decision network is the ideal GSS alternative for situations in which decision makers are located in the same building or geographic area and the decision makers are occasional users of the GSS approach. True or false?

10   A(n) _____ supports the actions of members of the board of directors, who are responsible to stockholders.

Review Questions

1   What is a 'satisficing model'? Describe a situation when it should be used.

2   What is the difference between a programmed decision and a non-programmed decision? Give several examples of each.

3   What are the basic kinds of reports produced by an MIS?

4   What are the functions performed by a financial MIS?

5   Describe the functions of a marketing MIS.

6 What is the difference between decision making and problem solving?

7 What is a geographic information system?

8 Describe the difference between a structured and an unstructured problem and give an example of each.

9 What is the difference between what-if analysis and goal-seeking analysis?

10 What is an executive support system? Identify three fundamental uses for such a system.

Discussion Questions

1 How can management information systems be used to support the objectives of the business organization?

2 How can a strong financial MIS provide strategic benefits to a firm?

3 You have been hired to develop a management information system and a decision support system for a manufacturing company. Describe what information you would include in printed reports and what information you would provide using a screen-based decision support system.

4 You have been hired to develop group support software. Describe the features you would include in your new GSS software.

5 The use of ESSs should not be limited to the executives of the company. Do you agree or disagree? Why?

Web Exercises

1 Use a search engine, such as Yahoo! or Google, to explore two or more companies that produce and sell MIS or DSS software. Describe what you found and any problems you had in using search engines on the Internet to find information. You might be asked to develop a report or send an email message to your instructor about what you found.

2 Use the Internet to explore two or more software packages that can be used to make group decisions easier. Summarize your findings in a report.

Case One

Decision Makers Gain Insight from BI Dashboards

Irish Life, founded in 1939, is Ireland's largest life insurer. In addition, the company also handles pensions for 200 000 Irish workers and is Ireland's largest investment manager, with over €31 billion in assets.

However, Irish Life had a problem. It collected vast amounts of data through its three major lines of business. It had business intelligence (BI) software to help analyze all this data, but that software wasn't doing the job. Paul Egan, business intelligence IT manager at Irish Life, explains that 'a lot of the tools were only IT tools and only IT people could use them, but [with those tools] we could never keep up with the appetite the business had for this'. Irish Life needed software that its business managers could use in their decision making without having to become technical specialists.

After looking at the available BI packages from its incumbent supplier and other software vendors, Irish Life sought advice from consultants at the Gartner Group. The life insurance provider then chose software from Tableau Software of Seattle, Washington, and engaged Tableau partner MXI Computing to help implement that software.

Using the Tableau software, Irish Life can represent data graphically across the organization, mapping patterns and trends more clearly than it could before the company began to use it. It will make Tableau dashboards available to about 300 users. These users will be able to build their own dashboards, to publish on the web, or distribute on mobile devices running Android or iOS software. The net result, Irish Life believes, will be improved decision making due to better availability of data and better insight into the data. The Intelligence and Design stages of decision making are especially well positioned to benefit from this insight.

For example, Irish Life recently announced the Personal Lifestyle Strategy programme for customized retirement planning within the framework of a corporate pension plan. Making the decisions that were involved in developing this programme required detailed analysis of workforce data – exactly what data visualization is suited for.

'Managers can come up with their own dashboards based on the numbers they know they need. There's less work for IT in the front end: IT now only have to worry about the data warehouse, which is where we can add value. We don't have to worry about the visuals as much,' added Egan. Insights from the BI tool have already led to Irish Life moving its management team's focus in certain cases to product lines or customer accounts that needed closer attention. 'It will make a difference in how effectively we manage the business,' Egan said.

The results that Irish Life expected to achieve are being realized. Gerry Hassett, CEO at Irish Life Retail, said, 'We can see that the return on investment is already being delivered. We can now see what is happening on a day-to-day and week-to-week basis, which means we can develop our business accordingly and further enhance our competitive edge.' He added that his dashboards 'took a few weeks to implement' and that it had been 'a seamless operation'.

Questions

1 What was the problem with the existing system?

2 How did the Tableau system help?

3 Why is flexibility in the interface important?

4 What sort of decisions can the system help managers make?

Case Two

End-User Computing, Spreadsheets and Errors

The term 'end-user computing' refers to non-programmers developing and using their own information systems. Ever since personal computers were widely adopted in businesses and the release of easy to use software such as Microsoft Excel, end-users have been developing systems for their own use. Excel and free alternatives such as OpenOffice are often used to calculate tax or perform what-if analyses, and are popular among end-users. However these systems have a big problem: they almost certainly contain errors.

Academic studies over the years have demonstrated that most corporate spreadsheets contain errors and that there is little that can be done about it. So what sorts of errors exist?

Firstly we should note that it is possible that spreadsheets contain deliberate errors. In a customer invoice it could happen that a crooked employee inputs a tax rate that overcharges a little, and in a complex order this could be very difficult for the customer to notice.

Putting deliberate mistakes aside, errors can be divided into qualitative and quantitative errors.

Qualitative errors come from poor spreadsheet design, and may not be errors at all in the first version of the spreadsheet. It may be that the errors only occur after the spreadsheet has been re-used a few times. One common qualitative error is known as `hardcoding`.

Hardcoding occurs when a value is introduced into a formula that gets copied/pasted about different cells. This means that the same value is stored multiple times in different cells. Let's say the value is a tax rate of 20 per cent. The formula might be `=F2*0.2`. This calculates 20 per cent of whatever is in cell F2. Now that formula gets copied about, and each time relative cell referencing changes the F2. Maybe somewhere the formula is now `=F23*0.2`, which gives the correct answer and all is well.

However, next year the tax rate changes to 21 per cent. To update the spreadsheet every instance of 0.2 as a tax rate needs to be changed to 0.21. But you can't just do a find and replace because that will change other values of 0.2 to 0.21 as well. It would be really easy to change `=F2*0.2` to `=F2*0.21` but accidentally leave `=F23*0.2` as it is, especially since it's been a year since the end-user designed the spreadsheet.

(To deal with hardcoding what you should do is separate the tax rate out into a cell on its own, say storing 0.2 in cell T1, and then use absolute cell referencing to refer to it. The formula above would become `=F2*$T$1`.)

The two main types of quantitative errors are logic errors and mechanical errors.

To illustrate the difference, let's say again that it's an accounting information system and we want to calculate the tax owed. A logic error happens when we enter a working formula but the formula is wrong because of a lack of knowledge about accounting rules or about mathematics. We might calculate 20 per cent tax as `=G1*20`. This formula will give an answer, but it won't be 20 per cent of whatever is in cell G1.

A mechanical error is a problem with our ability to use the software. Maybe we click on the wrong cell and enter G2 into our formula rather than G1. Maybe we type a £ when we mean to type $. Some mechanical errors are picked up immediately by the software – you will surely have seen something like this if you have used Excel or OpenOffice: 'There is an error in this formula' or 'Err559'.

The problems don't stop there. Even if an end-user has a working, error-free spreadsheet then they may still misinterpret its results. This is common when the output is a statistical result. It also can happen when the output is a chart that appears to show a trend that doesn't really exist. If a line in a chart is roughly straight, humans often perceive this as a causal relationship but in fact this rarely follows. For instance when you plot the line showing the number people who drowned each year by falling into a swimming-pool alongside the line showing the number of films Nicolas Cage appeared in each year, the two lines are almost identical. No one would suggest however that one causes the other to happen.

Questions

1 Given all of the above should end-users be banned from creating corporate spreadsheets?
2 How could a company mitigate logic errors?
3 Run a Google search for 'spreadsheet error detection software' and assess whether what you find could help.
4 How could end-user computing be improved?

Case Three

Tricked into learning CAD

Computer aided design software is used in manufacturing to help design new products. The process designers go through in product development is both extremely creative and highly technical. Using CAD software may not sound much like a game, but it can be. In 2009 Swedish software developer Markus Persson left his job at an established games development company to create his own game. Drawing inspiration from a game called Infiniminer, which made players collect resources from a randomly generated landscape, he began work on a new project called Cave Game, which would eventually evolve into Minecraft.

Minecraft allows users to create vast environments from blocks – 3-D cubes of various colours and textures – which they can share with their friends. Users have created well known landmarks and buildings, funfairs, homes, planes and boats. As we shall see, even entire countries have been re-created to scale. Cody Sumter, a graduate of the MIT Media Lab, thinks the Minecraft developers have tricked their 40 million users into learning to use a CAD program. To prove his point he has developed minecraft.print(), an attempt to bridge the structures made in Minecraft with the real world. His system outputs a standard model file which can be sent to a 3-D printer.

Minecraft has been an enormous success and is now available for numerous consoles and tablets. In 2014 the Danish Geodata Agency created a Minecraft version of the entire country of Denmark at a 1:1 scale. It's one of the biggest Minecraft creations ever, made up of about 4000 billion blocks and 1 terabyte of data. It was ingeniously built using the agency's 3-D elevation model and was meant to be used as a teaching tool. Unfortunately other players couldn't resist the temptation of blowing it up using Minecraft's TNT explosives. The Agency had disabled the use of explosives, but they forgot to disable an alternative form of TNT, the 'minecart with dynamite' item. 'We consider that as a nature of playing Minecraft – elements are broken down and new (space) ones are

being created,' Danish Geodata Agency spokesman Chris Hammeken told online publication The Register. 'Therefore we will not reboot the demonstration of Denmark in Minecraft. But occasionally we will rebuild minor areas if buildings are removed and nothing new is being created.'

The popularity of Minecraft has opened up all sorts of opportunities. British barman Joseph Garrett gave up his job when the videos he uploaded to YouTube of himself exploring Minecraft became more popular than the videos of Katy Perry, One Direction and Justin Bieber. Fans of Garrett, typically aged between 6 and 14, know him better as Stampy Longnose. Garrett said he decided to leave his job when he started earning the same amount in YouTube advertising revenue as he was in his day job. The same week this case was written, Microsoft bought Minecraft for over two billions euros.

Questions

1 Is Minecraft a game or something else?
2 How could Minecraft be used in education?
3 Discuss the actions of the 'griefers' who attacked the virtual Denmark. Were they playing, bullying, protesting or doing something else?
4 What serious applications, if any, can you think of for minecraft.print()?

Notes

1 Lacroix, Yvan, et al., 'Bombardier Flexjet Significantly Improves Its Fractional Aircraft Ownership Operations', *Interfaces*, January–February, 2005, p. 49.
2 Murty, Katta, et al., 'Hongkong International Terminals Gains Elastic Capacity', *Interfaces*, January–February, 2005, p. 61.
3 Troyer, Loren, et al., 'Improving Asset Management and Order Fulfillment at Deere', *Interfaces*, January–February, 2005, p. 76.
4 Tieto Website. Available from: www.tieto.com. Accessed 5 June 2011.
5 Kapoor, S., et al., 'A Technical Framework for Sense-and-Respond Business Management', *IBM Systems Journal*, Vol. 44, 2005, p. 5.
6 Port, Otis, 'Desktop Factories', *Business Week*, 2 May 2005, p. 22.
7 Wysocki, Bernard, et al., 'Just-In-Time Inventories Make US Vulnerable in a Pandemic', *The Wall Street Journal*, 12 January 2006, p. A1.
8 Richmond, Rita, 'Blogs Keep Internet Customers Coming Back', *The Wall Street Journal*, 1 March 2005, p. B8.
9 Peart, Mark, 'Service Excellence & CRM', *New Zealand Management*, May 2005, p. 68.
10 Forelle, Charles, 'IBM Tool Deploys Employees Efficiently', *The Wall Street Journal*, 14 July 2005, p. B3.
11 Anthes, Gary, 'Beyond Zip Codes', *Computerworld,* 19 September 2005, p. 56.
12 Sabuncuoglu, Ihsan, et al., 'The Turkish Army Uses Simulation to Model and Optimize Its Fuel-Supply System', *Interfaces*, November–December, 2005, p. 474.

[13] Havenstein, Heather, 'Celtics Turn to Data Analytics Tools for Help Pricing Tickets', *Computerworld*, 9 January 2006, p. 43.

[14] Havenstein, Heather, 'Business Intelligence Tools Help Nonprofit Group Make Loans to Tsunami Victims', *Computerworld*, 14 March 2005, p. 19.

[15] Rubenstein, Sarah, 'Next Step Toward Digitized Health Records', *The Wall Street Journal*, 9 May 2005, p. B1.

[16] Bhattacharya, K., et al., 'A Model-Driven Approach to Industrializing Discovery Processes in Pharmaceutical Research', *IBM Systems Journal*, Vol. 44, No. 1, 2005, p. 145.

[17] Anthes, Gary, 'Modelling Magic', *Computerworld*, 7 February 2005, p. 26.

[18] Port, Otis, 'Simple Solutions', *Business Week*, 3 October 2005, p. 24.

[19] Mitchell, Robert, 'Anticipation Game', *Computerworld*, 13 June 2005, p. 23.

[20] Aston, Adam, 'The Worst Isn't Over', *Business Week*, 16 January 2006, p. 29.

[21] Babcock, Charles, 'A New Model for Disasters', *Information Week*, 10 October 2005, p. 47.

[22] Majchrak, Ann, et al., 'Perceived Individual Collaboration Know-How Development Through Information Technology-Enabled Contextualization', *Information Systems Research*, March 2005, p. 9.

8

09

Knowledge Management and Specialized Information Systems

Principles

Knowledge management systems allow organizations to share knowledge and experience among their managers and employees.

Artificial intelligence systems form a broad and diverse set of systems that can replicate human decision making for certain types of well-defined problems.

Expert systems can enable a novice to perform at the level of an expert but must be developed and maintained very carefully.

Virtual reality systems can reshape the interface between people and information technology by offering new ways to communicate information, visualize processes and express ideas creatively.

Learning Objectives

- Describe the role of the chief knowledge officer (CKO).
- List some of the tools and techniques used in knowledge management.

- Define the term 'artificial intelligence' and state the objective of developing artificial intelligence systems.
- List the characteristics of intelligent behaviour and compare the performance of natural and artificial intelligence systems for each of these characteristics.
- Identify the major components of the artificial intelligence field and provide one example of each type of system.

- List the characteristics and basic components of expert systems.
- Identify at least three factors to consider in evaluating the development of an expert system.
- Outline and briefly explain the steps for developing an expert system.
- Identify the benefits associated with the use of expert systems.

- Define the term 'virtual reality' and provide three examples of virtual reality applications.
- Discuss examples of specialized systems for organizational and individual use.

Why Learn About Knowledge Management and Specialized Information Systems?

Knowledge management systems are used in almost every industry. If you are a manager, you might use a knowledge management system to support decisive action to help you correct a problem. If you are a production manager at a car company, you might oversee robots, a specialized information system, that attach windscreens to cars or paint body panels. As a young stock trader, you might use a system called a neural network to uncover patterns and make money trading stocks and stock options. As a marketing manager for a PC manufacturer, you might use virtual reality on a website to show customers your latest laptop and desktop computers. If you are in the military, you might use computer simulation as a training tool to prepare you for combat. In a petroleum company, you might use an expert system to determine where to drill for oil and gas. You will see many additional examples of using these information systems throughout this chapter. Learning about these systems will help you discover new ways to use information systems in your day-to-day work.

9.1 Knowledge Management Systems

Defining knowledge is difficult. One definition is that knowledge is the awareness and understanding of a set of information and the ways that information can be made useful to support a specific task or reach a decision. Knowing the procedures for ordering more inventory to avoid running out is an example of knowledge. In a sense, information tells you what has to be done (low inventory levels for some items), while knowledge tells you how to do it (make two important phone calls to the right people to get the needed inventory shipped overnight). A knowledge management system (KMS) is an organized collection of people, procedures, software, databases and devices used to create, store, share and use the organization's knowledge and experience.[1]

Overview of Knowledge Management Systems

Like the other systems discussed throughout this book, knowledge management systems attempt to help organizations achieve their goals. For businesses, this usually means increasing profits or reducing costs. For non-profit organizations, it can mean providing better customer service or providing special needs to people and groups. Many types of firms use KMSs to increase profits or reduce costs. According to a survey of CEOs, firms that use a KMS are more likely to innovate and perform better.[2]

A KMS stores and processes knowledge. This can involve different types of knowledge. Explicit knowledge is objective and can be measured and documented in reports, papers and rules. For example, knowing the best road to take to minimize drive time from home to the office when a major motorway is closed due to an accident is explicit knowledge. It can be documented in a report or a rule, as in 'If the A453 is closed, take the M1 to junction 25 and from there to the office'. Tacit knowledge, on the other hand, is hard to measure and document and typically is not objective or formalized. Knowing the best way to negotiate with a foreign government about nuclear disarmament or deal with a volatile hostage situation often requires a lifetime of experience and a high level of skill. These are examples of tacit knowledge. It is difficult to write a detailed report or a set of rules that would always work in every hostage situation. Many organizations actively attempt to convert tacit knowledge to explicit knowledge to make the knowledge easier to measure, document and share with others.

In a well-known *Harvard Business Review* paper called 'The Knowledge Creating Company' (from the November–December, 1991 issue), Ikujiro Nonaka describes four ways in which knowledge can be created.

1 When an individual learns directly from another individual, in an apprentice type relationship, tacit knowledge is created from tacit knowledge.

2 When two pieces of explicit knowledge are combined. For example, a website mash-up could be considered an example of this type of new knowledge. (Mash-ups were described in Chapter 6 as the combining of information from two or more web pages onto one web page.)

3 When an expert writes a book teaching others, explicit knowledge is being created from tacit knowledge.

4 When someone reads that book and (eventually) becomes an expert themselves, tacit knowledge has been created by explicit knowledge.

A diverse set of technologies can help capture, create and share knowledge. Expert systems (this chapter) can be used to share explicit knowledge. Blogs (Chapter 10) can be used to share tacit knowledge. Data mining algorithms (Chapter 5) can be used to discover new knowledge.

Obtaining, Storing, Sharing and Using Knowledge

Knowledge workers are people who create, use and disseminate knowledge. They are usually professionals in science, engineering or business, and belong to professional organizations. Other examples of knowledge workers include writers, researchers, educators and corporate designers. The **chief knowledge officer (CKO)** is a top-level executive who helps the organization work with a KMS to create, store and use knowledge to achieve organizational goals. The CKO is responsible for the organization's KMS, and typically works with other executives and directors, including the managing director, finance director and others. Obtaining, storing, sharing and using knowledge is the key to any KMS.[3] Using a KMS often leads to additional knowledge creation, storage, sharing and usage. A meteorologist, for example, might develop sophisticated mathematical models to predict the path and intensity of hurricanes. Business professors often conduct research in marketing strategies, management practices, corporate and individual investments and finance, effective accounting and auditing practices, and much more. Drug companies and medical researchers invest billions of pounds in creating knowledge on cures for diseases. Although knowledge workers can act alone, they often work in teams to create or obtain knowledge.

chief knowledge officer (CKO)
A top-level executive who helps the organization use a KMS to create, store and use knowledge to achieve organizational goals.

After knowledge is created, it is often stored in a 'knowledge repository'. The knowledge repository can be located both inside and outside the organization. Some types of software can store and share knowledge contained in documents and reports. Adobe Acrobat PDF files, for example, allow you to store corporate reports, tax returns and other documents, and send them to others over the Internet. You can use hardware devices and software to store and share audio and video material.[4] Traditional databases and data warehouses, discussed in Chapter 5, are often used to store the organization's knowledge. Specialized knowledge bases in expert systems, discussed later in the chapter, can also be used.

Because knowledge workers often work in groups or teams, they can use collaborative work software and group support systems to share knowledge. Intranets and password-protected Internet sites also provide ways to share knowledge. The social services department of Surrey Council in the UK, for example, use an intranet to help it create and manipulate knowledge.[5] Because knowledge can be critical in maintaining a competitive advantage, businesses should be careful in how they share it. Although they want important decision makers inside and outside the organization to have complete and easy access to knowledge, they also need to protect knowledge from competitors and others who shouldn't see it. As a result, many businesses use patents, copyrights, trade secrets, Internet firewalls and other measures to keep prying eyes from seeing important knowledge that is often expensive and hard to create.

In addition to using information systems and collaborative software tools to share knowledge, some organizations use non-technical approaches. These include corporate retreats and gatherings, sporting events, informal knowledge worker lounges or meeting places, kitchen facilities, day-care centres and comfortable workout centres.

Using a knowledge management system begins with locating the organization's knowledge. This is often done using a knowledge map or directory that points the knowledge worker to the needed knowledge. Drug companies have sophisticated knowledge maps that include database and file systems to allow scientists and drug researchers to locate previous medical studies. Lawyers can use powerful online knowledge maps, such as the legal section of Lexis-Nexis, to research legal opinions and the outcomes of previous cases. Medical researchers, university professors and even textbook authors use Lexis-Nexis to locate important knowledge. Organizations often use the Internet or corporate web portals to help their knowledge workers find knowledge stored in documents and reports. The following are examples of profit and non-profit organizations that use knowledge and knowledge management systems.

China Netcom Corporation uses KM software from Autonomy Corporation to search the records of up to 100 million telecommunications customers and create knowledge about its customers and marketing operations.[6]

Feilden, Clegg, Bradley, and Aedas, an architectural firm, uses KM to share best practices among its architects.[7] According to one designer, 'Knowledge management was one of those ideas that sprang up in the 1990s, along with fads such as total quality management and the concept of the learning organization. But knowledge management (KM) appears to have had staying power, and it is still firmly on the business agenda.'

Munich Re Group, a German insurance organization, uses KM to share best practices and knowledge.[8] 'It was always important to us that knowledge management isn't just an IT platform,' said Karen Edwards, knowledge management consultant in Munich Re's Knowledge Management Centre of Competence in Munich, Germany. 'The Munich Re people, they really were the assets. They're the things you try to bring together.'

Technology to Support Knowledge Management

KMSs use a number of tools discussed throughout this book. In Chapter 2, for example, we explored the importance of organizational learning and organizational change. An effective KMS is based on learning new knowledge and changing procedures and approaches as a result.[9] A manufacturing company, for example, might learn new ways to program robots on the factory floor to improve accuracy and reduce defective parts. The new knowledge will likely cause the manufacturing company to change how it programs and uses its robots. In Chapter 5 on database systems, we investigated the use of data mining and business intelligence. These powerful tools can be important in capturing and using knowledge. Enterprise resource planning tools, such as SAP, include knowledge management features.[10] We have also seen how groupware could improve group decision making and collaboration. Groupware can also be used to help capture, store and use knowledge. In the next chapter, we will examine more technology that could be used to share knowledge. Lastly, of course, hardware, software, databases, telecommunications and the Internet, discussed in Part 2, are important technologies used to support KMSs.

Hundreds of companies provide specific KM products and services.[11] In addition, researchers at colleges and universities have developed tools and technologies to support knowledge management.[12] Companies such as IBM have many knowledge management tools in a variety of products, including Lotus Notes and Domino.[13] Lotus Notes is a collection of software products that help people work together to create, share and store important knowledge and business documents. Its knowledge management features include domain search, content mapping and Lotus Sametime. Domain search allows people to perform sophisticated searches for knowledge in Domino databases using a single simple query. Content mapping organizes knowledge by categories, like a table of contents for a book. Lotus Sametime helps people communicate, collaborate and share ideas in real time. Lotus Domino Document Manager, formerly called Lotus Domino, helps people and organizations store, organize and retrieve documents.[14] The software can be used to write, review, archive and publish documents throughout the organization. Morphy Richards, a leading supplier of small home appliances in the UK, uses Domino for email, collaboration and document management.[15] According to one executive, 'Rather than relying on groups of employees emailing each other, we are putting in place a business application through which documents will formally flow – to improve the efficiency of the supply chain and create more transparent working practices.'

Microsoft offers a number of knowledge management tools, including Digital Dashboard, based on the Microsoft Office suite.[16] Digital Dashboard integrates information from different sources, including personal, group, enterprise and external information and documents. 'Microsoft has revolutionized the way that people use technology to create and share information. The company is the clear winner in the knowledge management business,' according to Rory Chase, managing director of Teleos, an independent knowledge management research company based in the UK. Other tools from Microsoft include Web Store Technology, which uses wireless technology to deliver knowledge to any location at any time; Access Workflow Designer, which helps database developers create effective systems to process transactions and keep work flowing through the organization; and related products.

In addition to these tools, several artificial intelligence, discussed next, can be used in a KMS.

9.2 Artificial Intelligence

At a Dartmouth College conference in 1956, John McCarthy proposed the use of the term artificial intelligence (AI) to describe computers with the ability to mimic or duplicate the functions of the human brain. Advances in AI have since led to systems that recognize complex patterns.[17] Many AI pioneers attended this first conference; a few predicted that computers would be as 'smart' as people by the 1960s. This prediction has not yet been realized and there is a debate about whether it actually ever could be; however, the benefits of AI in business and research can be seen today, and the research continues.

Artificial intelligence systems include the people, procedures, hardware, software, data and knowledge needed to develop computer systems and machines that demonstrate characteristics of intelligence. Researchers, scientists and experts on how human beings think are often involved in developing these systems.

artificial intelligence systems People, procedures, hardware, software, data and knowledge needed to develop computer systems and machines that demonstrate characteristics of intelligence.

The Nature of Intelligence

From the early AI pioneering stage, the research emphasis has been on developing machines with **intelligent behaviour**. Machine intelligence, however, is hard to achieve. Some of the specific characteristics of intelligent behaviour include the ability to do the following:

■ *Learn from experience and apply the knowledge acquired from experience.* Learning from past situations and events is a key component of

intelligent behaviour The ability to learn from experiences and apply knowledge acquired from experience, handle complex situations, solve problems when important information is missing, determine what is important, react quickly and correctly to a new situation, understand visual images, process and manipulate symbols, be creative and imaginative, and use heuristics.

intelligent behaviour and is a natural ability of humans, who learn by trial and error. This ability, however, must be carefully programmed into a computer system. Today, researchers are developing systems that can learn from experience. For instance, computerized AI chess software can learn to improve while playing human competitors. In one match, Garry Kasparov competed against a personal computer with AI software developed in Israel, called Deep Junior. This match was a 3–3 tie, but Kasparov picked up something the machine would have no interest in – €500 000. The 20 questions (20Q) website, www.20q.net, is another example of a system that learns.[18] The website is an artificial intelligence game that learns as people play.

■ *Handle complex situations.* People are often involved in complex situations. World leaders face difficult political decisions regarding terrorism, conflict, global economic conditions, hunger and poverty. In a business setting, top-level managers and executives must handle a complex market, challenging competitors, intricate government regulations and a demanding workforce. Even human experts make mistakes in dealing with these situations. Developing computer systems that can handle perplexing situations requires careful planning and elaborate computer programming.

■ *Solve problems when important information is missing.* The essence of decision making is dealing with uncertainty. Often, decisions must be made with too little information or inaccurate information because obtaining complete information is too costly or even impossible. Today, AI systems can make important calculations, comparisons and decisions even when information is missing.

■ *Determine what is important.* Knowing what is truly important is the mark of a good decision maker. Developing programs and approaches to allow computer systems and machines to identify important information is not a simple task.

■ *React quickly and correctly to a new situation.* A small child, for example, can look over a ledge or a drop-off and know not to venture too close. The child reacts quickly and correctly to a new situation. Computers, on the other hand, do not have this ability without complex programming.

■ *Understand visual images.* Interpreting visual images can be extremely difficult, even for sophisticated computers. Moving through a room of chairs, tables and other objects can be trivial for people but extremely complex for machines, robots and computers. Such machines require an extension of understanding visual images, called a **perceptive system**. Having a perceptive system allows a machine to approximate the way a person sees, hears and feels objects. Military robots, for example, use cameras and perceptive systems to conduct reconnaissance missions to detect enemy weapons and soldiers. Detecting and destroying them can save lives.

perceptive system A system that approximates the way a person sees, hears, and feels objects.

■ *Process and manipulate symbols.* People see, manipulate and process symbols every day. Visual images provide a constant stream of information to our brains. By contrast, computers have difficulty handling symbolic processing and reasoning. Although computers excel at numerical calculations, they aren't as good at dealing with symbols and 3-D objects. Recent developments in machine-vision hardware and software, however, allow some computers to process and manipulate symbols on a limited basis.

■ *Be creative and imaginative.* Throughout history, people have turned difficult situations into advantages by being creative and imaginative. For instance, when defective mints with holes in the middle were shipped, an enterprising entrepreneur decided to market these new mints as 'LifeSavers' instead of returning them to the manufacturer. Ice-cream cones were invented at the St Louis World's Fair when an imaginative store owner decided to wrap ice cream with a waffle from his grill for portability. Developing new and exciting products and services from an existing (perhaps negative) situation is a human characteristic. Computers cannot be imaginative or creative in this way, although software has been developed to enable a computer to write short stories.

■ *Use heuristics.* For some decisions, people use heuristics (rules of thumb arising from experience) or even guesses. In searching for a job, you might rank the companies you are considering according to profits per employee. Today, some computer systems, given the right programs, obtain good solutions that use approximations instead of trying to search for an optimal solution, which would be technically difficult or too time consuming.

This list of traits only partially defines intelligence. Unlike the terminology used in virtually every other field of IS research, in which the objectives can be clearly defined, the term 'intelligence' is a formidable stumbling block. One of the problems in AI is arriving at a working definition of real intelligence against which to compare the performance of an AI system.

The Difference Between Natural and Artificial Intelligence

Since the term 'artificial intelligence' was defined in the 1950s, experts have disagreed about the difference between natural and artificial intelligence. Can computers be programmed to have common sense? Profound differences separate natural from artificial intelligence, but they are declining in number (see Table 9.1). One of the driving forces behind AI research is an attempt to understand how people actually reason and think. Creating machines that can reason is possible only when we truly understand our own processes for doing so.

Table 9.1 A Comparison of Natural and Artificial Intelligence

Ability to	Natural Intelligence (Human)		Artificial Intelligence (Machine)	
	Low	High	Low	High
Use sensors (see hear, touch, smell)		√	√	
Be creative and imaginative		√	√	
Learn from experience		√	√	
Adapt to new situations		√	√	
Afford the cost of acquiring intelligence		√	√	
Acquire a large amount of external information		√		√
Use a variety of information sources		√		√
Make complex calculations	√			√
Transfer information	√			√
Make a series of calculations rapidly and accurately	√			√

9

Information Systems @ Work

Computer Game Captures the Knowledge of the Crowd

Crowdsourcing involves using information technology to access a large number of people who then work on a problem together. It has been used in a number of applications including classifying images to allow them to be found using Internet search engines, and in the search for extraterrestrial intelligence. But could crowdsourcing be used on more difficult, technically challenging problems?

Inside the cells in your body, proteins are at work helping you break down your food to give you energy, sending signals to your brain to control all your body functions, and transporting nutrients through your blood. Proteins are chains of amino acids, but they don't exist as a stretched out line. Instead they fold up into a compact blob, but it's a blob with a complex structure. For instance a protein will keep some of its amino acids at its centre and push others to its edges. This structure specifies the function of the protein. Therefore knowing the structure of a protein is key to both understanding how it works and to targeting it with drugs. A small protein can consist of 100 amino acids, while some human proteins can have many more (1000+ amino acids). The number of different ways even a small protein can fold is astronomical – just think of how many different patterns you can form by randomly scrunching up a piece of string. Figuring out which of the many possible structures is the best one is seen as one of the most difficult problems in biology today. Human beings are very good at spatial problem solving so could this creative power be harnessed through crowdsourcing and, if so, how? It turns out, the answer to the first question is yes, and one answer to the second is to turn folding into a computer game.

Foldit is an online puzzle game from the University of Washington which scores players' attempts to turn an amino-acid chain into a 'structured blob'. The best scoring blobs are then analyzed by

scientists to determine if the suggested structure is the one a real protein actually has. This knowledge can lead to new insights for the design of antiretroviral drugs. The structures suggested by players can also lead to the design of brand new proteins that could be created and used to prevent diseases.

The game has been a big success. Three years after it was launched, players solved a major scientific problem by modelling the crystal structure of something called 'M-PMV retroviral protease', a monkey virus that causes AIDS. The software developers and scientists said in their write-up that 'the critical role of Foldit players in the solution of the M-PMV PR structure shows the power of online games to channel human intuition and three-dimensional pattern-matching skills to solve challenging scientific problems'. They went on to suggest that their 'results indicate the potential for integrating video games into the real-world scientific process: the ingenuity of game players is a formidable force that, if properly directed, can be used to solve a wide range of scientific problems'. If you want to join in you can visit the foldit website, http://fold.it.

Questions

1 Why couldn't a computer just be programmed to fold proteins which are scored in the same way as the players' folds are?

2 Why do you think people play this game? What do they get out of it? What do people get out of playing normal computer games? Compare your answers to these last two questions.

3 How else could computer games be used in a serious way (hint: run an Internet search for 'serious games')?

4 Can you think of other problems that could be solved in a similar way?

9

The Major Branches of Artificial Intelligence

AI is a broad field that includes several specialty areas, such as expert systems, robotics, vision systems, natural language processing, learning systems and neural networks. Many of these areas are related; advances in one can occur simultaneously with or result in advances in others.

Expert Systems

An **expert system** consists of hardware and software that stores knowledge and makes inferences, similar to those of a human expert. Because of their many business applications, expert systems are discussed in more detail in their own section later in this chapter.

expert system Hardware and software that stores knowledge and makes inferences, similar to a human expert.

Robotics

Robotics involves developing mechanical or computer devices that can paint cars, make precision welds, and perform other tasks that require a high degree of precision or that are tedious or hazardous for human beings. Some robots are mechanical devices that don't use the AI features discussed in this chapter. Others are sophisticated systems that use one or more AI features or characteristics, such as the vision systems, learning systems or neural networks, discussed later in the chapter. For many businesses, robots are used to do the 'three Ds' – dull, dirty and dangerous jobs.[19] Manufacturers use robots to assemble and paint products. The NASA shuttle crash of the early 2000s, for example, has led some people to recommend using robots instead of people to explore space and perform scientific research (see Figure 9.1). Some robots, such as Sony's Aibo, can be used for companionship. Contemporary robotics combine both high-precision machine capabilities and sophisticated controlling software. The controlling software in robots is what is most important in terms of AI.

robotics Mechanical or computer devices that perform tasks requiring a high degree of precision or that are tedious or hazardous for humans.

The field of robotics has many applications, and research into these unique devices continues. The following are a few examples:

- IRobot is a company that builds a number of robots, including the Roomba Floorvac for cleaning floors and the PackBot, an unmanned vehicle used to assist and protect soldiers.[20] Manufacturers use robots to assemble and paint products.

- The Porter Adventist Hospital in Denver, Colorado, uses a €67 959 Da Vinci Surgical System to perform surgery on prostate cancer patients.[21] The robot has multiple arms that hold surgical tools. According to one doctor at Porter, 'The biggest advantage is it improves recovery time. Instead of having an eight-inch incision, the patient has a "band-aid" incision. It's much quicker.'

- DARPA (the Defence Advanced Research Project Agency) sponsors the DARPA Grand Challenge, a 212 km (132 mile) race over rugged terrain for computer-controlled cars.[22]

- Because of an age limit on camel jockeys, the state of Qatar decided to use robots in its camel races.[23] Developed in Switzerland, the robots have a human shape and only weigh 27 kg (59 lb). The robots use global positioning systems (GPS), a microphone to deliver voice commands to the camel and cameras. A camel trainer uses a joystick to control the robot's movements on the camel. Camel racing is very popular in Qatar.

- In military applications, robots are becoming real weapons. The US Air Force is developing a smart robotic jet fighter. Often called 'unmanned combat air vehicles' (UCAVs), these robotic war machines, such as the X-45A, will be able to identify and destroy targets without human pilots. UCAVs send pictures and information to a central command centre and can be directed to strike military targets. These new machines extend the current Predator and Global Hawk technologies the military used in Afghanistan after the September 11, 2001 terrorist attacks.

9

Figure 9.1 Robots in Space *Robots can be used in situations that are hazardous or inaccessible to humans. This is an artists impression of the European Space Agency's ExoMars Rover. Due to be launched in 2018, the rover will be able to navigate and drive autonomously across the surface of Mars.*

Although robots are essential components of today's automated manufacturing and military systems, future robots will find wider applications in banks, restaurants, homes, doctors' offices and hazardous working environments such as nuclear stations. The Repliee Q1 and Q2 robots from Japan are ultra-humanlike robots or androids that can blink, gesture, speak and even appear to breathe.[24] Microrobotics is a developing area. Also called micro-electro-mechanical systems (MEMSs), microrobots are the size of a grain of salt and can be used in a person's blood to monitor the body, and for other purposes in air bags, mobile phones, refrigerators and more.

If you would like to try to make a robot, LEGO Mindstorms is a good place to start (Figure 9.2).

Figure 9.2 Lego Mindstorms *This LEGO kit contains a programmable brick, motors and sensors so that users can build their own robots. The robot can be programmed in a range of languages, including Java and Visual Basic, as well as LEGO's own easy to use graphical environment.*

Vision Systems

Another area of AI involves **vision systems**. Vision systems include hardware and software that permit computers to capture, store and manipulate visual images.

For example, vision systems can be used with robots to give these machines 'sight'. Factory robots typically perform mechanical tasks with no visual stimuli. Robotic vision extends the capability of these systems, allowing the robot to make decisions based on visual input. Generally, robots with vision systems can recognize black and white and some grey shades but do not have good colour or 3-D vision. Other systems concentrate on only a few key features in an image, ignoring the rest. Another potential application of a vision system is fingerprint analysis.

Even with recent breakthroughs in vision systems, computers cannot see and understand visual images the way people can.

vision systems The hardware and software that permit computers to capture, store and manipulate visual images.

Natural Language Processing and Voice Recognition

As discussed in Chapter 4, **natural language processing** allows a computer to understand and react to statements and commands made in a 'natural' language, such as English. In some cases, voice recognition is used with natural language processing. Voice recognition involves converting sound waves into words. Dragon Systems' Naturally Speaking uses continuous voice recognition, or natural speech, allowing the user to input data into the computer by speaking at a normal pace without pausing between words. The spoken words are transcribed immediately onto the computer screen. After converting sounds into words, natural language processing systems can be used to react to the words or commands by performing a variety of tasks. Brokerage services are a perfect fit for voice-recognition and natural language processing technology to replace the existing 'press 1 to buy or sell shares' touchpad telephone menu system. People buying and selling use a vocabulary too varied for easy access through menus and touchpads, but still small enough for software to process in real time. Several brokerages – including Charles Schwab & Company, Fidelity Investments, DLJdirect, and TD Waterhouse Group – offer these services. These systems use voice recognition and natural language processing to let customers access retirement accounts, check balances and find stock quotes. Eventually, the technology may allow people to make transactions using voice commands over the phone and to use search engines to have their questions answered through the brokerage firm's call centre. One of the big advantages is that the number of calls routed to the customer service department drops considerably after new voice features are added. That is desirable to brokerages because it helps them staff their call centres correctly – even in volatile markets. Whereas a typical person uses a vocabulary of about 20 000 words or less, voice-recognition software can have a built-in vocabulary of 85 000 words. Some companies claim that voice-recognition and natural language processing software is so good that customers forget they are talking to a computer and start discussing the weather or sports results.

natural language processing Processing that allows the computer to understand and react to statements and commands made in a 'natural' language, such as English.

Learning Systems

Another part of AI deals with **learning systems**, a combination of software and hardware that allows a computer to change how it functions or reacts to situations based on feedback it receives. For example, some computerized games have learning abilities. If the computer does not win a game, it remembers not to make the same moves under the same conditions again. Tom Mitchell, director of the Center for Automated Learning and Discovery at Carnegie Mellon University, is experimenting with two learning software packages that help each other learn.[25] He believes that two learning software packages that cooperate are better than separate learning packages. Mitchell's learning software helps Internet search engines do a better job in finding information. Learning systems software requires feedback on the results of actions or decisions. At a minimum, the feedback needs to indicate whether the results are desirable (winning a game) or undesirable (losing a game). The feedback is then used to alter what the system will do in the future.

learning systems A combination of software and hardware that allows the computer to change how it functions or reacts to situations based on feedback it receives.

Neural Networks

neural network A computer system that attempts to simulate the functioning of a human brain.

An increasingly important aspect of AI involves **neural networks**, also called 'neural nets'. A neural network is a computer system that can act like or simulate the functioning of a human brain. The systems use massively parallel processors in an architecture that is based on the human brain's own mesh-like structure. In addition, neural network software simulates a neural network using standard computers. Neural networks can process many pieces of data at the same time and learn to recognize patterns. Some of the specific abilities of neural networks include discovering relationships and trends in large databases, and solving complex problems for which all the information is not present.

A particular skill of neural nets is analyzing detailed trends. Large amusement parks and banks use neural networks to determine staffing needs based on customer traffic – a task that requires precise analysis, down to the half-hour. Increasingly, businesses are using neural nets to help them navigate ever-thicker forests of data and make sense of a myriad of customer traits and buying habits. One application, for example, would be to track the habits of insurance customers and predict which ones will not renew a policy. Staff could then suggest to an insurance agent what changes to make in the policy to persuade the consumer to renew it. Some pattern-recognition software uses neural networks to analyze hundreds of millions of bank, brokerage and insurance accounts involving a trillion dollars to uncover money laundering and other suspicious money transfers.

Other Artificial Intelligence Applications

genetic algorithm An approach to solving large, complex problems in which a number of related operations or models change and evolve until the best one emerges.

A few other artificial intelligence applications exist in addition to those just discussed. A **genetic algorithm**, also called a genetic program, is an approach to solving large, complex problems in which many repeated operations or models change and evolve until the best one emerges. The first step is to change or vary competing solutions to the problem. This can be done by changing the parts of a program or by combining different program segments into a new program. The second step is to select only the best models or algorithms, which continue to evolve. Programs or program segments that are not as good as others are discarded, similar to natural selection or 'survival of the fittest', in which only the best species survive. This process of variation and natural selection continues until the genetic algorithm yields the best possible solution to the original problem. For example, some investment firms use genetic algorithms to help select the best stocks or bonds. Genetic algorithms are also used in computer science and mathematics. Genetic algorithms can help companies determine which orders to accept for maximum profit. This approach helps companies select the orders that will increase profits and take full advantage of the company's production facilities. Genetic algorithms are also being used to make better decisions in developing inputs to neural networks.

intelligent agent Programs and a knowledge base used to perform a specific task for a person, a process or another program; also called intelligent robot or bot.

An **intelligent agent** (also called an 'intelligent robot' or 'bot') consists of programs and a knowledge base used to perform a specific task for a person, a process, or another program. Like a sports agent who searches for the best sponsorship deals for a top athlete, an intelligent agent often searches to find the best price, schedule or solution to a problem. The programs used by an intelligent agent can search large amounts of data as the knowledge base refines the search or accommodates user preferences. Often used to search the vast resources of the Internet, intelligent agents can help people find information on an important topic or the best price for a new digital camera. Intelligent agents can also be used to make travel arrangements, monitor incoming email for viruses or junk mail, and coordinate meetings and schedules of busy executives. In the human resources field, intelligent agents help with online training. The software can look ahead in training materials and know what to start next.

Ethical and Societal Issues

A Match Made Online

Online dating is big business and today many specialist websites serve a range of niches including those looking for a partner in uniform, those of a certain age and those with certain religious beliefs. Two of the most famous sites are still Match.com and eHarmony. eHarmony has always tried to differentiate itself by using a 'scientific approach' to matching users. Greg Waldorf, eHarmony's chief executive says, 'at the time that we launched in 2000, people were really sceptical that you could bring technology or scientific research to something that had always been attributed in these magical terms to some unknowable quality about why two people connect'. They certainly have plenty of success stories on the web, as well as their fair share of complaints.

The eHarmony Compatibility Matching System is an expert system that has been programmed with co-founder Dr Neil Clark Warren's knowledge about what makes a good relationship. Its goal is to match partners for successful relationships using 29 key dimensions that help predict compatibility and the potential for relationship success. The 29 key dimensions are organized into two general categories: 'core traits' that include emotional temperament, social style, cognitive mode and physicality; and 'vital attributes' that include relationship skills, values and beliefs, and key experiences. An eHarmony applicant fills out a 436-item relationship questionnaire that allows the expert system to categorize that person's personality and build a compatibility profile. Heuristics are used to search the eHarmony database for compatible partners whose personality attributes make a good match according to Dr Warren's studies. An ordered list of potential partners is produced with the best candidates listed first. The service then provides methods to get in touch with prospective mates.

eHarmony uses artificial intelligence throughout its organization. Technology from SPSS, Inc., is used in various areas of the eHarmony business, including scientific research, brand development, product research, compatibility models, customer satisfaction and retention, and projective analysis. Artificial intelligence can be used to make predictions about the future based on historical data and to predict outcomes of events. eHarmony think it can be used to predict who someone will fall in love with.

eHarmony's senior director of research and product development is Steve Carter, a strong believer in AI for business. The numerous analytic and data management tools provided by the SPSS systems enable eHarmony to understand important information in more novel, forward-thinking ways. eHarmony is a prime example of how artificial intelligence and expert system tools are taking a lot of the guesswork out of life.

Something certainly seems to be working. Scientists who study social habits have found that the Internet may be altering the dynamics and outcomes of dating and marriage. Marriages that begin online, when compared with those that begin through traditional off-line venues, were slightly less likely to result in break-up, and are associated with slightly higher marital satisfaction.

Questions

1 What role does artificial intelligence play in the matchmaking process at eHarmony?

2 How does eHarmony use prediction in all of its business units?

3 Do you think the scientific methods provided by eHarmony are superior or inferior to traditional random chance encounters for finding a partner? Why?

4 What dangers to privacy and safety, if any, are involved in using a service like eHarmony?

9.3 Expert Systems

An expert system outputs a recommendation based on answers given to it by users (who are not experts in the field). The intention of the system is to capture the expert's knowledge and make it available to those who lack this knowledge. Expert systems have been developed to diagnose medical conditions, resolve engineering problems and solve energy problems. They have also been used to design new products and systems, develop innovative insurance products, determine the best use of timber and increase the quality of healthcare. Like human experts, expert systems use heuristics, or rules of thumb, to arrive at conclusions or make suggestions. The research conducted in AI during the past two decades is resulting in expert systems that explore new business possibilities, increase overall profitability, reduce costs, and provide superior service to customers and clients.

When to Use Expert Systems

Sophisticated expert systems can be difficult, expensive and time consuming to develop. The following is a list of factors that normally make expert systems worth the expenditure of time and money. Develop an expert system if it can do any of the following:

- Provide a high potential payoff or significantly reduce downside risk.
- Capture and preserve irreplaceable human expertise.
- Solve a problem that is not easily solved using traditional programming techniques.
- Develop a system which is more consistent than human experts.
- Provide expertise needed at a number of locations at the same time or in a hostile environment that is dangerous to human health.
- Provide expertise that is expensive or rare.
- Develop a solution faster than human experts can.
- Provide expertise needed for training and development to share the wisdom and experience of human experts with many people.

Components of Expert Systems

An expert system consists of a collection of integrated and related components, including a knowledge base, an inference engine, an explanation facility, a knowledge base acquisition facility and a user interface. A diagram of a typical expert system is shown in Figure 9.3.

Figure 9.3 Components of an Expert System

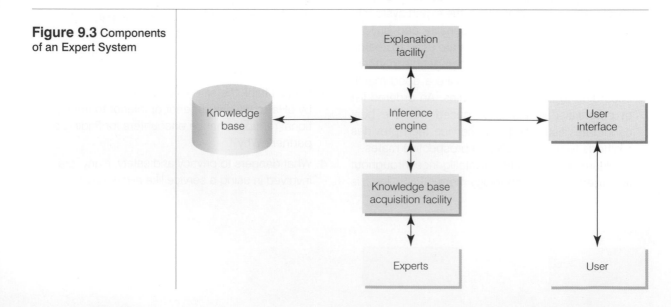

Today, specialized software allows users and decision makers to create and modify their own knowledge bases through the **knowledge acquisition facility**. The purpose of the knowledge acquisition facility is to provide a convenient and efficient means for capturing and storing all components of the knowledge base. Knowledge acquisition software can present users and decision makers with easy-to-use menus. After entering the appropriate attributes, the knowledge acquisition facility correctly stores information and relationships in the knowledge base, making the knowledge base easier and less expensive to set up and maintain. Knowledge acquisition can be a manual process or a mixture of manual and automated procedures. Regardless of how the knowledge is acquired, the knowledge base must be validated and updated frequently to make sure that it is still accurate.

knowledge acquisition facility Part of the expert system that provides convenient and efficient means of capturing and storing all the components of the knowledge base.

The User Interface

Specialized user interface software is employed for designing, creating, updating and using expert systems. The main purpose of the user interface is to make an expert system easier for users and decision makers to develop and use. At one time, skilled computer personnel created and operated most expert systems; today, the user interface permits decision makers to develop and use their own expert systems. Because expert systems place more emphasis on directing user activities than do other types of systems, text-oriented user interfaces (using menus, forms and scripts) might be more common in expert systems than the graphical interfaces often used with DSS. A typical user interface between a user and the expert system for a credit application.

EXPERT SYSTEM: Are there any previous credit problems?
USER: No.
EXPERT SYSTEM: Is the applicant's net income greater than four times the monthly loan payment?
USER: Yes.
EXPERT SYSTEM: Is the down payment greater than 15 per cent of the property value?
USER: Yes.
EXPERT SYSTEM: Are the net assets of the borrower greater than €25 000?
USER: Yes.
EXPERT SYSTEM: Has the borrower worked more than three years at the same company?
USER: Yes.
EXPERT SYSTEM: Accept the loan application.

Expert Systems Development

Like other computer systems, expert systems require a systematic development approach for best results. This approach includes determining the requirements for the expert system, identifying one or more experts in the area or discipline under investigation, constructing the components of the expert system, implementing the results, and maintaining and reviewing the complete system.

Participants in Developing and Using Expert Systems

Because of the time and effort involved in the task, an expert system is developed to address only a specific area of knowledge. This area of knowledge is called the **domain**. The **domain expert** is the person or group with the expertise or knowledge the expert system is trying to capture. The domain expert (individual or group) usually can do the following:

domain The area of knowledge addressed by the expert system.

domain expert The individual or group who has the expertise or knowledge one is trying to capture in the expert system.

■ Recognize the real problem.

■ Develop a general framework for problem solving.

■ Formulate theories about the situation.

■ Develop and use general rules to solve a problem.

■ Know when to break the rules or general principles.

■ Solve problems quickly and efficiently.

■ Learn from experience.

■ Know what is and is not important in solving a problem.

■ Explain the situation and solutions of problems to others.

knowledge engineer A person who has training or experience in the design, development, implementation and maintenance of an expert system.

knowledge user The person or group who uses and benefits from the expert system.

A **knowledge engineer** is a person who has training or experience in the design, development, implementation and maintenance of an expert system, including training or experience with expert system shells. The **knowledge user** is the person or group who uses and benefits from the expert system. Knowledge users do not need any previous training in computers or expert systems.

Expert Systems Development Tools and Techniques

Theoretically, expert systems can be developed from any programming language. Since the introduction of computer systems, programming languages have become easier to use, more powerful and increasingly able to handle specialized requirements. In the early days of expert systems development, traditional high-level languages, including Pascal, FORTRAN and COBOL, were used (see Figure 9.5). LISP was one of the first special languages developed and used for expert system applications. PROLOG was also developed to build expert systems. Since the 1990s, however, other expert system products (such as shells) have become available that remove the burden of programming, allowing non-programmers to develop and benefit from the use of expert systems.

Figure 9.5 Expert Systems Development

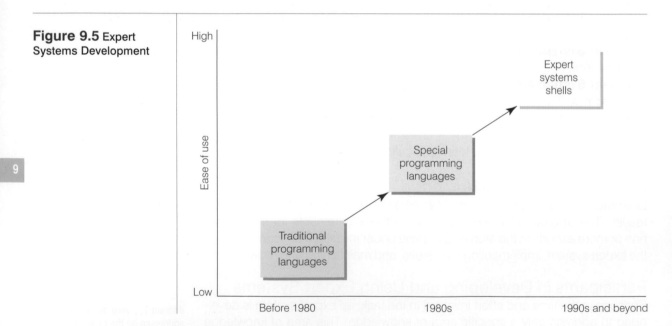

An expert system shell is a collection of software packages and tools used to design, develop, implement and maintain expert systems. Expert system shells are available for both personal computers and mainframe systems. Some shells are inexpensive, costing less than €400. In addition, off-the-shelf expert system shells are complete and ready to run. The user enters the appropriate data or parameters, and the expert system provides output to the problem or situation.

Some expert system products can analyze LAN networks, monitor air quality in commercial buildings, and evaluate oil and drilling operations. Table 9.2 lists a few expert system products.

Table 9.2 Popular Expert System Products

Name of Product	Application and Capabilities
Financial Adviser	Analyzes financial investments in new equipment, facilities, and the like; requests the appropriate data and performs a complete financial analysis
G2	Assists in oil and gas operations. Transco, a British company, uses it to help in the transport of gas to more than 20 million commercial and domestic customers
HazMat Loader	Analyzes hazardous materials in truck shipments
LSI Indicator	Helps determine property values; developed by one of the largest residential title and closing companies
MindWizard	Enables development of compact expert systems ranging from simple models that incorporate business decision rules to highly sophisticated models; PC-based and inexpensive
RAMPART	Analyzes risk. The US General Services Administration uses it to analyze risk to the approximately 8000 federal buildings it manages

Applications of Expert Systems and Artificial Intelligence

Expert systems and artificial intelligence have wide applications in business and government. A list of applications, some of which have already been mentioned, is given next.

■ *Credit granting and loan analysis.* Many banks employ expert systems to review a customer's credit application and credit history data from credit bureaus to make a decision on whether to grant a loan or approve a transaction. KPMG Peat Marwick uses an expert system called Loan Probe to review its reserves to determine whether sufficient funds have been set aside to cover the risk of some uncollectible loans.

■ *Stock picking.* Some expert systems help investment professionals pick stocks and other investments.

■ *Catching cheats and terrorists.* Some gambling casinos use expert system software to catch cheats. The CIA is testing the software to see whether it can detect possible terrorists when they make hotel or airline reservations.

■ *Budgeting.* Car companies can use expert systems to help budget, plan and coordinate prototype testing programs to save hundreds of millions of euros.

■ *Games.* Some expert systems are used for entertainment. For example, 20Q (www.20Q.net).

■ *Information management and retrieval.* The explosive growth of information available to decision makers has created a demand for devices to help manage the information. Bots can aid this process. Businesses might use a bot to retrieve information from large distributed databases or a vast network like the Internet.

■ *AI and expert systems embedded in products.* The antilock braking system on today's cars is an example of a rudimentary expert system. A processor senses when the tyres are beginning to skid and releases the brakes for a fraction of a second to prevent the skid. AI researchers are also finding ways to use neural networks and robotics in everyday devices, such as toasters, alarm clocks and televisions.

■ *Plant layout and manufacturing.* FLEXPERT is an expert system that uses fuzzy logic to perform plant layout. The software helps companies determine the best placement for equipment and manufacturing facilities. Expert systems can also spot defective welds during the manufacturing process. The expert system analyzes radiographic images and suggests which welds could be flawed.

9

- *Hospitals and medical facilities.* Some hospitals use expert systems to determine a patient's likelihood of contracting cancer or other diseases. Hospitals, pharmacies and other healthcare providers can use CaseAlert by MEDecision to determine possible high-risk or high-cost patients. MYCIN is an early expert system developed at Stanford University to analyze blood infections. UpToDate is another expert system used to diagnose patients. To help doctors in the diagnosis of thoracic pain, MatheMEDics has developed THORASK, a straightforward, easy-to-use program, requiring only the input of carefully obtained clinical information. The program helps the less experienced to distinguish the three principal categories of chest pain from each other. It does what a true medical expert system should do without the need for complicated user input. The user answers basic questions about the patient's history and directed physical findings, and the program immediately displays a list of diagnoses. The diagnoses are presented in decreasing order of likelihood, together with their estimated probabilities. The program also provides concise descriptions of relevant clinical conditions and their presentations, as well as brief suggestions for diagnostic approaches.

- *Help desk and assistance.* Customer service help desks use expert systems to provide timely and accurate assistance. The automated help desk frees up staff to handle more complex needs while still providing more timely assistance for routine calls.

- *Employee performance evaluation.* An expert system developed by Austin-Hayne, called Employee Appraiser, provides managers with expert advice for use in employee performance reviews and career development.

- *Virus detection.* IBM is using neural network technology to help create more advanced software for eradicating computer viruses, a major problem in businesses. IBM's neural network software deals with 'boot sector' viruses, the most prevalent type, using a form of artificial intelligence that generalizes by looking at examples. It requires a vast number of training samples, which in the case of antivirus software are fragments of virus code.

- *Repair and maintenance.* ACE is an expert system used by AT&T to analyze the maintenance of telephone networks. IET-Intelligent Electronics uses an expert system to diagnose maintenance problems related to aerospace equipment. General Electric Aircraft Engine Group uses an expert system to enhance maintenance performance levels at all sites and improve diagnostic accuracy.

- *Shipping.* CARGEX cargo expert system is used by Lufthansa, a German airline, to help determine the best shipping routes.

- *Marketing.* CoverStory is an expert system that extracts marketing information from a database and automatically writes marketing reports.

- *Warehouse optimization.* United Distillers uses an expert system to determine the best combinations of liquour stocks to produce its blends of Scotch whisky. This information is then supplemented with information about the location of the casks for each blend. The system optimizes the selection of required casks, keeping to a minimum the number of 'doors' (warehouse sections) from which the casks must be taken and the number of casks that need to be moved to clear the way. Other constraints must be satisfied, such as the current working capacity of each warehouse and the maintenance and restocking work that may be in progress.

9.4 Virtual Reality

The term 'virtual reality' was initially coined by Jaron Lanier, founder of VPL Research, in 1989. Originally, the term referred to immersive virtual reality in which the user becomes fully immersed in an artificial, 3-D world that is completely generated by a computer. Immersive virtual reality can represent any 3-D setting, real or abstract, such as a building, an archaeological excavation site, human anatomy, a sculpture or a crime scene reconstruction. Through immersion, the user can gain a deeper understanding of the virtual world's behaviour and functionality.

A virtual reality system enables one or more users to move and react in a computer-simulated environment. Virtual reality simulations require special interface devices that transmit the sights, sounds and sensations of the simulated world to the user. These devices can also record and send the speech and movements of the participants to the simulation program, enabling users to sense and manipulate virtual objects much as they would real objects. This natural style of interaction gives the participants the feeling that they are immersed in the simulated world. For example, a car manufacturer can use virtual reality to help it simulate and design factories.

A related term is 'augmented reality', which refers to the combination of computer generated data (images, sounds, etc.) with stimuli from the real world. For example, an augmented reality system might project instructions onto the user's eye, on top of the real world images they are seeing, so they could look at both at the same time.

Interface Devices

To see in a virtual world, often the user wears a head-mounted display (HMD) with screens directed at each eye. The HMD also contains a position tracker to monitor the location of the user's head and the direction in which the user is looking. Using this information, a computer generates images of the virtual world – a slightly different view for each eye – to match the direction that the user is looking and displays these images on the HMD. Many companies sell or rent virtual-reality interface devices, including Virtual Realities (www.vrealities.com), Amusitronix (www.amusitronix.com), I-O Display Systems (www.i-glassesstore.com) and others. With current technology, virtual-world scenes must be kept relatively simple so that the computer can update the visual imagery quickly enough (at least ten times per second) to prevent the user's view from appearing jerky and from lagging behind the user's movements.

The Electronic Visualization Laboratory at the University of Illinois at Chicago introduced a room constructed of large screens on three walls and the floor on which the graphics are projected. The CAVE®, as this room is called, provides the illusion of immersion by projecting stereo images on the walls and floor of a room-sized cube. Several persons wearing lightweight stereo glasses can enter and walk freely inside the CAVE®. A head-tracking system continuously adjusts the stereo projection to the current position of the leading viewer.

Users hear sounds in the virtual world through speakers mounted above or behind the screens. Spatial audio is possible, allowing for position tracking. When a sound source in virtual space is not directly in front of or behind the user, the computer transmits sounds to arrive at one ear a little earlier or later than at the other and to be a little louder or softer and slightly different in pitch.

The haptic interface, which relays the sense of touch and other physical sensations in the virtual world, is the least developed and perhaps the most challenging to create. Currently, with the use of a glove and position tracker, the computer locates the user's hand and measures finger movements. The user can reach into the virtual world and handle objects; however, it is difficult to realize sensations of a person tapping a hard surface, picking up an object, or running a finger across a textured surface. Touch sensations also have to be synchronized with the sights and sounds of the user's experience.

Forms of Virtual Reality

Aside from immersive virtual reality, which we just discussed, virtual reality can also refer to applications that are not fully immersive, such as mouse-controlled navigation through a

3-D environment on a graphics monitor, stereo viewing from the monitor via stereo glasses, stereo projection systems and others.

Some virtual reality applications allow views of real environments with superimposed virtual objects. Motion trackers monitor the movements of dancers or athletes for subsequent studies in immersive virtual reality. Telepresence systems (such as telemedicine and telerobotics) immerse a viewer in a real world that is captured by video cameras at a distant location and allow for the remote manipulation of real objects via robot arms and manipulators. Many believe that virtual reality will reshape the interface between people and information technology by offering new ways to communicate information, visualize processes and express ideas creatively.

Virtual Reality Applications

You can find hundreds of applications of virtual reality, with more being developed as the cost of hardware and software declines and people's imaginations are opened to the potential of virtual reality. Having been inspired by the 2002 movie *Minority Report*, Pamela Barry of Raytheon is experimenting with a virtual reality system that uses 'gesture technology',[26] and several commercial systems are now available from companies such as Solaris Labs. For example, by pointing an index finger towards a picture on a screen, the computer zooms in on the picture. Moving a hand in one direction causes the computer to scroll down through a video clip, and moving a hand in another direction clears the screen. Raytheon hopes 'gesture technology' will have applications in the military and space exploration. There are many other applications for virtual reality, including in the domains of medicine, education and entertainment.

Summary

Knowledge management systems allow organizations to share knowledge and experience among their managers and employees. Knowledge is an awareness and understanding of a set of information and the ways that information can be made useful to support a specific task or reach a decision. A knowledge management system (KMS) is an organized collection of people, procedures, software, databases and devices used to create, store, share and use the organization's knowledge and experience. Explicit knowledge is objective and can be measured and documented in reports, papers and rules. Tacit knowledge is hard to measure and document and is typically not objective or formalized.

Knowledge workers are people who create, use and disseminate knowledge. They are usually professionals in science, engineering, business and other areas. The chief knowledge officer (CKO) is a top-level executive who helps the organization use a KMS to create, store and use knowledge to achieve organizational goals. Obtaining, storing, sharing and using knowledge is the key to any KMS. The use of a KMS often leads to additional knowledge creation, storage, sharing and usage. Many tools and techniques can be used to create, store and use knowledge. These tools and techniques are available from IBM, Microsoft, and other companies and organizations.

Artificial intelligence systems form a broad and diverse set of systems that can replicate human decision making for certain types of well-defined problems. The term artificial intelligence is used to describe computers with the ability to mimic or duplicate the functions of the human brain. The objective of building AI systems is not to replace human decision making completely but to replicate it for certain types of well-defined problems.

Intelligent behaviour encompasses several characteristics, including the abilities to learn from experience and apply this knowledge to new experiences; handle complex situations and solve problems for which pieces of information might be missing; determine relevant information in a given situation, think in a logical and rational manner, and give a quick and correct response; and understand visual images and process symbols. Computers are better than people at transferring information, making a series of calculations rapidly and accurately, and making complex calculations, but human beings are better than computers at all other attributes of intelligence.

Artificial intelligence is a broad field that includes several key components, such as expert systems, robotics, vision systems, natural language processing, learning systems and neural networks. An expert system consists of the hardware and software used to produce systems that behave as a human expert would in a specialized field or area (e.g. credit analysis). Robotics uses mechanical or computer devices to perform tasks that require a high degree of precision or are tedious or hazardous for humans (e.g. stacking cartons on a pallet). Vision systems include hardware and software that permit computers to capture, store and manipulate images and pictures (e.g. face-recognition software). Natural language processing allows the computer to understand and react to statements and commands made in a 'natural' language, such as English. Learning systems use a combination of software and hardware to allow a computer to change how it functions or reacts to situations based on feedback it receives (e.g. a computerized chess game). A neural network is a computer system that can simulate the functioning of a human brain (e.g. disease diagnostics system). A genetic algorithm is an approach to solving large, complex problems in which a number of related operations or models change until the best one emerges.

Expert systems can enable a novice to perform at the level of an expert but must be developed and maintained very carefully. An expert system consists of a collection of integrated and related components, including a knowledge base, an inference engine, an explanation facility, a knowledge acquisition facility and a user interface. The knowledge base is an extension of a database, discussed in Chapter 5, and an information and decision support system, discussed in Chapter 8. It contains all the relevant data, rules and relationships used in the expert system. The rules are often composed of IF-THEN statements, which are used for drawing conclusions. Fuzzy logic allows expert systems to incorporate facts and relationships into expert system knowledge bases that might be imprecise or unknown.

The inference engine processes the rules, data and relationships stored in the knowledge base to provide answers, predictions and suggestions the way a human expert would. Two common methods for processing include backward and forward chaining. Backward chaining starts with a conclusion, then searches for facts to support it; forward chaining starts with a fact, then searches for a conclusion to support it.

The explanation facility of an expert system allows the user to understand what rules were used in arriving at a decision. The knowledge acquisition facility helps the user add or update knowledge in the knowledge base. The user interface makes it easier to develop and use the expert system.

The people involved in the development of an expert system include the domain expert, the knowledge engineer and the knowledge users. The domain expert is the person or group who has the expertise or knowledge being captured for the system. The knowledge engineer is the developer whose job is to extract the expertise from the domain expert. The knowledge user is the person who benefits from the use of the developed system.

The steps involved in the development of an expert system include: determining requirements, identifying experts, constructing expert system components, implementing results, and maintaining and reviewing the system.

Expert systems can be implemented in several ways. A fast way to acquire an expert system is to purchase an expert system shell or existing package. The shell program is a collection of software packages and tools used to design, develop, implement and maintain expert systems.

The benefits of using an expert system go beyond the typical reasons for using a computerized processing solution. Expert systems display 'intelligent' behaviour, manipulate symbolic information and draw conclusions, provide portable knowledge, and can deal with uncertainty. Expert systems can be used to solve problems in many fields or disciplines and can assist in all stages of the problem-solving process.

Virtual reality systems can reshape the interface between people and information technology by offering new ways to communicate information, visualize processes and express ideas creatively. A virtual reality system enables one or more users to move and react in a computer-simulated environment. Virtual reality simulations require special interface devices that transmit the sights, sounds and sensations of the simulated world to the user. These devices can also record and send the speech and movements of the participants to the simulation program. Thus, users can sense and manipulate virtual objects much as they would real objects. This natural style of interaction gives the participants the feeling that they are immersed in the simulated world.

Virtual reality can also refer to applications that are not fully immersive, such as mouse-controlled naviga-

tion through a 3-D environment on a graphics monitor, stereo viewing from the monitor via stereo glasses, stereo projection systems and others. Some virtual reality applications allow views of real environments with superimposed virtual objects. Virtual reality applications are found in medicine, education and training, and entertainment.

Self-Assessment Test

1 What type of knowledge is objective and can be measured and documented in reports, papers and rules?

a. tacit
b. descriptive
c. prescriptive
d. explicit

2 _____ are rules of thumb arising from experience or even guesses.

3 What is an important attribute for artificial intelligence?

a. the ability to use sensors
b. the ability to learn from experience
c. the ability to be creative
d. the ability to make complex calculations

4 _____ involves mechanical or computer devices that can paint cars, make precision welds, and perform other tasks that require a high degree of precision or are tedious or hazardous for human beings.

5 What is a disadvantage of an expert system?

a. the inability to solve complex problems
b. the inability to deal with uncertainty
c. limitations to relatively narrow problems
d. the inability to draw conclusions from complex relationships

6 A(n) _____ is a collection of software packages and tools used to develop expert systems that can be implemented on most popular PC platforms to reduce development time and costs.

7 What stores all relevant information, data, rules, cases and relationships used by the expert system?

a. the knowledge base
b. the data interface
c. the database
d. the acquisition facility

8 What allows a user or decision maker to understand how the expert system arrived at a certain conclusion or result?

a. domain expert
b. inference engine
c. knowledge base
d. explanation facility

9 A(n) _____ enables one or more users to move and react in a computer-simulated environment.

10 What type of virtual reality is used to make human beings feel as though they are in a 3-D setting, such as a building, an archaeological excavation site, the human anatomy, a sculpture or a crime scene reconstruction?

a. chaining
b. relative
c. immersive
d. visual

Review Questions

1 Define the term 'artificial intelligence'.

2 What is a vision system? Discuss two applications of such a system.

3 What is natural language processing? What are the three levels of voice recognition?

4 Describe three examples of the use of robotics. How can a microrobot be used?

5   What is an expert system shell?

6   Under what conditions is the development of an expert system likely to be worth the effort?

7   Identify the basic components of an expert system and describe the role of each.

8   What is virtual reality? Give several examples of its use.

9   Describe the roles of the domain expert, the knowledge engineer and the knowledge user in expert systems.

10 Describe three applications of expert systems or artificial intelligence.

Discussion Questions

1   What are the requirements for a computer to exhibit human-level intelligence? How long will it be before we have the technology to design such computers? Do you think we should push to try to accelerate such a development? Why or why not?

2   Describe how you might encourage your employees to share their knowledge with one another. What technologies might you use and why?

3   Describe how natural language processing could be used in a university setting.

4   What is the purpose of a knowledge base? How is one developed?

5   Imagine that you are developing the rules for an expert system to select the strongest candidates for a medical school. What rules or heuristics would you include?

Web Exercises

1   Use the Internet to find information about the use of robotics. Describe three examples of how this technology is used.

2   This chapter discussed several examples of expert systems. Search the Internet for two examples of the use of expert systems. Which one has the greatest potential to increase profits? Explain your choice.

Case One

Robots in Space

On 5 August 2012 the NASA Curiosity Rover successfully touched down on Mars. Using rockets to slow its descent in the upper Martian atmosphere, when it got closer to the ground it was lowered by a system called the Sky Crane. Basically Sky Crane is a robotic jet plane that floats in the sky while it lets the Rover down using cables. The Sky Crane was needed because a landing using only jets would blow up dust from the surface that could damage

Rover's sensors. The Sky Crane then flies off and crashes a safe distance away. NASA called the procedure 'seven minutes of terror'.

If you search on YouTube you can find actual footage of the Rover's landing (there are many animated versions available so you may have to search through a few). The first thing you'll see in the video is something falling away – that's the heat shield being discarded. After that you can see the Martian ground get closer and closer until touch down.

It's difficult to overstate how impressive this is. It's a video taken on another planet by a robot guiding itself to a predetermined landing site and then lowering another robot onto the ground. There is no human intervention – any signal sent by NASA would take too long to reach Mars to be useful. NASA sent the signal to start the landing procedure and from then on it was up to the robots.

The Sky Crane had to detect the landing site, control its jets to steer towards it, and then lower the Rover. When the Rover was down everyone in the control centre breathed a sigh of relief. Everyone, that is, except the Sky Crane team who knew that the crane still had to crash land. There was a small but real chance that it could crash on top of the Rover, obliterating it! That didn't happen and a few moments later they too could relax and celebrate.

According to NASA roboticist Linda Kobayashi, 'the hardest part of building robots is finding out

something didn't work the way you expected. When that happens, we usually have to go back to the drawing board and come up with some other creative way to do what we want.' NASA robots combine cutting edge mechanics, sensor technology and artificial intelligence and NASA encourage school children to get involved (there are links to stories about the LEGO Mindstorms on their website).

Questions

1 What applications for robots in your daily life can you think of?

2 The NASA robots described were autonomous – they controlled themselves. Can you think of any useful applications for robots that are controlled by humans?

3 Why do you think America and other countries spend so much money on space exploration?

4 Run an Internet search for LEGO Mindstorms projects. What is the most impressive project that you can find and why is it impressive?

Case Two

Cloud4Cancer Breast Cancer Detection

In 2012, 17-year-old Brittany Wenger won the Google Science Fair prize with her project Cloud4Cancer. Her project is an artificial neural network that takes data from a fine needle aspirate (a diagnostic procedure used to investigate lumps just under the skin) and then predicts whether a lump is malignant or benign. The network accepts nine fields of information including data on the size and shape of the lump, and a description of the cell activity.

Look at the illustration below. The database contains information on thousands of aspirates from the University of Wisconsin. The input layer is where the information contained in the nine fields is coded (turned into numbers) and sent to the hidden layer. In the figure there is only one hidden layer but in reality there would be more than this. The nodes in the hidden layers perform calculations on the data that is sent to them from the input layer. The results are then sent to the output layer which adds them all

up and outputs a decision. For example, if the result calculated by the output layer is greater than 0.5 it may predict that the lump is malignant; if it is less than 0.5 it might predict benign.

The neural network works by setting up the calculations performed by the hidden layers in such a way that important information from the input layer gets more 'say' in the result sent to the output layer. For instance, if it turns out that shape is more important than size, then the calculation on shape will make a bigger result than the one on size. The process to do this is called 'back propagation'.

The database from the University of Wisconsin also stores the correct result from each aspirate – whether or not each lump in the data was actually malignant or benign. The neural network therefore knows what result it should get for each of them. This data is the training data which is used to set the calculations performed by the hidden layers. The neural

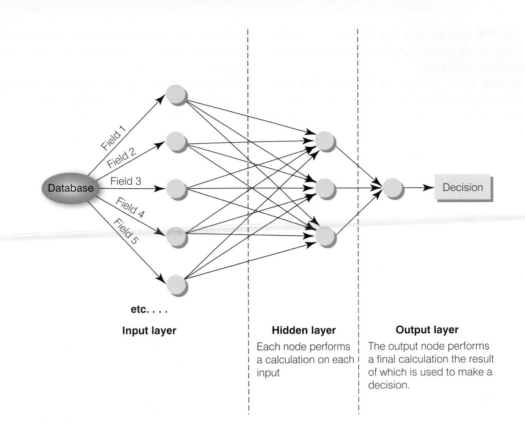

Input layer

etc. . . .

Hidden layer
Each node performs a calculation on each input

Output layer
The output node performs a final calculation the result of which is used to make a decision.

network looks at each of them over and over again until it reaches an optimum set of calculations. To get more training data, Brittany turned to the cloud (see the chapters on hardware and software for more information about cloud computing), uploading her project as a Google App which can be used to collect data from any hospital in the world.

Once trained, the neural network is ready to examine data from a new lump, one for which the correct result is not known. Brittany's neural network achieved predictive success of 97.4 per cent with 99.1 per cent sensitivity to malignancy – substantially better than existing commercial products. (However it has not yet been used to diagnose real patients.)

Questions

1 Who do you think would use this system?

2 Would you feel comfortable being diagnosed by a neural network?

3 What other applications for neural networks can you think of (remember training data has to be readily available). Run an Internet search – if no one has already implemented your idea, maybe you should! You could fairly easily use the programming language R and the free package Rattle to create it.

4 Do you think Brittany's network is actually intelligent? Why or why not?

Case Three

Google and BMW Train Cars to Drive Themselves

Artificial intelligence is defined in this chapter as computers having 'the ability to mimic or duplicate the functions of the human brain'. Driving a car in traffic is such an activity. By that definition vehicles that have begun to show the ability to drive in traffic have started to show intelligence.

Intelligent vehicle behaviour, is expected to become commonplace over the next few years. Alan

Taub, General Motors vice president for research and development, predicts that self-driving will be a standard feature by 2020.

In October 2010, Google disclosed its Autonomous Car program. The firm's cars are easily spotted in and around San Francisco: the base Toyota Prius has a funnel-shaped device on the roof to hold a 64-beam laser rangefinder. Additional inputs to the control computer come from high resolution maps of the area, two radar units on each bumper, a forward-facing camera to detect traffic lights, and GPS, inertial measurement unit, and wheel rotation counter to track vehicle motion.

Google's cars always travel with a licenced driver in the driver's seat. In the first 160 000 miles of operation, the driver had to take over twice: once when the car in front stopped and began to back into a parking space and once when a bicycle rider entered an intersection despite a red light. It would be fairly easy to program the cars' computers to check for cars starting to park but more difficult, though not impossible, to program them to handle cyclists running red lights. Situations in which a person has to take control should become rarer as time goes on.

The only accident involving a Google car in over 200 000 miles, by the way, came when one of the cars was rear ended while stopped at a traffic light. How many humans drive that far with only one minor fender-bender?

Google is not the only company studying autonomous driving technology. Vehicle manufacturers are investigating it, too. BMW is probably the furthest along: in January 2012, it demonstrated a self-driving car on Germany's no-speed-limits autobahns. The company's car looks like any other BMW since its radars, cameras, laser scanners and distance sensors are all inside the body. Nico Kaempchen, project manager of Highly Automated Driving at BMW Group Research and Technology, says 'the system works on all freeways that we have mapped out beforehand.'

Programming autonomous cars means studying driver behaviour to a detailed level. How do drivers alternate at an intersection with four stop signs? If other drivers don't yield to the driverless car, how should it inch into the intersection to show that it wants its turn? How large must an animal be before a car takes evasive action to avoid it?

Society must also resolve legal issues about this technology. How can police officers pull over driverless cars? Do they even have the right to? How can driverless cars recognize police officers directing traffic and ignore traffic lights over those officers' heads?

Despite such concerns, driverless vehicles were legalized in Nevada in 2011. Similar legislation is pending in Florida and Hawaii and may soon be introduced in California.

Like it or not, though, we will soon give our cars more control than our ancestors ever gave their most intelligent horses. 'It won't truly be an autonomous vehicle,' said Brad Templeton, a software designer and a consultant for the Google project, 'until you instruct it to drive to work and it heads to the beach instead.'

Questions

1 Suppose you saw a Google autonomous car driving along in front of you and going about 5 mph (or 10 km/hr) slower than you believe it is safe to go. There are two travel lanes in your direction. Would you pass the autonomous car? Do you think that is any riskier than passing a car controlled by a human driver?

2 As noted in the case, Google's autonomous cars are easily recognized but BMW's are not. Do you think this matters? If it does, which do you prefer and why?

3 Would you buy an autonomous car in the first year such cars are on the market? (Assume you were going to buy a new car anyhow, that the car itself appeals to you and that its price is reasonable.) If not, when do you think you would?

4 You are a lawyer. An autonomous car injures your client. What do you recommend your client do? If you recommend suing, who do you sue? What are some arguments you might use? What might the defendants argue?

Notes

1 Kimble, Chris, et al., 'Dualities, Distributed Communities of Practice and Knowledge Management', *Journal of Knowledge Management*, Vol. 9, 2005, p. 102.

2 Darroch, Jenny, 'Knowledge Management, Innovation, and Firm Performance', *Journal of Knowledge Management*, Vol. 9, 2005, p. 101.

3 Thurm, Scott, 'Companies Struggle to Pass on Knowledge that Workers Acquire', *The Wall Street Journal*, 23 January 2006, p. B1.

4 Woods, Ginny Parker, 'Sony Sets Its Sights on Digital Books', *The Wall Street Journal*, 16 February 2006, p. B3.

5 Skok, Walter, et al., 'Evaluating the Role and Effectiveness of an Intranet in Facilitating Knowledge Management: A Case Study at Surrey County Council', *Information and Management*, July 2005, p. 731.

6 Staff, 'Autonomy Links with Blinkx to Offer Search Facilities in China', *ComputerWire*, Issue 5228, 19 July 2005.

7 Staff, 'eArchitect: Share and Enjoy', *Building Design*, 17 June 2005, p. 24.

8 Zolkos, Rodd, 'Sharing the Intellectual Wealth', *BI Industry Focus*, 1 March 2005, p. 12.

9 Hsiu-Fen, Lin, et al., 'Impact of Organizational Learning and Knowledge Management Factors on E-Business Adoption', *Management Decision*, Vol. 43, 2005, p. 171.

10 Pelz-Sharpe, Alan, 'Document Management and Content Management Tucked Away in Several SAP Products', *Computer Weekly*, 2 August 2005, p. 26.

11 McKellar, Hugh, '100 Companies That Matter in Knowledge Management', *KM World*, March 2005, p. 18.

12 Sambamurthy, V., et al., 'Special Issue of Information Technologies and Knowledge Management', *MIS Quarterly*, June 2005, p. 193.

13 Kajmo, David, 'Knowledge Management in R5'. Retrieved from: www-128.ibm.com/developerworks/lotus/library/ls-Knowledge_Management/index.html.

14 Staff, 'IBM Lotus Domino Document Manager'. Retrieved from: www.lotus.com/lotus/offering4.nsf/wdocs/domdochome.

15 Staff, 'Morphy Richards Integrates Its Global Supply Chain with Lotus Domino'. Retrieved from: www-306.ibm.com/ software/success/cssdb.nsf/cs/DNSD-6EUNJ7? OpenDocument&Site=lotus.

16 Staff, 'Survey Rates Microsoft Number One in Knowledge Management Efforts. Retrieved from: www.microsoft.com/presspass/features/1999/11-22award.mspx.

17 Quain, John, 'Thinking Machines, Take Two', *PC Magazine*, 24 May 2005, p. 23.

18 20Q Website. Available from: www.20q.net.

19 Staff, 'Send in the Robots', *Fortune*, 24 January 2005, p. 140.

20 iRobot Website. Retrieved from: www.irobot.com.

21 Freeman, Diane, 'RobotDoc', *Rocky Mountain News*, 27 June 2005, p. 1B.

22 DARPA 'Grand Challenge'. Retrieved from: http://en.wikipedia.org/ wiki/Darpa_grand_challenge.

23 El-Rashidi, Yasime, 'Ride'em Robot', *The Wall Street Journal*, 3 October 2005, p. A1.

24 Chamberlain, Ted, 'Ultra-Lifelike Robot Debuts in Japan', *National Geographic News*, 10 June 2005.

25 Anthes, Gary, 'Self Taught', *Computerworld*, 6 February 2006, p. 28.

26 Karp, Jonathan, 'Minority Report Inspires Technology Aimed at Military', *The Wall Street Journal*, 12 April 2005, p. B1.

9

10

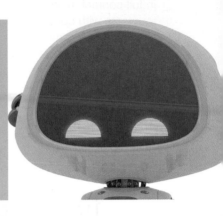

Pervasive Computing

Principles

The term 'computing' no longer refers to a computer on a desk. Mobile devices are letting employees access information from wherever they happen to be. In addition, these same technologies are allowing customers to interact with businesses in new ways.

Teams made up of people living in different geographical regions are able to work together efficiently and effectively, without ever having to meet. This work is facilitated by a range of technologies.

E-commerce and m-commerce can be used in many innovative ways to improve the operation of an organization.

Learning Objectives

- Identify the range of devices that now incorporate computing power.

- Describe the business benefits of mobile devices.
- Discuss and evaluate the technologies that can be used to support teamwork, when team members are separated by time and/or space.

- Describe how to select mobile systems to support business objectives.

The move of information systems from the office desktop into every aspect of our lives is well underway. Many businesses are exploiting this to their advantage, as are their customers. A mobile sales force can stay in touch with head office easily, and submit orders faster than before. Employees can take work with them on the plane or train, and remain in full contact, using text, audio and video. Potential customers are starting to expect to be able to communicate with companies in a number of ways, and if a business fails to recognize this fact it could lose customers to competitors who offer these communication channels. In addition, customers who have experienced poor service from a company are willing and able to communicate those experiences to other potential customers.

This chapter examines some of the technologies that are enabling all of this to happen. New ones are being introduced almost every month. It is important that businesses understand the potential benefits they can bring.

10.1   Introduction

Information systems are no longer tied to a desk in an office. As we saw in the chapter on hardware, mobile devices are allowing computing power to be taken on the move. Increasingly, computers look less and less like the familiar picture shown in Figure 10.1, of a tower unit, keyboard, monitor and mouse. This change is moving in two directions. New devices are being developed that people are happy to carry with them – tiny devices such as the iPod or a smartphone. Such devices do not have the functionality of a PC, but they are more convenient and can be taken anywhere. The other diection is that, rather than a new device, computing power is being incorporated into existing devices and objects that are already well known to us, such as a jacket, a pair of glasses or a car. This move away from the desktop is known as **pervasive computing**, or ubiquitous computing: ubiquitous because computers are all around us, even if we

pervasive computing A term meaning the move of the computer away from the desktop and towards something that is all around us, all the time.

Figure 10.1 The Conventional View of a Computer *The idea that computers must have a monitor, keyboard and mouse is being challenged by pervasive computing.*

10

don't always realize it. Perhaps from where you are sitting you can see a laptop, smartphone and a tablet computer. On any one of these devices you could read or post a blog entry, access the web, and pay for goods and services. People are using these devices to do all sorts of things on the move – buy cinema tickets to avoid queuing for them, check in for a flight, pay for a taxi journey. In this chapter we will look at some of these technologies and examine their business potential. We will also meet a particular class of system use, called **computer supported cooperative work**, which is allowing teams to work together on projects, regardless of where they happen to be. Many of the technologies described in this chapter are waiting for a 'killer application' that will allow them to take off. Maybe you'll be able to think of one!

> **computer supported cooperative work** A term that refers to technologies which allow groups to work together to achieve goals.

10.2 Wireless Internet Access

Central to being able to access information 'on the move' is wireless Internet access. The range of options available for wireless communication was described in Chapter 6 but for many people the options they have currently are wifi and 3G mobile communication, with 4G rapidly becoming more available. A wi-fi **hotspot** is an area where wireless access is available. Many bars and cafés provide their customers with wi-fi, often charging by the half-hour, although sometimes access is free. T-Mobile has set up wi-fi hotspots in many airports, coffee houses and bookshops.[1] Users can buy a pass for one hour, one day or one month costing around €7, €14 and €60 respectively, or can choose to take out a longer-term plan costing around €30 each month. This is useful for employees who are away from the office a lot. BT Fon uses wi-fi routers in its customer's homes to allow others to connect to the Internet. Fon works by having its routers broadcast two wi-fi signals – one private, just for use by the customer who owns the the router, and one public and accessible to registered members of the Fon community.[2] A wireless service is now expected by customers in major hotels. Many city centres have free wi-fi access. In the UK, both Norwich and Bristol have free wi-fi, as do other cities throughout Europe, such as Oulu in Finland.[3] In Norwich, over 200 antennae are used to provide a hotspot blanket over the city.[4] As a user walks out of range of one antenna and into the range of another, the system seamlessly hands over access between the two, in the same way that the mobile phone network does. Wi-fi access speeds are slightly slower than broadband, although this is perhaps made up for in convenience. The first entire nation to be given free wireless Internet access was the tiny Polynesian island of Niue with a population of just 2000.[5] The local authorities in the town of Knysna in South Africa have installed wi-fi to allow access to residents who have historically been cut off from Internet access because the town is so remote. Computers have been installed in the local library to give access to those who can't afford wi-fi-enabled devices.

> **hotspot** An area where wi-fi wireless Internet access is available.

The business benefits of wi-fi are clear – mobile access to information; employees away on business can easily send and receive email, using any one of a number of devices, some of which are discussed next. They can access information on company websites or read about local conditions on news services. They could also access sensitive information on company extranets.

10.3 Mobile Devices

The list of devices that can make use of wi-fi hotspots is growing. It now includes desktop computers (useful if you happen to live within a hotspot), laptops, tablet PCs, mobile phones, mobile game consoles such as the Nintendo DS, pocket PCs and VoIP phones. As we will see, other mobile devices are stand alone and do not require Internet access to make them useful.

Smartphone

Smartphones and tablet computers are now a viable alternative to laptops. Shown in Figure 10.2, these tiny devices are cheaper and more robust than laptops and can be combined with a range of accessories to increase their functionality.

Figure 10.2
A Smartphone *Users can now access a number of business related applications on their smartphone including email and even presentation software.*

Possibly the most useful accessory is a keyboard that can be attached to the smartphone so that data can be entered into it, as it could into a laptop or PC. Both fold up and roll up versions are available. These keyboards can be attached by a cable or wirelessly using the bluetooth protocol described in Chapter 6. South Korean company Celluon manufactures a device that projects a laser keyboard onto a surface such as the tray table on a plane, and detects when you press one of the virtual keys.[6] Attaching a keyboard to a smartphone provides an extremely portable word processor. Many workers in the western world would not be satisfied with such a tiny screen, however, such miniature devices are common in the Far East. It is true that you are unlikely to want to type at a smartphone for as long as you would a laptop, however many people do prefer the light weight of a smartphone and keyboard to that of a laptop. If a smartphone and keyboard combined with wi-fi access, the smartphone becomes a powerful tool to access all Internet services. Without the keyboard, a smartphone can be cumbersome to use.

Another useful accessory is a cable to enable the smartphone to be attached to a projector. Margi Presenter-to-Go[7] can be used to project Microsoft PowerPoint slides from a smartphone. The system even comes with a remote control so that the speaker can progress from one slide to the next without having to be beside the device – functionality that few PCs provide. This is an extremely convenient way for business people to take a presentation with them. For example, a salesperson could present to clients all over the world, and only have to carry a smartphone with accessories and, unless one was available at each location, a data projector.

One drawback to using a smartphone to give presentations is that it is difficult to create or edit PowerPoint slides on them. Therefore they only become an alternative to carrying a laptop if the presentation is not going to change. If it is known that the presentation will not change, and it is known that there is the appropriate hardware at the presentation location, it becomes more convenient to simply carry the presentation files on a flash drive, or even simply upload them to the web, where they can be downloaded for the presentation.

By connecting a **global positioning system (GPS)** receiver, and installing map software such as TomTom,[8] a smartphone can be used as a powerful navigational aid, either in a car or, if the GPS receiver is wireless (again using the bluetooth protocol), on foot. Fleet operators use GPS for vehicle tracking, safety and performance monitoring. GPS is also used by breakdown agencies such as the RAC and AA – the location of a broken down vehicle is fed into an information system which uses GPS information on the whereabouts of the fleet to make the decision on which patrol to send to the rescue.

global positioning system (GPS) A navigation system that enables a receiver to determine its precise location.

A smartphone can also be used to play audio and video files. Many people use one instead of a dedicated music device such as an MP3 player or an iPod. Some people download news clips each night from a provider such as the BBC, and watch them on the train on the way to work the next morning. The BBC has launched a service called 'iPlayer', from which almost all of their programmes can be downloaded and watched at any time within 30 days.[9]

Watching news programmes in this way could replace the traditional activity of reading the morning newspaper, plus it takes up less space on crowded public transport than a newspaper, is cleaner, and arguably easier to digest and more interesting.

When the functionality of a pocket PC is combined with the functionality of a mobile phone, that is, when you can make phone calls on it, it is known as a 'smartphone'.

Wearable Technology

Miniaturizing smartphone technology further allows it to become part of the clothes we wear, for example a jacket or belt. Coupled with other things we are comfortable wearing, for instance glasses with which to receive visual information or earphones for audio information, computing power can become a something we routinely take with us and use everywhere. The term 'wearable technology' usually refers to computers that are worn on the body, although it could also be used to encompass non-computing technology such as mechanical watches and glasses. The term **wearable computing** is used to distinguish between the two.

wearable computing A term that refers to computers and computing technology that are worn on the body.

When a smartphone is attached to a user's belt it is being 'worn' by that user. However, wearable computing refers to something more than this. The term really means the use of largely invisible computing technology, to seamlessly augment a human's task. So far, there are few everyday applications for wearable computing, and many of the commercial examples available have more novelty value than business value. However, one application, which is often mentioned, is navigation, where the clothes you wear somehow tell you where to go. For example, a GPS receiver could be built into a special jacket, which could apply pressure on one side of the body to guide the wearer in that direction. The interface for telling the jacket where you want to go could be a smartphone with a bluetooth link between it and the jacket. A research group at the Massachusetts Institute of Technology (MIT) developed an early platform which can be used to experiment with potential applications. MIThril had a number of ways of interacting with the body.

Suggested uses for MIThril included navigation and accessing the Internet on the move. However, neither of these take the unique nature of wearable computing into account and using it like this, gives little advantage over a smartphone. The most famous wearable computer is currently Google Glass, a product that they think will replace the smartphone. Google Glass uses voice input and transmits visual output directly into the eye of its user. It can also record everything that the user sees. However the next smartphone might not be glasses after all. Apple computers have recently launched a smart watch which has been described as an iPhone on the wrist. The launch follows a similar product from Samsung.

10

Some other potential applications for wearable computing are recording what the wearer sees and hears and how they move, and transmitting personal information between people, rather like an electronic business card. Indeed another device from MIT, the UberBadge, does exactly that. It can be worn as a name badge and used to transmit personal information. For instance, the system could be used at a business conference to collect information about all the people a delegate has spoken to throughout the day. The same device can collect information useful to conference organizers about where people spent the most time throughout the day. A business could adapt this to be able to locate its employees within its building, so that phone calls could be routed to the nearest phone. Perhaps wearable technology could be used to help judge a fencing or martial arts competition, or for recording dance moves, something that has been difficult in the past. There could also be applications for teaching – gloves that help teach someone how to play the piano. Another technology to come out of MIT, called Kameraflage, allows digital cameras to photograph colours in fabrics that the human eye cannot see. One possible use of this technology is to replace staff cards with invisible markers – a security guard could easily identify people who do not have authority to be in a certain area, by looking at his or her video monitor, which would pick up the marks on their clothes. Another wearable application is shown in Figure 10.3.

It should be noted that many people would resist wearable technology, for a variety of reasons, some of which are mentioned in the Ethical and Societal issues box, page 349.

Figure 10.3
Smartwatch *Modern smartwatches can be used to make and receive calls and can also run mobile apps.*

Ethical and Societal Issues

Never Hit a Man Wearing (Google) Glass

Sometimes described as the father of wearable computing, Canadian born Steve Mann has worn something very like Google Glass, which was described earlier in this chapter, every day for over 30 years. It is a device he refers to as the EyeTap and one that he invented himself. It can project images onto his eye and can record what he is looking at. Mann believes that the EyeTap will help many people see better, and improve their quality of lives through augmented reality (the ability to see virtual material overlaid on top of what a person is looking at). Over the years Mann has experimented with looking both forwards and backwards at the same time (something he says takes the human brain about four days to get used to), accessing the Internet for information during conversation (which has led some who have met him to call him a genius because he appears to know everything about any topic, or 'brain-damaged', presumably because he has left a person waiting for a response while he was reading a web page) and removing material from his vision that he deems offensive (such as adverts for cigarettes).

The EyeTap has allowed him to record his everyday experiences and he has become a proponent of something he calls 'sousveillance', the recording of an activity from the perspective of a participant in that activity. In other words, he thinks we should all be able to record our own experiences, thereby taking the power of surveillance away from authorities and putting it in the hands of individuals. This is exactly one of the things that Google Glass will achieve if the technology takes off.

But companies don't like it. The UK for instance has more CCTV cameras in its city centres per head than any other country in Europe. These cameras record what goes on and are used, among other things, to police crime. Steve Mann believes that everyone has the right to do the same by recording everything they see and hear. Whenever you go into a shop there is often a sign saying something like: 'video cameras are being used for your protection'. However Mann has repeatedly found that when he has gone into these shops wearing his sousveillance equipment he has been told to stop recording or asked to leave. It seems some businesses like to have the right to video people, but don't like people videoing them.

In June 2012, Mann was assaulted in a fast food restaurant in France. In an ironic twist, the assault happened because he was wearing his EyeTap and the fact that he was wearing it also meant that screen shots of the incident were captured. Mann has since published them online. Other more serious crimes have also been captured in the same way.

Royal Marines wear cameras on their helmets when they are in action in order to gather intelligence and record what they do. In October 2012, five Marines were charged with murder after one of their cameras captured footage of them in Helmand Province killing an injured Afghan insurgent. The film showed one of them shooting the prisoner with a 9 mm pistol saying, 'There, shuffle off this mortal coil … It's nothing you wouldn't do to us,' before adding, 'Obviously this doesn't go anywhere fellas – I just broke the Geneva Convention.' In another ironic twist the Marine who was unknowingly recording the event replies on the film, 'Yeah, Roger mate.' The Marine who pulled the trigger is currently in jail serving at least eight years and was dismissed with disgrace from the Army.

Questions

1 Would you wear (or have you worn) Google Glass? What applications can you think of for this technology?

2 What are some of the advantages in recording all of your experiences? Critically evaluate the disadvantages.

3 What is your opinion of the attitude of the shops who like to video you, but don't like you to video them? Why do you think this is? How would you combat this attitude?

4 Does having more CCTV cameras in city centres make the UK safer? Will having more Google Glass make cities safer? Explain your answer.

Information Systems @ Work

When Not to Use Wikipedia

Founded in 2001 by online entrepreneur Jimmy Wales and scholar Larry Sanger, Wikipedia is a free, online encyclopaedia which anyone can edit. Wikipedia is one of the most popular sites on the web and its pages often appear as the number one result in Internet searches. The English language version of Wikipedia contains an estimated 2.5 billion words and is 50 times larger than the Encyclopaedia Britannica. It is maintained across all languages by tens of thousands of editors – about 77 000 of whom make more than five edits a month.

Because anyone can make changes to its content, Wikipedia is constantly being targeted by vandals. A textbook would not normally quote Wikipedia (see the last paragraph of this case for more information on this) but as this Information Systems @ Work case is about Wikipedia itself, we will make an exception. Here is what Wikipedia currently says about vandalism (we say 'currently' because someone might change it tomorrow): 'On Wikipedia, vandalism is the act of editing the project in a malicious manner that is intentionally disruptive. Vandalism includes the addition, removal, or other modification of the text or other material that is either humorous, nonsensical, a hoax, or that is of an offensive, humiliating, or otherwise degrading nature.' Wikipedia editors are constantly fighting vandalism, but they are getting a little artificial intelligence help.

Computer programs called bots are used to perform repetitive tasks such as correcting common misspellings and fixing stylistic problems. Wikipedia uses bots for a wide range of reasons. 'We had a joke that one day all the bots should go on strike just to make everyone appreciate how much work they do,' says Chris Grant, a 19-year-old student in Australia who is on the Wikipedia committee that supervises the bots. 'The site would demand much more work from all of us and the editor burnout rate would be much higher.'

One example, a bot called ClueBot-NG, spends its time detecting and removing vandalism. ClueBot-NG uses machine learning methods to detect vandalism. Essentially humans in a computer lab give the computer examples of what is and what is not considered to be vandalism, and the bot learns on its own to recognize which is which. After it has learnt it starts work on real Wikipedia pages. At its heart is an Artificial Neural Network which takes as input a number of metrics about a sentence such as grammatical correctness, spelling and use of profanity, and outputs a score of how likely that sentence is to be vandalism. The score lies between 0 and 1, where 1 means the neural network is sure the sentence is vandalism. A threshold is set and if a sentence's score is above it, then that sentence is removed from Wikipedia by reverting to the most recent previous version of the article. 'Wikipedia has just grown so much that I don't know how well people would handle it if all the bots went away,' says Brad Jorsch, a computer programmer in North Carolina who runs a bot that tracks missing citations to articles.

At the start we said a textbook would not normally quote Wikipedia – so why not? Just imagine the article you are quoting has been vandalized and the bot doesn't get to it before you do. Would you really want a hoax showing up in one of your essays? If that did happen, however, you would not be alone – both BBC News and *The Times* newspaper have fallen victim to hoaxes in Wikipedia!

Questions

1 Outline a procedure you could use to allow you to draw on Wikipedia to research an essay you are writing.

2 It is one thing for a bot to correct vandalism, but another for it to write an article. However having a bot write an article is technically possible. Discuss the advantages and disadvantages of bots being put in charge of writing.

3 What could your university use a bot for?

4 List some reasons why people vandalize Wikipedia articles. How else could you combat vandalism?

E-Money

E-money refers to the transfer of funds happening electronically rather than by handing over physical coins and notes. It can be implemented in a number of ways. The most common is paying for goods and services over the Internet, however it does take other forms. Mobile phones are now also being used to pay for goods and services. Contactless payment using near field communication as described in Chapter 6 is becoming more common. Barclays Bank now offers customers a PayTag which they can stick on their wallet or phone and can be used to pay for goods costing less than about €20. The same technology is used to pay for public transport. An example is Hong Kong's Octopus card, originally intended to be used to pay for public transport, but now used throughout Hong Kong in a range of shops. When used on the city's train service, a passenger 'swipes' their card, when they enter the train station and they 'swipe' it again when they leave. The correct fare is then debited from their prepaid account. 'Swiping' the card merely involves waving it near a reader – direct contact is not required. In fact the card doesn't even have to be removed from the passenger's wallet! Octopus gadgets are now available such as the Octopus watch or Octopus ornaments. Whether using the card or a gadget, a chip in the device stores the amount that has been paid into the account. Similar systems have now been implemented throughout Europe and elsewhere, for example the Oyster Card in London (see Figure 10.4). Systems such as these that implement the concept of e-money make paying for goods fast and convenient. LUUP[10] is a payment system (the developers call it a 'digital wallet') that works using the text feature on mobile phones to transfer funds from buyer to seller (see Figure 10.4). The buyer sends LUUP a text with the format 'PAY USERNAME AMOUNT'. LUUP then transfers the specified amount from the buyer's account to the seller's account. For example a buyer might text 'PAY 10943933 EUR10'. This would cause a transfer of €10 to be transferred to account 10943933. Both buyer and seller then receive a text message when payment has been made.

LUUP and systems like it have the potential to negate the need for exact change when paying for things like taxi journeys. In Norway, where the system was developed, users can pay for food, public transport and shopping bills.

e-money The transfer of funds electronically rather than by handing over physical coins and notes.

Figure 10.4
Contactless payment
Payment is made just by waving the card near the reader.

10

A similar system is being used in developing countries to provide financial services to the least well off. While the physical infrastructure in Kenya (road and rail) is in a poor state, in contrast the country has excellent mobile phone coverage, provided by two companies, Celtel and Safricom. Safricom, part owned by Vodafone, provides a service called M-Pesa. M-Pesa lets customers borrow, withdraw and pay money using text messaging. In a culture where many people are unable to open bank accounts and must therefore carry cash, it has the potential to revolutionize lives.[11] The system gives security, and allows easy and safe transfer of cash from relatives in the first world. According to the World Bank, this happens a lot – over 200 million migrants worldwide sent €120 billion to their families in 2005, a figure which is more than double the volume of official aid.[12]

Another form of e-money is virtual currency such as Bitcoin. There is a debate whether virtual currencies are a form of money or more like valuable collectibles – like old Star Wars toys or bottles of wine or similar objects you might collect and trade. Some big websites do accept Bitcoins as a form of payment. Basically users are given Bitcoins in exchange for using their computer to process the system that records Bitcoin transactions. There is no physical unit – a bitcoin is literally just an entry in the transaction log (it's called a 'block chain'). Whether these actually have any value is decided by the market and Bitcoins have seen huge swings in what they are worth leading some economists to warn against them.

E-money has two implications for businesses. Firstly there is the convenience of employees using it themselves when on business trips. Perhaps more importantly, depending on the type of business, it may be that customers will come to expect to be able to pay for goods and services using e-money in the future. When this happens, the retailer needs to be ready for it.

Tangible Media

A new and interesting way to represent information stored on a computer is through the use of physical objects. Very few applications are currently commercially available; however, imagine that you have a bowl of plastic pebbles in your living room and each represents one of your favourite films. To view the film, you pick up one of the pebbles and wave it at your television screen. A moment later the film starts. This is more an artistic application than something most people would want, however a 'killer application' is perhaps just around the corner which will make this technology take off. Perhaps you could think of one yourself and capitalize on your idea.

Most people are comfortable with the concept of icons. An icon on your computer screen represents a file. The icon isn't the same thing as the file, it's more like a pointer to it. Double clicking on the icon opens up the file.

phicon Phicon stands for 'physical icon', and is a physical representation of digital data, in the same way that an icon on a computer screen represents a file.

The plastic pebble representing the film is the same idea, only the pebble is a physical icon, or **phicon** (pronounced fi-con). The technology has been available for several years but a 'killer application' for phicons has not yet been found. Some ideas are a business card which opens a personal home page automatically whenever it is held near a computer. Or a brochure, marketing literature for instance, that also contains additional electronic information within it. In the future your lecture handouts could also contain electronic resources built into them! This research area is known as tangible media.

Some companies are experimenting with sending touch over long distances. Such devices currently only have novelty value, but perhaps someone will soon come up with a useful business application. The Kiss Communicator and the Hug shirt are two such devices. The Kiss Communicator allows you to blow a kiss to someone wherever they are. The Hug Shirt allows you to send them a hug. To do this requires two hug shirts. You put on one of them and hug yourself. Sensors in the shirt detect what you have done and send the information needed to recreate this feeling via bluetooth, to your mobile phone. Your phone then transmits the information as a text message to the receiver of the hug. They get a text asking if they want to accept the hug. If they do, the signal gets passed to their hug shirt, again via bluetooth, which squeezes them in the same way that you hugged your own shirt. These devices both represent new ways of connecting people.

Personal Robotics

Robotics has been mentioned before in this text, mostly in the context of assembly plants, manufacturing and space exploration. In this section, we will look at some of the robots that are used, and could be used, in our everyday lives.

The Roomba is a robotic vacuum cleaner costing around €250. It can be released into a home where it spends its time continuously cleaning. When it needs a battery recharge, it can go to a base station and recharge itself. It cannot yet, however, empty itself, although it can navigate around furniture and other obstacles. A potential business application of this technology is in cleaning offices – an army of Roombas could be let loose overnight. However, at present, the technology is not really good enough for this. Those interested in studying robotics should consider that the Roomba gives a cheap platform to experiment with – the makers of the Roomba, who are products of MIT's Artificial Intelligence Lab, have made it so that you can install your own software on it, and modify its behaviour.

Quite a few attempts have been made to develop robots that have personality, to give them a more natural interface to interact with people. Minerva was a talking robot designed to accommodate people in public spaces. She was active in 1998 offering people at the Smithsonian's National Museum of American History tours and leading them from exhibit to exhibit. Minerva had moods – she could be happy and sing or get frustrated and blare her horn.

Minerva was a personal robot. One of the world's leading centres in **personal robotics** is the Robotic Life Group (also known as the Personal Robotics Group) at MIT, led by Cynthia Breazeal. This team builds robots to study our socialization with them. The term personal robotics refers to robots that become part of our everday lives. While currently of little relevance to

personal robotics A term which refers to robotic companions that people socialize with.

most businesses, we shall see in the next section that this might change, when we examine, among other things, one of the most loved personal robots, Sony's Aibo.

Virtual Pets

During the late 1990s, Sony released Aibo, a robotic puppy intended as a replacement for a real puppy. Aibo explored its environment, and got tried, hungry, grumpy, and sleepy. It sometimes craved attention and could get over excited. Sony sadly no longer manufacture Aibo, but many cheaper versions inspired by it remain on the market. Aibo is an example of a virtual pet.

Virtual pets started to gain worldwide popularity in the late 1990s when Japanese toy manufacturer Bandai released the Tamagotchi (Figure 10.5). About the size of a key ring, a typical Tamagotchi had a small black and white screen, three buttons, a speaker, a motion sensor and a microphone. Users could feed, clean and play with their Tamagotchi, call it via the microphone

virtual pet An artificial companion. Could be screen based, i.e. the pet is animated on a computer monitor, or a robot.

and chase away predators by shaking the unit. The pet would evolve over time and would eventually either die or fly away. Many users became emotionally attached to their pet, which was the ultimate goal of the software designers.

Virtual pets are perhaps unique among information systems in that their goal is to get users to feel a sense of responsibility towards the system and become attached in some way to it. Virtual pets are very popular at the moment. One of the most popular games for the Nintendo DS mobile games console is Nintendogs, which is essentially a more sophisticated version of the Tamagotchi.

Figure 10.5 The **Tamagotchi** *This virtual pet gained widespread popularity and notoriety in the 1990s.*

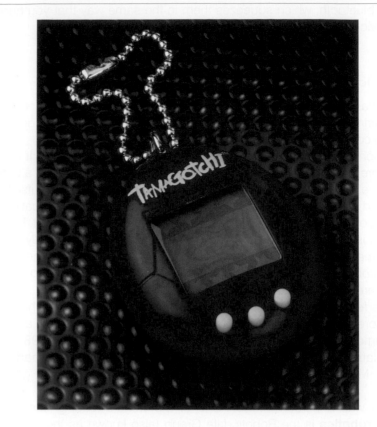

So why might businesses be interested in virtual pets? Some business tools (or at least software that could be used by businesses) have 'virtual-pet-like' personality built into them. 'Clippy' or 'Clipit', the Microsoft help agent, was one of the first. Clippy would cheerfully offer to help users with their tasks. It was almost universally hated, but it is clear that Microsoft and others have not yet given up on software with personality. Other attempts have been made to infuse personality into everyday software. PostPet by Sony was an email application where an on-screen puppy would fetch your mail, just as some real dogs do for their owners, but only if you were nice to it. The Nabaztag Rabbit is a personal companion that sits beside you and reads you the news and tells you when you have a new email. Mrs Dewey was a human interface to the Windows Live Search who would tell jokes to the user while they were running their search.

It is clear that some software developers are interested in giving their products personality. It is also clear that today's teenagers are perfectly comfortable interacting with devices that have personality. It may be that, in the future when they become employees, they will expect their business software to come with personality built in.

10.4 Computer Supported Cooperative Work

Computer supported cooperative work (CSCW) refers to technologies that allow groups to work together to achieve goals. Individuals in the groups can be co-located (in the same place) or geographically separated. The work can happen synchronously (individuals at work at the same time) or asynchronously (they work at different times). Different CSCW technologies exist to support these different modes of work. In global companies, CSCW technology is a powerful tool enabling a company to make the best of its human resources no matter where they are located. In this section, we will look at some CSCW tools.

Videoconferencing

For a long time in science fiction, the public has seen the future of the telephone call where both audio and video are transmitted. The technology now exists to achieve this easily and cheaply, yet while Skype video calls are popular they don't seem to have replaced phone calls in any great extent, at least in the home environment. A **videoconference** is a simultaneous communication between two or more parties where they both see and hear each other. A videoconference can be set up using instant messaging software. For businesses, videoconferences are useful to hold global meetings. Visual cues are available to help everyone understand what other people are really feeling – a yawn, a nod of the head, a smile, etc. None of these can be transmitted down a telephone line. However, running a videoconference does take discipline as it is easy for more than one person to talk at once and even a slight delay in transmission time can cause chaos. TKO Video Communications has video conferencing facilities all over the world which can be rented out by businesses who do not want to set up their own. A business in South Africa can hold a meeting with partners in Egypt and the United Arab Emirates by travelling to TKO offices in Cape Town, while their partners go to Cairo and Dubai. This is a shorter and cheaper journey than for them all having to physically meet.

> **videoconference** A videoconference is a simultaneous communication between two or more parties where they both see and hear each other.

Messaging

Messaging technology includes email, instant messaging and web chat rooms. Email has been discussed before. It is useful for asynchronous text-based communication. Instant messaging is used for synchronous communication – two (or more) people are communicating at the same time, usually typing short sentences to build up a conversation. Instant messaging is extremely useful and can be used by employees to work on a problem together. Instant messaging versus a telephone call is largely a matter of personal preference. One advantage messaging has is that the text can be easily saved and re-read at a later date. A chat room is a facility that enables two or more people to engage in interactive 'conversations' over the web. When you participate in a chat room, dozens of people might be participating from around the world. Multi-person chats are usually organized around specific topics, and participants often adopt nicknames to maintain anonymity.

Instant messaging technology is now being used by a diverse range of companies including Zurich Insurance and Ikea, as an alternative to making customers telephone a call centre. Customers often prefer clicking on the chat icon on a company website and waiting for the 'operator' to respond, than having to phone and wait in a queue. When phoning a call centre you often have to hold the phone to your ear, so at least one hand is tied up, and listen to (usually awful) music until someone answers. With messaging technology you can continue working at your computer until someone answers. You know when this happens as the task bar on your computer screen will start flashing.

Interactive Whiteboards

Essentially, an **interactive whiteboard** is a combination of a whiteboard and a PC. It can be used in a number of ways. Users can write on the whiteboard and then save what has been written as an image on their computer. This negates the need to take notes about what has been written after a meeting has finished. What is saved on the PC needn't be a static image – it could be an animation of everything that was written, including things that were

> **interactive whiteboard** This term can be used to mean slightly different technologies, but essentially it is a combination of a whiteboard and a desktop computer.

rubbed out. Alternatively, two whiteboards at different locations could be used by people at these different locations to see what each other is writing. Combined with videoconferencing, this can be a powerful way of running meetings when not everyone is present. An interactive whiteboard is shown in Figure 10.6.

Figure 10.6 Interactive Whiteboard *What gets written on the board can be saved, printed and sent to other whiteboards.*

Wikis

wiki A web page that can be edited by anyone with the proper authority.

A **wiki** is a web page that can be edited by anyone with the proper authority. The most famous example is Wikipedia, which can be edited by any web user – very few restrictions are put in place. To see the usefulness of wikis, have a look at Wikipedia. Its content is breathtaking, considering that all of it was created by volunteers. You might try editing an article you know something about, however consider this: there is no way to know if the information has been edited by an expert or by a joker, so think twice before you rely on anything you read there.

Wikis are clearly a good way of sharing knowledge and are being used by a large number of research groups and businesses, to allow employees to share their thoughts and ideas, and post up good practice. Read the first case at the end of the chapter (page 365) for more information.

MMOGs

Look for information about MMOGs using a search engine and you may be hit with a confusing array of acronyms including MMORTS, MMOFPS and MMORPGs. MMOG stands for 'massively multiplayer online game'. They have a long history, but today they exist as 3-D **virtual worlds**. Users are represented in the world by an avatar, which interacts with other avatars typically by text, but voice is starting to be used. From a business point of view, we are not primarily interested in virtual worlds as games, but as a platform for holding meetings and for their marketing potential. Probably the best virtual world for these activities is Second Life.

virtual world A computer-based environment where users' avatars can interact.

Owned by San Francisco-based Linden Lab, Second Life is a huge virtual world where residents meet socially and commercially. It has its own currency, the Linden dollar, which has a floating exchange rate with the US dollar. This means you can make (and spend) real money in Second Life. Several people are making a good living there (mostly by land speculation and by creating and selling animations) and big businesses are starting to get involved. IBM and Dell have already held global meetings in Second Life, and you can test drive Toyota cars there.[13] (Note, however, that IBM and Dell were researching the usefulness of using this platform to hold meetings – they were not actually holding a board meeting there; that has yet to happen.) Some commentators are saying that 3-D interfaces such as this will become the main way we access information over the Internet in the future. As an example of the direction Linden Lab may be planning for their technology, Jeff Bezos, the founder of Amazon, is one of the financial backers of Second Life, and Philip Rosedale, CEO of Linden Lab, has pointed out that whenever someone visits Amazon, there are thousands of other shoppers on the site with them. He has expressed the opinion that it would be a good thing if all those shoppers could both see and interact with each other. Business uses of virtual worlds have tailed off recently as the initial hype has worn off, but some commentators are still predicting they will play a part in future business communications.[14]

Blogs and Podcasts

While not strictly a CSCW technology, blogs still allow for the sharing of information from one to many people. A **blog**, short for 'weblog', is a website that people create and use to write about their observations, experiences and feelings on a wide range of topics. Technically it is identical to any other web page, although the content of a blog is updated much more frequently, typically every day. The community of blogs and bloggers is often called the 'blogosphere'. A 'blogger' is a person who creates a blog, while 'blogging' refers to the process of placing entries or 'posts' on a blog site. A blog is like a diary. When people post information to a blog, it is placed at the top of the blog. Blogs can contain links to other material, and people can usually comment on posts. Blogs are easy to post to, but they can cause problems when people tell or share too much.[15] People have been fired for blogging about work, and the daughter of a politician embarrassed her father when she made personal confessions on her blog.

> **blog** An online diary, a combination of the words 'web' and 'log'.

Blog sites, such as www.blogger.com, include information and tools to help people create and use weblogs. The way blogs are structured, with the most recent post appearing at the top, can make it extremely difficult to read and understand what it is all about – imagine you visit a blog, which you know (from an Internet search) talks about a product you are having problems with. Let's say the first post you come to starts: 'Today's fresh hell – ABC company rep John replied and said it would work. I tried it and ended up breaking the stupid thing. Just my luck.' The blogger is presumably making reference to something written about yesterday or before. It may take you a while to track down what they did to break the product, something you probably want to know about to avoid doing yourself. Go to blogger.com, select a blog at random (there is a feature to do this) and you will see the problem – it can be difficult to start reading a blog. If you keep a blog, you might want to think about this and how you can keep new and irregular readers interested.

Microblogs are currently extremely popular with Twitter being the most common example. They have much the same goals as the blogs described above except that posts are limited in size. In the case of Twitter's, the limit is 140 characters. Microblogs have many uses. They are often used by celebrities to keep in close contact with their fans. One of the end of chapter cases is about another use: Hashtag Activism.

A **podcast** is an audio broadcast over the Internet. The term 'podcast' comes from the word iPod, Apple's portable music player, and the word 'broadcast'. A podcast is essentially an audio blog, like a personal radio station on the Internet, and extends blogging by adding audio messages. Using a computer and microphone, you can record audio messages and place them on the Internet. You can then listen to the podcasts on your computer or download the audio material to a music player, such

> **podcast** An audio broadcast over the Internet.

as Apple's iPod. You can also use podcasting to listen to TV programmes, your favourite radio personalities, music, and messages from your friends and family at any time and place. Finding good podcasts, however, can be challenging. Apple's new version of iTunes allows you to download free software to search for podcasts by keyword.

People and corporations can use podcasts to listen to audio material, increase revenues, or advertise products and services.[16] Colleges and universities often use blogs and podcasts to deliver course material to students.

Many blogs and podcasts offer automatic updates to a computer using a technology called Really Simple Syndication (RSS). RSS is a collection of web formats to help provide web content or summaries of web content. With RSS, you can get a blog update without actually visiting the blog website. RSS can also be used to get other updates on the Internet from news websites and podcasts.

10.5 More Applications of Electronic and Mobile Commerce

Lastly in this chapter we will examine how e-commerce and m-commerce are being used in innovative and exciting ways. This section examines a few of the many B2B, B2C, C2C and m-commerce applications in the retail and wholesale, manufacturing, marketing, investment and finance, and auction arenas.

Retail and Wholesale

electronic retailing (e-tailing)
The direct sale from business to consumer through electronic storefronts, typically designed around an electronic catalogue and shopping cart model.

E-commerce is being used extensively in retailing and wholesaling. **Electronic retailing**, sometimes called e-tailing, is the direct sale of products or services by businesses to consumers through electronic shops, which are typically designed around the familiar electronic catalogue and shopping cart model. Tens of thousands of electronic retail websites sell a wide range. In addition, cyber shopping centres, or 'cybermalls', are another means to support retail shopping. A cybermall is a single website that offers many products and services at one Internet location. An Internet cybermall pulls multiple buyers and sellers into one virtual place, easily reachable through a web browser. For example, Cybermall New Zealand (www.cybermall.co.nz) is a virtual shopping mall that offers retail shopping, travel, and infotainment products and services.

A key sector of wholesale e-commerce is spending on manufacturing, repair and operations (MRO) of goods and services – from simple office supplies to mission-critical equipment, such as the motors, pumps, compressors and instruments that keep manufacturing facilities running smoothly. MRO purchases often approach 40 per cent of a manufacturing company's total revenues, but the purchasing system can be haphazard, without automated controls. In addition to these external purchase costs, companies face significant internal costs resulting from outdated and cumbersome MRO management processes. For example, studies show that a high percentage of manufacturing downtime is often caused by not having the right part at the right time in the right place. The result is lost productivity and capacity. E-commerce software for plant operations provides powerful comparative searching capabilities to enable managers to identify functionally equivalent items, helping them spot opportunities to combine purchases for cost savings. Comparing various suppliers, coupled with consolidating more spending with fewer suppliers, leads to decreased costs. In addition, automated workflows are typically based on industry best practices, which can streamline processes.

Manufacturing

One approach taken by many manufacturers to raise profitability and improve customer service is to move their supply chain operations onto the Internet. Here they can form an

electronic exchange to join with competitors and suppliers alike, using computers and websites to buy and sell goods, trade market information and run back-office operations, such as inventory control, as shown in Figure 10.7. With such an exchange, the business centre is not a physical building but a network-based location where business interactions occur. This approach has greatly speeded up the movement of raw materials and finished products among all members of the business community, thus reducing the amount of inventory that must be maintained. It has also led to a much more competitive marketplace and lower prices. Private exchanges are owned and operated by a single company. The owner uses the exchange to trade exclusively with established business partners. Public exchanges are owned and operated by industry groups. They provide

electronic exchange An electronic forum where manufacturers, suppliers and competitors buy and sell goods, trade market information and run back-office operations.

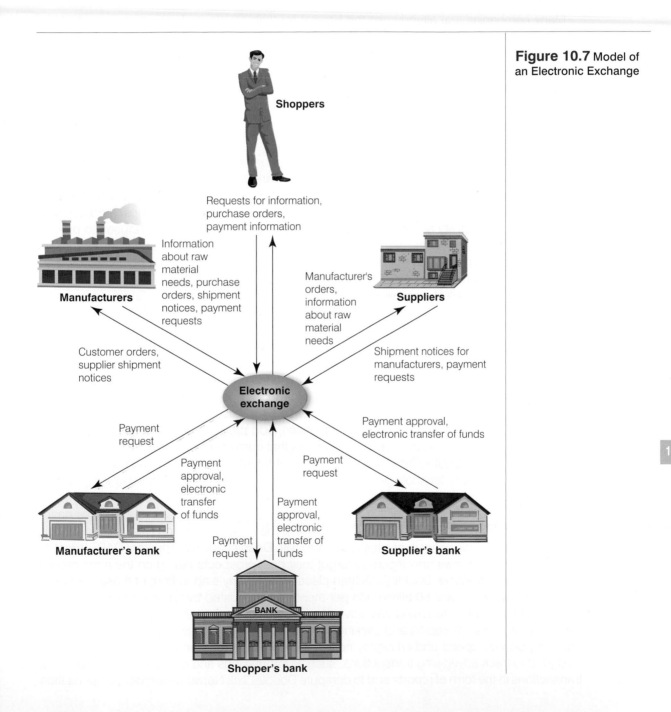

Figure 10.7 Model of an Electronic Exchange

Shoppers

Requests for information, purchase orders, payment information

Information about raw material needs, purchase orders, shipment notices, payment requests

Manufacturers

Manufacturer's orders, information about raw material needs

Suppliers

Customer orders, supplier shipment notices

Shipment notices for manufacturers, payment requests

Electronic exchange

Payment request

Payment approval, electronic transfer of funds

Payment approval, electronic transfer of funds

Payment request

Payment request

Payment approval, electronic transfer of funds

Manufacturer's bank

Supplier's bank

BANK

Shopper's bank

10

services and a common technology platform to their members and are open, usually for a fee, to any company that wants to use them.

Several strategic and competitive issues are associated with the use of exchanges. Many companies distrust their corporate rivals and fear they might lose trade secrets through participation in such exchanges. Suppliers worry that the online marketplaces and their auctions will drive down the prices of goods and favour buyers. Suppliers also can spend a great deal of money in the setup to participate in multiple exchanges. For example, more than a dozen new exchanges have appeared in the oil industry, and the printing industry has up to more than 20 online marketplaces. Until a clear winner emerges in particular industries, suppliers are more or less forced to sign on to several or all of them. Yet another issue is potential government scrutiny of exchange participants – when competitors get together to share information, it raises questions of collusion or antitrust behaviour.

Many companies that already use the Internet for their private exchanges have no desire to share their expertise with competitors. At the US shopping giant Wal-Mart, the world's number-one retail chain, executives turned down several invitations to join exchanges in the retail and consumer goods industries. Wal-Mart is pleased with its in-house exchange, Retail Link, which connects the company to 7000 worldwide suppliers that sell everything from toothpaste to furniture.

Marketing

The nature of the web allows firms to gather much more information about customer behaviour and preferences than they could using other marketing approaches. Marketing organizations can measure many online activities as customers and potential customers gather information and make their purchase decisions. Analysis of this data is complicated because of the web's interactivity and because each visitor voluntarily provides or refuses to provide personal data such as name, address, email address, telephone number and demographic data. Internet advertisers use the data they gather to identify specific portions of their markets and target them with tailored advertising messages. This practice, called **market segmentation**, divides the pool of potential customers into subgroups, which are usually defined in terms of demographic characteristics, such as age, gender, marital status, income level and geographic location.

market segmentation The identification of specific markets to target them with advertising messages.

technology-enabled relationship management Occurs when a firm obtains detailed information about a customer's behaviour, preferences, needs and buying patterns, and uses that information to set prices, negotiate terms, tailor promotions, add product features and otherwise customize its entire relationship with that customer.

Technology-enabled relationship management is a new twist on establishing direct customer relationships made possible when firms promote and sell on the web. Technology-enabled relationship management occurs when a firm obtains detailed information about a customer's behaviour, preferences, needs and buying patterns, and uses that information to set prices, negotiate terms, tailor promotions, add product features and otherwise customize its entire relationship with that customer.

DoubleClick is a leading global Internet advertising company that leverages technology and media expertise to help advertisers use the power of the web to build relationships with customers. The DoubleClick Network is its flagship product, a collection of high-traffic and well-recognized sites on the web, including MSN, Sports Illustrated, Continental Airlines, the Washington Post, CBS and more than 1500 others. This network of sites is coupled with DoubleClick's proprietary DART targeting technology, which allows advertisers to target their best prospects based on the most precise profiling criteria available. DoubleClick then places a company's ad in front of those best prospects. DART powers over 60 billion ads per month and is trusted by top advertising agencies. Comprehensive online reporting lets advertisers know how their campaign is performing and what type of users are seeing and clicking on their ads. This high-level targeting and real-time reporting provide speed and efficiency not available in any other medium. The system is also designed to track advertising transactions, such as impressions and clicks, to summarize these transactions in the form of reports and to compute DoubleClick Network member compensation.

Investment and Finance

The Internet has revolutionized the world of investment and finance. Perhaps the changes have been so great because this industry had so many built-in inefficiencies and so much opportunity for improvement.

The brokerage business adapted to the Internet faster than any other arm of finance. The allure of online trading that enables investors to do quick, thorough research and then buy shares in any company in a few seconds and at a fraction of the cost of a full-commission firm has brought many investors to the web. In spite of the wealth of information available online, the average consumer buys stocks based on a tip or a recommendation rather than as the result of research and analysis. It is the more sophisticated investor that really takes advantage of the data and tools available on the Internet.[17]

Online banking customers can check balances of their savings, chequing, and loan accounts; transfer money among accounts; and pay their bills. These customers enjoy the convenience of not writing cheques by hand, tracking their current balances, and reducing expenditures on envelopes and stamps.

All of the country's major banks and many of the smaller banks enable their customers to pay bills online; many support bill payment via a mobile phone or other wireless device. Banks are eager to gain more customers who pay bills online because such customers tend to stay with the bank longer, have higher cash balances, and use more of the bank's products.

The next advance in online bill paying is **electronic bill presentment**, which eliminates all paper, right down to the bill itself. With this process, the vendor posts an image of your statement on the Internet and alerts you by email that your bill has arrived. You then direct your bank to pay it.

electronic bill presentment
A method of billing whereby a vendor posts an image of your statement on the Internet and alerts you by email that your bill has arrived.

Auctions

eBay has become synonymous with online auctions for both private sellers and small companies. However, hundreds of online auction sites cater to newcomers to online auctions and to unhappy eBay customers. The most frequent complaints are increases in fees and problems with unscrupulous buyers. As a result, eBay is constantly trying to expand and improve its services. eBay spent €1.8 billion to acquire Skype, a pioneer in voice over IP (VoIP) services with the goal of improving communications between sellers and potential buyers for 'high-involvement' items such as automobiles, business equipment and high-end collectibles. eBay might also provide a pay-for-call service to provide a lead generation service for sellers based on the Skype technology. eBay purchased the payment gateway system of security company VeriSign to provide a payment solution to tens of thousands of new small and mid-sized businesses. Under the deal, eBay will also receive two million VeriSign security tokens, physical devices like keychain-sized USB plug-ins that are used to create two-factor security where users must provide both a security password and the physical token.[18]

Anywhere, Anytime Applications of Mobile Commerce

Because m-commerce devices usually have a single user, they are ideal for accessing personal information and receiving targeted messages for a particular consumer. Through m-commerce, companies can reach individual consumers to establish one-to-one marketing relationships and communicate whenever it is convenient – in short, anytime and anywhere. Following are just a few examples of potential m-commerce applications:

- Banking customers can use their wireless handheld devices to access their accounts and pay their bills.
- Clients of brokerage firms can view stock prices and company research as well as conduct trades to fit their schedules.

- Information services such as financial news, sports information and traffic updates can be delivered to people whenever they want.
- On-the-move retail consumers can place and pay for orders instantaneously.
- Telecommunications service users can view service changes, pay bills and customize their services.
- Retailers and service providers can send potential customers advertising, promotions or coupons to entice them to try their services as they move past their place of business.

The most successful m-commerce applications suit local conditions and people's habits and preferences. Most people do their research online and then buy offline at a local retailer. As a result, a growing market for local search engines is designed to answer the question, 'where do I buy product x at a brick-and-mortar retailer near me?' Consumers provide their post code and begin by asking a basic question – 'What local stores carry a particular category of items' (e.g. flat-screen televisions). Consumers typically don't start searching knowing that they want a specific model of Panasonic flat-screen TV. The local search engine then provides a list of local stores, including those with a website and those without, which sell this item.

As with any new technology, m-commerce will only succeed if it provides users with real benefits. Companies involved in m-commerce must think through their strategies carefully and ensure that they provide services that truly meet customers' needs.

Advantages of Electronic and Mobile Commerce

According to the Council of Supply Chain Management Professionals, 'Supply Chain Management encompasses the planning and management of all activities involved in sourcing and procurement, conversion, and all logistics management activities. Importantly, it also includes coordination and collaboration with channel partners, which can be suppliers, intermediaries, third-party service providers, and customers'.[19] Conversion to an e-commerce – driven supply chain provides businesses with an opportunity to achieve operational excellence by enabling consumers and companies to gain a global reach to worldwide markets, reduce the cost of doing business, speed the flow of goods and information, increase the accuracy of order processing and order fulfilment, and improve the level of customer service.

- *Global reach.* E-commerce offers enormous opportunities. It allows manufacturers to buy at a low cost worldwide, and it offers enterprises the chance to sell to a global market right from the very start-up of their business. Moreover, e-commerce offers great promise for developing countries, helping them to enter the prosperous global marketplace, and hence helping reduce the gap between rich and poor countries.
- *Reduce costs.* By eliminating or reducing time-consuming and labour-intensive steps throughout the order and delivery process, more sales can be completed in the same period and with increased accuracy. With increased speed and accuracy of customer order information, companies can reduce the need for inventory – from raw materials, to safety stocks, to finished goods – at all the intermediate manufacturing, storage and transportation points.
- *Speed the flow of goods and information.* When organizations are connected via e-commerce, the flow of information is accelerated because of the already established electronic connections and communications processes. As a result, information can flow easily, directly and rapidly from buyer to seller.
- *Increased accuracy*. By enabling buyers to enter their own product specifications and order information directly, human data-entry error on the part of the supplier is eliminated.
- *Improve customer service*. Increased and more detailed information about delivery dates and current status can increase customer loyalty. In addition, the ability to consistently meet customers' desired delivery dates with high-quality goods and services eliminates any incentive for customers to seek other sources of supply.

Summary

The term 'computing' no longer refers to a computer on a desk. Mobile devices are letting employees access information from wherever they happen to be. In addition, the same technologies are allowing customers to interact with businesses in new ways. A computer no longer has to look like a huge box with wires attached to a keyboard, monitor and mouse. Maybe people carry around several computer devices with them everyday – a smartphone and iPod are just two examples. Others include laptops and pocket PCs. Fewer people are using wearable technology, where computing power is built into, for example, the clothes that we wear. However, several research groups are interested in this area and if and when a company produces a 'killer application' for wearable technology, the market will grow substantially.

Central to any mobile computing is wireless networking, with wi-fi hotspots being an area where wireless access is available. Many bars and cafés provide their customers with wi-fi, often charging by the half-hour, although sometimes access is free. Tangible media takes concepts from the computer screen and embodies them. Phicons, or physical icons, are one early example. Phicons are used to represent something in the same way that icons on a computer screen represent a computer file. One example of phicons is using them to represent landmarks that can be used to interact with an electronic map.

Personal robotics attempts to make social robots that people want to interact with, as opposed to manufacturing robots which are used to assemble products. Again, several research groups have an interest in this area, but it has not yet really taken off. The robot puppy Aibo is an example of a personal robot. It is also an example of a virtual pet. Virtual pets are perhaps unique among information systems in that their goal is to get users to feel a sense of responsibility towards their pet and become attached in some way to them. Virtual pets are very popular at the moment. They are of interest to businesses as already we are seeing software tools that have been given personality by their developers. In the future, employees will be comfortable interacting with devices that have personality.

Teams made up of people living in different geographical regions are able to work together efficiently and effectively, without ever having to meet. This work is facilitated by a range of technologies. Computer supported cooperative work (CSCW) refers to technologies that allow groups to work together to achieve goals. Individuals in the groups can be co-located (in the same place) or geographically separated. The work can happen synchronously (individuals work at the same time) or asynchronously (they work at different times). Different CSCW technologies exist to support these different modes of work. In global companies, CSCW technology is a powerful tool enabling the company to make the best of its human resources no matter where it is located.

A videoconference is a simultaneous communication between two or more parties where they both see and hear each other. A video conference can be set up easily and cheaply using instant messenging. Videoconferencing is a powerful application, especially when combined with other CSCW tools, allowing people to hold useful meetings when they are geographically distant. Messaging technology includes email, instant messaging and web chat rooms. Each of these are used to communicate via text.

An interactive whiteboard is a combination of a whiteboard and a computer. Users can write on the whiteboard and then save what has been written as an image on their computer. This negates the need to take a note of what has been written after a meeting has finished. Two interactive whiteboards can be used to let people who are separated see what the others have written, and add to it. A wiki is a web page that can be edited by anyone with the proper authority. The most famous example is Wikipedia, which can be edited by any web user – very few restrictions are put in place. Wikis are clearly a good way of knowledge sharing. Virtual worlds are 3-D environments populated by avatars. Second Life is a good example. Second Life has been used to host global business meetings, and some large firms are now marketing their products there. Blogs and podcasts are another useful way of sharing knowledge. A blog is an online diary. A podcast is an audio broadcast over the Internet.

E-commerce and m-commerce can be used in many innovative ways to improve the operations of an organization. Electronic retailing (e-tailing) is the direct sale from a business to consumers through electronic storefronts designed around an electronic catalogue and shopping cart model.

A cybermall is a single website that offers many products and services at one Internet location.

Manufacturers are joining electronic exchanges, where they can work with competitors and suppliers to use computers and websites to buy and sell goods, trade market information, and run back-office operations such as inventory control. They are also using e-commerce to improve the efficiency of the selling process by moving customer queries about product availability and prices online.

The web allows firms to gather much more information about customer behaviour and preferences than they could using other marketing approaches.

This new technology has greatly enhanced the practice of market segmentation and enabled companies to establish closer relationships with their customers. Detailed information about a customer's behaviour, preferences, needs and buying patterns allow companies to set prices, negotiate terms, tailor promotions, add product features and otherwise customize a relationship with a customer.

The Internet has also revolutionized the world of investment and finance, especially online stock trading and online banking. The Internet has also created many options for electronic auctions, where geographically dispersed buyers and sellers can come together.

M-commerce transactions can be used in all these application arenas. M-commerce provides a unique opportunity to establish one-on-one marketing relationships and support communications anytime and anywhere.

Self-Assessment Test

1 A wi-fi _____ is an area where wireless access is available.

2 Keyboards can be wirelessly attached to a pocket PC using the _____ protocol.

3 _____ refers to the transfer of funds that happens electronically rather than by handing over physical coins and notes.

4 The Tamagotchi was an early example of a _____.

5 People only use CSCW tools if they are geographically distant. True or false?

6 A _____ is a web page that a group of users can easily edit.

7 The term 'blog' is an abbreviation of _____.

8 Buyers and sellers alike can use an electronic exchange to _____.
a. buy and sell goods
b. trade market information
c. run back-office operations
d. all of the above

9 The practice of _____ divides the pool of potential customers into subgroups, which are usually defined in terms of demographic characteristics.

10 An advancement in online bill payment that uses email for the company to post an image of your statement on the Internet so you can direct your bank to pay it is called _____.

Review Questions

1 What is wi-fi?

2 Explain the difference between a pocket PC and a smartphone. Is the distinction blurred?

3 List three ways of implementing e-money.

4 Suggest an application for wearable technology.

5 Define CSCW.

6 What is a videoconference?

7 What is the difference between a wiki and a blog?

8 What is e-tailing?

9 What is technology-enabled relationship management?

10 List some advantages of mobile commerce.

Discussion Questions

1 Explain some of the advantages of e-money. Are there any disadvantages? Which would you rather carry – notes and coins or e-money? Explain your answer.

2 Why do you think videoconferencing has not taken off in the home? Do you use videoconferencing to keep in touch with friends? Why or why not?

3 Do you keep a blog? If so, explain why and who you think you readers are. Outline an approach you could use to increase your readship.

4 Critically evaluate wiki software to determine whether it is a good way to share knowledge. Explain your answer.

5 What are some of the disadvantages of mobile technology? Is there anywhere you would not use a pocket PC, for instance? Why?

Web Exercises

1 Go to blogger.com and search for a blog by an information systems tutor (there are many!). Read the most recent posts and write a short summary of the experience.

2 Have a look at Wikipedia and read some of the articles about the technology discussed in this chapter. Can you spot any mistakes? Email a list of the articles you have read to your tutor.

Case One

Twitter Rallies Support for Kidnapped Girls

Hashtag activism refers to the use of Twitter hashtags to promote change, whether that change is social, political, economic or environmental. It involves using a hashtag to build public awareness and pressure on a particular issue. Jon Stewart of the Comedy Central TV programme The Daily Show says 'the thing about hashtag activism – it cannot force a crazy person to do something, but it can shame a less crazy person into not doing nothing.' He was referring to the kidnapping in 2014 of 200 Nigerian school girls by the terrorist group Boko Harem. For over a week the Nigerian authorities did little to find the girls and were accused of ignoring their plight, until two Nigerians sent out tweets that included the hashtag #bringbackourdaughters. At that point the story started to gather speed with the hashtag being changed along the way to #bringbackourgirls. Celebrities,

politicians and world leaders united behind the cause.

Notably, US First Lady Michelle Obama tweeted a photo of herself holding a placard showing the hashtag, an act which received an amount of criticism. Fox News contributors discussed if the hashtag could actually 'make progress' or was rather simply a tool to make people 'feel better about themselves.'

'It's an exercise in self-esteem,' commentator George Will said. 'I do not know how adults stand there, facing a camera, and say, "Bring back our girls". Are these barbarians in the wilds of Nigeria supposed to check their Twitter accounts and say, "Uh oh, Michelle Obama is very cross with us, we better change our behaviour"?'

If tweeting had been America's only response then perhaps this criticism might hold water, but

10

in fact the US did agree to send military and law enforcement experts who specialize in intelligence, investigations, hostage negotiation, information-sharing and victim assistance to help the Nigerian army. Certainly no one can say Mrs Obama didn't help raise awareness of the case.

At the time of writing the girls have not been recovered. The Nigerian army say that they have found their location but that it is currently too dangerous to attempt a rescue.

Questions

1 What do you think hashtag activism achieved in this case?

2 What are the limitations of hashtag activism?

3 Do you think hashtag activism is just an exercise in self-esteem?

4 How would you start a hashtag activism campaign?

Case Two

Killer Robots on the Loose

Fans of the Comedy Central TV programme The Colbert Report will know how frightened the show's writers are of killer robots, but when they started this running gag they probably did not know just how real a threat they actually are.

The International Committee for Robot Arms Control is a group of experts in robotics technology, robot ethics, international relations, international security, arms control, international humanitarian law and human rights law and human rights law who are concerned about the real dangers that military robots pose to peace and international security and to civilians in war. Their call is to 'Ban Autonomous Lethal Robots'.

Autonomous lethal robots are machines that can select and destroy targets without human intervention. America has recently relied on its fleet of drones in counter-insurgency, particularly in Pakistan where unmanned aircraft routinely venture to drop bombs on ground targets. But these drones are controlled in real time by a human or team of humans back at their base. However a team of Georgia Tech computer scientists at Fort Benning has demonstrated software that can – without human input – acquire and make life or death decisions about targets on the ground. Clay Dillow of Popular Science says, 'the only thing that's missing is the capability to fire. Add that, and you've got a killer robot.'

The International Committee for Robot Arms Control call is to have an outright ban on the development and deployment of weapon systems in which the decision to apply violent force is made autonomously. They are 'concerned about the potential of robots to undermine human responsibility in decisions to use force, and to obscure accountability for the consequences'. Some might argue that lethal autonomous weapons are the next step in modern warfare, a natural evolution beyond today's remotely operated drones and unmanned ground vehicles. The United Nations does not readily agree. Its Human Rights Council has, for now, called for a moratorium on the development of killer robots. But this is not enough for the International Committee for Robot Arms Control. Erik Schechte from LiveScience.com says 'the question is whether it is too early – or too late – for a blanket prohibition. Indeed, depending how one defines "autonomy," such systems are already in use.'

Questions

1 List the advantages and disadvantages – if you think there are any – of autonomous lethal robots.

2 The International Committee for Robot Arms Control is a group of experts, as are the Georgia Tech computer scientists. Does this suggest that the computer science community is split on this issue? What are your views?

3 Do you think it is too late for a blanket prohibition? Why or why not?

4 Can you think of any other applications for autonomous drones?

Case Three

Mother Manages the Home

The 'Internet of Things' is a phrase used to refer to connecting physical objects to the Internet. A basic example is sticking an RFID tag to a crate so that its location within a factory can be roughly determined. The same concept could be applied in the home – an RFID keyfob could mean that your computer will always know where your car keys are. For this to work you would need an RFID reader in every room.

A more advanced version of the Internet of Things is to embed technology into an object giving it the ability to interact with its own internal states and its external environment so that it can sense and communicate. The idea is that just as you can interact with other people via the Internet, and other computers via the Internet, you could also benefit from interacting with other objects ('things') via the Internet. Do you need to buy milk on the way home? Email your fridge and ask it. Are you going to arrive home early? Email your house and tell it to turn on the lights, the heating and the oven.

The Nabaztag Rabbit was mentioned in this chapter as a device that reads you the news, weather and your email. The people behind the rabbit have created a new company, Sen.se, and a new product range called Mother that is designed to bring the Internet of Things into the home. The company says, 'We are designing a world in which daily life can be continuously enhanced by the extra knowledge, comfort, fun and security, that sensors can bring but in which devices make the effort to understand us and have the courtesy to remain discreet.'

Mother consists of a series of mobile sensors called 'cookies' that sit in each room and detect location, movement and temperature. There is a 'parent device' that connects to the Internet in the same way that a PC does. The cookies wirelessly communicate with the parent device, and also with each other, via radio waves. The system can be used to tell who's at home, monitor their exercise such as walking or jogging distances, track a pet, tell you if you are drinking too much coffee, eating too many snacks or brushing your teeth enough, remind your to water the plants, measure the quality of everyone's sleep and, as the system is customizable, it has potentially many other applications.

'Mother is the first true advent of the Internet of Things in everyday life,' said Rafi Haladjian, Founder of Sen.se. 'We have made sensors that unobtrusively blend into your life. She offers the knowledge and comfort you want, when and how you want it, all while remaining discreet.'

A study by Pew Research has found that a large majority of the technology experts and engaged Internet users think that the Internet of Things and embedded and wearable computing will have widespread and beneficial effects by 2025.

Questions

1 What do you think the advantages and disadvantages are of the Mother system? Would you want one?

2 Can you think of other potential applications of Mother? What about in shared student accommodation? What about in a nursing home? Or school?

3 What other objects would you want to connect to the Internet and why?

4 What applications of the Internet of Things can you think of in a commercial setting?

Notes

1 T-Mobile Website. Retrieved from: www.t-mobile.co.uk.

2 www.btfon.com. Accessed 26 May 2014.

3 Head, W., 'Nokia Trials Wi-Fi Phones in Finland', *ITNews*. Retrieved from: www.itnews.com.au/News/35423, nokia-trials-wifi-phones-in-finland.aspx.

4 BBC Staff, bbc.co.uk, 'Norwich Pioneers Free City Wi-Fi'. Retrieved from: http://news.bbc.co.uk/1/hi/technology/ 5297884.stm.

5 BBC Staff, bbc.co.uk, 'Polynesians Get Free Wireless Web'. Retrieved from: http://news.bbc.co.uk/1/hi/technology/ 3020158.stm.

6 www.celluon.com/about.php. Accessed 26 May 2014.

7 Margi Website. Retrieved from: www.margi.com.

8 Tom Tom Website. Retrieved from: www.tomtom.com.

9 BBC iPlayer beta Website. Retrieved from: www.bbc.co.uk/iplayerbeta/.

10 LUUP Website. Retrieved from: www.luup.com.

11 Staff, bbc.co.uk, 'From Matatu to the Masai via Mobile'. Retrieved from: http://news.bbc.co.uk/1/hi/technology/ 6241603.stm.

12 World Bank Website. Retrieved from: web.worldbank.org/ WBSITE/EXTERNAL/EXTABOUTUS/EXTANNREP/EXTANNREP2K6/0,,contentMDK:21046759~menuPK:2915617~pagePK:64168445~piPK:64168309~theSitePK:2838572,00.html.

13 Rushe, D., 'Life in the Unreal World', *Sunday Times Magazine*, 10 December 2007.

14 Wasko, M., Teigland, R., Leidner, D. and Jarvenpaa, S., 2011. 'Stepping into the Internet: New Ventures in Virtual Worlds', *MIS Quarterly*, Vol. 35, No. 3 645–652.

15 Staff, 'Bloggers Learn the Price of Telling Too Much', CNN Online. Retrieved from http://edition.cnn.com/2005/TECH/internet/07/11/tell.all.blogs.ap/index.html, 11 July 2005.

16 McBride, Sarah, and Wingfield, Nick, 'As Podcasts Boom, Big Media Rushes to Stake a Claim', *The Wall Street Journal*, 10 October 2005, p. A1.

17 Rosencrance, Linda, 'Survey: User Satisfaction with E-Commerce Sites Rises Slightly', *Computerworld*, 21 February 2006.

18 Regan, Keith, 'Eyeing Expansion of PayPal, eBay Buys VeriSign Payment Gateway', *E-Commerce Times*, 11 October 2005.

19 Council of Supply Chain Management Professionals Website. Retrieved from: www.cscmp.org/Website/AboutCSCMP/Definitions/Definitions.asp.

World Views Case

Kulula.com: The Trials and Tribulations of a South African Online Airline

Anesh Maniraj Singh

University of Durban

Kulula.com was launched in August 2001 as the first online airline in South Africa. Kulula is one of two airlines that are operated by Comair Ltd. British Airways (BA), the other airline that Comair runs, is a full-service franchise operation that serves the South African domestic market. Kulula, unlike BA, is a limited-service operation aimed at providing low fares to a wider domestic market using five aircraft. Since its inception, Kulula has reinvented air travel in South Africa, making it possible for more people to fly than ever before.

Kulula is a true South African e-commerce success. The company boasts as one of its successes the fact that it has been profitable from day one. It is recognized internationally among the top low-cost airlines and participated in a conference attended by other such internationally known low-cost carriers as Virgin Blue, Ryanair and easyJet. Kulula also received an award from the South African Department of Trade and Industry for being a Technology Top 100 company.

Kulula's success is based on its clearly defined strategy of being the lowest-cost provider in the South African domestic air travel industry. To this end, Kulula has adopted a no-frills approach. Staff and cabin crew wear simple uniforms, and the company has no airport lounges. There are no business class seats and no frequent-flyer programmes. Customers pay for their food and drinks. In addition, Kulula does not issue paper tickets, and very few travel agents book its flights – 90 per cent of tickets are sold directly to customers. Furthermore, customers have to pay for ticket changes, and the company has a policy of 'no fly, no refund'. Yet, in its drive to keep costs down, Kulula does not compromise on maintenance and safety, and it employs the best pilots and meets the highest safety standards. Like all B2C companies, Kulula aims to create customer value by reducing overhead costs, including salaries, commissions, rent and consumables such as paper and paper-based documents. Furthermore, by cutting out the middleman such as travel agents, Kulula is able to keep prices low and save customers the time and inconvenience of having to pick up tickets from travel agents. Instead, customers control the entire shopping experience.

Kulula was the sole provider of low-cost flights in South Africa until early 2004, when One Time launched a no-frills service to compete head-on with Kulula. Due to the high price elasticity of demand within the industry, any lowering of price stimulates a higher demand for flights. The increase in competition in the low-price end of the market has seen Kulula decrease fares by up to 20 per cent while increasing passengers by over 40 per cent. There, however, has been no brand switching. Kulula has grown in the market at the expense of others.

Apart from its low-cost strategy, Kulula is successful because of its strong B2C business model. As previously mentioned, 90 per cent of its revenue is generated from direct sales. However, Kulula has ventured into the B2B market by collaborating with Computicket and a few travel agents, who can log on to the Kulula site from their company intranets. Kulula offers fares at substantial reductions to businesses that use it regularly. Furthermore, Kulula bases its success on three simple principles: Any decision taken must bring in additional revenue, save on costs, and/or enhance customer service. Technology contributes substantially to these three principles.

In its first year, Kulula used a locally developed reservation system, which soon ran out of functionality. The second-generation system was AirKiosk, which was developed in Boston for Kulula. The system change resulted in an improvement of functionality for passengers. For example, in 2003, Kulula ran a promotion during which tickets were sold at ridiculously low prices, and the system was overwhelmed.

10

Furthermore, Kulula experienced a system crash that lasted a day and a half, which severely hampered sales and customer service. As a result, year two saw a revamp in all technology: all the hardware was replaced, bandwidth was increased, new servers and database servers were installed, and web hosting was changed. In short, the entire system was replaced. According to IT Director Carl Scholtz, 'Our success depends on infrastructural stability; our current system has an output that is four times better than the best our systems could ever produce.' Kulula staff members are conscious of the security needs of customers and have invested in 128-bit encryption, giving customers peace of mind that their transactions and information are safe.

The success behind Kulula's systems lies in its branding – its strong identity in the marketplace, which includes its name and visual appeal. The term kulula means 'easy', and Kulula's website has been designed with a simple, no-fuss, user-friendly interface. When visiting the Kulula site, you are immediately aware that an airline ticket can be purchased in three easy steps. The first step allows customers to choose destinations and dates. The second step allows customers to choose the most convenient or cheapest flight based on their need. Kulula also allows customers to book cars and accommodations in step two. Step three is the transaction stage, which allows customers to choose the most suitable payment method. The confirmation and ticket can be printed after payment has been settled. Unlike other e-commerce sites, Kulula is uncluttered and simple to understand, enhancing customer service. Kulula is a fun brand – with offbeat advertising campaigns and bright green and blue corporate and aircraft colours – but behind the fun exterior is a group of people who are serious about business.

Kulula's future is extremely promising. Technology changes continually, and Kulula strives to have the best technology in place at all times. B2B e-commerce will continue to be a major focus of the company to develop additional distribution channels with little or no cost. In conjunction with bank partners, Kulula is developing additional methods of payment to replace credit card payments, allowing more people the opportunity to fly. These transactions will be free. Kulula is also involving customers in its marketing efforts by obtaining their permission to promote special offers by email and short message service to customers' mobile phones. The Kulula website will soon serve as a ticketing portal, where customers can also purchase British Airways tickets, in three easy steps. The company has many other developments in the pipeline that will enhance customer service. According to Scholtz, 'We are not an online airline, just an e-tailer that sells airline tickets.'

Questions

1 This case does not mention any back-up systems, either electronic or paper-based. What would you recommend to ensure that the business runs 24/7/365?

2 It is clear from this case that Kulula is a low-cost provider. What else could Kulula do with its technology to bring in additional revenue, save on cost and enhance customer service?

3 Does the approach taken by Kulula in terms of its strategy, its business model and the three principles of success lend itself to other businesses wanting to engage in e-commerce?

4 Kulula flights are almost always full. Do you think that by partnering with a company such as Lastminute.com the airline could fly to capacity at all times? What are the risks related to such a collaboration?

5 Kulula initially developed its systems in-house, which it later outsourced to AirKiosk in Boston. Do you think it is wise for an e-business to outsource its systems development? Is it strategically sound to outsource systems development to a company in a different country?

6 With the current trends in mobile commerce, could Kulula offer its services on mobile devices such as mobile phones? Would the company have to alter its strategic thinking to accommodate such a shift? Is it possible to develop a text-based interface that could facilitate a purchase in three easy steps?

PART 4

Systems Development

Systems Development

11

Systems Analysis

Principles

Effective systems development requires a team effort from stakeholders, users, managers, systems development specialists and various support personnel, and it starts with careful planning.

Systems development often uses tools to select, implement and monitor projects, including prototyping, rapid application development, CASE tools and object-oriented development.

Systems development starts with investigation and analysis of existing systems.

Learning Objectives

- Identify the key participants in the systems development process and discuss their roles.
- Define the term 'information systems' and 'planning' and list several reasons for initiating a systems project.
- Discuss three trends that illustrate the impact of enterprise resource planning software packages on systems development.

- Discuss the key features, advantages and disadvantages of the traditional, prototyping, rapid application development and end-user systems development lifecycles.
- Identify several factors that influence the success or failure of a systems development project.
- Discuss the use of CASE tools and the object-oriented approach to systems development.

- State the purpose of systems investigation.
- Discuss the importance of performance and cost objectives.
- State the purpose of systems analysis and discuss some of the tools and techniques used in this phase of systems development.

Why Learn About Systems Analysis?

Throughout this book, you have seen many examples of the use of information systems. But where do these systems come from? How can you work with IS personnel, such as systems analysts and computer programmers, to get what you need to succeed on the job? This chapter, the first of two chapters on systems development, gives you the answer. You will see how managers can initiate the systems development process and analyze end users' needs with the help of IS personnel. Systems investigation and systems analysis are the first two steps of the systems development process. This chapter provides specific examples of how new or modified systems are initiated and analyzed in a number of industries. In this chapter, you will learn how your project can be planned, aligned with corporate goals, rapidly developed and much more. The main thrust of this chapter and the next is about a company building its own information system from scratch. However, in the next chapter we will look at alternatives to this – buying in a system that someone else has already built.

We start with an overview of the systems development process.

11.1 An Overview of Systems Development

In today's businesses, managers and employees in all functional areas work together and use business information systems. Because they are central to project success, users are helping with development and, in many cases, leading the way. Users might request that a systems development team determine whether they should purchase a few PCs, update an existing order processing system, develop a new medical diagnostic, or design and implement a new website. In other cases, systems development might involve purchasing or leasing a systems such as an enterprise resource planning (ERP) package (discussed in Chapter 7).

This chapter and the next provide you with a deeper appreciation of the systems development process and show how businesses can avoid costly failures. Calculating the cost of an IT project is difficult and a number of high-profile mistakes have been made. Most of these are from the public sector (as any mistakes from the private sector are quickly covered up!). In the UK there have been IT problems and soaring costs with the system for issuing passports, the system managing benefit payments, and the system managing patient data in the National Health Service. Not all of these problems have been technical. The New National Health Service information sharing system has been delayed because of problems caused by a lack of communication with patients. There was widespread criticism that the public have been left in the dark about the project. Participants in systems development, in this case government health ministers, hospital managers, doctors and patient groups, are critical to systems development success.

Participants in Systems Development

Effective systems development requires a team effort. The team usually consists of users, managers, systems development specialists, various support personnel and other stakeholders. This team, called the development team, is responsible for determining the objectives of the new information system and delivering a system that meets these objectives. Many development teams use a project manager to head the systems development effort and to help coordinate the systems development process. A project is a planned collection of activities that achieves a goal, such as constructing a new manufacturing plant or developing a new decision support system.[2] All projects should have a defined starting point and ending point, normally given as a specific date. Most have a set budget, such as €150 000. The project manager is responsible for coordinating all people and resources needed to complete the project on time. In systems development, the project manager can be an IS person inside the organization or an external consultant hired to see the project to completion. Project managers need technical, business and people skills. In addition to completing the project on time and within the specified budget, the project manager is usually responsible for controlling project quality, training personnel, facilitating communication, managing risks and acquiring any necessary equipment, including office supplies and sophisticated computer systems. One study reported that almost 80 per cent of responding IS managers believe that it is critical to keep project planning skills in-house instead of outsourcing them.[3] Research studies have shown that project management success factors include good leadership from executives and project managers, a high level of trust in the project and its potential benefits, and the commitment of the project team and organization to successfully complete the project and implement its results.

In the context of systems development, stakeholders are people who, either themselves or through the area of the organization they represent, ultimately benefit from the systems development project. Users are people who will interact with the system regularly. They can be employees, managers or suppliers. For large-scale systems development projects, where the investment in, and value of, a system can be high, it is common for senior-level managers, including the heads of functional areas (finance, marketing and so on), to be part of the development team.

Depending on the nature of the systems project, the development team might include systems analysts and programmers, among others. A systems analyst is a professional who specializes in analyzing and designing business systems. Systems analysts play various roles while interacting with the users, management, vendors and suppliers, external companies, programmers and other IS support personnel (see Figure 11.1). Sometimes system analysts work with specialist business analysts, experts in the business who try to identify ways in which new information systems can improve the current business processes. Like an architect developing blueprints for a new building, a systems analyst develops detailed plans for the new or modified

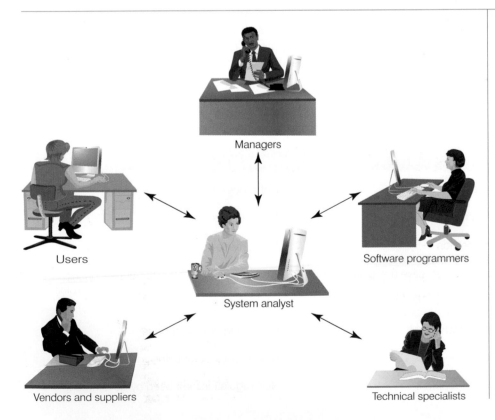

Figure 11.1 Role of the Systems Analyst
The systems analyst plays an important role in the development team and is often the only person who sees the system in its totality. The systems analyst is often called on to be a facilitator, moderator, negotiator and interpreter for development activities.

Managers

Users

Software programmers

System analyst

Vendors and suppliers

Technical specialists

system. The programmer is responsible for modifying or developing programs to satisfy user requirements. Like a contractor constructing a new building or renovating an existing one, the programmer takes the plans from the systems analyst and builds or modifies the necessary software.

The other support personnel on the development team are mostly technical specialists, including database and telecommunications experts, hardware engineers and supplier representatives. One or more of these roles might be outsourced to outside experts. Depending on the magnitude of the systems development project and the number of IS systems development specialists on the team, one or more IS managers might also belong to the team. The composition of a development team can vary over time and from project to project. For small businesses, the development team might consist of a systems analyst and the business owner as the primary stakeholder. For larger organizations, IS staff can include hundreds of people involved in a variety of activities, including systems development. Every development team should have a team leader. This person can be from the IS department, a manager from the company or a consultant from outside the company. The team leader needs both technical and people skills.

Regardless of the specific nature of a project, systems development creates or modifies systems, which ultimately means change. Managing this change effectively requires development team members to communicate well. Because you probably will participate in systems development during your career, you must learn communication skills. You might even be the individual who initiates systems development. Typical reasons for initiating IS projects are given in Table 11.1.

Information Systems Planning and Aligning Organization and IS Goals

The term information systems planning refers to translating strategic and organizational goals into systems development initiatives. The chief information officer (CIO) of the Marriott hotel chain, for example, attends board meetings and other top-level management meetings so that the he is familiar with, and can contribute to, the firm's strategic plan. According to Doug Lewis, former CIO for many Fortune 100 companies, 'Strategic goals must be finite, measurable and tangible.' Proper IS planning ensures that specific systems development objectives support organizational goals.

Table 11.1 Typical Reasons to Initiate a Systems Development Project

Reason	Example
Problems with existing system	Not processing orders fast enough
Desire to exploit new opportunities	M-commerce
Increasing competition	New competitor enters industry
Desire to make more effective use of information	Wanting to set up a customer relationship management system to expand and exploit information stored on customers
Organizational growth	Expanding customer base
Merger or acquisition	Buying out a competitor
Change in the environment	New regulations imposed by government

Aligning organizational goals and IS goals is critical for any successful systems development effort.[4] Because information systems support other business activities, IS staff and people in other departments need to understand each other's responsibilities and tasks. Determining whether organizational and IS goals are aligned can be difficult.

One of the primary benefits of IS planning and alignment of business goals is a long-range view of information systems use in the organization. The IS plan should guide the development of the IS infrastructure over time. IS planning should ensure better use of IS resources – including funds, personnel and time for scheduling specific projects. The steps of IS planning are shown in Figure 11.2.

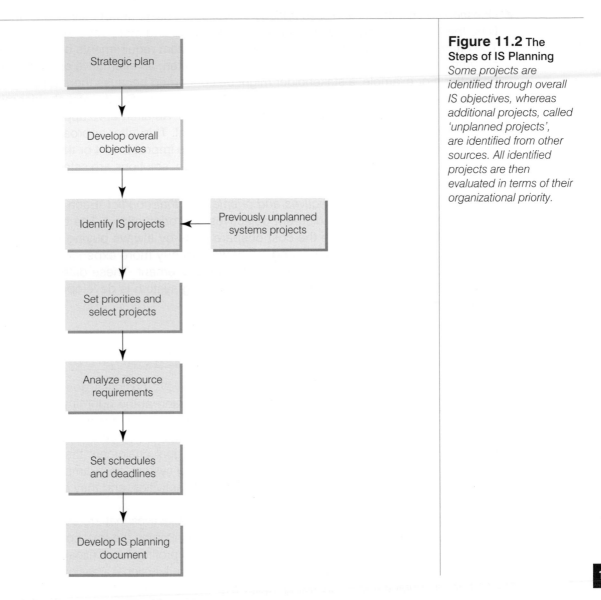

Figure 11.2 The Steps of IS Planning
Some projects are identified through overall IS objectives, whereas additional projects, called 'unplanned projects', are identified from other sources. All identified projects are then evaluated in terms of their organizational priority.

In today's business environment, many companies seek systems development projects that will provide them with a competitive advantage. Thinking competitively usually requires creative and critical analysis. For example, a company might want to achieve a competitive advantage by improving its customer–supplier relationship. Linking customers and suppliers electronically can result in more efficient communication and ultimately, superior products and services. By looking at problems in new or different ways and by introducing innovative methods to solve them, many organizations have gained significant advantages. In some cases, these new solutions are inspired by people and things not directly related to the problem.

11

creative analysis The investigation of new approaches to existing problems.

critical analysis The unbiased and careful questioning of whether system elements are related in the most effective ways.

Creative analysis involves investigating new approaches to existing problems. Typically, new solutions are inspired by people and events not directly related to the problem. **Critical analysis** requires unbiased and careful questioning of whether system elements are related in the most effective ways. It involves considering the establishment of new or different relationships among system elements and perhaps introducing new elements into the system. Critical analysis in systems development involves the following actions:

- *Questioning statements and assumptions*. Questioning users about their needs and clarifying their initial responses can result in better systems and more accurate predictions. Too often, stakeholders and users specify certain system requirements because they assume that their needs can only be met that way. Often, an alternative approach would be better. For example, a stakeholder might be concerned because there is always too much of some items in stock and not enough of other items. So, the stakeholder might request a new and improved inventory control system. An alternative approach is to identify the root cause for poor inventory management. This latter approach might determine that sales forecasting is inaccurate and needs improvement or that production cannot meet the set production schedule. All too often, solutions are selected before understanding the complete nature of the problem.

- *Identifying and resolving objectives and orientations that conflict*. Each department in an organization can have different objectives and orientations. The buying department might want to minimize the cost of spare parts by always buying from the lowest-cost supplier, but engineering might want to buy more expensive, higher quality spare parts to reduce the frequency of replacement. These differences must be identified and resolved before a new purchasing system is developed or an existing one modified.

Establishing Objectives for Systems Development

The overall objective of systems development is to achieve business goals, not technical goals, by delivering the right information to the right person at the right time. The impact a particular system has on an organization's ability to meet its goals determines the true value of that system to the organization. Although all systems should support business goals, some systems are more pivotal in continued operations and goal attainment than others. These systems are called 'key operational'. An order processing system, for example, is key operational. Without it, few organizations could continue daily activities, and they clearly would not meet set goals.

The goals defined for an organization also define the objectives that are set for a system. A manufacturing plant, for example, might determine that minimizing the total cost of owning and operating its equipment is critical to meet production and profit goals. Critical success factors (CSFs) are factors that are essential to the success of certain functional areas of an organization. The CSF for manufacturing – minimizing equipment maintenance and operating costs – would be converted into specific objectives for a proposed system. One specific objective might be to alert maintenance planners when a piece of equipment is due for routine preventative maintenance (e.g. cleaning and lubrication). Another objective might be to alert the maintenance planners when the necessary cleaning materials, lubrication oils or spare parts inventory levels are below specified limits. These objectives could be accomplished either through automatic stock replenishment or through the use of exception reports.

Regardless of the particular systems development effort, the development process should define a system with specific performance and cost objectives. The success or failure of the systems development effort will be measured against these objectives.

Performance Objectives

The extent to which a system performs as desired can be measured through its performance objectives. System performance is usually determined by factors such as the following:

■ *The quality or usefulness of the output.* Is the system generating the right information for a value-added business process or by a goal-oriented decision maker?

■ *The accuracy of the output.* Is the output accurate and does it reflect the true situation? As a result of the Enron accounting scandal in the US, and similar instances, when some companies overstated revenues or understated expenses, accuracy is becoming more important, and business leaders throughout the world are being held responsible for the accuracy of all corporate reports.

■ *The quality or usefulness of the format of the output.* Is the output generated in a form that is usable and easily understood? For example, objectives often concern the legibility of screen displays, the appearance of documents and the adherence to certain naming conventions.

■ *The speed at which output is generated.* Is the system generating output in time to meet organizational goals and operational objectives? Objectives such as customer response time, the time to determine product availability and throughput time are examples.

■ *The scalability of the resulting system.* Scalability allows an information system to handle business growth and increased business volume. For example, if a mid-sized business realizes an annual 10 per cent growth in sales for several years, an information system that is scalable will be able to efficiently handle the increase by adding processing, storage, software, database, telecommunications and other information systems resources to handle the growth.

■ *The degree to which business risk is reduced.* One important objective of many systems development projects is to reduce risk.[5] The BRE Bank in Poland, for example, used systems development to create a model-based decision support system to analyze and reduce loan risk and a variety of related risks associated with bank transactions. The new project uses a mathematical algorithm, called FIRST (financial institutions risk scenario trends), to reduce risk.

In some cases, the achievement of performance objectives can be easily measured (e.g. by tracking the time it takes to determine product availability). In other cases, it is sometimes more difficult to ascertain in the short term. For example, it might be difficult to determine how many customers are lost because of slow responses to customer enquiries regarding product availability. These outcomes, however, are often closely associated with business goals and are vital to the long-term success of the organization. Senior management usually dictates their attainment.

Cost Objectives

Organizations can spend more than is necessary during a systems development project. The benefits of achieving performance goals should be balanced with all costs associated with the system, including the following:

■ *Development costs.* All costs required to get the system up and running should be included. Some computer vendors give cash rewards to companies using their systems to reduce costs and as an incentive.[6]

■ *Costs related to the uniqueness of the system application.* A system's uniqueness has a profound effect on its cost. An expensive but reusable system might be preferable to a less costly system with limited use.

■ *Fixed investments in hardware and related equipment.* Developers should consider costs of such items as computers, network-related equipment and environmentally controlled data centres in which to operate the equipment.

■ *Ongoing operating costs of the system.* Operating costs include costs for personnel, software, supplies and resources such as the electricity required to run the system.

11

Balancing performance and cost objectives within the overall framework of organizational goals can be challenging. Setting objectives are important, however, because they allow an organization to allocate resources effectively and measure the success of a systems development effort.

11.2 Systems Development Lifecycles

The systems development process is also called the 'systems development lifecycle' (SDLC) because the activities associated with it are ongoing. As each system is built, the project has timelines and deadlines, until the system is installed and accepted. The life of the system then continues as it is maintained and reviewed. If the system needs significant improvement beyond the scope of maintenance, if it needs to be replaced because of a new generation of technology, or if the IS needs of the organization change significantly, a new project will be initiated and the cycle will start over.

A key fact of systems development is that the later in the SDLC an error is detected, the more expensive it is to correct (see Figure 11.3). One reason for the mounting costs is that if an error which occurred in a early stage of the SDLC isn't found until a later phase, the previous phases must be reworked to some extent. Another reason is that the errors found late in the SDLC affect more people. For example, an error found after a system is installed might require retraining users when a 'work-around' to the problem has been found. Thus, experienced systems developers prefer an approach that will catch errors early in the project lifecycle.

Figure 11.3
**Relationship Between
Timing of Errors and
Costs** *The later that system
changes are made in the
SDLC, the more expensive
these changes become.*

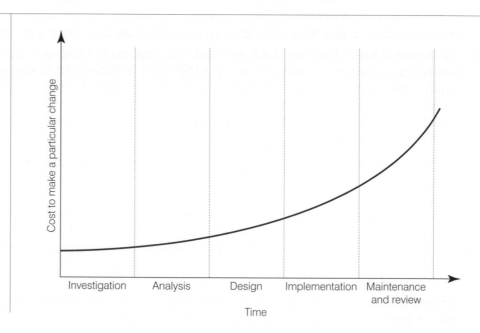

Several common systems development lifecycles exist: the traditional or waterfall approach, prototyping, rapid application development (RAD) and end-user development. In addition, companies can outsource the systems development process. With many companies, and most public sector organizations, these approaches are formalized and documented so that systems developers have a well-defined process to follow; in other companies, less formalized approaches are used. Keep Figure 11.3 in mind as you are introduced to alternative SDLCs in the sections that follow.

The Traditional Systems Development Lifecycle

Traditional systems development efforts, can range from a small project, such as purchasing an inexpensive computer program, to a major undertaking. The steps of traditional systems development might vary from one company to the next, but most approaches have five common phases: investigation, analysis, design, implementation, and maintenance and review (see Figure 11.4). Traditional systems development is also known as the waterfall approach.

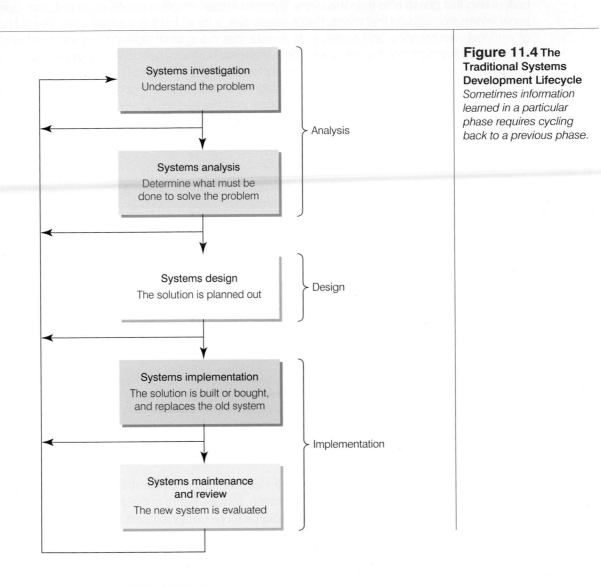

Figure 11.4 The Traditional Systems Development Lifecycle
Sometimes information learned in a particular phase requires cycling back to a previous phase.

In the systems investigation phase, potential problems and opportunities are identified and considered in light of the goals of the business. Systems investigation attempts to answer the questions 'what is the problem?' and 'is it worth solving?' The primary result of this phase is a defined development project for which business problems or opportunity statements have been created, to which some organizational resources have been committed, and for which systems analysis is recommended. Systems analysis attempts to answer the question 'what must the information system do to solve the problem?' This phase involves studying existing systems and work processes to identify strengths, weaknesses and opportunities for improvement. The major outcome of systems analysis is a list of requirements and priorities. Systems design seeks to answer the question 'how will the information system do what it must do to obtain the problem solution?' The primary result of this phase is a technical design that either describes the new system or describes how existing systems will be modified. The system design details system outputs, inputs and user interfaces; specifies hardware, software, database, telecommunications, personnel and procedure components; and shows how these components are related. Systems implementation involves creating or buying the various system components detailed in the systems design, assembling them and placing the new or modified system into operation. An important task during this phase is to train the users. Systems implementation results in an installed, operational information system that meets the business needs for which it was developed. The purpose of systems maintenance and review is to ensure that the system operates as intended and to modify the system so that it continues to meet changing business needs. As shown in Figure 11.4, a system under development moves from one phase of the traditional SDLC to the next.

The traditional SDLC allows for a large degree of management control. However, a major problem is that the user does not use the solution until the system is nearly complete. Table 11.2 lists advantages and disadvantages of the traditional SDLC.

Table 11.2 Advantages and Disadvantages of Traditional SDLC

Advantages	Disadvantages
Formal review at the end of each phase allows maximum management control	Users get a system that meets the needs as understood by the developers; this might not be what is really needed
This approach creates considerable system documentation	Documentation is expensive and time consuming to create. It is also difficult to keep current
Formal documentation ensures that system requirements can be traced back to stated business needs	Often, user needs go unstated or are misunderstood
It produces many intermediate products that can be reviewed to see whether they meet the users' needs and conform to standards	Users cannot easily review intermediate products and evaluate whether a particular product (e.g. data flow diagram) meets their business requirements

Prototyping

Prototyping, also known as the evolutionary lifecycle, takes an iterative approach to the systems development process. During each iteration, requirements and alternative solutions to the problem are identified and analyzed, new solutions are designed and a portion of the system is implemented. Users are then encouraged to try the prototype and provide feedback (see Figure 11.5). Prototyping begins with creating a preliminary model of a major subsystem or a scaled-down version of the entire system. For example, a prototype might show sample report formats and input screens. After they are developed and refined, the prototypical reports and input screens are used as models for the actual system, which can be developed using an end-user programming language such as Visual Basic. The first preliminary model is refined to form the second- and third-generation models, and so on until the complete system is developed. One potential problem with prototyping is knowing when the system is finished as people can always think of extra refinements they would like.

Prototypes can be classified as operational or non-operational. An operational prototype is a prototype that has functionality – it does something towards solving the problem. It may accept input, partially process it and output the results. Then, perhaps in the second iteration, the processing is refined and expanded. A non-operational prototype is a mock-up or model. It typically includes output and input specifications and formats. The outputs include mocked up reports to and the inputs include the layout of the user interface either on paper on a computer screen. The primary advantage of a non-operational prototype is that it can be developed much faster than an operational prototype. Non-operational prototypes can be discarded, and a fully operational system can be built based on what was learned from the prototypes. The

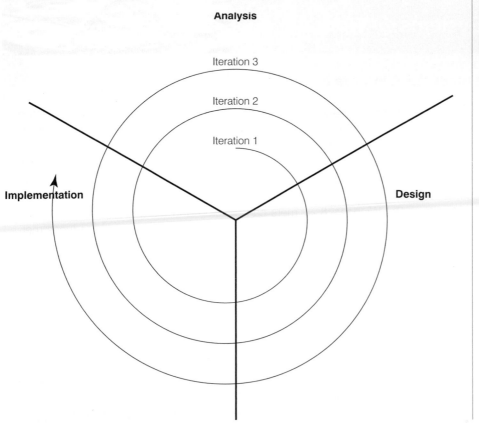

Figure 11.5 Prototyping
Prototyping is an iterative approach to systems development.

advantages and disadvantages of prototyping are summarized in Table 11.3. Prototypes can be useful communication tools – imagine asking a user what they need the new system to do. Many people may find it difficult to verbalize what they want. However, if you show them a prototype, they will soon be able to say what is right and wrong with it.

Table 11.3 Advantages and Disadvantages of Prototyping

Advantages	Disadvantages
Users can try the system and provide constructive feedback during development	Each iteration builds on the previous one. The final solution might be only incrementally better than the initial solution
An operational prototype can be produced in weeks	Formal end-of-phase reviews might not occur. Thus, it is very difficult to contain the scope of the prototype, and the project never seems to end
As solutions emerge, users become more positive about the process and the results	System documentation is often absent or incomplete because the primary focus is on development of the prototype
Prototyping enables early detection of errors and omissions	System backup and recovery, performance, and security issues can be overlooked in the haste to develop a prototype

11

Information Systems @ Work

Ten weeks to get ready for Windows 8

Dlala Studios is a young computer games company based near London. It was formed by two friends in June 2012 with a simple agenda: to 'make games we love, with people we love, for people to love'. The team wanted to take advantage of the Windows 8 operating system, which has touch screen features and the ability to run mobile apps. But Windows 8 was to be released in October 2012, which gave them less than ten weeks to develop their new game, Janksy. Janksy is an app game – with simple gameplay and short levels it's just the sort of thing a gamer can dip into when they have five minutes to spare. With such a tight schedule, Dlala joined the Microsoft BizSpark programme, and started to use Microsoft Visual Studio with Team Foundation Server.

BizSpark is a free service for small technology start-up companies like Dlala. It provides free software and support to a global community of over 100 000 start-ups in over 100 countries. Members can get hold of software development kits which come with sample code to help them write software for the Windows 8 platform. When developers have their software ready for release, BizSpark also helps them prepare for submission to Microsoft's online app store.

Visual Studio is an integrated development environment which facilitates rapid software development. It is named 'visual' because when using it, programmers start with the visual part of the software – the interface that users will see. They then add the code which gives each part of the interface its functionality. The Team Foundation Server is the part of Visual Studio which provides source code management to help developers manage different versions of the programs they are working on. The service helps groups of programmers to work together on one project. Using the suite of client-server tools in Team Foundation Server, programmers can develop and test their applications, plan projects and track their work. It also produces metrics for managing software development projects.

As a dispersed development team, Dlala found the tools to review code and check for conflicts invaluable. As soon as a team member had completed a task or tweaked some code, the code was immediately updated on the server. Dlala completed Janksy in time for the release of Windows 8 and was delighted to see it gain popularity in the Windows Store. Co-founder Aj Grand-Scrutton says, 'We completed the game in nine-and-a-half weeks. We were adamant about hitting the target of the Windows 8 launch. The support from Microsoft has been amazing.'

Questions

1 What metrics might be useful for managing software development projects?

2 Why is managing versions of code so difficult and also so important?

3 Why do you think Microsoft started the BizSpark programme? What benefits do the startups get? What does Microsoft get out of it?

4 Is the Team Foundation Server especially important for a small company?

11

Rapid Application Development, Agile Development, Joint Application Development and Other Systems Development Approaches

rapid application development (RAD) A systems development approach that employs tools, techniques, and methodologies designed to speed application development.

Rapid application development (RAD) employs tools, techniques and methodologies designed to speed up application development. Some people consider it to be the same as prototyping. Vendors, such as Computer Associates International, IBM and Oracle, market products targeting the RAD market. Rational Software, a division of IBM, has a RAD tool, called Rational Rapid Developer, to make developing large Java programs and applications easier and faster. Locus Systems, a program developer, used a RAD tool called OptimalJ to generate more than 60 per cent of the computer code for three applications it developed. Advantage Gen is a RAD tool from Computer Associates International. It can be used to rapidly generate computer code from business models and specifications.

RAD reduces paper-based documentation, automatically generates program source code, and facilitates user participation in design and development activities. It makes adapting to changing system requirements easier.

Other approaches to rapid development, such as agile development, allow the systems to change as they are being developed. Agile development requires frequent face-to-face meetings with the systems developers and users as they modify, refine and test how the system meets users' needs and what its capabilities are. Extreme programming (XP), a form of agile development, uses pairs of programmers who work together to design, test and code parts of the systems they develop. The iterative nature of XP helps companies develop robust systems, with fewer errors.

RAD makes extensive use of the joint application development (JAD) process for data collection and requirements analysis. Originally developed by IBM Canada in the 1970s, JAD involves group meetings in which users, stakeholders and IS professionals work together to analyze existing systems, propose possible solutions and define the requirements of a new or modified system. JAD groups consist of both problem holders and solution providers. A group normally requires one or more top-level executives who initiate the JAD process, a group leader for the meetings, potential users, and one or more individuals who act as secretaries and clerks to record what is accomplished and to provide general support for the sessions. Many companies have found that groups can develop better requirements than individuals working independently and have assessed JAD as a very successful development technique. Today, JAD often uses group support systems (GSS) software to foster positive group interactions, while suppressing negative group behaviour.

RAD should not be used on every software development project. In general, it is best suited for DSSs and MISs and less well suited for TPS. During a RAD project, the level of participation of stakeholders and users is much higher than in other approaches. Table 11.4 lists advantages and disadvantages of RAD.

The End-User Systems Development Lifecycle

The term end-user systems development describes any systems development project in which business managers and users assume the primary effort. Rather than ignoring these initiatives, astute IS professionals encourage them by offering guidance and support. Providing technical assistance, communicating standards and sharing 'best practices' throughout the organization are some ways IS professionals work with motivated managers and employees undertaking their own systems development. In this way, end-user-developed systems can be structured as complementary to,

Table 11.4 Advantages and Disadvantages of RAD

Advantages	Disadvantages
For appropriate projects, this approach puts an application into production sooner than any other approach	This intense SDLC can burn out systems developers and other project participants
Documentation is produced as a by-product of completing project tasks	This approach requires systems analysts and users to be skilled in RAD systems development tools and RAD techniques
RAD forces teamwork and lots of interaction between users and stakeholders	RAD requires a larger percentage of stakeholders' and users' time than other approaches

11

rather than in conflict with, existing and emerging information systems. In addition, this open communication among IS professionals, managers of the affected business area, and users allows the
IS professionals to identify specific initiatives so that additional organizational resources, beyond
those available to business managers or users, are provided for its development.

User-developed systems range from the very small (such as a software routine to merge
data from Microsoft Excel into Microsoft Word to produce a personalized letter for customers)
to those of significant organizational value (such as a customer contact database). Initially, IS
professionals discounted the value of these projects. As the number and magnitude of these
projects increased, however, IS professionals began to realize that, for the good of the entire
organization, their involvement with these projects needed to increase.

End-user systems development does have some disadvantages. Some end users don't have
the training to effectively develop and test a system. Expensive mistakes can be made using
faulty spreadsheets, for example, that have never been tested. Most end-user systems are also
poorly documented and therefore difficult to maintain. When these systems are updated, problems can be introduced that make the systems error-prone. In addition, some end users spend
time and corporate resources developing systems that are already available.

A survey of South African employers found that the IS skills they want in their new employees
are the ability to type, create documents, and a basic working knowledge of computer applications.

Outsourcing and On-Demand Computing

Many companies hire an outside consulting firm or computer company that specializes in systems development to take over some or all of its development and operations activities.[7] Some
companies, such as General Electric, have their own outsourcing subunits or have spun off
their outsourcing subunits as separate companies.[8] Outsourcing can be a good idea under the
following circumstances:

- When a company believes it can cut costs.
- When a firm has limited opportunity to distinguish itself competitively through a particular
  IS operation or application.
- When uninterrupted IS service is not crucial.
- When outsourcing does not strip the company of technical know-how required for future
  IS innovation.
- When the firm's existing IS capabilities are limited, ineffective or technically inferior.
- When a firm is downsizing.

The decision to outsource systems development is often a response to downsizing, which
reduces the number of employees or managers, equipment and systems, and even functions
and departments. Outsourcing allows companies to downsize their IS department and alleviate
difficult financial situations by reducing payroll and other expenses.

Organizations can outsource any aspect of their information system, including hardware maintenance and management, software development, database systems, networks and telecommunications, Internet and intranet operations, hiring and staffing, and the development of procedures and rules regarding the information system.[9] Eurostar, for example, hired the outsourcing
company Occam to develop a new website and back-end database to give its travel customers
greater travel information.[10] According to Scott Logie, managing director of Occam, 'The quality
and volume of data that Eurostar possesses is extremely valuable. By working together we will
allow the firm to develop real insight into its customers. This can be used to drive a strong customer acquisitions strategy, which will enhance its business and customer relationships.'

Reducing costs, obtaining state-of-the-art technology, eliminating staffing and personnel
problems, and increasing technological flexibility are reasons that companies have used the outsourcing and on-demand computing approaches.[11] A number of companies offer outsourcing

and on-demand computing services – from general systems development to specialized services. IBM's Global Services, for example, is one of the largest full-service outsourcing and consulting services.[12] IBM has consultants located in offices around the world. Electronic Data Systems (EDS) is another large company that specialises in consulting and outsourcing.[13] EDS has approximately 140 000 employees in almost 60 countries and more than 9000 clients worldwide. Accenture is another company that specializes in consulting and outsourcing.[14] The company has more than 75 000 employees in 47 countries.

Organizations can use a number of guidelines to make outsourcing a success, including the following:[15]

■ Keep tight controls on the outsourcing project.

■ Treat outsourcing companies as partners.

■ Start with smaller outsourcing jobs.

■ Create effective communications channels between the organization and the outsourcing company.

■ Carefully review legal outsourcing contracts, including rights and remedies clauses.[16]

Old Mutual South Africa has outsourced its IS infrastructure to T-Systems, to control its costs and access T-System's expertise.

Outsourcing has some disadvantages, however. Internal expertise can be lost and loyalty can suffer under an outsourcing arrangement. When a company outsources, key IS personnel with expertise in technical and business functions are no longer needed. When these IS employees leave, their experience with the organization and expertise in information systems are lost. For some companies, it can be difficult to achieve a competitive advantage when competitors are using the same computer or consulting company. When the outsourcing or on-demand computing is done offshore or in a foreign country, some people have raised security concerns. How will important data and trade secrets be guarded?

11.3 Factors Affecting System Development Success

Successful systems development means delivering a system that meets user and organizational needs – on time and within budget. There is no formula for achieving this, but the following factors are known to have an impact on success.

Involvement

Getting users and other stakeholders involved in systems development is critical for most systems development projects. Having the support of top-level managers is also important. The involvement of users throughout the development will mean they are less likely to resist the software when it is delivered. Historically, communication between people on the domain side (users, managers and other stakeholders) and on the systems side (systems analysts, programmers and other technical people) has been problematic, with there being little common ground between them. Each group has its own set of terminology and its own culture. Getting users and managers involved in systems development is one way of building bridges between the two and kick-starting dialogue. This may be done simply by inviting them to development meetings, organizing social gatherings, producing a questionnaire to survey user views, running interviews, etc., or by using joint application development (see page 385). If users have been involved throughout development they will be less likely to resist the changes the new system brings when it is implemented.

11

Degree of Change

A major factor that affects the quality of systems development is the degree of change associated with the project. The scope can vary from implementing minor enhancements to an existing system, up to major reengineering. The project team needs to recognize where they are on this spectrum of change.

As discussed in Chapter 2, continuous improvement projects do not require significant business process or IS changes, or retraining of people; thus, they have a high degree of success. Typically, because continuous improvement involves minor improvements, these projects also have relatively modest benefits. On the other hand, reengineering involves fundamental changes in how the organization conducts business and completes tasks. The factors associated with successful reengineering are similar to those of any development effort, including top management support, clearly defined corporate goals and systems development objectives, and careful management of change. Major reengineering projects tend to have a high degree of risk but also a high potential for major business benefits (see Figure 11.6).

Figure 11.6 Degree
of Change *The degree of
change can greatly affect
the probability of a project's
success.*

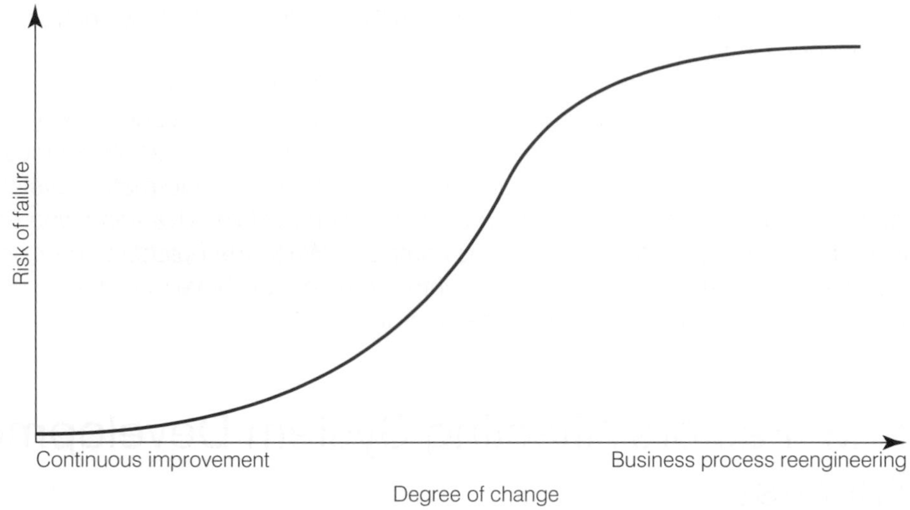

Risk of failure

Continuous improvement   Business process reengineering

Degree of change

Managing Change

The ability to manage change is critical to the success of systems development. New systems inevitably cause change. For example, the work environment and habits of users are invariably affected by the development of a new information system. Unfortunately, not everyone adapts easily, and the increasing complexity of systems can multiply the problems. Managing change requires the ability to recognize existing or potential problems (particularly the concerns of users) and deal with them before they become a serious threat to the success of the new or modified system. Here are several of the most common problems:

- Fear that the employee will lose his or her job, power or influence within the organization.
- Belief that the proposed system will create more work than it eliminates.
- Reluctance to work with 'computer people'.
- Anxiety that the proposed system will negatively alter the structure of the organization.
- Belief that other problems are more pressing than those solved by the proposed system or that the system is being developed by people unfamiliar with 'the way things need to get done'.
- Unwillingness to learn new procedures or approaches.

Preventing or dealing with these types of problems requires a coordinated effort from stakeholders and users, managers and IS personnel. One remedy is simply to talk with all people concerned and learn what their biggest concerns are. Management can then deal with those concerns and try to eliminate them. After immediate concerns are addressed, people can become part of the project team.

Quality and Standards

Another key success factor is the quality of project planning. The bigger the project, the more likely that poor planning will lead to significant problems. Many companies find that large systems projects fall behind schedule, go over budget and do not meet expectations. A systems development project for the UK Child Support Agency, for example, fell behind schedule and over £250 million over budget.[17] When it was delivered, two years late, there were interference problems – screens took too long to refresh and there was no delete key to undo accidental typing mistakes, staff training was also ineffective and inappropriate. The delayed project may have hurt the agency's ability to deliver important services to children. Although proper planning cannot guarantee that these types of problems will be avoided, it can minimize the likelihood of their occurrence. Good systems development is not automatic. Certain factors contribute to the failure of systems development projects. These factors and countermeasures to eliminate or alleviate the problem are summarized in Table 11.5.

The development of information systems requires a constant trade-off of schedule and cost versus quality. Historically, the development of application software has overemphasized

Table 11.5 Project Planning Issues Frequently Contributing to Project Failure

Factor	Countermeasure
Solving the wrong problem	Establish a clear connection between the project and organizational goals
Poor problem definition and analysis	Follow a standard systems development approach
Poor communication	There is no easy answer to this common problem
Project is too ambitious	Narrow the project focus to address only the most important business opportunities
Lack of top management support	Identify the senior manager who has the most to gain from the success of the project and recruit this person to champion the project
Lack of management and user involvement	Identify and recruit key stakeholders to be active participants in the project
Inadequate or improper system design	Follow a standard systems development approach
Lack of standards	Implement a standards system, such as ISO 9001
Poor testing and implementation	Plan sufficient time for this activity
Users cannot use the system effectively	Develop a rigorous user-training programme and budget sufficient time in the schedule to execute it
Lack of concern for maintenance	Include an estimate of employee effort and costs for maintenance in the original project justification

11

schedule and cost to the detriment of quality. Techniques, such as use of the ISO 9001 standards, have been developed to improve the quality of information systems. ISO 9001 is a set of international quality standards originally developed in Europe in 1987. These standards address customer satisfaction and are the only standards in the ISO 9000 family where third-party certification can be achieved. Adherence to ISO 9001 is a requirement in many international markets[18] (see Figure 11.7).

Figure 11.7 ISO Home
Page *ISO 9000 is a set of international quality standards used by IS and other organizations to ensure the quality of products and services.*

Organizational experience with the systems development process is also a key factor for systems development success.[19] The capability maturity model (CMM) is one way to measure this experience.[20] It is based on research done at Carnegie Mellon University and work by the Software Engineering Institute (SEI).[21] CMM is a measure of the maturity of the software development process in an organization. CMM grades an organization's systems development maturity using five levels: initial, repeatable, defined, managed, and optimized.

Use of Project Management Tools

Project management involves planning, scheduling, directing and controlling human, financial and technological resources for a defined task whose result is achievement of specific goals and objectives. Even small systems development projects must employ some type of project management.[22]

A project schedule is a detailed description of what is to be done. Each project activity, the use of personnel and other resources, and expected completion dates are described. A project milestone is a critical date for the completion of a major part of the project. The completion of program design, coding, testing and release are examples of milestones for a programming project. The project deadline is the date the entire project is to be completed and operational – when the organization can expect to begin to reap the benefits of the project.

In systems development, each activity has an earliest start time, earliest finish time and slack time, which is the amount of time an activity can be delayed without delaying the entire project. The critical path consists of all activities that, if delayed, would delay the entire project. These activities have zero slack time. Any problems with critical-path activities will cause problems for the entire project. To ensure that critical-path activities are completed in a timely fashion, formalized project management approaches have been developed. Tools such as Microsoft Project are available to help compute these critical project attributes.

Although the steps of systems development seem straightforward, larger projects can become complex, requiring hundreds or thousands of separate activities. For these systems development efforts, formal project management methods and tools become essential. A formalized approach called the **program evaluation and review technique (PERT)** creates three time estimates for an activity: shortest possible time, most likely time and longest possible time. A formula is then applied to determine a single PERT time estimate. A **Gantt chart** is a graphical tool used for planning, monitoring and coordinating projects; it is essentially a grid that lists activities and deadlines. Each time a task is completed, a marker such as a darkened line is placed in the proper grid cell to indicate the completion of a task (see Figure 11.8).

program evaluation and review technique (PERT) A formalized approach for developing a project schedule.

Gantt chart A graphical tool used for planning, monitoring, and coordinating projects.

Project planning documentation		Page 1 of 1													
System Warehouse inventory system (modification)		Date 12/10													
System — Scheduled activity ▬ Completed activity	Analyst Cecil Truman		Signature												

Activity*	Individual assigned	Week													
		1	2	3	4	5	6	7	8	9	10	11	12	13	14
R — Requirements definition															
R.1 Form project team	VP, Cecil, Bev	▬													
R.2 Define obj. and constraints	Cecil	▬													
R.3 Interview warehouse staff															
for requirements report	Bev			▬▬											
R.4 Organize requirements	Team				—▬										
R.5 VP review	VP, Team				—▬										
D — Design															
D.1 Revise program specs.	Bev					—▬									
D.2.1 Specify screens	Bev					—▬									
D.2.2 Specify reports	Bev						—▬								
D.2.3 Specify doc. changes	Cecil						▬								
D.4 Management review	Team						—								
I — Implementation															
I.1 Code program changes	Bev							—							
I.2.1 Build test file	Team							—							
I.2.2 Build production file	Bev								—						
I.3 Revise production file	Cecil								—						
I.4.1 Test short file	Bev							—							
I.4.2 Test production file	Cecil									—					
I.5 Management review	Team										—				
I.6 Install warehouse**															
I.6.1 Train new procedures	Bev										—				
I.6.2 Install	Bev											—			
I.6.3 Management review	Team												—		

*Weekly team reviews not shown here
**Report for warehouses 2 through 5

Figure 11.8 Sample Gantt Chart *A Gantt chart shows progress through systems development activities by putting a bar through appropriate cells.*

11

Both PERT and Gantt techniques can be automated using project management software. Several project management software packages are identified in Table 11.6. This software monitors all project activities and determines whether activities and the entire project are on time and within budget. Project management software also has workgroup capabilities to handle multiple projects and to allow a team to interact with the same software. Project management software helps managers determine the best way to reduce project completion time at the least cost. Many project managers, however, fear that the quality of a systems development project will suffer with shortened deadlines and think that slack time should be added back to the schedule as a result.

Table 11.6 Selected Project Management Software Packages

Software	Vendor
AboutTime	NetSQL Partners
Job Order	Management Software
OpenPlan	Welcom
Microsoft Project	Microsoft
Project Scheduler	Scitor
Super Project	Computer Associates

Use of Computer-Aided Software Engineering (CASE) Tools

Computer-aided software engineering (CASE) tools automate many of the tasks required in a systems development effort and encourage adherence to the SDLC, thus instilling a high degree of rigour and standardization to the entire systems development process. VRCASE, for example, is a CASE tool that a team of developers can use when developing applications in C++ and other languages. Prover Technology has developed a CASE tool that searches for programming bugs. The CASE tool searches for all possible design scenarios to make sure that the program is error free. Other CASE tools include Visible Systems (www.visible.com) and Popkin Software (www.popkin.com). Popkin Software, for example, can generate code in programming languages such as C++, Java and Visual Basic. Other CASE-related tools include Rational Rose from IBM and Visio, a charting and graphics program from Microsoft. Other companies that produce CASE tools include Accenture and Oracle. Oracle Designer and Developer CASE tools, for example, can help systems analysts automate and simplify the development process for database systems. See Table 11.7 for a list of CASE tools and their providers. The advantages and disadvantages of CASE tools are listed in Table 11.8. CASE tools that focus on activities associated with the early stages of systems development are often called 'upper-CASE tools'. These packages provide automated tools to assist with systems investigation, analysis and design activities. Other CASE packages, called 'lower-CASE tools', focus on the later implementation stage of systems development, and can automatically generate structured program code.

computer-aided software engineering (CASE) Tools that automate many of the tasks required in a systems development effort and encourage adherence to the SDLC.

11

Table 11.7 Typical CASE Tools

CASE Tool	Vendor
Oracle Designer	Oracle Corporation www.oracle.com
Visible Analyst	Visible Systems Corporation www.visible.com
Rational Rose	Rational Software www.ibm.com
Embarcadero Describe	Embarcadero Describe www.embarcadero.com

Table 11.8 Advantages and Disadvantages of CASE Tools

Advantages	Disadvantages
Produce systems with a longer effective operational life	Increase the initial costs of building and maintaining systems
Produce systems that more closely meet user needs and requirements	Require more extensive and accurate definition of user needs and requirements
Produce systems with excellent documentation	Can be difficult to customize
Produce systems that need less systems support	Require more training of maintenance staff
Produce more flexible systems	Can be difficult to use with existing systems

11.4 Systems Investigation

As discussed earlier in the chapter, systems investigation is the first phase in the traditional SDLC of a new or modified business information system. The purpose is to identify potential problems and opportunities and consider them in light of the goals of the company. In general, systems investigation attempts to uncover answers to the following questions:

■ What primary problems is the new system to solve?

■ What opportunities might a new or enhanced system provide?

■ What new hardware, software, databases, telecommunications, personnel or procedures will improve an existing system or are required in a new system?

■ What are the potential costs (variable and fixed)?

■ What are the associated risks?

Initiating Systems Investigation

Because systems development requests can require considerable time and effort to implement, many organizations have adopted a formal procedure for initiating systems development, beginning with systems investigation. The systems request form is a document that is filled out by someone who wants the IS department to initiate systems investigation. This form typically includes the following information:

■ Problems in or opportunities for the system.
■ Objectives of systems investigation.
■ Overview of the proposed system.
■ Expected costs and benefits of the proposed system.

The information in the systems request form helps to rationalize and prioritize the activities of the IS department. Based on the overall IS plan, the organization's needs and goals, and the estimated value and priority of the proposed projects, managers make decisions regarding the initiation of each systems investigation for such projects.

Participants in Systems Investigation

After a decision has been made to initiate systems investigation, the first step is to determine what members of the development team should participate in the investigation phase of the project. Members of the development team change from phase to phase (see Figure 11.9).

Figure 11.9 The Systems Investigation Team *The team consists of upper- and middle-level managers, a project manager, IS personnel, users and stakeholders.*

The investigation team

Managers, users and stakeholders ←→ IS personnel

• Undertakes feasibility analysis
• Establishes systems development goals
• Selects systems development methodology
• Prepares systems investigation report

Ideally, functional managers are heavily involved during the investigation phase. Other members could include users or stakeholders outside management, such as an employee who helps initiate systems development. The technical and financial expertise of others participating in investigation help the team determine whether the problem is worth solving. The members of the development team who participate in investigation are then responsible for gathering and analyzing data, preparing a report justifying systems development and presenting the results to top-level managers.

feasibility analysis Assessment of the technical, economic, legal, operational and schedule feasibility of a project.

technical feasibility Assessment of whether the hardware, software and other system components can be acquired or developed to solve the problem.

economic feasibility The determination of whether the project makes financial sense and whether predicted benefits offset the cost and time needed to obtain them.

Feasibility Analysis

A key step of the systems investigation phase is **feasibility analysis**, which assesses technical, economic, legal, operational and schedule feasibility. **Technical feasibility** is concerned with whether the hardware, software and other system components can be acquired or developed to solve the problem.

Economic feasibility determines whether the project makes financial sense and whether predicted benefits offset the cost and time needed to obtain them. One securities company, for example, investigated the economic feasibility of sending research reports electronically instead of through the mail. Economic analysis revealed that the new approach could save the company up to €370 000 per year. Economic feasibility can involve cash flow analysis such as that done in net present value or internal rate of return (IRR) calculations.

Net present value is an often-used approach for ranking competing projects and for determining economic feasibility. The net present value represents the net amount by which project savings exceed project expenses, after allowing for the cost of capital and the passage of time. The cost of capital is the average cost of funds used to finance the operations of the business. Net present value takes into account that a euro returned at a later date is not worth as much as one received today because the euro in hand can be invested to earn profits or interest in the interim. Spreadsheet programs, such as Lotus and Microsoft Excel, have built-in functions to compute the net present value and internal rate of return.

net present value The preferred approach for ranking competing projects and determining economic feasibility.

Legal feasibility determines whether laws or regulations can prevent or limit a systems development project. For example, some music sharing websites have been into trouble for infringement of copyright. If legal feasibility had been conducted, it would have identified this vulnerability during the website development phase. Legal feasibility involves an analysis of existing and future laws to determine the likelihood of legal action against the systems development project and the possible consequences.

legal feasibility The determination of whether laws or regulations may prevent or limit a systems development project.

Operational feasibility is a measure of whether the project can be put into action or operation. It can include logistical and motivational (acceptance of change) considerations. Motivational considerations are important because new systems affect people and data flows and can have unintended consequences. As a result, power and politics might come into play, and some people might resist the new system. On the other hand, recall that a new system can help avoid major problems. For example, because of deadly hospital errors, a healthcare consortium looks into the operational feasibility of developing a new computerized physician order-entry system to require that all prescriptions and every order a doctor gives to staff are entered into the computer. The computer then checks for drug allergies and interactions between drugs. If operationally feasible, the new system could save lives and help avoid lawsuits.

operational feasibility The measure of whether the project can be put into action or operation.

Schedule feasibility determines whether the project can be completed in a reasonable amount of time – a process that involves balancing the time and resource requirements of the project with other projects.

schedule feasibility The determination of whether the project can be completed in a reasonable amount of time.

The Systems Investigation Report

The primary outcome of systems investigation is a **systems investigation report**, also called a feasibility study. This report summarizes the results of systems investigation and the process of feasibility analysis and recommends a course of action: continue on into systems analysis, modify the project in some manner or drop it. A typical table of contents for the systems investigation report is shown in Figure 11.10.

systems investigation report A summary of the results of the systems investigation and the process of feasibility analysis and recommendation of a course of action.

Johnson & Florin Ltd
Systems investigation report

Contents

Executive summary
Review of goals and objectives
System problems and opportunities
Project feasibility
Project costs
Project benefits
Recommendations

Figure 11.10 A Typical Table of Contents for a Systems Investigation Report

11

Ethical and Societal Issues

South Africa's Green-preneurs

Wildlands Conservation Trust is creating a network of 'Green-preneurs' across four Provinces in South Africa by helping individuals to grow organic food and collect materials for recycling to sell or barter for goods such as food, clothes, education support, building material, water tanks, solar water heaters, solar powered lighting and bicycles. Their goal is to help people create viable small businesses.

Established in 2004, Wildlands is one of South Africa's foremost and widely recognized sustainable growth initiatives. To function effectively, Wildlands depends on consistent and reliable email access so that it can connect with employees in the field to keep up to date with their activities, give out instructions and receive feedback. This had always been done from a Microsoft Exchange server which was physically based at the headquarters in the small town of Hilton. The problem was Hilton's unreliable power. As Wildlands began to expand, intermittent email became a major problem and it began to investigate alternatives.

Microsoft Office 365 is an online service which allows users to access Office applications and their files through a web browser and is an example of cloud computing. It can therefore be accessed through a range of devices including PC, laptop and tablet computers. Office 365 includes applications for email and calendaring, and guarantees that they will be available 99.9 per cent of the time. (The guarantee refers to how frequently the Office 365 servers will be up and running – accessing them still depends on a working Internet connection.)

Microsoft has recently made Office 365 available for free to qualifying non-profit organizations in 41 countries, including South Africa. Microsoft South Africa's Office Business lead, Uriel Rootshtain, said that 'Non-profits and NGOs operate in the same way as any other organization or business, but many lack the resources to implement the latest technology. The donation of Office 365 allows them to be more effective and efficient in the work they do. The beauty of this program is there's no cap on the number of employees who can get on board, whether the organization has ten employees or thousands.'

During a two-week process which saw replacing the Exchange server with Office 365, Wildlands moved its email and file storage infrastructure into the cloud, immediately diminishing its dependence on connectivity and power availability at head office. Cloud computing can provide many benefits to users. Andrew Whitley, Strategic Manager of Ecological Restoration at the Wildlands Conservation Trust, says that many of his teams are located in remote areas across the country. 'As soon as we started using Office 365 across the organization, our problems with capturing data and storing it safely became a thing of the past. Our operations depend on collaboration, and we have been better able to upload and work off the same documents, whether you are in head office or in the field,' he said. 'In fact, our whole staff has found value in the many features such as calendar overlays, desktop sharing and group video conferencing that help them efficiently stay connected to each other and their work.'

Questions

1 How does Office 365 help Wildlands? Are there alternative solutions they could have used?

2 What are some of the benefits of cloud computing? What are some of the drawbacks?

3 Why do you think Microsoft has made Office 365 free for non-profit organizations?

4 What else could Wildlands do with Office 365?

11

The systems investigation report is reviewed by senior management, often organized as an advisory committee, or **steering committee**, consisting of senior management and users from the IS department and other functional areas. These people help IS personnel with their decisions about the use of information systems in the business and give authorization to pursue further systems development activities. After review, the steering committee might agree with the recommendation of the systems development team or suggest a change in project focus to concentrate more directly on meeting a specific company objective. Another alternative is that everyone might decide that the project is not feasible and cancel the project.

> **steering committee** An advisory group consisting of senior management and users from the IS department and other functional areas.

11.5 Systems Analysis

After a project has been approved for further study, the next step is to answer the question 'what must the information system do to solve the problem?'. The process needs to go beyond mere computerization of existing systems. The entire system, and the business process with which it is associated, should be evaluated. Often, a firm can make great gains if it restructures both business activities and the related information system simultaneously. The overall emphasis of analysis is gathering data on the existing system, determining the requirements for the new system, considering alternatives within these constraints and investigating the feasibility of the solutions. The primary outcome of systems analysis is a prioritized list of systems requirements.

General Considerations

Systems analysis starts by clarifying the overall goals of the organization and determining how the existing or proposed information system helps meet them. A manufacturing company, for example, might want to reduce the number of equipment breakdowns. This goal can be translated into one or more informational needs. One need might be to create and maintain an accurate list of each piece of equipment and a schedule for preventative maintenance. Another need might be a list of equipment failures and their causes.

Analysis of a small company's information system can be fairly straightforward. On the other hand, evaluating an existing information system for a large company can be a long, tedious process. As a result, large organizations evaluating a major information system normally follow a formalized analysis procedure, involving these steps:

1 Assembling the participants for systems analysis.
2 Collecting appropriate data and requirements.
3 Analyzing the data and requirements.
4 Preparing a report on the existing system, new system requirements and project priorities.

Participants in Systems Analysis

The first step in formal analysis is to assemble a team to study the existing system. This group includes members of the original investigation team – from users and stakeholders to IS personnel and management. Most organizations usually allow key members of the development team not only to analyze the condition of the existing system but also to perform other aspects of systems development, such as design and implementation.

After the participants in systems analysis are assembled, this group develops a list of specific objectives and activities. A schedule for meeting the objectives and completing the specific activities is also devised, along with deadlines for each stage and a statement of the resources required at each stage, such as administrative personnel, supplies and so forth. Major milestones are normally established to help the team monitor progress and determine whether problems or delays occur in performing systems analysis.

Data Collection and Analysis

direct observation Watching the existing system in action by one or more members of the analysis team.

questionnaires A method of gathering data when the data sources are spread over a wide geographic area.

structured interview An interview where the questions are prepared in advance.

unstructured interview An interview where the questions are not prepared in advance.

The purpose of data collection is to seek additional information about the problems or needs identified in the systems investigation report. During this process, the strengths and weaknesses of the existing system are emphasized.

Data collection begins by identifying and locating the various sources of data, including both internal and external sources (see Figure 11.11).

After data sources have been identified, data collection begins. Figure 11.12 shows the steps involved. Data collection might require a number of tools and techniques, such as interviews, **direct observation** and **questionnaires**.

Interviews can either be structured or unstructured. In a **structured interview**, the questions are written in advance. In an **unstructured interview**, the questions are not written in advance; the interviewer relies on experience in asking the best questions to uncover the inherent problems of the existing system. An advantage of the unstructured interview is that it allows the interviewer to ask follow-up or clarifying questions immediately.

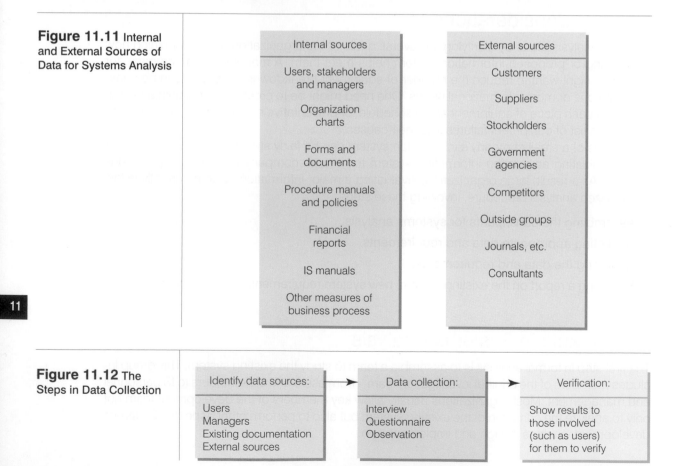

Figure 11.11 Internal and External Sources of Data for Systems Analysis

Figure 11.12 The Steps in Data Collection

With direct observation, one or more members of the analysis team directly observe the existing system in action. One of the best ways to understand how the existing system functions is to work with the users to discover how data flows in certain business tasks. Determining the data flow entails direct observation of users' work procedures, their reports, current screens (if automated already) and so on. From this observation, members of the analysis team determine which forms and procedures are adequate and which are inadequate and need improvement. Direct observation requires a certain amount of skill. The observer must be able to see what is really happening and not be influenced by attitudes or feelings. In addition, many people don't like being observed and may change their behaviour when they are. However, observation can reveal important problems and opportunities that would be difficult to obtain using other data collection methods.

When many data sources are spread over a wide geographic area, questionnaires sent to all stakeholders might be the best method. Like interviews, questionnaires can be either structured or unstructured. In most cases, a pilot study is conducted to fine-tune the questionnaire. A follow-up questionnaire can also capture the opinions of those who do not respond to the original questionnaire. Questionnaires can be used to collect data from a large number of users, and make them feel part of systems development. As stated earlier, this feeling of involvement will make users less likely to resist the new system when it is installed.

Other data collection techniques can also be employed. In some cases, telephone calls are an excellent method. Activities can also be simulated to see how the existing system reacts. Thus, fake sales orders, stock shortages, customer complaints and data-flow bottlenecks can be recreated to see how the existing system responds to these situations.

Statistical sampling, which involves taking a random sample of data, is another technique. For example, suppose that you want to collect data that describes 10 000 sales orders received over the last few years. Because it is too time consuming to analyze each of the 10 000 sales orders, you could collect a random sample of around 200 sales orders from the entire batch. You can assume that the characteristics of this sample apply to all 10 000 orders.

> **statistical sampling** Selecting a random sample of data and applying the characteristics of the sample to the whole group.

Data Analysis

The data collected in its raw form is usually not adequate to determine the effectiveness of the existing system or the requirements for the new system. The next step is to manipulate the collected data so that the development team members who are participating in systems analysis can use the data. This manipulation is called **data analysis**. Data and activity modelling and using data-flow diagrams and entity-relationship diagrams are useful during data analysis to show data flows and the relationships among various objects, associations and activities. Other common tools and techniques for data analysis include application flowcharts, grid charts, CASE tools and the object-oriented approach. Often two versions of the models are created – a version showing how things happen currently in the organization and another showing how they will happen after the new system has been installed.

> **data analysis** The manipulation of collected data so that the development team members who are participating in systems analysis can use the data.

Data Modelling

Data modelling was explained in Chapter 5, along with a technique you can use to create a data model. The purpose of this model is to visualize and structure the data that the organization stores. An example data model is shown in Figure 11.13a.

Activity (or Process) Modelling

To fully describe a business problem or solution, the related objects, associations and activities must be described. Activities in this sense are events or items that are necessary to fulfil the business relationship or that can be associated with the business relationship in a meaningful way.

Figure 11.13 Sample Data Model, Data-Flow Diagram and Description
This model shows a data model, data-flow diagram and brief description of the business relationship for a member of a golf club playing golf.

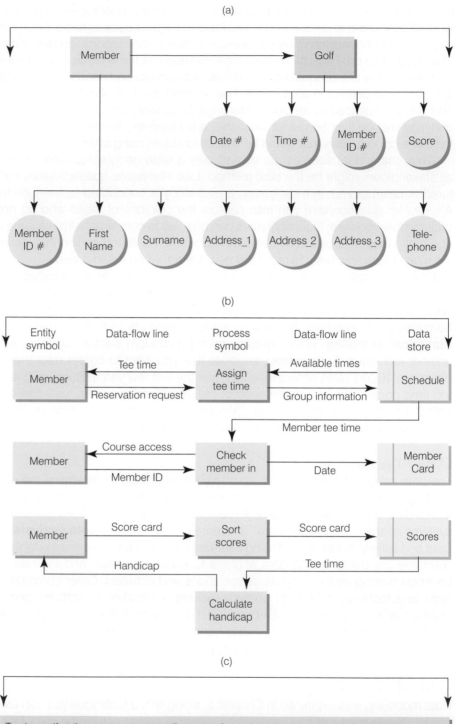

(a)

(b)

(c)

To play golf at the course, you must first pay a fee to become a member of the golf club. Members are issued member cards and are assigned member ID numbers. To reserve a tee time (a time to play golf), a member calls the club house at the golf course and arranges an available time slot with the reception clerk. The reception clerk reserves the tee time by writing the member's name and number of players in the group on the course schedule. When a member arrives at the course, he or she checks in at the reception desk where the reception clerk checks the course schedule and notes the date on the member's card. After a round of golf has been completed, the members leave their score card with the reception clerk. Member scores are tracked and member handicaps are updated on a monthly basis.

Activity modelling is sometimes accomplished through the use of data-flow diagrams or use case models. A **data-flow diagram (DFD)** models objects, associations and activities by describing how data can flow between and around various objects. DFDs work on the premise that every activity involves some communication, transference or flow that can be described as a data element. DFDs describe the activities that fulfil a business relationship or accomplish a business task, not how these activities are to be performed. That is, DFDs show the logical sequence of associations and activities, not the physical processes. A system modelled with a DFD could operate manually or could be computer based; if computer based, the system could operate with a variety of technologies.

> **data-flow diagram (DFD)** A model of objects, associations and activities that describes how data can flow between and around various objects.

A use case model consists of two parts – a diagram showing each process and the 'actors' who use the them. An actor is someone who gets something out of the process. Typical actors are customers and suppliers. 'Buy a product' is a typical process, or 'Reorder stock'. The second part of the model is a text description of each process broken down into numbered steps.

Comparing entity-relationship diagrams with data-flow diagrams provides insight into the concept of top-down design. Figures 11.13a and b show a data model and a data-flow diagram for the same business relationship – namely, a member of a golf club playing golf. Figure 11.13c provides a brief description of the business relationship for clarification.

Application Flowcharts

Application flowcharts show the relationships among applications or systems. Let's say that a small business has collected data about its order processing, inventory control, invoicing and marketing analysis applications. Management is thinking of modifying the inventory control application. The raw facts collected, however, do not help in determining how the applications are related to each other and the databases required for each. These relationships are established through data analysis with an application flowchart (see Figure 11.14). Using this tool for data analysis makes clear the relationships among the order processing functions.

In the simplified application flowchart in Figure 11.14, you can see that the telephone order administrator provides important data to the system about items such as versions, quantities and prices. The system calculates sales tax and order totals. Any changes made to this order processing system could affect the company's other systems, such as inventory control and marketing.

Grid Charts

A grid chart is a table that shows relationships among various aspects of a systems development effort. For example, a grid chart can reveal the databases used by the various applications (see Figure 11.15).

The simplified grid chart in Figure 11.15 shows that the customer database is used by the order processing, marketing analysis and invoicing applications. The inventory database is used by the order processing, inventory control and marketing analysis applications. The supplier database is used by the inventory control application, and the accounts receivable database is used by the invoicing application. This grid chart shows which applications use common databases and reveals that, for example, any changes to the inventory control application must investigate the inventory and supplier databases.

CASE Tools

As discussed earlier, many systems development projects use CASE tools to complete analysis tasks. Most computer-aided software engineering tools have generalized graphics programs that can generate a variety of diagrams and figures. Entity-relationship diagrams, data-flow diagrams, application flowcharts and other diagrams can be developed using CASE graphics programs to help describe the existing system. During the analysis phase, a CASE repository – a database of system descriptions, parameters and objectives – will be developed.

Figure 11.14 A Telephone Order Process Application Flowchart
The flowchart shows the relationships among various processes.

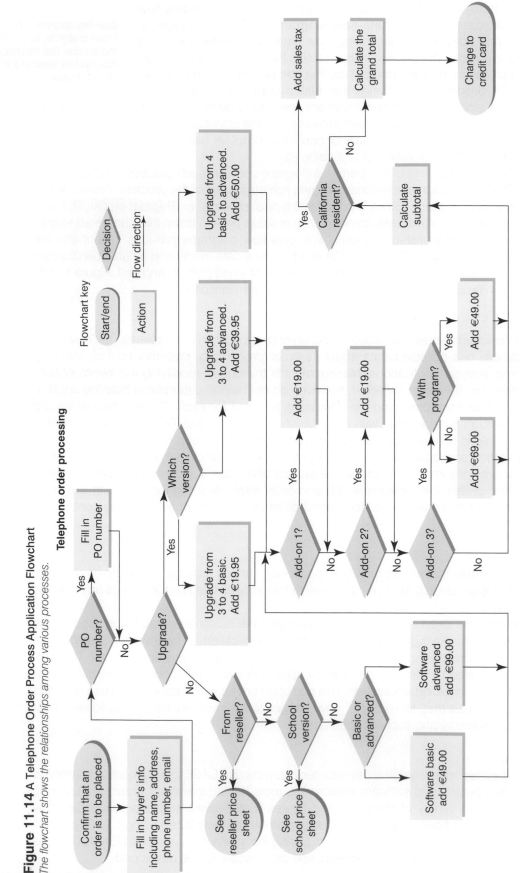

Telephone order processing

Flowchart key

Start/end

Action

Decision

Flow direction

Databases ➝ Applications ↓	Customer database	Inventory database	Supplier database	Accounts receivable database
Order processing application	X	X		
Inventory control application		X	X	
Marketing analysis application	X	X		
Invoicing application	X			X

Figure 11.15 A Grid Chart *The chart shows the relationships among applications and databases.*

Requirements Analysis

The overall purpose of requirements analysis is to determine user, stakeholder and organizational needs. For an accounts payable application, the stakeholders could include suppliers and members of the purchasing department. An accounts payable manager might want a better procedure for tracking the amount owed by customers. Specifically, the manager wants a weekly report that shows all customers who owe more than €1000 and are more than 90 days past due on their account. A financial manager might need a report that summarizes total amount owed by customers to consider whether to loosen or tighten credit limits. A sales manager might want to review the amount owed by a key customer relative to sales to that same customer. The purpose of requirements analysis is to capture these requests in detail. Questions that should be asked during requirements analysis include the following:

■ Are these stakeholders satisfied with the current accounts payable application?

■ What improvements could be made to satisfy suppliers and help the purchasing department?

One of the most difficult procedures in systems analysis is confirming user or systems requirements. In some cases, communications problems can interfere with determining these requirements. Numerous tools and techniques can be used to capture systems requirements. In addition to the data collection techniques already discussed (interview, questionnaire, etc.), others can be used in the context of a JAD session to determine system requirements.

Critical Success Factors

Managers and decision makers are asked to list only the factors that are critical to the success of their area of the organization. A critical success factor (CSF) for a production manager might be adequate raw materials from suppliers; a CSF for a sales representative could be a list of customers currently buying a certain type of product. Starting from these CSFs, the system inputs, outputs, performance and other specific requirements can be determined.

The IS Plan

As we have seen, the IS plan translates strategic and organizational goals into systems development initiatives. The IS planning process often generates strategic planning documents that can be used to define system requirements. Working from these documents ensures that

11

requirements analysis will address the goals set by top-level managers and decision makers (see Figure 11.16). There are unique benefits to applying the IS plan to define systems requirements. Because the IS plan takes a long-range approach to using information technology within the organization, the requirements for a system analyzed in terms of the IS plan are more likely to be compatible with future systems development initiatives.

Figure 11.16
Converting Organizational
Goals into Systems
Requirements

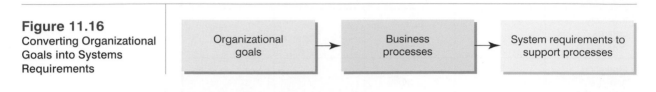

Screen and Report Layout

Developing formats for printed reports and screens to capture data and display information are some of the common tasks associated with developing systems. Screens and reports relating to systems output are specified first to verify that the desired solution is being delivered. Manual or computerized screen and report layout facilities are used to capture both input and output requirements.

Using a screen layout, a designer can quickly and efficiently design the features, layout and format of a display screen. In general, users who interact with the screen frequently can be presented with more data and less descriptive information; infrequent users should have more descriptive information presented to explain the data that they are viewing (see Figure 11.17).

Figure 11.17 Screen
Layouts *(a) A screen layout chart for frequent users who require little descriptive information.*
(b) A screen layout chart for infrequent users who require more descriptive information.

(a) ORDER ENTRY

ORDER NO.	CUSTOMER NO.	SALES PERSON	REGION	COMMISSION	NET DOLLARS
XXXXX	XXXXX	XXXXX	XXX	XXX	XXXXX

ITEM NO	QTY	UNIT	PRICE	DOLLARS	DISCOUNTS
XXXXXXXXX	XXXX	XX	XXXXX	XXXXXXX	XX XX XX
XXXXXXXXX	XXXX	XX	XXXXX	XXXXXXX	XX XX XX
XXXXXXXXX	XXXX	XX	XXXXX	XXXXXXX	XX XX XX
XXXXXXXXX	XXXX	XX	XXXXX	XXXXXXX	XX XX XX
XXXXXXXXX	XXXX	XX	XXXXX	XXXXXXX	XX XX XX
XXXXXXXXX	XXXX	XX	XXXXX	XXXXXXX	XX XX XX
XXXXXXXXX	XXXX	XX	XXXXX	XXXXXXX	XX XX XX
XXXXXXXXX	XXXX	XX	XXXXX	XXXXXXX	XX XX XX
XXXXXXXXX	XXXX	XX	XXXXX	XXXXXXX	XX XX XX
XXXXXXXXX	XXXX	XX	XXXXX	XXXXXXX	XX XX XX
XXXXXXXXX	XXXX	XX	XXXXX	XXXXXXX	XX XX XX
XXXXXXXXX	XXXX	XX	XXXXX	XXXXXXX	XX XX XX

(b)

Which online option would you like to perform?
(Please enter an X to make selection)

_DATA ENTRY -Enter transaction and report requests
for later processing.

_RETRIEVALS -Review online information from the
database: bill of materials,
where used, routing, item data.

Report layout allows designers to diagram and format printed reports. Reports can contain data, graphs or both. Graphic presentations allow managers and executives to quickly view trends and take appropriate action, if necessary.

Screen layout diagrams can document the screens users desire for the new or modified application. Report layout charts reveal the format and content of various reports that the application will prepare. Other diagrams and charts can be developed to reveal the relationship between the application and outputs from the application.

Requirements Analysis Tools

A number of tools can be used to document requirements analysis, including CASE tools. As requirements are developed and agreed on, entity-relationship diagrams, data-flow diagrams, screen and report layout forms, and other types of documentation are stored in the CASE repository. These requirements might also be used later as a reference during the rest of systems development or for a different systems development project.

Object-Oriented Systems Analysis

An alternative to analyzing the existing system using data-flow diagrams and flowcharts is the object-oriented approach to systems analysis. Like traditional analysis, problems or potential opportunities are identified during object-oriented analysis. Identifying key participants and collecting data are still performed.

With the object-oriented approach, systems analysts are looking for classes – things within the system that have data and action – rather than entities (see Chapter 5). These classes are then modelled with the messages and data that flow between them, and this model is used to capture the requirements of the new system. An order processing administrator might be a class – they have data (the order) and action (they input the data into the computer). The term 'object' refers to an instance of a class; in this case, the class is order processing administrator, whereas 'Bill Jones', who happens to be an order processing administrator, is an object.

In object-oriented systems, analysis all the classes in the system are identified and how they work together to solve a problem is documented. A class could be a piece of software or a human.

The Systems Analysis Report

Systems analysis concludes with a formal systems analysis report. It should cover the following elements:

■ The strengths and weaknesses of the existing system from a stakeholder's perspective.
■ The user/stakeholder requirements for the new system (also called the functional requirements).
■ The organizational requirements for the new system.
■ A description of what the new information system should do to solve the problem.

Suppose analysis reveals that a marketing manager thinks a weakness of the existing system is its inability to provide accurate reports on product availability. These requirements and a preliminary list of the corporate objectives for the new system will be in the systems analysis report. Particular attention is placed on areas of the existing system that could be improved to meet user requirements. The table of contents for a typical report is shown in Figure 11.18.

11

Figure 11.18 A Typical Table of Contents for a Report on an Existing System

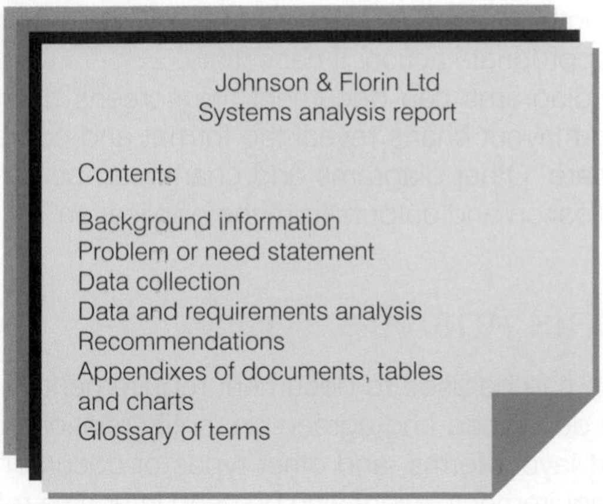

Johnson & Florin Ltd
Systems analysis report

Contents

Background information
Problem or need statement
Data collection
Data and requirements analysis
Recommendations
Appendixes of documents, tables and charts
Glossary of terms

The systems analysis report gives managers a good understanding of the problems and strengths of the existing system. If the existing system is operating better than expected or the necessary changes are too expensive relative to the benefits of a new or modified system, the systems development process can be stopped at this stage. If the report shows that changes to another part of the system might be the best solution, the development process might start over, beginning again with systems investigation. Or, if the systems analysis report shows that it will be beneficial to develop one or more new systems or to make changes to existing ones, systems design, which is discussed in the next chapter, begins.

Summary

Effective systems development requires a team effort from stakeholders, users, managers, systems development specialists and various support personnel, and it starts with careful planning. The systems development team consists of stakeholders: users, managers, systems development specialists and various support personnel. The development team determines the objectives of the information system and delivers to the organization a system that meets its objectives.

A systems analyst is a professional who specializes in analyzing and designing business systems. The programmer is responsible for modifying or developing programs to satisfy user requirements. Other support personnel on the development team include technical specialists, either IS department employees or outside consultants. Depending on the magnitude of the systems development project and the number of IS development specialists on

the team, the team might also include one or more IS managers. At some point in your career, you will likely be a participant in systems development. You could be involved in a systems development team – as a user, as a manager of a business area or project team, as a member of the IS department, or maybe even as a CIO.

Systems development projects are initiated for many reasons, including the need to solve problems with an existing system, to exploit opportunities to gain competitive advantage, to increase competition, to make use of effective information, to create organizational growth, to settle a merger or corporate acquisition, or to address a change in the market or external environment. External pressures, such as potential lawsuits or terrorist attacks, can also prompt an organization to initiate systems development.

Information systems planning refers to the translation of strategic and organizational goals into systems development initiatives. Benefits of IS planning include a long-range view of information technology use and better use of IS resources. Planning requires developing overall IS objectives; identifying IS projects; setting priorities and selecting projects; analyzing resource requirements; setting schedules, milestones and deadlines; and developing the IS planning document. IS planning can result in a competitive advantage through creative and critical analysis.

Establishing objectives for systems development is a key aspect of any successful development project. Critical success factors (CSFs) can identify important objectives. Systems development objectives can include performance goals (quality and usefulness of the output and the speed at which output is generated) and cost objectives (development costs, fixed costs and ongoing investment costs).

Systems development often uses tools to select, implement and monitor projects, including prototyping, rapid application development, CASE tools and object-oriented development. The five phases of the traditional SDLC are investigation, analysis, design, implementation, and maintenance and review. Systems investigation identifies potential problems and opportunities and considers them in light of organizational goals. Systems analysis seeks a general understanding of the solution required to solve the problem; the existing system is studied in detail and weaknesses are identified. Systems design creates new or modifies existing system requirements. Systems implementation encompasses programming, testing, training, conversion and operation of the system. Systems maintenance and review entails monitoring the system and performing enhancements or repairs.

Advantages of the traditional SDLC include the following: it provides for maximum management control, creates considerable system documentation, ensures that system requirements can be traced back to stated business needs, and produces many intermediate products for review. Its disadvantages include the following: users may get a system that meets the needs as understood by the developers, the documentation is expensive and difficult to maintain, users' needs go unstated or might not be met, and users cannot easily review the many intermediate products produced.

Prototyping is an iterative approach that involves defining the problem, building the initial version, having users work with and evaluate the initial version, providing feedback and incorporating suggestions into the second version. Prototypes can be fully operational or non-operational, depending on how critical the system under development is and how much time and money the organization has to spend on prototyping.

Rapid application development (RAD) uses tools and techniques designed to speed application development. Its use reduces paper-based documentation, automates program source code generation, and facilitates user participation in development activities. RAD can use newer programming techniques, such as agile development or extreme programming. RAD makes extensive use of the joint application development (JAD) process to gather data and perform requirements analysis. JAD involves group meetings in which users, stakeholders and IS professionals work together to analyze existing systems, propose possible solutions, and define the requirements for a new or modified system.

The term 'end-user systems development' describes any systems development project in which the primary effort is undertaken by a combination of business managers and users.

Many companies hire an outside consulting firm that specializes in systems development to take over some or all of its systems development activities. This approach is called 'outsourcing'. Reasons for outsourcing include companies' belief that they can cut costs, achieve a competitive advantage without having the necessary IS personnel in-house, obtain state-of-the-art technology, increase their technological flexibility and proceed with development despite downsizing. Many companies offer outsourcing services, including computer vendors and specialized consulting companies.

A number of factors affect systems development success. The degree of change introduced by the project, continuous improvement and reengineering, the use of quality programs and standards, organizational experience with systems development, the use of project management tools, and the use of CASE tools and the object-oriented approach are all factors that affect the success of a project. The greater the amount of change a system will endure, the greater the degree of risk and often the amount of reward. Continuous improvement projects do not require significant business process or IS changes, while reengineering involves fundamental changes in how the organization conducts business and completes tasks. Successful systems development projects often involve such factors as support from top management, strong user involvement, use of a proven methodology, clear project goals and objectives, concentration on key problems and straightforward designs, staying on schedule and within budget, good user training, and solid review and maintenance programs. Quality standards, such as ISO 9001, can also be used during the systems development process.

The use of automated project management tools enables detailed development, tracking and control of the project schedule. Effective use of a quality assurance process enables the project manager to deliver a high-quality system and to make intelligent trade-offs among cost, schedule and quality. CASE tools automate many of the systems development tasks, thus reducing an analyst's time and effort while ensuring good documentation. Object-oriented systems development can also be an important success factor. With the object-oriented systems development (OOSD) approach, a project can be broken down into a group of objects that interact. Instead of requiring thousands or millions of lines of detailed computer instructions or code, the systems development project might require a few dozen or maybe a hundred objects.

Systems development starts with investigation and analysis of existing systems. In most organizations, a systems request form initiates the investigation process. The systems investigation is designed to assess the feasibility of implementing solutions for business problems, including technical, economic, legal, operations and schedule feasibility. Net present value analysis is often used to help determine a project's economic feasibility. An investigation team follows up on the request and performs a feasibility analysis that addresses technical, economic, legal, operational and schedule feasibility.

If the project under investigation is feasible, major goals are set for the system's development, including performance, cost, managerial goals and procedural

goals. Many companies choose a popular methodology so that new IS employees, outside specialists and vendors will be familiar with the systems development tasks set forth in the approach. A systems development methodology must be selected. Object-oriented systems investigation is being used to a greater extent today.

Systems analysis is the examination of existing systems, which begins after a team receives approval for further study from management. Additional study of a selected system allows those involved to further understand the system's weaknesses and potential areas for improvement. An analysis team is assembled to collect and analyze data on the existing system.

Data collection methods include observation, interviews, questionnaires and statistical sampling. Data analysis manipulates the collected data to provide information. The analysis includes grid charts, application flowcharts and CASE tools. The overall purpose of requirements analysis is to determine user and organizational needs.

Data analysis and modelling is used to model organizational objects and associations using text and graphical diagrams. It is most often accomplished through the use of entity-relationship (ER) diagrams. Activity modelling is often accomplished through the use of data-flow diagrams (DFD), which model objects, associations and activities by describing how data can flow between and around various objects. DFD use symbols for data flows, processing, entities and data stores. Application flowcharts, grid charts and CASE tools are also used during systems analysis.

Requirements analysis determines the needs of users, stakeholders and the organization in general. Asking directly, using critical success factors, and determining requirements from the IS plan can be used. Often, screen and report layout charts are used to document requirements during systems analysis.

Like traditional analysis, problems or potential opportunities are identified during object-oriented analysis.

Self-Assessment Test

1 _____ is the activity of creating or modifying existing business systems. It refers to all aspects of the process – from identifying problems to be solved or opportunities to be exploited to the implementation and refinement of the chosen solution.

2 Which of the following people ultimately benefit from a systems development project?
   a. computer programmers
   b. systems analysts
   c. stakeholders
   d. senior-level manager

3 What factors are essential to the success of certain functional areas of an organization?
   a. critical success factors
   b. systems analysis factors
   c. creative goal factors
   d. systems development factors

4 What employs tools, techniques and methodologies designed to speed application development?
   a. rapid application development
   b. joint optimization
   c. prototyping
   d. extended application development

5 System performance is usually determined by factors such as fixed investments in hardware and related equipment. True or false?

6 _____ takes an iterative approach to the systems development process. During each iteration, requirements and alternative solutions to the problem are identified and analyzed, new solutions are designed, and a portion of the system is implemented.

7 Joint application development involves group meetings in which users, stakeholders and IS professionals work together to analyze existing systems, propose possible solutions, and define the requirements for a new or modified system. True or false?

8 Feasibility analysis is typically done during which systems development stage?
   a. investigation
   b. analysis
   c. design
   d. implementation

9 Data modelling is most often accomplished through the use of _____, whereas activity modelling is often accomplished through the use of _____.

10 The overall purpose of requirements analysis is to determine user, stakeholder and organizational needs. True or false?

Review Questions

1 What is an IS stakeholder?

2 What is the goal of IS planning? What steps are involved in IS planning?

3 What are the typical reasons to initiate systems development?

4 What is the difference between a programmer and a systems analyst?

5 Why is it important to identify and remove errors early in the systems development lifecycle?

6 Identify four reasons that a systems development project might be initiated.

7 List factors that have a strong influence on project success.

8 What is the difference between systems investigation and systems analysis?

9 How does the JAD technique support the RAD systems development lifecycle?

10 Describe some of the models that are used to document systems analysis.

11

Discussion Questions

1 Why is it important for business managers to have a basic understanding of the systems development process?

2 Briefly describe the role of a system user in the systems investigation and systems analysis stages of a project.

3 For what types of systems development projects might prototyping be especially useful? What are the characteristics of a system developed with a prototyping technique?

4 How important are communications skills to IS personnel? Consider this statement: 'IS personnel need a combination of skills – one-third technical skills, one-third business skills and one-third communications skills.' Do you think this is true? How would this affect the training of IS personnel?

5 Discuss three reasons why aligning overall business goals with IS goals is important.

Web Exercises

1 A number of tools can be used to develop a new web-based application. Describe the web development tools you would use and the steps you would complete to implement a website to rent movies and games over the Internet. You might be asked to develop a report or send an email message to your instructor about what you have found.

2 Using the Internet, locate an organization that is currently involved in a systems development project. Describe how it is using project management tools. Is project management software being used?

Case One

International Volunteering Management Needs ERP System

Austraining International is a project management company that works with clients all over the world, organizing volunteering programs to develop the skills of local people. Wholly owned by the Government of South Australia, the company extends its services throughout Asia, the Pacific, Latin America, Africa and the Caribbean, and can provide access to development specialists with local expertise and networks. Their vision is to enable people to positively change their world, resulting in empowered global communities and improved quality of life for program participants and recipients. Their volunteers have trained locals in Indonesia how to perform vaccinations and they have helped train English teachers in Bangladesh.

Austraining is a public/private partnership. 'It's a bit complicated,' says CFO Darren Hastings. 'The

organization operates around our social development mission, but we still aim to generate a surplus. Priorities shift often, and this is apparent at a strategic level, an operational level and at an individual level. We're constantly reconciling these two aspects of our strategy.'

The public/private business model combined with the diverse nature of its services leads to some complex financial management scenarios. It operates in more than 20 countries, each of which has its own currency and culture. It also must maintain personnel records for as many as 700 volunteers, and report different financial information to different public and private regulators. Of course the company must also track all of its funding.

As the company grew it became clear that their business model demanded the additional

11

capabilities of a full-featured enterprise resource planning system. 'We had secured several new clients and projects, which introduced more complex reporting requirements,' Hastings says. 'What had been a simple cost structure and account structure rapidly became much more complicated. As a result, we found ourselves performing a lot of manual manipulation of data.'

After an evaluation process, Austraining selected Microsoft Dynamics AX. Microsoft Dynamics AX is an ERP with features for multiple languages and multiple currencies, features for financial, human resources and operations management as well as additional industry capabilities for retailers, professional service industries, financial service businesses, manufacturers and public sector organizations. It is a comprehensive ERP solution for mid-size and larger organizations. It integrates with other Microsoft software which makes it easy to conduct business across different locations and countries. Similar to other ERP, it implements standard business processes which are seen as the best practice in one industry, helping a business to standardize processes and simplify compliance with any regulators.

Since deploying Microsoft Dynamics AX, everyone in the company uses the same data. Remote managers can run reports and retrieve information from the centralized data store. The new system

has eliminated several manual, paper-based processes, for example, reconciliation of expense reports and credit-card statements. Microsoft Dynamics AX also allows bank statements and local transactions to be recorded in their native currency, so that exchange rates no longer need to be calculated manually. Austraining plans to add additional functionality, including using the Microsoft Dynamics AX Human Capital Management module to manage its 700 volunteers. Hastings expects that bringing the volunteer database and financial information into a single system will allow Austraining to perform detailed performance analysis of expenses related to volunteer operations. The additional insight will enable it to forecast costs for volunteer programs, enabling it to optimize in-country operations by being able to prepare flexible and responsive long-term financial forecasting of program costs.

Questions

1 What are some of the benefits from employing an ERP system. Are there any drawbacks?

2 List some of the challenges a company like Austraining faces when managing its information.

3 What functionality does Austraining require from its ERP?

4 Explain how ERP vendors might design modules such as a human capital management module.

Case Two

Real Estate Classifieds in the Cloud

Established in 1998 in Durban, Johannesburg, Privateproperty is South Africa's most popular online classifieds service for real estate agents, private sellers, prospective buyers and landlords. With the goal of making property search an 'awesome experience', Privateproperty offers clearly displayed quality listings alongside simple mechanisms for contacting the seller or estate agent. The site boasts over 1 million visitors monthly, looking at over 120 000 properties spread across over 4000 suburbs in South Africa.

When it launched, Privateproperty relied on a modest technical infrastructure which provided a foundation for its website to grow. As its needs evolved, the technical team added additional functionality to the existing infrastructure. Properties were stored on a Microsoft SQL database with three web servers delivering access to the website. As traffic load increased Privateproperty simply added hardware. This worked until around 2012 when further expansion became difficult and even small problems resulted in downtime. It was also becoming expensive to host such a popular website. Privateproperty began to look for alternatives.

The team identified Microsoft Windows Azure, an 'open and flexible cloud platform that enables enterprises to swiftly build, deploy and administer applications across a global network of Microsoft-managed datacenters' as a possible solution. It is a cloud computing service. Using a cloud–based technology was a big change for the company but it offered several benefits from a scale, cost and us-ability perspective.

The technical team began recoding their online infrastructure with a view towards rolling out a revamped website six months later. In May 2013 they introduced their new web portal based on Windows Azure and decommissioned its old environment.

Simon Bray, Privateproperty's chief execu-tive officer said, 'The cost benefit associated with Windows Azure compared to local offerings is roughly eight times more affordable. This has al-lowed us to reallocate resources to other essential elements – enabling Privateproperty to grow as demand increases. This, I believe, has been the most important gain for Privateproperty. Azure's ability to scale our server resources on demand has allowed us to build a portal that can easily and cost-effectively handle the changing network load. Furthermore, Azure's unique platform as a service (PaaS) offering has enabled us to decrease our release cycle from once every two weeks down to once every two days. This rapid deployment model allows us to continuously improve the website and to respond quickly to any problems.'

Questions

1 What is 'platform as a service'?

2 Why might further expansion of Privateproperty's original infrastructure have become difficult?

3 How can Microsoft's cloud be so cheap compared with running a private web server?

4 Are there any disadvantages in running this website through the cloud?

Case Three

Requirements Tracking at Honeywell Technology Solutions Lab

As you read in this chapter, determining system re-quirements is a vital part of the development of any information system. Complex information systems have many sets of requirements. It is, therefore, essential to have a systematic way to determine them.

Honeywell Technology Solutions Lab (HTSL), through its IT Services and Solutions business unit, develops software solutions for other parts of Hon-eywell Inc. HTSL is based in Bengaluru (Bangalore), India, with centres in Beijing, Brno, Hyderabad, Madurai and Shanghai.

In 2010, the company identified a problem: at HTSL, various groups such as requirement writers and development, quality assurance (QA), and project management teams worked independently in separate 'silos'. It was difficult to track project requirements and the status of their implementa-tion. HTSL needed a system to manage the require-ments and its relationships to each other.

Beyond managing the requirements, HTSL needed an application that could coordinate test cases, design elements and defects. Requirement writers would create the requirements for software, and HTSL customers (other Honeywell divisions) would review and approve these requirements. Once approved, the development team would im-plement them, and the QA team would generate test cases based on them. Any defects found in ex-ecuting the test cases would also be tracked.

HTSL had a great deal of experience in develop-ing software for aerospace, automation and control, specialty materials, and transportation systems. However, they had no experience in developing software to manage the development process itself. The company recognized this deficit and turned to specialists.

Kovair, of Santa Clara, California, is such a specialist. Its Application Lifecycle Management (ALM) package is for 'implementing a software development life cycle (SDLC) process, collaborating on the entire development cycle and tracing implementations back to original specs. [It] ensures that all developers are working from the same playbook … and that there are no costly last minute surprises.'

One ALM module is Requirements Management. Using it, HTSL can gather requirements, rank them, manage their changes, and coordinate them with system test cases. The Requirements Management module can also produce a variety of reports, including formatted requirements specifications and reports showing the distribution of requirements by type, criticality, source or any other descriptor.

Honeywell already had a formal development process called 'Review, Approval, Baseline, Technical Design, Test Design, Implementation and Testing'. Kovair's ALM solution was customized to fit into this process. When a requirement is entered into ALM, it is marked 'Submitted', and the review process begins. ALM generates Review tasks for stakeholders, ensuring that they will give their views on the new requirement. When they approve it, perhaps after changes, its status is changed to 'Approved', and a task is entered for its owner to add it to the baseline system design. When this step is completed, two new tasks are created: one for the development team to develop technical specifications and then the software; and one for the quality assurance team to develop test cases. Development can then continue.

What were the results? HTSL has reduced rework due to incorrect requirements and sped up development. Development team productivity was improved by about 20 per cent, and requirements-related defects were reduced by at least 1 per cent.

Questions

1 What would have happened if HTSL tried to develop a system like ALM on its own instead of turning to Kovair? Discuss both pros and cons of the likely outcome.

2 The ALM software is intended to help companies manage the steps of software development. Software development is only one of the processes that businesses use every day. What are the characteristics of a process that make a software package like ALM useful? Identify criteria that can be used to decide whether a company should look for an ALM-like package for that process.

3 ALM is designed to manage the entire SDLC, not just requirements. Suppose you had to choose between

(a) a system that could manage the entire SDLC, and

(b) a system that only managed requirements but did that better. How would you choose between them?

4 This case is based in part on information from Kovair. Many organizations need to track software development projects, so other companies besides Kovair offer packages to do that. Suppose you were given the job of choosing such a package. List at least four criteria you would use in comparing different packages. Rank the items on your list from most to least important.

Notes

1 Triggle, N. 2014. 'Giant NHS Database Rollout Delayed'. BBC News. Available from: www.bbc.co.uk/news/health-26239532. Accessed 2 April 2014.

2 Brandel, Mary, 'Five Biggest Project Challenges for 2006', *Computerworld*, 2 January 2006, p. 16.

3 Kolbasuk, Marianne, 'Skills That Will Matter', *Information Week*, 2 January 2006, p. 53.

4 Hess, H.M., 'Aligning Technology and Business', *IBM Systems Journal*, Vol. 44, No. 1, 2005, p. 25.

5 Staff, 'BRE Bank Subscribes to Risk Management Database', *Asian Banker*, 15 January 2006.

6 Havenstein, Heather, 'Medical Groups Offered Rewards to IT Use', *Computerworld*, 6 February 2006, p. 14.

7 Engardio, Pete, 'The Future of Outsourcing', *Business Week*, 30 January 2006, p. 50.

8 Kripalani, Manjeet, 'Offshoring: Spreading the Gospel', *Business Week*, 6 March 2006, p. 46.

9 Shellenbarger, Sue, 'Outsourcing Jobs to the Den', *Wall Street Journal*, 12 January 2006, p. D1.

10 Staff, 'Eurostar Briefs Occam to Boost Traveler Insight', *Precision Marketing*, 6 January 2006, p. 6.

11 Arsanjani, A., 'Empowering the Business Analyst for On Demand Computing', *IBM Systems Journal*, Vol. 44, No. 1, 2005, p. 67.

12 IBM Website. Available from: www.ibm.com.

13 EDS Website. Available from: www.eds.com.

14 Accenture Website. Available from: www.accenture.com.

15 Vijayan, Jaikumar, 'Outsourcing Savvy', *Computerworld*, 3 January 2005, p. 16.

16 Hoffman, Thomas, 'Prenuptials for Outsourcing', *Computerworld*, 23 January 2006, p. 34.

17 Rohde, Laura, 'Report Details Flaws in UK Case Management IT System', *Computerworld*, 18 April 2005, p. 21.

18 ISO – International Standards Organization Website. Available from: www.iso.org.

19 Capability Maturity Model for Software home page Website. Available from: www.sei.cmu.edu.

20 Kay, Russell, 'CMMI', *Computerworld*, 24 January 2005, p. 28.

21 Software Engineering Institute (Website), 'Capability Maturity Model for Software'. Available from: www.sei.cmu.edu/cmm.

22 Glen, Paul, 'Detecting Disaster Projects', *Computerworld*, 6 February 2006, p. 39.

12

Systems Design and Implementation

Principles

Designing new systems or modifying existing ones should always help an organization achieve its goals.

The primary emphasis of systems implementation is to make sure that the right information is delivered to the right person in the right format at the right time.

Maintenance and review add to the useful life of a system but can consume large amounts of resources. These activities can benefit from the same rigorous methods and project management techniques applied to systems development.

Learning Objectives

■ State the purpose of systems design and discuss the differences between logical and physical systems design.

■ Describe some considerations in design modelling and the diagrams used during object-oriented design.

■ Outline key considerations in interface design and control and system security and control.

■ Define the term 'RFP' and discuss how this document is used to drive the acquisition of hardware and software.

■ Describe the techniques used to make systems selection evaluations.

■ State the purpose of systems implementation and discuss the activities associated with this phase of systems development.

■ List the advantages and disadvantages of purchasing versus developing software.

■ Discuss the software development process and some of the tools used in this process, including object-oriented program development tools.

■ State the importance of systems and software maintenance and discuss the activities involved.

■ Describe the systems review process.

Why Learn About Systems Design and Implementation?

The previous chapter talked about how problems are analyzed. This chapter looks at how this analysis can be used to design and build IT solutions. The chapter mainly looks at developing a new system but also examines solving a problem by buying an existing IS that has already been developed.

Information systems are used in every industry and almost every career. A manager at a hotel chain can use an information system to look up client preferences. An accountant at a manufacturing company can use an information system to analyze the costs of a new plant. A sales representative for a music store can use an information system to determine which CDs to order and which to discount because they are not selling. A computer engineer can use an information system to help determine why a computer system is running slowly. This chapter shows how you can be involved in designing and implementing an information system that will directly benefit you, and the options your company has for acquiring a new IS. It also shows how to avoid errors or recover from disasters. The way an information system is designed, implemented and maintained profoundly affects the daily functioning of an organization. Like systems investigation and analysis covered in the last chapter, design, implementation, maintenance and review (all covered in this chapter) strive to achieve organizational goals, such as reducing costs, increasing profits or improving customer service. The goal is to develop a new or modified system to deliver the right information to the right person at the right time.

12.1 Systems Design

systems design A stage of systems development where a solution to the problem is planned out and documented.

The purpose of **systems design** is to answer the question 'how will the information system solve the problem?' The primary result of the systems design phase is a technical design that details system inputs and the processing required to produce outputs, user interfaces, hardware, software, databases, telecommunications, personnel and procedures, and shows how these components are related.[1] The system that is designed should meet all the requirements specified during the analysis phase (explained in the previous chapter), overcome the shortcomings of the existing system and help the organization achieve its goals. Two key aspects of systems design are logical and physical design.

logical design A description of the functional requirements of a system.

The **logical design** refers to what the system will do. Logical design describes the functional requirements of a system. That is, it conceptualizes what the system will do to solve the problems identified through earlier analysis. Without this step, the technical details of the system (such as which hardware devices should be acquired) often obscure the best solution. Logical design involves planning the purpose of each system element, independent of hardware and software considerations. The logical design specifications that are determined and documented include output, input, process, file and database, telecommunications, procedures, controls and security, and personnel and job requirements.

physical design The specification of the characteristics of the system components necessary to put the logical design into action.

The **physical design** refers to how the tasks are accomplished, including how the components work together and what each component does. Physical design specifies the characteristics of the system components necessary to put the logical design into action. In this phase, the characteristics of the hardware, software, database, telecommunications, personnel, and procedure and control specifications must be detailed.

There are a number of notations that can be used to document the design stage. Data flow diagrams and class diagrams (mentioned in the previous chapter) are used, as is the notation shown in Chapter 5 for illustrating a data model. Sequence diagrams are used in object-oriented systems design to illustrate how messages pass between objects and to show the sequence of events in a process. Programmers use various notations to design the code that they will write.

Interface Design and Controls

Some special system characteristics should be considered during both logical and physical design. These characteristics relate to how users access and interact with the system. For example, with a **menu-driven system** (see Figure 12.1), users simply pick what they want to do from a list of alternatives. Most people can easily operate these types of systems and are familiar with them. They select an option or respond to questions (or prompts) from the system, and the system does the rest. An alternative is a command line interface such as that shown in Figure 12.2. **Command line interfaces** involve users typing commands at a prompt. For example, typing the name of a software package opens it.

menu-driven system A system in which users simply pick what they want to do from a list of alternatives.

command line interface An interface where the user types text commands to the computer.

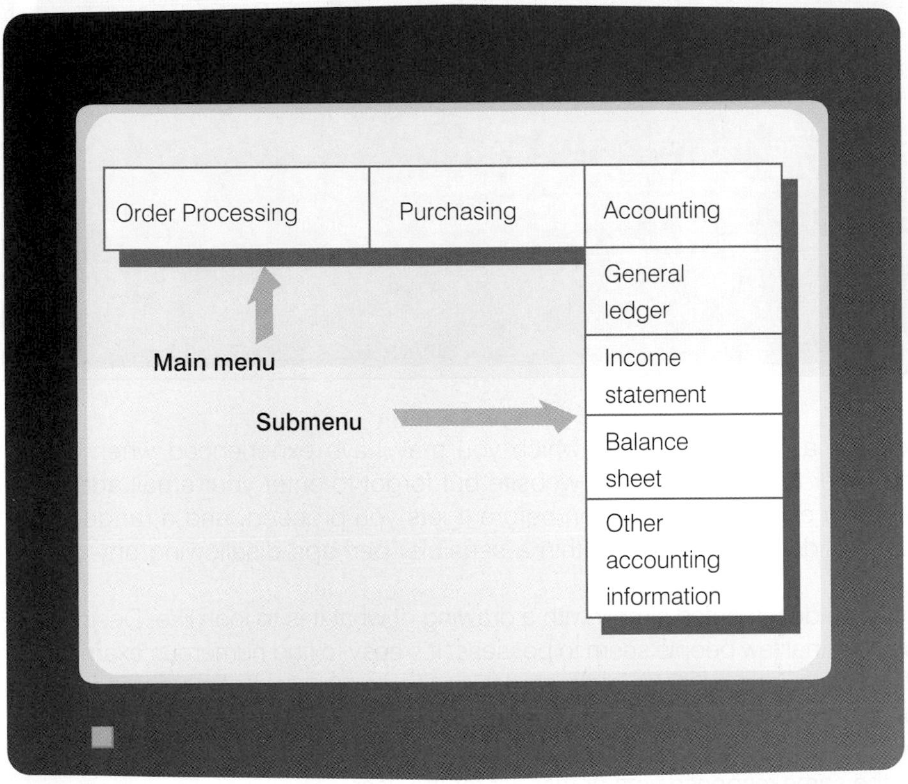

Figure 12.1
Menu-Driven System

Some other interface considerations are whether or not to include interactive help, whether the interface should be 2- or 3-D, whether or not to use virtual reality, a touch screen or a keyboard, and whether to include procedures to help with data entry. Such procedures include spell checking and lookup tables. For example, if you are entering a sales order for a company, you can type its abbreviation, such as ABCO. The program will then go to the customer table, normally stored on a disc, and look up all the information pertaining to the company abbreviated ABCO that you need to complete the sales order. Other data

12

Figure 12.2 Command Line Interface

```
PoSH - C:\

[C:\]
33 > Get-ChildItem 'H:\MediaCenterPC\My Music' -rec |
>>       where { -not $_.PSIsContainer -and $_.Extension -match "wma|mp3" } |
>>       Measure-Object -property length -sum -min -max -ave
>>

Count    : 1307
Average  : 5491276.09563887
Sum      : 7177097857
Maximum  : 22905267
Minimum  : 3235
Property : Length


[C:\]
34 > Get-WmiObject Win32_Bios

SMBIOSBIOSVersion : A07
Manufacturer      : Dell Computer Corporation
Name              : Phoenix ROM BIOS PLUS Version 1.10 A07
SerialNumber      : 40X6W31
Version           : DELL   - 8


[C:\]
35 > $rssUrl = "http://spaces.msn.com/keithhill/feed.rss"
[C:\]
36 > $blog = [xml](new-object System.Net.WebClient).DownloadString($rssUrl)
[C:\]
37 > $blog.rss.channel.item | select title -first 8

title
-----
New Name for Monad - Windows PowerShell!
MSH Community Extensions (MSH CX) Workspace is Up
Writing Cmdlets with PowerShell Script
Extracting Useful Info About Your Computer Using WMI
Monad Featured on This Week's Hanselminutes
Front Range Code Camp Presentation on Windows PowerShell
Find Modules That Have Been Rebased
Analyzing Visual C# Project Files


[C:\]
38 >
```

entry control includes a presence check, which you may have experienced when you've tried to submit an order to an e-commerce website but forgot to enter your email address – the system makes you enter this information before it lets you proceed, and a range check which makes sure the data you enter is within a sensible, perhaps disallowing any year of birth before 1910.

The interface can be documented simply with a drawing of what it is to look like. Designing a good interface is an art that few people seem to possess. It's easy to find numerous examples of bad (annoying, frustrating, non-intuitive) interface design. Table 12.1 lists some characteristics that many interfaces should have. This list however, does not apply to all systems. For example, in Chapter 10 we looked at virtual pets – to keep the user interested a virtual pet should not consistently have the same response time or respect for the user.

Design of System Security and Controls

In addition to considering the system's interface and user interactions, designers must also develop system security and controls for all aspects of the system, including hardware, software, database systems, telecommunications and Internet operations.[2] These key considerations involve error prevention, detection and correction; system controls; and disaster planning and recovery.[3]

12

Table 12.1 The Elements of Good Interactive Dialogue

Element	Description
Clarity	The computer system should ask for information using easily understood language. Whenever possible, the users themselves should help select the words and phrases used for dialogue with the computer system
Response time	Ideally, responses from the computer system should approximate a normal response time from a human being carrying on the same sort of dialogue
Consistency	The system should use the same commands, phrases, words, and function keys for all applications. After a user learns one application, all others will then be easier to use
Format	The system should use an attractive format and layout for all screens. The use of colour, highlighting, and the position of information on the screen should be considered carefully and applied consistently
Jargon	All dialogue should be written in easy-to-understand terms. Avoid jargon known only to IS specialists
Respect	All dialogue should be developed professionally and with respect. Dialogue should not talk down to or insult the user. Avoid statements such as 'You have made a fatal error'

Error Prevention, Detection and Correction

A new information system can be designed to check for certain errors itself. When users input values the system can check that the values entered make sense and if not the user is alerted. For instance the system can check whether the user enters a word when the system is expecting a number. Or if the user enters a number the computer can check it lies within a sensible range – that small items don't cost over €10 000 or that customers weren't born in the 18th century, for example. In these cases the user must fix the error themselves.

An alternative is to avoid the user entering data themselves. In a factory and many shops, for instance, workers will rarely enter product numbers manually – the number can be read from a barcode or an RFID chip. If the reader doesn't detect the number properly the user is alerted and must scan the item again – this will have happened to you many times at a supermarket check-out.

Disaster Planning and Recovery

Disaster planning is the process of anticipating and providing for disasters. A disaster can be an act of nature (a flood, fire or earthquake) or a human act (terrorism, error or a deliberate sabotage by a disgruntled employee). Disaster planning often focuses primarily on two issues: maintaining the integrity of corporate information, and keeping the information system running until normal operations can be resumed. **Disaster recovery** is the implementation of the disaster plan.[4] When Hurricane Katrina hit New Orleans in the US, investment and trading company Howard Weil Inc. had a plan to keep the firm operating[5] – it would move its employees to Houston, Texas. But when Houston also had to be evacuated, the company had to move its employees to another location – Stamford, Connecticut – according to its disaster plan. The company was able to rapidly recreate its trading desk and IS infrastructure to continue trading. According to Jefferson Parker, president of Howard Weil, 'You don't normally develop a backup plan for the backup plan.'

disaster planning The process of anticipating and providing for disasters.

disaster recovery The implementation of the disaster plan.

Although companies have known about the importance of disaster planning and recovery for decades, many do not adequately prepare. The primary tools used in disaster planning and recovery are back-ups. Hardware, software and data can all be 'backed up'.

For example, hot and cold sites can be used to back-up hardware and software. A **hot site** is a space, usually some distance away from the main operation, where spare computers with the appropriate telecommunication links set up, and software installed wait, along with any associated pereriphals such as printers, in case some problem occurs to disrupt the technology in the main location. The hot site is physically separate in case the problem is something like a flood, which would damage a wide area. If a disaster occurs, all that is needed is transportation to take staff to the hot site, along with the latest data back-up. As soon as the data is uploaded, operations can continue. Another approach is to use a **cold site**, also called a shell, which is a computer environment that includes rooms, electrical service, telecommunication links but no hardware. If a primary computer has a problem, back-up computer hardware is brought into the cold site, and the complete system is made operational. A warm site sits somewhere between the two (see Figure 12.3).

hot site A duplicate, operational hardware system or immediate access to one through a specialized vendor.

cold site A computer environment that includes rooms, electrical service, telecommunications links, data storage devices and the like; also called a 'shell'.

Figure 12.3 A Hot Site
A hot site waits, ready for action, in case it is needed.

Databases can be backed up by making a copy of all files and databases changed during the last few days or the last week, a technique called **incremental back-up**. One approach to back-up uses a transaction log, which is a separate file that contains only changes to the database and is backed up more frequently than the database itself (which is much bigger). If a problem occurs with a current database, the transaction log, and the last back-up of the database, can be used to recreate the current database.

incremental back-up Making a back-up copy of all files changed during the last few days or the last week.

Systems Controls

Security lapses, fraud and the invasion of privacy can present disastrous problems. For example, because of an inadequate security and control system, a futures and options trader for a British bank lost almost £1 billion. A simple systems control might have prevented a problem that caused the 200-year-old Bearings Bank to collapse. In addition, from time to time, tax officials have been caught looking at the returns of celebrities and others. Preventing and detecting these problems is an important part of systems design. Prevention includes the following:

- Determining potential problems.
- Ranking the importance of these problems.
- Planning the best place and approach to prevent problems.
- Deciding the best way to handle problems if they occur.

Every effort should be made to prevent problems, but companies must establish procedures to handle problems if they occur, including **system controls**.

systems controls Rules and procedures to maintain data security.

Most IS departments establish tight systems controls to maintain data security. Systems controls can help prevent computer misuse, crime and fraud by managers, employees and others. The accounting scandals in the early 2000s caused many IS departments to develop systems controls to make it more difficult for executives to mislead investors and employees. Some of these scandals involved billions of euros.

Most IS departments have a set of general operating rules that helps protect the system. Some of these are listed below.

- *Input controls:* Maintain input integrity and security. Their purpose is to reduce errors while protecting the computer system against improper or fraudulent input. Input controls range from using standardized input forms to eliminating data-entry errors and using tight password and identification controls.
- *Processing controls:* Deal with all aspects of processing and storage. The use of passwords and identification numbers, backup copies of data and storage rooms that have tight security systems are examples of processing and storage controls.
- *Output controls:* Ensure that output is handled correctly. In many cases, output generated from the computer system is recorded in a file that indicates the reports and documents that were generated, the time they were generated and their final destinations.
- *Database controls:* Deal with ensuring an efficient and effective database system. These controls include the use of identification numbers and passwords, without which a user is denied access to certain data and information. Many of these controls are provided by database management systems.
- *Telecommunications controls:* Provide accurate and reliable data and information transfer among systems. Telecommunications controls include firewalls and encryption to ensure correct communication while eliminating the potential for fraud and crime.
- *Personnel controls:* Make sure that only authorized personnel have access to certain systems to help prevent computer-related mistakes and crime. Personnel controls can involve the use of identification numbers and passwords that allow only certain people access to particular data and information. ID badges and other security devices (such as smart cards) can prevent unauthorized people from entering strategic areas in the information systems facility.

Generating Systems Design Alternatives

The development team will want to generate different designs. One approach is to come up with a basic, cheaper solution; a top-of-the-range solution at the edge of what can be afforded; and a mix solution sitting somewhere between the two. If the new system is complex, it might want to involve personnel from inside and outside the firm in generating alternative designs. If new hardware and software are to be acquired from an outside vendor, a formal request for proposal (RFP) can be made.

12

Request for Proposals

request for proposal (RFP) A
document that specifies in detail
required resources such as
hardware and software.

The **request for proposal (RFP)** is an important document for many organizations involved with large, complex systems development efforts. Smaller, less complex systems often do not require an RFP. A company that is purchasing an inexpensive piece of software that will run on existing hardware, for example, might not need to go through a formal RFP process.

When an RFP is used, it often results in a formal bid that is used to determine who gets a contract for new or modified systems. The RFP specifies in detail the required resources such as hardware and software.[6] Although it can take time and money to develop a high-quality RFP, it can save a company in the long run. Companies that frequently generate RFPs can automate the process. Software such as the RFP Machine from Pragmatech Software can be used to improve the quality of RFPs and reduce the time it takes to produce them. The RFP Machine stores important data needed to generate RFPs and automates the process of producing RFP documents.

In some cases, separate RFPs are developed for different needs. For example, a company might develop separate RFPs for hardware, software and database systems. The RFP also communicates these needs to one or more vendors, and it provides a way to evaluate whether the vendor has delivered what was expected. In some cases, the RFP is part of the vendor contract. The table of contents for a typical RFP is shown in Figure 12.4.

Figure 12.4 A Typical Table of Contents for a Request for Proposal

Johnson & Florin Ltd
Systems investigation report

Contents

Cover page (with company name and contact person)
Brief description of the company
Overview of the existing computer system
Summary of computer-related needs and/or problems
Objectives of the project
Description of what is needed
Hardware requirements
Personnel requirements
Communications requirements
Procedures to be developed
Training requirements
Maintenance requirements
Evaluation procedures (how vendors will be judged)
Proposal format (how vendors should respond)
Important dates (when tasks are to be completed)
Summary

Financial Options

When acquiring computer systems, several choices are available, including purchase, lease or rent. Cost objectives and constraints set for the system play a significant role in the choice, as do the advantages and disadvantages of each. In addition, traditional financial tools, including net present value and internal rate of return, can be used. Table 12.2 summarizes the advantages and disadvantages of these financial options.

Determining which option is best for a particular company in a given situation can be difficult. Financial considerations, tax laws, the organization's policies, its sales and transaction growth, marketplace dynamics, and the organization's financial resources are all important factors. In some cases, lease or rental fees can amount to more than the original purchase price after a few years. As a result, some companies prefer to purchase their equipment.

Table 12.2 Advantages and Disadvantages of Acquisition Options

Renting (Short-Term Option)	
Advantages	**Disadvantages**
No risk of obsolescence	No ownership of equipment
No long-term financial investment	High monthly costs
No initial investment of funds	Restrictive rental agreements
Maintenance usually included	

Leasing (Longer-Term Option)	
Advantages	**Disadvantages**
No risk of obsolescence	High cost of cancelling lease
No long-term financial investment	Longer time commitment than renting
No initial investment of funds	No ownership of equipment
Less expensive than renting	

Purchasing	
Advantages	**Disadvantages**
Total control over equipment	High initial investment
Can sell equipment at any time	Additional cost of maintenance
Can depreciate equipment	Possibility of obsolescence
Low cost if owned for a number of years	Other expenses, including taxes and insurance

On the other hand, constant advances in technology can make purchasing risky. A company would not want to purchase a new multimillion-dollar computer only to have newer and more powerful computers available a few months later at a lower price, unless the computer can be easily and inexpensively upgraded. Some servers, for example, are designed to be scalable to allow processors to be added or swapped, memory to be upgraded, and peripheral devices to be installed. Companies often employ several people to determine the best option based on all the factors. This staff can also help negotiate purchase, lease or rental contracts.

Evaluating and Selecting a Systems Design

The final step in systems design is to evaluate the various alternatives and select the one that will offer the best solution for organizational goals. Depending on their weight, any one of these objectives might result in the selection of one design over another. For example, financial concerns might make a company choose rental over equipment purchase. Specific performance objectives – for example, that the new system must perform online data processing – might result in a complex network design for which control procedures must be established. Evaluating and selecting the best design involves achieving a balance of system objectives that will best support organizational goals. Normally, evaluation and selection involves both a preliminary and a final evaluation before a design is selected.

The Preliminary Evaluation

preliminary evaluation An initial assessment whose purpose is to dismiss the unwanted proposals; begins after all proposals have been submitted.

A **preliminary evaluation** begins after all design proposals have been submitted. The purpose of this evaluation is to dismiss unwanted proposals. If external vendors have submitted proposals, some of them can usually be eliminated by investigating their proposals and comparing them with the original criteria. Those that compare favourably are often asked to make a formal presentation to the analysis team. The vendors should also be asked to supply a list of companies that use their equipment for a similar purpose. The organization then contacts these references and asks them to evaluate their hardware, their software and the vendor.

The Final Evaluation

final evaluation A detailed investigation of the proposals offered by the vendors remaining after the preliminary evaluation.

The **final evaluation** begins with a detailed investigation of the proposals offered by the remaining vendors. The vendors should be asked to make a final presentation and to fully demonstrate the system. The demonstration should be as close to actual operating conditions as possible. Applications such as payroll, inventory control and billing should be conducted using a large amount of test data.

After the final presentations and demonstrations have been given, the organization makes the final evaluation and selection. Cost comparisons, hardware performance, delivery dates, price, flexibility, back-up facilities, availability of software training and maintenance factors are considered. In addition to comparing computer speeds, storage capacities and other similar characteristics, companies should also carefully analyze whether the characteristics of the proposed systems meet the company's objectives. In most cases, the RFP captures these objectives and goals.

Group Consensus Evaluation

group consensus Decision making by a group that is appointed and given the responsibility of making the final evaluation and selection.

In **group consensus**, a decision-making group is appointed and given the responsibility of making the final evaluation and selection. Usually, this group includes the members of the development team who participated in either systems analysis or systems design. This approach might be used to evaluate which of several screen layouts or report formats is best.

Cost–Benefit Analysis Evaluation

cost–benefit analysis An approach that lists the costs and benefits of each proposed system. After they are expressed in monetary terms, all the costs are compared with all the benefits.

Cost–benefit analysis is an approach that lists the costs and benefits of each proposed system. After they are expressed in monetary terms, all the costs are compared with all the benefits. Table 12.3 lists some of the typical costs and benefits associated with the evaluation and selection procedure. This approach is used to evaluate options whose costs can be quantified, such as which hardware or software vendor to select.

Benchmark Test Evaluation

benchmark test An examination that compares computer systems operating under the same conditions.

A **benchmark test** is an examination that compares computer systems operating under the same conditions. Most computer companies publish their own benchmark tests, but some forbid disclosure of benchmark tests without prior written approval. Thus, one of the best approaches is for an organization to develop its own tests, and then use them to compare the equipment it is considering. This approach might be used to compare the end-user system response time on two similar systems. Several independent companies also rate computer systems. *Computerworld*, *PC Week* and many other publications, for example, not only summarize various systems, but also evaluate and compare computer systems and manufacturers according to a number of criteria.

Table 12.3 Cost–Benefit Analysis Table

Costs	Benefits
Development costs	Reduced costs
Personnel	Fewer personnel
Computer resources	Reduced manufacturing costs
	Reduced inventory costs
	More efficient use of equipment
	Faster response time
	Reduced downtime or crash time
	Less spoilage

Fixed costs	Increased Revenues
Computer equipment	New products and services
Software	New customers
One-time licence fees for software and maintenance	More business from existing customers
	Higher price as a result of better products and services

Operating costs	Intangible benefits
Equipment lease and/or rental fees	Better public image for the organization
Computer personnel (including salaries, benefits, etc.)	Higher employee morale
	Better service for new and existing customers
Electric and other utilities	The ability to recruit better employees
Computer paper, tape and discs	Position as a leader in the industry
Other computer supplies	System easier for programmers and users
Maintenance costs	
Insurance	

Point Evaluation

One of the disadvantages of cost–benefit analysis is the difficulty of determining the monetary values for all the benefits. An approach that does not employ monetary values is a **point evaluation system**. Each evaluation factor is assigned a weight, in percentage points, based on importance. Then each proposed information system is evaluated in terms of this factor and given a score, such as one ranging from 0 to 100, where 0 means that the alternative does not address the feature at all and 100 means that the alternative addresses that feature perfectly. The scores are totalled, and the system with the greatest total score is selected. When using point evaluation, an organization can list and evaluate literally hundreds of factors. Figure 12.5 shows a simplified version of this process. This approach is used when there are many options to be evaluated, such as which software best matches a particular business's needs.

point evaluation system An evaluation process in which each evaluation factor is assigned a weight, in percentage points, based on importance. Then each proposed system is evaluated in terms of this factor and given a score ranging from 0 to 100. The scores are totalled and the system with the greatest total score is selected.

12

Figure 12.5 An
Illustration of the Point
Evaluation System *In*
this example, software has
been given the most weight
(40 per cent), compared
with hardware (35 per cent)
and vendor support (25
per cent). When system A
is evaluated, the total of the
three factors amounts to
82.5 per cent. System B's
rating, on the other hand,
totals 86.75 per cent, which
is closer to 100 per cent.
Therefore, the firm chooses
system B.

		System A		System B			
Factor's importance		Evaluation		Weighted evaluation	Evaluation		Weighted evaluation
Hardware	35%	95	35%	33.25	75	35%	26.25
Software	40%	70	40%	28.00	95	40%	38.00
Vendor support	25%	85	25%	21.25	90	25%	22.50
Totals	100%			82.5			86.75

Freezing Design Specifications

Near the end of the design stage, some organizations prohibit further changes in the design of the system. Freezing systems design specifications means that the user agrees in writing that the design is acceptable. Other organizations, however, allow or even encourage design changes. These organizations often use the rapid systems development approaches, introduced in Chapter 11.

The Contract

One of the most important steps in systems design, if new computer facilities are being acquired, is to develop a good contract. Finding the best terms where everyone makes a profit can be difficult. Most computer vendors provide standard contracts; however, such contracts are designed to protect the vendor, not necessarily the organization buying the computer equipment.

Organizations often use outside consultants and legal firms to help them develop their contracts. Such contracts stipulate exactly what they expect from the system vendor and what interaction will occur between the vendor and the organization. All equipment specifications, software, training, installation, maintenance and so on are clearly stated. Also, the contract stipulates deadlines for the various stages or milestones of installation and implementation, as well as actions that the vendor will take in case of delays or problems. Some organizations include penalty clauses in the contract, in case the vendor does not meet its obligation by the specified date. Typically, the request for proposal becomes part of the contract. This saves a considerable amount of time in developing the contract, because the RFP specifies in detail what is expected from the vendors.

The Design Report

System specifications are the final results of systems design. They include a technical description that details system outputs, inputs and user interfaces, as well as all hardware, software, databases, telecommunications, personnel and procedure components, and the way these components are related. The specifications are contained in a **design report**, which is the primary result of systems design. The design report reflects the decisions made for systems design and prepares the way for systems implementation.

design report The primary result of systems design, reflecting the decisions made and preparing the way for systems implementation.

Information Systems @ Work

Has D-Wave Harnessed the Power of the Qubit to Revolutionize Computing?

Founded in 1999, D-Wave Systems plans to integrate new discoveries in physics, engineering and computer science to create new approaches to computation that will help solve some of the world's most complex challenges. Their D-Wave Two computer costs around €11 million, is the size of a shed, operates at temperatures lower than those found in deep space and is being used by NASA, Google and Lockheed Martin. The company claims that D-Wave Two is a working quantum computer.

The physics of small particles like a photon or electron seem strange to us. Particles can exist in more than one state at the same time, and can form partnerships with each other in a way that even if the two of them are separated by several miles, one still knows what state the other is in. If these particles could be reliably manipulated they could quickly perform computing tasks that would take normal computers many thousands of years, because they would be able to perform multiple calculations simultaneously. Some physicists believe that these calculations would actually be performed in other universes, although this is just one possible interpretation of how it might work. D-Wave's computers have been discussed at length in top scientific journals and it should be said that not everyone is convinced they have yet produced a real quantum computer.

Based in Burnaby on Canada's west coast, D-Wave has raised upwards of €100 million in venture capital from the likes of Amazon founder Jeff Bezos and In-Q-Tel, the venture capital arm of the Central Intelligence Agency. 'The original vision of the company was simple: build a commercially useful quantum computer as soon as possible,' says Vern Brownell, D-Wave's chief executive. 'We just want to provide quantum computing resources to researchers and businesses around the world so they can solve really hard problems, better than they can today.'

Scott Aaronson, professor of electrical engineering and computer science at the Massachusetts Institute of Technology is almost convinced. Another professor, Andrew Steane from the department of physics at Oxford University, says: 'If you go back five or ten years, the initial statements coming out of D-Wave, before they had a device to look at, were seen as something you could ignore, because it just didn't seem credible.

Then they produced this device, so they came up with the goods. And it's a non-negligible device – it has serious computing power. It's just a question of whether what it's achieving is beyond what could have been done with a system based on classical physics.'

Catherine McGeoch, a professor of computer science at Amherst College, has reported that in one test the D-Wave computer performed 3600 times faster than a conventional computer when solving an optimization problem.

D-Wave are not the only people trying to develop a quantum computer. Documents leaked by the whistle-blower Edward Snowden reveal that the US National Security Agency (NSA) has been conducting 'basic research' to determine whether it is possible to build a quantum computer that would be useful for cracking encrypted communications. This is because quantum computers should excel at factoring large numbers which could be used to break commonly used encryption methods, which derive their security from the fact that ordinary computers can't find factors quickly. So in principle, the NSA could use a quantum computer to read secret data. Another possible application is super-fast searches to sift through vast amounts of data. The Snowden documents state however that they are nowhere near reaching this goal.

Meanwhile D-Wave continues to improve its technology. Just as early digital systems were matched or outperformed in many respects by well-developed analogue computers, it is possible that D-Wave's first quantum computing efforts can be matched or exceeded by well-tuned classical systems. But then the company is only just getting started.

Questions

1 Do you think the traditional systems lifecycle applies to the development of D-Wave computer hardware or software?

2 Should we be fearful of organizations getting their hands on quantum computers?

3 Do you think there will be any applications for quantum computers in your day-to-day life?

4 If the D-Wave 2 computer is shown to not be a working quantum computer, does that mean the company has wasted its time and money?

12.2 Systems Implementation

systems implementation A stage
of systems development that
includes hardware acquisition,
software acquisition or
development, user preparation,
hiring and training of personnel,
site and data preparation,
installation, testing, start-up and
user acceptance.

After the information system has been designed, **systems implementation** involves a number of tasks which lead to the system being installed and ready to operate.[7] These include hardware acquisition, software acquisition or development (programming), user preparation, documentation preparation, hiring and training of personnel, site and data preparation, installation, testing, start-up and user acceptance. Spending on systems implementation is on the rise.[8]

The typical sequence of systems implementation activities is shown in Figure 12.6.

Figure 12.6 Typical
Steps in Systems
Implementation

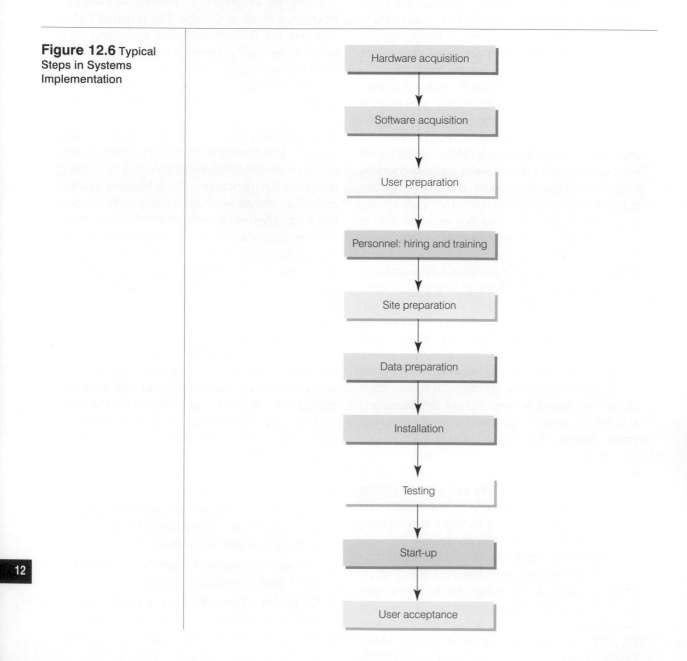

Acquiring Hardware from an IS Vendor

To obtain the components for an information system, organizations can purchase, lease or rent computer hardware and other resources from an IS vendor.[9] An IS vendor is a company that offers hardware, software, telecommunications systems, databases, IS personnel or other computer-related resources. Types of IS vendors include general computer manufacturers (such as IBM and Hewlett-Packard), small computer manufacturers (such as Dell and Gateway), peripheral equipment manufacturers (such as Epson and Cannon), computer dealers and distributors (such as PC World) and leasing companies (such as Hamilton Rentals and Hire Intelligence).

In addition to buying, leasing or renting computer hardware, companies can pay only for the computing services that they use. Called 'pay-as-you-go', 'on-demand' or 'utility' computing, this approach requires an organization to pay only for the computer power it uses, as it would pay for a utility such as electricity. Hewlett-Packard offers its clients a 'capacity-on-demand' approach, in which organizations pay according to the computer resources actually used, including processors, storage devices and network facilities.

Companies can also purchase used computer equipment. This option is especially attractive to firms that are experiencing an economic slowdown. Companies often use traditional Internet auctions to locate used or refurbished equipment. Popular Internet auction sites sometimes sell more than millions of euros of computer-related equipment annually. However, buyers need to beware: prices are not always low, and equipment selection can be limited on Internet auction sites.

In addition, companies are increasingly turning to service providers to implement some or all of the systems they need. As discussed in Chapter 4, an application service provider (ASP) can help companies implement software and other systems. The ASP can provide both user support and the computers on which to run the software. ASPs often focus on high-end applications, such as database systems and enterprise resource planning packages. As mentioned in Chapter 6, an Internet service provider (ISP) assists a company in gaining access to the Internet. ISPs can also help a company in setting up an Internet site. Some service providers specialize in specific systems or areas, such as marketing, finance or manufacturing.

Acquiring Software: Make or Buy?

As with hardware, application software can be acquired in several ways. As previously mentioned, it can be purchased from external developers or developed in-house.[10] This decision is often called the **make-or-buy decision**. A comparison of the two approaches is shown in Table 12.4. Today, most

make-or-buy decision The decision regarding whether to obtain the necessary software from internal or external sources.

Table 12.4 Comparison of Off the Shelf and Developed Software

Factor	Off the Shelf (Buy)	Bespoke (Make)
Cost	Lower cost	Higher cost
Needs	Might not exactly match needs	Software should exactly match needs
Quality	Usually high quality	Quality can vary depending on the programming team
Speed	Can acquire it now	Can take years to develop
Competitive advantage	Other organizations can have the same software and same advantage	Can develop a competitive advantage with good software

12

software is purchased 'off the shelf'. SAP, the large international software company headquartered in Germany, produces modular software which it sells to a variety of companies. The approach gives its customers using the software more flexibility in what they use and what they pay for SAP's modules.[11] The key is how the purchased systems are integrated into an effective system.

Off the shelf software should be of higher quality than developed, or 'bespoke', software, as it will have been tested 'in the field' by other users. Often those users form an online community, which can be of help to new users. New users often go to online discussion groups to ask questions about the software, rather than calling the developer's own hotline. The audio software Cakewalk, for example, used by amateur and professional musicians, has a thriving forum where beginers and experienced users can post questions, and answer other peoples' questions. Off the shelf software will likely be better documented than bespoke software.

In some cases, companies use a blend of external and internal software development. That is, in-house personnel modify or customize off the shelf or proprietary software programs. Software can also be rented. Salesforce.com, for example, rents software online that helps organizations manage their sales force and internal staff. Increasingly, software is being viewed as a utility or service, not a product you purchase.

System software, such as operating systems or utilities, is typically purchased from a software company. Increasingly, however, companies are obtaining open-source systems software, such as the Linux operating system, which can be obtained free or for a low cost.

Externally Acquired Software

A company planning to purchase or lease software from an outside company has many options. Commercial off the shelf development is often used. The commercial off the shelf (COTS) development process involves the use of commonly available products from software vendors. It combines software from various vendors into a finished system. In many cases, it is necessary to write some original software from scratch and combine it with purchased or leased software. For example, a company can purchase or lease software from several software vendors and combine it into a finished software program. COTS can be less expensive than developing an application from scratch. It can streamline and shorten the time needed to develop software. The other steps of the systems development lifecycle, such as requirements analysis, testing and implementation, must still be carefully done. A major challenge with COTS development is integrating all the off the shelf components into a unified software package. Other potential problems of the COTS development approach can include no access to the source code, the inability to make changes or updates, and the possibility of quality and security problems concerning the COTS software or components.

Developing Software

Another option is to develop software internally or hire a software house to develop it. Some advantages inherent with developing software include meeting user and organizational requirements and having more features and increased flexibility in terms of customization and changes. Such software programs also have greater potential for providing a competitive advantage because competitors cannot easily duplicate them in the short term.

chief programmer team A group of skilled IS professionals who design and implement a set of programs.

cross-platform development A development technique that allows programmers to develop programs that can run on computer systems having different hardware and operating systems or platforms.

If software is to be developed, there should be a **chief programmer team**. The chief programmer team is a group of skilled IS professionals with the task of designing and implementing a set of programs. This team has total responsibility for building the best software possible. Individuals on a chief programmer team often have excellent programming skills.

The following tools and techniques may also be used:

- *CASE and object-oriented approaches* (mentioned in Chapter 11).
- *Cross-platform development:* One software development technique, called **cross-platform development**, allows programmers to develop programs that can run on computer systems that have different

hardware and operating systems or platforms. Web service tools, such as .NET by Microsoft, are examples. With cross-platform development, for example, the same program can run on both a PC and a mainframe or on two different types of PCs.

- *Integrated development environment:* **Integrated development environments (IDEs)** combine the tools needed for programming with a programming language in one integrated package. An IDE allows programmers to use simple screens, customized pull-down menus and graphical user interfaces. Visual Studio 2005 from Microsoft is an example of an IDE. Oracle Designer, which is used with Oracle's database system, is another example of an IDE.

- *Structured walkthroughs:* As shown in Figure 12.7, a **structured walkthrough** is a planned and pre-announced review of the progress of a program or program module. The walkthrough helps team members review and evaluate the progress of components of a project. The structured walkthrough approach is also useful for programming projects that do not use the structured design approach.

integrated development environments (IDEs) A development approach that combines the tools needed for programming with a programming language into one integrated package.

structured walkthrough A planned and pre-announced review of the progress of a program module.

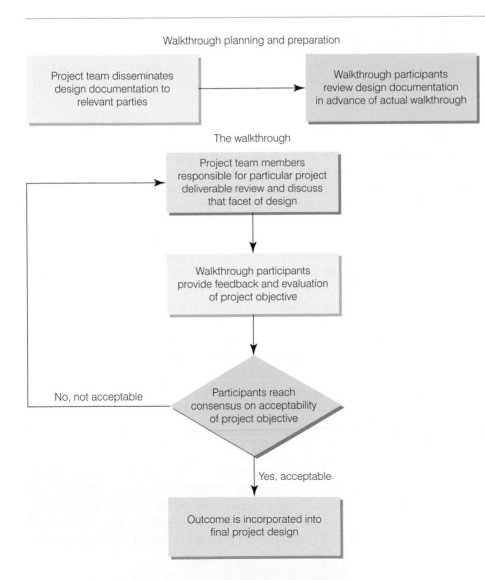

Figure 12.7 Structured Walkthrough *A structured walkthrough is a planned, pre-announced review of the progress of a particular project objective.*

technical documentation
Written details used by computer operators to execute the program and by analysts and programmers to solve problems or modify the program.

■ *Documentation:* With developed software, documentation is always important. **Technical documentation** is used by computer operators to execute the program and by analysts and programmers to solve problems or modify the program. In technical documentation, the purpose of every major piece of computer code is written out and explained. Key variables are also described. User documentation might be developed for the people who use the program. This type of documentation shows users, in easy-to-understand terms, how the program can and should be used, although an alternative such as a demonstration video may be created instead.

Acquiring Database and Telecommunications Systems

Because databases are a blend of hardware and software, many of the approaches discussed earlier for acquiring hardware and software also apply to database systems. For example, an upgraded inventory control system might require database capabilities, including more hard disc storage or a new DBMS. If so, additional storage hardware will have to be acquired from an IS vendor. New or upgraded software might also be purchased or developed in-house. With the increased use of e-commerce, the Internet, intranets and extranets, telecommunications is one of the fastest-growing applications for today's businesses and people. Over 200 e-commerce websites have implemented a new payment system.[12] Like database systems, telecommunications systems require a blend of hardware and software. Again, the earlier discussion on acquiring hardware and software also applies to the acquisition of telecommunications hardware and software.

User Preparation

user preparation The process of readying managers, decision makers, employees, other users and stakeholders for new systems.

User preparation is the process of readying managers, decision makers, employees, other users and stakeholders for the new systems. This activity is an important but often ignored area of systems implementation. For example, if a small airline does not adequately train employees with a new software package, the result could be a grounding of most of its flights and the need to find hotel rooms to accommodate unhappy travellers who are stranded.

Without question, training users is an essential part of user preparation, whether they are trained by internal personnel or by external training firms. In some cases, companies that provide software also train users at no charge or at a reasonable price. The cost of training can be negotiated during the selection of new software. Other companies conduct user training throughout the systems development process. Concerns and apprehensions about the new system must be eliminated through these training programs. Employees should be acquainted with the system's capabilities and limitations by the time they are ready to use it.

IS Personnel: Hiring and Training

Depending on the size of the new system, an organization might have to hire and, in some cases, train new IS personnel. An IS manager, systems analysts, computer programmers, data-entry operators and similar personnel might be needed for the new system.

As with users, the eventual success of any system depends on how it is used by the IS personnel within the organization. Training programs should be conducted for the IS personnel who will be looking after the new computer system. These programs are similar to those for the users, although they can be more detailed in the technical aspects of the systems. Effective training will help IS personnel use the new system to perform their jobs and support other users in the organization.

Site Preparation

The location of the new system needs to be prepared, a process called **site preparation**. For a small system, site preparation can be as simple as rearranging the furniture in an office to make room for a computer. With a larger system, this process is not so easy because it can require special wiring and air conditioning. One or two rooms might have to be completely renovated, and additional furniture might have to be purchased. A special floor might have to be built, under which the cables connecting the various computer components are placed, and a new security system might be needed to protect the equipment. For larger systems, additional power circuits might also be required.

site preparation Preparation of the location of a new system.

Data Preparation

Data preparation, or data conversion, involves making sure that all files and databases are ready to be used with the new computer software and systems. If an organization is installing a new payroll program, for instance, the old employee-payroll data might have to be converted into a format that can be used by the new computer software or system. After the data has been prepared or converted, the computerized database system or other software will then be used to maintain and update the computer files.

data preparation (data conversion) Ensuring all files and databases are ready to be used with new computer software and systems.

Installation

Installation is the process of physically placing the computer equipment on the site and making it operational. Although normally the hardware manufacturer is responsible for installing computer equipment, someone from the organization (usually the IS manager) should oversee the process, making sure that all equipment specified in the contract is installed at the proper location. After the system is installed, the manufacturer performs several tests to ensure that the equipment is operating as it should. After this, the acquired software can be installed on the new hardware and the system is again tested.

installation The process of physically placing the computer equipment on the site and making it operational.

Testing

Good testing procedures are essential to make sure that the new or modified information system operates as intended. Inadequate testing can result in mistakes and problems. A popular tax preparation company in the US, for example, implemented a web-based tax preparation system, but people could see one another's tax returns. The president of the tax preparation company called it 'our worst-case scenario'. Better testing can prevent these types of problems.

Several forms of testing should be used, including testing each program (**unit testing**), testing the entire system of programs (**system testing**), testing the application with a large amount of data (**volume testing**) and testing all related systems together (**integration testing**), as well as conducting any tests required by the user (**acceptance testing**).

Alpha testing involves testing an incomplete or early version of the system, while **beta testing** involves testing a complete and stable system by end-users. Alpha-unit testing, for example, is testing an individual program before it is completely finished. Beta-unit testing, on the other hand, is performed after alpha testing, when the individual program is complete and ready for use by end-users.

unit testing Testing of individual programs.

system testing Testing the entire system of programs.

volume testing Testing the application with a large amount of data.

integration testing Testing all related systems together.

acceptance testing Conducting any tests required by the user.

alpha testing Testing an incomplete or early version of the system.

beta testing Testing a complete and stable system by end-users.

12

Unit testing is accomplished by developing test data that will force the computer to execute every statement in the program. In addition, each program is tested with abnormal data to determine how it will handle problems.

System testing requires the testing of all the programs together. It is not uncommon for the output from one program to become the input for another. So, system testing ensures that the output from one program can be used as input for another program within the system. Volume testing ensures that the entire system can handle a large amount of data under normal operating conditions. Integration testing ensures that the new programs can interact with other major applications. It also ensures that data flows efficiently and without error to other applications. For example, a new inventory control application might require data input from an older order processing application. Integration testing would be done to ensure smooth data flow between the new and existing applications. Integration testing is typically done after unit and system testing. Metaserver, a software company for the insurance industry, has developed a tool called iConnect to perform integration testing for different insurance applications and databases.

Ethical and Societal Issues

Logistics Draws Inspiration from the Internet

One of the most important innovations in logistics over the last 100 years has been the standardized shipping container. Before that, men walked goods onto ships over gangplanks or hoisted nets into holds. The container changed all that. Now vehicles called straddle carriers that look like they belong in Star Wars, pick and carry containers to lifting points where they are stacked onto ships. Straddle carriers have the ability to stack up to four containers, and drivers are positioned sideways on, making them very difficult to drive. The standard container was adopted by the logistics industry in the 1980s. They are however confined to the sea – the dimensions are incompatible with road trucks. If that could be changed it would save loading and unloading time at ports.

Moving goods from here to there is a €60 billion a year industry, but things have changed little since the standard container was introduced. Lacking innovation, the logistics industry regularly ships containers that are not full and uses roads when they are congested, needlessly wasting energy and contributing to climate change. A group of researchers want to change this. They are developing something they refer to as the Physical Internet.

The Internet relies on a concept called Packet Switching. When data are sent over the Internet, they are spilt up into chunks called packets. These packets are given a header which essentially stores information on where they are going to and how they fit together with the other packets once they get there. Packets are then sent to their destination separately, and perhaps each will use a different route through the Internet, if a network error occurs along the way or if there is data congestion at one point. Once they all arrive, the packets are assembled by the receiving computer using the information in their headers. Packet switching means that there doesn't have to be a physical wire connecting two computers that are communicating. (This is in contrast to line or circuit switching where there was a physical connection – you may have seen this in old movies where a telephone operator plugs a wire into a switchboard, connecting two callers.)

The Physical Internet would use the standard containers and introduce common protocols and shared transport assets. Logistics professionals would have to collaborate but if they did then manufacturers, shippers, regulators and customers would be able to communicate seamlessly with each other. 'One reason there are so many trucks on the road is the inefficient way in which they are deployed,' says science journalist Jeffery Mervis. 'One 2004 British study, for instance, studied a 24-hour cycle for 1000 food delivery trucks and found that they were actually transporting goods only 10% of the time.' The rest of the time they were parked up somewhere, carrying empty loads or being loaded/uploaded. This means that logistics can account for 15 per cent of a product's cost. In fact sometimes it makes more economic sense to destroy containers rather than send them home empty, especially when home is on the other side of the world.

There is however big resistance to the idea of the Physical Internet. Many logistics companies are reluctant to share information about their routes, networks, markets or customers. Some see their supply chain as an integral part of their strategy. A recent simulation showed that the Physical Internet could achieve increased profits, lower prices,

reduced pollution and, since individual journeys were shorter, drivers were happier (as they could go home at night), which led to less staff turnover. This proof-of-concept could help convince companies of its advantages.

Questions

1 Why are standards so important?

2 How could the Physical Internet be organized? How would logistics companies have to change?

3 How could the logistics industry be persuaded to adopt the Physical Internet?

4 What information would be needed to make the Physical Internet work?

Finally, acceptance testing makes sure that the new or modified system is operating as intended. Run times, the amount of memory required, disc access methods and more can be tested during this phase. Acceptance testing ensures that all performance objectives defined for the system or application are satisfied. Involving users in acceptance testing can help them understand and effectively interact with the new system. Acceptance testing is the final check of the system before start-up.

Start-Up

Start-up, also called cutover, begins with the final tested information system. When start-up is finished, the system is fully operational. Start-up can be critical to the success of the organization. If not done properly, the results can be disastrous. One of the authors is aware of a small manufacturing company that decided to stop an accounting service used to send out bills on the same day they were going to start their own program to send out bills to customers. The manufacturing company wanted to save money by using their own billing program developed by an employee of the company. The new program didn't work, the accounting service wouldn't help because they were upset about being terminated, and the manufacturing company wasn't able to send out any bills to customers for more than three months. The company almost went bankrupt.

> **start-up** The process of making the final tested information system fully operational.

Various start-up approaches are available (see Figure 12.8). **Direct conversion** (also called plunge, big bang or direct cutover) involves stopping the old system and starting the new system on a given date. Direct conversion is usually the least desirable approach because of the potential for problems and errors when the old system is shut off and the new system is turned on at the same instant.

> **direct conversion** Stopping the old system and starting the new system on a given date.

The **phase-in approach** is a popular technique preferred by many organizations. In this approach, sometimes called a piecemeal approach, components of the new system are slowly phased in while components of the old one are slowly phased out. When everyone is confident that the new system is performing as expected, the old system is completely phased out. This gradual replacement is repeated for each application until the new system is running every application. In some cases, the phase-in approach can take months or years.

> **phase-in approach** Slowly replacing components of the old system with those of the new one. This process is repeated for each application until the new system is running every application and performing as expected; also called a piecemeal approach.

12

Figure 12.8 Start-Up Approaches

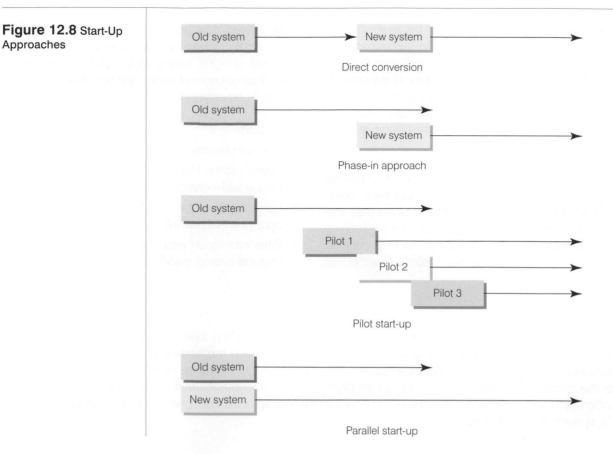

Old system → New system
Direct conversion

Old system
New system
Phase-in approach

Old system
Pilot 1
Pilot 2
Pilot 3
Pilot start-up

Old system
New system
Parallel start-up

pilot running Introducing the new system by direct conversion for one group of users rather than all users.

Pilot running involves introducing the new system with direct conversion for one group of users rather than all users. For example, a manufacturing company with many retail outlets throughout the country could use the pilot start-up approach and install a new inventory control system at one of the retail outlets. When this pilot retail outlet runs without problems, the new inventory control system can be implemented at other retail outlets. The National Health Service Cancer Registry in England, for example, used a pilot start-up approach to implement and test a new system to manage and integrate hundreds of cancer-related data sources.[13]

parallel running Running both the old and the new systems for a period of time.

Parallel running involves running both the old and new systems for a period of time. The output of the new system is compared closely with the output of the old system, and any differences are reconciled. When users are comfortable that the new system is working correctly, the old system is eliminated.

User Acceptance

user acceptance document A formal agreement signed by the user that states that a phase of the installation or the complete system is approved.

Most mainframe computer manufacturers use a formal **user acceptance document** – a formal agreement the user signs stating that a phase of the installation or the complete system is approved. This is a legal document that usually removes or reduces the IS vendor's liability for problems that occur after the user acceptance document has been signed. Because this document is so important, many companies get legal assistance before they sign it. Stakeholders can also be involved in acceptance testing to make sure that the benefits to them are indeed realized.

12.3 Systems Operation and Maintenance

Systems operation involves all aspects of using the new or modified system in all kinds of operating conditions. Getting the most out of a new or modified system during its operation is the most important aspect of systems operations for many organizations. Throughout this book, we have seen many examples of information systems operating in a variety of settings and industries. Thus, we will not cover the operation of an information system in detail in this section. The operation of any information system, however, does require adequate training and support before the system is used and continual support while the system is being operated. This training and support is required for all stakeholders, including employees, customers and others. Companies typically provide training through seminars, manuals and online documentation. To provide adequate support, many companies use a formal help desk. A help desk consists of people with technical expertise, computer systems, manuals and other resources needed to solve problems and give accurate answers to questions. With today's advances in telecommunications, help desks can be located around the world. If you are having trouble with your PC and call a freephone number for assistance, you might reach a help desk in India or China. For most organizations, operations costs over the life of a system are much greater than the development costs.

> **systems operation** Use of a new or modified system.

Systems maintenance involves checking, changing and enhancing the system to make it more useful in achieving user and organizational goals.[14] Maintenance is important for individuals, groups and organizations.[15] Organizations often have personnel dedicated to maintenance.

> **systems maintenance and review** The systems development phase that ensures the system operates as intended and modifies the system so that it continues to meet changing business needs.

The maintenance process can be especially difficult for older software. A legacy system is an old system that might have been patched or modified repeatedly over time. An old payroll program written in COBOL decades ago and frequently changed is an example of a legacy system. Legacy systems can be very expensive to maintain. At some point, it becomes less expensive to switch to new programs and applications than to repair and maintain the legacy system. Maintenance costs for older legacy systems can be 50 per cent of the total operating costs in some cases.

Software maintenance is a major concern for organizations. In some cases, organizations encounter major problems that require recycling the entire systems development process. In other situations, minor modifications are sufficient to remedy problems. Hardware maintenance is also important. Companies such as IBM are investigating autonomic computing, in which computers will be able to manage and maintain themselves.[16] The goal is for computers to be self-configuring, self-protecting, self-healing and self-optimizing. Being self-configuring allows a computer to handle new hardware, software or other changes to its operating environment. Being self-protecting means a computer can identify potential attacks, prevent them when possible and recover from attacks if they occur. Attacks can include viruses, worms, identity theft and industrial espionage. Being 'self-healing' means a computer can fix problems when they occur, and being 'self-optimizing' allows a computer to run faster and get more done in less time. Getting rid of old equipment is an important part of maintenance. The options include selling it on web auction sites such as eBay, recycling the equipment at a computer recycling centre, and donating it to a charitable organization, such as a school, library or religious organization. When discarding old computer systems, it is always a good idea to permanently remove sensitive files and programs. Companies, including McAfee, have software to help people remove data and programs from old computers and transfer them to new ones.[17]

Reasons for Maintenance

After a program is written, it will need ongoing maintenance. To some extent, a program is similar to a car that needs oil changes, tune-ups and repairs at certain times. Experience shows that frequent, minor maintenance to a program, if properly done, can prevent major system failures later. Some of the reasons for program maintenance are the following:

- Changes in business processes.
- New requests from stakeholders, users and managers.
- Bugs or errors in the program.
- Technical and hardware problems.
- Corporate mergers and acquisitions.
- Government regulations.
- Change in the operating system or hardware on which the application runs.
- Unexpected events, such as severe weather or terrorist attacks.

Most companies modify their existing programs instead of developing new ones because existing software performs many important functions, and companies can have millions of dollars invested in their old legacy systems. So, as new systems needs are identified, the burden of fulfilling the needs most often falls on the existing system. Old programs are repeatedly modified to meet ever-changing needs. Yet, over time, repeated modifications tend to interfere with the system's overall structure, reducing its efficiency and making further modifications more burdensome.

Types of Maintenance

slipstream upgrade A minor upgrade – typically a code adjustment or minor bug fix – not worth announcing. It usually requires recompiling all the code and, in so doing, it can create entirely new bugs.

patch A minor change to correct a problem or make a small enhancement. It is usually an addition to an existing program.

release A significant program change that often requires changes in the documentation of the software.

version A major program change, typically encompassing many new features.

Software companies and many other organizations use four generally accepted categories to signify the amount of change involved in maintenance. A **slipstream upgrade** is a minor upgrade – typically a code adjustment or minor bug fix. Many companies don't announce to users that a slipstream upgrade has been made. A slipstream upgrade usually requires recompiling all the code, so it can create entirely new bugs. This maintenance practice can explain why the same computers sometimes work differently with what is supposedly the same software. A **patch** is a minor change to correct a problem or make a small enhancement. It is usually an addition to an existing program. That is, the programming code representing the system enhancement is usually 'patched into', or added to, the existing code. Although slipstream upgrades and patches are minor changes, they can cause users and support personnel big problems if the programs do not run as before. A new **release** is a significant program change that often requires changes in the documentation of the software. Finally, a new **version** is a major program change, typically encompassing many new features.

The Request for Maintenance Form

request for maintenance form A form authorizing modification of programs.

Because of the amount of effort that can be spent on maintenance, many organizations require a **request for maintenance form** to authorize modification of programs. This form is usually signed by a business manager, who documents the need for the change and identifies the priority of the change relative to other work that has been requested. The IS group reviews the form and identifies the programs to be changed, determines the programmer who will be assigned to the project, estimates the expected completion date and develops a technical description of the change. A cost–benefit analysis might be required if the change requires substantial resources.

12

Performing Maintenance

Depending on organizational policies, the people who perform systems maintenance vary. In some cases, the team who designs and builds the system also performs maintenance. This ongoing responsibility gives the designers and programmers an incentive to build systems well from the outset: if there are problems, they will have to fix them. In other cases, organizations have a separate **maintenance team**. This team is responsible for modifying, fixing and updating existing software.

maintenance team A special IS team responsible for modifying, fixing and updating existing software.

In the past, companies had to maintain each computer system or server separately. With hundreds or thousands of computers scattered throughout an organization, this task could be very costly and time consuming. Today, the maintenance function is becoming more automated. Some companies, for example, use maintenance tools and software that will allow them to maintain and upgrade software centrally.

A number of vendors have developed tools to ease the software maintenance burden. Relativity Technologies has developed RescueWare, a product that converts third-generation code such as COBOL to highly maintainable C++, Java or Visual Basic object-oriented code. Using RescueWare, maintenance personnel download mainframe code to Windows NT or Windows 2000 workstations. They then use the product's graphical tools to analyze the original system's inner workings. RescueWare lets a programmer see the original system as a set of object views, which visually illustrate module functioning and program structures. IS personnel can choose one of three levels of transformation: revamping the user interface, converting the database access and transforming procedure logic.

The Financial Implications of Maintenance

The cost of maintenance is staggering. For older programs, the total cost of maintenance can be up to five times greater than the total cost of development. In other words, a program that originally cost €25 000 to develop might cost €125 000 to maintain over its lifetime. The average programmers can spend more than half their time on maintaining existing programs instead of developing new ones. In addition, as programs get older, total maintenance expenditures in time and money increase. With the use of newer programming languages and approaches, including object-oriented programming, maintenance costs are expected to decline. Even so, many organizations have literally millions of dollars invested in applications written in older languages (such as COBOL), which are both expensive and time consuming to maintain. The financial implications of maintenance mean companies must keep track of why systems are maintained, instead of simply keeping cost figures. This is another reason that documentation of maintenance tasks is so crucial. A determining factor in the decision to replace a system is the point at which it is costing more to fix it than to replace it.

The Relationship Between Maintenance and Design

Programs are expensive to develop, but they are even more expensive to maintain. Programs that are well designed and documented to be efficient, structured and flexible are less expensive to maintain in later years. Thus, there is a direct relationship between design and maintenance. More time spent on design up front can mean less time spent on maintenance later.

In most cases, it is worth the extra time and expense to design a good system. Consider a system that costs €250 000 to develop. Spending 10 per cent more on design would cost an additional €25 000, bringing the total design cost to €275 000. Maintenance costs over the life of the program could be €1 000 000. If this additional design expense can reduce maintenance costs by 10 per cent, the savings in maintenance costs would be €100 000. Over the life of the program, the net savings would be €75 000 (€100 000 − €25 000).

12

The need for good design goes beyond mere costs. Companies risk ignoring small system problems when they arise, but these small problems can become large in the future. As mentioned earlier, because maintenance programmers spend an estimated 50 per cent or more of their time deciphering poorly written, undocumented program code, they have little time to spend on developing new, more effective systems. If put to good use, the tools and techniques discussed in this chapter will allow organizations to build longer-lasting, more reliable systems.

12.4 Systems Review

systems review The final step of systems development, involving the analysis of systems to make sure that they are operating as intended.

Systems review, the final step of systems development, is the process of analyzing systems to make sure that they are operating as intended. This process often compares the performance and benefits of the system as it was designed with the actual performance and benefits of the system in operation.[18] A payroll application being developed for the Irish Health Service, for example, was almost €120 million over budget.[19] As a result, work on the application that serves about 37 000 workers was halted so the entire project could be reviewed in detail. The purpose of the systems review is to make sure that any additional work will result in a program that will work as intended.

Problems and opportunities uncovered during systems review trigger systems development and begin the process anew. For example, as the number of users of an interactive system increases, it is not unusual for system response time to increase. If the increase in response time is too great, it might be necessary to redesign some of the system, modify databases or increase the power of the computer hardware. When faced with a possible patent infringement problem, RIM, the maker of the popular BlackBerry phone and email service, developed back-up software that could be used in case the courts ruled against the company.[20] Even though RIM was able to settle the suit out of court, BlackBerry users were happy that the company had a back-up plan.

Internal employees, external consultants, or both, can perform systems review. When the problems or opportunities are industry-wide, people from several firms can get together. In some cases, they collaborate at an IS conference or in a private meeting involving several firms.

Types of Review Procedures

event-driven review A review triggered by a problem or opportunity such as an error, a corporate merger or a new market for products.

There are two types of review procedures: event driven and time driven (see Table 12.5). An **event-driven review** is triggered by a problem or opportunity such as an error, a corporate merger or a new market for products.[21] Natural disasters often revealed flaws in older systems, causing many companies and organizations to review their existing systems. Recent floods in the UK, for example, caused insurance companies to introduce flood maps to their quotation systems.

Table 12.5 Examples of Review Types

Event Driven	Time Driven
Problem with an existing system	Monthly review
Merger	Yearly review
New accounting system	Review every few years
Executive decision that an upgraded Internet site is needed to stay competitive	Five-year review

In contrast, some companies use a continuous improvement approach to systems development. With this approach, an organization makes changes to a system even when small problems or opportunities occur. Although continuous improvement can keep the system current and responsive, repeatedly designing and implementing changes can be both time consuming and expensive.

A **time-driven review** is performed after a specified amount of time. Many application programs are reviewed every six months to one year. With this approach, an existing system is monitored on a schedule. If problems or opportunities are uncovered, a new systems development cycle can be initiated. A payroll application, for example, can be reviewed once a year to make sure that it is still operating as expected. If it is not, changes are made.

> **time-driven review** Review performed after a specified amount of time.

Most companies use both approaches. A billing application, for example, might be reviewed once a year for errors, inefficiencies and opportunities to reduce operating costs. This is a time-driven approach. In addition, the billing application might be redone after a corporate merger, if one or more new managers require different information or reports, or if federal laws on bill collecting and privacy change. This is an event-driven approach.

Factors to Consider During Systems Review

Systems review should investigate a number of important factors, such as the following:

- *Mission:* Is the computer system helping the organization achieve its overall mission? Are stakeholder needs and desires satisfied or exceeded with the new or modified system?
- *Organizational goals:* Does the computer system support the specific goals of the various areas and departments of the organization?
- *Hardware and software:* Are hardware and software up to date and adequate to handle current and future processing needs?
- *Database:* Is the current database up to date and accurate? Is database storage space adequate to handle current and future needs?
- *Telecommunications:* Is the current telecommunications system fast enough, and does it allow managers and workers to send and receive timely messages? Does it allow for fast order processing and effective customer service?
- *Information systems personnel:* Are there sufficient IS personnel to perform current and projected processing tasks?
- *Control:* Are rules and procedures for system use and access acceptable? Are the existing control procedures adequate to protect against errors, invasion of privacy, fraud and other potential problems?
- *Training:* Are there adequate training programs and provisions for both users and IS personnel?
- *Costs:* Are development and operating costs in line with what is expected? Is there an adequate IS budget to support the organization?
- *Complexity:* Is the system overly complex and difficult to operate and maintain?
- *Reliability:* Is the system reliable? What is the mean time between failures (MTBF)?
- *Efficiency:* Is the computer system efficient? Are system outputs generated by the right amount of inputs, including personnel, hardware, software, budget and others?
- *Response time:* How long does it take the system to respond to users during peak processing times?
- *Documentation:* Is the documentation still valid? Are changes in documentation needed to reflect the current situation?

System Performance Measurement

Systems review often involves monitoring the system, called **system performance measurement**. The number of errors encountered, the amount of memory required, the amount of processing or CPU time needed and other problems should be closely observed.[22] If a particular system is not performing as expected, it should be modified, or a new system should be developed or acquired.

Setting up benchmarks for performance measurement can be critical. **System performance products** have been developed to measure all components of the information system, including hardware, software, database, telecommunications and network systems. When properly used, system performance products can quickly and efficiently locate actual or potential problems.

A number of products have been developed to assist in assessing system performance. OMEGAMON from IBM can monitor system performance in real time. Precise Software Solutions has system performance products that provide around-the-clock performance monitoring for Oracle database applications. Mercury Interactive offers a software tool called Diagnostic to help companies analyze the performance of their computer systems, diagnose potential problems and take corrective action if needed.[23]

Measuring a system is, in effect, the final task of systems development. The results of this process can bring the development team back to the beginning of the development lifecycle, where the process begins again.

Summary

Designing new systems or modifying existing ones should always help an organization achieve its goals. The purpose of systems design is to prepare the detailed design needs for a new system or modifications to the existing system. Logical systems design refers to the way that the various components of an information system will work together. The logical design includes data requirements for output and input, processing, files and databases, telecommunications, procedures, personnel and job design, and controls and security design. Physical systems design refers to the specification of the actual physical components. The physical design must specify characteristics for hardware and software design, database and telecommunications, and personnel and procedures design.

Logical and physical design can be accomplished using the traditional systems development lifecycle or the object-oriented approach. Using the object-oriented approach, analysts design key objects and classes of objects in the new or updated system. The

sequence of events that a new or modified system requires is often called a scenario, which can be diagrammed in a sequence diagram.

A number of special design considerations should be taken into account during both logical and physical system design. Interface design and control relates to how users access and interact with the system. A sign-on procedure consists of identification numbers, passwords and other safeguards needed for individuals to gain access to computer resources. If the system under development is interactive, the design must consider menus, help facilities, table lookup facilities and restart procedures. A good interactive dialogue will ask for information in a clear manner, respond rapidly, be consistent among applications and use an attractive format. Also, it will avoid use of computer jargon and treat the user with respect.

System security and control involves many aspects. Error prevention, detection and correction should be part of the system design process. Causes of errors include human activities, natural phenomena

12

and technical problems. Designers should be alert to prevention of fraud and invasion of privacy.

Disaster recovery is an important aspect of systems design. Disaster planning is the process of anticipating and providing for disasters. A disaster can be an act of nature (a flood, fire or earthquake) or a human act (terrorism, error, labour unrest or erasure of an important file). The primary tools used in disaster planning and recovery are hardware, software, database, telecommunications and personnel back-up.

Security, fraud and the invasion of privacy are also important design considerations. Most IS departments establish tight systems controls to maintain data security. Systems controls can help prevent computer misuse, crime and fraud by employees and others. Systems controls include input, output, processing, database, telecommunications and personnel controls.

Whether an individual is purchasing a personal computer or an experienced company is acquiring an expensive mainframe computer, the system could be obtained from one or more vendors. Some of the factors to consider in selecting a vendor are the vendor's reliability and financial stability, the type of service offered after the sale, the goods and services the vendor offers and keeps in stock, the vendor's willingness to demonstrate its products, the vendor's ability to repair hardware, the vendor's ability to modify its software, the availability of vendor-offered training of IS personnel and system users and evaluations of the vendor by independent organizations.

If new hardware or software will be purchased from a vendor, a formal request for proposal (RFP) is needed. The RFP outlines the company's needs; in response, the vendor provides a written reply. Financial options to consider include purchase, lease and rent.

RFPs from various vendors are reviewed and narrowed down to the few most likely candidates. In the final evaluation, a variety of techniques – including group consensus, cost–benefit analysis, point evaluation and benchmark tests – can be used. In group consensus, a decision-making group is appointed and given responsibility for making the final evaluation and selection. With cost–benefit analysis, all costs and benefits of the alternatives are expressed in monetary terms. Benchmarking involves comparing computer systems operating under the same condition. Point evaluation assigns weights to evaluation factors, and each alternative is evaluated in terms of each factor and given a score from 0 to 100. After the vendor is chosen, contract negotiations can begin.

One of the most important steps in systems design is to develop a good contract if new computer facilities are being acquired. A final design report is developed at the end of the systems design phase.

The primary emphasis of systems implementation is to make sure that the right information is delivered to the right person in the right format at the right time. The purpose of systems implementation is to install the system and make everything, including users, ready for its operation. Systems implementation includes hardware acquisition, software acquisition or development, user preparation, hiring and training of personnel, site and data preparation, installation, testing, start-up, and user acceptance. Hardware acquisition requires purchasing, leasing or renting computer resources from an IS vendor. Hardware is typically obtained from a computer hardware vendor.

Software can be purchased from vendors or developed in-house – a decision termed the make-or-buy decision. A purchased software package usually has a lower cost, less risk regarding the features and performance, and easy installation. The amount of development effort is also less when software is purchased. Developing software can result in a system that more closely meets the business needs and has increased flexibility in terms of customization and changes. Developing software also has greater potential for providing a competitive advantage. Increasingly, companies are using service providers to acquire software, Internet access and other IS resources. Software development is often performed by a chief programmer team – a group of IS professionals who design, develop and implement a software program. Structured design is a philosophy of designing and developing application software. Other tools, such as cross-platform development and integrated development environments (IDEs), make software development easier and more thorough. CASE tools are often used to automate some of these techniques.

Database and telecommunications software development involves acquiring the necessary databases, networks, telecommunications and Internet facilities. Companies have a wide array of choices, including newer object-oriented database systems.

Implementation must address personnel requirements. User preparation involves readying managers, employees and other users for the new system. New IS personnel might need to be hired, and users must be well trained in the system's functions. Preparation of the physical site of the system must be done, and any existing data to be used in the new system will require conversion to the new format. Hardware installation is done during the implementation step, as is testing. Testing includes program (unit) testing, systems testing, volume testing, integration testing and acceptance testing.

Start-up begins with the final tested information system. When start-up is finished, the system is fully operational. There are a number of different start-up approaches. Direct conversion involves stopping the old system and starting the new system on a given date. With the phase-in approach, sometimes called a piecemeal approach, components of the new system are slowly phased in while components of the old one are slowly phased out. When everyone is confident that the new system is performing as expected, the old system is completely phased out. Pilot start-up involves running the new system for one group of users rather than all users. Parallel start-up involves running both the old and new systems for a period of time. The output of the new system is compared closely with the output of the old system, and any differences are reconciled. When users are comfortable that the new system is working correctly, the old system is eliminated. Many IS vendors ask the user to sign a formal user acceptance document that releases the IS vendor from liability for problems that occur after the document is signed.

Maintenance and review add to the useful life of a system but can consume large amounts of resources. These activities can benefit from the same rigorous methods and project management techniques applied to systems development. Systems operation is the use of a new or modified system. Systems maintenance involves checking, changing and enhancing the system to make it more useful in obtaining user and organizational goals.

Maintenance is critical for the continued smooth operation of the system. The costs of performing maintenance can well exceed the original cost of acquiring the system. Some major causes of maintenance are new requests from stakeholders and managers, enhancement requests from users, bugs or errors, technical or hardware problems, newly added equipment, changes in organizational structure, and government regulations.

Maintenance can be as simple as a program patch to correct a small problem to the more complex upgrading of software with a new release from a vendor. For older programs, the total cost of maintenance can be greater than the total cost of development. Increased emphasis on design can often reduce maintenance costs. Requests for maintenance should be documented with a request for maintenance form, a document that formally authorizes modification of programs. The development team or a specialized maintenance team can then make approved changes. Maintenance can be greatly simplified with the object-oriented approach.

Systems review is the process of analyzing and monitoring systems to make sure that they are operating as intended. The two types of review procedures are the event-driven review and the time-driven review. An event-driven review is triggered by a problem or opportunity. A time-driven review is started after a specified amount of time.

Systems review involves measuring how well the system is supporting the mission and goals of the organization. System performance measurement monitors the system for number of errors, amount of memory and processing time required, and so on.

Self-Assessment Test

1 Determining the needed hardware and software for a new system is an example of _____.
   a. logical design
   b. physical design
   c. interactive design
   d. object-oriented design

2 Disaster planning is an important part of designing security and control systems. True or false?

3 The _____ often results in a formal bid that is used to determine who gets a contract for designing new or modifying existing systems. It specifies in detail the required resources such as hardware and software.

4 Near the end of the design stage, an organization prohibits further changes in the design of the system. This is called _____.

5 Software can be purchased from external developers or developed in house. This decision is often called the _____ decision.

6 What type of documentation is used by computer operators to execute a program and by analysts and programmers?
   a. unit documentation
   b. integrated documentation
   c. technical documentation
   d. user documentation

7 _____ testing involves testing the entire system of programs.

8 The phase-in approach to conversion involves running both the old system and the new system for three months or longer. True or false?

9 A(n) _____ is a minor change to correct a problem or make a small enhancement to a program or system.

10 Corporate mergers and acquisitions can be a reason for systems maintenance. True or false?

Review Questions

1 What is the purpose of systems design?

2 What is interactive processing? What design factors should be taken into account for this type of processing?

3 What is the difference between logical and physical design?

4 What are the different types of software and database back-up? Describe the procedure you use to back-up your homework files.

5 Identify specific controls that are used to maintain input integrity and security.

6 What is an RFP? What is typically included in one? How is it used?

7 What are the major steps of systems implementation?

8 What are some tools and techniques for software development?

9 Describe how you back-up the files you use on your PC.

10 What are the steps involved in testing the information system?

Discussion Questions

1 Describe the participants in the systems design stage. How do these participants compare with the participants of systems investigation?

2 Assume that you want to start a new DVD rental business for students at your college or university. Go through logical design for a new information system to help you keep track of the videos in your inventory.

3 Assume that you are the owner of an online stock-trading company. Describe how you could design the trading system to recover from a disaster.

4 Identify some of the advantages and disadvantages of purchasing versus developing software.

5 Is it equally important for all systems to have a disaster recovery plan? Why or why not?

Web Exercises

1 Use the Internet to find two different systems development projects that failed to meet cost or performance objectives. Summarize the problems and what should have been done. You might be asked to develop a report or send an email message to your instructor about what you found.

2 Using the web, search for information on structured design and programming. Also search the web for information about the object-oriented approach to systems design and implementation. Write a report on what you found. Under what conditions would you use these approaches to systems development and implementation?

Case One

Processing Petabytes at CERN and Around the World

Founded in 1954, the CERN laboratory sits astride the Franco-Swiss border near Geneva. CERN, the European Organization for Nuclear Research, is one of the world's largest and most respected centres for scientific research. Its business is fundamental physics, finding out what the universe is made of and how it works. CERN is the home of the Large Hadron Collider, a 27-km-long particle accelerator used in physics experiments to study the basic constituents of matter and learn about the laws of Nature. A by-product of these experiments is data. Lots of data.

When particles collide, a 7000-tonne device called the ATLAS detector monitors what happens, looking at the new particles that are created. In July 2012, CERN scientists reported that ATLAS had detected the Higgs boson particle, the only particle predicted by the standard model of particle physics that had not already been observed.

According to the parameters set by the physicists, particles pass through ATLAS while microprocessors convert their path and energies into electronic signals, discarding the majority (199 999 out of every 200 000) and keeping only those that look promising. Even by discarding this many, ATLAS still creates 19 GB of data every minute. In 2010, ATLAS generated enough data to fill a stack of CDs 14 km long. That rate of data production outstrips any other scientific effort.

Physicists deal with this data flood with a divide-and-conquer approach. Data from ATLAS are sent to a vast global network known as the Worldwide LHC Computer Grid. *Nature* magazine's Geoff Brumfiel says that the grid is as great a technological advance as the collider itself. Distributed across 34 countries and with 150 petabytes of disc space, the grid allows for analyses that would push the most powerful supercomputers to the edge.

From the ATLAS detector, the data is sent to CERN's computing centre where selected collisions are reconstructed. Dedicated fibre-optic links then carry the data to 11 data centres spread across the globe, one of which is in the Rutherford Appleton Laboratory at Oxford, UK. Here, scientists divide up the data by the kinds of particles they want to study. 'Particle physics is a bit like investigating a mid-air collision. Nobody is there to witness it; instead the debris is painstakingly collected and reassembled to give investigators hints as to what happened', says Mr Brumfiel. At the next level down, more computer centres request data analyses from the 11 data centres so that they can provide storage and access to the data for other users. When a request for an analysis is made, the grid pulls the data from centres like the one at Oxford, then parcels the data into thousands of separate pieces and spreads it across the network. The actual analyses are run at many computing centres. When complete, an email is sent to the person who made the request telling him or her that the results are ready.

Things don't always run smoothly. Air-conditioning units have become clogged up shutting down centres, road workers have severed the fibre-optic cable, and a fire brought down a data centre in Taiwan for months. The entire system relies on goodwill: 'We have no line management over these people whatsoever', says Jamie Shiers, a group leader in CERN's computing centre, in reference to the people who work at the data centres and smaller computer centres.

Questions

1 How could a project as complex as the Worldwide LHC Computer Grid operate 'on goodwill'?

2 What are some of the challenges the designers of the Worldwide LHC Computer Grid faced when creating it?

3 This project was created mostly using public funding. Do you feel this was money well spent?

4 How could the data produced be archived for future generations of scientists and historians to examine?

Case Two

Failover at Amazon

As one of the most recognized Internet brands in the world, it is not surprising that Amazon takes the availability of its website to its customers very seriously. Any disruption would have a massive impact on sales and could damage its hard won reputation.

When you search for a product on Amazon, the web page that you see was created 'dynamically'. A split second before the page appeared on your computer screen it didn't exist – it was created just for you. The way this works depends on a series of databases. In one is stored information about products. For books this includes the title and author, the publisher, a picture of the front cover and product reviews. In another is information about you, including what past purchases you made and what products to recommend you. These are used to create the recommended products that appear at the bottom of the page. When you search for a product the Amazon computers search these databases and assemble the information extracted into the web page that you get to see. The entire process is extremely fast and most people don't appreciate what's going on behind the scenes.

Amazon's databases have to be bullet proof. If one of them fails, a back-up should kick in immediately, something referred to as 'failover'. Fast-start failover is a feature developed by Oracle for its database management system. It automatically switches to a synchronized stand-by database in the event of loss of the primary database. The old primary database is then automatically reconfigured as a new stand-by database as soon as it is fixed. The system, part of a product called Data Guard, allows for disaster recovery with zero data loss. The failover process takes less than 30 seconds.

The way this works is that a piece of software referred to as the Observer monitors two databases

at all times looking for problems with either of them. Problems include input/output errors, loss of network connection such that the Observer can no longer communicate with them, or a database shutdown. If a problem is detected with the primary database the Observer first of all checks that the standby database is fully synchronized, that is, that it's fully up to date. If it's not fully up to date, for instance if it doesn't store the most recent transaction, then that transaction would be lost after failover. If the standby database is synchronized then failover goes ahead. If it's not then failover does not happen and the engineers are alerted.

Following a fast-start failover, the Observer periodically attempts to contact the old primary database. If a reconnection to the old primary database is made, the Observer automatically reinstates the old primary database so that it can become a new stand-by database to the new primary database. This quickly restores high availability to the Data Guard configuration. The stand-by database is usually physically located away from the primary database. An automatic failover system is important when information technology is critical – where any downtime results in lost production, lost business, lost revenue generation and reduced customer satisfaction. Products like Data Guard provide good business continuity.

Questions

1 Why is the stand-by database located physically separate from the primary database?

2 List some industries where automatic failover is important.

3 What are some of the problems Amazon would face if their databases went down?

4 Do you think this system would be suitable for a small business?

Case Three

IBM Grades Programmer Productivity

As you read in this chapter, computer programs are written by people. As with any type of work, some people are better at programming than others. Employers need a fair, objective way to find out who the excellent programmers are so as to recognize their superior work, to figure out what will help the others improve, and to learn what makes the excellent programmers better so the employers can try to duplicate this 'secret sauce' throughout their workforce.

Superior programming is a composite of several measures. One is productivity: how much code a programmer produces. Another is quality: how error-free that code is. Other measures include the performance and security of the resulting program and its clarity for future modifications by people who were not involved in writing it.

Because it is difficult to measure these factors, most managers end up measuring the process by which software is built and the effort put into that process rather than its outcomes. As Jitendra Subramanyam, director of research at CAST, Inc., writes, 'It's as if Michael Phelps tracks his time in the gym, the time it takes him to eat his meals, the time he spends on his Xbox, time walking his dog ... but bizarrely, not the time it takes him to swim the 100 meter butterfly!' IBM recognizes the need to focus on people and their output. 'At the end of the day, people are in the middle of application development,' says Pat Howard, vice president and cloud leader in IBM's global business services division. 'It's really important to have great investments, great energy focused around the talent.'

Howard's department uses the Applications Intelligence Platform from French software firm CAST to quantify performance. 'Essentially it permitted our people to walk around with a scorecard. They could begin to earn points, based on the results or the value they were driving for the business,' Howard says.

The program also helps to identify performance shortfalls and skill deficiencies. 'We use it to identify where more training is needed,' Howard says. Training budgets are tight, so 'when you spend it, you've got to spend it really smartly, aim it at the right place.'

The Bank of New York Mellon is another CAST user. The bank uses CAST to control the quality of the software produced by offshore contract software developers. Vice president for systems and technology Robert-Michel Lejeune says, 'You provide specifications, the offshorer has a process in place, but when they deliver, you don't know the level of quality. Using an automated tool provides you with facts and figures on the go.'

A system such as this can never be the entire answer to employee or contractor performance evaluation. Systems cannot measure important employee efforts such as contributing ideas in team meetings, mentoring junior employees and willingly taking on jobs that nobody else wants. However, CAST or something like it will be part of the answer at more and more companies in the future.

Questions

1 How would you feel as a programmer if your company announced that it was going to start using CAST Applications Intelligence Platform to measure your productivity and that of your colleagues? Would it matter to you if the firm said that 20 per cent of your performance evaluation, which determines your salary increases, would be based on CAST's reports? What about 50 per cent? 80 per cent?

2 Consider other intellectual activities with a defined end product, such as writing a movie script based on a book or designing a university dormitory. Would such tools be useful for measuring the productivity of people who do those things and the quality of their output? If you don't think it would, how is programming different?

3 Are there any drawbacks to using a programmer productivity measurement tool such as CAST's Applications Intelligence Platform? If there are, what are they?

4 Should software development managers be required to use a program such as CAST to measure the productivity of their teams?

Notes

1 Arnott, David, 'Cognitive Biases and Decision Support Systems Development: A Design Science Approach', *Information Systems Journal*, January 2006, p. 55.

2 Greenemeier, Larry, 'Wanted: Up-Front Security', *Information Week*, 2 January 2006, p. 35.

3 Cavusoglu, Huseyin, et al., 'The Value of Intrusion Detection Systems in Information Technology Security Architecture', *Information Systems Research*, March 2005, p. 28.

4 Mearian, Lucas, 'CNL Financial Updates Disaster Recovery Plan', *Computerworld*, 9 January 2006, p. 8.

5 Hadi, Mohammed, 'New Orleans Firm Fled Houston for Stamford', *The Wall Street Journal,* 27 September 2005, p. C3.

6 Brandel, Mary, 'Getting to Know You', *Computerworld*, 21 February 2005, p. 36.

7 Zha, Xuan, 'Knowledge-Intensive Collaborative Design Modeling and Support: System Implementation and Application', *Computers in Industry*, January 2006, p. 56.

8 McGee, Marianne, 'Outlook 2006', *Information Week*, 2 January 2006, p. 28.

9 Thibodeau, Patrick, 'HP Gives Reprieve on Support to e300 Users', *Computerworld*, 2 January 2006, p. 8.

10 Hoffman, Thomas, 'Return on Software', *Computerworld*, 31 January 2005, p. 39.

11 Reinhardt, Andy, 'SAP: A Sea of Change in Software', *Business Week*, 11 July 2005, p. 46.

12 Burrows, Peter, 'Bill Me Later', *Business Week*, 16 January 2006, p. 38.

13 Havenstein, Heather, 'Pilot Project Aims to Improve Analysis and Delivery of Cancer Treatment', *Computerworld*, 30 January 2006, p. 24.

14 Koten, C., Gray, A.R., 'An Application of Bayesian Network for Predicting Object-Oriented Software Maintainability', *Information and Software Technology*, January 2006, p. 59.

15 Pratt, Mark, 'Shining a Light on Maintenance', *Computerworld*, 13 February 2006, p. 41.

16 Thibodeau, Patrick, 'IBM Adds Autonomic Tools to Speed Up Error Detection', *Computerworld*, 4 July 2005, p. 7.

17 Nuzu, Christine M., 'Before You Throw It Out', *The Wall Street Journal*, 12 September 2005, p. R9.

18 Songini, Marc, 'Buggy App Causes Tax Problems in Wisconsin', *Computerworld*, 9 January 2006, p. 12.

19 Songini, Marc, 'Irish Agency Halts Work on Two SAP Application Projects', *Computerworld*, 17 October 2005, p. 12.

20 Malykhina, Elena, 'BlackBerry Backup Plan', *Information Week*, 13 February 2006, p. 28.

21 Hayashi, Yuka, 'Tokyo Exchange to Retool Trading System', *The Wall Street Journal*, January 21 2006, p. B1.

22 Yang, Ching-Chien, et al., 'A Study of the Factors Impacting ERP System Performance – From the User's Perspective', *Journal of American Academy of Business*, March 2006, p. 161.

23 Havenstein, Heather, 'Tools Bridge IT, Operations', *Computerworld*, 4 April, 2005, p. 12.

World Views Case

Making Robots that Interact with their Environment

In Chapter 3 we looked at the use of robots in the home, at work and in specialist settings such as exploring space. One of the case studies at the end of Chapter 9 even looked at military killer robots, a concept that we should not readily dismiss. In Chapter 9 we also mentioned LEGO Mindstorms, a LEGO kit which you can use at home to explore robotics and learn to computer program. In this case we will look at how you can make a robot do what you want it to using the Mindstorms kit. Even if you have no interest in robotics the following may be of interest as it shows you the fundamentals of breaking down a task into smaller tasks and assembling those smaller tasks in efficient ways to solve problems. What you are about to learn is how all computer programs work.

If you've ever seen the television programme Robot Wars, the machines that they use are not what we mean when we use the term 'robot' because they are being remote controlled by a human operator. What we mean by 'robot' is an autonomous machine that interacts with, and reacts to, its environment without human intervention. To do this a robot will need motors to give it movement – this is the robot's behaviour — and sensors to detect its environment. The Mindstorms kit comes with a number of sensors – you can get LEGO sensors that detect light, sound and distance from an object. Let's keep it simple and just use a button to detect touch – when the button is pressed it means our robot is touching something. Then we'll give our robot wheels and use two motors to control its movement. Using both motors will move the robot forwards and backwards, and putting one motor in reverse and one going forwards will turn the robot. There are instructions in the Mindstorms kit to build a robot like this. The following sketch shows how it's going to work. Let's see if we can get this robot to navigate about its environment.

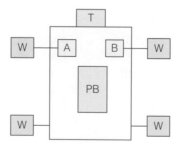

A and B are the two motors. The parts marked W are the wheels and T is the button. PB is the LEGO programmable brick, essentially the on-board computer. When our robot bumps into something T will be pressed. At that point the robot will stop and make a turn.

When a big task is broken down into smaller tasks there are three ways that the smaller tasks can be assembled in order to efficiently solve a problem. The three are called: Sequence, Selection and Iteration.

Sequence just means doing one task after another. For example, the sequence that we are going to use to turn our robot to the left is:

Turn both motors on in reverse for half a second.
Stop both motors.
Turn Motor A on in reverse for one second.
Turn Motor B on forward for one second.
Stop both motors.

The timings would have been decided by experimenting with the motors but one second will do for now. The reason we reverse a bit at the start is to give the robot room to make its move.

Selection means choosing between two paths in our program. It is used when our robot will have to decide between two or more options. Let's say when our robot bumps into something it randomly chooses whether to turn left or right. The sequence and selection of the tasks (we need both sequence and selection together) will be as follows:

Randomly generate a number between 0 and 1.

If the number is less than 0.5 turn left, otherwise turn right.

Instead of the using the word 'otherwise' most programming languages use the word 'else'. A selection statement always has a condition. In this case the condition is 'number is less than 0.5'.

That just leaves iteration. Iteration means doing same tasks over and over again. We could program our robot like this:

When there is a bump, make a turn.
When there is a bump, make a turn.
When there is a bump, make a turn.
When there is a bump, make a turn.
When there is a bump, make a turn.
When there is a bump, make a turn.

This would allow the robot to explore its environment until it had bumped into objects six times. Instead we can use iteration:

Keep doing the following: when there is a bump, make a turn.

In many programming languages the phrase 'Keep doing the following' is written as 'Do'. Usually there is another condition. To re-create the six times code above we could use:

Do six times: when there is a bump, make a turn.

Instead we're going to let our robot explore until someone turns it off – so we're not going to have a condition, we're just going to use 'Do'.

That's pretty much all there is to it. Putting it all together our program is as follows:

Do
{
Turn on both motors going forward
If Button T is pressed
   {
   Stop both motors
   Randomly generate a number between 0 and 1
   If the number is less than 0.5 turn left, else turn right
   }
}

The brackets are to keep the separate parts of the program together. The first and last brackets keep together all the code that is iterated. The inner brackets keep together the code that happens if the button is pressed. In the above we have simplified the code by using 'turn left' and 'turn right'. It is not as readable but the full program would be as follows:

Do
{
Turn on both motors forward
If Button T is pressed
   {
   Stop both motors
   Randomly generate a number between 0 and 1
   If the number is less than 0.5
      {
      Turn both motors on in reverse for half a second
      Stop both motors

12

Turn Motor A on in reverse for one second
Turn Motor B on forward for one second
Stop both motors
}
else
{
Turn both motors on in reverse for half a second
Stop both motors
Turn Motor B on in reverse for one second
Turn Motor A on forward for one second
Stop both motors
}
}
}

This code won't run on any system – it's an example of 'pseudocode': a description of a program rather than the program itself. It would have to be converted into a particular programming language, and there are several available for Mindstorms. The following is the first few lines of the above pseudo-code in real code. You can see that it's much less readable, but pretty much it is line-by-line the same.

task main()
{
while(true)
{
OnFor(OUT_A + OUT_C)
if(SENSOR_1)
{
Off(OUT_A + OUT_B)
ran_num = Random(1)
if(ran_num < 0.5)
...and so on.

Unfortunately this robot will not be very reliable if you use it in your front room. There will be bumps on the floor that it might get stuck on or small objects that it bangs up against and the button doesn't get pressed so it doesn't know to turn away. Many successful industrial robots are built to interact with one well known and fully controlled environment, like in a specially designed factory. The most advanced robots are those that can cope with an uncontrolled environment, like those that NASA have sent to Mars. However everything these advanced robots do is built up from sequence, selection and iteration.

Questions

1 See if you can work your way through the full program.

2 How would you edit the above code to make the robot follow a sound? (You could assume the sound will be loudest when the sound sensor is pointing right at it.)

3 Can you design code that would allow a robot to navigate a maze? What sensors would you need?

4 Design some code that will sort a list of words into alphabetical order. If you haven't programmed before you might find this challenging, but literally just get a list of words and sort them yourself. Then take what you have done and break it down into smaller tasks. Then assemble the tasks using sequence, selection and iteration.

12

World Views Case

Strategic Enterprise Management at International Manufacturing Corporation (IMC)

Bernd Heesen

University of Applied Sciences Furtwangen, Germany

The International Manufacturing Corporation (IMC), with 3000 employees worldwide, is a supplier of automotive parts and is headquartered in the US. Given the increasing market pressure and the need to operate internationally, IMC has recently made three acquisitions. The acquisition of one company in the UK and two companies in Germany is expected to leverage the companies' complementary manufacturing and sales capabilities to gain a stronger market presence in North America and Europe. The subsidiaries are still managed by their former management teams, who are now reporting to the US headquarters. Each of the subsidiaries still operates its own management information system because the system fulfilled the requirements in the past and at the time of the acquisition there was no visible benefit to change what was working. A couple of interfaces were created to facilitate the monthly financial reporting to the headquarters.

Recently, the CEO of IMC realized some disadvantages of the diversity of hardware and software platforms. When one IT expert from one German subsidiary terminated her employment, no other IT expert within IMC had detailed knowledge of the local system, which threatened regular operations in that plant. The company needed to seek external consulting support to maintain the system until a new IT expert could be hired. This dependency on individual experts in each location was expensive and caused problems during periods when the experts were on leave. In addition, the interfaces between the subsidiaries' systems and the headquarters' system that were created right after the acquisition had to be modified whenever a change or upgrade was made to one of the subsidiary systems. Even minor changes, such as the reorganization of product codes or sales organizations, required reprogramming, maintenance of conversion tables and subsequent testing of the related business processes in the system. The IT departments worked overtime and still did not find the time to invest in new initiatives such as enabling mobile computing for the sales force and developing a strategic enterprise management system that would allow consolidated planning and monitoring of all key performance indicators for the organization, a project long requested by the CEO. The two German subsidiaries had recently upgraded their systems, and problems identified during the testing of the interfaces could not be corrected in time for the submission of the monthly reports to headquarters. The data was finally corrected, but the monthly reporting was several days late. This was not the first time that the monthly financial reporting had been delayed or that the data needed to be corrected because of system-related problems, which caused other problems at headquarters.

The CEO finally requested consolidation of the systems in the coming year to allow for an integrated strategic enterprise management system that would provide current information from all legal entities and support a consolidated budgeting and planning process. He compared the company's current system with the cockpit of an aeroplane and stated that 'no one would expect a pilot to fly an aeroplane with malfunctioning instruments; hence nobody can expect management to run a company based on incomplete or incorrect information'. The CIO was asked to develop a business case for the implementation of such a system, considering the savings from personnel, hardware and software, as well as process improvements.

After IMC's board approved the business case to implement enterprise resource planning (ERP) software from SAP, the CIO established a project in January 1999. The project schedule called for completion of the financial, human resource, supply chain management and customer relationship management functions for the complete organization – called the Big Bang – in January 2000. A prototype of the application was planned to be ready by July 1999 so that the departments could test all functionality with a set of converted data extracted from the current systems. The plan also called for complete conversion of live data by the end of November 1999 so that in December both the current system and the new system could be used in parallel before making the decision to switch systems. Consultants from SAP were hired to support the implementation – for project management and configuration of the system – and an independent training organization was charged with planning the end-user training and developing computer-based training (CBT) programs for ongoing use. The project plan allowed for hiring temporary staff to help with the cutover and redundant data entry in December 1999.

The project started with a kickoff meeting in February, after which nearly all team members began their project work. The complete prototype of the application could only be made available in September because some of the team members had to fulfill their regular jobs while providing their expertise to the project. Some of the early project decisions had to be revised to accommodate the best-practice business model from IMC, after the IMC team members better understood how the SAP system worked and the consultants had gained a better understanding of how IMC wanted to operate. The CIO still wanted to maintain the timeline and called weekly meetings of the project's team leaders for finance, human resources, supply chain management and customer relationship management. Those meetings led to the decision to delay rollout of some of the functionality and to reduce the functionality to what was really needed (eliminating nice-to-have functionality). The prototype testing produced additional feedback from the departments that needed to be incorporated in the design of the final solution prior to the conversion. Many of the department heads, who had not been part of the core project team, only then became aware of the changes and started to talk about the new software, saying that it was not working properly yet and some of the team members were scared they would not make the deadline. In November, the data conversion revealed some additional problems (e.g. with data-entry errors made by the temporary staff who were keying data into the new system in instances in which an automated conversion was not cost-effective). As a result, the parallel use of the current and new system, which depended on all data being available, was delayed. To add to the pressure, the CIO believed that delaying the project's completion could be perceived as his failure. The CIO and steering committee of the project needed to make a decision on how to move forward: (1) continue with the project's completion in January 2000 as planned or (2) delay conversion to the new system until a proper parallel test could be completed.

Questions

1 How would you develop a business case to justify an investment in an integrated strategic enterprise management system?

2 What are the essential requirements for a strategic management system?

3 Which tasks would you consider when developing the original project plan for the implementation?

4 Given IMC's current situation, what would you decide if you were the CIO?

Note: The name International Manufacturing Corporation was selected to protect the identity of the real company featured in the case.

PART 5

Information Systems in Business and Society

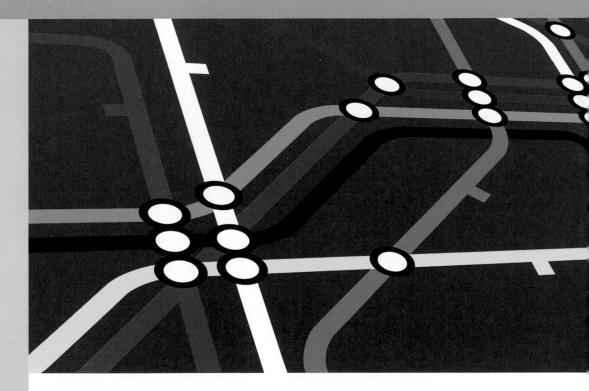

13

Security, Privacy and Ethical Issues in Information Systems

Principles	Learning Objectives
Policies and procedures must be established to avoid computer waste and mistakes.	■ Describe some examples of waste and mistakes in an IS environment, their causes and possible solutions.
	■ Identify policies and procedures useful in eliminating waste and mistakes.
	■ Discuss the principles and limits of an individual's right to privacy.
Computer crime is a serious and rapidly growing area of concern requiring management attention.	■ Explain the types and effects of computer crime.
	■ Identify specific measures to prevent computer crime.
Jobs, equipment and working conditions must be designed to avoid negative health effects.	■ List the important effects of computers on the work environment.
	■ Identify specific actions that must be taken to ensure the health and safety of employees.
	■ Outline criteria for the ethical use of information systems.

Why Learn About
Security, Privacy
and Ethical Issues in
Information Systems?

Our last chapter will look at security, privacy and ethical issues, something that has been in the background right throughout this book. A wide range of non-technical issues associated with the use of information systems provide both opportunities and threats to modern organizations. The issues span the full spectrum – from preventing computer waste and mistakes, to avoiding violations of privacy, to complying with laws on collecting data about customers, to monitoring employees. If you become a member of a human resources, information systems or legal department within an organization, you will likely be charged with leading the rest of the organization in dealing with these and other issues covered in this chapter. As a user of information systems, especially the Internet, it is in your own self-interest to become well versed on these issues. You need to know about the topics in this chapter to help avoid or recover from crime, fraud, privacy invasion or other potential problems.

13.1 Computer Waste and Mistakes

Computer-related waste and mistakes are major causes of computer problems, contributing as they do to unnecessarily high costs and lost profits. Computer waste involves the inappropriate use of computer technology and resources. It includes employees wasting computer resources and time by playing games and surfing the web, sending unnecessary email, printing documents and other material that is then not read, developing systems that are not used to their full extent, and discarding old hardware when it could be recycled or given to charity. UK-based Computers for Charities, for instance, will collect old technology, wipe clean any data stored on them and deliver them to charities where they are still useful. Junk email, also called spam, and junk faxes also cause waste. People receive hundreds of email messages and faxes advertising products and services not wanted or requested. Not only does this waste time, but it also wastes paper and computer resources. Worse yet, spam messages often carry attached files with embedded viruses that can cause networks and computers to crash or allow hackers to gain unauthorized access to systems and data.[1] Image-based spam is a new tactic spammers use to circumvent spam-filtering software that rejects email based on the content of messages and the use of keywords. The message is presented in a graphic form that can be read by people but not computers. This form of spam can be quite offensive and may contain pornographic photos and extremely graphic language.[2] When waste is identified, it typically points to one common cause: the improper management of information systems and resources.

Computer-related mistakes refer to errors, failures and other computer problems that make computer output incorrect or not useful, caused mostly by human error. Despite many people's distrust, computers themselves rarely make mistakes. Even the most sophisticated hardware cannot produce meaningful output if users do not follow proper procedures. Mistakes can be caused by unclear expectations and a lack of feedback. Or a programmer might develop a program that contains errors. In other cases, a data-entry administrator might enter the wrong data. Unless errors are caught early and prevented, the speed of computers can intensify mistakes. As information technology becomes faster, more complex and more powerful, organizations and computer users face increased risks of experiencing the results of computer-related mistakes.

Preventing Computer-Related Waste and Mistakes

To remain profitable in a competitive environment, organizations must use all resources wisely. Preventing computer-related waste and mistakes like those just described should therefore be a goal. To achieve it involves (1) establishing, (2) implementing, (3) monitoring, and (4) reviewing effective policies and procedures.

Establishing Policies and Procedures

The first step to prevent computer-related waste is to establish policies and procedures regarding efficient acquisition, use, and disposal of systems and devices. Most companies have implemented stringent policies on the acquisition of computer systems and equipment, including requiring a formal justification statement before computer equipment is purchased, definition of standard computing platforms (operating system, type of computer chip, minimum amount of RAM, etc.) and the use of preferred vendors for all acquisitions.

Prevention of computer-related mistakes begins by identifying the most common types of errors, of which there are surprisingly few. Types of computer-related mistakes include the following:

- Data-entry or data-capture errors.
- Errors in computer programs.
- Errors in handling files, including formatting a disc by mistake, copying an old file over a newer one and deleting a file by mistake.
- Mishandling of computer output.
- Inadequate planning for and control of equipment malfunctions.
- Inadequate planning for and control of environmental difficulties (electrical problems, humidity problems, etc.).
- Installing computing capacity inadequate for the level of activity on corporate websites.
- Failure to provide access to the most current information by not adding new and not deleting old URL links.

Training programmes for individuals and workgroups, and manuals and documents on how computer systems are to be maintained and used can help prevent problems. Other preventative measures include needing approval of certain systems and applications before they are implemented and used to ensure compatibility and cost-effectiveness, and a requirement that documentation and descriptions of certain applications be submitted to a central office, including all cell formulas for spreadsheets and a description of all data elements and relationships in a database system (which, as we saw in Chapter 5, is already recorded in the data dictionary). After companies have planned and developed policies and procedures, they must consider how best to implement them.

Sometimes, computer error combines with human procedural errors to lead to the loss of human life. In March 2003, a Patriot missile battery on the Kuwait border accidentally shot down a British Royal Air Force Tornado GR-4 aircraft that was returning from a mission over Iraq. Two British pilots were killed in the incident. Many defence industry experts think the accident was caused by problems with the Patriot's radar combined with human error.

Implementing Policies and Procedures

Implementing policies and procedures to minimize waste and mistakes varies according to the type of business. Most companies develop such policies and procedures with advice from the firm's internal auditing group or its external auditing firm. The policies often focus on the implementation of source data automation and the use of data editing to ensure data accuracy and completeness, and the assignment of responsibility for data accuracy within each information system. Some useful policies to minimize waste and mistakes include the following:

- Changes to critical tables, HTML and URLs should be tightly controlled, with all changes authorized by responsible owners and documented.
- A user manual should be available that covers operating procedures and documents the management and control of the application.

- Each system report should indicate its general content in its title and specify the time period it covers.
- The system should have controls to prevent invalid and unreasonable data entry.
- Controls should exist to ensure that data input, HTML and URLs are valid, applicable and posted in the right time frame.
- Users should implement proper procedures to ensure correct input data.

Training is another key aspect of implementation. Many users are not properly trained in using applications, and their mistakes can be very costly. One home in the small town of Valparaiso, in the US, fairly valued at $88 550 was incorrectly recorded in the county's computer system as being worth over $290 million. The erroneous figure was used to forecast future income from property taxes. When the error was uncovered, the local school district and government agencies were forced to slash their budgets by €1.5 million when they found they wouldn't be getting the tax money after all.[3]

Monitoring Policies and Procedures

To ensure that users throughout an organization are following established procedures, the next step is to monitor routine practices and take corrective action if necessary. By understanding what is happening in day-to-day activities, organizations can make adjustments or develop new procedures. Many organizations implement internal audits to measure actual results against established goals, such as percentage of end-user reports produced on time, percentage of data-input errors detected, number of input transactions entered per eight-hour shift and so on.

Reviewing Policies and Procedures

The final step is to review existing policies and procedures and determine whether they are adequate. During review, people should ask the following questions:

- Do current policies cover existing practices adequately? Were any problems or opportunities uncovered during monitoring?
- Is the organization planning any new activities in the future? If so, does it need new policies or procedures on who will handle them and what must be done?
- Are contingencies and disasters covered?

This review and planning allows companies to take a proactive approach to problem solving, which can enhance a company's performance, such as by increasing productivity and improving customer service. Information systems professionals and users still need to be aware of the misuse of resources throughout an organization. Preventing errors and mistakes is one way to do so. Another is implementing in-house security measures and legal protections to detect and prevent a dangerous type of misuse: computer crime.

Information Systems @ Work

Artwork Lost in an Obsolete File Format

In 2011, Cory Arcangel stumbled upon an old video of the artist Andy Warhol in 1985 that had been uploaded to YouTube. Warhol was using a Commodore Amiga computer to paint a portrait of Debbie Harry, the lead singer of Blondie. Arcangel became intrigued by the possibility that Warhol had created other works this way and contacted the Andy Warhol Museum to find out. Chief archivist Matt Wrbican gave him permission to search the archives for floppy discs. They soon found some discs but then faced a problem that is now all too common – how to access obsolete hardware and software formats.

The team enlisted the help of the Carnegie Mellon University's computer club who used a system known as Kyroflux-specialist hardware and software that was built specifically to read old floppy discs. The team began by making copies of the 40 or so discs. Some of these could then be read by an Amiga emulator, a modern piece of software that mimics the older computer. Other discs were in a non-standard format and could not be read. This was often done to protect commercial software. The team had to painstakingly reverse engineer the graphics format used. This involved reading the technical specification of the formats used at the time, analyzing how the files were stored and comparing the two.

Eventually several images were recovered showing works electronically signed by Warhol. In total 18 images were recovered, a dozen of which are signed. These were then saved into a modern file format. Arcangel said, 'What's amazing is

that by looking at these images, we can see how quickly Warhol seemed to intuit the essence of what it meant to express oneself, in what then was a brand-new medium: the digital.'

Some will wonder whether another computer club will have to re-analyze these images again in 30 years' time.

Questions

1 How could you ensure that you will be able to access the files you created today in 15 years' time?

2 In this case both hardware and software became obsolete. Which do you think is a bigger problem for companies today?

3 Is obsolescence a particular problem for museums and archives?

4 Explain why a software company would use a non-standard format. Is this approach suitable for any other types of company?

13.2 Computer Crime

According to Financial Fraud Action UK, in 2012 credit card fraudsters stole nearly €400 million in the UK alone, with €163 million of this happening through e-commerce transactions.[4] In 2013, Internet security experts Kaspersky Lab detected almost 3 billion malware attacks on user computers and 104 427 new malicious programs aimed at mobile devices.[5] The term computer crime covers a wide variety of activities, including these. Some more examples are listed next and then some types of computer crime are discussed.

- The largest consumer fraud in the US was committed by the Gambino crime family involving two different computer-related ploys and resulted in a loss to the public of over €200 million. One of the schemes offered 'free' tours of adult Internet sites but required the victim to provide a credit card supposedly for age-verification purposes. Victims took the free tours and then their credit cards were hit for charges over and over again. The second prong to this scheme involved the use of a third-party billing provider to add charges on people's telephone bills for services not provided.[6]

- A 20-year-old man was sentenced to 57 months in prison for hijacking more than 400 000 PCs over the Internet and turning them into a 'botnet' or 'zombie network', a network of personal computers used to perform a task without the owner's knowledge. He then would rent the zombie network out to spyware distributors, hackers and spammers to use in performing their work.[7]

- Russian organized crime extorted untold thousands of dollars from firms doing business on the Internet by demanding €7000 or more for protection from being hit by a denial-of-service attack on their website. Some firms bought the 'protection'; some of those that did not were attacked.[8]

13

- A British information systems expert accessed a series of computer networks used by the US Army, Navy, Air Force and Department of Defense, searching for what he called 'suppressed technology'. US authorities claimed he caused more than $700 000 of damage.[9]

- The UK government's tax credit website, which allowed qualifying citizens to claim tax benefits, was shut down in 2005 because it was being targeted by organized gangs claiming many millions of pounds from the government.[10]

Identify Theft

Identity theft is one of the fastest growing crimes. It is a crime where an imposter obtains key pieces of personal identification information, such as date of birth, address, national insurance number and mother's maiden name, and uses them to open bank accounts, get credit cards, loans, benefits and documents such as passports and driving licences in the victim's name. In other cases, the identity thief uses personal information to gain access to the person's existing accounts. Typically, the thief changes the mailing address on an account and runs up a huge bill before the person whose identity has been stolen realizes there is a problem. The Internet has made it easier for an identity thief to use the stolen information because transactions can be made without any personal interaction. The UK Home Office has a website, www.identitytheft.org.uk/, to advise its citizens and help victims. A wide range of methods are used by the perpetrators of these crimes that it makes investigating them difficult. Frequently, a critical computer password has been talked out of a person, or guessed based on a knowledge of the person, a practice called **social engineering**. For example, many people use the name of their pet as their password. Many teenagers use the name of their favourite pop artist. Alternatively, the attackers might simply go through the person's rubbish, looking for a disgarded utility bill or bank statement. In addition, over 2000 websites offer the digital tools – for free – that will let people snoop, crash computers, hijack control of a machine or retrieve a copy of every keystroke.

social engineering Using one's social skills to get computer users to provide you with information to access an information system or its data.

Another popular method to get information is 'shoulder surfing' – the identity thief simply stands next to someone at a public office, such as the passport office or even when filling in a form to join a customer loyalty programme, and watches as the person fills out personal information on a form. The same thing can happen at a bank ATM where the attacker simply watches the person enter their PIN, or at a shop when the victim is using their credit card to make a purchase (see Figure 13.1).

Consumers can help protect themselves by regularly checking their credit reports, following up with creditors if their bills do not arrive on time, not revealing any personal information in response to unsolicited email or phone calls, and shredding bills and other documents that contain sensitive information.[11]

Cyberterrorism

Government officials and IS security specialists have documented a significant increase in Internet probes and server scans since early 2001. A growing concern among authorities is that such intrusions are part of an organized effort by cyberterrorists to map potential security holes in critical systems. A **cyberterrorist** is someone who intimidates or coerces a government or organization to advance their political or social objectives by launching computer-based attacks against computers, networks and the information stored on them. Attacks would likely be aimed at critical infrastructure, which includes telecommunications, energy, banking and finance, water systems, government operations and emergency services. Successful cyberattacks against the facilities that provide these services could cause widespread and massive disruptions to the normal function of a society.

cyberterrorist Someone who intimidates or coerces a government or organization to advance his or her political or social objectives by launching computer-based attacks against computers, networks and the information stored on them.

13

Figure 13.1 Shoulder Surfing *Always take care when using an ATM that no one can see you enter your PIN.*

A similar term, 'cyberwar', is arguably not a crime but involves a country or state attacking another, using the same techniques as a cyberterrorist.

Illegal Access and Use

Crimes involving illegal system access and use of computer services are a concern to both government and business. Since the outset of information technology, computers have been plagued by criminal crackers. A **cracker**, often called a hacker, although this term has a range of meanings, is a computer-savvy person who attempts to gain unauthorized or illegal access to computer systems. Often they are 'just looking' but could also be trying to corrupt files, steal data or even transfer money. In many cases, crackers are people who are looking for fun and excitement – the challenge of beating the system. **Script kiddies** admire crackers, but have little technical savvy. They are crackers who download programs called 'scripts' that automate the job of breaking into computers. **Insiders** are employees, disgruntled or otherwise, working solo or in concert with outsiders to compromise corporate systems.

cracker A person who enjoys computer technology and spends time learning and using computer systems.

script kiddie A cracker with little technical savvy who downloads programs called scripts, which automate the job of breaking into computers.

insider An employee, disgruntled or otherwise, working solo or in concert with outsiders to compromise corporate systems.

Catching and convicting criminal hackers remains a difficult task. The method behind these crimes is often hard to determine. Even if the method behind the crime is known, tracking down the criminals can take a lot of time.

Data and information are valuable corporate assets. The intentional use of illegal and destructive programs to alter or destroy data is as much a crime as destroying tangible goods. The most common of these programs are viruses and worms, which are software programs that, when loaded into a computer system, will destroy, interrupt or cause errors in processing. Such programs are also called 'malware'.

13

virus A computer program file capable of attaching to discs or other files and replicating itself repeatedly, typically without the user's knowledge or permission.

A **virus** is a computer program file capable of attaching to discs or other files and replicating itself repeatedly, typically without the user's knowledge or permission. Some viruses attach to files, so when the infected file executes, the virus also executes. Other viruses sit in a computer's memory and infect files as the computer opens, modifies or creates the files. They are often disguised as games or images with clever or attention-grabbing titles such as 'Boss, naked'. Some viruses display symptoms, and some viruses damage files and computer systems. The m00p virus gang, for example, conspired to infect computers with a virus that would turn each infected machine into a zombie machine under their control. The zombie network could then be used to spread viruses and other malware across the Internet, without the owners of the compromised computers even being aware.[12] Hoax viruses can also be a problem. A hoax virus is a message, usually distributed by email, warning recipients to carry out a procedure on their computer to protect themselves from a 'virus threat', when the procedure itself is actually doing the damage. Typically a hoax virus encourages people to delete an important systems file. The message will encourage people to forward it on to all their contacts.

worm A parasitic computer program that can create copies of itself on the infected computer or send copies to other computers via a network.

Worms are computer programs that replicate but, unlike viruses, do not infect other computer program files. Worms can create copies on the same computer or can send the copies to other computers via a network. Worms often spread via Internet Relay Chat (IRC). For example, the MyDoom worm, also known as Shimgapi and Novarg, started spreading in January 2004 and quickly became the most virulent email worm ever. The worm arrived as an email with an attachment with various names and extensions, including .exe, .scr, .zip and .pif. When the attachment executed, the worm sent copies of itself to other email addresses stored in the infected computer. The first version of the virus, MyDoom.A, was designed to attack The SCO Group Inc.'s website. A later variant, dubbed MyDoom.B, was designed to enable similar denial-of-service attacks against the Microsoft website. The B variant also included a particularly nasty feature in that it blocked infected computers from accessing sites belonging to vendors of antivirus products. Infected email messages carrying the MyDoom worm have been intercepted from over 142 countries and at one time accounted for 1 in every 12 email messages.

Trojan horse A malicious program that disguises itself as a useful application and purposefully does something the user does not expect.

A **Trojan horse** program is a malicious program that disguises itself as a useful application and purposefully does something the user does not expect. Trojans are not viruses because they do not replicate, but they can be just as destructive. Many people use the term to refer only to non-replicating malicious programs, thus making a distinction between Trojans and viruses. A German language email, for example, was used to spread a Trojan horse that steals passwords and logon details of customers' online bank accounts and then relays them back to a remote server. The malware tried to get users to install the Trojan horse by disguising itself as a software patch for a new flaw in Microsoft software.[13] Spyware is often spread using the Trojan horse method. Spyware is software which records all manner of personal information about users and forwards it to the spyware's owner, all without the user's consent. Name, address, credit card numbers and passwords can all be collected by spyware, as can information on web browsing behaviour, which would be valuable for marketing.

A logic bomb is a type of Trojan horse that executes when specific conditions occur. Triggers for logic bombs can include a change in a file by a particular series of keystrokes or at a specific time or date.

A variant is a modified version of a virus that is produced by the virus's author or another person who amends the original virus code. If changes are small, most antivirus products will also detect variants. However, if the changes are significant, the variant might go undetected by antivirus software.

In some cases, a virus or a worm can completely halt the operation of a computer system or network for days or longer until the problem is found and repaired. In other cases, a virus or a worm can destroy important data and programs. If back-ups are inadequate, the data and programs might never be fully functional again. The costs include the effort required to identify and neutralize the virus or worm and to restore computer files and data, as well as the value of business lost because of unscheduled computer downtime.

As a result of the increasing threat of viruses and worms, most computer users and organizations have installed **antivirus programs** on their computers. Such software runs in the background to protect your computer from dangers lurking on the Internet and other possible sources of infected files. Some antivirus software is even capable of repairing common virus infections automatically, without interrupting your work. The latest virus definitions are downloaded automatically when you connect to the Internet, ensuring that your PC's protection is current. To safeguard your PC and prevent it from spreading viruses to your friends and coworkers, some antivirus software scans and cleans both incoming and outgoing email messages. Table 13.1 lists some of the most popular antivirus software.

> **antivirus program** Software that runs in the background to protect your computer from dangers lurking on the Internet and other possible sources of infected files.

Table 13.1 Antivirus Software

Antivirus Software	Software Manufacturer	Website
Symantec's Norton AntiVirus	Symantec	www.symantec.com
McAfee Virus Scan	McAfee	www.mcafee.com
Panda Antivirus Platinum	Panda Software	www.pandasoftware.com
Vexira Antivirus	Central Command	www.centralcommand.com
Sophos Antivirus	Sophos	www.sophos.com
PC-cillin	Trend Micro	www.trendmicro.com

Proper use of antivirus software requires the following steps:

1 Install antivirus software. These programs should automatically check for viruses each time you boot up your computer or insert a disc or CD, and some even monitor all e-mail and file transmissions and copying operations.

2 Ensure the antivirus software updates often. New viruses are created all the time, and antivirus software suppliers are constantly updating their software to detect and take action against these new viruses. The software should itself check for updates regularly, without the need for an instruction from the user.

3 Scan all removable media, including CDs, before copying or running programs from them. Hiding on discs or CDs, viruses often move between systems. If you carry document or program files on removable media between computers at school or work and your home system, always scan them.

4 Install software only from a sealed package or secure website of a known software company. Even software publishers can unknowingly distribute viruses on their program discs or software downloads. Most scan their own systems, but viruses might still remain.

5 Follow careful downloading practices. If you download software from the Internet or a bulletin board, check your computer for viruses immediately after completing the transmission.

6 If you detect a virus, take immediate action. Early detection often allows you to remove a virus before it does any serious damage.

Despite careful precautions, viruses can still cause problems. They can elude virus-scanning software by lurking almost anywhere in a system. Future antivirus programs might incorporate 'nature-based models' that check for unusual or unfamiliar computer code. The advantage of this type of virus program is the ability to detect new viruses that are not part of an antivirus database.

Hoax, or false, viruses are another problem. Crackers sometimes warn the public of a new and devastating virus that doesn't actually exist just to create fear. Companies sometimes spend hundreds of hours warning employees and taking preventative action against a non-existent virus. Security specialists recommend that IS personnel establish a formal paranoia policy to thwart virus panic among gullible end users. Such policies should stress that before users forward an e-mail alert to colleagues, they should send it to the help desk or the security team. The corporate intranet can be used to explain the difference between real viruses and fakes, and it can provide links to websites to set the record straight.

Be aware that virus writers also use known hoaxes to their advantage. For example, AOL4FREE began as a hoax virus warning. Then, a hacker distributed a destructive Trojan attached to the original hoax virus warning. Always remain vigilant and never open a suspicious attachment.[14]

Equipment Theft

During illegal access to computer systems, data can be stolen. In addition to theft of data and software, all types of computer systems and equipment have been stolen from offices. Mobile computers such as laptops and smartphones are especially easy for thieves to take. Very often the data stored on these devices is more valuable than the device itself. An MI5 agent's laptop containing sensitive government information was stolen at Paddington train station in London, and a senior British Army official's laptop was taken at Heathrow Airport.[15] To fight computer crime, many companies use devices that disable the disc drive and/or lock the computer to the desk.

Software and Internet Software Piracy

Like books and movies – other intellectual properties – software is protected by copyright laws. Often, people who would never think of plagiarizing another author's written work have no qualms about using and copying software programs they have not paid for. Such illegal duplicators are called 'pirates'; the act of illegally duplicating software is called **software piracy**.

software piracy The act of illegally duplicating software.

Technically, software purchasers are granted the right only to use the software under certain conditions; they don't really own the software. Licences vary from program to program and can authorize as few as one computer or one person to use the software or as many as several hundred network users to share the application across the system. Making additional copies, or loading the software onto more than one machine, might violate copyright law and be considered piracy.

The Business Software Alliance estimates that the software industry loses over €8 billion per year in revenue to software piracy annually. Half the loss comes from Asia, where China and Indonesia are the biggest offenders. In Western Europe, annual piracy losses range between 1.5 and 2 billion euros. Although the rate of software piracy is quite high in Latin America and Central Europe, those software markets are so small that the monetary losses are considerably lower. Overall, it is estimated that 35 per cent of the world's software is pirated.[16]

Internet-based software piracy occurs when software is illegally downloaded from the Internet. It is the most rapidly expanding type of software piracy and the most difficult form to combat. The same purchasing rules apply to online software purchases as for traditional purchases. Internet piracy can take several forms, including the following:

■ Pirate websites that make software available for free or in exchange for uploaded programs.

■ Internet auction sites that offer counterfeit software, which infringes copyrights.

■ Peer-to-peer networks, which enable unauthorized transfer of copyrighted programs.

Computer-Related Scams

People have lost hundreds of thousands of euros on property, travel, stock, and other business scams. Now, many of these scams are being perpetrated with computers. Using the Internet, scam artists offer get-rich-quick schemes involving bogus property deals, tout 'free' holidays with huge hidden costs, commit bank fraud, offer fake telephone lotteries, sell worthless penny stocks and promote illegal tax-avoidance schemes.

Over the past few years, credit card customers of various banks have been targeted by scam artists trying to get personal information needed to use their credit cards. The scam typically works by sending an email to many thousands of people, asking them to click on a link that seems to direct users to a bank's website, to fill in essential security information. Some of the recipients will probably be customers of the bank. At the site, they are asked for their full debit and credit card numbers and expiration dates, their name, address and other personal information. The problem is that the website customers are directed to is a fake site operated by someone trying to gain access to that information. As discussed previously, this form of scam is called 'phishing'. The website used is often extremely similar to the bank's real website and may contain links to the real site. During March 2014, the Anti-Phishing Working Group detected 44 212 phishing websites.[17]

In the weeks following Hurricane Katrina in the US, the FBI warned that over half the Hurricane Katrina aid sites it checked were registered to people outside the US and likely to be fraudulent. A 20-year-old man was charged with setting up websites designed to look like those of the American Red Cross and other organizations accepting donations to help the victims. He then sold these to 'would-be scammers' for about $140 each. For his trouble, this person is facing 50 years in prison and a fine of $1 million.[18]

The following is a list of tips to help you avoid becoming a scam victim:

- Don't agree to anything in a high-pressure meeting or seminar. Insist on having time to think it over and to discuss things with your spouse, your partner or even your solicitor. If a company won't give you the time you need to check it out and think things over, you don't want to do business with it. A good deal now will be a good deal tomorrow; the only reason for rushing you is if the company has something to hide.

- Don't judge a company based on appearances. Professional-looking websites can be created and published in a matter of days. After a few weeks of taking money, a site can vanish without a trace in just a few minutes. You might find that the perfect money-making opportunity offered on a website was a money-maker for the crook and a money-loser for you.

- Avoid any plan that pays commissions simply for recruiting additional distributors. Your primary source of income should be your own product sales. If the earnings are not made primarily by sales of goods or services to consumers or sales by distributors under you, you might be dealing with an illegal pyramid.

- Beware of 'shills', people paid by a company to lie about how much they've earned and how easy the plan was to operate. Check with an independent source to make sure that you aren't having the wool pulled over your eyes.

- Beware of a company's claim that it can set you up in a profitable home-based business but that you must first pay up front to attend a seminar and buy expensive materials. Frequently, seminars are high-pressure sales pitches, and the material is so general that it is worthless.

- If you are interested in starting a home-based business, get a complete description of the work involved before you send any money. You might find that what you are asked to do after you pay is far different from what was stated in the ad. You should never have to pay for a job description or for needed materials.

■ Get in writing the refund, buy-back and cancellation policies of any company you deal with. Do not depend on oral promises.

■ If you need advice about an online solicitation, or if you want to report a possible scam, contact your country's computer crime unit. In the UK, you can find more information at www.direct.gov.uk or www.met.police.uk/computercrime.

13.3 Preventing Computer-Related Crime

Because of increased computer use, greater emphasis is placed on the prevention and detection of computer crime. Many countries have passed data laws governing how data can be stored, processed and transferred, and laws on computer crime. Some believe that these laws are not effective because companies do not always actively detect and pursue computer crime, security is inadequate and convicted criminals are not severely punished. However, all over the world, private users, companies, employees and public officials are making individual and group efforts to curb computer crime, and recent efforts have met with some success.

Crime Prevention by the State

In the UK, the Computer Misuse Act of 1990, which criminalizes unauthorized access to computer systems, and the Data Protection Act of 1984 (expanded in 1998), which governs when and how data about individuals can be stored and processed, have been passed. Many countries have passed similar laws.

In the UK, the Home Office is charged with tackling computer crime with some police forces having a 'cyber crime' unit. The Information Commissioner's Office is in charge of the UK's independent authority set up to protect personal information (and as we shall see later in this chapter, to promote access to official information). The UK also has an organization dedicated to fighting specific types of computer crime. The Child Exploitation and Online Protection Centre (CEOP) tackles child sex abuse, especially where it has been facilitated in some way by the Internet.

Crime Prevention by Organizations

Companies are also taking crime-fighting efforts seriously. Many businesses have designed procedures and specialized hardware and software to protect their corporate data and systems. Specialized hardware and software, such as encryption devices, can be used to encode data and information to help prevent unauthorized use. Encryption is the process of converting an original electronic message into a form that can be understood only by the intended recipients. A key is a variable value that is applied using an algorithm to a string or block of unencrypted text to produce encrypted text or to decrypt encrypted text. Encryption methods rely on the limitations of computing power for their effectiveness – if breaking a code requires too much computing power, even the most determined code crackers will not be successful. The length of the key used to encode and decode messages determines the strength of the encryption algorithm.

public-key infrastructure (PKI) A means to enable users of an unsecured public network such as the Internet to securely and privately exchange data through the use of a public and a private cryptographic key pair that is obtained and shared through a trusted authority.

Public-key infrastructure (PKI) enables users of an unsecured public network such as the Internet to securely and privately exchange data through the use of a public and a private cryptographic key pair that is obtained and shared through a trusted authority. PKI is the most common method on the Internet for authenticating a message sender or encrypting a message. PKI uses two keys to encode and decode messages. One key of the pair, the message receiver's public key, is readily available to the public and is used by anyone to send that individual encrypted messages. The second key, the message receiver's private key, is kept secret and is known only by the message receiver. Its owner uses the private key to decrypt messages – convert encoded messages back into the original message. Knowing a person's public key does not enable you to decrypt an encoded message to that person.

Using **biometrics** is another way to protect important data and information systems. Biometrics involves the measurement of one of a person's traits, whether physical or behavioural. Biometric techniques compare a person's unique characteristics against a stored set to detect differences between

biometrics The measurement of one of a person's traits, whether physical or behavioural.

them. Biometric systems can scan fingerprints, faces, handprints, irises and retinal images to prevent unauthorized access to important data and computer resources. Most of the interest among corporate users is in fingerprint technology, followed by face recognition. Fingerprint scans hit the middle ground between price and effectiveness (see Figure 13.2). Iris and retina scans are more accurate, but they are more expensive and involve more equipment.

Figure 13.2 Fingerprint Authentication *Fingerprint authentication devices provide security in the PC environment by using fingerprint information instead of passwords.*

Co-op Mid Counties is the first UK retailer to implement a payment by biometrics system with fingerprint readers supplied by the US company Pay By Touch. The system is installed in just three of its stores in Oxford, but, if successful, the system will be expanded to all of its 150 stores. To use the system, customers must register with Co-op Mid Counties by providing a photo ID and submit to fingerprinting. In addition to providing improved security, the system takes less time to process a payment – three seconds compared with seven seconds for traditional payment approval methods.[19]

As employees move from one position to another at a company, they can build up access to multiple systems if inadequate security procedures fail to revoke access privileges. It is clearly not appropriate for people who have changed positions and responsibilities to still have access to systems they no longer use. To avoid this problem, many organizations create role-based system access lists so that only people filling a particular role (e.g. line manager) can access a specific system.

Crime-fighting procedures usually require additional controls on the information system. Before designing and implementing controls, organizations must consider the types of computer-related crime that might occur, the consequences of these crimes, and the cost and complexity of needed controls. In most cases, organizations conclude that the trade-off between crime and the additional cost and complexity weighs in favour of better system controls. Having knowledge of some of the methods used to commit crime is also helpful in preventing, detecting and developing systems resistant to computer crime (see Table 13.2). Some companies actually hire former criminals to thwart other criminals.

Table 13.2 Common Methods Used to Commit Computer Crimes

Methods	Examples
Add, delete or change inputs to the computer system	Delete records of absences from class in a student's school records
Modify or develop computer programs that commit the crime	Change a bank's program for calculating interest to make it deposit rounded amounts in the criminal's account
Alter or modify the data files used by the computer system	Change a student's grade from C to A
Operate the computer system in such a way as to commit computer crime	Access a restricted government computer system
Divert or misuse valid output from the computer system	Steal discarded printouts of customer records from a company trash bin
Steal computer resources, including hardware, software and time on computer equipment	Make illegal copies of a software program without paying for its use
Offer worthless products for sale over the Internet	Send email requesting money for worthless hair growth product
Blackmail executives to prevent release of harmful information	Eavesdrop on organization's wireless network to capture competitive data or scandalous information
Blackmail company to prevent loss of computer-based information	Plant logic bomb and send letter threatening to set it off unless paid considerable sum

Although the number of potential computer crimes appears to be limitless, the actual methods used to commit crime are limited. The following list provides a set of useful guidelines to protect your computer from criminal hackers.

- Install strong user authentication and encryption capabilities on your firewall.
- Install the latest security patches, which are often available at the vendor's Internet site.
- Disable guest accounts and null user accounts that let intruders access the network without a password.
- Do not provide overfriendly logon procedures for remote users (e.g. an organization that used the word 'welcome' on their initial logon screen found they had difficulty prosecuting a criminal hacker).
- Restrict physical access to the server and configure it so that breaking into one server won't compromise the whole network.
- Give each application (email, FTP and domain name server) its own dedicated server.
- Turn audit trails on.
- Consider using caller ID.
- Install a corporate firewall between your corporate network and the Internet.

■ Install antivirus software on all computers and regularly download vendor updates.

■ Conduct regular IS security audits.

■ Verify and exercise frequent data back-ups for critical data.

Companies are also joining together to fight crime. The Software and Information Industry Alliance (SIIA) was the original antipiracy organization, formed and financed by many of the large software publishers. Microsoft financed the formation of a second antipiracy organization, the Business Software Alliance (BSA). The BSA, through intense publicity, has become the more prominent organization. Other software companies, including Apple, Adobe, Hewlett-Packard and IBM, now contribute to the BSA.

Crime Prevention by Individuals

A number of individuals – victims, former criminals, concerned parents – have set up websites offering support for those worried about computer crime, and advice on how to fight it.

Using Intrusion Detection Software

An **intrusion detection system (IDS)** monitors system and network resources and notifies network security personnel when it senses a possible intrusion. Examples of suspicious activities include repeated failed logon attempts, attempts to download a program to a server and access to a system at unusual hours. Such activities generate alarms that are captured on log files. Intrusion detection systems send an alarm, often by email or pager, to network security personnel when they detect an apparent attack. Unfortunately, many IDSs frequently provide false alarms that result in wasted effort. If the attack is real, network security personnel must make a decision about what to do to resist the attack. Any delay in response increases the probability of damage from a criminal hacker attack. Use of an IDS provides another layer of protection in the event that an intruder gets past the outer security layers – passwords, security procedures and corporate firewall.

> **intrusion detection system (IDS)** Software that monitors system and network resources and notifies network security personnel when it senses a possible intrusion.

The following story is true, but the company's name has been changed to protect its identity. The ABC company employs more than 25 IDS sensors across its worldwide network, enabling it to monitor 90 per cent of the company's internal network traffic. The remaining 10 per cent comes from its engineering labs and remote sales offices, which are not monitored because of a lack of resources. The company's IDS worked very well in providing an early warning of an impending SQL Slammer attack. The Slammer worm had entered the network via a server in one of the engineering labs. The person monitoring the IDS noticed outbound traffic consistent with SQL Slammer at about 7:30 a.m. He contacted the network operations group by email and followed up with a phone call and a voice mail message. Unfortunately, the operations group gets so many emails that if a message is not highlighted as URGENT, the message might be missed. That is exactly what happened – the email alert wasn't read, and the voice message wasn't retrieved in time to block the attack. A few hours later, the ABC company found itself dealing with a massive number of reports of network and server problems.

Using Managed Security Service Providers (MSSPs)

Keeping up with computer criminals – and with new regulations – can be daunting for organizations. Criminal hackers are constantly poking and prodding, trying to breach the security defences of companies. For most small and mid-sized organizations, the level of in-house network security expertise needed to protect their business operations can be quite costly to acquire and maintain. As a result, many are outsourcing their network security operations to managed security service providers (MSSPs) such as Counterpane, Guardent, Internet Security Services, Riptech and Symantec. MSSPs monitor, manage and maintain network security for both hardware and software. These companies provide a valuable service for IS departments drowning in reams of alerts and false alarms coming from virtual private networks (VPNs); antivirus, firewall and intrusion detection systems; and other security monitoring systems. In addition, some provide vulnerability scanning and web blocking/filtering capabilities.

Preventing Crime on the Internet

As mentioned in Chapter 6, Internet security can include firewalls and many methods to secure financial transactions. A firewall can include both hardware and software that act as a barrier between an organization's information system and the outside world. Some systems have been developed to safeguard financial transactions on the Internet.

To help prevent crime on the Internet, the following steps can be taken:

1 Develop effective Internet usage and security policies for all employees.
2 Use a stand-alone firewall (hardware and software) with network monitoring capabilities.
3 Deploy intrusion detection systems, monitor them and follow up on their alarms.
4 Monitor managers and employees to make sure that they are using the Internet for business purposes.
5 Use Internet security specialists to perform audits of all Internet and network activities.

Even with these precautions, computers and networks can never be completely protected against crime. One of the biggest threats is from employees. Although firewalls provide good perimeter control to prevent crime from the outside, procedures and protection measures are needed to protect against computer crime by employees. Passwords, identification numbers, and tighter control of employees and managers also help prevent Internet-related crime.

13.4 Privacy

Privacy is a big issue for many people. When information is computerized and can be processed and transferred easily, augmented and collated, summarized and reported, privacy concerns grow. The European Union has a data-protection directive that requires firms transporting data across national boundaries to have certain privacy procedures in place. This directive affects virtually any company doing business in Europe, and it is driving much of the attention being given to privacy in the US.

Privacy and the Government

Many people are suspicious of the government when it comes to information that is stored about them. In the UK, the government is currently introducing an identity card scheme which, it is claimed, will help fight international terrorism and identify theft and other fraud. The card would be linked to a database, which would hold names, addresses and biometric information on all citzens. Expected to cost many billions of euros, some people have pledged never to carry them, claiming that the scheme would create a 'big brother' society. Many of these fears are unfounded, although the debate does highlight a lack of trust in the state.

Many governments are in fact quite open about the information that they store. Numerous countries have implemented some sort of freedom of information legistration. In South Africa, it is the Promotion of Access to Information Act. In the UK it is the Freedom of Information Act. Similar laws have been passed throughout Europe.

The UK Freedom of Information Act governs all data that is not about an individual, in any public organization including government, local councils, schools, universities and hospitals. The Act basically states that all such organizations must give out whatever information is requested of them, as long as it is not about an individual (which is protected under the Data Protection Act) or some other sensitive information. So, for example, you would be able to ask your university how many people achieved A grades in one of your modules last year (this information is probably published on the students' portal anyway). However, you couldn't request information about a professor's salary. You could, though, ask for information about lecturers' pay scales (which again is already freely available from the relevant union's website).

Privacy at Work

The right to privacy at work is an important issue. Currently, the rights of workers who want their privacy and the interests of companies that demand to know more about their employees are in conflict. Recently, companies that have been monitoring their workers have raised concerns. For example, workers might find that they are being closely monitored via computer technology. These computer-monitoring systems tie directly into workstations; specialized computer programs can track every keystroke made by a user. This type of system can determine what workers are doing while at the keyboard. The system also knows when the worker is not using the keyboard or computer system. These systems can estimate what people are doing and how many breaks they are taking. Needless to say, many workers consider this close supervision very dehumanizing.

Email Privacy

Email also raises some interesting issues about work privacy. A company has the right to look at any data stored on its servers, which includes its email servers and therefore all messages sent by or to its employees. Many companies routinely store all emails sent or received for several years and many employees have lost their jobs for forwarding inappropriate messages. Others have sent embarassing messages that have been forwarded exponentially by recipients who pass the 'joke' on to their friends. A solicitor at a London firm, for example, sent one message to some friends about his girlfriend's sexual preferences and a week later the message had been distributed to over a million people, through many blue chip firms.[20]

Privacy and the Internet

Some people assume that there is no privacy on the Internet and that you use it at your own risk. Others believe that companies with websites should have strict privacy procedures and be accountable for privacy invasion. Regardless of your view, the potential for privacy invasion on the Internet is huge. People wanting to invade your privacy could be anyone from criminal hackers to marketing companies to corporate bosses. Email is a prime target, as discussed previously. When you visit a website, information about you and your computer can be captured. When this information is combined with other information, companies can know what you read, what products you buy and what your interests are. According to an executive of an Internet software monitoring company, 'It's a marketing person's dream'.

Most people who buy products on the web say it's very important for a site to have a policy explaining how personal information is used, and the policy statement must make people feel comfortable and be extremely clear about what information is collected and what will and will not be done with it. However, many websites still do not prominently display their privacy policy or implement practices completely consistent with that policy. The real issue that Internet users need to be concerned with is 'what do content providers want with their personal information?'

If a site requests that you provide your name and address, you have every right to know why and what will be done with it. If you buy something and provide a shipping address, will it be sold to other retailers? Will your email address be sold on a list of active Internet shoppers? And, if so, you should realize that it's no different than the lists compiled from the orders you place with catalogue retailers – you have the right to be taken off any mailing list.

These same questions can be asked of Internet chat rooms that require you to register before you can post messages. It is important for the forum moderators to know who is posting, but users should also have confidence that their information will not be misused.

Platform for Privacy Preferences (P3P) A screening technology that shields users from websites that don't provide the level of privacy protection they desire.

A potential solution to some consumer privacy concerns is the screening technology called the **Platform for Privacy Preferences (P3P)** being proposed to shield users from sites that don't provide the level of privacy protection they desire. Instead of forcing users to find and read through the privacy policy for each site they visit, P3P software in a computer's browser will download the privacy policy from each site, scan it and notify the user if the policy does not match his or her preferences. (Of course, unethical marketers can post a privacy policy that does not accurately reflect the manner in which the data is treated.) The World Wide Web Consortium (W3C), an international industry group whose members include Apple, Commerce One, Ericsson and Microsoft, is supporting the development of P3P.

A social network service employs the web and software to connect people for whatever purpose. There are thousands of such networks, which have become popular among teenagers. Some of the more popular social networking websites include Bebo, Classmates.com, Facebook, Hi5, Imbee, MySpace, Namesdatabase.com, Tagged and XuQa. Most of these allow one to easily create a user profile that provides personal details, photos, even videos that can be viewed by other visitors to the website. Some of the websites have age restrictions or require that a parent register their pre-teen by providing a credit card to validate the parent's identity. Teens can provide information about where they live, go to school, their favourite music and interests in the hopes of meeting new friends. Unfortunately, they can also meet ill-intentioned strangers at these sites. Many documented encounters involve adults masquerading as teens attempting to meet young people for illicit purposes. Parents are advised to discuss potential dangers, check their children's profiles and monitor their activities at such websites.

Whenever someone registers a domain name such as www.mydomain.co.uk, the name and address given during registration become public information and can be seen by simply running a 'whois' query, which can be easily done on many websites. Parents should be aware of this before they let their children have their own web page.

Fairness in Information Use

Selling information to other companies can be so lucrative that many companies will continue to store and sell the data they collect on customers, employees and others. When is this information storage and use fair and reasonable to the people whose data is stored and sold? Do people have a right to know about data stored about them and to decide what data is stored and used? As shown in Table 13.3, these questions can be broken down into four issues that should be addressed: knowledge, control, notice and consent.

In the UK, the Data Protection Act governs the answers to these questions. The act relates to data about individuals and states that:

1 Personal data shall be processed fairly and lawfully.

2 Companies must have a reason for collecting and storing the data – they can't arbitrarily start hoarding it, and they cannot process it in any manner incompatible with that reason.

3 The data collected shall be adequate, relevant and not excessive in relation to the reason for collecting it.

Table 13.3 The Right to Know and the Ability to Decide

Fairness Issues	Database Storage	Database Usage
The right to know	Knowledge	Notice
The ability to decide	Control	Consent

Knowledge: Should people know what data is stored about them? In some cases, people are informed that information about them is stored in a corporate database. In others, they do not know that their personal information is stored in corporate databases

Control: Should people be able to correct errors in corporate database systems? This is possible with most organizations, although it can be difficult in some cases

Notice: Should an organization that uses personal data for a purpose other than the original purpose notify individuals in advance? Most companies don't do this

Consent: If information on people is to be used for other purposes, should these people be asked to give their consent before data on them is used? Many companies do not give people the ability to decide if information on them will be sold or used for other purposes

4 Companies must make an effort to ensure the data is accurate and, where necessary, up to date.

5 The data will not be stored for longer than necessary.

6 All of the above applies to processing the data, not just collecting and storing it.

7 Companies must take steps to ensure that the data is secure.

8 The data must not be transferred to somewhere that does not have a similar law on processing it.

The act allows individuals to access information stored about them and, if necessary, have the data updated or deleted. Similar laws have been implemented throughout Europe.

Even though privacy laws for private organizations are not very restrictive, most organizations are very sensitive to privacy issues and fairness. They realize that invasions of privacy can hurt their business, turn away customers, and dramatically reduce revenues and profits. Consider a major international credit card company. If the company sold confidential financial information on millions of customers to other companies, the results could be disastrous. In a matter of days, the firm's business and revenues could be reduced dramatically. Therefore, most organizations maintain privacy policies, even though they are not required by law. Corporate privacy policies should address a customer's knowledge, control, notice, and consent over the storage and use of information. They can also cover who has access to private data and when it can be used.

Multinational companies face an extremely difficult challenge in implementing data-collection and dissemination processes and policies because of the multitude of differing country or regional statutes. A good database design practice is to assign a single unique identifier to each customer – so that each has a single record describing all relationships with the company across all its business units. That way, the organization can apply customer privacy preferences consistently throughout all databases. Failure to do so can expose the organization to legal risks – aside from upsetting customers who opted out of some collection practices.

Right to Forget

In May 2014, an EU court ruling took a step towards giving people the 'right to be forgotten' by forcing Google and other search engines to remove certain links from search results.

The content itself will still be available on the web, but it will just be more difficult to find. The implications of this have not yet sunk in, and Google's response has been to produce a form that people can use to request that search results be removed. Each request they receive will be assessed and a balance sought between the 'privacy rights of the individual and the public's right to know and distribute information'. It is thought that among those most likely to use the form will be people with spent convictions, victims of domestic violence and students wishing to tidy up their online image before submitting job applications.[21]

Individual Efforts to Protect Privacy

Many people are taking steps to increase their own privacy protection. Some of the steps that you can take to protect personal privacy include the following:

- If you are concerned about what information a company is holding on you, use the Data Protection Act (or your country's equivalent) to find out what is stored about you in existing databases.
- Be careful when you share information about yourself. Don't share information unless it is absolutely necessary.
- Be vigilant in insisting that your doctor, bank or financial institution does not share information about you with others without your written consent.
- Be proactive to protect your privacy. For instance, you could get an unlisted phone number and think twice about registering for a service if it means you must supply a postal address. Consider registering for the telephone preference and mail preference services in your country (which stops commercial calls and post). In the UK the address is www.tpsonline.org.uk.
- When purchasing anything from a website, make sure that you safeguard your credit card numbers, passwords and personal information. Do not do business with a site unless you know that it handles credit card information securely (look for https:// in the address bar). Do not provide personal information without reviewing the site's data privacy policy.

When some people give over personal information, they change it slightly somehow, maybe changing their name from John T. Smith to John R. Smith. Then, in the future, if they get contacted as John R. Smith from an unknown source, they know which company the information must have come from, and can take the appropriate steps.

13.5 The Work Environment

The use of computer-based information systems has changed the makeup of the workforce. Jobs that require IS literacy have increased, and many less-skilled positions have been eliminated. Corporate programs, such as reengineering and continuous improvement, bring with them the concern that, as business processes are restructured and information systems are integrated within them, the people involved in these processes will be removed.

However, the growing field of computer technology and information systems has opened up numerous avenues to professionals and nonprofessionals of all backgrounds. Enhanced telecommunications has been the impetus for new types of business and has created global markets in industries once limited to domestic markets. Even the simplest tasks have been aided by computers, making cash registers faster, smoothing order processing, and allowing people with disabilities to participate more actively in the workforce. As computers and other IS components drop in cost and become easier to use, more workers will benefit from the increased productivity and efficiency provided by computers. However, information systems can raise other concerns.

Health Concerns

Organizations can increase employee effectiveness by paying attention to the health concerns in today's work environment. For some people, working with computers can cause occupational stress. Anxieties about job insecurity, loss of control, incompetence and demotion are just a few of the fears workers might experience. In some cases, the stress can become so severe that workers might sabotage computer systems and equipment. Monitoring employee stress can alert companies to potential problems. Training and counselling can often help the employee and deter problems.

Computer use can affect physical health as well. Strains, sprains, tendonitis, tennis elbow, the inability to hold objects and sharp pain in the fingers can result. Also common is repetitive strain injuries (RSI), including carpal tunnel syndrome (CTS), which is the aggravation of the pathway for nerves that travel through the wrist (the carpal tunnel). CTS involves wrist pain, a feeling of tingling and numbness, and difficulty grasping and holding objects. It can be caused by many factors, such as stress, lack of exercise and the repetitive motion of typing on a computer keyboard. Decisions on workers' compensation related to repetitive stress injuries have been made both for and against employees.

Other work-related health hazards involve emissions from improperly maintained and used equipment. Some studies show that poorly maintained laser printers can release ozone into the air; others dispute the claim. Numerous studies on the impact of emissions from display screens have also resulted in conflicting theories. Although some medical authorities believe that long-term exposure can cause cancer, studies are not conclusive at this time. In any case, many organizations are developing conservative and cautious policies.

Most computer manufacturers publish technical information on radiation emissions from their CRT monitors, and many companies pay close attention to this information. In addition, adjustable chairs and workstations should be supplied if employees request them.

In April 2014, French labour unions and employers in the high-tech and consulting field signed an agreement that employees must be able to disconnect communications tools. The agreement was widely reported as a ban on reading work-related emails after 6 p.m. although this is not the case. However the move does show that the French recognize the negative impact that being always online can have on wellbeing.[22]

Avoiding Health and Environmental Problems

Many computer-related health problems are caused by a poorly designed work environment. The computer screen can be hard to read, with glare and poor contrast. Desks and chairs can also be uncomfortable. Keyboards and computer screens might be fixed in place or difficult to move. The hazardous activities associated with these unfavourable conditions are collectively referred to as 'work stressors'. Although these problems might not be of major concern to casual users of computer systems, continued stressors such as repetitive motion, awkward posture and eyestrain can cause more serious and long-term injuries. If nothing else, these problems can severely limit productivity and performance.

The science of designing machines, products and systems to maximize the safety, comfort and efficiency of the people who use them, called **ergonomics**, has suggested some approaches to reducing these health problems. The slope of the keyboard, the positioning and design of display screens, and the placement and design of computer tables and chairs have been carefully studied. Flexibility is a major component of ergonomics and an important feature of computer devices. People come in many sizes, have differing preferences and require different positioning of equipment for best results. Some people, for example, want to place the keyboard in their laps; others prefer it on a solid table. Because

ergonomics The science of designing machines, products and systems to maximize the safety, comfort and efficiency of the people who use them.

of these individual differences, computer designers are attempting to develop systems that provide a great deal of flexibility. In fact, the revolutionary design of Apple's iMac computer came about through concerns for users' comfort, and after using basically the same keyboard design for over a decade, Microsoft introduced a new split keyboard called the Natural Ergonomic Keyboard 4000. The keyboard provides improved ergonomic features such as improved angles that reduce motion and how much you must stretch your fingers when you type. The design of the keyboard also provides more convenient wrist and arm postures, which make typing more convenient for users.[23]

Computer users who work at their machines for more than an hour per day should consider using LCD screens, which are much easier on your eyes than CRT screens. If you stare at a CRT screen all day long, your eye muscles can get fatigued from all the screen flicker and bright backlighting of the monitor. LCD screens provide a much better viewing experience for your eyes by virtually eliminating flicker and still being bright without harsh incandescence.[24]

In addition to steps taken by hardware manufacturing companies, computer users must also take action to reduce strain injury and develop a better work environment. For example, when working at a workstation, the top of the monitor should be at or just below eye level. Your wrists and hands should be in line with your forearms, with your elbows close to your body and supported. Your lower back needs to be well supported. Your feet should be flat on the floor. Take an occasional break to get away from the keyboard and screen. Stand up and stretch while at your workplace. Do not ignore pain or discomfort. Many workers ignore early signs of strain injury, and, as a result, the problem becomes much worse and more difficult to treat.

Ethical and Societal Issues

Internet Searches by Hand

A human flesh search (translated from the Chinese 人肉搜索) is a search organized online but conducted with help from people, unlike a Google search which is entirely automated. Often it is used to identify a human being. Professor Fei-Yue Wang, of the Chinese Academy of Sciences, and colleagues trace the first human flesh search back to 2001 when a user posted a photo of a beautiful woman to an Internet forum and claimed she was his girlfriend. A number of users then worked together to find out who she was, using a range of online and offline searches. She was eventually identified and in the process the user's claim of knowing her was discredited.

In another case, two students started a human flesh search when they were each overcharged for a haircut. The staff at the barbershop claimed that they had 'deep connections' with people the students would not want to cross and tried to intimidate them into paying up and forgetting about it. Instead the two launched a human flesh search to identify who these 'deep connections' might be. A local group was formed to conduct physical investigations in offline settings and other net citizens started a demonstration in front of the barbershop. The government investigated the case and fined the barber owner a half million RMB (Chinese yuan, about €60 000) for illegal pricing schemes.

However a human flesh search doesn't always get it right. In March 2013, taxi driver Yin Feng's phone started to ring. As soon as he had hung up on one angry caller, another would contact him. 'All of my private information was made public. My ID card number, name, phone number, address, even my mother-in-law's phone number was dug out and posted online,' he says. It turns out that someone had seen a taxi driver abusing an elderly homeless person. Witnesses managed to get the first few digits of the driver's licence plate. Thousands then banded together online to track him down. Yin insists the Internet vigilantes were wrong.

In another famous case, a Communist official in China's central Shaanxi province was spotted at the scene of a deadly traffic accident. A human flesh search soon discovered the man was the province's health and safety chief. The search also revealed that in every official photograph he was wearing a different designer watch, worth far more than he could afford on his official salary. Days after his face was spotted, he found himself without a job. Since then several officials have attracted attention with photos of them revealing tan lines indicating they had removed their watches just before the picture was taken.

Chinese officials are taking action against human flesh searches with an announcement from those in charge of Internet surveillance that mobs of web users who turn on individuals and make their lives a misery will not be tolerated. Some doubt this will make a difference. By using the Internet in this way, officials and others such as the owner of the barber shop will be forced to improve their behaviour argues Wu Zuolai, a scholar with the Chinese Academy of Arts in Beijing. 'They get criticized every day, and it will become a regular routine,' he says.

It's not just a Chinese phenomenon. A human flesh search was used in 2013 to identify the bombers who disrupted the Boston marathon and hacker group Anonymous is well known for its human flesh searches. It should be noted that the Boston search initially turned up the wrong answer, and the wrong people appeared on the front of several newspapers.

Questions

1 Why do you think people get involved in human flesh searches?

2 What are the benefits and dangers of this sort of activity?

3 Do you consider a human flesh search to be a form of citizen journalism?

4 Can you identify good applications for human flesh search?

13.6 Ethical Issues in Information Systems

As you've seen throughout the book in our Ethical and Societal Issues boxes, ethical issues deal with what is generally considered right or wrong. As we have seen, laws do not provide a complete guide to ethical behaviour. Just because an activity is defined as legal does not mean that it is ethical. As a result, practitioners in many professions subscribe to a **code of ethics** that states the principles and core values that are essential to their work and, therefore, govern their behaviour. The code can become a reference point for weighing what is legal and what is ethical. For example, doctors adhere to varying versions of the 2000-year-old Hippocratic Oath, which medical schools offer as an affirmation to their graduating classes.

code of ethics A code that states the principles and core values that are essential to a set of people and, therefore, govern their behaviour.

Some IS professionals believe that their field offers many opportunities for unethical behaviour. They also believe that unethical behaviour can be reduced by top-level managers developing, discussing and enforcing codes of ethics. Various IS-related organizations and associations promote ethically responsible use of information systems and have developed useful codes of ethics. The British Computer Society has a code of ethics and professional conduct that can be used to help guide the actions of IS professionals. These guidelines can also be used for those who employ or hire IS professionals to monitor and guide their work and can be seen at www.bcs.org. The international professional association ISACA (the Information Systems Audit and Control Association) which focuses on IT Governance, includes recognition of ethical issues in its governance framework COBIT (Control Objectives for Information and Related Technology). COBIT governs all aspects of IT development and management and is used to meet government regulations on reporting information, such as those set out for instance in the US Sarbanes-Oxley Act and the South African King III code of corporate governance. For more information see: http://www.isaca.org/COBIT.

The mishandling of the social issues discussed in this chapter – including waste and mistakes, crime, privacy, health and ethics – can devastate an organization. The prevention of these problems and recovery from them are important aspects of managing information and information systems as critical corporate assets. Increasingly, organizations are recognizing that people are the most important component of a computer-based information system and that long-term competitive advantage can be found in a well-trained, motivated and knowledgeable workforce.

Summary

Policies and procedures must be established to avoid computer waste and mistakes. Computer waste is the inappropriate use of computer technology and resources in both the public and private sectors. Computer mistakes relate to errors, failures and other problems that result in output that is incorrect and without value. Waste and mistakes occur in government agencies as well as corporations. At the corporate level, computer waste and mistakes impose unnecessarily high costs for an information system and drag down profits. Waste often results from poor integration of IS components, leading to duplication of efforts and overcapacity. Inefficient procedures also waste IS resources, as do thoughtless disposal of useful resources and misuse of computer time for games and personal processing jobs. Inappropriate processing instructions, inaccurate data entry, mishandling of IS output and poor systems design all cause computer mistakes.

A less dramatic, yet still relevant, example of waste is the amount of company time and money employees can waste playing computer games, sending unimportant email or accessing the Internet. Junk email, also called spam, and junk faxes also cause waste.

Preventing waste and mistakes involves establishing, implementing, monitoring and reviewing effective policies and procedures. Careful programming practices, thorough testing, flexible network interconnections, and rigorous back-up procedures can help an information system prevent and recover from many kinds of mistakes. Companies should develop manuals and training programs to avoid waste and mistakes. Company policies should specify criteria for new resource purchases and user-developed processing tools to help guard against waste and mistakes.

Computer crime is a serious and rapidly growing area of concern requiring management attention. Some crimes use computers as tools (e.g. to manipulate records, counterfeit money and documents, commit fraud via telecommunications links and make unauthorized electronic transfers of money). Identity theft is a crime in which an imposter obtains key pieces of personal identification information to impersonate someone else. The information is then used to obtain credit, merchandise and services in the name of the victim, or to provide the thief with false credentials.

A cyberterrorist is someone who intimidates or coerces a government or organization to advance his or her political or social objectives by launching computer-based attacks against computers, networks and the information stored on them. A cracker, or criminal hacker, is a computer-savvy person who attempts to gain unauthorized access to computer systems to steal passwords, corrupt files and programs, and even transfer money. Script kiddies are crackers with little technical savvy. Insiders are employees, disgruntled or otherwise, working solo or in concert with outsiders to compromise corporate systems.

Computer crimes target computer systems and include illegal access to computer systems, alteration and destruction of data and programs by viruses (system, application and document), and simple theft of computer resources. A virus is a program that attaches itself to other programs. A worm functions as an independent program, replicating its own program files until it destroys other systems and programs or interrupts the operation of computer systems and networks. Malware is a general term for software that is harmful or destructive. A Trojan horse program is a malicious program that disguises itself as a useful application and purposefully does something the user does not expect. A logic bomb is designed to 'explode' or execute at a specified time and date.

Because of increased computer use, greater emphasis is placed on the prevention and detection of computer crime. Antivirus software is used to detect the presence of viruses, worms and logic bombs. Use of an intrusion detection system (IDS) provides another layer of protection in the event that an intruder gets past the outer security layers – passwords, security procedures and corporate firewall. It monitors system and network resources and notifies network security personnel when it senses a possible intrusion. Many small and mid-sized organizations are outsourcing their network security operations to managed security service providers (MSSPs), which monitor, manage and maintain network security hardware and software.

Software and Internet piracy might represent the most common computer crime. Computer scams have cost people and companies thousands of dollars. Computer crime is also an international issue.

Many organizations and people help prevent computer crime. Security measures, such as using passwords, identification numbers and data encryption, help to guard against illegal computer access, especially when supported by effective control procedures. Public-key infrastructure (PKI) enables users of an unsecured public network such as the Internet to securely and privately exchange data through the use of a public and a private cryptographic key pair that is obtained and shared through a trusted authority. The use of biometrics, involving the measurement of a person's unique characteristics, such as the iris, retina or voice pattern, is another way to protect important data and information systems. Virus-scanning software identifies and removes damaging computer programs. Although most companies use data files for legitimate, justifiable purposes, opportunities for invasion of privacy abound. Privacy issues are a concern with government agencies, e-mail use, corporations, and the Internet. A business should develop a clear and thorough policy about privacy rights for customers, including database access. That policy should also address the rights of employees, including electronic monitoring systems and email. Fairness in information use for privacy rights emphasizes knowledge, control, notice and consent for people profiled in databases. People should know about the data that is stored about them and be able to correct errors in corporate database systems. If information on people is to be used for other purposes, they should be asked to give their consent beforehand. Each person has the right to know and the ability to decide. Platform for Privacy Preferences (P3P) is a screening technology that shields users from websites that don't provide the level of privacy protection they desire.

Jobs, equipment and working conditions must be designed to avoid negative health effects. Computers have changed the makeup of the workforce and even eliminated some jobs, but they have also expanded and enriched employment opportunities in many ways. Computers and related devices can affect employees' emotional and physical health. Some critics blame computer systems for emissions of ozone and electromagnetic radiation.

The study of designing and positioning computer equipment, called ergonomics, has suggested some approaches to reducing these health problems. Ergonomic design principles help to reduce harmful effects and increase the efficiency of an information system. The slope of the keyboard, the positioning and design of display screens, and the placement and design of computer tables and chairs are essential for good health. Good practice includes keeping good posture, not ignoring pain or problems, performing stretching and strengthening exercises, and seeking proper treatment. Although they can cause negative health consequences, information systems can also be used to provide a wealth of information on health topics through the Internet and other sources.

Ethics determine generally accepted and discouraged activities within a company and society at large. Ethical computer users define acceptable practices more strictly than just refraining from committing crimes; they also consider the effects of their IS activities, including Internet usage, on other people and organizations. Many IS professionals join computer-related associations and agree to abide by detailed ethical codes.

Self-Assessment Test

1   It is solely up to IS professionals to implement and follow proper IS usages policies to ensure effective use of company resources. True or false?

2   Preventing waste and mistakes involves establishing, implementing, _____ and reviewing effective policies and procedures.

3   Computer crime is frequently easily detected and the amount of money involved is often quite small. True or false?

4   _____ is a crime in which an imposter obtains key pieces of personal identification information, such as National Insurance or driving licence numbers, to impersonate someone else.

5   Someone who intimidates or coerces a government to advance his or her political objectives by launching computer-based attacks against computers, networks and the information stored on them is called a _____.
   a. cyberterrorist
   b. hacker
   c. criminal hacker or cracker
   d. social engineer

6   A logic bomb is a type of Trojan horse that executes when specific conditions occur. True or false?

7   Malware capable of spreading itself from one computer to another is called a _____.
   a. logic bomb
   b. Trojan horse
   c. virus
   d. worm

8   Phishing is a computer scam that seems to direct users to a bank's website but actually captures key personal information about its victims. True or false?

9   CTS, or _____, is the aggravation of the pathway of nerves that travel through the wrist.

10   The study of designing and positioning computer equipment to improve worker productivity and minimize worker injuries is called _____.

Review Questions

1   What special issues are associated with the prevention of image-based spam?

2   Identify three types of common computer-related mistakes.

3   What is a variant? What dangers are associated with such malware?

4   What is phishing? What actions can you take to reduce the likelihood that you will be a victim of this crime?

5   What is a virus? What is a worm? How are they different?

6   Outline measures you should take to protect yourself against viruses and worms.

7   Identify at least five tips to follow to avoid becoming a victim of a computer scam.

8   What is biometrics, and how can it be used to protect sensitive data?

9   What is the difference between antivirus software and an intrusion detection system?

10   What is a code of ethics? Give an example.

Discussion Questions

1 Outline an approach, including specific techniques, that you could employ to gain personal data about the members of your class. Explain how they could protect themselves from what you have suggested.

2 Your 12-year-old niece shows you a profile of her male maths teacher posted on Facebook that includes a list of dozens of students as the instructor's friends and a quote: 'I hope to make lots of new friends and, who knows, maybe find Miss Right.' What would you do?

3 Imagine that you are a hacker and have developed a Trojan horse program. What tactics might you use to get unsuspecting victims to load the program onto their computer?

4 Briefly discuss the potential for cyberterrorism to cause a major disruption in your daily life. What are some likely targets of a cyberterrorist? What sort of action could a cyberterrorist take against these targets?

5 You travel a lot in your role as vice president of sales and carry a laptop containing customer data, budget information, product development plans and promotion information. What measures should you take to ensure against potential theft of your laptop and its critical data?

Web Exercises

1 Search the web for a site that provides software to detect and remove spyware. Write a short report for your instructor summarizing your findings.

2 Do research on the web to find evidence of an increase or decrease in the number of viruses being developed and released. To what is the change attributed? Write a brief memo to your instructor identifying your sources and summarizing your findings.

Case One

Global Industrial Espionage or Deceitful Double Standards?

In May 2014, the US Department of Justice issued a most unusual indictment. A jury in the Western District of Pennsylvania charged five Chinese military personnel with computer hacking, economic espionage and other offences directed at six American corporations in the nuclear power, metals and solar products industries. It was the first time 'known state actors' had been charged with 'infiltrating US commercial targets by cyber means'.

The details of the charge are that the Chinese allegedly hacked into the computers of the six companies to gain access to their computers and to steal important commercial information that would be useful to competitors in China, including state-owned enterprises. The Americans allege that they also stole 'sensitive, internal communications that would provide a competitor, or an adversary in litigation, with insight into the strategy and vulnerabilities of the American companies'.

US Attorney General Eric Holder said, 'this is a case alleging economic espionage by members of the Chinese military and represents the first ever charges against a state actor for this type of hacking. The range of trade secrets and other sensitive business information stolen in this case is significant and demands an aggressive response. Success in the global market place should be based solely on a company's ability to innovate and compete, not on a sponsor government's ability to spy and steal business secrets. This Administration will not tolerate actions by any nation that seeks to illegally sabotage American companies and undermine the integrity of fair competition in the operation of the free market.'

China's defence ministry immediately put out a strongly worded statement on its website denying that their government or military had ever engaged in any cyber espionage activities. 'For a long time,' it said, 'the US has possessed the technology and essential infrastructure needed to conduct large-scale systematic cyber thefts and surveillance on foreign government leaders, businesses and individuals. This is a fact which the whole world knows. The US's deceitful nature and its practice of double standards when it comes to cyber security have long been exposed, from the Wikileaks incident to the Edward Snowden affair.'

Referencing CIA whistleblower Edward Snowden was appropriate. Snowden has claimed that the US regularly hacks Chinese networks and that targets have included Chinese universities, public officials and businesses. The Chinese defence ministry agrees,

stating that China's military has been the target of many online attacks, and 'a fair number' of those had been launched from American IP addresses. It said the arrest of the five Chinese army officers had 'severely damaged mutual trust'. The BBC's John Sudworth in Shanghai says it is extremely unlikely that any of the accused will ever be handed over to the US.

Just one month before all this happened, Defence Secretary Chuck Hagel said the Pentagon planned to more than triple its cyber-security capabilities in the next few years to defend against future Internet attacks.

Questions

1 How could US companies protect themselves from corporate espionage?

2 Why do you think the US Department of Justice issued this indictment if it is extremely unlikely that any of the accused will be handed over to the US?

3 Do you think the US has 'deceitful double standards' or is it right to protect its corporations?

4 Is all fair in love and cyber war?

Case Two

The Cult of Less

Late in 2009, software engineer Kelly Sutton came to a life-changing conclusion: more stuff equals more stress. 'Each thing I own came with a small expectation of responsibility. I look into my closet and feel guilt. I glance into my desk drawers and see my neglect. When was the last time I wore this? Have I ever even used that?' He landed on a radical solution: he decided to get rid of it all, or most of it at least: 'I will eliminate a large part of stress in my life and I will truly cherish the few things that I own.'

Many of the things we collect have digital alternatives. Books, movies and music can all be stored electronically with almost no space requirements. Mr Sutton founded CultofLess.com, a website which has helped him sell or give away his possessions – apart from his laptop, an iPad, an Amazon Kindle, two external hard drives, a 'few' articles of

clothing and bed sheets for a mattress that was left in his newly rented apartment. 'I think cutting down on physical commodities in general might be a trend of my generation. Cutting down on physical commodities that can be replaced by digital counterparts will be a fact,' he said.

He is not alone. Chris Yurista from Washington, DC, left his rented apartment and decided to use the Internet as his address. His possessions include a backpack full of designer clothing, a laptop, an external hard drive, a small piano keyboard and a bicycle. The decision wasn't about money – he earns a significant income as a travel agent, but feels he no longer has to worry about dusting, organizing and cleaning his possessions. 'I don't feel a void living the way I'm living because I've figured out a way to use digital technology to my advantage,' he said. Mr Yurista has substituted his bed for friends' couches, paper bills for online banking, and a record collection containing nearly 2000 albums for an external hard drive and nearly 13 000 MP3s.

Mr Yurista says he frequently worries he may lose his new digital life to a hard drive crash or downed server. 'You have to really make sure you have back-ups of your digital goods everywhere,' he said. Data recovery engineer Chris Bross at recovery company Drive Savers believes as individuals grow increasingly dependent on digital storage technology for holding assets, data recovery services will become rather like the firefighters of the twenty-first century – responders who save your valuables. And like a house fire that rips through a family's prized possessions, when someone loses their digital goods to a computer crash, they can be devastated.

Kelly Chessen, a 36-year-old former suicide hotline counsellor is Drive Savers' official 'data crisis counsellor'. Ms Chessen's role is to try to calm people down when they lose their digital possessions to failed drives. She says some people have gone as far as to threaten suicide over their lost digital possessions and data. In 2014 Mr Sutton says he still lives like this, but that he now owns a sofa too!

Questions

1 Make a list of your possessions. Tick off those that could be digitized and those that you could live without. What is left?

2 What would some of the challenges be in living with less?

3 Is it valuable to society that more people live with less? Is it valuable to humanity? To planet Earth?

4 Kelly Sutton and Chris Yurista have gone to an extreme. Can you describe a more moderate version of living with less that more people could go along with?

Case Three

Websites, Wikis and Whistleblowing

A 'wiki' is a website that anyone – or a selected group of people – can edit. Wikis are an excellent knowledge management tool. They allow people to document and disseminate their knowledge, and add to the knowledge other people have documented. The most famous example is Wikipedia, 'the free encyclopaedia that anyone can edit'.

Almost as famous is another site, WikiLeaks. Citizens have always desired accountability and transparency in their elected officials, to be secure in the knowledge that they are doing a good job and working for the good of their nation. Use of new information laws such as the Freedom of Information Act in the UK has raised public awareness that this does not always appear to be the case. One Freedom of Information request revealed the frivolous expenses claimed by members of parliament, and WikiLeaks aims to bring important news and information like this to the public by providing an innovative, secure and anonymous way for sources to 'leak' information.

WikiLeaks is no longer a wiki like Wikipedia in that it is not edited directly and collaboratively (although that is how it was originally designed). Instead the name is probably kept for historical reasons, and now refers to the fact that members of the public can anonymously submit material they wish to make public. The material is vetted and verified by WikiLeaks' accredited journalists and then published as downloadable files. In that sense the WikiLeaks website is a knowledge sharing site. WikiLeaks itself however is more than a website. It is a not-for-profit media organization whose members base their work on the defence of freedom of speech and improving humanity's common historical record. It was supposedly started by Chinese dissidents, journalists, mathematicians and start-up company technologists, based in the US, Asia,

Europe, Australia and South Africa, but is now represented in the media by Julian Assange.

Whoever they are, they certainly know how to create headlines. They have received a number of media awards and have published sensitive information on torture, suppression of free speech, financial corruption, abuse and religious cults. More famously in 2010 they released detailed correspondence between the US State Department and its diplomats. The content included unguarded comments from diplomats about the host countries of their embassies and information about US intelligence and counterintelligence actions. Since this happened, lawyers for WikiLeaks have stated that they believe they are being watched by security services, and several companies have severed ties with WikiLeaks, including the company that provided its web server. (In a twist, Internet activist group Anonymous then targeted these companies with denial of service attacks.)

Julian Assange has been living in the Embassy of Ecuador in London since 2012 after seeking asylum there when he skipped bail fearing extradition to Sweden to face charges of rape. From there he still represents WikiLeaks and the organization is still in the news. WikiLeaks helped whistleblower Edward Snowden after he published details of the extent of US National Security Agency's Internet surveillance. After fleeing the US for Hong Kong, Snowden contacted WikiLeaks who subsequently paid for his hotel and sent an advisor to help him.

The US has charged Snowden with two counts of violating the Espionage Act and theft of government property, and has revoked his passport. US government staff have been blocked from viewing WikiLeaks and the US has considered prosecuting WikiLeaks and Assange 'on grounds

they encouraged the theft of government property', although they later indicated this would be unlikely to happen. The army Private who leaked the diplomatic cables is now in military jail.

So, given the potential cost, why would anyone blow the whistle?

The people involved appear to passionately believe in their cause and they have certainly had some positive impact. However, according to BBC reporter Bill Thompson, their ultimate impact might be something they did not want: `WikiLeaks has exposed the inadequacies in the way governments control their internal flow of information, and organizations dedicated to transparency and disclosure will observe the tactics used to shut it down and adapt accordingly. But the state can learn too, and has the resources to implement what it learns. I fear that WikiLeaks is as likely to usher in an era of more effective control as it is to sweep away the authoritarian regimes that Julian Assange opposes.'

Questions

1 What do you feel the impact of whistleblowing organizations such as WikiLeaks will be?

2 Should governments be worried by organizations such as WikiLeaks?

3 What role has the Internet played in empowering citizens? Many governments claim to have e-government initiatives. Review what is available in your country – does this put power into the hands of the people? What more could your government do?

4 Can you think of a way in which people can be given accountability and transparency from their elected officials without going to the extremes WikiLeaks has?

Notes

1 McGillicuddy, Shamus, 'Thwarting Spam from the Inside and the Outside', ComputerWeekly. com. Retrieved from www.networksasia.net/article/thwarting-spam-inside-and-outside-1152547200?qt-breaking_news_most_read=0? qt-breaking_news_most_read=0 11 July 2006.

2 McGillicuddy, Shamus, 'Image-Based Spam on the Rise', ComputerWeekly.com, 3 August 2006.

3 Whiting, Rick, 'Hamstrung by Defective Data', *Information Week*, 8 May 2006.

4 www.financialfraudaction.org.uk. Accessed 16 July 2014.

5 http://securelist.com/analysis/kaspersky-security-bulletin/58265/kaspersky-security-bulletin-2013-overall-statistics-for-2013/#01. Accessed 16 July 2014.

6 Mitchell, Robert, 'Q&A: Making A Federal Case – How the FBI Collars Cybercriminals', *Computerworld*, 28 July 2006.

7 Koprowski, Gene J., 'Study: Nearly a Quarter Million PCs Turned into "Zombies" Daily', *E-commerce Times*, 14 January 2006.

8 McMillian, Robert, 'Internet Sieges Can Cost Businesses a Bundle', *Computerworld*, 25 August 2005.

9 BBC News Website, 'UK Hacker "Should be Extradited"', 10 May 2006. Available from: http://news.bbc.co.uk/ 1/hi/technology/4757375.stm.

10 BBC News Website, 'Tax Credit Errors "Waste £1.4bn"', 8 May 2007. Available from: http://news.bbc.co.uk/1/hi/ business/6634843.stm.

11 Keizer, Gregg, 'US Consumers Taking Steps to Stymie ID Theft', *Information Week*, 19 May 2006.

12 Savvas, Antony, 'Police Arrest m00p Gang Suspects', ComputerWeekly.com, 28 June 2006.

13 Savvas, Antony, 'Trojan Steals Bank Details After Pretending to Be Microsoft Patch', ComputerWeekly.com, 31 May 2006.

14 McAfee Website, 'Virus Hoaxes', 24 August 2006. Available from: http://vil.mcafee.com/hoax.asp.

15 BBC News Website, 'Defence Consultant's Laptop Stolen', 16 April 2001. Available from: http://news.bbc.co.uk/1/hi/ uk/1279584.stm.

16 Business Software Alliance Website home page. Available from: www.bsa.org/usa.

17 http://docs.apwg.org/reports/apwg_trends_report_q1_2014.pdf. Accessed 16 July 2014.

18 McMillan, Robert, 'Man Charged in Hurricane Katrina Phishing Scams', *Computerworld*, 18 August 2006.

19 Hadfield, Will, 'Co-op Goes Live with First Payment by Biometrics System', ComputerWeekly.com, 10 March 2006.

20 Wakefield, J., 'E-mail Embarrassment for City Lawyer', ZDNet UK, 14 December 2000, http://news.zdnet.co.uk/internet/0,1000000097,2083185,00.htm.

21 BBC News, 2014, 'Google Sets Up "Right to be Forgotten" Form after EU Ruling. Available from: www.bbc.co.uk/news/technology-27631001. Accessed 3 May 2014.

22 The Economist, 2014. 'Not What it Seemed'. Available from: www.economist.com/blogs/charlemagne/2014/04/frances-6pm-e-mail-ban. Accessed 3 May 2014.

23 Shah, Agam, 'Microsoft Revamps Keyboards and Mice', *Computerworld*, 6 September 2005.

24 Merrin, John, 'Review: Six 19-inch LCD Monitors', *Information Week*, 8 June 2005.

World Views Case

Coping with a Major IT Security Breach

Alan Hogarth
Glasgow Caledonian University

'Legal pressures, not to mention your moral obligation to assist unwitting victims, means that you should never delay when disclosing IT security incidents,' says Martin Allen of Pointsec.

Computer security breaches are becoming increasingly common. One need look no further than the recent misplacing of the UK Government's Revenue discs containing personal information on approximately 25 million people. However this was by no means the first example of such a breach.

Another high profile example was in November 2005 when a laptop belonging to an employee of the Boeing Corporation was stolen. The information held on this machine was essentially personal finance details on about 161 000 current and former employees. As none of the confidential information was encrypted the thieves would have had easy access to the information to exploit as they saw fit. This serves to highlight Boeing's IT security failings, but furthermore to compound the situation they did not own up to the incident. Boeing still will not explain the precise timings but has admitted that it was 'several days' after the theft before the 161 000 'victims' were officially informed that their personal details were now in the public domain. Boeing is not alone, companies across the world have always preferred to keep silent on any security breaches that have affected them. Because the problem is so bad the UK Metropolitan Police guaranteed anonymity if a company were to report a breach of its system. Basically, without such a scheme, police were unable to prosecute the hackers because officers were unaware that the incidents had taken place. The dilemma of the targeted organization is understandable. A simple breach of security could cost a typical bank £250 000 in terms of lost productivity, replacement hardware or system downtime. However, if the attack is reported to the police and the perpetrators are subsequently tried the whole episode could then become public knowledge, which results in customers losing trust in the bank concerned.

There are many and varied types of issues, ranging from loss of key information, adverse publicity, loss of trust, legal action by customers and official censure by regulators. All of which can be avoided with a little forethought and a professional attitude to the use of data encryption. Where once key data was held on a few PCs, now the information is far more portable and prone to all manner of mishaps intentional or otherwise. Laptops, which we have seen, are particularly easy to lose or steal.

Furthermore, unscrupulous staff or dishonest visitors can easily download information from a bank's main systems to a multitude of external storage devices. These include USB flash drives, digital cameras, MP3 players or even mobile phones. All of which then become vulnerable if subsequently lost, stolen or re-copied. Although Windows provides some encryption with its Encrypting File System, EFS is difficult to manage and impossible to enforce. Importantly, if files are copied from a Windows PC to these devices they invariably lose their encryption, often without the user being aware that this has happened. As such, an effective encryption policy needs to encompass every device onto which employees might wish to copy files. It also needs to be transparent to users, so that it can be centrally controlled without any user action being required. And it should be impossible to disable, except by authorized administrators.

Ideally it should also have the selective ability to block files from being copied to external devices at all, or if the target device doesn't support the same level of encryption as that which protects the source data. If you choose a proprietary encryption system if anyone discovers the secret mathematical formula behind it all of the files that you have every encrypted instantly become public knowledge. Therefore, use a known international standard such as the Advanced Encryption System, or AES, with a key length of at least 256 bits.

Another situation relevant to the above discussion is one where a director of a company attended a conference last week, during which his briefcase was stolen. This case held his laptop and on the laptop were a list of the top 10 000 accounts by revenue. The information was not encrypted. This happened on a Friday afternoon, but the loss was not reported until Monday morning. This is an obviously unacceptable situation for any company.

The trust of one's customers and investors is among the greatest assets that your organization owns. Lose it, and you're well on your way to being out of business. But failing to protect key information and data, or to introduce unnecessary delays in making losses public, could make such a situation a reality. Therefore a full disc encryption should be mandatory to all organizations.

Questions

1 What IT security measures should have been implemented to prevent an occurrence like the Boeing incident referred to in the case study?

2 How important is it to an organization that the measures discussed in Question 1 should form part of an IT Security Policy? Who should be responsible for this policy and who should have access to it?

3 If you were a Director of a company whose 10 000 client accounts went missing during a laptop theft, how would you ensure that those clients are discreetly informed as soon as possible?

4 What action should the marketing department take to help regain the trust of new customers who have decided to take their accounts elsewhere?

Answers to Self-Assessment Tests

Chapter 1

1 information system
2 system
3 a
4 False
5 computer-based information system (CBIS)

6 c
7 d
8 Mobile commerce (m-commerce)
9 d
10 Information systems

Chapter 2

1 True
2 organization
3 True
4 a
5 Outsourcing
6 False

7 process redesign
8 c
9 Return on investment
10 d
11 True
12 chief information officer (CIO)

Chapter 3

1 False
2 True
3 objectives
4 exabyte
5 b
6 instruction

7 Source data automation
8 computer downsizing
9 True
10 False
11 hazardous materials

Chapter 4

1 c
2 True
3 Linux
4 False
5 d
6 False
7 a
8 a
9 Proprietary
10 a
11 d
12 object-oriented
13 syntax
14 False
15 c
16 site licence

Chapter 5

1 c
2 entity
3 enterprise rules
4 primary key
5 cardinality
6 b
7 a
8 data warehouse
9 b
10 Online analytical processing (OLAP)

Chapter 6

1 False
2 a
3 broadband over power lines
4 d
5 multiplexer
6 personal area network
7 Internet service provider (ISP)
8 d
9 extranet
10 True

Chapter 7

1 correction
2 True
3 d
4 source data automation
5 purchasing
6 d
7 c
8 True
9 d
10 False

Chapter 8

1 d

2 False

3 d

4 optimization

5 True

6 True

7 c

8 b

9 False

10 executive information system (EIS)

Chapter 9

1 d

2 Heuristics

3 d

4 Robotics

5 c

6 expert system shell

7 a

8 d

9 virtual reality system

10 c

Chapter 10

1 hotspot

2 bluetooth

3 E-money

4 virtual pet

5 False

6 wiki

7 weblog

8 d

9 market segmentation

10 electronic bill presentment

Chapter 11

1 Systems development

2 c

3 a

4 a

5 False

6 Prototyping

7 True

8 a

9 entity-relationship (ER) diagrams; data-flow diagrams

10 True

Chapter 12

1 b

2 True

3 request for proposal (RFP)

4 freezing design specifications

5 make-or-buy

6 c

7 System

8 False

9 patch

10 True

Chapter 13

1 False

2 monitoring

3 False

4 Identity theft

5 a

6 True

7 d

8 True

9 carpal tunnel syndrome

10 ergonomics

Credits

Chapter 1

Information Systems @ Work References: www.cybernest.co.za/cn/index.jsp. Accessed January 6, 2011; www.telkom.co.za. Accessed 13 January 2014; Data Center Knowledge, 'Smart Approaches to Free-Cooling in Data Centers', 2 June, 2010. Available from: www.datacenterknowledge.com/archives/2010/06/02/smart-approaches-to-free-cooling-in-data-centers/

Ethical and Societal Issues References: Anderson, N. 2013. "MOOCS – Here Come the Credentials". *The Washington Post.* Available from: www.washingtonpost.com/blogs/college-inc/post/moocs-here-come-the-credentials/2013/01/09/a1db85a2-5a67-11e2-88d0-c4cf65c3ad15_blog.html. Accessed 2 July 2014; Coughlan, S. 2012. 'How do you Stop Online Students Cheating?' BBC News. Available from: www.bbc.co.uk/news/business-19661899. Accessed 2 July 2014; Moskovitch, R., et al., 2009. 'Identity Theft, Computers and Behavioral Biometrics', IEEE International Conference on Intelligence and Security Informatics, 13 January 2009.

Case One References: Jones, N. 2014. 'The Learning Machines', *Nature* 505 (7482) pp. 146–148, Le, Q.V. et al., 2012. 'Building High-level Features Using Large Scale Unsupervised Learning'. Available from: http://arxiv.org/pdf/1112.6209v5.pdf; Stone, B. 2013. 'Inside Google's Secret Lab,' *Business Week.* Available from: www.businessweek.com/articles/2013-05-22/inside-googles-secret-lab

Case Two References: Government Site of Castilla-La Mancha, www.jccm.es (in Spanish). Accessed 29 October 2011; Government of Castilla-La Mancha, Case Study: Castilla-La Mancha Government', submitted as Computerworld case study, www.eiseverywhere.com/file_uploads/eedce33bed14338d4f98066e49364b82_Castila_la_Mancha_Government_-_Vblock_Castilla_la_Mancha.pdf. Accessed 27 October 2011; VCE, 'Regional Government Creates New Collaborative Cloud Model'. Available from: www.vce.com/pdf/solutions/vcecase-study-castilla-la-mancha.pdf. Accessed 27 October 2011; VCE, the Virtual Computing Environment Company Website. Available from: www.vce.com, accessed 29 October 2011; VCE, Castilla-La Mancha project video (partly in English, partly in Spanish). Available from: www.vce.com/media/videos/vce-customer-castilla-la-mancha.htm. Accessed 27 October 2011.

Case Three References: www.pendahealth.com, accessed 2 July 2014; Graham, F. 2012. 'Technology Opens the Doors of Africa's Health Sector.' BBC News. Available from: www.bbc.co.uk/news/business-18969646. Accessed 2 July 2014; ChangeMakers. 'Penda Health: Quality Healthcare for all Kenyans'. Available from: www.changemakers.com/project/penda-health-quality-healthcare-all-kenyans'. Accessed 2 July 2014; IndieGoGo. 'Build a New Penda Health Clinic in Nairobi!' Available from: www.indiegogo.com/projects/build-a-new-penda-health-clinic-in-nairobi. Accessed 2 July 2014.

Chapter 2

Ethical and Societal Issues References: Ward, M. 2012. 'For Sale: Cheap Access to Corporate Computers'. BBC News. Available from: www.bbc.co.uk/news/technology-20209012; http://krebsonsecurity.com/tag/dedicatexpress-com/ Accessed 27 January 2014; http://404hack.blogspot.co.uk/2012/10/dedicatexpresscom-is-selling-access-to.html. Accessed 27 January 2014.

Information Systems @ Work References: Preston, R. 2014. "Virtual Mannequins" Promise Better Fit for Online Shoppers'. BBC News. Available from: www.bbc.co.uk/news/technology-25812130.

Accessed 2 July 2014; Morgan, H. 2014. 'Arden Reed's "Tailor Truck" Uses 3D Scanning to Create Bespoke Suits'. Available from: www.ecouterre.com/arden-reeds-tailor-truck-uses-3d-scanning-to-create-bespoke-suits. Accessed 2 July 2014; http://fits.me. Accessed 2 July 2014; http://newyork.arden-reed.com/tailor-truck. Accessed 2 July 2014.

Case One References: Grant, I., 'Tesco Uses Customer Data to Stride ahead of Competition', Computer Weekly. Available from: www.computerweekly.com/news/1280095684/Tesco-uses-customer-data-to-stride-ahead-ofcompetition, 12 April 2011. Accessed

2 December 2011; Kishino A.R., 'Kishino Augmented Reality for Tesco' (video). Available from: www.youtube.com/watch?v=S5QDRoxuHtk, 15 November 2011. Accessed 2 December, 2011; Sillitoe, B., 'Tesco Trials Virtual Store in South Korea'. *Retail Gazette*. Available from: www.retailgazette.co.uk/articles/43224-tesco-trials-virtual-storein-south-korea, 26 August 2011. Accessed 2 December 2011; Taylor, G., 'Tesco Launches Big Price Drop Facebook App', *Retail Gazette*. Available from: www.retailgazette.co.uk/articles/41023-tescolaunches-big-price-drop-facebook-app, 19 October 2011. Accessed 2 December 2011; Tesco PLC, 'Interim Results 2011/12', 5 October 2011. Available from: www.tescoplc.com/investors/results-and-events; Whiteaker, J., 'Tesco to Trial Augmented Reality In-store', *Retail Gazette*. Available from: www.retailgazette.co.uk/articles/44432-tesco-to-trial-augmentedreality-instore, 17 November 2011. Accessed 2 December 2011.

Case Two References: Schonfeld, E. 2010. 'Huffington Post Buys Adaptive Semantics to Keep Up With 100 000 Comments a Day'. Techcrunch. Available from: http://techcrunch.com/2010/06/17/huffington-post-buys-adapative-semantics/ Accessed 7 February 2010; Sonderman, J. 2012. 'How the Huffington Post Handles 70+ Million Comments a Year'. Available from: www.poynter.org/latest-news/top-stories/190492/how-the-huffington-post-handles-70-million-comments-a-year/. Accessed 7 February 2010.

Case Three References: Berg, Oscar, 'Creating Competitive Advantage with Social Software'. The Content Economy (blog). Available from: www.thecontenteconomy.com/2011/06/creating-competitive-advantage-with.html, 9 June 2011. Accessed 6 November 2011; IBM: 'Getting the Price Right', IBM Success Stories. Available from: www.01.ibm.com/software/success/cssdb.nsf/CS/STRD-8MQLX4, 31 October 2011. Accessed 6 November 2011; IBM, 'Netezza Mediamath – A Nucleus ROI Case Study', IBM Success Stories. Available from www01.ibm.com/software/success/cssdb.nsf/CS/JHUN-8N748A, 31 October 2011. Accessed 6 November 2011; Porter, Michael E., 'How Competitive Forces Shape Strategy'. *Harvard Business Review*. Available from: http://hbr.org/1979/03/how-competitive-forces-shape-strategy/ar/1 (free registration required to read beyond the first page), March/April 1979. Accessed 6 November 2011.

World Views Case References: Alan Hogarth, Glasgow Caledonian University; Adam, R., de la Rey, C., Naidoo, K. and Reddy, D. 'High Performance Computing in South Africa: Computing in Support of African Development', *CTWatch Quarterly*, Vol. 2, No. 1, February 2006.

Chapter 3

Table 3.2: Office Depot website, www.officedepot.com, October 2011.
Information Systems @ Work References: Metz, C., 'Facebook Hacks Shipping Dock into World-Class Server Lab', Wired. Available from: www.wired.com/wiredenterprise/2012/01/facebook-server-lab, 9 January 2012; Michael, Amir, 'Inside the Open Compute Project Server', Facebook Engineering Notes. Available from: www.facebook.com/notes/facebook-engineering/inside-the-open-computer-project-server/10150144796738920, 8 April 2011; Chang, E., 'Facebook Shares Technology to Build Data Centers'. Bloomberg TV. Available from: www.bloomberg.com/video/73907872, 12 August 2011; Open Compute Project Website, http://opencompute.org. Accessed 9 January 2012.

Ethical and Societal Issues References: www.explainingthefuture.com/3dprinting.html. Accessed 28 February 2014; RT News, 2013. '3D-printed Gun Malfunctions "Will Kill at Both Ends" – Australian police. Available from: http://rt.com/news/3d-gun-australia-police-758/. Accessed 28 February 2014; Gibbs, S. 2014. "First Metal 3D Printed Gun is Capable of Firing 50 Shots". *The Guardian*. Available from: www.theguardian.com/technology/2013/nov/08/metal-3d-printed-gun-50-shots. Accessed 28 February 2014.

Case One References: King, L. 2011. 'Deutsche Bank Completes Could Computing Overhaul'. Available from: www.computerworlduk.com/news/cloud-computing/3322339/deutsche-bank-completes-cloud-computing-overhaul. Accessed 10 March 2014. McLaurin, A. 'Identity Management in the New Hybrid Cloud World'. Available from: www.opendatacenteralliance.org/docs/vote_pdfs/Identity_Management_in_the_New_Hybrid_Cloud_World.pdf. Accessed 10 March 2014. Morgan, G. 2011. 'Deutsche Bank Lifts the Hood on Cloud Transition'. Available from: www.computing.co.uk/

ctg/news/2128892/deutsche-bank-lifts-hood-cloud-transition. Accessed 10 March 2014.

Case Two References: Brandon, J., 'Storage Tips from Heavy-Duty Users'. Computerworld. Available from: www.computerworld.com/s/article/358624/Extreme_Storage, 10 October 2011; Fuller, D., "NAS Shoot-out: 5 Storage Servers Battle for Business'. Computerworld. Available from: www.computerworld.com/s/article/9220996/NAS_shoot_out_5_storage_servers_battle_for_business, 19 October 2011; Vijayan, J., 'New Tools Driving Big Data Analytics, Survey Finds'. Computerworld. Available from: www

.computerworld.com/s/article/9219487/New_tools_driving_big_data_analytics_survey_finds, 25 August 2011; Williams, N., 'Blackpool and the Fylde College Achieves Business Continuity and Saves Cost with NetApp SAN Storage'. Available from: www.computerweekly.com/Articles/2011/01/24/245031/Case-study-NetApp-storage-solution-gains-top-results-for-Blackpool-and-the-Fylde-College.htm (free registration required to download full paper), 24 January 2011.

Case Three References: www.techsolution.co.za. Accessed 10 March 2014; www.webopedia.com/TERM/R/RFID.html. Accessed 10 March 2014.

Chapter 4

Information Systems @ Work References: Endsley, R., 'How Small Business PrintedArt Uses Linux and Open Source'. Available from: www.linux.com/learn/tutorials/539523-case-study-how-small-business-print-edart-uses-linux-and-open-source, 25 January 2012; Staff, 'Gompute Harnesses Sophisticated IBM High Performance Computing', IBM, www-01.ibm.com/software/success/cssdb.nsf/CS/STRD-8SYJ2K, 3 April 2012; Metz, C., 'Microsoft Preps for Public Embrace of Linux', Wired. Available from: www.wired.com/wiredenterprise/2012/05/microsoft-linux, 30 May 2012; Meyer, D., 'Microsoft Azure Starts Embracing Linux and Python'. ZDNet UK. Available from: www.zdnet.co.uk/news/cloud/2012/06/07/microsoft-azure-starts-embracing-linux-and-python-40155346, 7 June 2012; Staff, May 2012 Web Server Survey, Netcraft. Available from: news.netcraft.com/archives/2012/05/02/may-2012-web-server-survey.html, 2 May 2012; PrintedArt Website. Available from: www.printedart.com. Accessed 31 May 2012.

Ethical and Societal Issues References: Areva Website. Available from: www.areva.com. Accessed 31 May 2012; Collins, J., 'S.C. Nuke Plant First in US to Go Digital'. *Herald-Sun* (Durham, NC). Available from: www.heraldsun.com/view/full_story/13488870/article-S-C–nuke-plant-first-in-U-S–to-go-digital, 29 May 2011; Staff, 'Oconee Nuclear Station Projects Honored with Three Awards by the Nuclear Energy Institute'. Duke Energy. Available from: www.duke-energy.com/news/releases/2012052301.asp, 23 May 2012; Hashemian, H., 'USA's First Fully Digital Station'. Nuclear Engineering

International. Available from: www.neimagazine.com/story.asp?storyCode=2058654, 21 January 2011; Staff, 'Duke Energy Employees Win Top Nuclear Industry Award for Improving Safety With Digital Milestone'. Nuclear Energy Institute. Available from: www.nei.org/newsandevents/newsreleases/duke-energy-employees-win-top-nuclear-industry-award-for-improving-safety-with-digital-milestone, 23 May 2012.

Case One References: Staff, 'Tendring Saves £150 000 per Annum with Idox e-Planning. Available from: www.idoxgroup.com/downloads/news/Idox_case_study_Tendring_e-Planning.pdf, 17 May 2011; Idox Group Website. Available from: www.idoxgroup.com. Accessed 31 May 2012; Tendring District Council Website. Available from: www.tendringdc.gov.uk. Accessed 31 May 2012.

Case Two References: 'What is Microfinance?' CGAP. Available from: www/cgap.org/p/site/c/template.rc/1.26.1302. Accessed 14 June 2012; www.equitas.in. Accessed 3 January 2012. Equitas Micro – case study, 2011, Temenos. Available from: www.temenos.com/equitas-micro-case-study.

Case Three References: https://bugcrowd.com/. Accessed 11 March 2014. Ward, M. 2014. 'How to Make Money Finding Bugs in Software'. BBC News. Available from: http://www.bbc.co.uk/news/technology-25258620.

Chapter 5

Ethical and Societal Issues References: Triggle, N. 2014. 'Giant NHS Database Rollout Delayed.' BBC News. Available from: http://www.bbc.co.uk/news/health-26239532. Accessed 2 April 2014; www.nhs.uk/NHSEngland/thenhs/records/healthrecords/Pages/care-data.aspx. Accessed 2 April 2014; National Health Service. The care.data programme – better information means better care. Available from: www.england.nhs.uk/ourwork/tsd/care-data. Accessed 2 July 2014; National Health Service. 'Your Records.' Available from: www.nhs.uk/nhsengland/thenhs/records/healthrecords/pages/care-data.aspx. Accessed 2 July 2014.

Information Systems @ Work References: 'Oracle Enterprise Manager 12c for Database Management'. Available from: www.oracle.com/technetwork/oem/db-mgmt/db-mgmt-093445.html. Accessed 5 May 2012; Staff, 'Vodafone Group plc Embraces Proactive Support, Improving Pan-European Database Performance to Ensure Reliable Mobile Communications for 391 Million Customers'. Oracle. Available from: www.oracle.com/us/corporate/customers/customersearch/vodafonegroup-1-db-ss-1530452.html, 22 February 2012; Vodafone Website, www.vodafone.com. Accessed 5 May 2012.

Case One References: 'People Prefer Perks They Can Share.' Marketing. 10 February 2014. Available from: www.marketingmag.com.au/news/people-prefer-perks-they-can-share-australias-top-10-loyalty-programs-revealed-49081/#.UzKZIyh5kUU. Accessed 26 March 2014. O'Hear, S. 2012. 'Stocard Raises $850K to Take On Apple's Passbook and Force Loyalty Cards to Go Mobile'. Techcrunch. Available from: http://techcrunch.com/2012/12/11/stocard. Accessed 26 March 2014.

Case Two References: Preis, T., et al. 2013. Quantifying Trading Behavior in Financial Markets Using Google Trends. Scientific Reports 3, Article number: 1684, doi:10.1038/srep01684.

Case Three References: www.bipractice.co.za. Accessed 4 May 2012. www.medihelp.co.za. Accessed 4 May 2012. www.eiseverywhere.com/file_uploads/8af b2148c7782bb37e9ae1fa220b9824_Medihelp_-_Business_Critical_High_Performance_Data_Warehouse.pdf. Accessed 16 January 2012. Medihelp Customer Case Study. Available from: www.sybase.com/files/Success_Stories/Medihelp-CS.pdf, 14 October 2011.

Chapter 6

Ethical and Societal Issues References: Staff, 'Poland – Impact of the Regulations on the Stimulation of the Infrastructural Investments and Actions Concerning Development of the Information Society'. International Telecommunications Union. Available from: www.itu.int/ITU-D/eur/NLP-BBI/CaseStudy/CaseStudy_POL_Impact_of_Regulation.html, 29 June 2011; Staff, 'Poland Broadband Overview'. Point-Topic. Available from: point-topic.com/content/operatorSource/profiles2/poland-broadband-overview.htm, 26 August 2011; Staff, 'Broadband Network in Eastern Poland'. Polish Information and Foreign Investment Agency. Available from: www.paiz.gov.pl/20111114/broadband_network_in_eastern_poland, 14 November 2011; Internet World Stats, 'Internet Usage in Europe'. Available from: www.internetworldstats.com/stats4.htm, 11 April 2012.

Information Systems @ Work References: Savvas, A., 'Atos Origin Abandoning Email'. Computerworld UK. Available from: www.computerworlduk.com/news/it-business/3260053/atos-originabandoning-email, 9 February 2011; Savvas, A., 'Defiant Atos Sticks with Company-wide Email Ban'. Computerworld UK. Available from: www.computerworlduk.com/news/it-business/3323504/defiant-atos-sticks-withcompany-wide-email-ban, 7 December 2011; Prentice, B., 'Why Will "Zero Email" Policies Fail? Bureaucracy!' Gartner blog: blogs.gartner.com/brian_prentice/2011/12/11/why-will-zero-email-policies-failbureaucracy, 11 December 2011; Tardieu, H., 'Achieving a Zero Email Culture: Is Bureaucracy a Showstopper?', Atos blog, blog.atos.net/sc/2011/12/21/achieving-a-zero-email-culture-is-bureaucracy-ashowstopper, 21 December 2011; Atos S.A. Website. Available from: www.atos.net. Accessed 27 January 2012.

Case One References: Staff, 'University of Sydney Makes the Grade with Autonomy'. Autonomy. Available from: publications.autonomy.com/pdfs/Promote/Case%20Studies/Education/20111110_CI_CS_University_of_Sydney_web.pdf (requires free registration), 10 November 2011; Autonomy Website. Available from: www.autonomy.com. Accessed 7 June 2012; Gartner Group Website. Available from: www.gartner.com. Accessed 8 June 2012; University of Sydney Website. Available from: sydney.edu.au. Accessed 7 June 2012.

Case Two References: Microsoft SharePoint Website. Available from: sharepoint.microsoft.com. Accessed 6 June 2012; PepsiCo Europe Webpage. Available from: www.pepsico.com. Accessed 6 June 2012; Schwartz, J. 'What to Expect in SharePoint 15'. Redmond. Available from: redmondmag.com/articles/2012/04/01/whats-next-for-sharepoint, 4 April 2012; Ward, T. 'Social Intranet Case Study: PepsiCo Russia'. Available from: www.intranetblog.com/social-intranet-case-study-pepsico-russia/2012/03/28, 28 March 2012; Weis, R.T. 'How Pepsi Won the Cola Wars in Russia'. Available from: www.frumforum.com/how-pepsi-won-the-cola-wars-in-russia, 28 October 2011; WSS Consulting Website (in Russian). Available from: www.wss-consulting.ru. Accessed 7 June 2012.

Case Three References: Microsoft case study, 'Microsoft Disaster Response', Computerworld Honours Awards, 2011. Available from: www.eiseverywhere.com/file_uploads/1731e3ed9282e5b481db8572c9d5e4f_microsoft_coropration_-_microsoft_disaster_response.pdf. Accessed 28 January 2012; Microsoft Website, 'Microsoft Supports Relief Efforts in Haiti' (video), 19 August 2012; Microsoft Citizenship Team, 'How Technology is Helping Distribute Food in Japan'. Available from: http://blogs.technet.com/b/microsoftupblog/archive/2011/03/18/how-technology-is-helping-distribute-food-in-japan.aspx. Accessed 30 April 2014; Microsoft Website, 'Serving Communities: Disaster and Humanitarian Response'. Available from: www.microsoft.com/about/corporatecitizenship/en-us/serving-communities/disaster-and-humanitarian-response. Accessed 30 April 2014; NetHope Website. Available from: www.nethope.org. Accessed 31 January 2012.

World View Case References: Mitchell, R.L. 2002. 'Microsoft Days: Transforming the Desktop'. ComputerWorld. Available from: www.computerworld.com/s/article/76413/Microsoft_Days_Transforming_the_Desktop?taxonomyId=063. Accessed 2 July; www.youtube.com/watch?v=OpLU__bhu2w. Accessed 2 July 2014; www.youtube.com/watch?v=INuPyr1GuQ. Accessed 2 July 2014.

Chapter 7

Information Systems @ Work References: Staff, 2014. 'Inside the Supermarkets' Dark Stores' *The Guardian*. Available from: www.theguardian.com/business/shortcuts/2014/jan/07/inside-supermarkets-dark-stores-online-shopping. Accessed 11 April, 2014; Jacobs, E. 2014. 'Shedding Light on Dark Stores. *Financial Times*. Available from: www.ft.com/cms/s/0/af7034e0-bfda-11e3-b6e8-00144feabdc0.html. Accessed 11 April 2014; 'Building a Multi-channel Tesco'. Available from: www.youtube.com/watch?v=QONyKR0KdYs. Accessed 11 April 2014.

Ethical and Societal Issues References: CiviCRM Website. Available from: civicrm.org. Accessed 2 May 2012; Foundation for Prader-Willi Research Website. Available from: www.fpwr.org. Accessed 2 May 2012; Nomensa, '47% of Donors Not Completing Their Journey to Give'. Available from: www.nomensa.com/about/news-items/47-donors-not-completing-their-journey-give, 1 November 2011; Norris, S. and Potts, J., 'Designing the Perfect Donation Experience'. Nomensa Ltd. Available from: www.nomensa.com/insights/designing-perfect-donation-process-part-1 (requires free registration), October 2011; Sheridan, A., 'Getting to Know You: CRM for the Charity Sector', Fundraising. Available from: www.civilsociety.co.uk/fundraising/opinion/content/8759/getting_to_know_you_crm_for_the_sector, 6 April 2011.

Case Two References: Masary Website. Available from: www.e-masary.com. Accessed 1 March 2012; MobiKash Afrika, 'The First Intra-region Mobile Network and Bank Agnostic Mobile Commerce Solution'. Computerworld case study. Available from: www.eiseverywhere.com/file_uploads/e1bfbec2f385506b3890cbd7eb7e9dd9_MobiKash_Afrika_-_The_First_Intra-region_Mobile_Network_and_Bank_Agnostic_Mobile_Commerce_Solution.pdf. Accessed 1 March 2012; MobiKash Africa Website. Available from: www.mobikash.com. Accessed 1 March 2012; 'Reaching the Unbanked in a MobiKash

World', interview with CEO Duncan Otieno, Mobile-World. Available from: www.mobileworldmag.com/reachingthe-unbanked-in-a-mobikash-world.html, 28 December 2011; Sybase, 'MobiKash Africa: Customer Case Study'. Available from: www.sybase.com/files/Success_Stories/Mobikash-CS.pdf. Accessed 1 March 2012.

Case Three References: Kerry Group Website. Available from: www.kerrygroup.com. Accessed 2 May 2012; Staff, 'Kerry's SAP Transformation Measures Up to Their L&D Beliefs'. Olas. Available from: olas.ie/olas/Files/DRAFT%20KErry%20synopsis%20RB07.pdf, 18 May 2011; Staff, 'Kerry Group Transforms Its Global Procurement Group in Weeks With SAP Sourcing OnDemand Solution'. SAP. Available from: www.sap.com/news-reader/index.epx?pressid=18809, 1 May 2012.

Chapter 8

Information Systems @ Work References: Shadbolt, P. 2013. 'Hong Kong's Light Pollution "Worst in the World".' CNN. Available from: http://edition.cnn.com/2013/03/21/world/asia/hong-kong-light-pollution; http://lossofthe-night.blogspot.co.uk. Accessed 7 May 2014; https://play.google.com/store/apps/details?id=com.cosalux.welovestars. Accessed 7 May 2014; www.globeatnight.org/about.php. Accessed 7 May 2014; www.nature.com/srep/2013/130516/srep01835/full/srep01835.html. Accessed 7 May 2014; www.verlustdernacht.de/research.html. Accessed 7 May 2014.

Ethical and Societal Issues References: Australia Chicken Meat Federation Website. Available from: www.chicken.org.au. Accessed 11 April 2012; Department of Local Government and Planning, Queensland Government, 'Rural Planning: The Identification and Constraint Mapping of Potential Poultry Farming Industry Locations within Southern Queensland'. OZRI 2011 conference. Available from: www10.giscafe.com/link/Esri-Australia-Rural-Planning-identification-constraint-mapping-potential-poultry-farming-industry-locations-within-Southern-Queensland./36838/view.html, 14 October 2011; Queensland Government Website. Available from: www.qld.gov.au. Accessed 11 April 2012; ESRI ArcGIS software Website. Available from: www.esri.com/software/arcgis. Accessed 11 April 2012.

Case One References: Savvas, A. 'Irish Life Deploys New BI System'. Computerworld UK. Available from: www.computerworlduk.com/news/applications/3321944/irish-life-deploys-new-bi-system. Accessed 30 November 2011; Smith, G. 'Irish Life Chooses Tableau to Deliver Business Intelligence Dashboards. Available from: www.siliconrepublic.com/enterprise/item/25782-irish-life-chooses-tableau. Accessed 14 February 2012; www.tableausoftware.com. Accessed 4 April 2012; www.irishlife.ie. Accessed 4 April 2012.

Case Two References: Panko, R.R. 2009, Spreadsheet Research Website. Available from: http://panko.shidler.hawaii.edu/SSR. Accessed 16 July 2014; Panko, R.R. and Aurigemma, S. 2010. 'Revising the Panko–Halverson Taxonomy of Spreadsheet Errors', *Decision Support Systems* 49, pp. 235–244; Spurious Correlations Website. Available from: www.tylervigen.com. Accessed 16 July 2014.

Case Three References: Cheshire. T. 2012. 'Want to Learn Computer-Aided Design (CAD)? Play Minecraft.' Wired. Available from: www.wired.co.uk/magazine/archive/2012/11/play/minecrafted. Accessed May 7 2014; Mailbery, E. 2014. 'Danish Government Creates Entire Country in Minecraft, Users Promptly Blow it Up and Plant American Flag. Available from: www.gamespot.com/articles/danish-government-creates-entire-country-in-minecraft-users-promptly-blow-it-up-and-plant-american-flag/1100-6419412/. Accessed 7 May 2014; Woollaston, V. 2014. 'Making Money Out of MINECRAFT: Barman Gives Up Job to Upload Tips on the Game – and Now his YouTube Channel Gets More Hits than One Direction and Justin Bieber.' *Daily Mail*. Available from: www.dailymail.co.uk/sciencetech/article-2573860/Making-money-MINECRAFT-Barman-gives-job-play-game-professionally-Youtube-channel-gets-hits-One-Direction-Justin-Bieber.html. Accessed 7 May 2014; www.codysumter.com. Accessed 7 May 2014; https://minecraft.net/game. Accessed 7 May 2014.

Chapter 9

Information Systems @ Work References: Khatib, F., et al. 2011. *Nature Structural & Molecular Biology,* 18, 1175–1177; Foldit Website. Available from: http://fold.it/portal. Accessed 9 May 2014.

Ethical and Societal Issues References: Cacioppo, J.T., et al., 2013. 'Marital Satisfaction and Break-ups Differ Across On-line and Off-line Meeting Venues'. *Proceedings of the National Academy of Sciences,* doi: 10.1073/pnas.1222447110; Palmer, J. 2008. 'How to Live and Love Online'. BBC. Available from: http://news.bbc.co.uk/1/hi/technology/7651293.stm; DM Review Editorial Staff, 'eHarmony Expands SPSS Deployment Company-Wide for Research and Development'; DM Direct Newsletter. Available from: www.dmreview.com/article_sub.cfm?articleID=1055723, 9 June 2006; eHarmony website. Available from: www.eharmony.com. Accessed 14 May 2014.

Case One References: Kerr, R.A. 2012. 'Hang On! Curiosity is Plunging Onto Mars', *Science,* Vol. 336, No. 6088, pp. 1498–1499; Wall, M., 2012. 'NASA: Huge Mars Rover's Sky Crane Landing Was "Least Crazy" Idea'. Space.com. Available from: www.space.com/16889-mars-rover-curiosity-sky-crane-landing.html. Accessed 14 May 2014; NASA Robotics Website. Available from: http://robotics.nasa.gov/students/faq.php. Accessed 14 May 2014.

Case Two References: Google, 2012. 'Neural Network for Breast Cancer Data Built on Google App Engine. Available from: http://googleappengine.blogspot.co.uk/2012/08/neural-network-for-breast-cancer-data.html. Accessed 14 May 2014; www.youtube.com/watch?v=n-YbJi4EPxc. Accessed 14 May 2014; http://cloud4cancer.appspot.com. Accessed 14 May 2014

Case Three References: Guizzo, E., 'How Google's Self-Driving Car Works'. IEEE Spectrum. Available from: spectrum.ieee.org/automaton/robotics/artificial-intelligence/how-google-self-driving-car-works, 18 October 2011; Hachman, M., 'Google's Self-Driving Car Challenge: 1 Million Miles, by Itself', *PC Magazine.* Available from: www.pcmag.com/article2/0,2817,2395049,00.asp, 20 October 2011; Kelly, T., 'BMW Self Driving Car: Carmaker Shows off Hands-Free Car on Autobahn', *Huffington Post.* Available from: www.huffingtonpost.com/2012/01/26/bmw-self-driving-car_n_1234362.html, 26 January 2012; Trei, M., 'BMW Challenges Google's Self-Driving Car'. NBC Bay Area News. Available from: www.nbcbayarea.com/blogs/press-here/BMW-Challenges-Googles-Self-Driving-Car-137892303.html, 23 January 2012; Vanderbilt, T., 'Five Reasons the Robo-Car Haters Are Wrong'." Wired. Available from: www.wired.com/autopia/2012/02/robo-car-haters-are-wrong, 9 February 2012; Vanderbilt, T., 'Let the Robot Drive: The Autonomous Car of the Future is Here'. Wired. Available from: www.wired.com/magazine/2012/01/ff_autonomous-cars, 20 January 2012.

Chapter 10

Ethical and Societal Issues References: Furness, H., 2012. 'Five Royal Marines Charged with Murder Following Video Footage Discovery. *The Telegraph.* Available from: www.telegraph.co.uk/news/uknews/defence/9607343/Five-Royal-Marines-charged-with-murder-following-video-footage-discovery.html. Accessed 26 May 2014; BBC News. 2014. 'Jailed Ex-Marine Loses Appeal Against Afghan Murder Conviction. Available from: www.bbc.co.uk/news/uk-27514493. Accessed 26 May 2014; BBC News, 2013. 'Marine Guilty of Afghanistan Murder. Available from: www.bbc.co.uk/news/uk-24870699. Accessed 26 May 2014; Staff, 2012. 'Google Project Glass: Will We Really Wear Digital Goggles' Available from: www.theguardian.com/technology/2012/apr/05/google-project-glass-digital-goggles. Accessed 26 May 2014; http://eyetap.blogspot.co.uk/2012/07/physical-assault-by-mcdonalds-for.html. Accessed 26 May 2014.

Information Systems @ Work References: Dick, M., 2008. 'Is the future in bits?' BBC News. Available from: http://news.bbc.co.uk/1/hi/technology/7761153.stm. Accessed 20 May 2014; Miliard, M.,

2008. 'Who Are These Devoted, Even Obsessive Contributors to Wikipedia?' *City Weekly*. Available from: www.cityweekly.net/utah/article-5129-feature-wikipediots-who-are-these-devoted-even-obsessive-contributors-to-wikipedia.html. Accessed 20 May 2014; Nasaw, D., 2012. 'Meet the "Bots" that Edit Wikipedia'. BBC News. Available from www.bbc.co.uk/news/magazine-18892510. Accessed 20 May 2014; http://en.wikipedia.org/wiki/User:ClueBot_NG. Accessed 20 May 2014; http://en.wikipedia.org/wiki/Vandalism_on_Wikipedia. Accessed 20 May 2014.

Case One References: Taibi, C., 2014. 'Fox News Panel Slams #BringBackOurGirls Hashtag Activism,' *Huffington Post*. Available from: www.huffingtonpost.com/2014/05/11/fox-news-bringbackourgirls-hashtag-activism-brit-hume-george-will_n_5305749.html. Accessed 4 June 2014; BBC News, 2014., 'Nigeria Army "Knows Where Boko Haram are Holding girls".' Available from: www.bbc.co.uk/news/world-africa-27582873. Accessed 4 June 2014; Staff, 2014. 'Kidnapped Schoolgirls: British Experts to Fly to Nigeria "as Soon as Possible".' *The Guardian*. Available from: www.theguardian.com/world/2014/may/07/kidnapped-schoolgirls-british-experts-nigeria-boko-haram. Accessed 4 June 2014; The Daily Show, 12 May 2014.

Case Two References: Dillow, C., 2014., 'Killer Drones: When Will Our Weaponized Robots Become Autonomous?' *Popular Science*. Available from: www.popsci.com/technology/article/2011-09/killer-drones-when-will-our-weaponized-robots-become-autonomous. Accessed 4 June 2014; Schechter, E., 2014. 'Killer Robots: Natural Evolution, or Abomination?' Live Science. Available from: www.livescience.com/44161-killer-robot-drones-debate.html. Accessed 4 June 2014; International Committee for Robot Arms Control Website. Available from: http://icrac.net. Accessed 4 June 2014.

Case Three References: Anderson, J. and Rainie, L. 2014. 'Main Report: An In-depth Look at Expert Responses'. Available from: www.pewinternet.org/2014/05/14/main-report-an-in-depth-look-at-expert-responses. Accessed 28 May 2014; Robarts, S. 2014. 'Sen.se Launches "Mother" Home and Family Monitoring System.' Gizmag. Available from: www.gizmag.com/sense-mother-home-family-monitor/30313. Accessed 28 May 2014; Sisco Website. Available from: www.cisco.com/web/solutions/trends/iot/overview.html. Accessed 28 May 2014; Sen.se Website. Available from: https://sen.se/about/who. Accessed 28 May 2014; Sen.se Website. Available from: https://sen.se/store/cookie. Accessed 28 May 2014.

Chapter 11

Information Systems @ Work References: Dlala Website. Available from: http://dlalastudios.com/company. Accessed 16 May 2014; Pocketgamer. Available from: www.pocketgamer.co.uk/r/Windows+8/Janksy/review.asp?c=47641. Accessed 16 May 2014; www.microsoft.com/bizspark/. Accessed 16 May 2014; http://msdn.microsoft.com/en-us/library/vstudio/fda2bad5(v=vs.120).aspx. Accessed 16 May 2014.

Ethical and Societal Issues References: Wildlands Website. Available from: www.wildlands.co.za. Accessed 29 May 2014; IT News Africa, 'Microsoft Makes Office 365 Freely Available to NGOs.' Available from: www.itnews-africa.com/2013/09/microsoft-makes-office-365-freely-available-to-ngos. Accessed 29 May 2014; Microsoft case studies, 'Wildlands Enhances Business Continuity in the Bush by Moving to Office 365.' Available from: www.microsoft.com/casestudies/Case_Study_Detail.aspx?casestudyid=710000003628. Accessed 29 May, 2014; http://office.microsoft.com/en-gb/business/office-365-online-business-software-programs-FX102997619.aspx. Accessed 29 May 2014; http://office.microsoft.com/en-gb/business/office-365-business-email-and-shared-calendar-services-FX102996755.aspx. Accessed 29 May 2014.

Case One References: International Agency Consolidates Global Operations. Microsoft Case Studies. Available from: www.microsoft.com/en-gb/dynamics/customer-success-stories-detail.aspx?casestudyid=710000003775. Accessed 16 May 2014; www.microsoft.com/en-gb/dynamics/erp-ax-overview.aspx. Accessed 16 May 2014; www.microsoft.com/en-gb/business/products/dynamics-ax.aspx. Accessed 16 May 2014, Austraining Website. Available from: www.austraining.com.au/purpose/our-purpose. Accessed 16 May 2014.

Case Two References: Azure Website, azure. microsoft.com. Accessed 4 June 2014. Microsoft Case Studies, 2013. Private Property Breaks New Ground With Microsoft Windows Azure. www. google.co.uk/search?client=safari&rls=en& q=Private+Property+Breaks+New+Ground+With +Microsoft+Windows+Azure&ie=UTF-8&oe=UTF-8&gfe_rd=cr&ei=ORiPU_jWEarR8gf7z4HQCA. Privateproperty Website, www.privateproperty.co.za/ AboutUs.aspx. Accessed 4 June 2014. *Redmond Magazine*, 2014. http://redmondmag.com/blogs/the-schwartz-report/2014/06/microsoft-azure-gaining-on-aws.aspx. Accessed 4 June 2014.

Case Three References: Kovair, Inc., 'Requirements Management Case Study for Honeywell'. Available from: www.kovair.com/whitepapers/Requirements-Management-Case-Study-for-Honeywell.pdf, August 2011; HTSL Website. Available from: www.honeywell. com/sites/htsl. Accessed 26 January 2012; Kovair ALM Website. Available from: www.kovair.com/ alm/application-lifecycle-management-description .aspx. Accessed 27 January 2012.

Chapter 12

Information Systems @ Work References: Aron, J., 2014. 'Entangled Spies: Why the NSA Wants a Quantum Computer.' *New Scientist*, Available from: www.newscientist.com/article/dn24812-entangled-spies-why-the-nsa-wants-a-quantum-computer. html#.U4hCYRw0gpc. Accessed 30 May 2014; Deutsch, D. *The Fabric of Reality* (London: Penguin, 1998); Grossman, L., 2014. 'The Quantum Quest for a Revolutionary Computer'. Time. Available from: http://time.com/4802/quantum-leap. Accessed 30 May 2014; McGeoch, C.C. and Wang, C., 2013. 'Experimental Evaluation of an Adiabatic Quantum System for Combinatorial Optimization'. CFÕ13, May 14Ð16, 2013, Ischia, Italy; Rincon, P. 2014. 'D-Wave: Is $15m Machine a Glimpse of Future Computing?' BBC News. Available from: www .bbc.co.uk/news/science-environment-27264552. accessed 30 May, 2014; D-Wave Website. Available from: www.dwavesys.com. Accessed 30 May 2014.

Ethical and Societal Issues References: Donovan, A. and Bonney, J., 2006. 'The Box That Changed the World: Fifty Years of Container Shipping – An Illustrated History, Commonwealth Business Media; Mervis, J., 2014. 'The Information Highway Gets Physical.' *Science*, Vol. 334, No. 6188, pp. 1104–1107.

Case One References: Brumfiel, Geoff, 'Down the Petabyte Highway', *Nature*, Vol. 469, No. 7330, 20 January 2011;Cho, A., 2012. 'Higgs Boson Makes Its Debut After Decades-Long Search'. *Science*, Vol. 337,

No. 6091, pp. 141–143; European Organization for Nuclear Research. Available from: http://public.web. cern.ch/public/. Accessed 28 January 2011.

Case Two References: Amazon Website. Available from: www.amazon.co.uk. Accessed 25 May 2014; Oracle Case Study, 'OTN Case Study: Automatic Failover With Oracle Data Guard Fast-Start Failover'. Available from: www.oracleimg.com/technetwork/ database/features/availability/faststartfailoverprofile-132336.pdf. Accessed 25 May 2014; Oracle Data Guard, 'Oracle Data Guard.' Available from: www. oracle.com/technology/deploy/availability/htdocs/ DataGuardOverview.html. Accessed 25 May 2014.

Case Three References: Bednarz, A., 'How IBM Started Grading Its Developers' Productivity'. Computerworld. Available from: www.computerworld.com/s/ article/9221566/How_IBM_started_grading_its_developers_prproductivi, 7 November 2011; CAST Website. Available from: www.castsoftware.com. Accessed 4 March 2012; Lejeune, R.-M., 'Bank of New York Mellon Interview' (video). Available from: www.youtube.com/ watch?v=zLb7pCwA4rE, 7 February 2012; Subramanyam, J., '5 Requirements for Measuring Application Quality'. Network World. Accessed from: www.network-world.com/news/tech/2011/061611-application-quality. html, 7 June 2011.

World View Case References: Sato, J. 2002. 'Jim Sato's Lego Mindstorms: The Master's Technique.' No Starch Press; Mindstorms NXT 2.0. Lego Kit 8547.

Chapter 13

Information Systems @ Work References: Chacos, B., 2014. 'Lost Andy Warhol Art Recovered From 1980's Amiga Floppy Disks'. PC World. Available from: www.pcworld.com/article/2146903/lost-andy-warhol-art-recovered-from-1980s-amiga-floppy-disks.html. Accessed 4 June 2014; BBC News, 2014. 'Warhol Works Recovered From Old Amiga Disks'. Available from: www.bbc.co.uk/news/technology-27141201. Accessed 4 June 2014; http://studioforcreativeinquiry.org/public/warhol_amiga_report_v10.pdf. Accessed 4 June 2014; www.kryoflux.com. Accessed 4 June 2014.

Ethical and Societal Issues References: Hatton, C., 2014. 'China's Internet Vigilantes and the "Human Flesh Search Engine".' BBC News. Available from: www.bbc.co.uk/news/magazine-25913472. Accessed 20 May 2014; Wang, F. et al., 2010. 'A Study of the Human Flesh Search Engine: Crowd Powered Expansion of Online Knowledge.' Computer, Vol. 42, No. 8, pp. 45–53; 'The China Story, Human Flesh Search Engine'. Available from: www.thechinastory.org/yearbooks/yearbook-2013/chapter-6-chinas-internet-a-civilising-process/human-flesh-search-engine-renrou-sousuo-yinqing-人肉搜索引擎/. Accessed 20 May 2014; Hutchinson, B., 2013. 'New York Post Sued for Labeling Two Young Men as Boston Marathon Bombers.' Daily News. Available from: www.nydailynews.com/new-york/post-sued-misidentifying-boston-marathon-bombers-article-1.1365726. Accessed 23 May 2014.

Case One References: US Department of Juctice, 2014. 'US Charges Five Chinese Military Hackers for Cyber Espionage Against US Corporations and a Labor Organization for Commercial Advantage.' Available from: www.justice.gov/opa/pr/2014/May/14-ag-528.html. Accessed 23 May 2014; BBC News, 2014. 'China Denounces US Cyber-Theft Charges'. Retrieved from: www.bbc.co.uk/news/world-us-canada-27477601. Accessed 23 May 2014; BBC News, 2014. 'US Justice Department Charges Chinese with Hacking.' Available from: www.bbc.co.uk/news/world-us-canada-27475324. Accessed 23 May 2014; BBC News, 2014. 'Edward Snowden: Leaks that Exposed US Spy Programme'. Available from: www.bbc.co.uk/news/world-us-canada-23123964. Accessed 23 May 2014.

Case Two References: http://cultofless.tumblr.com/post/182833987/is-it-possible-to-own-nothing. Accessed 28 January 2011; Danzico, M. 2010. Cult of less: Living out of a hard drive. BBC News. Retrieved from www.bbc.co.uk/news/world-us-canada-10928032

Case Three References: Entous, A. and Perez, E., 2010. 'Prosecutors Eye WikiLeaks Charges.' The Wall Street Journal. Available from: http://online.wsj.com/news/articles/SB10001424052748704488404575441673460880204. Accessed 6 May 2014; Horwitz, S., 2013. 'Julian Assange Unlikely to Face US Charges Over Publishing Classified Documents.' Washington Post. Available from: www.washingtonpost.com/world/national-security/julian-assange-unlikely-to-face-us-charges-over-publishing-classified-documents/2013/11/25/dd27decc-55f1-11e3-8304-caf30787c0a9_story.html. Accessed 6 May 2014; Jones, S., 2010. 'Julian Assange's Lawyers Say They are Being Watched.' The Guardian. Available from: www.guardian.co.uk/media/2010/dec/05/julian-assange-lawyers-being-watched. Accessed 16 January 2011; Kelley, M.B., 2014. 'Edward Snowden's Relationship with WikiLeaks Should Concern Everyone.' Business Insider. Available from: www.businessinsider.com/edward-snowden-and-wikileaks-2014-1. Accessed 6 May 2014; MacAskill, E., 2010. 'US Blocks Access to WikiLeaks for Federal Workers.' The Guardian. Available from: www.theguardian.com/world/2010/dec/03/wikileaks-cables-blocks-access-federal. Accessed 6 May 2014; Pilkington, E., 2013.' Julian Assange Lawyer Calls on US to Make Formal Decision on Prosecution.' The Guardian. Available from: www.theguardian.com/media/2013/nov/26/julian-assange-lawyer-us-prosecution-decision. Accessed 6 May, 2014; web.archive.org/web/20080314204422/www.wikileaks.org/wiki/Wikileaks:About. Accessed 16 January 2011; BBC News, 2010. 'A World After Wikileaks. Available from: www.bbc.co.uk/news/technology-12007616. Accessed 16 January 2011.

Glossary

acceptance testing Conducting any tests required by the user.

accounting systems Systems that include budget, accounts receivable, payroll, asset management and general ledger.

ad hoc DSS A DSS concerned with situations or decisions that come up only a few times during the life of the organization.

alignment When the output from an information system is exactly what is needed to help a company achieve its strategic goals, the two are said to be in alignment.

alpha testing Testing an incomplete or early version of the system.

analogue signal A variable signal continuous in both time and amplitude so that any small fluctuations in the signal are meaningful.

antivirus program Software that runs in the background to protect your computer from dangers lurking on the Internet and other possible sources of infected files.

applet A small program embedded in web pages.

application program interface (API) An interface that allows applications to make use of the operating system.

application service provider (ASP) A company that provides software, support and the computer hardware on which to run the software from the user's facilities.

applications portfolio A scheme for classifying information systems according to the contribution they make to the organization.

arithmetic/logic unit (ALU) The part of the CPU that performs mathematical calculations and makes logical comparisons.

ARPANET A project started by the US Department of Defense (DoD) in 1969 as both an experiment in reliable networking and a means to link DoD and military research contractors, including many universities doing military-funded research.

artificial intelligence (AI) The ability of computer systems to mimic or duplicate the functions or characteristics of the human brain or intelligence.

artificial intelligence systems People, procedures, hardware, software, data and knowledge needed to develop computer systems and machines that demonstrate characteristics of intelligence.

auditing Analyzing the financial condition of an organization and determining whether financial statements and reports produced by the financial MIS are accurate.

B2Me A form of e-commerce where the business treats each customer as a separate market segment. Typical B2Me features include customizing a website for each customer, perhaps based on their previous purchases and personalized (electronic) marketing literature.

backbone One of the Internet's high-speed, long-distance communications links.

backward chaining The process of starting with conclusions and working backwards to the supporting facts.

batch processing system A form of data processing where business transactions are accumulated over a period of time and prepared for processing as a single unit or batch.

benchmark test An examination that compares computer systems operating under the same conditions.

beta testing Testing a complete and stable system by end users.

biometrics The measurement of one of a person's traits, whether physical or behavioural.

blade server A server that houses many individual computer motherboards that include one or more processors, computer memory, computer storage and computer network connections.

blog An online diary, a combination of the words 'web' and 'log'.

bluetooth A wireless communications specification that describes how smartphones, computers, printers and other electronic devices can be interconnected over distances of a few metres at a rate of about 2Mbps.

brainstorming A decision-making approach that often consists of members offering ideas 'off the top of their heads'.

bridge A telecommunications device that connects one LAN to another LAN that uses the same telecommunications protocol.

broadband communications A telecommunications system in which a very high rate of data exchange is possible.

business intelligence The process of gathering enough of the right information in a timely manner and usable form and analyzing it to have a positive impact on business strategy, tactics or operations.

business-to-business (B2B) e-commerce A subset of e-commerce where all the participants are organizations.

business-to-consumer (B2C) e-commerce A form of e-commerce in which customers deal directly with an organization and avoid intermediaries.

byte (B) Eight bits that together represent a single character of data.

cache memory A type of high-speed memory that a processor can access more rapidly than main memory.

cardinality In a relationship, cardinality is the number of one entity that can be related to another entity.

central processing unit (CPU) The part of the computer that consists of three associated elements: the arithmetic/logic unit, the control unit and the register areas.

centralized processing Processing alternative in which all processing occurs at a single location or facility.

certification A process for testing skills and knowledge, which results in a statement by the certifying authority that states an individual is capable of performing a particular kind of job.

channel bandwidth The rate at which data is exchanged over a communications channel, usually measured in bits per second (bps).

chief knowledge officer (CKO) A top-level executive who helps the organization use a KMS to create, store and use knowledge to achieve organizational goals.

chief programmer team A group of skilled IS professionals who design and implement a set of programs.

chip-and-PIN card A type of card that employs a computer chip that communicates with a card reader using radio frequencies; it does not need to be swiped at a terminal.

choice stage The third stage of decision making, which requires selecting a course of action.

client/server An architecture in which multiple computer platforms are dedicated to special functions such as database management, printing, communications and program execution.

clock speed A series of electronic pulses produced at a predetermined rate that affects machine cycle time.

cloud computing A computing environment where software and storage are provided as an Internet service and are accessed via a web browser.

code of ethics A code that states the principles and core values that are essential to a set of people and, therefore, govern their behaviour.

cold site A computer environment that includes rooms, electrical service, telecommunications links, data storage devices and the like; also called a 'shell'.

command line interface An interface where the user types text commands to the computer.

command-based user interface A user interface that requires you to give text commands to the computer to perform basic activities.

compact disc read-only memory (CD-ROM) A common form of optical disc on which data, once it has been recorded, cannot be modified.

competitive advantage The ability of a firm to outperform its industry; that is, to earn a higher rate of profit than the industry norm.

competitive intelligence One aspect of business intelligence limited to information about competitors and the ways that knowledge affects strategy, tactics and operations.

compiler A special software program that converts the programmer's source code into the machine-language instructions consisting of binary digits.

computer literacy Knowledge of computer systems and equipment and the ways they function; it stresses equipment and devices (hardware), programs and instructions (software), databases and telecommunications.

computer network The communications media, devices and software needed to connect two or more computer systems and/or devices.

computer programs Sequences of instructions for the computer.

computer supported cooperative work A term that refers to technologies which allow groups to work together to achieve goals.

computer-aided manufacturing (CAM) A system that directly controls manufacturing equipment.

computer-aided software engineering (CASE) Tools that automate many of the tasks required in a systems development effort and encourage adherence to the SDLC.

computer-based information system (CBIS) A single set of hardware, software, databases, telecommunications, people and procedures that are configured to collect, manipulate, store and process data into information.

computer-integrated manufacturing (CIM) Using computers to link the components of the production process into an effective system.

concurrency control A method of dealing with a situation in which two or more people need to access the same record in a database at the same time.

consumer-to-consumer (C2C) e-commerce A subset of e-commerce that involves consumers selling directly to other consumers.

contactless card A card with an embedded chip that only needs to be held close to a terminal to transfer its data; no PIN needs to be entered.

continuous improvement Constantly seeking ways to improve business processes to add value to products and services.

control unit The part of the CPU that sequentially accesses program instructions, decodes them and coordinates the flow of data in and out of the ALU, registers, primary storage, and even secondary storage and various output devices.

coprocessor The part of the computer that speeds processing by executing specific types of instructions while the CPU works on another processing activity.

cost–benefit analysis An approach that lists the costs and benefits of each proposed system. After they are expressed in monetary terms, all the costs are compared with all the benefits.

counterintelligence The steps an organization takes to protect information sought by 'hostile' intelligence gatherers.

cracker A person who enjoys computer technology and spends time learning and using computer systems.

creative analysis The investigation of new approaches to existing problems.

critical analysis The unbiased and careful questioning of whether system elements are related in the most effective ways.

critical path Activities that, if delayed, would delay the entire project.

cross-platform development A development technique that allows programmers to develop programs that can run on computer systems having different hardware and operating systems or platforms.

customer relationship management (CRM) system A system that helps a company manage all aspects of customer encounters, including marketing and advertising, sales, customer service after the sale and programmes to retain loyal customers.

cyberterrorist Someone who intimidates or coerces a government or organization to advance his or her political or social objectives by launching computer-based attacks against computers, networks and the information stored on them.

data administrator A non-technical position responsible for defining and implementing consistent principles for a variety of data issues.

data analysis The manipulation of collected data so that the development team members who are participating in systems analysis can use the data.

database An organized collection of information.

database administrator (DBA) The role of the database administrator is to plan, design, create, operate, secure, monitor and maintain databases.

data collection Capturing and gathering all data necessary to complete the processing of transactions.

data correction The process of re-entering data that was not typed or scanned properly.

data definition language (DDL) A collection of instructions and commands used to define and describe data and relationships in a specific database.

data dictionary A detailed description of all the data used in the database.

data editing The process of checking data for validity and completeness.

data entry Converting human-readable data into a machine-readable form.

data-flow diagram (DFD) A model of objects, associations and activities that describes how data can flow between and around various objects.

data input Transferring machine-readable data into the system.

data manipulation The process of performing calculations and other data transformations related to business transactions.

data manipulation language (DML) The commands that are used to manipulate the data in a database.

data mining The process of analyzing data to try to discover patterns and relationships within the data.

data preparation (data conversion) Ensuring all files and databases are ready to be used with new computer software and systems.

data storage The process of updating one or more databases with new transactions.

data warehouse A database or collection of databases that collects business information from many sources in the enterprise, covering all aspects of the company's processes, products and customers.

database administrator (DBA) The role of the database administrator is to plan, design, create, operate, secure, monitor and maintain databases.

decentralized processing Processing alternative in which processing devices are placed at various remote locations.

decision-making phase The first part of problem solving, including three stages: intelligence, design and choice.

decision support system (DSS) An organized collection of people, procedures, software, databases and devices used to support problem-specific decision making.

degree The number of entities involved in a relationship.

demand report A report developed to give certain information at someone's request.

design report The primary result of systems design, reflecting the decisions made and preparing the way for systems implementation.

design stage The second stage of decision making, in which alternative solutions to the problem are developed.

desktop computer A nonportable computer that fits on a desktop and that provides sufficient computing power, memory and storage for most business computing tasks.

dialogue manager A user interface that allows decision makers to easily access and manipulate the DSS and to use common business terms and phrases.

digital audio player A device that can store, organize and play digital music files.

digital camera An input device used with a PC to record and store images and video in digital form.

digital signal A signal that represents bits.

digital video disc (DVD) A storage medium used to store software, video games and movies.

direct access A retrieval method in which data can be retrieved without the need to read and discard other data.

direct access storage device (DASD) A device used for direct access of secondary storage data.

direct conversion Stopping the old system and starting the new system on a given date.

direct observation Watching the existing system in action by one or more members of the analysis team.

disaster planning The process of anticipating and providing for disasters.

disaster recovery The implementation of the disaster plan.

disc mirroring A process of storing data that provides an exact copy that protects users fully in the event of data loss.

distributed database A database in which the data is spread across several smaller databases connected via telecommunications devices.

document production The process of generating output records and reports.

documentation Text that describes the program functions to help the user operate the computer system.

domain The area of knowledge addressed by the expert system.

domain expert The individual or group who has the expertise or knowledge one is trying to capture in the expert system.

downsizing Reducing the number of employees to cut costs.

drill-down report A report providing increasingly detailed data about a situation.

e-commerce Any business transaction executed electronically between companies (business-to-business), companies and consumers (business-to-consumer), consumers and other consumers (consumer-to-consumer), business and the public sector, and consumers and the public sector.

economic feasibility The determination of whether the project makes financial sense and whether predicted benefits offset the cost and time needed to obtain them.

economic order quantity (EOQ) The quantity that should be reordered to minimize total inventory costs.

effectiveness A measure of the extent to which a system achieves its goals; it can be computed by dividing the goals actually achieved by the total of the stated goals.

efficiency A measure of what is produced divided by what is consumed.

e-government The use of information and communications technology to simplify the sharing of information, speed formerly paper-based processes, and improve the relationship between citizen and government.

electronic bill presentment A method of billing whereby a vendor posts an image of your statement on the Internet and alerts you by email that your bill has arrived.

electronic business (e-business) Using information systems and the Internet to perform all business-related tasks and functions.

electronic commerce Conducting business transactions (e.g. distribution, buying, selling and servicing) electronically over computer networks such as the Internet, extranets and corporate networks.

electronic exchange An electronic forum where manufacturers, suppliers and competitors buy and sell goods, trade market information and run back-office operations.

electronic retailing (e-tailing) The direct sale from business to consumer through electronic storefronts, typically designed around an electronic catalogue and shopping cart model.

e-money The transfer of funds electronically rather than by handing over physical coins and notes.

empowerment Giving employees and their managers more responsibility and authority to make decisions, take certain actions, and have more control over their jobs.

encryption The process of converting an original message into a form that can be understood only by the intended receiver.

encryption key A variable value that is applied (using an algorithm) to a set of unencrypted text to produce encrypted text or to decrypt encrypted text.

enterprise resource planning (ERP) system A set of integrated programs capable of managing a company's vital business operations for an entire multi-site, global organization.

enterprise rules The rules governing relationships between entities.

enterprise sphere of influence The sphere of influence that serves the needs of the firm in its interaction with its environment.

entity A person, place or thing about whom or about which an organization wants to store data.

ergonomics The science of designing machines, products and systems to maximize the safety, comfort and efficiency of the people who use them.

event-driven review A review triggered by a problem or opportunity such as an error, a corporate merger or a new market for products.

exception report A report automatically produced when a situation is unusual or requires management action.

execution time (e-time) The time it takes to execute an instruction and store the results.

executive support system (ESS) Specialized DSS that includes all hardware, software, data, procedures and people used to assist senior-level executives within the organization.

expert system Hardware and software that stores knowledge and makes inferences, similar to a human expert.

explanation facility Component of an expert system that allows a user or decision maker to understand how the expert system arrived at certain conclusions or results.

Extensible Markup Language (XML) The markup language for web documents containing structured information, including words, pictures and other elements.

extranet A network based on web technologies that allows selected outsiders, such as business partners, suppliers, or customers, to access authorized resources of a company's intranet.

feasibility analysis Assessment of the technical, economic, legal, operational and schedule feasibility of a project.

feedback Output that is used to make changes to input or processing activities.

field A characteristic or attribute of an entity that is stored in the database

File Transfer Protocol (FTP) A protocol that describes a file transfer process between a host and a remote computer and allows users to copy files from one computer to another.

final evaluation A detailed investigation of the proposals offered by the vendors remaining after the preliminary evaluation.

financial MIS A management information system that provides financial information not only for executives but also for a broader set of people who need to make better decisions on a daily basis.

five-forces model A widely accepted model that identifies five key factors that can lead to attainment of competitive advantage, including (1) the rivalry among existing competitors, (2) the threat of new entrants, (3) the threat of substitute products and services, (4) the bargaining power of buyers, and (5) the bargaining power of suppliers.

flat organizational structure An organizational structure with a reduced number of management layers.

flexible manufacturing system (FMS) An approach that allows manufacturing facilities to rapidly and efficiently change from making one product to making another.

forecasting Predicting future events.

foreign key When a primary key is posted into another table to create a relationship between the two, it is known as a foreign key.

forward chaining The process of starting with the facts and working forwards to the conclusions.

front-end processor A special-purpose computer that manages communications to and from a computer system serving hundreds or even thousands of users.

future strategic application Future strategic applications are ideas for systems which, if fully developed and deployed, might one day become strategic applications.

Gantt chart A graphical tool used for planning, monitoring and coordinating projects.

gateway A telecommunications device that serves as an entrance to another network.

genetic algorithm An approach to solving large, complex problems in which a number of related operations or models change and evolve until the best one emerges.

geographic information system (GIS) A computer system capable of assembling, storing, manipulating and displaying geographic information; that is, data identified according to its location.

gigahertz (GHz) Billions of cycles per second, a measure of clock speed.

global positioning system (GPS) A navigation system that enables a receiver to determine its precise location.

goal-seeking analysis The process of determining the problem data required for a given result.

graphical user interface (GUI) An interface that allows users to manipulate icons and menus displayed on screen to send commands to the computer system.

graphics processing unit (GPU) A specialized circuit that is very efficient at manipulating computer graphics and is much faster than the typical CPU chip at performing floating point operations and executing algorithms for which processing of large blocks of data is done in parallel.

green computing A program concerned with the efficient and environmentally responsible design, manufacture, operation and disposal of IS-related products.

grid computing The use of a collection of computers, often owned by multiple individuals or organizations, to work in a coordinated manner to solve a common problem.

group consensus Decision making by a group that is appointed and given the responsibility of making the final evaluation and selection.

group consensus approach A decision-making approach that forces members in the group to reach a unanimous decision.

group support system (GSS) Software application that consists of most elements in a DSS, plus software to provide effective support in group decision making; also called 'group decision support system'.

handheld computer A single-user computer that provides ease of portability because of its small size.

hardware Any machinery (most of which uses digital circuits) that assists in the input, processing, storage and output activities of an information system.

heuristics Commonly accepted guidelines or procedures that usually find a good solution.

highly structured problems Problems that are straightforward and require known facts and relationships.

home page A cover page for a website that has graphics, titles and text.

hot site A duplicate, operational hardware system or immediate access to one through a specialized vendor.

hotspot An area where wi-fi wireless Internet access is available.

HTML tags Codes that let the web browser know how to format text – as a heading, as a list or as body text – and whether images, sound or other elements should be inserted.

human resource MIS (HRMIS) An information system that is concerned with activities related to employees and potential employees of an organization, also called a personnel MIS.

hypermedia An extension of hypertext where the data, including text, images, video and other media, on web pages is connected allowing users to access information in whatever order they wish.

hyptertext Text used to connect web pages, allowing users to access information in whatever order they wish.

Hypertext Markup Language (HTML) The standard page description language for web pages.

IF-THEN statements Rules that suggest certain conclusions.

implementation stage A stage of problem solving in which a solution is put into effect.

incremental back-up Making a back-up copy of all files changed during the last few days or the last week.

inference engine Part of the expert system that seeks information and relationships from the knowledge base and provides answers, predictions and suggestions the way a human expert would.

information system (IS) A set of interrelated components that collect, manipulate, store, and disseminate information and provide a feedback mechanism to meet an objective.

information systems literacy Knowledge of how data and information are used by individuals, groups and organizations.

input The activity of gathering and capturing data.

insider An employee, disgruntled or otherwise, working solo or in concert with outsiders to compromise corporate systems.

installation The process of physically placing the computer equipment on the site and making it operational.

institutional DSS A DSS that handles situations or decisions that occur more than once, usually several times per year or more. An institutional DSS is used repeatedly and refined over the years.

instruction time (I-time) The time it takes to perform the fetch-instruction and decode-instruction steps of the instruction phase.

integrated development environments (IDEs) A development approach that combines the tools needed for programming with a programming language into one integrated package.

integration testing Testing all related systems together.

intelligence stage The first stage of decision making, in which potential problems or opportunities are identified and defined.

intelligent agent Programs and a knowledge base used to perform a specific task for a person, a process or another program; also called intelligent robot or bot.

intelligent behaviour The ability to learn from experiences and apply knowledge acquired from experience, handle complex situations, solve problems when important information is missing, determine what is important, react quickly and correctly to a new situation, understand visual images, process and manipulate symbols, be creative and imaginative, and use heuristics.

interactive whiteboard This term can be used to mean slightly different technologies, but essentially it is a combination of a whiteboard and a desktop computer.

international network A network that links users and systems in more than one country.

Internet The world's largest computer network, actually consisting of thousands of interconnected networks, all freely exchanging information.

Internet Protocol (IP) A communication standard that enables traffic to be routed from one network to another as needed.

Internet service provider (ISP) Any company that provides people or organizations with access to the Internet.

intranet An internal company network built using Internet and World Wide Web standards and products that allows people within an organization to exchange information and work on projects.

intrusion detection system (IDS) Software that monitors system and network resources and notifies network security personnel when it senses a possible intrusion.

Java An object-oriented programming language from Sun Microsystems based on C++ that allows small programs (applets) to be embedded within an HTML document.

just-in-time (JIT) inventory A philosophy of inventory management in which inventory and materials are delivered just before they are used in manufacturing a product.

kernel The heart of the operating system, which controls the most critical processes.

key-indicator report A summary of the previous day's critical activities; typically available at the beginning of each workday.

key operational application Key operational applications are essential. Without them the organization could not conduct business.

knowledge acquisition facility Part of the expert system that provides convenient and efficient means of capturing and storing all the components of the knowledge base.

knowledge base A component of an expert system that stores all relevant information, data, rules, cases and relationships used by the expert system.

knowledge engineer A person who has training or experience in the design, development, implementation and maintenance of an expert system.

knowledge user The person or group who uses and benefits from the expert system.

laptop computer A personal computer designed for use by mobile users, being small and light enough to sit comfortably on a user's lap.

LCD display Flat display that uses liquid crystals – organic, oil-like material placed between two polarizers – to form characters and graphic images on a backlit screen.

learning systems A combination of software and hardware that allows the computer to change how it functions or reacts to situations based on feedback it receives.

legal feasibility The determination of whether laws or regulations may prevent or limit a systems development project.

local area network (LAN) A computer network that connects computer systems and devices within a small area, such as an office, home or several floors in a building.

logical design A description of the functional requirements of a system.

machine cycle The instruction phase followed by the execution phase.

magnetic stripe card A type of card that stores limited amounts of data by modifying the magnetism of tiny iron-based particles contained in a band on the card.

magnetic tape A secondary storage medium; Mylar film coated with iron oxide with portions of the tape magnetized to represent bits.

mainframe computer A large, powerful computer often shared by hundreds of concurrent users connected to the machine via terminals.

maintenance team A special IS team responsible for modifying, fixing and updating existing software.

make-or-buy decision The decision regarding whether to obtain the necessary software from internal or external sources.

management information system (MIS) An organized collection of people, procedures, software, databases and devices that provides routine information to managers and decision makers.

market segmentation The identification of specific markets to target them with advertising messages.

marketing MIS An information system that supports managerial activities in product development, distribution, pricing decisions and promotional effectiveness.

massively parallel processing systems A form of multiprocessing that speeds processing by linking hundreds or thousands of processors to operate at the same time, or in parallel, with each processor having its own bus, memory, discs, copy of the operating system and applications.

material requirements planning (MRP) A set of inventory-control techniques that help coordinate thousands of inventory items when the demand of one item is dependent on the demand for another.

megahertz (MHz) Millions of cycles per second.

menu-driven system A system in which users simply pick what they want to do from a list of alternatives.

mesh networking A way to route communications between network nodes (computers or other device) by allowing for continuous connections and reconfiguration around blocked paths by 'hopping' from node to node until a connection can be established.

metropolitan area network (MAN) A telecommunications network that connects users and their devices in a geographical area that spans a campus or city.

middleware Software that allows different systems to communicate and exchange data.

MIPS Millions of instructions per second, a measure of machine cycle time.

mobile commerce (m-commerce) Conducting business transactions electronically using mobile devices such as smartphones.

model base Part of a DSS that provides decision makers access to a variety of models and assists them in decision making.

model management software Software that coordinates the use of models in a DSS.

modem A telecommunications hardware device that converts (modulates and demodulates) communications signals so they can be transmitted over the communication media.

monitoring stage The final stage of the problem-solving process, in which decision makers evaluate the implementation.

Moore's Law A hypothesis that states that transistor densities on a single chip double every 18 months.

MP3 A standard format for compressing a sound sequence into a small file.

multicore microprocessor A microprocessor that combines two or more independent processors into a single computer so they can share the workload and deliver a big boost in processing capacity.

multiple instruction/multiple data (MIMD) A form of parallel computing in which the processors all execute different instructions.

multiplexer A device that encodes data from two or more data sources onto a single communications channel, thus reducing the number of communications channels needed and therefore lowering telecommunications costs.

multiprocessing The simultaneous execution of two or more instructions at the same time.

narrowband communications A telecommunications system that supports a much lower rate of data exchange than broadband.

natural language processing Processing that allows the computer to understand and react to statements and commands made in a 'natural' language, such as English.

near field communication (NFC) A very short-range wireless connectivity technology designed for consumer electronics, smartphones and credit cards.

netbook computer A small, light, inexpensive member of the laptop computer family.

net present value The preferred approach for ranking competing projects and determining economic feasibility.

nettop computer An inexpensive desktop computer designed to be smaller, lighter and consume much less power than a traditional desktop computer.

network Computers and equipment that are connected in a building, around the country or around the world to enable electronic communications.

network-attached storage (NAS) Hard disc storage that is set up with its own network address rather than being attached to a computer.

network-management software Software that enables a manager on a networked desktop to monitor the use of individual computers and shared hardware (such as printers), scan for viruses and ensure compliance with software licences.

network operating system (NOS) Systems software that controls the computer systems and devices on a network and allows them to communicate with each other.

neural network A computer system that attempts to simulate the functioning of a human brain.

nominal group technique A decision-making approach that encourages feedback from individual group members, and the final decision is made by voting, similar to the way public officials are elected.

non-programmed decision A decision that deals with unusual or exceptional situations that can be difficult to quantify.

notebook computer Smaller than a laptop computer, an extremely lightweight computer that weighs less than 4 pounds and can easily fit in a briefcase.

off-the-shelf software Software mass-produced by software vendors to address needs that are common across businesses, organizations or individuals.

on-demand computing Contracting for computer resources to rapidly respond to an organization's varying workflow. Also called 'on-demand business' and 'utility computing'.

online analytical processing (OLAP) Software that allows users to explore data from a number of perspectives.

online transaction processing (OLTP) A form of data processing where each transaction is processed immediately, without the delay of accumulating transactions into a batch.

open-source software Software that is distributed, typically for free, with the source code also available so that it can be studied, changed and improved by its users.

operating system (OS) A set of computer programs that controls the computer hardware and acts as an interface with application programs.

operational feasibility The measure of whether the project can be put into action or operation.

optical storage device A form of data storage that uses lasers to read and write data.

optionality If a binary relationship is optional for an entity, that entity doesn't have to be related to the other.

organic light-emitting diode (OLED) display Flat display that uses a layer of organic material sandwiched between two conductors, which in turn are sandwiched between a glass top plate and a glass bottom plate so that when electric current is applied to the two conductors, a bright, electroluminescent light is produced directly from organic material.

organization A formal collection of people and other resources established to accomplish a set of goals.

organizational change The responses that are necessary so that for-profit and non-profit organizations can plan for, implement and handle change.

organizational learning The adaptations to new conditions or alterations of organizational practices over time.

organizational structure Organizational subunits and the way they relate to the overall organization.

output Production of useful information, often in the form of documents and reports.

outsourcing Contracting with outside professional services to meet specific business needs.

parallel computing The simultaneous execution of the same task on multiple processors to obtain results faster.

parallel running Running both the old and the new systems for a period of time.

patch A minor change to correct a problem or make a small enhancement. It is usually an addition to an existing program.

perceptive system A system that approximates the way a person sees, hears and feels objects.

personal area network (PAN) A network that supports the interconnection of information technology within a range of three metres or so.

personal productivity software The software that enables users to improve their personal effectiveness, increasing the amount of work and quality of work they can do.

personal robotics A term which refers to robotic companions that people socialize with.

personal sphere of influence The sphere of influence that serves the needs of an individual user.

pervasive computing A term meaning the move of the computer away from the desktop and towards something that is all around us, all the time.

phase-in approach Slowly replacing components of the old system with those of the new one. This process is repeated for each application until the new system is running every application and performing as expected; also called a piecemeal approach.

phicon Phicon stands for 'physical icon', and is a physical representation of digital data, in the same way that an icon on a computer screen represents a file.

physical design The specification of the characteristics of the system components necessary to put the logical design into action.

pilot running Introducing the new system by direct conversion for one group of users rather than all users.

pipelining A form of CPU operation in which multiple execution phases are performed in a single machine cycle.

pixel A dot of colour on a photo image or a point of light on a display screen.

plasma display A type of display using thousands of smart cells (pixels) consisting of electrodes and neon and xenon gases that are electrically turned into plasma (electrically charged atoms and negatively charged particles) to emit light.

Platform for Privacy Preferences (P3P) A screening technology that shields users from websites that don't provide the level of privacy protection they desire.

podcast An audio broadcast over the Internet.

point evaluation system An evaluation process in which each evaluation factor is assigned a weight, in percentage points, based on importance. Then each proposed system is evaluated in terms of this factor and given a score ranging from 0 to 100. The scores are totalled and the system with the greatest total score is selected.

point-of-sale (POS) device A terminal used in retail operations to enter sales information into the computer system.

policy-based storage management Automation of storage using previously defined policies.

portable computer A computer small enough to be carried easily.

preliminary evaluation An initial assessment whose purpose is to dismiss the unwanted proposals; begins after all proposals have been submitted.

primary key A field in a table that is unique – each record in that table has a different value in the primary key field. The primary key is used to uniquely identify each record, and to create relationships between tables.

primary storage (main memory; memory) The part of the computer that holds program instructions and data. Primary storage, also called main memory or memory, is closely associated with the CPU. Memory holds program instructions and data immediately before or after the registers.

private branch exchange (PBX) A telephone switching exchange that serves a single organization.

problem solving A process that goes beyond decision making to include the implementation and monitoring stages.

procedures The strategies, policies, methods, and rules for using a CBIS.

processing Converting or transforming input into useful outputs.

productivity A measure of the output achieved divided by the input required. Productivity = (Output / Input) × 100%.

program evaluation and review technique (PERT) A formalized approach for developing a project schedule.

programmed decision A decision made using a rule, procedure or quantitative method.

programming language Sets of keywords, symbols and a system of rules for constructing statements by which humans can communicate instructions to be executed by a computer.

project organizational structure A structure centred on major products or services.

proprietary software One-of-a-kind software designed for a specific application and owned by the company, organization, or person that uses it.

public-key infrastructure (PKI) A means to enable users of an unsecured public network such as the Internet to securely and privately exchange data through the use of a public and a private cryptographic key pair that is obtained and shared through a trusted authority.

quality control A process that ensures that the finished product meets the customers' needs.

questionnaires A method of gathering data when the data sources are spread over a wide geographic area.

radio frequency identification (RFID) A technology that employs a microchip with an antenna that broadcasts its unique identifier and location to receivers.

random access memory (RAM) A form of memory in which instructions or data can be temporarily stored.

rapid application development (RAD) A systems development approach that employs tools, techniques and methodologies designed to speed application development.

read-only memory (ROM) A non-volatile form of memory.

record A row in a table; all the data pertaining to one instance of an entity.

redundant array of independent/inexpensive discs (RAID) A method of storing data that generates extra bits of data from existing data, allowing the system to create a 'reconstruction map' so that, if a hard drive fails, the system can rebuild lost data.

reengineering Also known as 'process redesign' and 'business process reengineering' (BPR). The radical redesign of business processes, organizational structures, information systems and values of the organization to achieve a breakthrough in business results.

register A high-speed storage area in the CPU used to temporarily hold small units of program instructions and data immediately before, during and after execution by the CPU.

relational database A series of related tables, stored together with a minimum of duplication to achieve consistent and controlled pool of data.

release A significant program change that often requires changes in the documentation of the software.

reorder point (ROP) A critical inventory quantity level.

replicated database A database that holds a duplicate set of frequently used data.

request for maintenance form A form authorizing modification of programs.

request for proposal (RFP) A document that specifies in detail required resources such as hardware and software.

requirements engineering Also known as 'requirements analysis' and 'requirements capture'. Identifying what an information systems is needed (required) to do. Once the requirements have been identified, a solution can then be designed.

return on investment (ROI) One measure of IS value that investigates the additional profits or benefits that are generated as a percentage of the investment in IS technology.

robotics Mechanical or computer devices that perform tasks requiring a high degree of precision or that are tedious or hazardous for humans.

router A telecommunications device that forwards data packets across two or more distinct networks towards their destinations, through a process known as routing.

satisficing model A model that will find a good – but not necessarily the best – problem solution.

scalability The ability to increase the processing capability of a computer system so that it can handle more users, more data or more transactions in a given period.

schedule feasibility The determination of whether the project can be completed in a reasonable amount of time.

scheduled report A report produced periodically, or on a schedule, such as daily, weekly or monthly.

script kiddie A cracker with little technical savvy who downloads programs called scripts, which automate the job of breaking into computers.

search engine A web search tool.

secondary storage (permanent storage) Devices that store larger amounts of data, instructions and information more permanently than allowed with main memory.

semi-structured or unstructured problems More complex problems in which the relationships among the pieces of data are not always clear, the data might be in a variety of formats, and the data is often difficult to manipulate or obtain.

sequential access A retrieval method in which data must be accessed in the order in which it is stored.

sequential access storage device (SASD) A device used to sequentially access secondary storage data.

server A computer employed by many users to perform a specific task, such as running network or Internet applications.

service-oriented architecture (SOA) A modular method of developing software and systems that allows users to interact with systems and systems to interact with each other.

simulation The ability of the DSS to duplicate the features of a real system.

single-user license A software license that permits you to install the software on one or more computers, used by one person.

site preparation Preparation of the location of a new system.

slipstream upgrade A minor upgrade – typically a code adjustment or minor bug fix – not worth announcing. It usually requires recompiling all the code and, in so doing, it can create entirely new bugs.

smartphone A phone that combines the functionality of a mobile phone, camera, web browser, email tool and other devices into a single handheld device.

social engineering Using one's social skills to get computer users to provide you with information to access an information system or its data.

software The computer programs that govern the operation of the computer.

software as a service (SaaS) A service that allows businesses to subscribe to web-delivered application software.

software piracy The act of illegally duplicating software.

software suite A collection of single application programs packaged in a bundle.

source data automation Capturing and editing data where the data is initially created and in a form that can be directly input to a computer, thus ensuring accuracy and timeliness.

speech-recognition technology Input devices that recognize human speech.

start-up The process of making the final tested information system fully operational.

statistical sampling Selecting a random sample of data and applying the characteristics of the sample to the whole group.

steering committee An advisory group consisting of senior management and users from the IS department and other functional areas.

storage area network (SAN) A special-purpose, high-speed network that provides high-speed connections among data storage devices and computers over a network.

storage as a service A data storage model where a data storage service provider rents space to individuals and organizations.

strategic alliance (strategic partnership) An agreement between two or more companies that involves the joint production and distribution of goods and services.

strategic application A strategic application gives a firm a competitive advantage.

strategic planning Determining long-term objectives by analyzing the strengths and weaknesses of the organization, predicting future trends and projecting the development of new product lines.

structured interview An interview where the questions are prepared in advance.

structured walkthrough A planned and pre-announced review of the progress of a program module.

supercomputers The most powerful computer systems with the fastest processing speeds.

support application Support applications make work more convenient but are not essential.

switch A telecommunications device that uses the physical device address in each incoming message on the network to determine to which output port it should forward the message to reach another device on the same network.

syntax A set of rules associated with a programming language.

system A set of elements or components that interact to accomplish goals.

system performance measurement Monitoring the system – the number of errors encountered, the amount of memory required, the amount of processing or CPU time needed and other problems.

system performance products Software that measures all components of the computer-based information system, including hardware, software, database, telecommunications and network systems.

system performance standard A specific objective of the system.

system testing Testing the entire system of programs.

systems controls Rules and procedures to maintain data security.

systems design A stage of systems development where a solution to the problem is planned out and documented.

systems development The activity of creating or modifying existing business systems.

systems implementation A stage of systems development that includes hardware acquisition, software acquisition or development, user preparation, hiring and training of personnel, site and data preparation, installation, testing, start-up and user acceptance.

systems investigation report A summary of the results of the systems investigation and the process of feasibility analysis and recommendation of a course of action.

systems maintenance and review The systems development phase that ensures the system operates as intended and modifies the system so that it continues to meet changing business needs.

systems operation Use of a new or modified system.

systems review The final step of systems development, involving the analysis of systems to make sure that they are operating as intended.

tablet computer A portable, lightweight computer with no keyboard that allows you to roam the office, home or factory floor, carrying the device like a clipboard.

team organizational structure A structure centred on work teams or groups.

technical documentation Written details used by computer operators to execute the program and by analysts and programmers to solve problems or modify the program.

technical feasibility Assessment of whether the hardware, software and other system components can be acquired or developed to solve the problem.

technology diffusion A measure of how widely technology is spread throughout the organization.

technology-enabled relationship management Occurs when a firm obtains detailed information about a customer's behaviour, preferences, needs and buying patterns, and uses that information to set prices, negotiate terms, tailor promotions, add product features and otherwise customize its entire relationship with that customer.

technology infrastructure All the hardware, software, databases, telecommunications, people and procedures that are configured to collect, manipulate, store and process data into information.

technology infusion The extent to which technology is deeply integrated into an area or department.

telecommunications The electronic transmission of signals for communications; enables organizations to carry out their processes and tasks through effective computer networks.

Telnet A terminal emulation protocol that enables users to log on to other computers on the Internet to gain access to public files.

thin client A low-cost, centrally managed computer with essential but limited capabilities and no extra drives, such as a CD or DVD drive or expansion slots.

time-driven review Review performed after a specified amount of time.

total cost of ownership (TCO) The measurement of the total cost of owning computer equipment, including desktop computers, networks and large computers.

traditional organizational structure An organizational structure similar to a managerial pyramid, where the hierarchy of decision making and authority flows from strategic management at the top down to operational management and non-management employees. Also called a hierarchical structure.

transaction Any business-related exchange, such as payments to employees, sales to customers and payments to suppliers.

transaction processing cycle The process of data collection, data editing, data correction, data manipulation, data storage and document production.

transaction processing system (TPS) An organized collection of people, procedures, software, databases and devices used to record completed business transactions.

Transmission Control Protocol (TCP) The widely used transport-layer protocol that most Internet applications use with IP.

Trojan horse A malicious program that disguises itself as a useful application and purposefully does something the user does not expect.

tunnelling The process by which VPNs transfer information by encapsulating traffic in IP packets over the Internet.

ultra wideband (UWB) A form of short-range communications that employs extremely short electromagnetic pulses lasting 50 to 1000 picoseconds that are transmitted across a broad range of radio frequencies or several gigahertz.

uniform resource locator (URL) An assigned address on the Internet for each computer.

unit testing Testing of individual programs.

unstructured interview An interview where the questions are not prepared in advance.

user Person who will interact with the system regularly.

user acceptance document A formal agreement signed by the user that states that a phase of the installation or the complete system is approved.

user interface The element of the operating system that allows you to access and command the computer system.

user preparation The process of readying managers, decision makers, employees, other users and stakeholders for new systems.

utility program Program that helps to perform maintenance or correct problems with a computer system.

value chain A series (chain) of activities that includes inbound logistics, warehouse and storage, production, finished product storage, outbound logistics, marketing and sales and customer service.

version A major program change, typically encompassing many new features.

videoconference A videoconference is a simultaneous communication between two or more parties where they both see and hear each other.

virtual organizational structure A structure that employs individuals, groups or complete business units in geographically dispersed areas that can last for a few weeks or years, often requiring telecommunications or the Internet.

virtual pet An artificial companion. Could be screen based, i.e. the pet is animated on a computer monitor, or a robot.

virtual private network (VPN) A secure connection between two points on the Internet.

virtual reality The simulation of a real or imagined environment that can be experienced visually in three dimensions.

virtual tape A storage device that manages less frequently needed data so that it appears to be stored entirely on tape cartridges, although some parts of it might actually be located on faster hard discs.

virtual world A computer-based environment where users' avatars can interact.

virus A computer program file capable of attaching to discs or other files and replicating itself repeatedly, typically without the user's knowledge or permission.

vision systems The hardware and software that permit computers to capture, store and manipulate visual images.

volume testing Testing the application with a large amount of data.

wearable computing A term that refers to computers and computing technology that are worn on the body.

web browser Software that creates a unique, hypermedia-based menu on a computer screen, providing a graphical interface to the web.

web services Standards and tools that streamline and simplify communication among websites for business and personal purposes.

what-if analysis The process of making hypothetical changes to problem data and observing the impact on the results.

wide area network (WAN) A telecommunications network that ties together large geographic regions.

wi-fi A medium-range wireless telecommunications technology brand owned by the Wi-Fi Alliance.

wiki A web page that can be edited by anyone with the proper authority.

workgroup Two or more people who work together to achieve a common goal.

workgroup application software Software that supports teamwork, whether team members are in the same location or dispersed around the world.

workgroup sphere of influence The sphere of influence that elps workgroup members attain their common goals.

workstation A more powerful personal computer used for mathematical computing, computer-assisted design and other high-end processing, but still small enough to fit on a desktop.

World Wide Web (WWW or W3) A collection of tens of thousands of independently owned computers that work together as one in an Internet service.

worm A parasitic computer program that can create copies of itself on the infected computer or send copies to other computers via a network.

Index